Other Titles in the Jossey-Bass Nonprofit and Public Management Series:

Strategic Planning for Public and Nonprofit Organizations, Revised Edition
John M. Bryson

Handbook of Public Administration, Second Edition
James L. Perry

Creating and Implementing Your Strategic Plan Workbook
John M. Bryson, Farnum K. Alston

Handbook of Practical Program Evaluation
Joseph S. Wholey, Harry P. Hatry, Kathryn E. Newcomer

Handbook of Training and Development for the Public Sector
Montgomery Van Wart, N. Joseph Cayer, Steve Cook

Strategic Management of Public and Third Sector Organizations
Paul C. Nutt, Robert W. Backoff

The Search Conference
Merrelyn Emery, Ronald E. Purser

Seamless Government
Russell M. Linden

Authentic Leadership
Robert W. Terry

Planners on Planning
Bruce W. McClendon, Anthony James Catanese

Benchmarking for Best Practices in the Public Sector
Patricia Keehley, Steven Medlin, Sue MacBride, Laura Longmire

Transforming Government
Patricia W. Ingraham, James R. Thompson, Ronald P. Sanders, Editors

Transforming Public Policy
Nancy C. Roberts, Paula J. King

The Spirit of Public Administration
H. George Frederickson

Understanding and Managing Public Organizations, Second Edition
Hal G. Rainey

New Strategies for Public Pay
Howard Risher, Charles Fay

Grassroots Leaders for a New Economy
Douglas Henton, John Melville, Kimberly Walesh

Human Resources Management for Public and Nonprofit Organizations
Joan E. Pynes

How Do Public Managers Manage?
Carolyn Ban

Leading Without Power: Finding Hope in Serving Community
Max De Pree

The Leader of the Future
Frances Hesselbein, Marshall Goldsmith, Richard Beckhard, Editors

The Organization of the Future
Frances Hesselbein, Marshall Goldsmith, Richard Beckhard, Editors

Handbook of Public Law and Administration

Handbook of Public Law and Administration

Phillip J. Cooper
Chester A. Newland
Editors

Jossey-Bass Publishers
San Francisco

The quote from Clarence Page on page 303 (from the *Rocky Mountain News*) is reprinted by permission of Tribune Media Services.

Substantial discounts on bulk quantities of Jossey-Bass books are available to corporations, professional associations, and other organizations. For details and discount information, contact the special sales department at Jossey-Bass Inc., Publishers (415) 433–1740; Fax (800) 605–2665.

For sales outside the United States, please contact your local Simon & Schuster International Office.

Jossey-Bass Web address: http://www.josseybass.com

 Manufactured in the United States of America on Lyons Falls Turin Book. This paper is acid-free and 100 percent totally chlorine-free.

Library of Congress Cataloging-in-Publication Data

Handbook of public law and administration / Phillip J. Cooper, Chester A. Newland, editors. — 1st ed.
   p.   cm. — (The Jossey-Bass nonprofit and public management series)
Includes bibliographical references and index.
ISBN 0-7879-0930-0
1. Administrative law—United States. 2. Public administration—United States. I. Cooper, Phillip J. II. Newland, Chester A. III. Series.
KF5402.H356   1997
342.73'06—dc21   97-28390

FIRST EDITION

HC Printing   10 9 8 7 6 5 4 3 2 1

The Jossey-Bass
Nonprofit and Public Management Series

CONTENTS

FIGURE AND TABLES

Figure

Tables

PREFACE

For many public administrators, legal issues rank at the bottom of the list of desirable professional activities. Too often, law is chiefly associated with expensive, years-long lawsuits and unreasonably legalistic red tape. Risk management requirements that arise out of feared liabilities, personnel grievances that mushroom into disruptive litigation, legal constraints on management discretion, and concerns about court orders mandating new or different agency obligations often render the subject of law in public administration about as popular as personal tax audits and coincidental root canals.

Yet no dimension of public administration is more important than public law. At the least, public law should be a positive framework of constitutional democracy that sustains responsible practice, and certainly at its best it is. Elected officials, managers, and other civil and military personnel who try to operate without informed awareness of public law and of its consequences place themselves, their organizations, their missions, and the people they serve at risk. Most crucially, positive qualities of responsible civilization may be lost.

POSITIVE PURPOSES OF LAW AND ADMINISTRATION

In short, legal dimensions of public administration are, at their core, not solely or even primarily about avoiding lawsuits or other such perceived negatives. The ultimate point is that public law provides the positive foundation on which agencies are grounded and from which basic authorities of public officers, whether elected or appointed, are derived. Both civil and military agencies are primarily creatures of law; they carry out public responsibilities on the basis of legal delegations of authority and within boundaries that are refined through differentiated professional expertise and experience, underpinned and connected by shared constitutional values and legal processes that sustain them.

Law and public administration share deep roots in the most fundamental ideals of constitutionally democratic civilization: the disciplined *search for reasonableness* in pursuit of human dignity, and the rule of law. In Western civilization, early insights into the searching processes that underpin such responsible public life are found in Plato's well-known *Allegory of the Cave*. The unending search for universally binding law, reflected in religious, philosophical, political, and jurisprudential thinking, remains the strongest framework that sustains responsible public administrators. Experience in reflective practice in the field yields a mature balance of humility and professionally disciplined self confidence to keep the search for reasonableness alive in the face of endlessly hard challenges and opportunities for public service.

This positive nexus of law and public administration is the chief concern of this handbook.

LAW IN THE WORLD OF NOT-FOR-PROFITS AND CONTRACTORS

Volunteers, managers, and other contributors to the important not-for-profit organizations that constitute much of today's public administration also find their offices and authorities defined or constrained by law or by quasi-legal documents, including corporate charters, bylaws, and contracts; and to the extent that these organizations administer public programs through grants or contracts with one or more levels of government, they are an integral part of the public law community. Of course, since major portions of public services are now delivered by not-for-profit organizations, increasing numbers of third-sector administrators, including volunteers, find themselves in this situation. Like their government colleagues, managers in these organizations must learn to use legal resources effectively and positively, rather than working in fear of law as a constraint or even as a hazard.

Of course, the long-established and expanding roles of contracting in the overall scheme of governance and service delivery raises important questions about the status and operations of profit-seeking as well as not-for-profit organizations today. As major for-profit firms, including some well-established defense contractors that have "done government" for decades, bid to perform other public services, additional challenges arise. Consider, for example, the

Lockheed-Martin attempt in 1996 and 1997 to win a contract to operate Texas welfare programs.

PRACTICAL TOOLS OF PUBLIC ADMINISTRATION

While positive uses of public law are essential to success in public administration, managers are also confronted on a regular basis by conflicts and other legal challenges. Often the realities of law and administration degenerate to destructive levels. This handbook deals with that practical reality. A challenge for administrators, lawyers, judges, and others who are engaged together in these processes is how to shape substantive and procedural issues constructively for the long-term civic good in the face of often hard complexities. Given that responsibility, the significant issue often is not whether administrators win or lose in a given case. After all, few people other than those involved in particular cases pay attention to the many thousands of challenges that get resolved in informal proceedings or that are dismissed by courts or dealt with in chambers. What matters, ultimately, is how such legal matters, taken together as larger wholes, shape the ongoing contexts and operations of public administration.

In the pages that follow, the authors address how legal battles have reshaped and continue to alter separation of powers and checks and balances, federalism and intergovernmental relations, human resources management, public finance and budgeting, and organizational management. Anyone who thinks that such fundamental matters as the nature of federalism and shared powers of government among different branches are settled has not paid attention to the tremendous dynamism in these institutions, driven in no small part by legal contests at all levels of government and private enterprise. And important structural changes in governance do not even begin to address the turmoil in such obviously controversial topics as affirmative action, gender equality, racial discrimination, and regulation. Discussions of the legal struggles that have shaped and reshaped public administration in such matters fill the pages of this handbook.

Of course, these tensions come as no surprise to any experienced public administrator. In an environment in which it has become necessary to assemble national groups to discuss the meaning of civility and how to restore it, at a time when thousands have been butchered in ethnic and religious violence around the world, in a world where a sensationalized murder trial is the medium by which many Americans have learned what they feel they know about the legal system, and in an era in which resources are decreasing even as needs and pressures are growing exponentially, the significance of serious legal challenges is to be expected. Whether one looks at the failure of political systems, the weaknesses of human nature, the tenor of the times, or the need to find ways to wage emotionally challenging battles short of armed conflict, there is every reason to think that high levels of legal conflict will continue in the years to come. *The hope is that, over-all, those struggles will be disciplined by a search for reasonableness.* Both today's hard realities and this lingering high hope are the subjects of this handbook.

Hope is sustained through responsible efforts. Presently, for example, important attempts are under way to create and refine approaches to freedom of information balanced with privacy rights, alternative dispute resolution and facilitation of shared creativity, and integrative collective bargaining and other employee-management processes. While participative, high-involvement management, which has dominated the literature and much of the practice of leading North American enterprises since the start of the human relations movement three generations ago, is challenged today by the rising dominance of international markets, the search for reasonable principles of organizational justice survives in public law and administration. But challenges abound, and they are addressed in the chapters of this handbook.

Public administrators need survival mechanisms, and more. Both because law provides the tools of public administration and because it offers the legal shields and weapons necessary to advance the public interest in a world that is often more confrontational than reasonable, public administrators need mastery of public law concepts and processes. Hired legal thinkers are generally more useful than hired guns to help achieve such mastery, but neither can substitute for administrators' internalized understanding of the basics of constitutions, charters, statutes, executive orders, regulations, ordinances, and contracts. Likewise, it is essential for administrators to know something about what is termed the "black letter law" of rulemaking, adjudication, judicial review, and information management and privacy law. Public managers must be clear about what kinds of remedies courts issue, whether these are money damage awards in tort cases or remedial decrees mandating institutional or procedural reforms. All of these practical subjects are given considerable attention in this volume.

A USER'S GUIDE TO THE HANDBOOK

Handbooks are useful devices, and certainly Jossey-Bass has pioneered in the development of entire series of modern collections for public administrators and related professionals. These handbooks have many uses. They can serve as single-volume texts for familiarizing students with large amounts of information prepared by a wide range of authoritative authors. They can serve as reference works to be consulted for explanations and updates, and as guides to facilitate more detailed reading on specific topics. They can be read chapter by chapter or in sections as needs require. This volume can be used in all of these ways.

Still, a few helpful hints may facilitate use of this handbook. Consider its organization. Part One presents quite different but equally fundamental discussions of the public law foundations of public administration. These are not simply alternative frameworks for thinking about the nature of public law and its role in public management, though they would be valuable if that were all they did. Beyond that function, however, these three chapters explain the basic relationships among the central processes of law and public management and why they sometimes function effectively together but at other times clash. Even experienced readers will find that these discussions offer different ways of understanding law and public management than are readily available elsewhere.

Part Two addresses the practical frameworks, techniques, and tools of law and administration. The chapters explain how various actors in all branches of government play roles in the interpretation and application of law. They consider the nature and uses of the legal authorities an administrator is likely to encounter. They explain techniques most commonly used to interpret such authorities as constitutions and statutes.

The chapters in Part Three consider the roles of various types of participants in the process, with particular attention to separated and shared powers and modern intergovernmental relations, which are rooted in the basic notions of federalism. Variations are discussed that the constitutional founders, prescient though they were, could never have anticipated.

The chapters in Part Four go beyond the usual introduction to legal authorities and techniques of interpretation to address more specific elements of practical administrative law. Thus they examine devices used by presidents and governors to mandate actions, such as executive orders and proclamations; the relationships of statutes and ordinances at the local level; the operation of rule-making processes, including contemporary attempts to extend negotiated rule-making; and the essential elements of administrative adjudication as well as their relationships to effective management practices.

The chapters in Part Five address the kinds of issues that arise in human resources management and personnel systems. These include such topics as the constitutional free speech rights of public servants; labor-relations authorities, techniques, and resolutions; privacy and integrity protection processes for public employees; issues of race, gender, and other diversity in today's administration; and how these issues come together or sometimes fail to connect in reconceptualizations of public personnel systems.

Of course, no discussion of public law would be complete without attention to issues of accountability. Nothing is more essential to constitutional democracy. Thus, the chapters in Part Six consider the relationships between law and ethics; the fishbowl phenomenon and its legal analogue of privacy protection and freedom of information; debates over tort liability as a mechanism of accountability and remediation; the use of equitable decrees to address problems in a range of settings from prisons to schools; and the broad problem of ensuring adequate judicial review without interfering in the basic purposes of public administration.

The chapters in Part Seven attempt to engage, more directly than is usual in the literature, critical facets of relationships between law and public policy. In particular, they consider who represents government and why people should care; what interactions of law and public decision-making processes look like in the toughest of circumstances in real life; how law and legal processes affect budgets and financial management; which forces of law in government contracting are becoming more important as privatization increases; and how alternative dispute resolution techniques have been fashioned and implemented to reconcile some of the tensions without destructive conflicts.

Finally, this book attempts to look forward into the dynamics of changes and developments in the relationship between law and administration. Just as it is important not to neglect foundations and frameworks, so it would be a mistake to ignore probable future trends, especially since many are evident in developments that are already affecting important processes, tools, techniques, and management practices.

WHAT IS NEW AND DIFFERENT HERE?

In sum, this volume is an effort to provide a broad resource in support of efforts to learn about, understand, and develop tools for responsible and effective performance within the public law arena of public administration. All of the chapters were drafted with the perspectives of public administrators clearly in mind. It is hoped that the volume will also be useful for lawyers in public affairs, precisely because of its practical orientation to public administrators and the institutions and people served by them. That concern guided the design and governed the selection of authors.

This is not a book written by the usual suspects in the particular fields. Rather, it has been marked by an effort to ensure that, while it contains pieces by leading scholars in public law, it also includes key chapters by highly experienced practitioners, young scholars with new perspectives, and senior academicians and "pracademics" in public administration who do not routinely work in public law but who are established experts in fields as diverse as intergovernmental relations, human resources management, and organizational behavior. In all cases, attempts have been made not only to produce chapters that are topical and that provide foundation knowledge in the key issues but also to provide useful knowledge for readers with general interest in the legal basics of administration.

The chapters that follow thus provide foundation perspectives that can be read by thoughtful practitioners, experienced researchers, and students who are fresh to the fields of law and administration. They present tools required to understand the building blocks of these interconnected fields, whether they be constitutions, statutes, regulations, ordinances, or principles and practices.

ACKNOWLEDGMENTS

It is always a difficult privilege to acknowledge all of the people who performed helpful roles in the development of a book, especially an edited collection. Acknowledgment is also an especially humbling responsibility in preparation of a volume that bridges two core fields of constitutional democracy. In a very real sense, this volume derives in part from a heritage of constitutional government.

Many influences over several years lead to this sort of broadly based volume. Acknowledgment of those influences usually begins with gratitude to authors and other colleagues who stimulated thinking and work. But in this case appreciation first goes to Alan Shrader and his colleagues at Jossey-Bass, without whom this volume would never have been written. Even before the first edition of the *Handbook of Public Administration* was published in 1989, Jossey-Bass's professionals were encouraging production of the *Handbook of Public Law and Administration.* They stayed with the idea through the editors' standard excuses and warnings about other commitments and obstacles. Alan Shrader worked with series editor James Perry to go beyond the first attempt at a book design to make something unique, useful, and special. That sort of dedication by a publisher and its people to book development in public administration in this day and age is rare and greatly appreciated.

All that having been said, of course, the real work of writing this book was done by literally dozens of authors. These authors represent many disciplinary backgrounds and bring varied career experiences to their writing. That is completely appropriate to a volume that concerns itself with such a broad subject as public law in public institutions. This project includes some writers not ordinarily encountered in the literature of public law. In addition, the writers who are active in law were asked to examine new topics or to consider approaches different from ones taken in the past. Thus these contributors have met important challenges with fresh perspectives. Sadly, one author, Judge Roger Miner of the United States Circuit Court of Appeals for the Second Circuit, suffered a serious health problem during the late months of the project and was unable to continue participation, despite efforts to do so. The editors' wishes are for his rapid recovery.

The efforts of the many referees who reviewed and commented on chapter manuscripts are appreciated. Their suggestions and editorial ideas were most helpful. Thanks to the staffs of the Sacramento Center and the Washington Public Affairs Center of the University of Southern California and to the MPA Program at the University of Vermont for their support. Also, Phil Cooper does not want this opportunity to pass without expressing his special appreciation to Claudia for her understanding and support throughout this long project.

July 1997

Phillip J. Cooper
Burlington, Vermont

Chester A. Newland
Sacramento, California

EDITORS AND CONTRIBUTORS

HOWARD BALL is professor of political science and University Scholar at the University of Vermont. He received his B.A. degree (1960) in history from the City University of New York, Hunter College, and his M.A. (1963) and Ph.D. (1970) degrees in political science from Rutgers University. His scholarship and teaching are in the field of public law and judicial process. He is the author of twenty-one books and of dozens of articles published in political science, public administration, and law journals. He is presently at work on a major biography of the late Associate Justice Marshall of the U.S. Supreme Court, *A Defiant Life: Thurgood Marshall and the Persistence of Racism in America.*

LISA B. BINGHAM is assistant professor of public and environmental affairs in the School of Public and Environmental Affairs at Indiana University. She received her B.A. degree (1976) magna cum laude in philosophy and with high honors in ancient Greek from Smith College, and her J.D. degree (1979) with high honors from the University of Connecticut School of Law. She is a member of Phi Beta Kappa. Bingham practiced labor and employment law from 1979 to 1989 as a partner in the Hartford law firm Shipman & Goodwin, representing public sector employees in collective bargaining. She served as a lecturer in law at the Indiana University School of Law from 1989 to 1992. She is a labor arbitrator on the American Arbitration Association and Federal Mediation and Conciliation Service panels, and a mediator on the Indiana Education Employment Relations Board *ad hoc* panel. She has published articles on dispute resolution in *Arbitration Journal,* the

International Journal of Conflict Management, the *Journal of Public Administration Research and Theory, Labor Law Journal,* and the second edition of *The Handbook of Public Administration.*

STACEY SIMPSON CALVERT is a law student at the University of Alabama School of Law, where she will receive her J.D. degree in 1998. She plans to work in the field of employment law. She is a 1995 graduate of the Master of Public Administration program at the University of Alabama at Birmingham. She earned her B.A. degree (1989) in music at the University of North Texas.

N. JOSEPH CAYER is professor at the School of Public Affairs, Arizona State University. He received his B.A. degree (1964) in political science and his M.P.A. degree (1966) from the University of Colorado, Boulder, and his Ph.D. degree (1972) in political science from the University of Massachusetts, Amherst. He is the author of *Public Personnel Administration in the United States,* now in its third edition (1996), and author or coauthor of six other books on public administration and public policy. Cayer is also the author or coauthor of numerous articles published in journals, including *Public Administration Review, Review of Public Personnel Administration, Public Personnel Management, Social Science Quarterly, Employee Assistance Quarterly,* and *American Review of Public Administration.*

BEVERLY A. CIGLER is professor of public policy and administration at the School of Public Affairs, Pennsylvania State University, Harrisburg. She holds a B.A. degree (1968) from Thiel College and M.A. (1972) and Ph.D. (1977) degrees from Penn State, all in political science. Her work focuses on state and local politics, policy, and management. She received the Donald Stone Award for distinguished scholarship in intergovernmental relations from the American Society for Public Administration's Section on Intergovernmental Administration and Management in 1994, and the Friend of County Government Award from the County Commissioners Association of Pennsylvania in 1995. She has presented more than ninety speeches to national and state organizations of government officials.

CORNELL W. CLAYTON is associate professor of political science at Washington State University. He received his D.Phil. degree (1990) in politics from Oxford University. He is the author of *The Politics of Justice: The Attorney General and the Making of Legal Policy* (1992) and the editor of *Government Lawyers: The Federal Legal Bureaucracy and Presidential Politics* (1995).

PHILLIP J. COOPER is Gund Professor of Liberal Arts and director of the Master of Public Administration Program at the University of Vermont. He received his

B.A. degree (1972) in government at California State University, Sacramento, and his M.A. (1977) and Ph.D. (1978) degrees from the Maxwell School of Citizenship and Public Affairs at Syracuse University. Before going to the University of Vermont in 1995, Cooper was chair of the Department of Public Administration at the University of Kansas. He has been a consultant to state and federal agencies, Congress, the White House, and the United Nations. He is the author of numerous books and articles on public administration, administrative law, constitutional law, law and public policy, and environmental administration.

DAVID L. CORLISS is director of legal services for the city of Lawrence, Kansas. He received his B.A. degree (1983) with honors in political science, an M.P.A. degree (1985), and a J.D. degree (1987) from the University of Kansas. Prior to his service with the city of Lawrence, Corliss served in the city manager's office in Wichita, Kansas; in the county administrator's office in Douglas County, Kansas; and as research attorney for the League of Kansas Municipalities. He has taught the law and public management course for the Edwin O. Stene Graduate Program in Public Administration at the University of Kansas.

RUTH HOOGLAND DEHOOG is associate professor of political science and director of the M.P.A. Program at the University of North Carolina, Greensboro. She holds a B.A. degree (1975) from Calvin College and M.A. (1978) and Ph.D. (1981) degrees from Michigan State University, all in political science. She is author of *Contracting Out for Human Services* (1984) and coauthor of *The Politics of Dissatisfaction* (1991), as well as author and coauthor of book chapters and journal articles in the fields of urban administration, privatization, and public service delivery.

LOTTE E. FEINBERG is professor in the Department of Public Management at John Jay College of Criminal Justice, New York City. She received her B.A. degree (1964) from Brooklyn College, her Ed.M. degree (1965) from Harvard University, and her Ph.D. degree (1977) from New York University. Her research into the Freedom of Information Act (FOIA) has been supported in part by a National Endowment for the Humanities research fellowship, by research grants from the Lyndon Baines Johnson and Gerald R. Ford Presidential Libraries, and by grants from the Research Foundation of the City University of New York. Feinberg coedited a symposium on the FOIA for the *Public Administration Review (PAR)* (1986) and has published articles on FOIA and information policy in *PAR, Government Information Quarterly, The Investigative Reporters and Editors Journal,* and *Quill.* She is currently completing a book on the history and politics of the FOIA.

LOUIS FISHER is senior specialist in separation of powers with the Congressional Research Service of the Library of Congress. He is a fellow of the National Academy of Public Administration and testifies frequently before Congress on such issues as executive privilege, the item veto, the pocket veto, presidential reorganization authority, executive spending discretion, and presidential impoundment powers. He served in 1987 as research director of the House Iran-Contra Committee and wrote major sections of the final report. He received his B.S. degree (1956) from the College of William and Mary and his Ph.D. degree (1967) from the New School for Social Research. His books include *President and Congress* (1972); *Presidential Spending Power* (1975, Brownlow Book Award); *The Constitution Between Friends: Congress, the President, and the Law* (1978); *The Politics of Shared Power: Congress and the Executive* (3rd ed., 1991); *Constitutional Dialogues* (1988, Brownlow Book Award); *American Constitutional Law* (1990); *Constitutional Conflicts between Congress and the President* (3rd ed., 1991); *Political Dynamics of Constitutional Law* (1992, with Neal Devins); and *Presidential War Power* (1995). He is coeditor with Leonard Levy of the four-volume *Encyclopedia of the American Presidency* (1994), and author of more than 150 articles. He has participated with the American Bar Association in providing assistance to constitution drafters in eastern Europe and Russia.

ROBERT S. GILMOUR is professor of political science at the University of Connecticut, Storrs, where he specializes in the relationships between public law, administration, and public policy. He has been a consultant and legal counselor to both federal and state governments and has served as a professional staff member on the U.S. Senate Committee on Governmental Affairs. He received both his B.A. (1962) and M.A. (1963) degrees from the University of Florida and his Ph.D. (1968) in public law and government from Columbia University. He also studied at the University of Connecticut School of Law and was admitted to practice in Vermont (1977) and the District of Columbia (1986). Gilmour is author, with Alexis A. Halley, of *Who Makes Public Policy? The Struggle Between Congress and the Executive* (1995) and, with Harold Seidman, of *Politics, Position, and Power: From the Positive to the Regulatory State* (4th ed., 1986).

MARY E. GUY is Jerry Collins Eminent Scholar in Public Administration and Policy at the Reubin O. D. Askew School of Public Administration and Policy, Florida State University. She received her B.A. degree (1969) in psychology from Jacksonville University, an M.R.C. degree (1971) from the University of Florida (1971), and an M.A. degree (1976) in psychology and a Ph.D. degree (1981) in political science from the University of South Carolina. Her research interests include public management and the difference gender makes. Recent works include *Women and Men of the States: Public Administrators at the State Level* (1992), as well as numerous articles and book chapters on the subject.

BRUCE S. JENKINS is a U.S. senior district judge. Appointed to the federal district bench in 1978, Judge Jenkins served as chief judge of the U.S. District Court for the District of Utah from 1984 through 1993. He graduated magna cum laude with a B.A. degree (1949) in political science from the University of Utah and was admitted to the Phi Beta Kappa and Phi Kappa Phi honorary fraternities. He received his J.D. degree (1952) from the University of Utah College of Law, where he served on the board of editors of the *Utah Law Review*. In addition to the private practice of law, Judge Jenkins has actively pursued interests in government. He was twice reelected to the state legislature and was elected president of the Utah State Senate in 1965. He then served for thirteen years as a U.S. bankruptcy judge before moving to the district bench. Judge Jenkins is the author of numerous opinions and articles. He is also adjunct professor at the University of Utah College of Law.

RUSSELL C. KEARL currently serves as a judicial law clerk for U.S. Senior District Judge Bruce S. Jenkins, U.S. District Court, District of Utah. Kearl graduated magna cum laude with a B.A. degree (1977) in political science from the University of Utah and was admitted to the Phi Beta Kappa and Phi Kappa Phi honorary fraternities. He received his J.D. degree (1980) from the University of Utah College of Law, where he served as associate editor of the *Journal of Contemporary Law*. A member of the Utah State Bar, Kearl has nine years of experience as a trial lawyer in private practice, particularly in civil trial and appellate practice in federal and state courts. He has served since 1981 as adjunct instructor at Westminster College of Salt Lake City.

CORNELIUS M. KERWIN is dean of the School of Public Affairs and professor of public administration at American University. He specializes in regulatory affairs and other aspects of public policy. His B.A. degree (1971) is from the American University; his M.A. degree (1973), from the University of Rhode Island; and his Ph.D. degree (1978), from Johns Hopkins University, all in political science. He is a member of the Federal Affairs Committee of the Greater Washington Board of Trade. He was founding chair of the Section on Public Law and Administration of the American Society for Public Administration. He is a member of the National Council of the National Association of Schools of Public Affairs and Administration, and a fellow of the National Academy of Public Administration. His publications include *Rulemaking: How Government Agencies Write Law and Make Policy* (1994) and *How Washington Works* (3rd ed., 1997).

MAXINE KURTZ is currently a personnel and human resources consultant and an attorney specializing in employment law. She retired from the city and county of Denver after forty-three years in executive positions, including five years on the mayor's staff as program administrator and as evaluation administrator with the Denver Model Cities Program, and nineteen years with the Denver Career Service Authority. She is serving her sixth two-year term as a member of the Colorado Advisory Committee to the U.S. Commission on Civil Rights, including the statutory maximum of two terms as the committee chair. Kurtz has testified on civil rights and related issues before committees of the U.S. House of Representatives and the U.S. Senate. Her honors include being named to Pi Alpha Alpha, the honorary public administration society, in the outstanding public administrator category. She has also served on the National Council of the American Society for Public Administration.

THOMAS P. LAUTH is professor and department head, Department of Political Science, University of Georgia. He is a member of the Executive Council of the National Association of Schools of Public Affairs and Administration. He has served as president of the Georgia Political Science Association and as a member of the National Council of the American Society for Public Administration. Lauth earned his B.A. degree (1960) in government at the University of Notre Dame and his Ph.D. degree (1976) in political science from the Maxwell School at Syracuse University. His articles on governmental budgeting and on state and city administration have appeared in several academic journals, and he is coauthor of the *Politics of State and City Administration* (1986) and coeditor of *Governors, Legislatures, and Budgets: Diversity Across the American States* (1991).

RONALD C. MOE is currently specialist in government organization and management with the Congressional Research Service (CRS) of the Library of Congress. He received his Ph.D. degree (1968) in public law and government from Columbia University. Prior to joining CRS in 1973, he served in various positions in the executive branch, including senior policy advisor to the Cost of Living Council in the executive office of the president. Over the years, Moe has taught at various universities, including Columbia University, City University of New York, San Diego State University, and American University. His writings include books and articles in professional journals. In 1988, 1992, 1995, and 1996 he received the Louis Brownlow Award from the American Society for Public Administration for the annual best practitioner article in the *Public Administration Review*. In 1992, the secretary of state appointed Moe as commissioner to the Department of State's congressionally mandated Commission on Personnel. In 1993, Moe became a fellow at the Center for the Study of American Government at the Johns Hopkins University. He is also a fellow of the National Academy of Public Administration and is currently working on a book on institutional politics in the contemporary administrative state.

CHESTER A. NEWLAND is a teacher at the University of Southern California, where he is Frances R. and John J. Duggan Distinguished Professor of Public Administration. He is a member of the National Academy of Public Administration, an honorary member of the International City/County Management Association, a past national president of the American Society for Public Administration, and past editor in chief of the *Public Administration Review.* Previous government service included director of the Lyndon Baines Johnson Library; twice director of the Federal Executive Institute; city council member in Denton, Texas; and museum trustee in Sacramento, California. He received his B.A. degree (1954) in government from the University of North Texas and his M.A. (1955) and Ph.D. (1958) degrees in political science from the University of Kansas.

LLOYD G. NIGRO is professor in the Department of Public Administration and Urban Studies at Georgia State University, Atlanta. He received his B.A. degree (1965) from San Diego State College and his M.P.A. (1968) and Ph.D. (1972) degrees in public administration from the University of Southern California, Los Angeles. In addition to articles on varied aspects of public personnel policy, civil service management and reform, and administrative theory and ethics, Nigro has coauthored and edited several books, including *Modern Public Administration* (1990) and *The New Public Personnel Administration* (4th ed., 1994).

DAVID M. O'BRIEN is professor in the Department of Government and Foreign Affairs at the University of Virginia. He received his B.A. (1973), M.A. (1974), and Ph.D. (1977) degrees in political science from the University of California, Santa Barbara. He has been a judicial fellow at the U.S. Supreme Court, a visiting fellow at the Russell Sage Foundation, a Fulbright lecturer at Oxford University, and a Fulbright researcher in Japan. Among his many books and articles is *Storm Center: The Supreme Court in American Politics* (1992), which won the American Bar Association's Silver Gavel Award, and *To Dream of Dreams: Religious Freedom and Constitutional Politics in Postwar Japan* (1996).

ROSEMARY O'LEARY is associate professor of Public and Environmental Affairs at Indiana University. Previously she was on the faculty of the Department of Public Administration at the Maxwell School of Citizenship and Public Affairs at Syracuse University. She has won five national research awards and has published two books, a monograph, and nearly fifty articles on public management, law and public policy, bureaucratic politics, and environment and natural resources policy. She has served as chair of the Public Administration Section of the American Political Science Association.

LAURENCE J. O'TOOLE JR. is professor in the Department of Political Science and senior research associate of the Institute of Community and Area Development at the University of Georgia. He is the editor of *American Intergovernmental Relations* (1993), now in its second edition, and recipient of the Burchfield

(1979) and Moshers (1987) awards of the American Society for Public Administration. He received his B.S. degree (1970) in chemistry with high honors from Clarkson University and his M.P.A. (1972) and Ph.D. (1975) degrees in public administration from the Maxwell School of Syracuse University.

HAL G. RAINEY is professor of political science at the University of Georgia. He received his B.A. degree (1968) in English and psychology from the University of North Carolina at Chapel Hill and his M.A. degree (1972) in psychology and Ph.D. degree (1978) in public administration from the Ohio State University. In 1995, he received the Charles Levine Award for excellence in teaching, research, and service, conferred jointly by the American Society for Public Administration and the National Association of Schools of Public Affairs and Administration. His book *Understanding and Managing Public Organizations* (1991) won the 1992 Best Book Award of the Public and Nonprofit Sectors Division of the Academy of Management. A second edition was published in 1997.

NORMA M. RICCUCCI is associate professor of public administration and policy at the Rockefeller College of the University at Albany, State University of New York. She has published extensively in the areas of public personnel management, affirmative action, and public-sector labor relations. She is author of *Unsung Heroes: Federal Execucrats Making a Difference* (1995); coeditor of *Public Personnel Management: Current Concerns, Future Challenges* (1991, 1997); and coauthor of *Personnel Management in Government* (4th ed., 1992).

WILLIAM D. RICHARDSON is associate professor of political science and public administration at Georgia State University in Atlanta. He received his B.A. (1973), M.A. (1975), and Ph.D. (1979) degrees from the State University of New York at Buffalo. His articles on aspects of American government, political thought, and ethics have appeared in numerous journals and books, including *Administration and Society, Public Administration Review, Polity, Interpretation,* and *Public Voices.* His most recent book, *Democracy, Bureaucracy, and Character: Founding Thought,* is forthcoming from the University Press of Kansas.

HOLLY Taylor SELLERS is a doctoral candidate in political science at the University of Connecticut, Storrs, where her studies and research focus on public law, public administration, and public policy. She has published on human resources issues in the *Public Administration Review* and in *Judicature.* She served as Connecticut Superior Court Law Clerk from 1983 to 1984; as legal services counsel, office of the chief court administrator of Connecticut from 1984 to 1989; and as judicial performance evaluation administrator from 1992 to 1995. She received her B.A. degree (1978) from the State University of New York in Albany, her J.D. degree (1983) from Albany Law School, and her M.P.A. degree (1996) from the

University of Connecticut, Storrs. She was admitted to law practice in Connecticut (1983) and New York (1984).

JENNIFER A. UTTER is a Ph.D. candidate at the University of Kansas, Lawrence, and a law student at the University of Texas School of Law, Austin. She earned her B.A. degree (1992) in political science magna cum laude and her M.P.A. degree (1993) at the State University of New York, Albany.

CHARLES W. WASHINGTON is professor of public administration at Florida Atlantic University, former director of the John C. Stennis Institute of Government, and holder of the John C. Stennis Chair in Political Science at Mississippi State University. He is former associate dean, assistant dean for undergraduate and graduate programs, and chair of the Department of Public Administration, School of Government and Business Administration, George Washington University. He received his B.A. degree (1968) in political science and his M.P.A. degree (1970) from Florida Atlantic University. He received his Ph.D. degree (1976) in public administration from the Maxwell School, Syracuse University, and is a fellow of the National Academy of Public Administration.

PAUL WEILAND is a J.D. candidate at Harvard Law School. He received his B.A. degree (1992) in international relations and political science from the University of Southern California and his Ph.D. degree (1996) from the Joint Program in Public Policy of the School of Public and Environmental Affairs and the Department of Political Science at Indiana University, Bloomington. He has published a number of journal articles and book chapters on environmental law and policy.

CHARLES R. WISE is professor of public affairs in the School of Public and Environmental Affairs of Indiana University. He is currently president of the National Association of Schools of Public Affairs and Administration. He was formerly managing editor of the *Public Administration Review (PAR)*. He was awarded the William and Frederick Mosher Award in 1985, 1991, and 1992 for the best academic article published by *PAR*. Wise has also served in the U.S. Department of Justice, first as special assistant for policy analysis in the office of legislative affairs and later as director of intergovernmental relations (coordinating relationships with state and local officials). Wise's research is in the areas of public law and administration, public organization design and analysis, and legislative process. He is the author of *The Dynamics of Legislation: Leadership and Policy Change in the Congressional Process* (1991) and has published articles in *PAR*, *Journal of Public Administration Research and Theory (J-PART)*, the *Administrative Law Review*, *Public Administration Quarterly*, *Public Administration and Development*, the *Journal of Legislative Studies*, *Policy Studies Journal*, *Public Productivity Review*, and *Scandinavian Political Studies*.

Handbook of Public Law and Administration

PUBLIC LAW FOUNDATIONS OF AMERICAN PUBLIC ADMINISTRATION

Justice Oliver Wendell Holmes argued persuasively that theory is to the law what the foundation is to a building. That informed perspective defines theory as eminently practical. This handbook begins exactly there—with practical, basic foundations of law and public administration.

The chapters in Part One present three quite different but complementary discussions of basics. The frameworks presented are not simply alternative ways of thinking about the nature of law and its role in public administration, though they would be valuable if that were their only use. The authors go beyond that, however, and explain relationships among the central institutions and processes of law and public administration and why they sometimes function effectively together but at other times clash.

In the first chapter, Chet Newland revives discussion of the enduring principle that, paired with human dignity, is at the core of the American constitutional heritage: the *rule of law*. This principle refers especially to government under law and to an unending search for reasonableness as law's most basic norm. Such rule of law is at the heart of constitutionally based civilization. Without it, constitutions are mere words on paper, as they have been in many places. In such situations, judicial and administrative systems that are charged with facilitation of popular self governance through maintenance of reasonable law can be nothing more than political arms of the state and devices to enforce instruments of economic and other powers. However, in a fast-changing contemporary civilization with an informed sense of a rule of law, concepts like human

1

dignity, rights and liberties, and reasonableness can remain dynamic yet solidly based in practical theory.

Newland first examines the constitutional duty of the chief executive to "take care that the Laws be faithfully executed" (U.S. Constitution, Art. II, Sec. 3). Glaring failures in faithful execution have challenged the principle of a rule of law during the last third of the twentieth century. Even violations by top officials of laws and the rules of governmental institutions have become commonplace. These failures are associated with shifting paradigms of partisan and personal politics. Both law and public administration have been impacted adversely by the changed political culture.

Newland then analyzes the Americanization of law throughout the nation's history to demonstrate changing frameworks in the past and present. He probes the interconnections of law and culture, along with the emergence of the field of law as a relatively autonomous cultural force in the larger American context. A key question today is whether the nation functions essentially under its heritage of a rule of law or whether many norms now conflict with that ideal. Newland examines the cultures of today's politics and administration in that realistic context. Clearly, the conditions that contributed to emergence of public administration as a relatively autonomous field have greatly changed. Deterioration of shared cultural norms—the disciplines of democracy, including a rule of law— now threatens public administration as a field of expertise and professionalism.

In Chapter Two, Cornelius M. Kerwin also makes the case that law is not a force that threatens public administration; rather, it is central to the management task. Indeed, he argues, public management is about the business of carrying out and also shaping the law. Much of what administrative agencies do is concerned with accepting and understanding legal mandates, clarifying and explaining legal obligations and rights, enforcing the law in particular cases, and resolving disputes that come from those processes.

These are extremely dynamic processes in which public managers play many roles, from policymaker in rulemaking to investigator and enforcement officer to adjudicator in both formal and, more often, informal dispute resolution processes. Of these roles, Kerwin argues, probably the least well-understood dimension is how participation in and effects of the rulemaking process involve public managers. In fact, he contends, one of the great contemporary challenges for many public administrators is to manage the legal processes that agencies are charged by the legislature to operate. This challenge is all the more important when political leaders are pressing for reinvention and reengineering of government. Under these conditions, it is more important than ever for administrators not only to accept their legal roles and responsibilities but also to make diligent efforts to remain current on legal developments.

The waves of contemporary change include the need to develop ways to administer benefits and permit or licensing programs more acceptably and effectively, without sacrificing the basic concept of fundamental fairness and the more specific requirements of due process of law. Here, too, a challenge is to manage the legal process—in this case, adjudications. Achieving a mix of attitudes and process refinements is not a simple task in a time when contrary pressures exist to treat people with issues pending before agencies as customers and, at the same time, to develop and enforce provisions for such needs as environmental protection or prevention of welfare or Medicaid abuses.

Ronald C. Moe cautions in Chapter Three that the issues of balance and principle highlighted by Newland and Kerwin have not, in fact, been maintained at the forefront of public administration. It is precisely that problem, he contends, that has led to a host of difficulties. Ironically, at the very time when many advocates of public management reform have called for less attention to law, and even pointed at law as the core of contemporary problems in administration, it is more important than ever, Moe argues, to reinforce informed public law foundations of the field.

The fundamental public law cornerstones of public administration are constitutionally empowered and limited government. Sovereignty is distinctive in authority and commensurate responsibility. Moe argues that those who have popularized the concept of reinventing government, like David Osborne and Ted Gaebler, have created a false dichotomy between faithfulness to the public law cornerstones of public administration and responsiveness to contemporary needs and opportunities in public affairs.

Public agencies are, by their very nature, creatures of public law. Moe explains that neither performance nor accountability are ultimately achieved by establishing a framework of public law on the one hand and then making manifold exceptions to it in the interests of political or superficial managerial expediency on the other hand. There has been, Moe argues, a considerable history of that kind of parallel and inconsistent treatment of public law in public administration in recent decades, with unfortunate results. In the end, public law ought to be a creative instrument of constitutional government and, as such, a deeply ingrained part of the culture of public administration.

CHAPTER ONE

Faithful Execution of the Laws, Rule of Law, and Autonomy of Public Administration

Chester A. Newland

Public law and public administration ideally share common purposes: pursuit of effective constitutional government and facilitation of responsible self governance. Both fields seek to balance authority that is commensurate with desired social accomplishment with disciplines that assure broad responsibility and accountability to shared standards of reasonableness. Beyond these large purposes, compartmentalization of roles—both methods and norms—has characterized these fields within the frameworks of federalism and separation of powers in American government. Law has been ideally associated with well-reasoned adjudicatory fairness, defined according to standards of the times. Public administration has traditionally been identified more with scientifically objective and technical expertise associated with economy, efficiency, and effectiveness (including equity), which are also contingently defined.

Public law and public administration are both concerned with policy—its formulation, implementation, and other dynamics. And both are affected by and more or less embrace paradigms that acknowledge distinct arenas of politics for confirmation of performance and for interest accommodation through such democratic disciplines as participation, responsiveness, electoral accountability, and openness.

As dimensions of American constitutional democracy, both law and public administration are most fundamentally joined by norms of government under law (classically termed "rule of law") and popular self governance, at least in terms of jurisprudence and political theory. That connection was stronger before

5

the 1920s, when principal public administration leaders attempted to establish boundaries for the field apart from those of law. In the first through fourth editions of the textbook that dominated the field for decades, *Introduction to Public Administration,* Leonard White defined methods and norms that nearly isolated academic public administration from cutting-edge legal thought: "The book . . . assumes that the study of public administration should start from the base of management rather than the foundation of law, and is therefore more absorbed in the affairs of the American Management Association than the decisions of the courts" (White, 1926, p. xvi).

Today, methods and norms of both law and politics are considerably changed from what they were in the era when public administration emerged to become a relatively autonomous field. Public administration especially has changed dramatically since the 1960s, and it is now confronted with fundamental problems. Connections among changes in all three fields—law, politics, and public administration—are crucial. These connections are cogently illustrated in historical contexts of implementation of Article II, Section 3, of the Constitution, which directs the president to "take Care that the Laws be faithfully executed," and this chapter begins with a discussion of that directive. Contemporary failures in faithful execution may in turn be best understood in terms of applied theory of government under a rule of law and shifting paradigms of politics. In the next sections of the chapter, the Americanization of law and politics is the core subject, and it is connected to the most fundamental developments in public administration. A recurrent theme is that conditions, including respect for law by government officials, that once supported public administration as a relatively autonomous field are now greatly diminished and sometimes absent, especially at the national level of government. Another theme is that *the culture of a rule of law* in American society generally is gravely weakened.

FAITHFUL EXECUTION OF THE LAWS

The framers of the Constitution of the United States struggled thoughtfully about how to reconcile enhanced executive power and responsible government under law. Experience during the last third of the twentieth century demonstrates that they were wise to worry. Presidential government is a label frequently attached today to the American national political system, just as it was described in the nineteenth century as congressional government. Neither tag is correct in the American system of separated and shared powers. But persistent use of such labels highlights the durability of the founders' concerns: how to facilitate democratic self governance and effective representative government under a rule of law.

Practical Origins and Early Interpretations

Creation of an executive branch under the Constitution of the United States was not aimed at establishing a president with authority to act independently as the government. Addition of an executive branch was simply designed to remedy the great defect of government under the Articles of Confederation, which lacked effective means to enforce laws. The executive branch, in short, was created as a practical means to facilitate action within legal limits by one national government of the United States.

This practical purpose gave rise to the Constitution's Faithful Execution of the Laws Clause. At the constitutional convention in Philadelphia in 1787, the initial language of the Virginia Plan (the Randolph Plan) proposed "that a National Executive be instituted; to be chosen by the National Legislature," with "a general authority to execute the National Laws" (Madison, 1787, p. 21).The plan made clear the circumscribed character of the proposed officer: "to execute such powers, not legislative or judiciary in their nature, as may from time to time be delegated by the national legislative"(Madison, 1787, p. 63). Roger Sherman said that he "considered the Executive magistracy as nothing more than an institution for carrying the will of the Legislature into effect, that the person or persons ought to be appointed by and accountable to the Legislative only, which was the depository of the supreme will of the Society" (Madison, 1787, p. 65). The New Jersey Plan called for a plural executive with general authority to execute national laws. Greatest executive authority was proposed by the Hamilton Plan: "to have a negative on all laws about to be passed, and the execution of all laws passed" (Madison, 1787, p. 292). Finally, after all deliberations and stylistic drafting, the constitutional language emerged: "he shall take Care that the Laws be faithfully executed."

Presidential authority under this provision has been interpreted throughout American history as constrained, particularly by responsibilities and powers assigned by Congress to other governmental officers. In the First Congress, Madison stated that presidential responsibility is to ensure "good behavior" and to "superintend" executive officers for that purpose (U.S. Congress, 1789, pp. 379, 387). In 1823, President James Monroe wished to alter decisions of Treasury Department auditors and comptrollers. Attorney General William Wirt advised: "If the laws, then, require a particular officer by name to perform a duty, not only is that officer bound to perform it, but no other officer can perform it without a violation of law; and were the President to perform it, he would not only be not taking care that the laws be faithfully executed, but he would be violating them himself." Wirt concluded: "The Constitution assigns to Congress the power of designating the duties of particular officers: the President is only required to take care that they execute them faithfully" (U.S. Department of Justice, 1823, p. 625).

Contemporary Challenges and Controversies

The question of whether the president has all executive powers or whether others have such powers as are provided by law, with presidential authority limited to taking care that others execute the laws faithfully, has been answered by the courts mostly on the side of limitations of presidential power, with large exceptions in foreign and military affairs. A relatively recent example that relies on long-established doctrine is *Morrison v. Olson* (1988), in which the Supreme Court upheld provisions of the Ethics in Government Act of 1978 for appointment of independent counsel by a three-judge panel. Another best-known example is *United States v. Nixon* (1974), in which the Court allowed a special prosecutor, an employee of the executive branch, to sue his hierarchical superior, the president. Yet in spite of these examples, the twentieth-century history of American government has been one of presidential aggrandizement, and many court rulings have condoned that trend.

Arising out of that development, a large question today that would never even have been considered until recent decades is whether a president may ignore or refuse to obey statutes or court decisions. One aspect of this question has been clearly settled: the Department of Justice, representing the president, may challenge the constitutionality of statutes, as it successfully did in *Immigration and Naturalization Service v. Chadha* (1983). However, according to general interpretation, the president is not supposed to refuse to obey a statute. Yet questions from President Nixon's time remain today. In 1973, Nixon claimed an absolutely clear constitutional power to impound funds appropriated by Congress in the Clean Water Act of 1972. He had vetoed the Federal Water Pollution Act of 1972, and Congress overrode the veto. In *Train v. City of New York* (1975), the Supreme Court held that the president lacked authority to withhold funds mandated by Congress as public expenditures. However, the Court's statutory construction avoided a specific constitutional ruling.

Impoundment authority claimed by Nixon was traced back to Jefferson's decision in 1803 to inform Congress that he would not spend a $50,000 appropriation for gunboats after peace prevailed. After World War II, Presidents Truman, Eisenhower, and Kennedy invoked Jefferson's precedent to control defense spending. Lyndon Johnson went further, impounding funds upon advice of the attorney general that an appropriation act in itself is not a mandate to spend. Congress acquiesced in such presidential actions, allowing legislators to respond to pressures of special interests, knowing that the president might exercise discretion to correct some of the most egregious of congressional wastefulness. Nixon's acts went beyond the relatively benignly stylized game that preceded him, and the House briefly considered whether they were impeachable offenses. Congress finally sought, in the Budget and Impoundment Control Act of 1974, to limit impoundments.

The Reagan administration went further than ever before or since in assert-ing presidential power to ignore statutory provisions. The president's White House counsel, Fred F. Fielding, presented the administration's views as fol-lows: "There are times when the Administration has been accused of ignoring the law. But remember that the President is sworn to uphold both the Consti-tution and the laws. We seek to resolve conflicts. Strong Presidents especially are mindful of their responsibilities to those who come after them and seek to assure that they do not erode any executive prerogatives" (Tolchin, 1985, p. 19). Pursuant to such thinking, Reagan's director of the Office of Management and Budget acted on advice of the attorney general to direct executive depart-ments and agencies to disregard selected provisions of the Competition in Con-tracting Act. As observed later by the Court of Appeals, Third Circuit, Attorney General Meese asserted the "power of the executive branch . . . not to follow court decisions in this case. According to the Attorney General's testimony be-fore the House's Committee on the Judiciary on April 18, 1985, the district court is not a 'court of competent jurisdiction' to decide constitutional ques-tions" (*Ameron, Inc.* v. *United States Army Corps of Engineers,* 1986, pp. 889–890). With respect to judicial authority, the Court of Appeals said, "It should be too obvious even to require restating that the district court, as an Article III court, has the power to rule on the constitutionality of an act of Congress and to impose appropriate remedies to compel compliance with an act found to be constitutional (p. 890). With respect to the Reagan administration's assertions of executive power, the Court of Appeals said: "This claim of right for the Pres-ident to *declare* statutes unconstitutional and to declare his refusal to execute them, as distinguished from his undisputed right to veto, criticize, or even re-fuse to defend in court, statutes which he regards as unconstitutional is dubi-ous at best" (p. 889).

In essence, President Reagan sought in this instance to exercise a nonexis-tent item veto power well after a statute became law, and his administration sought a writ of certiorari from the U.S. Supreme Court, which was granted March 21, 1988. That writ was dismissed October 19, 1988, however, upon the government's embarrassed withdrawal, leaving the forceful language of the Court of Appeals standing.

Nonetheless, other means of executive aggrandizement have persisted, including enactment of a so-called Line Item Veto Act, signed April 9, 1996, which grants enhanced budget-recision authority to the president. While that act faces a certain constitutional challenge in the courts, other inventive appli-cations of presidential authority are exercised. Increasingly, upon approving enacted legislation, presidents have sought through commentary to stamp it with their own meanings. This has included taking exceptions to enforceability of particular provisions.

Faithfulness to a Rule of Law?

As indicated in the foregoing discussion, questions about faithful execution of the laws have commonly concerned means of enforcement of laws and management of conflicts among the three branches over their respective powers. Since the Nixon years, however, concerns have focused increasingly on failures by public officials to observe a rule of law as an underlying norm of American constitutional government. Failures to observe standards of reasonableness that define a government under law have come to characterize the national government to such an extent that a traditional focus on constitutional interpretation of faithful execution of the laws no longer suffices to explain governmental realities. In the 1970s and 1980s, questions increasingly arose about whether officials may properly put self interests and partisan loyalties, especially to the president, above responsibility to a rule of law (Newland, 1987).

Spoils and corruption during the final three decades of the twentieth century ranged from Vice President Spiro Agnew accepting bagman payoffs at his office to the illegal or unethical use of public authority by numerous appointees of President Reagan and some appointees of President Clinton to pursue self interests. Defense contract scandals were large and sustained over many years. Major scandals of the Executive Office of the President (EOP) and the White House Office included Watergate under Nixon and the Iran-Contra Affair under Reagan. During the 1996 presidential race, several violations of campaign finance laws by the Clinton campaign involved close, long-time associates of the president who were given influential governmental and party appointments and frequent White House access. Crime and ethical failures ran deeply in Congress as well, from corrupt aides to former Speaker of the House John McCormack to later Speaker Jim Wright, and to a great multitude of members of Congress in the House Bank and Post Office scandals of the 1990s, not to mention senatorial misdeeds. Admitted ethical failures by Speaker Newt Gingrich, aired during 1996 and 1997, kept alive concerns about endemic corruption of the political system.

The changed norm with respect to a rule of law was reflected in a stark difference between the Johnson and Carter administrations in loyalty expected of career civil servants. As recently as the Johnson administration, first loyalty to the law was the espoused standard, in a framework of expertise, professionalism, and political neutrality. In the Carter administration, building on Nixon's precedents, first loyalty to the president defined common expectations, in line with control of civil service norms by the newly created, partisanly directed Office of Personnel Management (OPM). Communications between the presidentially controlled bureaucracy and Congress became centralized in partisan appointees. Such presidentially partisan developments have increased ever since.

Essentially, these changes reflect conflicts between norms and methods associated with government under a rule of law and the norms and methods of today's fragmented, partisan, demolition politics, characterized by Robert A. Dahl as political disorder (Dahl, 1994). Public administration is caught between these forces, and all three fields—law, politics, and administration—are in some turbulence.

CHANGING FRAMEWORKS OF AMERICAN LAW

To comprehend contemporary issues of faithful execution of the laws and a rule of law, it is useful to review norms and methods of law, especially observing the interconnections of law to culture and how those interconnections relate to politics and administration. For that purpose, it is important first to recall America's initial vision of constitutional fundamentals. It is also especially useful to understand Americanization of law during the industrial revolution, including the development of frameworks of analytical jurisprudence. The impacts of legal realism, sociological jurisprudence, and related political theory on American perceptions of law are also crucial. Ultimately, it is necessary to understand interactions of law as a relatively autonomous cultural force in the larger American culture. Today a key question is, Does the nation function essentially under a rule of law or do many of its components behave in some conflict with that fundamental norm?

America's Initial Constitutional Vision

Popular sovereignty and limited government emerged as America's fundamental political vision out of the revolutionary era during the last third of the eighteenth century. Limited government had been established earlier as an ideal, beginning in Magna Carta. Its foundations were greatly strengthened four hundred years later in seventeenth-century England and the Glorious Revolution. But *popular sovereignty developed in America as the most revolutionary principle of government ever conceived.* The idea that took root during the American Revolution grew quickly, branching in two directions. The first idea was that people are capable of *self governance,* without need of much government, let alone oversight by royalty, nobility, or an officially established church. The second idea was that people are capable of exercising ultimate (if not direct) control over the limited government required to facilitate self governance to accomplish community and individual needs.

Thus, popular sovereignty and limited government became two branches of one constitutional principle—America's most basic legal framework. This two-part principle became, in turn, a defining cultural foundation of American law, characterized by an endless struggle to balance freedom and responsibility and to reconcile change and stability. But it also came to be dealt with sometimes as an equation of disorder and order, and often, in practical fact, as repetitive conflict between lawlessness and keeping the peace.

The struggle for public law in America, in short, started most crucially as a search for legal means both to empower and to limit responsibly effective government, rather than to use government as a means to limit people, either as individuals or as communities. The post-Enlightenment culture of America later moved far from these roots, followed, not led, by its law. Nonetheless, these fundamental ideas remained vital in the nation's continuing revolutionary and frontier mythologies, and they survive in space-age memory and imagination.

Nineteenth-Century Americanization of Law

The Enlightenment that culminated in the American Revolution was soon displaced by the commerce, technology, and urban settlement of the Industrial Revolution. Unprecedented aggregations of resources—capital, labor, and other means of production and trade—were embraced as necessary, and creativity to match these new aspirations became the challenge of law and its "Americanization." In response, the life of the law for more than a century became largely acculturated to industry and demographic concerns (Hall, Wiecek, and Finkelman, 1991).

As this new era started, both states and the newly formed U.S. government involved themselves directly in the economy, supporting commercial developments. New York's Erie Canal was merely the most visible of widespread state encouragement of commercial economies. The new federal government joined these efforts, adopting protective tariffs, supporting transportation, and establishing a national bank. But by the 1830s, advocates of laissez faire started displacing the older laws of states and Congress with "the laws of the marketplace." Within the next two decades, contracts came out of relative obscurity to dominate private law. In the same period, certain wrongful acts moved to the forefront as torts, becoming a distinctive practice of law. During the next two antebellum decades, courts commonly limited business liabilities for industrial accidents, lost or damaged goods, and harmful products and practices.

Despite the rapid rise of industrialization, agriculture remained the dominant economic force until after the Civil War. But market agriculture increasingly dominated, displacing the economic importance of family farms, which often functioned as relatively self-sufficient units. Before the end of the nineteenth century, manufacturing became the greatest force of economic growth. Men increasingly worked *separate and apart* from women and children, who became identified more often as family dependents and less as economic assets. Following the changing workplace demography, law expanded into domestic relations, formerly an arena of quite limited government involvement.

The end of bond slavery following the Civil War also fundamentally affected workplace and social demography, jolting a culture built on legal protection of slavery through turbulent reconstruction and into an era of *separate but equal* statutes, sanctioned by the U.S. Supreme Court in *Plessy* v. *Ferguson* (1896). White supremacy and inferior public accommodations for nonwhites followed throughout most of the South and in many other places. Race, always central in American law, thus continued as a strong basis for separating people, who were also being driven apart according to gender and generations by industrial workplace demography and its proliferating legal frameworks.

Problems of culture and law became further compounded by changes in immigration. In the 1880s, more than 40 percent of the nation's population growth was from a great influx of foreign-born people, most from cultures visibly different from the American past. Many late-nineteenth-century immigrants became ghettoized in cities. This separation became associated with urban poverty, disease, crime, and some rioting. Control through criminal justice systems became one approach to cope with these problems, initiating what has become one of the largest and most costly fields of public law. Private and public social services, especially parochial and public education and epidemiological health, constituted other strategies, associated in part with the melting-pot ideal of ethnic assimilation and Americanization. But a new separation—by class—became an embedded idea, intensifying in the first third of the twentieth century, the global era of "isms."

Thus, the nineteenth century left a heritage of diversity, growing social contentiousness, and contradictory commitments to individual inequality and economic and social separation. Stimulus and response characterized relationships of law, the economy, and society, as Americans increasingly sought to solve social problems through legal force. Analytical jurisprudence dominated the nineteenth century and the first decades of the next one, defining law as a command of a political superior (none so forceful as the popular sovereign) to a political inferior (none so weak as the segregated), enforced by material sanctions. In the hands of legislators and judges, this most often translated into economic laissez faire and negative social controls. Nationwide, but most often chronicled memorably in culture-defining frontier history and fiction of the Wild West, this approach often translated into gunsmoke mixed with sweat from hard toil, considerable entrepreneurial adventure, and frequent private and public greed and corruption. These images became mythical symbols of American culture that still serve today as mainstays of movies and television and affect the culture of private and public law. They were among the roots from which public administration grew, and they remain important.

Changed Rhetoric About Law: Realism and Purpose

Historical jurisprudence and new empiricism combined to challenge analytical thinking, as in Oliver Wendell Holmes Jr.'s observation in *The Common Law* that the life of the law has not been logic but experience (Holmes, 1881). But in response to the inherited culture and reactions to it, the most dramatic change in the rhetoric of law during the first half of the twentieth century was a movement toward realism and, more substantially, toward sociological jurisprudence.

Louis Brandeis most notably signaled coming changes in his successful legal assault on laissez faire in *Muller* v. *Oregon* (1908), arguing *ex facto jus oritur* to win judicial notice of findings advanced by the social sciences (also the stuff of the new field of public administration), reaching beyond narrow facts about hours of female employment in this particular case. Through reliance on scientific research, the famous Brandeis brief in the Muller case established enormously new directions in Americanization of law that were not embraced in such Commonwealth countries as Australia and Canada until the 1950s (Newland, 1961). The sociological jurisprudence that followed struggled to achieve important influence by the late 1930s in the New Deal revolution in decisions of the Supreme Court, becoming dominant later in such cases as *Brown* v. *Board of Education of Topeka* (1954), ending approval of the "separate but equal" doctrine for public schools.

Legal realism, at its origins, was shocking in its frankness. Even Benjamin Nathan Cardozo, no far-out militant despite some perceptions, described conscious and unconscious processes by which judges decide cases as follows: "I take judge-made law as one of the existing realities of life. There, before us, is the brew. Not a judge on the bench but has had a hand in the making" (Cardozo, 1921, pp. 10–11). Such a metaphor in the midst of Prohibition! That aside, Cardozo's more fundamental point, lost upon militant activists and other inattentive readers, was that, while it is inevitable that judges make law, no judge has authority intentionally to decide cases subjectively. Cardozo embraced the new sociological jurisprudence with restraint, also clinging to historical, philosophical, and analytical standards as essential guides in decision making. He sought to sustain authoritative boundaries of law in a socially turbulent era by stressing disciplines to justify autonomy of the judicial process.

Such conceptions of a distinctive identity of law as a relatively autonomous force of civilized culture persisted through the remainder of the twentieth century. Cardozo addressed the judicial process. However, roles and disciplines of public administrators and others with responsibilities for interpretation and application of law fit similarly within the boundaries of this discourse. It is fundamental rhetoric of constitutional democracy that addresses legitimacy questions directly but that also probes more deeply, as Cardozo did, into the authority of actions of public officials. This rhetoric confronts political and moral questions in terms of their reasonableness, based broadly in disciplined human experience.

Political Theory: Shared Culture and a Rule of Law

The foregoing sketch of earlier American conceptions of law highlights both fundamental roots in culture generally and law's relative autonomy as an importantly differentiated cultural methodology—a distinctive field of the humanities and social sciences. Public administration shares those characteristics, but with some of its own distinctive differentiations as a field.

Both law and public administration draw on political theory beyond jurisprudence to define a rule of law that is basic to both. Each reaches beyond defining the boundary and legitimacy questions of its field to deeper issues of authority and purpose. And political theory informs both fields similarly as to meanings of a rule of law.

Law and public administration both find basic understanding, for example, in Plato's allegory of the cave. That broadly shared story goes as far as any in Western civilization to explain *the search for reasonableness* that is now widely accepted as fundamental to procedural and substantive dimensions of a rule of law. It also conveys appreciation of humility as a human virtue in the continuous discipline of inquiry that ideally characterizes both law and public administration. As classical philosophy aspired to disciplines of science, art, and politics, law and public administration ideally draw on those and more in today's aspirations for reasonableness in their struggles for constitutional government and facilitation of self governance. The effort to do so is an endless struggle in which problems need to be and commonly are solved, at costs of time, effort, and other resources. But the struggle—the problem—remains unresolved, caught in convictions of those informed by experience and other relevant disciplines that a rule of law is elusive. Any judge or public administrator who thinks that that ideal has been finally accomplished beyond disciplined efforts to be reasonable in each case at hand has only achieved standing as a gold-plated egotist.

These understandings of a rule of law in today's political theory draw on many successors to Plato, particularly such Enlightenment thinkers as John Locke, Thomas Jefferson, and James Madison and such later philosopher-historians as Alexis de Tocqueville ([1835] 1966), Carl Friedrich (1963), and James MacGregor Burns (1978). These understandings are also advisedly tested and refined, however, against contemporary cases, both those that remain invisibly routine and such dramatic examples as those identified earlier. Consider Watergate and Iran-Contra in the 1970s and 1980s and examples from the 1990s, such as the Rodney King and O. J. Simpson cases in Los Angeles, the 1995 Packwood case in the U.S. Senate, the 1995 federal building bombing case in Oklahoma (not even tried until 1997, and then in Colorado, far from the most affected victims), the 1996–1997 Kaczynski Unabomer cases, and contemporary congressional and private militia criticisms of the Federal Bureau of Investigation and the Bureau of Alcohol, Tobacco, and Firearms for their handling of illegal armaments cases in Waco, Texas, in Ruby Ridge, Idaho, and around Jordan, Montana.

To appreciate such complexities in America's contemporary struggles for a rule of law, reflect again on when popular sovereignty and limited government became joined as one fundamental principle in creation of the Constitution of the United States. As noted earlier, popular sovereignty emerged over a relatively short period of years as the most revolutionary idea ever in political theory. Diversity among the original thirteen states and their populations added to inherent challenges in that principle in the creation of one nation. But compared to multicultural America today, the original United States shared a relatively common culture, including embrace of Enlightenment standards for a rule of law. As complexities among the popular base of sovereignty increased with demographic changes in the nineteenth century, standards in law shifted toward freedom for commerce and social controls over people.

Greater demographic changes and exceptions to shared culture pose today's large challenges:

- In the absence of more or less broadly shared culture, as illustrated in the examples cited earlier, is a constitutional system based in significant part on popular sovereignty viable?

- Given its cultural dimensions, illustrated in the earlier discussion of nineteenth-century Americanization of law, is a rule of law viable in the absence of shared cultural values and disciplines of self governance and constitutionally empowered and limited government?

- More specifically, is it possible today for politicians, street people, students, businesspeople, immigrants, beach people, public administrators, and others of diverse cultures to share in a rule of law?

CULTURES OF POLITICS AND ADMINISTRATION

During the fifty years after its acknowledged emergence in the 1880s, American public administration, like law at the time, became more or less idealized as an autonomous field occupied at key points by politically neutral experts and disciplined by authoritative standards of professional discourse that justified a distinct identity and legitimated its actions. But by the last decades of the twentieth century, some bets on those assumptions were off. A form of realism, both theoretical and practical, started to overtake public administration by the late 1940s

respect by the 1930s and continuing into the late 1960s were penetrated by group-based politics of a new age.

Several factors contributed to the renewed domination by transactional politics in pursuit of self interests and its negative impacts on civic culture through the 1990s. Clearly, politics as a marketlike exchange in support of special interests and personal aggrandizement had persisted throughout reform decades, often exercising decisive power, just as transformational ideals persist today, though relatively neglected in political practice. But starting in the elections of the 1950s, then dominating in the national elections of 1968 and mushrooming thereafter, expensive costly primary and general election campaigns, voter mistrust and independence, and political action committees combined with other negative forces to subject politicians and their parties to tradition-shattering pressures.

An inheritance from the 1960s was Balkanization of Congress in a period of dramatic rise of expensive, special-interest-dominated politics. Congressional campaign committees of each party slightly moderated that development in the 1980s for some individuals but not for the institution. The Republican takeover of the House in 1995, along with control of the Senate, followed by continued GOP leadership in the 105th Congress dramatically reduced fragmentation on the Hill. High-cost exchange politics continued, however.

Presidential electoral politics changed more dramatically than electoral politics at other levels, starting with John Kennedy's nomination through primaries, and the impacts have been greatest on public administration and on the culture of a rule of law. Presidential primaries drastically changed the nominating process by 1960, subsequently converting national party conventions into media extravaganzas for previously anointed candidates (as in both the Republican and Democratic conventions of 1996). Every presidential candidate since 1960 has been forced, in competition with others of the same ostensible party (not to mention multiple ventures of opposing party candidates), to raise enormous funds or draw on personal and family wealth, and to manage means of continuous and shifting coalition formation and maintenance. To win, in short, an electoral finance and campaign machine that is largely the loyal property of the candidate (or vice versa) is required. Upon winning, not only the newly elected president but the machine takes over the executive branch, and the next campaign starts in today's context of relatively nondeliberative, plebiscitary politics (Dahl, 1994). As a result, a new spoils era of presidential partisanship now characterizes American national government, driving presidents to seek to govern by campaigning, trapped in what Charles Jones has described as a "distorted view of the president as the government" (Jones, 1996, p. 6).

Two dimensions of today's presidential spoils are most crucial for public administration and for prospects of a rule of law. First, increasing numbers of presidential loyalists now occupy the ranks of public service. Paul Light, in his book, *Thickening Government,* documented expansion of positions over which the president is the "one true master" from "451 in 1960 to 2,393 in 1992, a 430 percent increase" (Light, 1995, p. 7). Furthermore, Light found thickening layers of political appointees: "thirty-two layers, of which seventeen existed in at least half of the departments" (p. 7). Second, unlike the congressionally dominated spoils that early national reformers fought, presidential spoils are rarely for ongoing tenure in executive branch jobs. These political appointees commonly seek briefer power to direct the policies and resources of today's enormous government. Financial impacts on special interests of policy alternatives are often worth millions and billions of dollars; procurement and service contracts are also worth millions and billions; visible access to power and glory are worth something to many; presidential loyalists now preside over these affairs not only at top policy levels but increasingly at operating levels once occupied by politically neutral, expert, professional civil servants; and gratitude is easy to express with or without violations of existing laws and rules, including politically written campaign finance provisions and "ethical" codes. Recall the shabby reelection finances of President Clinton, noted earlier. This is today's tune of presidential exchange politics. While it continuously plays, harmonics resound from Capitol Hill and from similar transactional politics at other levels across the country.

The U.S. Supreme Court has contributed importantly to the impoverishment of political parties' former powers over primaries, ballot access, districting, and finance. The Court has embraced notions of group-based politics and representation that came to dominate American political science and politics by the 1950s and 1960s. This endorsement has supported compartmentalization rather than connectedness in political representation and leadership (Ryden, 1996).

Failed Boundaries and Authority of Public Administration

Today's exchange politics and its new spoils negatively affect both public administration and a rule of law. The boundaries of public administration have been penetrated, greatly diminishing its autonomy. Although relative autonomy of the field of law remains strong, the culture of a rule of law has been greatly diminished in politics and in the nation generally, as discussed in the first section of this chapter.

In its creation, public administration gained autonomy as a field in large part because of the politics-administration dichotomy (notwithstanding its complexity and contradictions) and the associated principle of civil service neutrality. As noted, these boundary setters were not embraced by reformers as an escape from politics; realists understood necessities of ongoing politics of reform. But a formula was required to facilitate public administration by professional experts within the constitutional framework of separation of powers (O'Toole, 1987). At local government levels, that formula became possible in many places through elimination of the separation-of-powers principle in favor of council-manager government—a modified parliamentary structure with ultimate authority concentrated in the hands of elected legislators (Newland, 1995). At the state and national levels, such fundamental institutional change was impossible. But the practice of relatively autonomous public administration within the executive branch was possible if its culture was politically neutral, if it functioned under shared legislative and executive oversight, and if administration was characterized as implementation of authoritatively established policies.

That last condition was seldom narrowly limiting in practice. Even early on, authoritative sources included not only constitutional provisions, statutes, court cases, and administrative rules and precedents but also scientific and technical expertise, as reflected in Justice Holmes's empiricism and later thinking in sociological jurisprudence. Unfortunately, academic public administration increasingly cut itself off from cutting-edge thinking in law, even administrative law, limiting understanding of such practically applied theory. That, in turn, eventually limited the field's authoritative base. On top of that, lawyers filled many of the catbird seats of expanding, positive government.

More visibly serious were assaults on the boundaries that defined public administration and allowed it relative autonomy. These onslaughts initially came in three waves from within the field itself. First, public administration leaders stressed separation of powers rather than shared legislative-executive authority, and they identified themselves and the field with *the executive* (as in the Brownlow Report and in the behaviors of careerists in the Bureau of the Budget inner sanctum of the EOP, where Congress, with its alleged meddling, often seemed cast as the enemy in routine rhetoric). Eventually, this left the field wide open to a new era of presidentially dominant spoils. Another assault on public administration's boundaries came as rejection of the dichotomy of politics-administration, starting in the late 1940s when inquiry increasingly turned to effectiveness issues and continuities in policy formulation and implementation (Newland, 1987, 1991, 1995). It became easy for critics to misinterpret new theory and its applications—and to conclude that if public administration consists most essentially of policy and politics, politicians, not career bureaucrats, should dominate the field. A third wave from within the field, developing in the 1950s and moving to the forefront in the 1960s, was public employee militancy and unionization, followed by collective bargaining and rejection of political neutrality and such limits as the Hatch Acts. This internal assault had strong allies from outside public administration, and it was more telling in local and state governments than nationally. But at all levels it was a major cultural change away from public service values in the field of public administration, and important old boundaries of autonomy largely crumbled.

With its former boundaries of autonomy in growing disarray by the end of the 1960s, public administration became easy pickings for the new spoils of transactional presidential politics—and that made assault on the culture of a rule of law easy also. The onslaught at the national level started visibly under President Nixon; under EOP reorganization, the Office of Management and Budget as successor to the Bureau of Budget became staffed with presidential partisans four levels down; the newly created Office of Policy Development, "Hatched" in law, was nonetheless partisanly political under John Ehrlichman; and appointments of presidential partisans became accepted at both headquarters and field levels of agencies. Documents released by the National Archives in late 1996 and early 1997 revealed, for example, Nixon's instructions on May 13, 1971, to appoint a new commissioner of Internal Revenue: "I want to be sure he is a ruthless son of a bitch, that he will do what he's told, that every income-tax return I want to see I see, that he will go after our enemies and not go after our friends" (Lardner, 1997, p. A8). All of that was just for starters, along with illegal impoundment of Clean Water Act funds for presidentially partisan purposes. That in turn was a warmup of sorts for Watergate. *So much for a rule of law!*

The Civil Service Reform Act (CSRA) of 1978 eliminated bipartisan leadership of national civil service and reduced the effectiveness of shared congressional-presidential oversight. The newly created OPM, headed by presidential partisans, quickly became politically dominated. Only five bipartisan political positions were in the former U.S. Civil Service Commission; no partisans were in the management or operating structures. More than thirty partisans were present in OPM under Carter and Reagan following implementation of the 1978 law, and that partisan tendency continued under a greatly diminished agency thereafter.

The Senior Executive Service (SES), created by Title IV of CSRA, erased most boundaries between career executives and noncareerists, including partisan and limited-term appointees. It did provide that no less than 85 percent of SES positions must be held by careerists, but it left to mostly political decisions which positions are to be reserved for careerists, facilitating placement of partisan appointees in positions to maximize partisan political advantage.

WEAKENED CULTURES OF PUBLIC ADMINISTRATION AND A RULE OF LAW

America's vision of self-governing people exercising ultimate sovereignty over constitutionally empowered and limited government has been challenged by complexities throughout history. Inherent contradictions in the ideals combined in this and other constitutional principles have been reconciled during most periods through *a shared culture of a rule of law.* The nineteenth century greatly tested durability of government of a large nation based on such idealism, and enormous changes followed the Industrial Revolution, the Civil War, and post-centennial reform movements. Americanization of law established it as a relatively autonomous field—a subculture ideally in support of a rule of law, variously defined according to times that often included corruption in politics, business, and government.

The centennial era introduced renewed vision of transformational idealism, and reform periods that followed ushered in important changes. These were largely complimentary movements in politics and law. The reformers also created public administration as a new field to facilitate practical government attuned to transformational ideals. Boundaries were established to make possible relative autonomy of public administration, different from both law and electoral politics, but as one among these three integrally related fields.

By the 1970s, conditions that supported the development and practice of professionally expert public administration deteriorated. Both politics and law became increasingly group-based and focused on winning by almost any means and costs, and less oriented to civic transformation and reasonableness. From within the field, the boundaries of public administration had already been made permeable by the close of the 1960s, and they fell in the next thirty years under pressures of transactional politics. These changes are dramatically evident with respect to the constitutional provision for faithful execution of the law. But they are also present in business, government, and American society in general, reflecting an absence of shared disciplines of constitutional democracy.

Self governance and a rule of law survive as theoretical ideals of American culture in support of human dignity and a search for reasonableness. However, disorderly contemporary practices in politics, law, and public administration gravely challenge the durability of these fundamentals of constitutional democracy.

Cases Cited

Ameron, Inc. v. *United States Army Corps of Engineers,* 787 F2d 875 (3d Circ.) (1986).

Brown v. *Board of Education of Topeka,* 347 U.S. 483 (1954).

Immigration and Naturalization Service (INS) v. *Chadha,* 462 U.S. 919 (1983).

Morrison v. *Olson,* 487 U.S. 654 (1988).

Muller v. *Oregon,* 408 U.S. 412 (1908).

Plessy v. *Ferguson,* 163 U.S. 537 (1896).

Train v. *City of New York,* 420 U.S. 35 (1975).

United States v. *Nixon,* 418 U.S. 683 (1974).

References

Burns, J. M. *Leadership.* New York: HarperCollins, 1978.

Cardozo, B. N. *The Nature of the Judicial Process.* New Haven, Conn.: Yale University Press, 1921.

Dahl, R. A. *The New American Political (Dis)order.* Berkeley: Institute of Governmental Studies, University of California, 1994.

Friedrich, C. J. *Philosophy of Law in Historical Perspective.* Chicago: University of Chicago Press, 1963.

Hall, K. L., Wiecek, W. M., and Finkelman, P. *American Legal History.* New York: Oxford University Press, 1991.

Holmes, O. W. Jr. *The Common Law.* Cambridge, Mass.: Lowell Lectures, Harvard University, 1881.

Jones, C. O. "The Clinton Administration in a Separated System: A Presidency at Risk?" *extensions* (Journal of the Carl Albert Research and Studies Center, University of Oklahoma), Spring 1996, pp. 3–9.

Lardner, G. Jr. "Nixon Sought Hatchet Man to Run IRS, Tapes Reveal." *Sacramento Bee,* Jan. 4, 1997, p. A8.

Light, P. C. *Thickening Government: Federal Hierarchy and the Diffusion of Accountability.* Washington, D.C.: Brookings Institution, 1995.

Madison, J. *Journal: Records of the Federal Convention,* Vol. 1. Philadelphia: Convention Records, 1787.

Newland, C. A. "Innovation in Judicial Technique." *Southwestern Social Science Quarterly,* 1961, *42,* 22–31.

Newland, C. A., "Public Executives: Bicentennial Leadership Challenges." *Public Administration Review,* 1987, *47,* 45–56.

Newland, C. A. "Faithful Execution of the Law and Empowering Public Confidence." *Presidential Studies Quarterly,* 1991, *21,* 673–686.

Newland, C. A. "Managing from the Future in Council-Manager Government." In H. G. Frederickson (ed.), *Ideal and Practice in Council-Manager Government.* (2nd ed.) Washington, D.C.: International City Management Association, 1995.

O'Toole, L. J. Jr. "Doctrines and Developments: Separation of Powers, the Politics-Administration Dichotomy, and the Rise of the Administrative State." *Public Administration Review,* 1987, *47,* 17–25.

Ryden, D. K. *Representation in Crisis: The Constitution, Interest Groups, and Political Parties.* Albany: State University of New York Press, 1996.

Tocqueville, A. de. *Democracy in America* (G. Lawrence, trans.; J. P. Mayer, ed.). New York: Doubleday, 1966. (Originally published 1835.)

Tolchin, M. "As Laws Are Flouted, Congress Seethes." *New York Times,* Nov. 13, 1985, p. 19, col. 3.

U.S. Congress. *Annals of Congress,* Vol. 1, 1789.

U.S. Department of Justice. *Opinions of the Attorney General,* Vol. 1, 1823.

White, L. D. *Introduction to Public Administration.* (1st–4th eds.) Old Tappan, N.J.: Macmillan, 1926, 1939, 1948, 1954.

CHAPTER TWO

Public Law and Public Management

A Conceptual Framework

Cornelius M. Kerwin

It is useful for public managers to adopt vantage points different from those most often presented in public law treatises, casebooks, and texts. When the common ground that joins administrative law and public management is explored, one usually considers how legal obligations come to reside with agencies of government, how agencies have responded, what conflicts their stewardship of these responsibilities have fostered, and how, if at all, they have been resolved, most often by courts but with important roles for the other constitutional branches. This general framework is not the only approach one can find in the literature, but it has dominated consideration of the meeting ground between law and administration (Rosenbloom and O'Leary, 1996). It enjoys high status for a variety of reasons, the most compelling being the profoundly important insights it has yielded about fundamental mechanisms of a representative democracy grounded in the rule of law.

The framework offered here is more instrumental than the dominating framework because it concentrates heavily (but not solely) on the managerial and administrative infrastructures in agencies of government that receive and process the legal obligations transferred to them. While it may be less profound than the perspectives that go to the very heart of the constitutional system, the view offered here may also promote a fuller understanding of the sometimes titanic clashes of interests and authority from which the political and legal systems have grown. This view starts with the critical and sometimes ignored fact that law is, after all, what the whole of public administration is about. America's ongoing experiment in self governance depends heavily on the ability of structures and processes housed in and sometimes fashioned by bureaucracies to achieve the constitutional goals. The sometimes homely, occasionally obscure and underappreciated functions of the law of public management are easily lost in the midst of broad theoretical debates about the role of law and government in personal and national lives. Still, the symbiosis of law and management expresses itself innumerable times in the daily activities of thousands of government agencies. This framework describes the legal boundaries of public managers' working environments.

The perspective offered here is best termed *the management of law*. The term is inspired by John Rohr's phrase, "to run a constitution" (Rohr, 1986). It suggests that the law is a function performed by public agencies, albeit their most important activity. As an agency function, the management of law occurs in stages and has definable results. At its roots, the framework consists of four interrelated agency functions that require managerial direction and administrative support if an agency is to meet its legal obligations. These are:

1. Receipt and comprehension of legal authority
2. Clarification and specification of legal authority, obligations, and rights
3. Application of the law to appropriate persons and actions
4. Resolution of disputes that arise under legal authority

The relationships among these subjects and more familiar topics in administrative law and public management will soon be apparent, if they are not already. Space and the current state of knowledge do not allow full explanation of all the major subjects and issues. Instead, the endeavor here is to produce a reasonably complete inventory of the main activities associated with each of the four functions agencies must perform to manage the law.

RECEIPT AND COMPREHENSION OF LEGAL AUTHORITY

Agencies of government commonly receive legal authority and obligations from statutes written by legislators, whether they are creating agencies, authorizing new programs, establishing standards and procedures, or appropriating funds to get the job done. They may also be required to respond to mandates found in judicial decisions and executive orders, both of which carry the force of law. The question of delegation and the use of delegated authority has long been a prominent topic in the literature and discourse devoted to administrative law (Davis, 1975). A new framework for the study of the relationship between public law and administration should not sacrifice any understanding of delegation, but it should also include aspects of the transfer of legal authority by legislatures to agencies that usually command less attention than their current importance merits. Such a framework must direct considerable attention to certain aspects of the transfer of legal obligations to agencies from courts, and it must treat all elements of executive orders, that is, directions from the chief executive (president, governor, mayor, city manager, and so on).

The standard treatment of delegation includes a general definition of the term and some coverage of the famous New Deal cases that led to Supreme Court repudiation of the delegation scheme contained in the National Industrial Recovery Act. Briefly, these decisions found legislative delegations unconstitutional because they transferred authority without sufficient definition or constraints to prevent misunderstanding or abuse by the receiving agencies (*Schechter Poultry Corporation* v. *United States,* 1935; *Panama Refining Company* v. *Ryan,* 1935). The standard frameworks then focus on the factors that contributed to the eventual judicial acceptance of quite broad and frequently ill-defined grants of authority by legislatures, and conclude with contemporary standards that emphasize the responsibilities of receiving agencies when delegations of authority lack sufficient definition (*Amalgamated Meat Cutters and Butcher Workmen* v. *Connally,* 1971). Clear statements of policy that inform the public by the agency charged with filling the gaps in statutes and implementing legal mandates become extremely important. A full understanding of these elements of delegation is critical but insufficient context to prepare today's public managers for many issues that agencies confront as they receive and attempt to comprehend their legal obligations.

New or altered legal responsibilities that emanate from Congress or other legislative bodies arrive at agencies in distinctive forms. The content of statutes and the forces that produce them are essential parts of a practitioner's framework because of the influence they exert on the ability of agencies to understand and then work with legal authority and obligations. To be more precise, a useful framework must take account of the range of specificity found in statutes. The trend, urged by Lowi (1987) and evident in some laws, is that basic statutes evolve from the general to the more specific over long periods of time through serial amendments. Laws are works in progress that frequently begin with sweeping but vague mandates. They are revisited regularly by legislatures that learn from experience and amend the laws to give more specific direction to agencies. The important issue here, of course, is the extent and type of discretion agencies exercise as a result of delegated authority, and the instruments, or "tools," of law and policy with which they are expected to work.

Whether broad and vague or focused and directive, statutory authority establishes a rich variety of discretion for the receiving agency. At the same time, however, each type of policy instrument dictates distinctive patterns in an agency's implementation activity. Traditional command and control regulation, for example, operates quite differently than market-type mechanisms. A useful framework should also be alert to the forces that structure legislative choice and lead elected representatives to select a given form of statutory authority (McCubbins, Noll, and Weingart, 1987). These forces frequently migrate along with the statutory authority to the receiving agency and profoundly affect the policy implementation process.

Accounting for the arrival of additional legal obligations in the forms of judicial decisions and executive orders is an important element in any framework. Both forms are common, and for some agencies they are highly significant. Agencies whose statutory authorities require significant amounts of rulemaking have been strongly influenced by a series of executive orders issued by presidents from Nixon through Clinton. Executive orders have received only limited attention from scholars, but these "power tools" of presidential management, as Phillip Cooper has termed them (see Chapters Seven and Eleven), substantially affect how agencies use the legal authorities they are granted and meet their legal obligations.

Perhaps the best known and most studied of the executive orders are those concerned with the conduct of regulatory responsibilities by agencies of government (E.O. 12291; E.O. 12866). Recent presidents have used executive orders to articulate overarching regulatory policies that can be enforced directly by the White House staff. They have also mandated certain types of cost-benefit analysis. Guidance associated with these executive orders also specified procedures for Office of Management and Budget (OMB) review of proposed and final rules. Executive orders mandating OMB review of rules constitutes a major development in both administrative law and public management (National Academy of Public Administration, 1987). Other executive orders call for special considerations, such as that which called for special attention to the impact of regulation on state governments (E.O. 12612). These orders have proved to be sources of considerable power for presidents seeking to affect the course of public policy, because rules and regulations frequently contain the most specific statements of legal obligations and rights articulated by any branch of government (Kerwin, 1994).

Judicial decisions also affect how agencies carry out their legal responsibilities (Cooper, 1988). The treatment of judicial review of agency actions is appropriately a major element in any framework for the study of law and public administration. This dimension of the role of courts is examined in Chapter Twenty-Five and elsewhere in this collection. Cases that direct the choice of administrative decision-making forms, set boundaries and requirements for public participation, establish rights of due process for those who are affected by government actions, and establish the proper relationship between the branches when dealing with the administrative process immediately come to mind when the topic of judicial review is raised. A useful framework might also consider judicial decisions that apply more narrowly. Many decisions have effects that are less monumental than those that are most frequently explored in administrative law courses but whose collective impacts on agencies are truly dramatic. Many agencies are sued quite frequently, and the legal challenges in such cases are most often not major constitutional issues but are confined to the appropriateness of a given rule, the process by which it was developed, or the manner in which it was applied to an individual person, firm, or organization. An understanding of law and management must draw on and benefits from recent research that focuses on such cases and classifies them according to the types of actions the resulting judicial decision caused the agency to take (O'Leary, 1993). This research provides an efficient presentation of the more typical and mundane forms of judicial decision in the consideration of the sources from which agencies receive their legal obligations.

Once all the sources of agencies' legal authorities and obligations are accounted for, a framework should also take account of the means by which agencies come to understand what these legal responsibilities require them to accomplish. Three of the most important decisions that administrators make are (1) What must be done? (2) What is the priority order of the tasks to be performed? and (3) What activities will be delayed or removed entirely from the agenda? This set of decisions includes the ways agencies review new statutes, amendments to existing laws, executive orders, and judicial decisions, and how they make decisions about needed actions. In some federal agencies, for example, these early decisions help to give a broad structure to what may develop into massive programs of regulation or service delivery. Many documents illustrate how agencies communicate a plan for implementing new legal responsibilities. These documents provide important insights into the types of deliberations that agencies undertake and the types of officials who are involved (see, for example, Office of Air and Radiation, Environmental Protection Agency, 1991). A decision not to act or to delay action can be of high importance. Witness the controversy associated with the timing of the actions of the Federal Aviation Administration (FAA) in 1996 against ValueJet in the wake of that airline's fatal accident in the Everglades. Certainly various offices of general counsel, or their equivalent, play pivotal roles in these initial reviews and interpretations of the law and related instruments. Agency attorneys conduct these activities in consultation with others in the agency responsible for policy, as well as with those who have detailed knowledge of how the new responsibility affects other areas of the agency's jurisdiction. Executive orders and judicial decisions require varying levels of analysis before an agency can begin to put them into effect. Further, when they arrive, these new mandates join a complex mix of existing agency responsibilities with which many must interact, with synergy or otherwise. Responsible officials must attempt to anticipate varied conflicts and other possibilities.

CLARIFICATION AND SPECIFICATION OF LEGAL RESPONSIBILITIES

When legal mandates have been received and comprehended, the most likely next step is the development of rules and supporting documents by agencies that explain how the requirements of statutes, executive orders, or judicial decisions will be met. Treatments of this topic are quite common in existing frameworks (Cooper, 1983). Most administrative law texts do this by examining the choices of given forms of action by agencies, usually taking care to distinguish rulemaking as a general governmental activity from other forms of agency action, such as adjudication. The rulemaking provisions of the Administrative Procedure Act (APA) are reviewed, followed by summaries of the major steps that have been added to the APA's minimalist requirements, which have been adopted during over fifty years since passage of the original act in 1946. The rise of hybrid rulemaking techniques, with their enhanced opportunities for public participation, and the changes wrought by executive orders (mentioned earlier) are frequent subjects when the discussion of rulemaking is extended beyond the basics of the APA. Most administrative law texts discuss the subject of rulemaking with an eye toward judicial review, which commonly follows adoption of major rules.

Elsewhere I have argued forcefully that rulemaking is the single most important function performed by agencies of government (Kerwin, 1994). It is not necessary to linger over the reasons here. However, as an indispensable form of lawmaking, the development of rules vests agencies with the most important power of government granted by the Constitution. In accounting for this fact, a law and management conceptual framework must cover the administration of rulemaking by agencies, patterns of actual participation by the public, and oversight by the constitutional branches of government.

Federal and many state agencies of government maintain sophisticated rulemaking management systems that determine, to a considerable extent, how and how well this fundamental legal function is performed. Management of contemporary rulemaking includes the following (Kerwin, 1994, ch. 4):

1. Setting priorities
2. Creating mechanisms for approving the start of individual rules
3. Planning key activities

4. Assigning resources
5. Coordinating internal participation
6. Collecting and analyzing essential primary information
7. Conducting required secondary analyses
8. Drafting the preamble and proposed rule
9. Structuring opportunities for public participation
10. Ensuring that essential public participation occurs
11. Evaluating the results of public participation
12. Securing necessary approvals within the agency
13. Maintaining liaison with the White House and possibly the Congress (or state or local legislative bodies)
14. Publishing the final rule
15. Preparing essential postrulemaking activities

It is not necessary to explore all of these management tasks here, but several are so frequently absent from the standard treatments of rulemaking that some additional explanation is useful.

Priority Setting

To meet legal requirements, agencies of government with broad-ranging jurisdictions must set priorities among the many potential rulemaking projects they could undertake given their statutory responsibilities. Many of these agencies confront far more opportunities for rulemaking than they have the time and resources to accomplish. Sometimes the priority-setting process is effectively preempted by quite specific statutory mandates, frequently accompanied by deadlines and so-called hammer provisions, or by a court decision that obligates the agency to produce a new or altered rule and even to do so under a judicial deadline. A "hammer" is a legislative provision, usually quite stringent or burdensome, that automatically takes effect if a legislative deadline is missed. Other, less explicit external forces can affect priority setting, such as pressure from the White House, key Hill figures, and interest groups that have the option of using formal petitions to prod reluctant agencies into the development of a regulation. On their own, agencies have developed a number of different priority-setting mechanisms. Some agencies, such as the FAA, limit the number of major rulemaking projects that can be under way at any one time to those deemed by senior officials to be of greatest importance to the agency's mission. Other agencies are less proactive in their priority setting, relying instead on systems in which rules are initiated at lower levels and subject to high-level

Agency Phase

Systems of public management touch most people in some ways every day, and some of those contacts are sufficiently irritating to trigger disputes. The sheer volume of interactions combined with the high value placed on due process ensures that dispute resolution will continue to be central to the management of law in government agencies. Therefore, it is also essential to consider the management systems that have grown up to provide appropriate procedural protections to those who consider themselves aggrieved by the actions of entitlement-, benefit-, and service-providing agencies. Of course, the same is true of those affected by decisions of regulatory officials. Here, the loss of business, profit, and property may be very substantial. Massive systems of administrative due process exist in agencies such as the U.S. Department of Health and Human Services, the Department of Veterans Affairs, the Environmental Protection Agency, and the U.S. Department of Labor, to name a few. How they function and their effects on agency management and basic program operations are worthy of consideration (Lubbers, 1994).

The 1990s movement to reinvent government and governmental processes persistently stresses the importance of treating those who come into contact with government as customers. It is important to acknowledge the significance of this movement and to explore the legal implications of transforming beneficiaries of entitlement and service programs and regulated parties into customers. Of particular concern is the ability of newly designed outreach or service programs to deliver benefits and services in manners that more effectively strike balances between satisfying the customers and promoting the larger public interest, be it through regulation or some other form of action. It is especially important here to consider whether and how reinvented or reengineered programs and policies have been able to avoid the disconnect between general program rules and actual operating conditions and imperatives that have vexed both benefit and regulatory programs. Privatization is an older movement also deserving of attention in the framework. This includes exploring the legal aspects of privatization's numerous forms, including coproduction, contracting out, and full transfer. In these areas, contract management and liability issues are frequent and significant. Whether the vehicle for the delivery of benefits or regulation is a public agency or its private contractor, conflict is inevitable. A conceptual framework must include means of dispute resolution.

Judicial Phase

The role of the judicial system in dispute resolution begins when administrative resolutions are unacceptable and one or more parties seek a formal declaration of the law and an enforcement order or remedy against an agency under the principles of judicial review established in the APA. The degree of deference that courts pay to administrative decisions of various sorts is a matter of enormous importance. Among other things, it profoundly influences how agencies manage their legal responsibilities. Their willingness to exercise discretion is often tied to the extent and tenor of the scrutiny they expect from judges (O'Leary, 1993). However, in addition to this common concern about who wins or what judicial orders contain, it is important to have management systems in place in agencies to support litigation once it ensues; these clarify the roles played by nonattorneys in court cases in which an agency action is challenged. Exploration of the policies and management relationships that govern agency appeals of unfavorable decisions is important. The complex interactions between agencies and the various offices in the Department of Justice, and their state analogs, that effectively control litigation by government are also important for both administrative and legal practitioners. In the end, courts and administrative agencies are locked in a permanent relationship that agencies must manage as actively as they do any other function they perform.

CONCLUSION

Law is central to the work of public managers. It remains the ultimate manifestation of collective self governance in America's constitutionally democratic society. In arguing that public management is, at base, the management of law, this chapter is a reminder that this is a period when public administration has been the target of withering attacks. This framework stresses that people in the United States, whether citizens or not, enjoy legal status aside from being customers and that, under the principles of popular sovereignty and limited government, citizens are ultimately the sources of law and only secondarily the judges of service quality. At its best, public management facilitates effective citizenship by easing the path of law in all its contemporary manifestations.

Cases Cited

Amalgamated Meat Cutters and Butcher Workmen v. *Connally,* 337 F. Supp. 737 (1971).

Motor Vehicle Manufacturers Association v. *State Farm Mutual,* 463 U.S. 29 (1983).

Panama Refining Company v. *Ryan,* 293 U.S. 388 (1935).

Schechter Poultry Corporation v. *United States,* 295 U.S. 495 (1935).

References

Administrative Procedure Act, 5 U.S.C. 551 et seq.

Anthony, R. "Interpretative Rules, Policy Statements, Guidelines, Manuals and the Like: Should Agencies Use Them to Bind the Public?" *Duke University Law Review,* 1992, *41,* 1131–1384.

Cooper, P. J. *Public Law and Public Administration.* Mountain View, Calif.: Mayfield, 1983.

Cooper, P. J. *Hard Judicial Choices.* New York: Oxford University Press, 1988.

Davis, K. C. *Administrative Law and Government.* (2nd ed.) St. Paul, Minn.: West, 1975.

Gore, A. Jr. *From Red Tape to Results: Creating a Government That Works Better and Costs Less.* Report of the National Performance Review. Washington, D.C.: U.S. Government Printing Office, 1993.

Gore, A. Jr. *Commonsense Government: Third Report of the National Performance Review.* Washington, D.C.: U.S. Government Printing Office, 1995.

Kagan, R. "Regulatory Enforcement." In D. H. Rosenbloom and B. Schwartz (eds.), *Handbook of Regulation and Administrative Law.* New York: Dekker, 1994.

Kerwin, C. M. "Transforming Regulation: A Case Study of Hydropower Licensing." *Public Administration Review,* 1990, *51,* 91–100.

Kerwin, C. M. *Rulemaking: How Government Agencies Write Law and Make Policy.* Washington, D.C.: Congressional Quarterly Press, 1994.

Lipsky, M. *Street-Level Bureaucracy: Dilemmas of the Individual in the Public Services.* New York: Russell Sage Foundation, 1980.

Lowi, T. "Two Roads to Serfdom: Liberalism, Conservativism and Administrative Power." *American University Law Review,* 1987, *36,* 295–322.

Lubbers, J. "Management of Federal Agency Adjudication." In D. Rosenbloom and B. Schwartz (eds.), *Handbook of Regulation and Administrative Law.* New York: Dekker, 1994.

McCubbins, M., Noll, R., and Weingart, B. "Administrative Procedures as Instruments of Political Control." Paper presented at the Midwest Political Science Association Conference, Chicago, Mar. 1987.

McGarrity, T. "Some Thoughts on Deossifying the Rulemaking Process." *Duke University Law Review,* 1992, *41,* 1385–1462.

National Academy of Public Administration. *Presidential Management of Rulemaking.* Washington, D.C.: National Academy of Public Administration, 1987.

Office of Air and Radiation, Environmental Protection Agency. *Implementation Strategy for the Clean Air Act Amendments of 1990.* Washington, D.C.: Environmental Protection Agency, 1991.

O'Leary, R. *Environmental Change: The Federal Courts and the EPA.* Philadelphia: Temple University Press, 1993.

Rohr, J. A. *To Run a Constitution: The Legitimacy of the Administrative State.* Lawrence: University of Kansas Press, 1986.

Rosenbloom, D. H., and O'Leary, R. *Public Administration and Law.* (2nd ed.) New York: Dekker, 1996.

Scholz, J. "Managing Regulatory Enforcement in the United States." In D. H. Rosenbloom and B. Schwartz (eds.), *Handbook of Regulation and Administrative Law.* New York: Dekker, 1994.

CHAPTER THREE

The Importance of Public Law

New and Old Paradigms of Government Management

Ronald C. Moe

This is an age of new and competing government management paradigms (or worldviews). At least that is what those who profit from the sale of books on the subject urge people to believe. These latter-day Machiavellis and Webers do have interesting points to make, of course, and they follow in a heady tradition of theorists ready to advise rulers how to rule and the masses how to accommodate and direct the forces beyond their individual control. But is this search for a new management paradigm really as intellectually sound as the promoters would lead people to believe? Or is there more to the story?

While much of the contemporary paradigm building has its origin in the discipline of economics, no scholarly field has been immune. Nothing is modest in the claims of these new paradigm builders. The title of James Pinkerton's 1995 book *What Comes Next: The End of Big Government and the New Paradigm Ahead* literally says it all. Government as it is now known, asserts Pinkerton, is scheduled for extinction. The current, and thus "old," paradigm is based on laws and accountable structures (the latter are referred to both clinically and pejoratively as "bureaucracy"), and this paradigm is not flexible enough to accommodate the "cyberfuture" portrayed by Pinkerton and others who share his views. What is needed, they opine, is a new paradigm, a radically streamlined government guided by a worldview of choice, empowerment, inclusiveness, decentralization, and communitarian healing.

In hopes of heading off the Pinkertonian deconstruction of the state, political liberals have preferred a watered down version of the new paradigm under

41

the rubric of "reinventing government." Their "bible" is to be found in Osborne and Gaebler's popular journalistic treatise, *Reinventing Government: How the Entrepreneurial Spirit Is Transforming the Public Sector from Schoolhouse to State-house, City Hall to the Pentagon* (1992). (For some reason, these paradigm builders prefer long titles.) Osborne and Gaebler adopt the business school methodology of designing organizations and programs by replicating "success stories." Success stories, however, are not equivalents of tested theory and are—particularly in the hands of Osborne and Gaebler and their disciple Vice President Albert Gore—little more than managerial anecdotes.

As for the social scientists, many have pinned their future on the abandonment of long-tested administrative-management theory (paradigm), with its reliance on law. In its place they have also sought a generic management paradigm that in large measure is based on an economic model of behavior sweetened with a dollop of public policy analysis to justify their academic pretensions. By emphasizing the blend of economics and public policy over laws, public management, as defined by Barry Bozeman (1993, p. 3), "runs away from public administration."

While the seekers of new paradigms have different motives, objectives, and prescriptions, they share one crucial assumption: they believe that the governmental sector and the private sector are alike in their fundamental characteristics, and subject to essentially the same behavioral incentives. This fundamental assumption is faulty, however, and from this faulty assumption follows much intellectual mischief.

DISTINCTIVENESS OF GOVERNMENTAL AND PRIVATE SECTORS

The working assumption of this chapter is that the governmental and private sectors are fundamentally distinctive, and the distinctions are based in legal theory of constitutional government, not economic theory. Assignment of functions between the sectors is not simply an economic exercise to find the most "economical" choice, but first and foremost it is a legal exercise in which the values of accountability of officers of the United States are spelled out in law.

This country has two distinctive forms of law: public law, which governs the activities of governmental bodies in their capacity as agents of the sovereign (for example, officers of the United States must follow due process in performing their duties); and private law, which governs the relations of private parties with one another (private parties are not subject to due process requirements). Historically, the political institutions and judiciary have kept these streams of legal doctrine and the two sectors largely distinct in practice and separate organizationally—and with good cause.

With respect to management, the distinctions between the sectors are manifest. *The distinguishing characteristic of governmental management, in contrast to private management, is that the actions of the governmental officials must have their bases in public law, not in the pecuniary interest of private entrepreneurs and owners or in the fiduciary concerns of private managers* (Moe and Gilmour, 1995). This point is critical, for when the sectors are blended or meshed in some fashion, the fundamental lines of accountability, the managerial culture and its internal incentives, and the relationship of this activity to the citizenry are changed, and the latter designation is often replaced in the new paradigms by the term *customer.*

The management paradigms currently competing for favor among political and career managers and the scholarly community all possess their own brands of insight, but none is wholly satisfactory because they all fail to provide the theoretical comprehensiveness necessary to ensure that the basic political values of American democracy are met. That is, the various paradigms being hailed ignore the essential character of the governmental sector, a character determined by law, not by economic, sociological, or technological axioms. It is law that determines the mission, structure, financing, human resources, policies, procedures, and ultimately the incentive parameters in which managers function within governmental institutions. The thesis of this chapter is that the quality of these institutional and managerial laws has deteriorated in recent decades, resulting in decreased capacity of governmental agencies to perform basic functions in an accountable and effective manner.

Implicit in the arguments of Pinkerton, Osborne and Gaebler, and Bozeman is that the sectors are alike in their essentials and that "sector blurring" is not only present and inevitable but also the desired way to plan and manage for the future. While allowing for a modest amount of distinctiveness between government organizations and private organizations, the overwhelming contemporary reality, in their view, is that there are similarities between the public and private sectors of American life. That public administration theory still equates public organizations with government organizations is, according to Bozeman, "a puzzling and even disappointing approach to an organizational world" (1987, pp. xi–xii).

Do not forget, however, that when people talk about government, they are not simply talking about another service provider. Certainly governments provide services, both directly and indirectly through third parties, but service provision is not essential to the character of government. What is essential to governmental character is its exercise of sovereign authority under the Constitution, its interactions with citizens in a framework of popular sovereignty and limited government. The concept of sovereignty is the single most important characteristic that separates the public and private sectors, particularly at the federal level. The federal government exercises the rights and immunities of the sovereign and possesses the legitimate right to use coercion to enforce the public will through law, while organizations functioning in the private sector do not, or at least ought not, possess such sovereign rights and immunities (Moe, 1987).

IT ALL BEGINS WITH LAW

Paradigm builders, insofar as they recognize its existence, tend to dismiss legally based administrative theory as part of the "old paradigm." The administrative management paradigm, with its emphasis on the Constitution, its statutory controls, its hierarchical lines of responsibility to the president, its distinctive legal character of governmental and private sectors, and its need for a cadre of nonpartisan professional managers ultimately responsible not only to the president but also to Congress, is depicted as the paradigm that failed. This paradigm is the cause of the government being "broken"—the term used by President Clinton upon accepting "the Gore Report" of the National Performance Review (NPR) (Gore, 1993)—in the eyes of the reinventors and deconstructivists. The paradigm has not proven flexible enough to permit change to occur at the speed considered necessary in the new, information-driven, technological world. The administrative management paradigm is even viewed as out-of-date in the realm of power politics. Vice President Gore asserts that his entrepreneurial management paradigm is deterministically correct and no longer subject to debate: "Chief Executive Officers—from the White House to agency heads—must ensure that everyone understands that power will never flow through the old channels again. That's how GE did it; that's how we must do it as well" (Gore, 1993, p. 86). The vice president later expounded these views, as applied to federal managers, in the *Public Administration Review* (Gore, 1994).

Donald Kettl, a sympathetic observer of the new paradigm scene, nonetheless is cognizant that behind the rhetoric of generic management paradigms is a political agenda: "First, 'reinventing government' seeks the transfer of power from the legislative to the executive branch. In the Vice President's report, Congress is notable principally for its rare appearance. When it does appear, it is usually as an unindicted co-conspirator responsible for undermining effective management. The NPR criticizes Congress for micromanagement and for unpredictable budgetary decisions. Almost all of what the NPR recommends, in fact, requires that Congress give up power" (Kettl, 1994, p. 309).

The NPR posits that the purpose of government management is to achieve four objectives: (1) cast aside red tape, (2) maximize customer satisfaction, (3) decentralize authority, and (4) work better and cost less. Entrepreneurial governments of the future will rely on constant reengineering and downsizing, and on managers who are "performance" oriented. Peter Drucker (1995), who is as responsible as anyone for this era of new paradigms, nonetheless has his misgivings and suggests it is time for another *-ing* word: *rethinking.* In his mind, we have not rethought the purposes of government for five centuries—a bit of an exaggeration, but the point is still worth making. Downsizing, he attests, has rarely made the corporations that practice it more effective or profitable, a result he sees being replicated in the forced downsizing of the federal government. Patchwork approaches to systemic problems merely exacerbate management problems. Downsizing government and bragging about it, as President Clinton does when he claims he has made the federal government the smallest it has been since 1933, merely adds to public cynicism (Barnes, 1995). Drucker (1995) sees the problem of government as a matter of selecting the right functions to perform. But even selecting the right functions does not ensure that the management of the function will be effective. There tends to be an intellectual disconnection between selecting the proper functions for government and the proper management of those functions.

May I suggest that most of this theorizing (actually it is not so much theorizing as the stringing together of aphorisms) misses the basic truth about government management? In the federal government, the purpose of agency management is to implement the laws, both the wise and the less wise, passed by Congress as elected representatives of the people. As a matter of direct delegation under Article I of the Constitution, Congress makes the laws, establishes offices and departments, and appropriates necessary funding. The missions and priorities of agencies are determined by law, not by the president or by agency heads, either collectively or separately. While comity and cooperation among Congress, the president, and the agencies are the bases for most relationships among the branches, the authoritative element in the relationship is clear. Management of the executive branch, in terms of both process and behavior, is ultimately dependent upon Congress and the law (Moe and Gilmour, 1995, p. 138). And Congress is not like the compliant boards of directors that characterize most private corporations. Repeatedly, outside CEOs brought in to "reinvent" or "reengineer" a federal program along private sector lines are shocked to find that they must meticulously obey laws and regulations, and that they are answerable to Congress for their actions.

GENERAL MANAGEMENT LAWS

Congressional involvement in the detailed direction of executive management is not aberrational behavior, nor is it part of some larger political strategy employed by an imperialistic Congress. Because of Congress's immense legislative powers to organize and control the orientation, even the very existence, of every aspect of executive branch management, Congress has always had the potential—frequently realized in contemporary practice—to be a veritable comanager of policy and program implementation (Gilmour and Halley, 1994).

The interests of Congress and the president, however, are not necessarily at odds or confrontational. Indeed, there is a high degree of congruence of institutional interests in managing the executive agencies. The most important elements in this cooperative exercise are the general management laws that provide the overall direction and rules for the executive branch. These laws are the glue that keeps the naturally disparate parts of the executive branch tied together as a whole. The quality of the general management laws, therefore, largely determines the quality of institutional management.

The basis for management of the executive branch, viewed comprehensively, is to be found in the one hundred or so general management laws (U.S. Congress, 1986). These laws specify crosscutting provisions that regulate the activities, procedures, and administration of all agencies of government. The operative word with respect to general management laws is *agency* as defined in Title 5 of the U.S. Code. All entities of the federal government are considered to be agencies of the United States and therefore are covered by all provisions of the U.S. Code, except where exempted either organizationally by class or individually by enabling statute.

General management laws come in various guises and may be dramatic in their impacts, as are the Budget and Accounting Act, the Government Corporation Control Act, the Paperwork Reduction Act, the Inspector General Act, and the Freedom of Information Act. Or they may be of relatively low visibility (although visibility is not necessarily equatable with importance), such as the Miscellaneous Receipts Act, the Federal Advisory Committee Act, the Federal Tort Claims Act, and the Anti-Deficiency Act. The purpose of these general management laws, and of the host of additional similar acts, is to shift the focus of deliberation and decision to the general rather than the exceptional. The politics of general applicability is a politics by which the president, central management agencies, and Congress have the authority and leverage to keep the natural centrifugal forces of administrative practices within accountable limits. That is, the laws and regulations apply to all agencies, with the supplicants for exemption carrying the burden of proof. Exceptional politics occurs when there are no applicable general management laws or when those that exist have been permitted to atrophy or, conversely, have become cumbersome or obsolete through extraneous amendments.

In the arena of exceptional politics, where the management of each agency tends to be viewed sui generis and is the sum of exceptional circumstances, interest groups and agency leadership have the advantage in making policy and in agency management. The logical result of an executive branch functioning under a culture of exceptional politics is an executive branch that is disaggregated and largely unaccountable to both the president and Congress, especially the former, for its activities. The national government is closer to this logical end of exceptional politics than is generally appreciated even by otherwise sophisticated observers of the governmental scene.

In recent years, a number of additional central management laws have been enacted, each supported and justified by its own definition of a problem, with little or no consideration of its probable impact upon other related general management laws. The typical agency head today must contend with such laws as the Federal Managers Financial Integrity Act, the Prompt Payment Act, the Government Performance and Results Act, and the Chief Financial Officers Act, as well as with directives and decisions from the Office of Management and Budget (OMB), the Office of Personnel Management, the Office of Federal Procurement Policy, the Office of Information and Regulatory Analysis, the Office of Federal Ethics—and the list goes on.

The plethora of management acts has been a major contributing factor in the fragmentation of executive management and the increase in involvement by Congress in detailed management issues. In the absence of a comprehensive management theory or an institution in the executive branch responsible for keeping the general management laws clean and creative, management issues naturally tend to be approached on a case-by-case basis, with bits and pieces finding their way into law, usually accompanied by the phrase "notwithstanding any provision of law to the contrary, the following shall occur." Nearly everyone now seems involved in management of the executive branch, even the appropriations committees of Congress.

In the Department of Transportation Appropriations Act of 1996 (PL. 104–50), for instance, an inconspicuous provision was inserted that has little to do with appropriations and much to do with institutional management: "That, notwithstanding 5 U.S.C. 905(b), the President may prepare and transmit to Congress not later than the date for transmittal to Congress of the Budget Request for FY 1997, a reorganization plan pursuant to chapter 9 of title 5, U.S. Code, for the reorganization of the surface transportation activities of the Department of Transportation (DOT) and the relationship of the St. Lawrence Seaway Development Corporation to the Department" (Sec. 311). The act limited DOT to no more than one hundred political and presidential appointees.

What this 1996 provision did was renew the president's reorganization plan authority as it applies to this one department. The law had been allowed to lapse in 1984, in part as a consequence of the decision in *Immigration and Naturalization Service* v. *Chadha* (462 U.S. 919, 1983) that made the legislative veto unconstitutional. On eighteen occasions between 1932 and 1984, Congress delegated to the president the authority to submit reorganization plans that have the effect of establishing, abolishing, or reorganizing agencies and functions. Under provisions that varied over the years, reorganization authority provided for an expedited deliberation and approval/disapproval process by Congress (hence, the legislative veto). The most recent extension of the Reorganization Act covered the short period from November 8, 1983, through December 31, 1984 (P.L. 98–614). As with most of the prior extensions of the act, substantive and procedural amendments limited its coverage and made it more nearly like the regular legislative process. Indeed, by the 1980s, it was difficult to determine what advantages accrued to the president and the executive branch from the act (Fisher and Moe, 1981). In October 1984, as a consequence of the *Chadha* decision, Congress took the precaution of retroactively ratifying all the reorganization plans enacted under the Reorganization Act prior to that date by reaffirming that reorganization plans are statutes (P.L. 98–532).

In deliberations on the Transportation Act of 1996, the committees charged with general oversight of departmental organization (and reorganizations) were reportedly not consulted, nor were the committees charged with legislative responsibility for the Department of Transportation. It was, according to critics, an "end run" exercised by the department, with the apparent agreement of the appropriations committees, to permit the department to submit a reorganization plan that would enjoy some sort of fast-track approval process, thus permitting minimal amendments. It is not clear from the record whether OMB approved or even knew of this provision to reactivate the reorganization plan authority for this one department alone, but it is clear that such specific actions weaken OMB's authority over other departments and agencies seeking similar dispensation from the normal legislative process.

THE PRESIDENTIAL RETREAT

As additional general management laws have been passed, one after another, each arguably necessary at the time of passage but collectively approaching incoherence, the institutions responsible for overseeing the administration of the laws have been retreating from their responsibilities. Presidents, at least since Dwight Eisenhower, have heeded the warnings of political scientists and pundits that they should avoid becoming managers (Moe, 1990; Rose, 1988). In 1960, Richard Neustadt's *Presidential Power* appeared and launched a broadside against the institutional/legalist view of the presidency. While never fully rejecting the role of law in the armory of presidential powers, the emphasis was clearly in the opposite direction, toward the president's political role. "Laws and customs," Neustadt wrote, "tell us little about leadership in fact" (p. 6). The message of the book was that "presidential power is the power to persuade" (p. 10). Forget the law, Neustadt was saying. Peek behind the decision-making curtain if you want to find out what is really happening. Presidents should love power and know how to use it. They should avoid mere clerkship functions or they will miss their opportunity for heroic destiny.

This theme has been repeated over and over again in the prescriptive literature on the presidency. In 1976, Stephen Hess wrote for a new, incoming president: "Presidents have made a serious mistake, starting with Roosevelt, in asserting that they are chief managers of the federal government. . . . Rather than chief manager, the President is the chief political officer of the United States" (p. 6).

The presidential retreat from managerial responsibilities was offset in part by the retention of neutrally competent management capacity in the Bureau of the Budget (called the Office of Management and Budget after 1970) (Heclo, 1975). But after President Richard Nixon found it impossible to reorganize the executive branch following the regular legislative process, he turned toward an administrative-president strategy, one that included politicizing OMB (Moe, 1985). Richard Nathan wrote approvingly that "this administrative presidency strategy is appropriate and desirable for both liberals and conservatives" (1983, p. 1). The politicization process of OMB and the departments has been largely accepted by today's public management school (influenced by rational choice concepts) as both inevitable and desirable. That acceptance constitutes a major element in the development within the social science community of their version of a new paradigm of public management to fit with the paradigms offered by economists and business executives.

Recent presidents have sought not so much to manage the executive branch through properly conceptualized management laws and trained professional managers as to control government through short-term political appointees placed deep within agencies, and through the budgetary process.

The sheer number of political appointees today and the extraordinary political constraints in effect in regard to their selection place obvious limits on the quality of agency management (Garcia, 1995; Weko, 1995). Under the best of circumstances it is difficult to imagine major long-term commitments to management improvements by short-term appointees whose personal agendas often run counter to those of the White House and to agency interests. After viewing the top management in the executive branch in 1988, the National Commission on the Public Service—commonly called the Volcker Commission, after the chairman—reported: "From 1964 to 1984, the proportion of political appointees who stayed in position 1.5 years or less was 41.7 percent for cabinet secretaries, 62 percent for deputy secretaries, and 46.3 percent for under secretaries. From 1979 to 1986, noncareer members (political appointees) of the Senior Executive Service remained in office an average of 20 months. Fully 40 percent of the political executives throughout government stayed in their positions less than one year. In contrast, 70 percent of the career executives have been with their agencies for 10 years and 50 percent of them for 15 years" (Volcker, 1989, p. 168).

The Volcker Commission concluded that the president would be better served by a substantial reduction in the number of political and presidential appointees.

It recommended that although "a reduction in the total number of Presidential appointees must be based on a position-by-position assessment, the Commission is confident that a substantial cut is possible, and believes a cut from the current 3,000 to more than 2,000 is a reasonable target" (Volcker, 1989, pp. 18, 50; see also Light, 1995).

As the institutional capacity for management declined in OMB, both absolutely and relative to congressionally initiated management, the president and his political aides came to rely more on the budget as a management tool. While the new management paradigms publicly espouse a more decentralized, more participatory management culture than the old paradigm, in practice they promote greater control through the budgetary process and by budget analysts. Thus, the Government Performance and Results Act passed in 1993 (31 U.S.C. 1101) and hailed as the vehicle to implement the new, business-oriented public management paradigm is subsumed for implementation under the budgetary process and is centrally subject to budget analysts (OMB Circular A–11). As much of the executive branch as possible will be placed under relatively stringent performance agreements, with "nonperforming" managers and agencies being penalized in budgetary terms. Management in the executive branch is increasingly subordinate to budget control and priorities, and that is the way the "reinventors" intended it to be.

The reinventing-government exercise was deliberately not assigned to the management side of OMB. The decision by Vice President Gore, supported by President Clinton, was to displace the legally based management paradigm and OMB staff through the use of ad hoc, nonstatutory, noninstitutionalized bodies under the direction of the vice president's political staff. The NPR staff, a counter-OMB if you will, consisted mostly of private consultants and lower-level detailees from the departments. However, they not only wrote the various reports and publicity sheets, they also wrote some of the executive orders signed by the president.

The objective of the reinventing-government exercise was not to rewrite management laws or reorganize institutions but to change the culture of the governmental sector to more closely resemble that of a large, private corporation. Central management agencies (such as the Office of Personnel Management, the General Services Administration, and the management side of OMB) were downgraded and stripped of much of their capacity to manage through laws. In any of the versions of the new management paradigm, laws are the rejected element.

The presidential retreat from hands-on managerial responsibilities for the executive branch coupled with neglect for maintaining the currency and integrity of general management laws and topped off with wholesale abandonment of the professional corps of government managers are the ingredients of an unintended major shift of political power away from the institutional presidency and toward Congress, departments and agencies, and interest groups. Ironically, although it is the intent of the new paradigm designers and the reinventors to strip Congress of its powers and authorities, because they are playing the politics of exceptional management rather than general management, the ultimate institutional loser will in all likelihood be the presidency.

IS ANYONE MINDING THE STORE?

While there are those among the economists who recognize that proper limits exist for market management and that there is need for properly designed, legally based institutions to protect both democratic values and the private market sector itself (North, 1990), their voices tend to be drowned in the sea of those calling for nostrums rather than tested theory. On a very practical level, the question increasingly being raised is, Is anyone minding the store? What is OMB doing to protect the general interests of the president and the government writ large, as distinguished from the particularistic interests of departments, agencies, government corporations, and other instrumentalities of the executive branch?

Throughout the 1970s and 1980s, there was an implicit policy of disinvestment in the management side of government generally and OMB in particular (Bowsher, 1988). This decline in management capacity in OMB was striking and was a major contributing factor to the mismanagement and scandals that plagued the Department of Housing and Urban Development (HUD) during the 1980s, according to a 1990 Senate Banking Committee study: "Given the mismanagement and abuse of certain HUD programs during the 1980s, it is important to inquire why OMB oversight of HUD management failed to uncover and prevent it. The answer has been evident since OMB's creation in 1970. OMB's management efforts have been largely unable to compete for resources or attention with the high-priority budget process, and have therefore been minimal. Even when certain management oversight strategies have received attention and resources from OMB, their effects have been adversely influenced by the short-term budget mind-set and highly politicized nature of the organization" (U.S. Congress, 1990, p. 194).

Although recommendations have repeatedly been made from various sources, most recently from the House Government Reform and Oversight Committee, to strengthen the management capacity of OMB or, more directly, to create a separate Office of Federal Management (U.S. Congress, 1991; U.S. Congress, 1995; National Academy of Public Administration, 1988), presidents and directors of OMB have shown little interest.

The NPR "Gore Report" in 1993 rejected earlier recommendations to rebuild OMB's management capacity and indirectly proposed that OMB not have a separate management component. A subsequent OMB reorganization, commonly termed the OMB 2000 Review, largely implemented the NPR suggestion by integrating the staff of the General Management Division and the existing budget analysts into five Resource Management Offices structured along budgetary and functional lines. Insofar as designated management functions remain in OMB, they are located in much-reduced statutory elements of the agency (for example, the Office of Federal Procurement Policy) (U.S. Office of Management and Budget, 1994). The integration (critics argue that a better term is "subordination"; see Dean, Ink, and Seidman, 1994) of management functions and personnel within the larger budgetary side of the agency is permanent and represents recognition that a reinvented (new-paradigm) government is one in which general management laws are no longer viewed as constituting the basis for a politically accountable executive branch. In defending the 1994 reorganization of OMB, then OMB director Leon Panetta stated: "Critics of these recommendations may say the effort to 'integrate' management and budget will end in merely bigger budget divisions, whose management responsibilities will be driven out by daily fire-fighting on budget issues. . . . We believe this criticism is based on a false premise that 'management' and 'budget' issues can be thought of separately" ("Executive Memo," 1994, p. 8).

The nub of the current debate is whether there is a subject field, properly defined, of government management separable from budgetary priorities and from generic private management concepts. Clearly, the new paradigm promoters and their cousins, the reinventors, do not think so. Just as clearly, the author of this chapter believes that government management is a separable field with its own long-tested theoretical basis and its own call upon the president for attention and support. To believe otherwise is to weaken the values of the Constitution, of legislative control, and of the presidency itself.

If OMB, for reasons sufficient unto itself, no longer desires or has the capacity to provide coherent management leadership for the executive branch based on the general management statutes, the answer to the question, Who is minding the store? appears to be, No one.

John Koskinen, deputy director for management in OMB during the Clinton Administration's first term, viewed himself as a "crisis manager" (for example, managing government shutdowns) and new-paradigm player, not as guardian of the general management laws of government. In an interview, Koskinen provided a glimpse of his philosophy when he noted that government has a number of "factories," or business-like agencies, that could be run more like private corporations. He referred to these agencies as *performance-based organizations* (PBOs). As PBOs, the agencies would still retain a political appointee to set policy, but their day-to-day operations would be turned over to an outside executive, hired under a three-to-five-year contract. If the executive failed to meet performance objectives, he or she could be fired. If successful, the executive would receive a financial reward, much like private sector managers (Barr, 1995).

This philosophy of replacing a public service ethic with a private sector, pecuniary-based ethic for managers is not without its risks. The new paradigm, promoting as it does the meshing of the governmental and private sectors, largely replaces political accountability with economic accountability. In effect, the executive branch gets to define and reward its own success without direct accountability to Congress. Turning government functions over to "outside executives" (meaning persons who are not officers of the United States) raises extraordinary issues of constitutional law as well as simple issues of accountability. How could Congress exercise supervision over these outside executives? Would these persons be called to testify before committees? Would they be subject to subpoenas, contempt actions, and impeachment? Would these "contract managers" be concerned with implementing public laws or with maximizing revenues and personal financial rewards? What is the point of a "political officer" who is essentially a contract officer? Who would determine the adequacy of the contract with the managers or the level of financial reward? Would not a special class of manager emerge to manage entities having, in effect, their own "patronage" systems apart from the civil service?

The federal government is facing a management crisis, but it is not the sort of challenge described by the new-paradigm promoters. While most of the writing on the topic and most of the present political executive leadership accepts one or more of the new management paradigms, there is a "real world" of management issues that raises its head at awkward moments. The administrative management paradigm, based as it is on the Constitution, statutes, judicial rulings, and the like, continues to be the foundation of most federal management, no matter what others may write or do. The problem is that as this legal framework deteriorates through neglect and misuse, the entire political system is placed in jeopardy. No longer will the laws be considered fully legitimate or subject to comprehensive applicability. The legal symmetry of political accountability reaching to the president and through the president to Congress is rapidly becoming frayed with exceptions and compromised processes.

The line that distinguishes between the governmental and private sectors, once viewed as critical to the protection of both public and private rights, is today breached not only by exceptional behavior but also by the prescriptive name of "principle." Some say that the governmental sector is being privatized, while others argue that the private sector is being governmentalized. On balance, the danger appears to be that, in the name of "downsizing government" and other business sector practices, increasing amounts of governmental authority and funds are being assigned to third parties, usually contractors, with less-than-adequate assurances that the citizens' interests are being served and protected. Don Kettl wrote in 1993: "In its eager pursuit of the competition prescription, government has—for a remarkable number of reasons—too often surrendered its basic policy making powers to contractors" (p. 13). It is too often

Bowsher, C. A., Comptroller General of the United States. "The Emerging Crisis: The Disinvestment in Government." Webb Lecture, National Academy of Public Administration, Washington, D.C., Dec. 2, 1988.

Bozeman, B. *All Organizations Are Public: Bridging Public and Private Organizational Theories.* San Francisco: Jossey-Bass, 1987.

Bozeman, B. (ed). *Public Management: The State of the Art.* San Francisco: Jossey-Bass, 1993.

Dean, A., Ink, D., and Seidman, H. "OMB's 'M' Fading Away." *Government Executive,* June 26, 1994, pp. 62–64.

Drucker, P. F. *"Really* Reinventing Government." *Atlantic Monthly,* Feb. 1995, pp. 49–61.

"Executive Memo: OMB Management Merger." *Government Executive,* Apr. 26, 1994, p. 8.

Fisher, L., and Moe, R. C. "Presidential Reorganization Authority: Is It Worth the Cost?" *Political Science Quarterly,* 1981, *96,* 301–318.

Garcia, R. "Growth in the Number of Full-Time Political Appointees in the Executive Branch, 1980–1992." *Congressional Research Service Memorandum.* Washington, D.C.: Congressional Research Service, June 29, 1995.

Gilmour, R. S., and Halley, A. A. *Who Makes Public Policy? The Struggle for Control Between Congress and the Executive.* Chatham, N.J.: Chatham House, 1994.

Gore, A. Jr. *From Red Tape to Results: Creating a Government That Works Better and Costs Less.* Report of the National Performance Review. Washington, D.C.: U.S. Government Printing Office, 1993.

Gore, A. Jr. "The Job of the Federal Executive." *Public Administration Review,* 1994, *54,* 317–321.

Heclo, H. "The OMB and the Presidency: The Problem of 'Neutral Competence.'" *Public Interest,* 1975, *38,* 80–85.

Hess, S. *Organizing the Presidency.* Washington, D.C.: Brookings Institution, 1976.

Kettl, D. F. *Sharing Power: Public Governance and Private Markets.* Washington, D.C.: Brookings Institution, 1993.

Kettl, D. F. "Beyond the Rhetoric of Reinvention: Driving Themes of the Clinton Administration's Management Reforms." *Governance,* 1994, *7,* 309.

Light, P. C. *Thickening Government: Federal Hierarchy and the Diffusion of Accountability.* Washington, D.C.: Brookings Institution, 1995.

Moe, R. C. "Exploring the Limits of Privatization." *Public Administration Review,* 1987, *47,* 456–457.

Moe, R. C. "Traditional Organizational Principles and the Managerial Presidency: From Phoenix to Ashes." *Public Administration Review,* 1990, *50,* 129–140.

Moe, R. C., and Gilmour, R. S. "Rediscovering Principles of Public Administration: The Neglected Foundation of Public Law." *Public Administration Review,* 1995, *55,* 135–146.

Moe, T. M. "The Politicized Presidency." In J. E. Chubb and P. Peterson (eds.), *The New Direction in American Politics.* Washington, D.C.: Brookings Institution, 1985.

Nathan, R. *The Administrative Presidency.* New York: Wiley, 1983.

National Academy of Public Administration. *Strengthening Presidential Leadership by Establishing an Office of Federal Management.* Washington, D.C.: National Academy of Public Administration, 1988.

Neustadt, R. E. *Presidential Power: The Politics of Leadership.* New York: Wiley, 1960.

North, D. C. *Institutions, Institutional Change, and Economic Performance.* Cambridge, Mass.: Cambridge University Press, 1990.

Osborne, D., and Gaebler, T. *Reinventing Government: How the Entrepreneurial Spirit Is Transforming the Public Sector from Schoolhouse to Statehouse, City Hall to the Pentagon.* Reading, Mass.: Addison Wesley Longman, 1992.

Pinkerton, J. P. *What Comes Next: The End of Big Government and the New Paradigm Ahead.* New York: Hyperion, 1995.

Rose, R. *The Postmodern President: The White House Meets the World.* Chatham, N.J.: Chatham House, 1988.

Stanton, T. H. "Assessing Institutional Development: The Legal Framework That Shapes Public Institutions." In R. Picciotto and R. C. Rist (eds.), *Evaluating Country Development Policies and Programs: New Approaches for a New Agenda.* San Francisco: Jossey-Bass, 1995.

U.S. Congress, Senate Committee on Governmental Affairs. *Office of Management and Budget: Evolving Roles and Future Issues.* Senate Print 134, 99th Cong., 2nd Sess. Washington, D.C.: U.S. Government Printing Office, 1986.

U.S. Congress, Senate Committee on Banking, Housing and Urban Affairs, HUD/MOD Rehab Investigating Subcommittee. *Final Report and Recommendations.* Committee Print 124, 101st Cong., 2nd Sess. Washington, D.C.: U.S. Government Printing Office, 1990.

U.S. Congress, House Committee on the Budget. *Management Reform: A Top Priority for the Federal Executive Branch.* Committee Print, 102nd Cong., 1st Sess. Washington, D.C.: U.S. Government Printing Office, 1991.

U.S. Congress, House Committee on Government Reform and Oversight. *Making Government Work: Fulfilling the Mandate for Change.* House Report 435, 104th Cong., 1st Sess. Washington, D.C.: U.S. Government Printing Office, 1995.

U.S. Office of Management and Budget. *Making OMB More Effective in Serving the Presidency: Changes in OMB as a Result of OMB 2000 Review.* OMB Memorandum No. 94–16. Washington, D.C.: Office of Management and Budget, Mar. 1, 1994.

Volcker, P. *Rebuilding the Public Service.* Washington, D.C.: National Commission on the Public Service, 1989.

Weko, T. J. *The Politicizing Presidency: The White House Personnel Office, 1948–1994.* Lawrence: University of Kansas Press, 1995.

PART TWO

PRACTICAL FRAMEWORKS
OF PUBLIC LAW
AND ADMINISTRATION

While Part One emphasized fundamental constitutional and societal concerns in public law, politics, and public administration, Part Two addresses applied frameworks, techniques, and tools of law and administration. It explains how various actors in all branches of government play roles in the interpretation and application of law. It considers the legal authorities that an administrator is likely to encounter. And it explains the techniques most commonly used to interpret such authorities as constitutions and statutes.

In Chapter Four, Louis Fisher reminds public administrators that in considering the real operation of law in the legal system, one of the most fundamental facts of life is that courts, including the Supreme Court of the United States, are only some of the key decision makers. He argues that in reality, rather than participating in a process in which legislatures make the law, executives enforce it, and courts interpret it, all three sets of actors share in an ongoing dialogue about law and politics. This reality is clear where constitutional issues are involved, but it is even more obviously the case when statutes are under discussion. And on a day-to-day basis, discussions of law and administration are far more often about the nature and meaning of statutes than about bedrock constitutional debates.

Fisher explains that one of the problems with observers of contemporary legal controversies is that many take a linear and limited perspective. They look at developments up to the point where a high court, perhaps even the Supreme Court, renders a ruling in a dispute, and then they assume the matter is settled.

Not true, Fisher notes, citing examples of the ways in which executives and legislators respond to court rulings. New legislation or new administrative positions arise following court actions, and they may then go back to the courts for further consideration. This happens all the time. Failure to recognize these ongoing, multiparty conversations conveys an unreal and partial understanding of how the institutions of government operate, which is at the very heart of public administration.

That having been said, public administrators must understand that a complex body of law exists within which they must operate, even as elected officials continue to debate the need for dramatic changes in specific legal provisions and their implementation. Robert S. Gilmour and Holly Taylor Sellers (Chapter Five) get down to the business of explaining how to access important rules of law—what are termed legal authorities. Whether the authority at issue is a constitutional provision, a statute, a regulation, or a judicial precedent, logical and accessible tools are available to facilitate analysis and informed actions.

Gilmour and Sellers take a street-level view of the events that might trigger the need to locate a legal authority and the processes for doing so. They point out that much helpful information is available in sources other than the words of rules, statutes, and legislative history, and that before administrators refer to these very formal, standard legal sources, they first consider such sources as past practice, guidelines, manuals, and agency memoranda. When these sources prove not to be enough, administrators then move to the more standardized tools like regulations and statutes. Finally, the authors explain why and how precedent cases are used.

To use legal precedents, it is necessary to understand the techniques of legal interpretation. This is the subject of Chapter Six. In this chapter, Howard Ball focuses first on the techniques that are employed in dealing with constitutional issues. These techniques are unique because of the nature of the Constitution, the open-textured language with which it was written, and the difficulty of amending the document should courts render inappropriate and incorrect interpretations of its provisions. In addition to these relatively practical considerations, Ball points to constitutionalism—a commitment to the maintenance of and obedience to a written fundamental charter of government—as a basic American public value.

All that having been said, however, Ball notes that there have historically been several different perspectives on constitutional interpretation, ranging from the so-called literalist view, that the document means precisely what it says and nothing else, to the living document approach, which calls for efforts to keep the Constitution current by interpreting its words in light of contemporary social needs. Ball addresses these and other perspectives on interpretation so that administrators may better understand how other participants in what Fisher earlier termed the constitutional dialogue approach the problem of applying the terms of the document.

Ball then explains why and how the processes of statutory interpretation differ from the constitutional task, and he introduces the additional elements that come into play when administrators work to translate the terms of legislative enactments into action. While a fundamental obligation is to read statutes closely and accurately, that task must be accomplished against a background that calls for an important process of reconciliation. Ball indicates that courts that review the way agencies implement statutes must grant sufficient deference to administrative expertise and experience in order to achieve effectiveness and efficiency and, simultaneously, to the need to maintain a close-enough oversight of agency interpretations to ensure accountability.

With this body of authority and interpretation in mind, as well as an appreciation for Cornelius M. Kerwin's concern for the management of legal processes, Phillip J. Cooper turns in Chapter Seven to the use of legal tools to carry out administrative obligations. In particular, he focuses on public law as a set of tools for policy and management.

Cooper considers the different devices employed to issue authoritative pronouncements of policy, including statutes, executive orders, treaties, and regulations, as well as the different types and uses of each device. The type of statute or regulation that is at issue matters, not only because devices operate in different ways but also because the process for generating and changing them differs. And while it is true that the processes of policymaking and administration are interconnected in many respects, primary uses of some other tools are management oriented. In addition to the management uses of rules, the chapter considers management perspectives on adjudication, contracts, interjurisdictional agreements, and even judicial review. For example, although many substantive rules are created to regulate firms or individuals in the community, procedural rules are issued to bind the agency internally and thereby enhance efficiency and effectiveness and avoid arbitrariness.

The chapter argues that it is not just the device itself that provides tools for management but also the processes associated with that instrument. Thus rulemaking procedures can be used to enhance participation and ensure feedback—important goals for any modern manager.

The chapter also argues that a variety of contemporary political leaders and would-be administrative reformers have attacked both the devices and the processes. In the bargain, the critics have, ironically enough, undermined public management efforts rather than enhancing them. Thus those who have made regulations and rulemaking the great evil to be eliminated, as well as those who have attacked adjudicative mechanisms as a burdensome judicialization of administration, have pressed criticisms to dangerous extremes that have undermined important mechanisms that are necessary to do the people's business effectively, fairly, and in an accountable manner.

CHAPTER FOUR

The Law-Politics Dialogue

It's Not All Courts!

Louis Fisher

Administrators and practitioners play a vital, creative, and continuing role in defining public law, both through initiatives within their agencies and in their interactions with the legislative branch and the courts. There is no reason for agency officials to be overly deferential either to the authority or to the expertise of the legislative and judicial branches. The experience of working within an agency—of applying legislative language to concrete problems—yields information and understanding that are indispensable to the work of legislators and judges.

Agency participation has a circular quality in the sense that rarely is there a "final word" on a legal matter. Instead, all three branches of government are involved in a dialogue that constantly defines and redefines legal boundaries and legal rights. Justice Felix Frankfurter put the role of the judiciary into proper perspective by reminding us that the Supreme Court "can only hope to set limits and point the way. It falls to the lot of legislative bodies and administrative officials to find practical solutions within the frame of our decisions" (*Niemotko* v. *Maryland,* 1961, pp. 275–276). At times the legislative and executive branches work within the broad contours of a judicial decision. On other occasions it is the judiciary that seeks practical solutions within the frame of congressional statutes and executive precedents.

EFFORTS TO SEPARATE LAW AND POLITICS

Although courts like to pretend that politics is something set apart from the rigors of legal analysis, law and politics not only intermesh but are often two sides of the same coin. For many years judges attempted to convince the public that their decisions originated from a pristine search for legal truth, undeterred by political considerations. Thus judges "found" the law rather than made it. The doctrine of mechanical jurisprudence, joined with the supposedly nonpolitical nature of the judiciary, provided convenient reasons for separating courts from the rest of government. A perceptive essay by political scientist C. Herman Pritchett noted that the disciplines of law and political science drifted apart for semantic, philosophical, and practical reasons: "Law is a prestigious symbol, whereas politics tends to be a dirty word. Law is stability; politics is chaos. Law is impersonal; politics is personal. Law is given; politics is free choice. Law is reason; politics is prejudice and self interest. Law is justice; politics is who gets there first with the most" (Pritchett, 1969, p. 31).

No one watching government today can find hermetically sealed categories of law and politics. There are differences, often significant differences, but more often they represent matters of shadings and nuance, not issues of black and white.

Justices of the Supreme Court have often encouraged the belief that a gulf separates law from politics. Chief Justice John Marshall insisted in *Marbury* v. *Madison* (1803) that "questions in their nature political . . . can never be made in this court" (p. 170). In that very same decision, however, he established a precedent of far-reaching political importance: the power of the judiciary to review and overturn the actions of Congress and the executive. As noted by one scholar, Marshall "more closely associated the art of judging with the positive qualities of impartiality and disinterestedness, and yet he had made his office a vehicle for the expression of his views about the proper foundations of American government" (White, 1976, p. 35).

Marshall closely tracked the path established by Alexander Hamilton's essay in *Federalist* No. 78. According to Hamilton, the judiciary, "from the very nature of its functions," would also be the "least dangerous" to the political rights of the Constitution. The executive, he noted, holds the sword and the legislature commands the purse. Because the judiciary has "no influence over either the sword or the purse, . . . It may truly be said to have neither FORCE nor WILL, but merely judgment; and must ultimately depend upon the aid of the executive arm even for the efficacy of its judgments." There is something to be said for Hamilton's analysis. Certainly Justice Marshall knew, in the *Marbury* case, that any effort by the Court to order President Jefferson to deliver the disputed commissions would be not only ignored but ignored with impunity. But to confine the judiciary to matters of "judgment" is to misinterpret the manner in which the courts go about their business.

During his days as law school professor, Felix Frankfurter referred to constitutional law as "applied politics" (MacLeish and Prichard, [1962] 1990). The "simple truth of the matter," he said, "is that decisions of the Court denying or sanctioning the exercise of federal power, as in the first child labor case, largely involve a judgment about practical matters, and not at all any esoteric knowledge of the Constitution" (p. 12). Frankfurter regarded courts as "less than ever technical expounders of technical provisions of the Constitution. They are arbiters of the economic and social life of vast regions and at times of the whole country" (Frankfurter and Landis, 1928, p. 173).

Once on the bench, however, Frankfurter did his part to perpetuate the law-politics dichotomy. Refusing to take a reapportionment case in 1946, he said it was "hostile to a democratic system to involve the judiciary in the politics of the people" (*Colegrove* v. *Green*, 1946, pp. 553–554). In *Baker* v. *Carr* (1962) the Supreme Court liberated itself from this narrow holding, and it has demonstrated throughout its history a sensitivity to the political system in which it must operate. Writing in 1921, Justice Benjamin Nathan Cardozo dismissed the idea that judges "stand aloof" from the "great tides and currents" that engulf the rest of mankind (Cardozo, 1921, p. 168).

Although the Supreme Court is an independent branch, it is not isolated. It is buffeted by the same social winds that press upon the executive and legislative branches, even if it does not respond in precisely the same way. It does not, and cannot, operate in a vacuum.

Chief Justice Earl Warren believed that law could be distinguished from politics. Progress in politics "could be made and most often was made by compromising and taking half a loaf where a whole loaf could not be obtained." He insisted that the "opposite is true so far as the judicial process was concerned." Through the judicial process, "and particularly in the Supreme Court, the basic ingredient of decision is principle, and it should not be compromised and parceled out a little in one case, a little more in another, until eventually someone receives the full benefit" (Warren, 1977, p. 6).

However, the piecemeal and incremental approach describes the judicial process quite well. The Supreme Court prefers to avoid general rules that exceed the necessities of a particular case. Especially in the field of constitutional law, it recognizes the "embarrassment" that may result from formulating rules or deciding questions "beyond the necessities of the immediate issue" (*Euclid* v. *Ambler Company*, 1926, p. 397). Compromise, expediency, and ad hoc action are a part of the process by which a multimember Court gropes incrementally toward a consensus and decision. The desegregation case, *Brown* v. *Board of Education of Topeka* (1954), was preceded by two decades of halting progress toward the eventual abandonment of the "separate but equal" doctrine enunciated in 1896.

It is typical of the Court to make a series of exploratory movements followed by backing and filling—a prudent and sensible policy for resolving constitutional issues that have profound political, social, and economic ramifications.

The desegregation case of 1954 plunged the Court into a political maelstrom that pitted blacks against whites, the North against the South, and states righters against advocates of national power. Justice Robert Jackson, who regarded the briefs for this case as sociology rather than law, was reluctant to rule segregation as unconstitutional. When he finally decided to join the majority, the case still seemed to him basically a question of politics: "I don't know how to justify the abolition of segregation as a judicial act. Our problem is to make a judicial decision out of a political conclusion . . ." (Schwartz, 1983, p. 89).

Chief Justice Warren came closer to the truth when he examined the Court's role with regard to the treatment of Japanese-Americans during World War II. The Court upheld both the curfew order against Japanese-Americans and their eventual detention in inland camps. In a remarkable sentence, Warren said that the fact that the Court upheld that action as constitutional "does not necessarily answer the question whether, in a broader sense, it actually is" (Warren, 1962, p. 193). In other words, when the courts fail to strike down a governmental action, that does not mean that constitutional standards have been followed. Warren concluded that under our political system the judiciary must play a limited role: "In our democracy it is still the Legislature and the elected Executive who have the primary responsibility for fashioning and executing policy consistent with the Constitution" (p. 202). Even here he warned against excessive reliance on the political branches: "The day-to-day job of upholding the Constitution really lies elsewhere. It rests, realistically, on the shoulders of every citizen" (p. 202). Agency officials, who are in touch with issues that affect both citizens and aliens, must remain sensitive to constitutional standards and democratic rights.

After he left the Court, Justice Potter Stewart reflected on the decision to exclude from the courtroom evidence that had been illegally obtained: "Looking back, the exclusionary rule seems a bit jerry-built—like a roller coaster track constructed while the roller coaster sped along. Each new piece of track was attached hastily and imperfectly to the one before it, just in time to prevent the roller coaster from crashing, but without an opportunity to measure the curves and dips preceding it or to contemplate the twists and turns that inevitably lay ahead" (Stewart, 1983, p. 1366).

Court orders must be obeyed, but obedience here relates only to the orderly and expeditious administration of justice, not to the soundness and finality of a court order. Upon appeal, erroneous court orders may be reversed. The fact that the judiciary has acted does not relieve members of the political branches or the public from exercising independent judgment.

THE POLITICS OF LITIGATION

Especially in the twentieth century, issues that reach the state and federal courts embody disputes that are of vital importance to individual citizens, corporations and trade unions, and the elected branches of government. Constitutions do not govern by text alone, even as interpreted by a supreme body of judges. Constitutions draw their life from forces outside the law: from ideas, customs, society, and the constant dialogue among political institutions. In *South Carolina* v. *United States* (1905, p. 448), the Supreme Court stated that the Constitution "is a written instrument. As such its meaning does not alter. That which it meant when adopted it means now." Having delivered the conventional formula, the Court immediately came to terms with reality: "Being a grant of powers to a government its language is general, and as changes come in social and political life it embraces in its grasp all new conditions which are within the scope of the powers in terms conferred."

Just as the Supreme Court leaves its mark on American society, so do social forces determine constitutional law. As part of government, courts are buffeted by social and political pressures. To what extent is difficult to say. We see the final result in a decision but can only speculate how the court got there. For their own institutional protection, courts must take account of social movements and public opinion.

It is tempting to concentrate on decisional law and ignore the political, historical, and social framework in which decisions are handed down. Textbooks in constitutional law generally separate the courts from the rest of government and make unrealistic claims of judicial independence. Morris Raphael Cohen, one of the early students of legal realism, denied that the law is a "closed, independent system having nothing to do with economic, political, social, or philosophical science" (Cohen, 1933, pp. 380–381). It was Lord Ratcliffe (1960) who counseled that "we cannot learn law by learning law." This tantalizing phrase meant that law must be "a part of history, a part of economics and sociology, a part of ethics and a philosophy of life. It is not strong enough in itself to be a philosophy of itself" (pp. 92–93).

It is too flippant to accept the fictional Mr. Dooley's pronouncement that the Supreme Court follows the elections' returns, but careful studies by Robert Dahl (1957), David Adamany (1973), and Richard Funston (1975) show that the Court generally stays within the political boundaries of its times. The judiciary is most likely to be out of step with the legislative and executive branches during periods of electoral and partisan realignment, when the country undergoes sharp shifts in political directions while the courts retain the orientation of an age gone by.

When judges stray outside and oppose the policy of elected leaders, they do so at substantial risk to their legitimacy, effectiveness, and independence. Courts maintain their strength by steering a course that fits within the permissible limits of public opinion. This reality does not make the courts a political body in the same sense as the legislative and executive branches, but pragmatism and statesmanship must temper abstract legal analysis. Tocqueville noted in the 1830s that the power of the Supreme Court "is enormous, but it is the power of public opinion. They are all-powerful as long as the people respect the law; but they would be impotent against popular neglect or contempt of the law." Judges "must be statesmen, wise to discern the signs of the times, not afraid to brave the obstacles that can be subdued, nor slow to turn away from the current when it threatens to sweep them off . . ." (Tocqueville, [1835] 1951, pp. 151–152).

The responsiveness of courts to the social community is even more immediate at the local level. Federal district courts have regularly reflected public opinion on such matters as civil rights, labor relations, and the sentencing of Vietnam resisters. A conference of federal judges in 1961 agreed that public opinion "should not materially affect sentences" and that the judiciary "must stand firm against undue public opinion." Nevertheless, the judges cautioned that resistance to public opinion "should not mean that the community's attitude must be completely ignored in sentencing: although judges should be leaders of public opinion, they must never get so far out in front that the public loses sight of them" (35 F.R.D. 398, p. 1964).

Social and political forces affect the process by which courts decide a case. In such contentious areas as civil rights, sex discrimination, church and state, and criminal procedures, judges move with a series of half steps, disposing of the particular issue at hand while preparing for the next case. Through installments they lay the groundwork for a more comprehensive solution, always sensitive to the response of society and the institutions of government that must enforce judicial rulings. This social and political framework sets the boundaries for judicial activity and helps influence the substance of specific decisions—if not immediately, then within a few years. A purely technical approach to the law misses the constant, creative interplay that takes place between the judiciary and society at large.

From the late nineteenth century to the 1930s, federal and state courts struck down a number of legislative efforts to ameliorate industrial conditions. Laws that established maximum hours or minimum wages were declared an unconstitutional interference with the "liberty of contract" (a phrase that does not appear in the Constitution). Lawyers from the corporate sector helped translate the economic philosophy of laissez faire into legal terms and constitutional doctrines. These judicial rulings were so spiced with conservative business values that Justice Oliver Wendell Holmes protested that cases were "decided upon an economic theory which a large part of the country does not entertain." He chided his brethren: "The Fourteenth Amendment does not enact Mr. Herbert Spencer's Social Statics" (*Lochner* v. *New York*, 1905, p. 75). When it was evident that the country would no longer tolerate interference by the courts, the judiciary retreated. After retiring from the Court, Justice Owen Roberts explained the expansion of national power over economic conditions: "Looking back, it is difficult to see how the Court could have resisted the popular urge for uniform standards throughout the country—for what in effect was a unified economy" (Roberts, 1951, p. 61).

To associate litigation with social forces is not meant to demean the courts or reduce adjudication to just another form of politics. Judges make policy, but not in the same manner as legislators and executives. Unlike the elected branches, the judiciary is not expected to satisfy the needs of the majority or respond to electoral pressures. Instead, it has a special responsibility to protect minority interests and constitutional rights. Although judges have an opportunity to engage in their own form of lobbying, they are not supposed to publicly debate a pending issue or participate in ex parte meetings that are open to only one party—privileges routinely exercised by legislators and administrators. Most lobbying by the executive and legislative branches is open and direct; lobbying by the judiciary is filtered through legal briefs, professional meetings, and law review articles.

The executive and legislative branches have elaborate mechanisms for handling public relations, self promotion, and contacts with the press. For the most part, judges release their opinions and remain silent. If executive officials and legislators are criticized in the press, they can respond in kind. Judges, with rare exceptions, take their lumps without retaliation.

Even so, the operations of the judiciary are sometimes difficult to distinguish from those of the legislative and executive branches. Although responsive to majoritarian pressures, legislators and executive officials are also sensitive to minority rights, often to a greater extent than the courts (Fisher, 1993). The political branches are more at liberty to engage in ad hoc and random actions, but they usually follow general principles and precedents of their own and feel an obligation to present a reasoned explanation for their decisions.

New appointments to the courts allow the judiciary to incorporate contemporary social and political attitudes. New judges bring fresh ideas and philosophies to the courts. It was Justice Robert Jackson's view that changes in the Court's composition enable it to absorb ideas and attitudes from the public. He denied that this admission did violence to the notion of an independent, nonpolitical judiciary: "let us not deceive ourselves; long-sustained public opinion does influence the process of constitutional interpretation. Each new member of the ever-changing personnel of our courts brings to his task the assumptions and accustomed thought of a later period. The practical play of the forces of politics is such that judicial power has often delayed but never permanently defeated the persistent will of a substantial majority" (Jackson, 1953, p. 761).

LOBBYING THE COURTS

Private organizations accept litigation as part of the political process. They may conclude that their interests are better served by seeking court action than by approaching the legislative and executive branches. Many of the major labor-management struggles were initially fought in the courts, with unions and employers hiring counsel to represent their interests. In 1963, Justice William Brennan referred to litigation as a form of political expression. Groups unable to achieve their objectives through the electoral process, Brennan said, often turn to the judiciary: "Under the conditions of modern government, litigation may well be the sole practicable avenue open to a minority to petition for a redress of grievances" (*NAACP* v. *Button*, 1963, pp. 429–430). For groups such as the National Association for the Advancement of Colored People (NAACP) and the American Civil Liberties Union, litigation is not merely a technique for resolving private differences. It is a form of political expression and association (*In re Primus*, 1978, p. 428).

In an article in 1969, Justice Thurgood Marshall explained the importance of individual and group efforts to pressure the courts and the elected branches. Since constitutional protections are not self enforcing, citizens have to act: "No matter how solemn and profound the declarations of principle contained in our charter of government, no matter how dedicated and independent our judiciary, true justice can only be obtained through the actions of committed individuals, individuals acting both independently and through organized groups." Rights guaranteed by the Constitution "can be made meaningful only by legislative or judicial action. . . . Legislation does not pass itself and the courts cannot act in the absence of a controversy" (Marshall, 1969, pp. 662–663). It is therefore crucial for citizens to organize and press their interests upon the branches of government.

The use of litigation in the 1940s and 1950s to shape social policy led to broader public participation and produced fundamental changes in the amicus curiae (friend of the court) brief. Originally, such briefs permitted third parties—people who had no direct interest in the case—to bring certain facts to the attention of the court to avoid judicial error. Over the years these briefs lost their innocent quality and became an instrument used by private groups to advance their causes. The amicus curiae brief moved "from neutrality to partisanship, from friendship to advocacy." It stopped being "a neutral, amorphous embodiment of justice" and became an active participant in the interest group struggle (Krislov, 1963, p. 694).

The political nature of litigation is underscored by many familiar examples. Through dozens of court actions, the Jehovah's Witnesses secured such rights as the refusal to salute or pledge allegiance to the American flag, the right to solicit from house to house, and the right to preach in the streets without a license. Those objectives were not available from legislatures responsive to majoritarian pressures. The NAACP created a Legal Defense and Educational Fund to pursue rights denied blacks by Congress and state legislatures. A series of victories in the courts established basic rights for blacks in voting, housing, education, and jury service. The National Consumers' League channeled its resources into litigation and won important protections for factory workers. The American Liberty League, organized by conservative businessmen, turned to litigation in an effort to prevent the enactment of economic regulation by Congress.

Through the publication of articles, books, and commission reports, authors have hoped to influence public opinion and a future court decision. Judicial reliance on this body of literature has become of deep concern to many legislators who fear that the judiciary indiscriminately considers "unknown, unrecognized and nonauthoritative text books, law review articles, and other writings of propaganda artists and lobbyists" (Patman, 1957). The author of this statement, Congressman Wright Patman, complained that the Supreme Court had turned increasingly for guidance to private publications and studies that were promoted by the administration. The research was designed, he said, not to study an issue objectively but to advance the particular views of private interests trying, through the medium of publication, to influence the judiciary's disposition of public policy questions. Experts pointed out in reply that the members of study committees and commissions are aware that lawyers will cite the reports in their briefs "and that the real impact of this might very well be in the decisions made by courts and administrative agencies" (Schwartz, 1957).

Since court opinions frequently turn on the "reasonableness" of governmental actions, legal briefs attempt to amass sociological data and scientific findings. The "Brandeis brief" of 1908 was the forerunner of this strategy, and it is now a common tactic for both sides of a lawsuit. Authors hope to see their writings cited in briefs and footnoted in court decisions. The practice of citing professional journals goes back at least to Justice Louis Brandeis in the 1920s. Other justices, like Benjamin Cardozo and Harlan Stone, adopted this technique as a way of keeping law current with changes in American society. Brandeis's opinions introduced a new meaning to the word "authority." He believed that an opinion "derives its authority, just as law derives its existence, from all the facts of life. The judge is free to draw upon these facts wherever he can find them, if only they are helpful" (Newland, 1959, p. 140).

INDEPENDENT STATE ACTION

By interpreting their own constitutions and statutes, states can reach constitutional decisions that differ markedly from U.S. Supreme Court rulings. The federal Constitution provides only a minimum, or a floor, for the protection of individual rights and liberties. As noted by the Supreme Court in 1980, each state has the "sovereign right to adopt in its own Constitution individual liberties more expansive than those conferred by the Federal Constitution" (*Prune-Yard Shopping Center* v. *Robins,* 1980, p. 81). When states want to express these independent views, they must make clear that their rulings depend exclusively on the constitution and laws of the state. If state courts base their decisions on "bona fide separate, adequate and independent grounds," the U.S. Supreme Court will not undertake a review (*Michigan* v. *Long,* 1983). Under these circumstances, the "final word" on certain constitutional issues rests with the states, not with the U.S. Supreme Court.

State independence is strengthened at times because state constitutions may contain language far more explicit and precise than the U.S. Constitution. Although the Supreme Court has accepted the use of public funds for sectarian schools to pay for such expenses as transportation and textbooks, many state courts have denied that type of assistance because of highly restrictive language in their constitutions that prohibits the appropriation of public funds for any religious worship or instruction (Fisher, 1995, pp. 772–773). Similarly, state constitutions are often far more explicit in protecting the rights of speech, assembly, and privacy. By interpreting these provisions, state courts and state legislatures can act in ways that depart dramatically from U.S. Supreme Court doctrines. Independent constitutional interpretations by the states can satisfy the values we place on diversity, pluralism, and a distrust of centralized government.

WHO HAS THE "LAST WORD"?

The notion that the Constitution is somehow equivalent to Supreme Court decisions is a curious product of the twentieth century. One searches previous periods in vain for evidence that the judiciary wields a monopoly on constitutional law. During the history of two centuries, the three branches have insisted on independent interpretations of the Constitution, and the nation is none the worse for it. On the whole, that model is preferable to the belief that the Supreme Court can somehow resolve all the fractious disputes that come its way. It has never done that successfully. At times the Court has issued decisions of great harm to itself and to the country. For the most part, Court decisions are tentative and reversible like other political events. To equate the Court with the Constitution is to place on the Court an institutional burden it should not, and cannot, carry.

In a masterful phrase, rendered almost hypnotic by its elegance, Justice Jackson said: "We are not final because we are infallible, but we are infallible only because we are final" (*Brown* v. *Allen,* 1953, p. 540). The historical record demonstrates convincingly that the Court is neither final nor infallible. Judicial decisions rest undisturbed only to the extent that the elected branches and the general public find the decisions convincing, reasonable, and acceptable. Otherwise, the debate on constitutional principles will continue. Justice Byron White was more realistic about judicial power when he said that the Supreme Court "is not alone in being obliged to construe the Constitution in the course of its work; nor does it even approach having a monopoly on the wisdom and insight appropriate to the task" (*Welsh* v. *United States,* 1970, p. 370).

Many constitutional issues are resolved without a lawsuit. The legislative and executive branches are constantly involved in constitutional interpretation through the passage of bills, through agency implementation, and through executive-legislative conflicts. Even when a legal dispute is brought before a court, there is no assurance that it will be settled there. The judiciary can avoid the constitutional issue by disposing of the case on statutory grounds or by raising threshold barriers of jurisdiction, standing, mootness, ripeness, political questions, and prudential considerations. If the constitutional question is decided, more likely than not the courts will defer to the interpretation previously reached by other branches. On those rare occasions when the courts invalidate a legislative or executive action, usually it is only a matter of time before the statute or administrative action is revised slightly to trigger another dialogue with the judiciary.

It is through this rich and dynamic political process that the Constitution is constantly adapted to seek harmony between legal principles and the needs of a changing society. This process of give and take and mutual respect permits the unelected judiciary to function in a democratic system. Court decisions are always subject to scrutiny by the elected branches and the people. Chief Justice Roger Taney once noted that an opinion by the Supreme Court on the construction of the Constitution "is always open to discussion when it is supposed to have been founded in error, and that its judicial authority should hereafter depend altogether on the force of the reasoning by which it is supported" (*Passenger Cases,* 1849, p. 470).

Just because the Court issues its judgment does not mean that others must suspend theirs. Constitutional determinations are not matters that can be left exclusively to the judiciary. Individuals outside the courts have their own judgments to make. As the seventeenth-century philosopher Baruch Spinoza advised, "no one can willingly transfer his natural right of free reason and judgment" (Spinoza, 1954, p. 333). Even with their own consent, people cannot abdicate the duty to think for themselves. What is constitutional or unconstitutional must be left for people to explore, ponder, and come to terms with. The courts are an important element, but not the only element, in maintaining a constitutional order. That task is necessarily shared with Congress, the president, executive agencies, the states, and the general public.

Cases Cited

Baker v. *Carr,* 369 U.S. 186 (1962).

Brown v. *Allen,* 344 U.S. 443 (1953).

Brown v. *Board of Education of Topeka,* 347 U.S. 483, (1954).

Colegrove v. *Green,* 328 U.S. 549 (1946).

Euclid v. *Ambler Company,* 272 U.S. 365 (1926).

In re Primus, 436 U.S. 412 (1978).

Lochner v. *New York,* 198 U.S. 45 (1905).

Marbury v. *Madison,* 5 U.S. 137 (1803).

Michigan v. *Long,* 463 U.S. 1032 (1983).

NAACP v. *Button,* 371 U.S. 415 (1963).

Niemotko v. *Maryland,* 340 U.S. 268 (1961).

Passenger Cases, 48 U.S. [7 How.] 283 (1849).

PruneYard Shopping Center v. *Robins,* 447 U.S. 74 (1980).

South Carolina v. *United States,* 199 U.S. 437 (1905).

Welsh v. *United States,* 398 U.S. 333 (1970).

References

Adamany, D. "Legitimacy, Realigning Elections, and the Supreme Court." *Wisconsin Law Review,* 1973, *1973,* 790–846.

Cardozo, B. N. *The Nature of the Judicial Process.* New Haven, Conn.: Yale University Press, 1921.

Cohen, M. R. *Law and the Social Order.* Orlando, Fla.: Harcourt Brace, 1933.

Dahl, R. A. "Decision-Making in a Democracy: The Supreme Court as a National Policy-Maker." *Journal of Public Law,* 1957, *6,* 279–295.

Fisher, L. "One of the Guardians, Some of the Time." In R. A. Licht (ed.), *Is the Supreme Court the Guardian of the Constitution?* Washington, D.C.: American Enterprise Institute Press, 1993.

Fisher, L. *American Constitutional Law.* New York: McGraw-Hill, 1995.

Frankfurter, F., and Landis, F. M. *The Business of the Supreme Court.* Old Tappan, N.J.: Macmillan, 1928.

Funston, R. "The Supreme Court and Critical Elections." *American Political Science Review,* 1975, *69,* 795–811.

Jackson, R. H. "Maintaining Our Freedoms: The Role of the Judiciary." *Vital Speeches,* 1953, *19*(24), 761.

Krislov, S. "The Amicus Curiae Brief: From Friendship to Advocacy." *Yale Law Journal,* 1963, *72,* 694.

MacLeish, A., and Prichard, E. F. (eds.). *Law and Politics.* Magnolia, Mass.: Smith, 1990. (Originally published 1962.)

Marshall, T. "Group Action in the Pursuit of Justice." *New York University Law Review,* 1969, *44,* 661–672.

Newland, C. A. "The Supreme Court and Legal Writing: Learned Journals as Vehicles of an Anti-Antitrust Lobby? *Georgetown Law Journal,* 1959, *48,* 105–143.

Patman, W. *Congressional Record,* 1957, *103,* 16160.

Pritchett, C. H. In J. B. Grossman and J. Tanenhaus (eds.), *Frontiers of Judicial Research.* Iowa City: University of Iowa, 1969.

Ratcliffe, C.J.R. *The Law and Its Compass.* Evanston, Ill.: Northwestern University Press, 1960.

Roberts, O. J. *The Court and the Constitution.* Cambridge, Mass.: Harvard University Law School, 1951.

Schwartz, B. *Super Chief: Earl Warren and His Supreme Court.* New York: New York University Press, 1983.

Schwartz, L. B. *Congressional Record,* 1957, *103,* 16167.

Spinoza, B. *Spinoza.* New York: Modern Library, 1954.

Stewart, P. "The Road to *Mapp* v. *Ohio* and Beyond: The Origins, Development and Future of the Exclusionary Rule in Search and Seizure Cases." *Columbia Law Review,* 1983, *83,* 1365–1404.

Tocqueville, A. de. *Democracy in America,* ed. P. Bradley. New York: Knopf, 1951. (Originally published 1835.)

Warren, E. "The Bill of Rights and the Military." *New York University Law Review,* 1962, *37,* 181–203.

Warren, E. *The Memoirs of Earl Warren.* New York: Doubleday, 1977.

White, G. E. *The American Judicial Tradition.* New York: Oxford University Press, 1976.

CHAPTER FIVE

Legal Authorities and Administrative Actions

Robert S. Gilmour
Holly Taylor Sellers

American public administrators make decisions daily that affect the lives of individual citizens and, more broadly, the course of public policy. In doing so they act on the basis of legal authority granted them by the public. Ultimately, administrators and their legal advisors cast their gaze upwards to the U.S. Constitution and to U.S. Supreme Court rulings and opinions as sources for such authority. Accordingly, much of the law-oriented public administration literature and practice understands proper policy and administrative behavior in much the same way, from the "top down." In practice, however, administrators generally should and are far more likely to make their decisions from the "bottom up," relying on legal cues and imperatives that are more immediately relevant, more readily accessible, or both. In response to these practical legal needs, this chapter examines how public administrators themselves are most likely to search for the sources or bases of legal authority for administrative action when decision-making questions—from the immediate to the ultimate—arise.

Important differences in relevant sources of legal authority occur as the result of differences in organizational structure, particularly relative to the location, level, function, and character of the governmental (or quasi-governmental) unit involved. While federal and state executive branch agencies are essentially hierarchical by design, there are numerous exceptions and anomalies (Meyer, 1972; Seidman and Gilmour, 1986). Moreover, pronounced constitutional and other structural differences are found among the states: gubernatorial powers, number and scope of agency powers, legislative size and resources, statutory specificity and sophistication, and the nature of oversight activity. Variations also occur with respect to judicial doctrines and activism of courts in their review of agency actions. Local governments are even more varied in their administrative arrangements, activities, and resources (Graham and Hays, 1986). Despite these differences, however, enough similarities remain to provide a general framework.

TRIGGERS FOR LEGAL INQUIRY

This discussion presupposes the emergence of an issue leading to legal review of an official action. In many instances, such reviews are initiated by decision makers themselves, though potentially there are numerous—and ultimately more compelling—additional reviewers. For a thoughtful though inexperienced official, nearly every event or decision point presents legal questions about how to proceed. Experience may decrease the frequency of such questions but will never (and should never) eliminate them. For one thing, legal answers, even to precisely the same questions, may change dramatically over time. For example, legally required procedures for the addition or deletion of a client to local welfare rolls may be revised summarily by the adoption of new internal policy guidelines; the promulgation of an agency rule; the passage of a new statute, such as the Welfare Reform Act of 1996; or the announcement of an appellate court decision in either state or federal court, such as when the U.S. Supreme Court required pretermination hearings for welfare recipients (*Goldberg* v. *Kelly,* 1970).

It is difficult to predict with certainty just which issues will launch a legal inquiry. In some settings, legal issues are raised internally, almost as matters of routine (Are we doing the right thing? Are we doing it in the appropriate way?), and if not by the decision maker in the field, then by a coworker or supervisor. In other instances issues may be raised by a client, a clientele organization, a public interest group, or the communications media. In still other instances, issues are raised pointedly in a legal complaint to enjoin imminent administrative action or in a suit for relief from action already taken (see, for example, Wood, 1990). Whatever the genesis of legal issues, the need for administrators to anticipate them, to address them during the decision-making process, and to avoid obvious, unnecessary, and costly mistakes is imperative.

SOURCES OF AUTHORITY: PRIORITIES FROM THE STREET LEVEL

Starting from the premise that street-level administrators rely first and most heavily on legal touchstones closest to their operating level, several sources of authority become immediately identifiable and accessible. Other sources that are unfamiliar to many administrators and seemingly more distant and arcane are nonetheless reasonably accessible as well.

Past Practice

As matters of daily routine, many if not most actions are taken on the basis of past practice. The ancient justification "We've always done it that way" is not only generally acceptable but also encouraged. A few agencies that base their formal decisions on precedent may actually be required, on changing their course of action, to "supply a reasoned analysis indicating that prior policies and standards are being deliberately changed, not casually ignored . . ." (*Greater Boston Television Corporation* v. *FCC*, 1971, p. 852). Even when faithful adherence to past practice is not legally obligated, it ensures consistency of action—the very antithesis of arbitrariness.

The presumption embraced by a preference for consistency is that the initial rationale for a given course of action was legally appropriate when first taken, and that it remains so in the present (*Motor Vehicle Manufacturers Association of the United States* v. *State Farm Mutual Automobile Insurance Company, Inc.,* 1983). However, changes in legal standards over the past few decades, particularly with regard to procedural fairness and completeness, have made we've-always-done-it procedures of many years' duration suspect and ripe for thoroughgoing review. Many long-standing summary arrangements for the discipline or dismissal of municipal and state employees, for example, were changed literally overnight from Washington with the announcement in 1985 of the U.S. Supreme Court decision in *Cleveland Board of Education* v. *Loudermill,* which required that when a government employer dismisses a subordinate, "the tenured public employee is entitled to oral or written notice of the charges against him, an explanation of the employer's evidence, and an opportunity to present his side of the story" (p. 546).

Agency Memoranda, Guidelines, and Manuals

Perpetuation of a legitimate course of action may eventually lead to commemoration of a procedure in an office memorandum, in agency guidelines, or in a manual. Whether this is done will depend upon multiple factors, including the size and resources of the office, the likelihood that a particular scenario will be repeated, informal traditions and past experience of the office, and internal procedures for generating such a memo or policy statement.

Another element important to the adoption of internal guidelines is the applicability of statutory procedural requirements in an agency's enabling legislation (the statute that created and empowers an agency) or in a generic administrative procedure act. In the federal example, rulemaking provisions of the U.S. Administrative Procedure Act (APA) exempt agency adoption of "interpretative rules, general statements of policy, or rules of agency organization, procedure, or practice" from notice-and-comment prerequisites demanded by the APA for promulgation of an agency rule, "except when notice or hearing is required by [another] statute . . ." (5 U.S.C. §553b). The Model State Administrative Procedure Act and the "little" APAs of a number of states offer no such exemption. Moreover, even federal agency "guidelines" and "general statements of policy" that "affect substantial individual rights and obligations" must "remain consistent with the governing legislation [and must also] employ procedures that conform to the law" (*Morton* v. *Ruiz,* 1974, pp. 230–232). In short, federal agency policies affecting the legal rights of those outside the agency must be adopted according to the same procedures required of other agency-made law.

Despite these requirements, the more burdensome procedural requirements have been added to rulemaking (see for example, E.O. 12291 and E.O. 12498), the more tempting it is for agencies to use internal procedural rules, interpretations, and so-called policy statements to avoid APA rulemaking obligations (Kerwin, 1994, pp. 72–75). The legitimate reason for agency issuance of such statements and interpretations (sometimes referred to as "interpretative rules") is to provide additional information as a means of improving compliance without changing basic policy. Thus the Federal Trade Commission issued interpretative guidelines, including sample pricing and disclosure materials, to funeral directors and used-car dealers in order to encourage compliance with the commission's consumer protection rules, even though those industries were free to make legal challenges to the regulations themselves.

Once a decision is made to commit informal organizational norms and tenets of practice to the more formal language of a practice-and-procedure manual, thus promulgating them as rules, it should be understood that the organization is then bound by such a manual as a matter of law for as long as it remains in effect (*United States* v. *Nixon,* 1974, pp. 964–966). In fact, the existence of such a manual may actually encourage judicial review of official policy in such a way that agency discretion is reduced (*United States ex rel. Accardi* v. *Shaughnessy,* 1954), though it may also give the agency a more defensible position if its actions are challenged as arbitrary and capricious.

Additional problems with respect to agency manual writing also lie in the interpretation of generic policies to cover specific circumstances. It is the rare policy that foresees and addresses all possible scenarios; thus officials are left to interpret policy in light of the particular circumstances at hand. Augmenting existing policy statements with the addition and examination of relevant past decisions and memos that do not constitute official policy statements may yield a coherent pattern. But more likely it will not. In such a case, a plausible argument will have to be made for the most consistent body of actions or, if inconsistent, the most recent decisions and pronouncements. An example of this is agency or departmental policies governing sexual harassment. Typically such policies provide for reporting, investigation, and resolution of complaints.

Should a determination be made that harassment has occurred, a variety of remedies may be available, including counseling, change of work assignment, suspension from employment, or termination from employment. Administrators faced with fashioning an appropriate remedy under the circumstances may want to supplement their judgment with information regarding prior infractions and resolutions. In addition to providing guidance in the immediate case, such consultation has the salutary effect of contributing to a consistent agency response to such incidents.

Regulations

The preceding discussion accounts for much of the legal authority relied upon for informal decision-making processes in many organizations, both public and private, on a daily basis. In the public sector, however, an executive official or administrator is far more likely to be faced with issues implicating agency regulations (rules), local ordinances, state statutes and constitutions, executive orders, and ultimately federal statutes and the U.S. Constitution.

In theory, at least, statutes passed by legislatures set out the purposes and powers of administrative agencies (also of municipalities and other public authorities) and define their overall policies, leaving to them the tasks of filling in the specifics through regulation. In turn, the regulatory (rulemaking) process is defined and structured by the federal APA and its counterparts in the states, and often also by particularized requirements of an agency's enabling legislation. Fundamentals of the informal rulemaking process are almost universally the same: placing a notice of proposed rulemaking (often referred to by the initials NPR or NPRM) in the *Federal Register* (or in a state equivalent, such as the *Connecticut Law Journal*); creating an opportunity for the public to comment on the proposed regulation in writing, orally, or both; and finally, promulgating and publishing the final regulation (legally binding rule), consistent with the record, including public comments received (see also Chapter Two).

Though regulations tend to be quite detailed, given the complexity of some of the subject matter, such as the control of toxic chemicals, detail does not necessarily imply clarity. What is clear, however, is that a regulation will bind the agency that issues it. As the Supreme Court has stated quite plainly: "So long as [a] regulation is extant it has the force of law. . . . So long as [a] regulation remains in force the Executive Branch is bound by it, and indeed the United States as the sovereign composed of the three branches is bound to respect and enforce it" (*United States* v. *Nixon*, 1974, pp. 694–696).

Where a regulation is ambiguous, the administrator's interpretation "becomes of controlling weight unless it is plainly erroneous or inconsistent with the regulation" (*Bowles* v. *Seminole Rock Company*, 1945, pp. 413–414; *Ford Motor Company* v. *Milhollin*, 1980, pp. 565–567). Consequently, self-conscious interpretations and other memoranda that can be understood as interpretations of regulations (also of agency orders) should be considered carefully before final drafts are released. By way of illustration, the U.S. Supreme Court, in ruling on the intent of a circular issued by the Department of Housing and Urban Development (HUD), based its determination on letters of HUD staff members and contrasting language in another HUD circular (*Thorpe* v. *Housing Authority,* 1969, p. 276). In another case that involved orders issued by the Secretary of the Interior, the Court held: "The Secretary's interpretation may not be the only one permitted by the language of the orders, but it is quite clearly a reasonable interpretation; courts must therefore respect it" (*Udall* v. *Tallman,* 1965, p. 4).

Such judicial deference to administrative articulation of its rules and orders makes it obvious that primary legal authority for regulatory interpretation, apart from controlling statutes, is to be found in the agency itself. Accordingly, care should be taken not only in preparing interpretative materials but also in collecting and cataloging them. At the very least, materials supporting such interpretations should be filed, along with an agency rationale or statement of reasons, and indexed in such a way that they can be readily retrieved.

Statutes and Legislative History

Although at first blush it may be comforting to locate a statute (or local ordinance) directly on the point of a question, statutory interpretation is a complicated and controversial area (see Dickerson, 1975; Scalia, 1997). Cases abound with interpretations of the "clear language" of a statute that are not at all clear once applied to a specific set of facts. In other situations, statutes may be ambiguous by design as masks for unresolved legislative differences or as reflections of legislative uncertainty as to matters of established fact, scientific feasibility, and general practicality. One of the most famous instances of this type of statute occurred when Congress passed the Occupational Safety and Health Act of 1970 (29 U.S.C. §651 *et seq.*), authorizing the Secretary of Labor to promulgate legal standards regulating exposure to "harmful physical agents" so that "to the extent feasible . . . no employee will suffer material impairment of health or functional capacity. . . ." The critical term, "extent feasible," was left undefined. Having developed an equally indeterminate (also conflicted) legislative record, Congress consequently left it to the Department of Labor and the courts to determine effective policy (see *Industrial Union Department, AFL-CIO* v. *American Petroleum Institute,* 1980).

As a rule, if legislation is clear on its face, in context courts will not look beyond the statutory language for purposes of interpretation even if that language leads to questionable results (*Tennessee Valley Authority* v. *Hill,* 1978). For example, in *Los Angeles Department of Water and Power* v. *Manhart* (1978), the U.S. Supreme Court struck down the use of gender-based retirement annuity calculations for contributions or payouts. While recognizing that such a decision could wreak havoc on the actuarial soundness of such programs, the Court nevertheless said that the controlling statute (the Civil Rights Act of 1964) plainly prohibited actions with regard to a particular pension based on class characteristics such as sex-differentiated longevity patterns. If Congress wanted to change the law, it could do so, but the court would not.

In the absence of legislative clarity, however, courts may well resort to other sources—hearing statements, floor debate, report language, signing statements, and other records—to determine legislative purpose and intent. With regard to federal law, the place to begin a search for such materials is in the *U.S. Code Congressional and Administrative News,* which provides a detailed history of each major statutory provision as well as critical documentation, including committee reports. (Historical materials on legislation may also be found in compilations by the Congressional Research Service; see U.S. Senate, 1986.) Unfortunately, no similar compendium of documents exists for state and local jurisdictions. These must usually be ferreted out from state libraries and legislative archives.

When carrying out the law, agencies (as well as reviewing courts) often find it advisable, even necessary, to delve beyond the black letter of statute. Under the doctrine of "primary jurisdiction" agencies administering statutes are commonly deferred to by courts as the appropriate authorities to make initial determinations of statutory meaning (*Eastex, Inc.* v. *NLRB,* 1978, p. 568). It is ordinarily expected that in doing so federal agencies will conscientiously attend to the commands of the committee report language that accompanies bills, even though such instructions may travel well beyond the confines of enacted statute (Ripley and Franklin, 1991, p. 63). Legislative histories answer such questions as whether a statute is reviewable (*Block* v. *Community Nutrition Institute,* 1984) or whether judicial review may be triggered by a private citizen rather than by government alone, in what are called "implied private rights of action" (*Middlesex County Sewerage Authority* v. *National Sea Clammers Association,* 1981). Agency attention is particularly important when committee report language, however extensive and detailed, accompanies appropriations laws. These reports explain the nature and bases for prohibitory provisions (for example, "No funds appropriated hereunder shall be expended for . . .") or for mandatory expenditures. The special power of appropriations committee report provisions reflects the political reality that willful agency disobedience of their terms may well result in swift retribution by appropriators during the succeeding annual budget cycle (Harris, 1964, p. 97; Schick, 1995, p. 162). In situations of this sort (which may also be found at the state and local levels), the political imperatives of such "legal authority" may outweigh even the importance of judicial review.

Case Law

Despite the detailed information provided in statutes, committee reports, regulations, and agency policy memos, many issues fall outside such provisions. Even when a provision is seemingly on point, there may have been further action on such an issue. Specifically, some of these matters may have been addressed and reported as the results of decided litigation. Most searches for appropriate legal authority will, in fact, only begin with a review of related statutory and regulatory provisions. Statutory searches commencing with the *United States Code Annotated* or with a state's annotated statutes, for example, will quickly locate judicial case notes explicating particular statutory provisions.

American common law, developed by judge-decided cases on the basis of precedent, may be trumped at any time by enactment of a statute. Immediately thereafter, however, such a statute is subject to challenge as to its constitutionality, meaning, and applicability. Moreover, contemporary problems may arise with regard to very old statutes. Thus, when cable television arrived on the scene, a court had to determine whether cable TV was a part of "broadcasting," as defined by an aging statute (the Communications Act of 1934), in deciding whether the Federal Communications Commission had regulatory jurisdiction over the newly emerging industry (*United States* v. *Southwestern Cable Company*, 1968). Consequently, it is a rare statute that may be read without reference to case law, particularly if it has been on the books for any length of time.

Mandatory Judicial Precedents. In the absence of statute, judicial decisions may alone provide legal answers to specific sets of problems or, where relevant legislation exists, a definitive interpretation of an existing statute. Unlike statutes, binding court precedents (holdings in official judicial reports of specific legal relevance) are virtually impossible to locate without recourse to privately printed annotations, digests, and citators. Straightforward access to mandatory precedents is further confounded by the American dual court system, in which fifty state judicial hierarchies exist parallel to but jurisdictionally separate from each other and from the federal court system. On an issue arising at the local level in which there is any imputation of a federal issue, both state and federal case law must be searched for effective authority.

West Publishing Company produces digests (indexed summaries of judicial holdings) of all American case law since 1658. These digests are published on a state-by-state basis (such as *West's Indiana Digest*) for all but three states (Delaware, Nevada, and Utah) and decennially for all jurisdictions combined (for instance, the *Ninth Decennial Digest*, Part Two, 1981–1986). They include all reported cases, are updated annually by pocket parts (literally, a leaflet attached to a publication by insertion in a "pocket" in the back of a volume), and are organized by case-holding topics according to West's Key Number System (a subject-based indexing system unique to that publisher's legal publications). These same topical headings and subheadings are cross-referenced with West's National Reporter System, which includes reported state cases by region (such as the *Southern Reporter, 2nd Series,* which reports Alabama, Florida, Louisiana, and Mississippi cases) and various federal reporters (such as the *Federal Reporter,* which includes the decisions of U.S. District Courts and U.S. Circuit Courts of Appeals, and the *Supreme Court Reporter* of U.S. Supreme Court opinions).

While this chapter does not purport to be a short course on "how to search the law" (see Cohen, Berring, and Olson, 1989; Corbin, 1989; and Cohen and Olson, 1992), at least one caveat is in order: legal interpretation is a continuous process. Mandatory precedents are only those directly on the point of inquiry that are issued most recently by the highest appellate court of jurisdictionally relevant authority. Heeding this warning requires that any search for controlling authority must extend to careful "Shepardizing" of relevant opinions in the appropriate Shepard's citators (see Cohen and Olson, 1992, chap. 3), consultation of the most recent pocket parts of relevant digests, and review of current slip opinions from relevant appellate courts. For many public managers, the starting point from which to access this kind of information may be very current law review articles or professional newsletters.

Persuasive Precedents. When no immediate state or federal precedents apply, cases from sister states with the same factual situations, legal claims, and judicial holdings may be highly persuasive if not controlling. Because legal reasoning proceeds by way of analogy, the objective of a search for persuasive authority is to find judicial answers to fact patterns so similar that logical distinctions cannot reasonably be drawn.

This approach may be most useful when states have adopted similar laws, or versions of uniform laws, such as the Uniform Commercial Code of the Model State Administrative Procedure Act. If substantially similar—or identical—statutes have been adopted, a precedent established under similar circumstances in another jurisdiction may provide a persuasive argument in favor of adoption of that interpretation.

Such an approach can also be taken when no uniform law provides a common denominator. One area in which states are continually struggling to find guidance is in defining "state action" in an ever-changing environment. While U.S. Supreme Court cases provide some guidance (such as *West* v. *Adkins*, 1988), the determination of when an action is attributed to the state, or is taken "under color of" state law, is necessarily made on a case-by-case basis. Thus, in *West*, the part-time physician providing services at a state hospital under contract with the state who was deemed a state actor could next be providing services at a different type of institution or under different contractual terms as a "private" actor. The efficacy of the analogy determines the persuasiveness of the precedent.

Persuasive precedents and assistance with the logical analysis for their understanding and application may most easily be located in the same sources in which many preliminary searches for mandatory precedents begin: in the leading legal reference works. An excellent place to begin virtually any search of

American common law is in one or both of the competing encyclopedias, *American Jurisprudence 2d* (Am.Jur.2d), published by the Lawyers Co-Operative Publishing Company/Bancroft-Whitney Company, and *Corpus Juris Secundum* (C.J.S.), produced by West Publishing Company. Both volumes are vast, copiously indexed, heavily footnoted, and frequently cited compendiums of law. Similar nonauthoritative but highly useful overview treatments of specific subareas of the law, often cited in judicial opinions, may be found in such multivolume works as Kenneth Culp Davis's *Administrative Law Treatise.* Loose-leaf reporting services such as the *Government Employee Relations Report* and the *Administrative Law Reporter Second* may also offer updated information in these rapidly changing areas of law.

In addition to the encyclopedias, treatises, and reporting services, the extensive annotated reports produced in the *American Law Reports* series *(A.L.R., A.L.R. 2d, A.L.R. 3d, A.L.R. 4th, A.L.R. 5th,* and *A.L.R. Fed.)* are especially useful, not only in finding appropriate law but in understanding varied approaches to the analysis of specialized legal problems in different jurisdictions. Additional analysis and persuasive authority is to be found in leading articles, notes, and commentaries published in the substantial number of legal periodicals produced through the law schools in the form of law reviews or journals. These may be located through the *Index to Legal Periodicals* or, even more efficiently, through computerized legal research engines such as Lexis/Nexis.

Constitutions

For some organizations, depending on the issue, a municipal charter, the state constitution, or even the U.S. Constitution may provide critical guidance. This may be true for questions involving both the general scope of agency authority and authority to act in a specific instance. While it is unusual for a case at the trial court level to be decided on the basis of constitutional authority, it is not at all unusual to face issues with constitutional ramifications. Obviously such situations make it difficult for administrators to proceed without expert counsel, but this is not to say that administrators need not be knowledgeable in this area.

Modern judicial decisions such as the Kent State case (*Scheuer* v. *Rhodes,* 1974), which involved state officials, and *Butz* v. *Economou* (1978), which affected federal officers, make it plain that the doctrine of "governmental immunity" is no longer absolute with respect to either the government (at any level) or its employees. An ensuing triad of cases (*Monell* v. *New York City Department of Social Services,* 1978; *Owen* v. *City of Independence, Missouri,* 1980; and *Maine* v. *Thiboutot,* 1980) demonstrated even more pointedly that local governments and their employees are no longer afforded unqualified immunity from law suits (Lee, 1987). Even a cursory review of such cases makes a compelling argument for public administrators to develop what David Rosenbloom (1992) terms a "constitutional competence," which comprehends the content and logical structure of the constitutional rights of those persons, including their subordinates, upon whom administrators act in their official capacities. This competence, it is argued, should be achieved through training, especially for those officials engaged in personnel actions and those in law enforcement (pp. 125, 128–129).

Even from a less instrumental perspective, public administrators may be regarded, ultimately, as constitutional officers who have, as such, a duty to exercise discretion in support of this role (Rohr, 1986, p. 181). Clearly the incentive is for officials "to err on the side of protecting citizens' rights" (*Owen* v. *City of Independence, Missouri,* 1980, p. 652). Unlike private actors, government officials are agents of the sovereign and are thus constrained by an enormous body of statutory, regulatory, and case law stemming from the Constitution as the means of protecting the rights and freedoms of citizens at the hands of the state (see Moe and Gilmour, 1995).

FINDING HELP: GUIDANCE ON LEGAL AUTHORITIES

The most accessible—and therefore most common—source of legal guidance is the administrative decision maker's peer group. Essentially, when a novel issue presents itself, the first inclination is to ask how to handle an issue or whether it has been encountered before. Failure to resolve such a question in the first instance is typically followed by inquiry up the chain of agency authority.

Another possible route is a lateral move to subject-matter or procedural specialists. These people may be available within an organization unit responsible for a particular area, such as a human resources management department or an affirmative action office for personnel issues. Some organizations have a standing committee or an ombudsman to whom inquiries and anomalous situations concerning specific policies may be referred for resolution.

Many administrative policymaking bodies also gather representative policies from other organizations as examples before attempting to create their own, just as legislatures examine other state (or national) statutes and model codes. At the very least, a prior policy adopted by an agency subject to similar constraints holds the advantage of having been thought through by experienced administrators elsewhere.

Local governments are typically involved in statewide support associations, such as the Connecticut Council of Municipalities, and national support organizations, such as the International City/County Management Association and the National League of Cities, which have research resources relevant to legal problems. State officials, similarly, may consult resources of the Council of State Governments in Lexington, Kentucky, and the State-Local Legal Center in Washington, D.C.

Extraordinary though it may seem, in view of the growing legions of American lawyers, there are still too few to go around—or more accurately, too few resources to hire them—for the awesome array of legal questions that arise in administrative settings. Large organizations typically have an in-house counsel, even a legal department. Or the attorney general may assign staff to an agency. Even so, legal advisors are likely to be accessible only through hierarchical channels, when and if questions raised are understood to merit expert attention. Smaller organizations and units of local government may not have regular access to legal counsel except when major, budget-straining legal issues can no longer be avoided or ignored. In either case, the prevalence of legal challenges in routine administrative practice argues strongly for the development, by nonlawyer administrators, of basic competence in the legal authorities most immediately relevant to agency operations and internal processes.

Cases Cited

Block v. *Community Nutrition Institute*, 467 U.S. 340 (1984).

Bowles v. *Seminole Rock Company*, 325 U.S. 410 (1945).

Butz v. *Economou*, 438 U.S. 478 (1978).

Cleveland Board of Education v. *Loudermill*, 470 U.S. 532 (1985).

Eastex, Inc. v. *NLRB*, 437 U.S. 556 (1978).

Ford Motor Company v. *Milhollin*, 444 U.S. 555 (1980).

Goldberg v. *Kelly*, 397 U.S. 254 (1970).

Greater Boston Television Corporation v. *FCC*, 444 F.2d 841 (D.C., Cir.), cert. denied 403 U.S. 923 (1971).

Industrial Union Department, AFL-CIO v. *American Petroleum Institute*, 448 U.S. 607 (1980).

Los Angeles Department of Water and Power v. *Manhart*, 435 U.S. 702 (1978).

Maine v. *Thiboutot*, 448 U.S. 1 (1980).

Middlesex County Sewerage Authority v. *National Sea Clammers Association*, 453 U.S. 1 (1981).

Monell v. *New York City Department of Social Services*, 436 U.S. 658 (1978).

Morton v. *Ruiz*, 415 U.S. 199 (1974).

Motor Vehicle Manufacturers Association of the United States v. *State Farm Mutual Automobile Insurance Company, Inc.*, 463 U.S. 29 (1983).

Owen v. *City of Independence, Missouri*, 445 U.S. 622 (1980).

Scheuer v. *Rhodes*, 416 U.S. 232 (1974).

Tennessee Valley Authority v. *Hill*, 437 U.S. 153 (1978).

Thorpe v. *Housing Authority*, 393 U.S. 268 (1969).

Udall v. *Tallman*, 380 U.S. 1 (1965).

United States ex rel. Accardi v. *Shaughnessy*, 347 U.S. 260 (1954).

United States v. *Nixon*, 418 U.S. 683 (1974).

United States v. *Southwestern Cable Company*, 392 U.S. 157 (1968).

West v. *Adkins*, 108 S.Ct. 2250 (1988).

References

Cohen, M. L., Berring, R. C., and Olson, K. C. *How to Find the Law.* (9th ed.) St. Paul, Minn.: West, 1989.

Cohen, M. L., and Olson, K. C. *Legal Research in a Nutshell.* (5th ed.) St. Paul, Minn.: West, 1992.

Corbin, J. *Find the Law in the Library.* Chicago: American Library Association, 1989.

Davis, K. C. *Administrative Law Treatise.* 5 vols. (2nd ed.) San Diego: Davis, 1978–1989.

Dickerson, F. R. *The Interpretation and Application of Statutes.* New York: Little, Brown, 1975.

Graham, C. B., and Hays, S. W. *Managing the Public Organization.* Washington, D.C.: Congressional Quarterly Press, 1986.

Harris, J. P. *Congressional Control of Administration.* Washington, D.C.: Brookings Institution, 1964.

Kerwin, C. M. *Rulemaking: How Government Agencies Write Law and Make Policy.* Washington, D.C.: Congressional Quarterly Press, 1994.

Lee, Y. S. "Civil Liability of State and Local Governments: Myth and Reality." *Public Administration Review,* 1987, *47,* 160–170.

Meyer, M. W. *Bureaucratic Structure and Authority.* New York: HarperCollins, 1972.

Moe, R. C., and Gilmour, R. S. "Rediscovering Principles of Public Administration: The Neglected Foundation of Public Law." *Public Administration Review,* 1995, *55,* 135–146.

Ripley, R. B., and Franklin, G. A. *Congress, the Bureaucracy, and Public Policy.* (5th ed.) Pacific Grove, Calif.: Brooks/Cole, 1991.

Rohr, J. A. *To Run a Constitution: The Legitimacy of the Administrative State.* Lawrence: University of Kansas Press, 1986.

Rosenbloom, D. H. "Public Administrative Liability for Constitutional Torts, the Rehnquist Court, and Public Administration." *Public Administration Review,* 1992, *42,* 115–131.

Scalia, A. *A Matter of Interpretation: Federal Courts and the Law.* Princeton, N.J.: Princeton University Press, 1997.

Schick, A. *The Federal Budget: Politics, Policy, Process—From the Positive to the Regulatory State.* Washington, D.C.: Brookings Institution, 1995.

Seidman, H., and Gilmour, R. S. *Politics, Position, and Power.* (4th ed.) New York: Oxford University Press, 1986.

U.S. Senate, Committee on Governmental Affairs (Congressional Research Service, Library of Congress). *Office of Management and Budget: Evolving Roles and Future Issues.* Washington, D.C.: 99th Cong., 2nd sess., Feb. 1986. (Committee print.)

Wood, R. *Remedial Law.* Amherst: University of Massachusetts Press, 1990.

CHAPTER SIX

Techniques of Legal Interpretation and Why They Matter

Howard Ball

In a highly perceptive recent essay on the state of public administration in the United States in the last decade of the twentieth century, Ronald Moe and Robert Gilmour bring the public administrator back to the profession's fundamentals—principles that generally have been ignored in the political community's rush to reinvent government (Moe and Gilmour, 1995). They discuss what they believe are the ten primary norms of the discipline, norms "which have been historically fundamental" to public administration and should continue to be essential principles of the profession (p. 135). At least four of them are appropriate for this chapter on the relationship between administrative action and the law:

1. "The purpose of agency management is to implement the laws passed by Congress as elected representatives of the people."

2. "The president is the chief executive officer of the executive department and Commander-in-Chief of the armed forces and as such is responsible for the execution of the laws."

3. "Executive branch managers are held legally accountable by reviewing courts for maintaining procedural safeguards in dealing with both citizens and employees and for conforming to legislative deadlines and substantive standards."

4. "Policy and program objectives specifically agreed to and incorporated into enabling legislation, subject to reasonable and articulate standards

of measurement and compliance, facilitate effective implementation"
(pp. 138–140).

These normative perceptions of public administration underscore a number
of important constitutional questions for public administration and public law.
Congress has the constitutional power to pass laws. American legal and political history, however, is dotted with hundreds of constitutional challenges to the
congressional enactments that create the public law that must be administered
by agencies of the government. Since the beginning of the republic, courts have
been asked to determine whether or not the actions of legislatures are constitutional, and judges have developed legal techniques to address these important questions. The cases that arise involve interpreting constitutional clauses
and statutory language, as well as determining the constitutionality of many
hundreds of ordinances, rules, regulations, and orders. Cases and controversies
(the constitutional term for a properly presented legal challenge) have been
brought into courts alleging either the arbitrariness of the substance of the laws
or that discrimination has occurred in their application by agency personnel.
Courts are also asked to address controversies regarding procedural safeguards
for the conduct of public administrators as they go about the task of implementing these statutes. There are, as well, legal questions as to whether an
agency's actions conform to the substantive standards established by the
enabling legislation.

In each of these types of cases, judges apply specialized techniques of interpretation to resolve the conflict. This chapter examines techniques of legal interpretation applied by the reviewing judges to resolve both constitutional and
statutory controversies. Specifically, it considers constitutional interpretation
and statutory construction, as well as the issue of the relationship of judicial
review to administrative discretion in interpretation.

THE CONSTITUTIONAL FOUNDATIONS FOR
ALL PUBLIC ADMINISTRATION ACTIONS

Public administrators employ a set of tools in the performance of their official
duties (see Chapter Seven). Drawing upon these tools, the executive, the legis-
lator, and the public administrator go about the task of creating and fairly
administering public policy. All public administrators—indeed, all those
involved in the political process—must accept a basic premise about working
in a democratic republic: "All legal authority [for administrative action] flows
from a constitutional foundation" (Cooper, 1996, p. 118). The concept of *constitutionalism* is fundamental in a democracy, at least as that concept is understood in the United States. Authoritative power to develop and to implement

public policy is granted but at the same time is constrained and proscribed in such a political system by a written constitution. The constitution, also known as the fundamental or organic law of a political community, whether national or state, both authorizes the legitimate use of power and sets limits on the use of power by public officials.

Constitutional grants of power have enabled legislatures to create administrative agencies, define their powers, and establish the political and legal parameters within which such powers are exercised (Cooper, 1996). Persons or groups adversely affected, who are injured in some way, by the legislation and the ensuing administrative activity can challenge it in the courts, seeking reversal of the administrative action or asking to have an agency act in a fair, non-capricious manner. Petitioners commonly make the following charges:

- The agency has been created in an unconstitutional manner.
- Agency powers, given by the legislators, are unauthorized and therefore unconstitutional grants of power made by the legislature.
- The interpretations given a statute by an agency are erroneous.
- The process used to turn agency decisions into regulations are arbitrary and capricious.
- The record used to support an agency interpretation, taken as a whole, fails to provide substantial evidence to support an administrative action (Cooper, 1983, pp. 184–186).

When contests over legislative, executive, or administrative agency actions are heard in courts, the expectation by the litigating parties is that the judiciary, whether national or state, will resolve the conflict by issuing (1) findings of fact, (2) conclusions of law, and (3) a remedy in the form of an order of the court if redress is warranted. It matters a great deal that the formal interpretation of law is issued, not only because such rulings explain legal rights and set the boundaries beyond which government may not act but also because it may legitimate legislative or administrative action.

When a suit is brought but settled by agreement of the parties before it is submitted for decision by the court, a consent decree may be entered. Consent decrees and remedial orders (like those used in prison conditions or school desegregation cases) are addressed in Chapter Seven of this book. This chapter is concerned with the process and character of authoritatively stated conclusions of law and not agreements between litigants.

These rulings may be issued in cases that challenge a statute or regulation as written—referred to as a challenge to the facial validity of the provision in question. Such a challenge may be based on the idea that the provision is vague or excessively broad. Decisions in such cases are often issued when a court is convinced that the challenged statute is unconstitutional or otherwise invalid, and when waiting until after actual enforcement would result in irreparable harm. An example would be a case in which newly passed legislation is alleged to violate freedom of speech and waiting for implementation could lead to self censorship or interference with the free flow of communication.

In most cases, however, judges normally do not entertain challenges unless a case is ripe—that is, fully ready for adjudication. In general, for a case to be considered ripe, the policy must have been implemented and the party bringing the challenge must show that he or she has suffered actual injury to a legally protected interest, such as liberty or property. That injury must have been caused by the policy being attacked.

In American society, the imprimatur of a court goes a long way toward resolving a dispute. Alexander Bickel, a noted constitutional scholar, once wrote: "The Court's prestige, the spell it casts as a symbol, enables it to entrench and solidify measures [by executives, legislators, or administrators] that may have been tentative in the conception or that are on the verge of abandonment in the execution" (Bickel, 1978, p. 48). This legitimation of a challenged policy, or of its implementation, is a highly important function of the judiciary in the constitutional system.

CONSTITUTIONAL INTERPRETATION

Some challenges that move into the judicial system contend that the executive or the legislature acted beyond the grants of power given to them in the Constitution. Alternatively, the court may be asked to find that even if administrators had the authority to act in a given subject area, they did so in a manner that violated another part of the Constitution, such as the Fifth and Fourteenth Amendments, which prohibit deprivation of due process and discrimination. The belief generally accepted in the American system of government is that "when Congress passes a bill and that bill is duly approved by the President, . . . the law that results also contains rules. In a constitutional system, it is imperative that we distinguish between two sets of rules. The rules contained in the Constitution are superior; the rules embodied in the legislation are inferior. In the event that legislation . . . conflicts with the Constitution, the inferior rules must give way to the superior ones" (Ducat, 1996, p. 94).

Typically, cases call for the judiciary to determine whether, in interpreting constitutional powers to pass legislation or to issue an executive order, the legislature or the executive has exceeded its powers as specified or implied in the Constitution and as interpreted by the judiciary (Ball, 1996).

It is extremely important to recognize that, in these challenges, judges are asked to determine the scope of a constitutional clause initially interpreted by the executive or the legislature (Fisher, 1991, p. 88). For example, Congress employed its Commerce Clause powers (Art. I, Sec. 8, Cl. 3) to pass legislation ending discrimination in places of public accommodation whose activities affected commerce. Challenges immediately arose from an Atlanta motel and, of all things, a Birmingham, Alabama, barbecue restaurant, alleging that the Civil Rights Act of 1964 was unconstitutional because of allegedly unwarranted and unconstitutional use of the Commerce Clause by Congress (*Heart of Atlanta Motel* v. *United States,* 1964; *Katzenbach* v. *McClung,* 1964). This type of case is one that asks judges to open the Constitution and give meaning to its words even though Congress and the president already made their views known when the law was enacted. As Ducat (1996, p. 97) noted, "It remains for doctrines created by the Justices [of the U.S. Supreme Court] to flesh out constitutional principles and connect them to the facts of a case."

In so doing, lawyers, and the judges with whom they interact, have traditionally "consulted the plain or historic meaning of the language in the text; the intent of the drafters of the constitutional provision at issue; the structure of the Constitution as a whole; the purposes sought to be accomplished by the constitutional provision; precedent; and deeply held values or notions of social policy" (Garvey and Aleinikoff, 1994, p. 94).

Although these elements of statutory interpretation are touchstones for constitutional interpretation, it goes too far to suggest that this is a mechanical process based solely or even primarily on clearly subjective criteria. Walter Murphy (1978), a respected political scientist, captured the nature of the process when he wrote: "[It is] an art, an art that must sometimes be both creative and political in the highest sense of the word, for it must apply imperfectly stated general principles to concrete and complex problems of human life and it must produce an authoritative solution. A [constitutional] interpreter . . . cannot rationally treat it as a detailed code or as a compact computer whose machine language is locked in the minds of men long dead" (Murphy, 1978, p. 1771).

The Constitution was designed to endure. Therefore the framers used broad language for many of its most important provisions. James Madison made it clear that the decision to use such language was deliberate. And if some provisions of the basic document are open textured, provisions enshrined in the amendments are even more subject to interpretive judgment. Words like *unreasonable search* or *excessive fines* are clearly subject to manifold interpretations.

So, because the American tradition is of a written constitution, the judge necessarily begins from the language of the applicable part of the Constitution, the clause or section whose initial interpretation by legislators or executives forms the essence of the litigation (Fisher, 1988, p. 97; Tarr, 1994, p. 269). But given that the words are often only a starting point, it is necessary to move on to other tools of interpretation (Fisher, 1988, pp. 64–69). The following techniques of constitutional interpretation have traditionally been used by jurists who are asked to resolve the difficult questions placed before them.

The Original Intent of the Framers

Edwin Meese III, U.S. attorney general during the Ronald Reagan administration (1981 to 1989), argued vigorously that courts should resolve constitutional cases by following the original intent of the Constitution's fathers (Meese, 1985, p. 701). In buttressing his argument for a particular type of legal interpretation, Meese liked to quote from an infamous 1857 Supreme Court opinion, *Dred Scott* v. *Sandford* (1857), in which the Court refused to recognize blacks as persons or citizens but concluded that they were considered property. In an opinion characterized as a "self-inflicted wound," Chief Justice Roger Taney wrote for the U.S. Supreme Court that "[Constitutional language] must be construed now as it was understood at the time of its adoption. It is not only the same in words, but the same in meaning" (p. 426).

The writer for a court majority, Meese argued, must base the justification for the decision on the intent of the Constitution's framers. Inherent in this technique of legal reasoning, called *interpretivism* by some (Ducat, 1996, pp. 93–94), is the assertion that a judgment by a court involving the language of the Constitution must faithfully reflect the original values and perceptions of those who wrote the basic document in 1787. The attorney general, in his broadside on this issue, wrote that the sole task of a court in constitutional adjudication is to "resurrect the original meaning of constitutional provisions . . . as the only reliable guide to judgment, . . . [one] which would produce defensible principles of government that would not be tainted by ideological predilection" (Meese, 1985, p. 702).

William Rehnquist, at the time an associate justice, in his dissent in the First Amendment case of *Wallace* v. *Jaffree* (1985), gave judicial voice to Meese's arguments. Reciting his understanding of the debates during ratification and in Congress and the letters and correspondence of leading political figures, specifically James Madison, Thomas Jefferson, Benjamin Huntington, and Samuel Livermore, Rehnquist concluded that the men who wrote the Constitution "saw the [First] Amendment as designed to prohibit the establishment of a national religion. . . . [They] did not see it as requiring neutrality on the part of government between religion and irreligion" (p. 98).

Rehnquist's conclusions in his *Jaffree* dissent were in fundamental opposition to almost forty years of Supreme Court precedent in the area of civil liberties (see, for example, Justice Hugo Black's opinion for the Court in *Everson* v. *Board of Education*, 1947). His views were based on his own reading of the original intent of the writers of the Constitution and of the Bill of Rights, adopted in 1791. From this reading Rehnquist determined that the First Amendment's Establishment of Religion Clause was constructed to address a very particular evil: "The evil to be aimed at would require that the Government be absolutely neutral as between religion and irreligion. The evil to be aimed at, so far as those who spoke were concerned, appears to have been the establishment of a national church, and perhaps the preference of one religious sect over another; but it was definitely not concern about whether the Government might aid all religions even handedly" (p. 99).

An important corollary to Meese's intent-of-the-framers standard is the *strict constructionism* standard used by judges in deciding constitutional controversies (Edley, 1990, p. 68). This concept underscores present-day judicial continuity with the past. The judge understands the constitutional clause involved in the litigation by examining the "plain meaning"—that is, the ordinary meaning of its language—as amplified by the framers' intent and then applying it to the controversy presently facing the judges (Ducat, 1996, p. 95). This "strict construction" by the judges is a technique of legal interpretation that is supposedly true to the original intent of the framers.

But as U.S. Supreme Court Justice Robert Jackson observed in a 1952 concurrence: "Just what our forefathers did envision, or would have envisioned had they foreseen modern conditions, must be divined from materials almost as enigmatic as the dreams Joseph was called upon to interpret for Pharaoh" (*Youngstown Steel and Tube Corporation* v. *Sawyer,* 1952, p. 634).

A majority of presently sitting judges are in agreement with Jackson's observations. As Justice Sandra Day O'Connor noted, "in general . . . we have only limited evidence of exactly how the Framers intended the First Amendment to apply." Even though she recognized the danger of excessive reliance on original intent, she added: *"But when we do have evidence that a particular law would have offended the Framers, we have not hesitated to invalidate it on that ground alone"* (*Minneapolis Star and Tribune* v. *Minnesota Commission of Revenue,* 1983, p. 584, n. 6, emphasis added). Thus, the original-intent approach usually prevails only when it is crystal clear to the jurist who is writing that the framers would have rejected the challenged use of a constitutional grant of power.

Yet another corollary to the intent-of-the-framers principle of adjudication is the *literalism* standard, the chief judicial proponent of which was Hugo L. Black (Ball, 1996). He argued for over half a century, as a U.S. senator and as an associate justice of the U.S. Supreme Court, that the Constitution must be interpreted within its "four corners" by a judge, especially a justice of the U.S. Supreme Court (Black, 1968). Thus, when the First Amendment says that "Congress shall make no law . . . abridging the freedom of the press," to a literalist it means precisely that—no law!

Black's commitment to literalism as a standard for resolving constitutional controversies involved literally applying the Constitution's words to answer the constitutional questions raised by the parties to the dispute. Black believed that judges were "required to confine [interpretation] to the words and phrases contained in the Constitution" (quoted in Magee, 1980, p. 19). Nothing more, and nothing less, was an appropriate legal technique for resolving such legal controversies.

The Constitution as a Living Document

Contrary to the first set of concepts, some judges have employed the standard of the Constitution as a living, evolving document. This principle of constitutional interpretation has at its base a broad flexibility in interpreting the words of the Constitution (Fisher, 1988, p. 79). It calls upon the judge to adapt the Constitution's "majestic generalities" to contemporary problems (Jackson, 1941, p. xi). Thus, for example, a modern court must interpret the Interstate Commerce Clause in Article I of the Constitution to validate a congressional bill that establishes regulations for the transmission of radio and television communications. The "Constitution as an evolving document" is a form of eclecticism. It blends "in varying proportions the methods of philosophy, history, tradition, logic and sociology" (Cardozo, 1921, p. 57).

This technique has been used by judges who have been labeled "non-interpretivists" (Ely, 1980) because they produce opinions based on other factors beyond the literal four corners of the Constitution.

Judges who use this approach have sometimes been associated with the creation of "new rights." That is, they have discovered new rights of privacy and abortion through expansive assessment of the Due Process Clauses in the Fifth and Fourteenth Amendments and the Equal Protection Clause in the Fourteenth Amendment (see *Griswold* v. *Connecticut,* 1965; *Roe* v. *Wade,* 1973). As Justice William Brennan, a major figure in the defense and implementation of this approach, wrote: "The genius of the Constitution . . . is [in its] adaptability of its great principles to cope with current problems and current needs" (Brennan, 1985, p. A1). In a 1983 dissent, he wrote: "The Constitution is not a static document whose meaning on every detail is fixed for all time by the life experience of the Framers. . . . To be truly faithful to the Framers, 'our use of history of their time must limit itself to broad purposes, not specific practices.' . . . Indeed, a proper respect for the Framers themselves forbids us to give so static and lifeless a meaning to their work" (*Marsh* v. *Chambers,* 1983, pp. 816–817).

The Constitution as Embodiment of
Principles of Human Decency

A third approach used by judges in rendering judgment in constitutional cases is the principles-of-human-decency standard (Fisher, 1988, pp. 71–77). This perspective is one that reflects the "higher law" background of the Constitution, that is, that the Constitution's principles were based on long-standing principles of natural law found in western political philosophy (Corwin, 1928). Its usage can be seen in a classic case of constitutional litigation, *Rochin* v. *California* (1952), decided by the U.S. Supreme Court.

Law enforcement officers broke into Antonio Rochin's home without a warrant and saw him swallow what they believed to be illegal drugs. After failing to extract them from his mouth, they took Rochin to a local hospital where his stomach was pumped, against his will, and two pills were retrieved and found to be morphine. The seized evidence was used to convict him and he appealed his conviction, arguing that the officials violated the Fourth Amendment's prohibition against unreasonable searches and seizures.

The Supreme Court reversed the conviction, with Justice Felix Frankfurter writing the opinion for the majority. His opinion is a classic statement of the Constitution-as-embodiment-of-human-decency standard of legal interpretation. He wrote, in part, that the behavior of the police "offends those canons of decency and fairness which express the notions of justice of English-speaking peoples . . . so rooted in the traditions and conscience of our people as to be ranked as fundamental" (*Rochin* v. *California,* 1952, pp. 168–169). The police, Frankfurter concluded, had acted in a way "that shocks the conscience" and that "offended the community's sense of fair play and decency" (p. 172).

While this famous example is about a criminal case, the issue also arises in conjunction with cases that affect administrators who must implement local government policy. For example, East Cleveland, Ohio, enacted a zoning ordinance that limited people living in residential units to family members. It defined family members so as to eliminate many children and relatives who were members of the extended family. In overturning the ordinance, the Supreme Court warned that despite the fact that no specific provision of the Constitution spoke directly to the matter, the Constitution would not allow a community to impose a middle-class suburban lifestyle and rule out the extended family (*Moore* v. *East Cleveland,* 1977).

The Constitution Viewed in its Historical Development

A final approach used by some judges to adjudicate cases that call for constitutional interpretation is the historical (economic, social, cultural, political) development standard. When the intent of the framers is unclear and there is a rejection of the Brennan standard of the Constitution as an evolving document, judges can view the constitutional language in a historical context. That is, they may examine historical trends in an effort to interpret the constitutional language in the dispute before them (Fisher, 1988, pp. 73–79). Using this legal technique of constitutional interpretation, Justice O'Connor says that the court "must employ both history and reason in [the] analysis (*Wallace* v. *Jaffree,* 1985, p. 81). She observed that "this uncertainty as to the intent of the Framers of the Bill of Rights does not mean that we should ignore history for guidance on the role of religion in public education. This Court has not done so. . . . When the intent of the Framers is unclear, I believe we must employ both history and reason in our analysis. . . . When we are interpreting the Constitution, a page of history is worth a volume of logic" (pp. 80–81).

These, then, are the basic legal techniques, or approaches, used by judges when they review cases asking them to examine the language of the Constitution in light of legislative or executive actions that, it is alleged, go beyond constitutional grants of power and are therefore unconstitutional or invalid. What is seen, first and foremost, are judicial efforts to create reasonable conceptual devices to assist judges in answering the thorny legal questions raised by parties and *amici* (friends of the court briefs) in these constitutional controversies.

STATUTORY CONSTRUCTION

There are, in addition to cases and controversies requiring constitutional interpretation by the judges, legal clashes in which public administrators are challenged for taking action beyond statutory authority or based on misinterpretations of statute, failing to take action when required by statute, or violating procedural requirements imposed by statute. These legal questions revolve around the legitimate scope of administrative actions or the behavior of administrators as they implement the public policy.

When such legal controversies emerge, a primary task of a court is to assess the administrative action in light of the legislation that empowered the administrator. In this type of legal controversy, involving judicial examination of statutes, ordinances, rules, or administrative orders, injured parties bring suit claiming either that an agency action has exceeded the grant of power and authority given to that agency by the legislature and that its action is *ultra vires,* that is, beyond its authority, or that proper statutory procedures were not followed by the agency (Cooper, 1996, p. 130).

Generally, in American jurisprudential history the judiciary interprets provisions of statutes and local ordinances strictly on grounds that the legislature can remedy erroneous interpretations without great difficulty. In the process of statutory construction, judges begin with the text of the applicable statute or ordinance (Frankfurter, 1947). If the statute's meaning is clear on its face and the administrator has acted consistent with the statute's guidelines, then the judges end their search. This is the so-called "plain meaning" rule (*Lake County* v. *Rollins,* 1889, p. 670).

However, if the plain meaning is not obvious, as is so often true, then the judge must analyze the language of the statute more closely to determine whether an administrator has acted correctly or reasonably. Contemporary courts generally show deference to the expert knowledge and experience of the administrator with respect to the area governed by the statute. However, in its

1995 term, the Supreme Court extended the concept of deference to an even broader notion and even to circumstances in which no particular reason exists for a claim to expertise. It said that "it is our practice to defer to the reasonable judgments of agencies with regard to the meaning of ambiguous terms in the statutes that they are charged with administering" (*Smiley* v. *Citibank,* 1996, p. 30). Continuing, the majority noted that "we accord deference to agencies . . . because of a presumption that Congress, when it left ambiguity in a statute, meant for implementation by an agency, understood that the ambiguity would be resolved, first and foremost, by the agency, and desired the agency [rather than the courts] to possess whatever degree of discretion the ambiguity allows" (p. 31).

How does the judge interpret statutes the implementation of which is challenged when there is no plain meaning? How does a court resolve a conflict in which it is alleged that the administrator's interpretation is erroneous, either because it is not reasonable or because the act does not leave room for wide deference in interpretation?

First, when adjudicating, a judge accepts certain critically important presumptions:

1. *The challenged administrative application of the statute is a coherent effort to accomplish a general purpose, consistent with a grant of constitutional power* (Murphy, 1964). As the U.S. Supreme Court said in *Citizens to Preserve Overton Park* v. *Volpe* (1971), the agency head's "decision [being challenged in court] is entitled to a presumption of regularity." However, the Court added: "but that presumption is not to shield his action from a thorough, probing review" (p. 415).

2. *The scope of the statute's words, words that lead to administrative actions that have been challenged, will be read in a historical context rather than being given a cold and artificial dictionary meaning.* Treating the words in that fashion gives specificity to the written language in the enactment (Tarr, 1994, p. 271). U.S. Supreme Court Justice Oliver Wendell Holmes correctly observed that "a word is not a crystal, transparent and unchanged; it is the skin of a living thought and may vary greatly in color and content, according to the circumstances and the time in which it is used" (*Towne* v. *Eisner,* 1918, p. 425).

3. *The judge must also examine the challenged administrative application of the statutory text as an integrated whole, which means that she or he must understand its purpose and whether there are clashes in the statute's various sections.* If uncertainty remains in the judge's mind about the statute's meaning and application, then she or he will consult the legislative history of the statute, that is, the materials used by legislators in the course of adopting the statute (Dickerson, 1975). When determining the purpose of the statute, the judge, and his or her clerks, must trace the evolution of the statute through records of committee hearings. They may also have to examine committee reports summarizing

the legislation, as well as comments of legislators in floor debates regarding the purposes of the challenged statute (Tarr, 1994, p. 271).

Doing so might enable the judge to determine better the purpose of the legislation and how the legislature believed it should be interpreted and applied by administrators responsible for its enforcement. A judge's interpretation of the legislation must "coincide with the intentions of the legislators" (Tarr, 1994, p. 271).

However, given the "unreliability of legislative history, [some] argue that judges should ignore it in favor of analysis of the enactment and of judicial rulings interpreting it" (Tarr, 1994, p. 272). Furthermore, the judicial use of precedent, *stare decisis,* in determining meaning of a challenged statute is another tactic for the jurist to employ in attempting to resolve the legal conflict. Use of prior decisions of a court can be authoritative and persuasive in determining the meaning, within a context, of a statute and of the expected kinds of administrative behavior that should follow from it.

WHY THESE INTERPRETIVE APPROACHES MATTER

These processes and techniques used by courts to resolve conflicts matter because they generate, over time, a set of guidelines for correct—that is, constitutional—administrative behavior. These judicial decisions also provide a public rationale for their judgments, and generally lead to the judiciary's placing its imprimatur on the great majority of agency actions. The expectation on the part of the litigants is that the judiciary, using such legal techniques in either constitutional or statutory litigation, will decide cases according to law, justified by understood and announced processes of legal reasoning. In so doing, judges not only provide support for administrative action but also support the legitimacy of the judiciary at the same time.

A well-written opinion clearly explains the rationale for the decision of the court. It is a well-crafted essay containing the facts in the controversy, an analysis of the legal claims made by the parties to the dispute, a laying out of the legal questions that the court found appropriate in the resolution of the dispute, and finally, the justification for the judgment of the court (van Geel, 1991, p. 47). To the degree that administrators follow the same practices, their own decisions are that much more convincing and legally defensible.

Finally, there is an open-ended character to this process of adjudication, just as there are similar qualities in the use of language in the law, whether constitutional or statutory. The judge has wide latitude when judging. Justice Frankfurter, in *Universal Camera* v. *NLRB* (1951), addressed these "limits of language and the irrepressibility of discretion" (p. 488), which is a reality confronted by administrators and judges alike. He spoke about the character of judicial behavior when examining agency actions taken in light of constitutional, statutory, or executive department principles, bills, or rules: "It cannot too often be repeated that judges are not automata. The ultimate reliance for the fair operation of any standard is a judiciary of high competence and character and the constant play of an informed professional critique upon its work. . . . *There are no talismanic words that can avoid the process of judgment.* The difficulty is that we cannot escape, in relation to this problem, the use of undefined defining terms" (p. 488).

In the final analysis, judges, much like legislators, executives, and agency personnel, wrestle with language in the resolution of disputes before them. When judges reach judgment, it is a public message that provides a rationale for their decision, one that can be challenged and changed by others in this never-ending process of constitutional and statutory decision making.

Cases Cited

Citizens to Preserve Overton Park v. *Volpe,* 401 U.S. 402 (1971).

Dred Scott v. *Sandford,* 60 U.S. (19 Howard) 393 (1857).

Everson v. *Board of Education,* 330 U.S. 1 (1947).

Griswold v. *Connecticut,* 381 U.S. 479 (1965).

Heart of Atlanta Motel v. *United States,* 379 U.S. 241 (1964).

Katzenbach v. *McClung,* 379 U.S. 294 (1964).

Lake County v. *Rollins,* 130 U.S. 662 (1889).

Marsh v. *Chambers,* 463 U.S. 783 (1983).

Minneapolis Star and Tribune v. *Minnesota Commission of Revenue,* 460 U.S. 575 (1983).

Moore v. *East Cleveland,* 431 U.S. 494 (1977).

Rochin v. *California,* 342 U.S. 165 (1952).

Roe v. *Wade,* 410 U.S. 113 (1973).

Smiley v. *Citibank,* 135 L.Ed.2d 25 (1996).

Towne v. *Eisner,* 245 U.S. 418 (1918).

Universal Camera v. *NLRB,* 340 U.S. 474 (1951).

Wallace v. *Jaffree,* 472 U.S. 38 (1985).

Youngstown Steel and Tube Corporation v. *Sawyer,* 343 U.S. 579 (1952).

References

Ball, H. *Hugo L. Black: Cold Steel Warrior.* New York: Oxford University Press, 1996.

Bickel, A. "Foreword: The Passive Virtues—The Supreme Court, 1960 Term." *Harvard Law Review,* 1978, *75,* 40–79.

Black, H. L. *A Constitutional Faith.* New York: Knopf, 1968.

Brennan, W. J. Jr. "Address Given at Georgetown University, Washington, October 12, 1985." *New York Times,* Oct. 13, 1985, p. A1.

Cardozo, B. N. *The Nature of the Judicial Process.* New Haven, Conn.: Yale University Press, 1921.

Cooper, P. J. *Public Law and Public Administration.* Mountain View, Calif.: Mayfield, 1983.

Cooper, P. J. "Understanding What the Law Says About Administrative Responsibility." In J. Perry (ed.), *Handbook of Public Administration.* (2nd ed.) San Francisco: Jossey-Bass, 1996.

Corwin, E. S. *The "Higher Law" Background of American Constitutional Law.* Ithaca, N.Y.: Cornell University Press, 1928.

Dickerson, R. *The Interpretation and Application of Statutes.* New York: Little, Brown, 1975.

Ducat, C. *Constitutional Interpretation.* St. Paul, Minn.: West, 1996.

Edley, C. *Administrative Law: Rethinking Judicial Control of Bureaucracy.* New Haven, Conn.: Yale University Press, 1990.

Ely, J. H. *Democracy and Distrust: A Theory of Judicial Review.* Cambridge, Mass.: Harvard University Press, 1980.

Fisher, L. *Constitutional Dialogues: Interpretation as Political Process.* Princeton, N.J.: Princeton University Press, 1988.

Fisher, L. "The Curious Belief in Judicial Supremacy." *Suffolk University Law Review,* 1991, *25,* 85–116.

Frankfurter, F. "Some Reflections on the Reading of Statutes." *Columbia Law Review,* 1947, *47,* 527–546.

Garvey, J., and Aleinikoff, T. A. *Modern Constitutional Theory.* St. Paul, Minn.: West, 1994.

Jackson, R. H. *The Struggle for Judicial Supremacy.* New York: Knopf, 1941.

Magee, J. J. *Mr. Justice Black: Absolutist on the Court.* Charlottesville: University of Virginia Press, 1980.

Meese, E. III. "The Attorney General's View of the Supreme Court: Toward a Jurisprudence of Original Intention." *Public Administration Review,* 1985, *45,* 701–704.

Moe, R. C., and Gilmour, R. S. "Rediscovering Principles of Public Administration: The Neglected Foundation of Public Law." *Public Administration Review,* 1995, *55,* 135–146.

Murphy, W. *Elements of Judicial Strategy.* Chicago: University of Chicago Press, 1964.

Murphy, W. "Constitutional Interpretation: The Art of Historian, Magician, or Statesman?" *Yale Law Journal,* 1978, *87,* 1752–1771.

Tarr, G. A. *Judicial Process and Judicial Policymaking.* St. Paul, Minn.: West, 1994.

van Geel, T. R. *Understanding Supreme Court Opinions.* Reading, Mass.: Addison Wesley Longman, 1991.

CHAPTER SEVEN

Public Law as a Set
of Tools for Management

Phillip J. Cooper

If one term engenders more antagonism in the contemporary world than *bureaucracy*, it is probably *law*. Among the most frequent critics of the law governing the public sector are those whose job it is to govern. Indeed, much of the effort to reinvent government and a good deal of the rhetoric associated with the Clinton administration's National Performance Review has focused on the problems engendered by law in general and regulations in particular (Gore, 1993; Osborne and Gaebler, 1992). While that sort of rhetoric may be popular with the voters, it is a dangerous and self-defeating fallacy for public managers to internalize in their professional lives and day-to-day operations.

To be sure, many people have been taught to fear the law and to regard it as a negative force in their lives. It is no accident that when one threatens to throw the book at them, it means a law book. It is also true that most people have known of someone who has been involved in litigation, and most do not want to face that kind of experience. Thus, many administrators spend much of their time attempting to avoid lawsuits. One who has worked with someone like that is reminded of the picture of a person walking down a sidewalk looking over his or her shoulder all the time instead of watching what he or she is approaching. But there is no way to avoid the importance of law in public management and, as this chapter shows, it would be a bad idea even if it were possible.

The law of public administration—what is here loosely termed *administrative law*—is essential to public managers as a set of foundations on which administrative authority is based and as a set of tools for public management. It is the purpose of this chapter to consider just how and why this law of administration is such a positive fact of public administration life. The chapter considers the nature of public law as a set of tools, the role of rulemaking and standard setting, the importance of adjudicative action, and the role of judicial review in the overall framework of administrative operations. It concludes with a consideration of tools based on legal authority and those grounded on contract.

THE TWO-EDGED SWORD

Kenneth Culp Davis said that the discretion that administrators possess under law is very like an axe, a tool that may be used for constructive purposes or as a weapon to cause mayhem (Davis, 1969). However, the fact that legal tools might be dangerous if they are improperly used is no reason to reject or ignore their necessity in public administration. They are devices used to implement and operate the policies mandated by legislatures and chief executives. Elements of rulemaking and adjudication, for example, are present in most aspects of public administration, whether they are identified as such or not.

Beyond the question of legal tools, public law also provides a foundation for administration and is essential to the infrastructure on which administrative institutions, and most other institutions of society for that matter, operate. In Article I, Section 8, the United States Constitution establishes the foundation for the economy, governmental institutions, and other elements of the country's infrastructure. It provides authority for Congress to raise and collect taxes, coin money, set a system of weights and measures, build post roads, raise and equip a military for national security, and "make all laws which shall be necessary and proper for carrying into Execution the foregoing Powers, and all other Powers vested by this Constitution in the Government of the United States, or in any Department or Officer thereof." It establishes the relationships among units and departments of government, sets forth the foundations for the processes of government, and provides for recourse to the rule of law as a mechanism for the resolution of problems. Article VI provides a coherence to the several aspects of law by indicating that "this Constitution, and the Laws of the United States which shall be made in Pursuance thereof; and all Treaties made, or which shall be made under the Authority of the United States, shall be the supreme Law of the Land; and the Judges in every State shall be bound thereby, any Thing in the Constitution or Laws in any State to the Contrary notwithstanding." And contrary to attempts by revisionist historians and ideologues to rewrite history, that same Constitution and the debates surrounding it make clear the importance of public administration in the life of the nation (Rohr, 1987).

The maintenance of this infrastructure requires a continuous reexamination of its constitutional foundations. As the economy changes and governments alter their organization and operation, the courts are frequently asked to consider anew just how to reconcile the changes with constitutional foundations. Other chapters in this volume address aspects of both the rule of law and constitutional foundations. This chapter concentrates on the facet of public law that provides tools for public policy and public management.

POLICY TOOLS AND MANAGEMENT TOOLS

Varied legal tools are used not only to administer public sector organizations but also to fashion the policies for which those agencies were created. Of course, administrative organizations, as well as chief executives and legislators at various levels, participate in policymaking.

It has been understood for more than half a century that no simple or neat lines separate policymaking activities from administration (Appleby, 1949; Waldo, 1948). Clearly, the manner in which policy is made shapes the way managers can administer it (Sabatier, 1985). In fact, many policies are aimed at the internal structures, procedures, resources, and operations of administrative agencies. Still others, like laws concerning contracting, govern the ways in which public agencies form working partnerships with private or not-for-profit organizations (De Hoog, 1984; Kettl, 1993). It is also plainly true that administrators play key roles in a good deal of policy formulation, including drafting bills that are ultimately adopted by the legislature and executive orders that emanate from the White House, the Governors' offices, and county and city governments.

Notwithstanding these interrelationships, the tasks and tools used in policymaking differ somewhat from those employed in day-to-day management. The term *policy tools* applies not only to the legal devices used to issue authoritative positions on issues, but also refers to the different types of devices that can be combined to create policies. In addition to the classical formulations of statutes and the regulations issued to implement them, policy tools can include such mechanisms as incentive devices, permit systems, marketable rights, user fees, special taxes, disclosure requirements, liability or insurance requirements, and a number of others (Salamon, 1989; Organization for Economic Cooperation and Development, 1989; Mosher, 1968, 1980). But whatever the components of a policy statement might be, whether traditional command and control or more contemporary market-oriented devices, at some point a legal tool must be used to issue the authoritative statement of the policy, the one that is binding on both administrators and citizens.

Policy Tools

Legal policy tools include statutes, executive orders, treaties, and regulations. There are three basic types of statutes: (1) *enabling acts* (also referred to as organic acts) that create agencies, explain their powers, and establish their jurisdiction (the circumstances in which the agency can invoke authority); (2) *authorization statutes,* which create programs or direct agencies to undertake any of a variety of responsibilities; and (3) *appropriations statutes,* which provide funds but may also contain provisions that mandate or prohibit certain types of agency actions.

Agencies may function under any number of authorization statutes that are adopted over the years. Indeed, administrators may find themselves implementing legislation that imposes contradictory or at least incompatible mandates that have come from different legislatures at different points in time. One of the tasks of legislative relations offices at state and federal levels is to be alert to potential conflicts and to inform legislators in time to avoid impossible situations when policies must be implemented. State Leagues of Cities and similar organizations of county officials serve this function on behalf of local governments.

Theoretically, appropriations legislation is the mechanism by which finances are conveyed to administrators to operate their organizations and carry out policy obligations. However, appropriations bills are frequently used to affect the substance of policies as well as to support them. Because appropriations committees are supposed to exercise a watchdog function to protect the public purse against fraud, abuse, and waste, they may add mandatory or prohibitive provisions to their bills. These committees often use such devices to pressure agencies to undertake or avoid certain types of activities. It is a fact that such mandates can engender conflict between authorization committees and appropriations committees that put the administrator squarely in the middle. In addition to the reconnaissance function (see Green, 1978) that agencies undertake, the other technique used to avoid such conflicts is communications between agency staffs and committee staffs.

In recent years, this task has become more complex. As the political environment shifts substantially and significant turnover occurs among legislators and staff, these efforts at coordination and communication become more difficult. If the legislature sees itself as having a stern mandate for dramatic change, the chance of mutually contradictory statutory mandates increases. Similar tension occurs when a sharp division exists between the views of the legislative leadership and the positions of the chief executive. Another situation that should signal a manager to be alert is when political officials in the executive branch seek to undertake a substantial amount of change in a limited period either by reorganization or through direct action in the form of executive orders. In such circumstances, the executive may put an agency into a conflict situation. In short, high-intensity change periods require increased efforts at coordination and communication to avoid serious problems. Such efforts are especially difficult but even more necessary when change occurs during periods of funding cuts and downsizing, as has been true in recent years. Problems arise because agency leaders are busier and fewer people are available to take responsibility for the statutory reconnaissance effort.

In addition to these types of statutes aimed at individual agencies, many other statutes cover all or most public agencies. They include administrative procedures laws, civil rights legislation protecting citizens from administrative abuse, and administrative support and management legislation. The procedure laws provide for such mechanisms as freedom of information and open meetings requirements, standard rulemaking processes, and due process protocols when agencies make important decisions involving individual citizens. They also establish routines according to which judicial review may be carried out to ensure agency compliance with legal obligations. Civil rights statutes apply antidiscrimination requirements to agencies in terms of both how they deal with their own employees and what their interactions are with citizens who come to their agencies for action. Administrative support and management legislation ranges from laws establishing the civil service to statutes governing the use of contracts.

Difficulties occur in some jurisdictions because contracting laws historically have been quite separate from other legislation applying to administrative agencies. Contracting has been treated separately because of great concern about the risks of corruption in the purchasing of goods and services needed by public agencies. That historical reality has presented difficulties for contemporary public managers. First, because contracts have been treated separately, there are often discontinuities, if not outright conflicts, between the manner in which agencies operate in all of their other activities and what they do in contract situations. That is a difficulty because both agencies (particularly state human service organizations) and local governments have increasingly relied upon contract operations to carry out service operations. This makes it increasingly untenable to separate contract operations completely from other processes. States principally rely on contractors, often not-for-profit organizations, to perform many health care, mental health, counseling, and youth services activities. Contracting, which was once seen as a special activity, is now often the core activity for many agencies. The second problem is related to the first. Most contracting legislation was written to facilitate heavy construction and procurement of goods rather than provision of services. While the federal government has been engaged for decades in efforts to adapt contracting processes to changed realities, the contracting laws are very much a work in progress. Some states have not even made a good start at the process, except to satisfy federal requirements. It is true that sporadic attention has been paid to contracting, but it is often aimed principally at bidding processes, where one finds the greatest traditional concerns about corruption or conflicts of interest. Contract administration has not received as much attention as it deserves, either legislatively or from a management perspective (see Kettl, 1993). This promises to be an area of legislative development for the foreseeable future as government by contract increases in importance at all levels.

Increasingly, one of the tools used to develop policy is direct promulgation of executive orders, proclamations, and memoranda. Not only is it tempting for presidents—or for that matter, governors—simply to announce policies having the force of law, but the politics of divided government in recent years has rendered the use of regular legislative channels so difficult that the temptation is even greater than before. Legislatures have sometimes permitted executive orders when they could have overturned them because it is a way for the legislature to avoid difficult political choices and because it seems more expedient in some situations. Thus, the National Performance Review (NPR), led by Vice President Albert Gore, urged the Clinton administration from the very beginning to use "presidential directives" to implement its recommendations (Gore, 1993). Executive orders are legally binding as long as they are consistent with executive authority to issue them and provided that they do not violate the Constitution or existing statutes. While these devices are not well known or understood even by many experienced administrators, what is even less well understood is the fact that some of these orders are crafted in executive departments for promulgation by the president.

The White House also uses treaties, executive agreements, and other devices of international relations to promulgate policy. While treaties normally require ratification by the Senate, the Supreme Court has held that executive agreements, which are negotiated between the president and representatives of other nations, may enjoy the same status as treaties and carry similar legal force (*Dames and Moore* v. *Reagan*, 1981). As the number of international agreements increases, the importance of these devices to domestic agencies and state and local governments grows. That importance has become more apparent since the ratification of the North American Free Trade Agreement and the General Agreement on Tariffs and Trade, but these are only two of the most visible international accords.

Regulations are commonly known but not always well-understood mechanisms for the promulgation of policy. While the subjects of rules and the process by which they are made are addressed in more detail later in the chapter, it is important to note here that they are used both as policy tools and as management tools. When rules are directed outward toward those served or regulated by an agency, the kinds of rules used are referred to as substantive or legislative rules, but agencies also issue what are termed interpretative rules and policy statements. Substantive rules carry the force of law so long as the agency that made them had the authority to issue that type of rule, and provided that they were made in the process required by the Administrative Procedure Act or other applicable legislation.

Management Tools

In addition to announcing policy, rules are used as mechanisms to manage the implementation and operation of policy. But other legal tools are also used in management, including adjudication, contracts, interjurisdictional agreements, and judicial review.

Traditionally, agencies are considered to have inherent authority to issue procedural rules governing internal organization and operation. Indeed, many agencies have a wide array of guidelines, standard operating procedures, and other regulations that are used to maintain effective operations. These types of rules can be made without the complex procedural requirements necessary for the promulgation of substantive rules. Procedural rules are intended to be more flexible than substantive rules and adaptable to changing management needs.

Adjudication and other forms of conflict management are also important legal tools for administrators. They vary in level of formality but are intended to provide for a measure of fairness and orderliness in the resolution of disputes. The essential distinction between the promulgation of rules and the applicability of adjudication is that rules are usually intended to apply in the future to a number of people while adjudications take place when a public agency makes a decision about a named individual regarding the person's current or past situation. An adjudication involves important decisions that affect a person's rights, duties, or status under the law.

Contracts, which were discussed in a slightly different context earlier, represent another kind of legal tool for management. They are as binding as any other legal tool, though the process for their enforcement is different from that of an agency rule or adjudication. It is commonly assumed in contemporary management literature that negotiated instruments such as contracts or alternative dispute resolution are to be preferred to rules or formal adjudications. Thus, pressure is growing to make wider use of contracts as standard mechanisms for the administration of people and programs (Osborne and Gaebler, 1992).

Interjurisdictional agreements are essentially contractual relationships between two or more governmental units to share or exchange services or to create governing arrangements. Certain types of interjurisdictional agreements, such as interstate compacts, must be approved by the legislature. They therefore involve both the status of a legislative mandate and a negotiated agreement.

Litigation is itself a management tool. It is used for enforcement of rules or contracts. It is a normal and expected extension of administrative adjudication. Conversely, experienced public managers understand that judicial review is a normal and expected aspect of life in public administration.

The decision to use a particular legal tool in public management has consequences, not only because each tool has its own characteristics, but also because many tools serve distinctive purposes and have their own dynamics. The next sections consider rules and standard setting, the process of administrative adjudication, negotiated reality, and the surprising usefulness of judicial review.

Rulemaking and Standard Setting. The usefulness of rules as policy or as management tools involves more than simply their substantive value. Rules are useful in themselves, to be sure, but they are issued through a process that is itself a constructive management mechanism.

Rulemaking as a Tool. The foundations of the concept of rulemaking are simple enough, but they raise important issues of legitimacy. Issues arise both in those situations in which unelected administrators establish legally binding policy in the form of rules that govern members of the community outside the agency, and in those cases in which managers set forth internal rules as procedural devices to facilitate efficiency, agency requirements to ensure accountability, or personnel requirements to mandate behaviors of employees. To address such concerns and enhance decision making, administrative procedures acts, both state and federal, set forth procedures to ensure that rulemaking is open, orderly, and participative (see Chapter Thirteen of this book and Kerwin, 1994). In recent years, however, political gamesmanship by both major parties has led to efforts to cripple the rulemaking process. Consider first the basic idea of the way the process could be used as a tool, the difficulties presented by so-called rulemaking reforms and administrative reactions to them, and the reasons why it is worth reconsidering the process.

The original approach taken in the administrative procedure acts was simply to ensure that a regular process was prescribed by a statute to be followed by most agencies of government (some were exempted because of their particular nature, such as the military). It was to be an open process in that it was to begin with public notice of proposed rulemaking, to be followed by an opportunity for public comment before decisions were ultimately made by administrators. When a rule was adopted, public notice was to be provided before it was enforced. Those who thought that these requirements were not followed or that the decision was arbitrary and capricious or in violation of the Constitution or statutory constraints could then have the rulemaking reviewed in court.

It is somewhat ironic in the 1990s to hear the steady drum beat against rules as principal barriers to good administration (see Osborne and Gaebler, 1992; Gore, 1993) when one considers that most of the criticism from the 1930s to the late 1960s was that agencies were not using rulemaking procedures but were more or less making up the rules as they played the game. That is, people brought before agencies in enforcement proceedings often learned for the first time how an agency construed a statute. Virtually every serious observer of administrative law matters challenged that arbitrary and unfair process and urged agencies to use rulemaking both to help structure their own discretion in order to avoid arbitrariness, and to provide fair notice and opportunity for participation to people affected by agency decision making (see Friendly, 1962; Davis, 1969). In fact, in the early 1970s, Congress began mandating that federal agencies must adopt rules; by the 1980s it regularly mandated that the rules required in legislation had to be issued within a fixed time limit, usually 180 days.

It is in large part for these reasons that rulemaking increased significantly during the decade of the 1970s. During this period there was also some degree of change in the process that stemmed from both legislative and judicial mandates. Courts faced with challenges to rulemaking during the 1970s were troubled by the fact that some agencies seemed to be honoring the procedural requirements in form but not substance. Notice was provided only in the *Federal Register*, with little more than a few days opportunity to file comments. That meant that only well-organized lobbying groups that could afford to monitor agency activities and mobilize resources to respond instantly were able to play effective participative roles in the process. There was often little or no evidence that comments that had been submitted were seriously considered by agencies beyond creating a docket sheet and filing the comments away in the record. When challenged, some agencies were unable to produce rulemaking records providing any evidence that they had really undertaken any systematic and participative decision-making process.

In response to these problems, courts, led by the United States Circuit Court of Appeals for the D.C. Circuit, issued a series of rulings indicating that the notice, participation, and consideration requirements of the Administrative Procedure Act meant exactly what they said and were to be honored in substance as well as in form (see, for example, *Mobil Oil* v. *Federal Power Commission*, 1973; *International Harvester* v. *Ruckelshaus*, 1973; *Appalachian Power Company* v. *EPA*, 1973; *Walter Holm and Company* v. *Hardin*, 1971). At root, these rulings required that notice had to be sufficient to allow a serious opportunity for participation, that participation had to be sufficient to ensure a "thorough ventilation of the issues" (*National Resources Defense Council* v. *U.S. Nuclear Regulatory Commission*, 1976, p. 644), and that there had to be evidence of serious consideration of comments submitted when the rulemaking decision was announced. Satisfaction of these requirements can be assured by the development of an adequate rulemaking record that contains evidence of the kinds of notice, participation, and decision-making factors required by the law. Although the Supreme Court eventually ruled that the courts could not mandate procedures not otherwise required by statute (*Vermont Yankee Nuclear Power Corporation* v. *Natural Resources Defense Council*, 1978), political bodies, including Congress and the executive, had already seen the wisdom of what the court had done. Thus, virtually all new legislation that contained rulemaking provisions required what had come to be known as hybrid rulemaking. President Jimmy Carter imposed it on all executive branch agencies by executive order (E.O. 12044).

The fact that more agencies were required to make more rules than ever before and that the process for rulemaking had been expanded provided a tempting target for politicians bent on running against the bureaucracy, a perennial practice by both Democrats and Republicans since at least 1976. The Carter administration favored deregulation in general and a more cautious approach to rulemaking if regulations were to be issued. President Ronald Reagan—who ran against what he termed the intrusive regulatory state, and in particular rulemaking by the Environmental Protection Agency and the Occupational Safety and Health Administration (OSHA)—imposed draconian requirements on rulemaking by executive order (E.O. 12291; E.O. 12498). These included a range of preclearance requirements within the Office of Management and Budget, severe cost-benefit requirements, and a variety of other restrictions (see Kerwin, 1994). President George Bush went so far as to issue a ninety-day moratorium on all rulemaking by executive branch agencies (Bush, 1992).

If anyone thought the attack on rulemaking would end with the election of a Democratic president, they were sorely mistaken. The Clinton administration made the attack on rules and rulemaking just as important as its Republican predecessors, though it claimed that it could accomplish the feat without harming the environment or creating health and safety concerns. Not only did Vice President Gore's National Performance Review attack the regulations that applied to the public, but the NPR also sought and received the president's support for an executive order mandating the elimination of half of all rules governing internal agency operations (E.O. 12866).

Thus, the formal requirements on federal agencies for rulemaking have been significantly increased since the late 1970s and presently seem very burdensome. However, as Kerwin (1994) has found, rulemaking procedures can be regularized and planning can be done to reduce some of the burdens. Unfortunately, some administrators have been tempted to avoid rulemaking processes by issuing other kinds of statements that they try to avoid calling substantive or legislative rules, or by reverting to the practice of using enforcement actions to announce rules in order to avoid the burdens and costs involved in contemporary rulemaking. Reviewing courts have not been patient with such games, however understandable the motivations for them might be (*Community Nutrition Institute* v. *Young*, 1987; *Ford Motor Company* v. *Federal Trade Commission*, 1981; *General Motors* v. *Ruckelshaus*, 1983).

The Positive Aspects of Rules. So why, in the face of all of these developments, should public managers seek to use rules and rulemaking as tools? The advantages to those outside the agency should be obvious. They are the same reasons that pressures arose for rulemaking in the first place. The major advantages are fairness in terms of the ability to know the rules ahead of time and the opportunity to express one's concerns about potential agency actions through participation in rulemaking. When politicians engage in cheap theatrics, like showing stacks of rules about to be eliminated, they neglect to point out that rules bind agencies and are mechanisms for holding them accountable. That is not to defend useless or outdated rules, but to reject mindless attacks on rules.

For managers, a number of reasons exist not to jump onto the antirule bandwagon. Rules are mechanisms that enhance predictability and efficiency. There has been considerable discussion about the success of the National Performance Review in having local offices avoid standard rules and negotiate alternatives in such practices as OSHA workplace enforcement. However, the discretion to set aside national standards in one case is only the flip side of the opportunity to be arbitrary. There is also a problem of inconsistency across jurisdictions. For large programs like Social Security, the dangers of inconsistencies and arbitrariness argue in favor of some degree of standardization and against excessive local deviations, however attractive they may seem. Standardization has its downside, but it may also enhance efficiency and fairness. Moreover, the use of rules avoids the dangers of having to make similar decisions many times; a complex decision made once may take time when it is initially done but save time and effort in the long run. The continuing use and adjustment of standards rather than starting from the beginning each time a judgment is needed also allows for a kind of calibration of administrative process and policy action. Finally, the plain fact is that many statutes mandate rulemaking, so a clear obligation exists to develop a system of lawful rules according to proper procedures.

Of course, effective management also involves a concern with internal morale. From an employee's perspective, rules and standards mean that behavior and consequences are predictable. If the manner of evaluation, decisions about pay, or promotions are not supported by some kind of foundation in policy, fear of arbitrariness and favoritism may grow. If the concept of notice and opportunity for participation is extended within an organization even when it is not mandated by law, it supports the general trend in contemporary management to empower employees.

Existence of reasonable internal rules and policies also means that the world does not end when one particularly experienced or knowledgeable individual leaves the agency or is away for a time. Rules also mean that if an employee challenges management, a fair foundation exists from which management may defend itself. Any manager who thinks that the elimination of rules will make disgruntled employees less likely to sue is living in a dangerous fantasy world. One need not make hostile assumptions about employees, in the sense of theory X versus theory Y approaches to management, to realize that no agency can count on having excellent employees all the time. Besides, some degree of guidance and advance notice helps good employees to know what is expected of them, and well-executed procedures for the development of such guidelines allow those employees to play more active roles in management.

Clearly, there are dangers of overdoing rule systems. Plainly, some rules are unnecessary. Some kind of regular effort is needed, as an element of effective management, to review rules and other kinds of guidelines in order to adjust them to contemporary conditions and eliminate those that are unnecessary. However, neither these acknowledgments nor the fact that rules have been made the favorite target of would-be management reformers, stump politicians, or wags ignorant of the real worlds of public and private management should prevent managers from using these important tools to carry out their responsibilities and operate agency organizations more effectively.

Adjudication and Dispute Resolution. If politicians often make rulemaking a favorite target, many administrators see due process requirements as a significant cause of many managers' problems. It is true that when important decisions are made concerning a person's job, government benefits, or legal status, the requirements of due process of law must be satisfied. It is also true that due process requires procedures that can be time-consuming and difficult. There are three answers to these realities.

First, since the mid–1970s, the Supreme Court and other federal courts have demanded increased or new due process requirements less often than was true in earlier times. Beginning with a series of important rulings in the 1970s, the Supreme Court held that the due process required was that imposed by the particular statute or regulations involved and that the Constitution does not require more unless a balancing test is satisfied. That test requires the Court to consider "first, the private interest that will be affected by the official action; second, the risk of an erroneous deprivation of such interest through the procedures used, and the probable value, if any, of additional or substitute safeguards; and, finally, the Government's interest, including the function involved and the fiscal and administrative burdens that the additional or substitute procedural requirements would entail" (*Mathews* v. *Eldridge*, 1976, p. 335). Relatively few cases brought to the Court following *Eldridge* were able to meet that test.

Public employees who have demanded due process protections beyond the provisions available to them under statute or collective bargaining agreements have not fared well in recent years. It has become clear that the Court has moved to reimpose a right/privilege approach (*Arnett* v. *Kennedy*, 1974) to public employment, though a majority refuses to admit directly to doing so. As Justice William Rehnquist put it in a 1985 case, "one who avails himself of government entitlements accepts the grant of tenure along with its inherent [procedural] limitations" (*Cleveland Board of Education* v. *Loudermill*, 1985, p. 536). Justice Antonin Scalia agrees, but the Court has generally continued the use of the balancing test to determine when a hearing is due even for tenured public employees, as set forth in *Loudermill*. Indeed, in more recent rulings, the Court has allowed termination of employees even in the absence of a showing that their speech or conduct actually caused organizational disruption (*Waters* v. *Churchill*, 1994; see also *Connick* v. *Myers*, 1983). Thus, there is currently no growing threat of being overwhelmed by court-imposed due process.

Second, the requirement for due process does not mean that every decision requires the equivalent of a court trial. In most instances, it requires notice of what is being done, a statement of the authority under which the action is being taken, a statement of the reasons supporting the action, an opportunity to reply, a written decision based on the record, and some kind of opportunity to appeal. In more formal situations, it may mean the right to a hearing before an unbiased decision maker before final action is taken. However, the trend is away from requiring formal trial-type hearings except in the most serious of situations unless a statute or regulation specifically requires such a proceeding.

Third, despite the apparent burdens involved, the effective use of due process techniques enhances management effectiveness. Recent efforts to delayer and decentralize organizations notwithstanding, it remains necessary for managers to make key decisions about performance appraisals, pay raises, promotions, and adverse personnel actions, including, on occasion, decisions to terminate employees. Looking outside the organization, no amount of effort to portray clients of social service or regulatory agencies as customers, as is the current fashion, will change the fact the agencies will continue to make critically important decisions that affect people's lives and businesses. And whether the decisions involve determinations about clients or management judgments about employees, due process helps with the task.

It should also be noted that calls for increased use of alternative dispute resolution procedures do not mean less procedure, merely different types of processes. Moreover, the use of such techniques normally does not preclude the possibility of adjudication at some future point. It also requires the development of skills in negotiations as well as in the drafting of the kinds of agreements that emerge from negotiation or mediation.

At root, due process is about the need to ensure fundamental fairness in administrative decision making. Clients and employees can deal with losing, but they have much more difficulty accepting unfairness. People do not want to work in an organization where they are likely to be treated arbitrarily. No one wants to operate in a setting in which coworkers or superiors are permitted to conduct whispering campaigns to decision makers without giving the accused person an opportunity to respond before a judgment is reached. Such events are called *ex parte* communications. They are efforts at unfair influence. The sense that decisions will not be made by innuendo or behind closed doors but in a manner that permits an opportunity to make one's case enhances a sense of integrity and sensitivity to individual needs.

Negotiated Reality. Despite these relatively simple facts about the usefulness of rulemaking and due process principles, there have been strong reactions against such processes, with critics denouncing them as remnants of a command-and-control approach to governing that is outdated (Osborne and Gaebler, 1992). These reformers urge that, instead, negotiation should be used and resolutions of problems should look more like distinctive contractual agreements rather than like decisions based on general rules or adjudicative decisions (Gore, 1993).

It is predictable, for a variety of reasons, that the use of contractual agreements will increase over time. However, contracts are not substitutes for more generally applicable processes, and they present their own important problems. First, contracts are every bit as binding as general rules or adjudicative decisions. Further, enforcement discretion in regard to rules rests with administrators and is presumptively unreviewable in court (*Heckler* v. *Chaney*, 1985). In a contractual relationship, either party holds the discretion to trigger enforcement processes. Moreover, the mechanisms for the resolution of disputes are commonly specified in the contracts themselves. Where a jurisdiction has several contracts, it may find it necessary to proceed under several different types of dispute resolution procedures if disagreements arise, rather than have a standard mode of proceeding. The obvious conclusion is that skills in negotiation, drafting, administration, and the management of disputes under contracts are needed. Few jurisdictions have many people adequately trained in these skills (Kettl, 1993). These abilities are all the more critical because contracts are interpreted strictly if challenged in court, compared to the flexibility that is accorded in the application of rules or in adjudications.

The Utility of Judicial Review. Few phenomena of modern public administration history are calculated to raise the blood pressure of public managers faster than the mention of the judicial evaluation of their actions. Indeed, many managers seem to spend a great deal of their time and energy preparing for court challenges. First of all, relatively few day-to-day administrative decisions are likely ever to make it to a court. Administrators do not seem to be aware that most presumptions in most situations are in favor of public managers if and when they are taken to court.

While it is understandable that managers fear litigation, it is nevertheless useful to keep a number of factors in mind. Courts are normal participants in the world of public administration and always have been. State courts were declaring legislative actions unconstitutional and upholding others even before the U.S. Constitution was written in 1787. Court challenges are brought by the rich and the poor, the young and the old, businesses and private individuals. These are facts of administrative life that will not change. While winning in court is always preferable to losing, it is sometimes better to get an authoritative resolution of a problem, even if it is an adverse ruling, than to function under continuing uncertainty. The courts also represent a kind of protection from attempts at inappropriate influence and corruption. The law protects administrative discretion as well as constraining it. Viewing the courts as adversaries makes no more sense than viewing the legislature in the same way. Such antagonism is an understandable but self-defeating and ultimately illegitimate behavior in a constitutional democracy that purports to operate under the rule of law.

CONCLUSION

The simple truth is that reinventing, reengineering, delayering, and decentralizing have not changed the fact that the authority of public administrators stems from law. The law provides the tools that are used to make the most important, and often the most challenging, public decisions. The secret is to understand the legal tools and learn how to use them most effectively in changing management contexts.

Efforts to attack rulemaking and adjudication as techniques used in public administration are not only illegal in many situations but dangerously wrong-headed from a management standpoint. The key is to learn enough about these tools to know when and how to use them, and to exercise the kinds of discretion that are available in these mechanisms. It is equally important to consider how to integrate other tools, like contracting, so that they work effectively rather than operating in conflict with other devices.

Even what seem to be the most difficult and antagonistic of situations, such as judicial review, play critical roles in maintaining not only the effectiveness but also the legitimacy of public administration. Such situations are normal and expected aspects of the enterprise of public administration. They are fundamental institutions of constitutional democracy.

Cases Cited

Appalachian Power Company v. *EPA*, 477 F.2d 495 (D.C. Cir., 1973).

Arnett v. *Kennedy*, 416 U.S. 134 (1974).

Cleveland Board of Education v. *Loudermill*, 470 U.S. 532 (1985).

Community Nutrition Institute v. *Young*, 818 F.2d 943 (D.C. Cir., 1987).

Connick v. *Myers*, 461 U.S. 138 (1983).

Dames and Moore v. *Reagan*, 453 U.S. 654 (1981).

Ford Motor Company v. *Federal Trade Commission*, 673 F.2d 1008 (9th Cir., 1981).

General Motors v. *Ruckelshaus*, 724 F.2d 979 (D.C. Cir., 1983).

Heckler v. *Chaney*, 470 U.S. 821 (1985).

International Harvester v. *Ruckelshaus*, 478 F.2d 615 (D.C. Cir., 1973).

Mathews v. *Eldridge*, 424 U.S. 319 (1976).

Mobil Oil v. *Federal Power Commission*, 483 F.2d 1238 (D.C. Cir., 1973).

Natural Resources Defense Council v. *U.S. Nuclear Regulatory Commission*, 547 F.2d 633 (D.C. Cir. 1976).

Vermont Yankee Nuclear Power Corporation v. *Natural Resources Defense Council*, 435 U.S. 519 (1978).

Walter Holm and Company v. *Hardin*, 449 F.2d 1009 (D.C. Cir., 1971).

Waters v. *Churchill*, 128 L.Ed 2d 686 (1994).

References

Appleby, P. *Policy and Administration.* University: University of Alabama Press, 1949.

Bush, G. "Reducing the Burden of Government Regulations." Presidential memorandum, Jan. 28, 1992.

Davis, K. C. *Discretionary Justice.* Baton Rouge: Louisiana State University Press, 1969.

De Hoog, R. H. *Contracting for Social Services.* Albany: State University of New York Press, 1984.

Friendly, H. *The Federal Administrative Agencies.* Cambridge, Mass.: Harvard University Press, 1962.

Gore, A. Jr. *From Red Tape to Results: Creating a Government That Works Better and Costs Less.* Report of the National Performance Review. Washington, D.C.: U.S. Government Printing Office, 1993.

Green, M. *The Other Government.* New York: Norton, 1978.

Kerwin, C. M. *Rulemaking: How Government Agencies Write Law and Make Policy.* Washington, D.C.: Congressional Quarterly Press, 1994.

Kettl, D. F. *Sharing Power: Public Governance and Private Markets.* Washington, D.C.: Brookings Institution, 1993.

Mosher, F. C. *Democracy and the Public Service.* New York: Oxford University Press, 1968.

Mosher, F. C. "The Changing Responsibilities and Tactics of the Federal Government." *Public Administration Review,* 1980, *40,* 541–547.

Organization for Economic Cooperation and Development. *Economic Instruments for Environmental Protection.* Paris: Organization for Economic Cooperation and Development, 1989.

Osborne, D., and Gaebler, T. *Reinventing Government.* Reading, Mass.: Addison Wesley Longman, 1992.

Rohr, J. A. *To Run a Constitution: The Legitimacy of the Administrative State.* Lawrence: University Press of Kansas, 1987.

Sabatier, P. "Top-Down and Bottom-Up Approaches to Implementation Research: A Critical Analysis and Suggested Synthesis." Paper presented at the Thirteenth World Congress of the International Political Science Association, Paris, July 15–20, 1985.

Salamon, L. *Beyond Privatization: The Tools of Government Action.* Washington, D.C.: Urban Institute, 1989.

Waldo, D. *The Administrative State.* Somerset, N.J.: Ronald Press, 1948.

PART THREE

WHO HAS THE POWER AND WHERE ARE THE LIMITS?

art Three considers more directly the roles of varied types of participants in public law and administrative processes. Particular attention is devoted to separation of powers with checks and balances and to contemporary intergovernmental relations, rooted in the basic notions of federalism. The creators of the Constitution, prescient though they were, could never have anticipated many of today's variations. In fact, one contemporary difficulty is that those who learned years ago about these constitutional principles and related institutions now live in a world where much is very different. So much has changed, in fact, that what were regarded as truisms in the 1970s are often no longer true at all.

Chester A. Newland begins this discussion in Chapter Eight with a new look at the search for workability of separation of powers with checks and balances. He emphasizes three sets of ongoing conversations: (1) the basic framework of separate and shared powers, (2) modes of interpretation used to address interbranch conflicts, and (3) contemporary political failures associated with separation of powers standoffs. A problem with many academic frameworks for understanding separation of powers, he argues, is that they emphasize disconnected, specialized disciplines and the maintenance of distinct institutions rather than considering actual interrelated processes and the interwoven nature of the relationships of law and administration. It is these interstices that present the most important and often the most vexing challenges for today's public officials.

Newland points out that at the local level, where much of public administration operates, the forms of professionally managed government often resemble the parliamentary model more than the national model of separate institutions and perpetual conflicts. The existence of multiple commissions and boards, as well as a tradition of weak governors in many states, has also resulted in important departures from the national textbook model of separation of powers.

Among the principal problems today, Newland notes, is a breakdown in the historic norm under which the political branches often sought to work out accommodations that facilitated more or less reasonable working relationships, at least on major matters of state. Increased willingness of executive and legislative leaders to fight, in contexts of narrowly transactional politics, rather than to share responsibilities for transformational government has persisted in recent decades in such visibly crucial areas as budgets and international affairs. That orientation is symptomatic of a wider set of tensions. Clearly, law can only partially correct the consequences of irresponsible partisanship. If disintegrative politics continues to dominate, that is a formula for failure of constitutional government. Without delay, the object must be to restore political efforts to make separation of powers with checks and balances work, even as courts also search more successfully for reasonable understanding.

One of the most important changes in public administration over the past quarter century is the shift of attention away from Washington to the more than eighty thousand other governmental units at the state, regional, and local levels, where the vast majority of public administrators live and work. Just as Newland emphasized interrelationships, Laurence J. O'Toole addresses in Chapter Nine the changing nature of intergovernmental relations after what he terms the "ghost of 'dual federalism'" has been put to rest.

O'Toole warns, however, that the legal dimensions of intergovernmental relations have often been ignored in favor of an overwhelmingly fiscal framework that emphasizes various kinds of grants-in-aid as the linchpins of cross-governmental cooperation. Dollars matter, to be sure, but that does not mean that there are not also important legal aspects at issue. Thus, tax policy, grants-in-aid, and contracts issued under those grants by states and localities all present both fiscal and legal features that must be understood by those who manage intergovernmental programs.

One of the reasons that the legal features of intergovernmental relations have resurfaced in the contemporary era is the growth of unfunded mandates—obligations issued to states or local governments that do not carry with them the resources necessary for implementation and operation of the new functions and programs. O'Toole points out that while some of these are obvious, as in the case of direct preemptions of authority by the federal government, others are less obvious, as in the case of administrative regulations that impose significant compliance requirements. In fact, most regulatory programs have evolved, he notes, so as to operate under an intergovernmental design that calls upon states to develop and administer their own standards within limits set by Washington.

Thus much environmental legislation by Congress is actually administered by the states, or even, in some cases, by localities.

For many public administrators, one of the most important sets of intergovernmental relationships involves personnel management in which many of the policies that affect day-to-day operations are driven by Washington. Thus, the legal dimensions of intergovernmental relationships reach into virtually every office in the nation.

Beverly A. Cigler takes some of the issues raised by O'Toole to a more specific level in her discussion of state and local government operations in Chapter Ten. Recognizing the forces described by O'Toole, Cigler explains that the cumulative results of intergovernmental mandates are demands on state and local government managers to make real the policy goals that are (or were) pet projects of Washington politicians, including various agency heads. While legal challenges continue over these mandates, she notes, principal efforts have been to move toward incentive approaches and alternative dispute resolution.

Starting with the premise that the relationship between the states and their local governments is not the same as that between the national government and the states, Cigler points to the importance of understanding the nature and authority of local governments. While they possess more authority than many recognize, local governments are essentially at the crunch points of judicially imposed obligations and national and state policy mandates.

Cigler points out, however, that in the end, the judiciary in issues of federalism is not moving totally in the direction of granting greater power to Washington and constraining localities. As is true in other fields, debates over federalism continue in the courts as well as in politics, with indications of a desire to restore to state and local officials the authority and discretion they need to accomplish the tasks for which their governments were created.

CHAPTER EIGHT

Separation of Powers with Checks and Balances

The Search for Workability

Chester A. Newland

The constitutional framework of separation of powers with checks and balances is a formula for gridlock, absent the lubrication of transformational politics. This framework is analyzed here relative to law and public administration. The focus is on the national level, but state and local institutions are touched upon. Contemporary issues during the movement into the twenty-first century are principal concerns, but these are framed in historical contexts of jurisprudence, politics, and applied theory of the American administrative state, which are probed as basic foundations in the practice of public administration.

Three interrelated sets of dynamics are chief concerns in this chapter. Examined first is the search for workable conceptualization. The discussion initially notes the fragmented research and analysis associated with separation of powers, but it focuses chiefly on basic constitutional doctrines. Frameworks of interpretation are examined next, with examples of two enduring sets of issues of legislative-executive-judicial relationships: powers of appointment and removal, and powers of executive privilege and congressional oversight. The final section deals with contemporary political failures of government under the separation of powers, focusing on budgeting and war powers. These examples illustrate that, at best, law is only a partial corrective for irresponsible politics.

SEPARATION OF POWERS DOCTRINES AND APPLICATIONS

The framework of separation of powers with checks and balances has inspired varied interpretations in political science, constitutional law, and public administration. Competing perspectives have flourished during the closing decades of the twentieth century. These perspectives are the focus here, following note of practical origins and disconnected scholarship that subsequently became associated with the three branches of government.

Practical Origins and Disconnected Scholarship

America's constitutional founders sought to create within a federal structure an empowered national government while protecting valued liberties and properties. They tried to achieve that balance through addition of an effective executive within a framework of well-limited national institutions. To that end, although they never used the words *separation of powers* in the Constitution, they chose to combine that structure with checks and balances as a practical means that was buttressed by a somewhat fashionable theory of the time.

That theory, presented in 1748 by Charles-Louis de Montesquieu in *The Spirit of the Laws,* especially cautioned against a union of legislative and executive powers while viewing the judiciary as relatively less significant. To the American constitutional framers, practical experience was a much stronger force than theory, and judicial institutions were important to them. The founders' experience included eighteenth-century ideas of "mixed government," consisting of a balance among monarchy, aristocracy, and democracy. However, given that the developing American culture rejected both monarchy and traditional aristocracy, a different division of power was sought to protect valued interests. Thus, on a practical level the states moved toward a three-branch separation of powers in their early constitutions, complete in most cases with strong judiciaries, although many had weak executive branches.

James Madison's *Federalist* No. 51 is the clearest starting point for understanding the constitutional framers' intentions and decisions. In that essay, Madison analyzed separation of powers, checks and balances among the proposed branches, the bicameral Congress, and the federal system of division of state and national authorities. Nothing was said at that point in *The Federalist Papers* about what later developed as administrative bureaucracy, but Hamilton separately considered the need for an effective executive. Much was said to demonstrate an intention to create an empowered central government—a republican form with capacities to govern but encumbered by constitutional safeguards against tyranny.

Dealing with this framework ever since, practice and scholarship have often tended to become preoccupied with the "separate institutions" (Jones, 1995), neglecting the practical constitutional purposes: to create an empowered government limited by law. Within both government and universities, researchers from narrow specialties have commonly focused distinctly on Congress, the president, or the Supreme Court, with further disconnected study of the executive branch, public administration, lower-level courts, and politics and elections. A purpose of this book is to escape such separated scholarship by focusing on interrelated processes and contents of law and administration that ultimately give practical meaning to constitutional democracy.

As an interdisciplinary field of practice from its beginnings, public administration has been less insular than more narrow disciplines. But the field has nonetheless suffered from partly self-imposed limitations. Most notably, for decades public administration has seemed almost to seek escape from politics, neglecting its essential roots in the reform of political corruption and incapacity. Also, the field early on embraced a presidential-executive bias from which it has not escaped. Until the 1960s and 1970s, the essential connectedness of policy and its implementation was largely neglected. By the 1980s and 1990s, following entrepreneurial fashions of a newly rediscovered importance of management, foundations in law and institutional relationships under separation of powers seemed somewhat abandoned (Newland, 1994, 1996). But despite such failings, as a broadly inclusive field long before today's dominance of interdisciplinary inquiry and practice, public administration retains some orientation to integrative, collaborative performance of governmental functions.

Separated Powers Versus Shared Authority

In political science theory and practice, constitutional perspectives have tended to emphasize more or less either a separation between the branches or shared responsibility among them. Those who stress separation focus on the distinct powers of the three branches and the boundaries *between* them. Prime examples are the extreme doctrines of separate presidential powers espoused by Attorney General Edwin Meese III and White House Counsel Fred Fielding in the Reagan administration (Meese, 1985). Other perspectives stress checks and balances and shared responsibilities *among* the branches (Fisher, 1991). While separationist doctrine reached an all-time high influence through presidential advocates in the 1980s, contrary but mixed perspectives were common in Congress and in the U.S. Supreme Court.

The two best-known Supreme Court decisions on the subject during the 1980s, *Immigration and Naturalization Service* v. *Chadha* (1983) and *Bowsher* v. *Synar* (1986), illustrate the complexities involved in contemporary interbranch relations (Fisher, 1987). These cases attest to both the original and flip side of Justice Oliver Wendell Holmes's caution that hard cases make bad law. In *Chadha*, the legislative veto case, the Supreme Court majority expressed views of separation that were seen among congressional branch experts (Fisher, 1991) as matching or reaching even beyond the following dicta by Justice George Sutherland in 1935 in *Humphrey's Executor* v. *United States* (1935, pp. 629–630): "The fundamental necessity of maintaining each of the three general departments of government entirely free from the control or coercive influence, direct or indirect, of either of the others, has often been stressed and is hardly open to serious question. So much is implied in the very fact of the separation of powers of these departments by the Constitution; and in the rule which recognizes their essential coequality."

In *Chadha*, the Court was confronted with a most unusual case. It involved what amounted to a one-house legislative veto of a quasi-judicial action involving a number of named parties, as contrasted to rulemaking action and a response by both houses. Thus bicameralism and Presentation Clause issues were important. Yet, the legislative veto, while a jerry-rigged device, had grown important since the New Deal era as a means to allow Congress to maintain some checks over administrative interpretation and applications of often-fuzzy statutory language (see Chapter Three). Faced with this, the Court majority reached an understandable outcome with a most poorly constructed opinion. Peculiarly narrow dicta asserted that Congress can only control executive agencies through the full lawmaking process of passage of a joint resolution or of a bill presented for presidential signature or veto. This process overlooked all sorts of theretofore unchallenged congressional oversight and other roles.

Three years later, in *Bowsher,* the Supreme Court was again confronted with a hard case, created out of legislation designed to shift political responsibility for budgeting policy from Congress and the president. The Court was virtually forced again to make bad and hard doctrine. Once more, the majority stretched separationist doctrine beyond common realities, asserting that the Constitution "does not contemplate an active role for Congress in the supervision of officers charged with the execution of the laws it enacts" (*Bowsher* v. *Synar,* 1986, p. 722).

Separationist doctrine, commonly less farfetched than dicta expressed in the *Chadha* and *Synar* cases, has built heavily in recent years on widely accepted "coequality" doctrine. In the 1990s, leading political science proponents have stressed separation as a correction to sixty years of stress on a presidency-centered, responsible-party government. Charles O. Jones, as president of the American Political Science Association, is a chief example: "It is widely accepted that the separation of powers is a defining mark of the American government. It features coequal branches, sometimes sharing powers, sometimes competing for shares of power" (Jones, 1995, p. 3). A year earlier, in his book *The Presidency in a Separated System,* Jones concluded that "most grasp the purposes of a diffused-responsibility system of mixed representation and shared powers, but some believe that the president is the presidency, the presidency is the government, and ours is a presidential system." He continued that those with such beliefs "will be proven to be wrong" (1994, p. 298).

The shared responsibility perspective, building on checks and balances, persisted through decades of preoccupation with presidential empowerment, long before its latter-day embrace as fashionable political science. Justice Robert Jackson, while supporting clearly separate powers, summarized a balanced perspective, saying that while the Constitution "diffuses power the better to secure liberty, it also contemplates that the practice will integrate the dispersed powers into a workable government. It enjoins upon its branches separateness but interdependence, autonomy but reciprocity" (*Youngstown Steel and Tube Corporation v. Sawyer*, 1952, p. 635).

Shared constitutional authority of Congress and the presidency has been probed most persuasively since the 1970s by Louis Fisher, senior specialist in separation of powers in the Congressional Research Service, Library of Congress. Against long-sustained tides of theory of presidential government, Fisher has stressed the constitutional framers' search for balance among political institutions and "various patterns of cooperation and conflict" (1991, p. 22) as the governmental branches have interacted through two centuries of changes.

Executive leadership in a framework of hierarchical bureaucracy became a tenet of public administration as a means to reform political corruption. Legislatures at all levels and fragmented executive structures resulting from long ballots were run through with corrupt politics, becoming the nemesis of reform movements that stretched from Centennial Era agrarian revolt through the Progressive Era and into the New Deal. The short ballot became a means of reform at local and state levels, and presidential government became the formula at the national level to escape defects of congressional government.

At local levels, separation of powers was rejected by reformers in favor of a variation on parliamentary experience: concentration of political authority in a small, elected council and assignment by charter of executive authority to a professionally expert manager, subject only to law and removal authority of the council upon loss of confidence. This remains the favored local government framework in a majority of American cities, although separation of powers under strong-mayor models persists in many larger cities as well as in the smallest ones (Newland, 1995).

At the state level, reform favored a governor empowered both by authority over financial and other administrative resources and by elimination of most other separately elected executive officers and independent boards and commissions. While this movement has made some headway, multiple executives and numerous boards and commissions have continued in states, reflecting the durability of a dispersed executive model with a relatively weak governor. Orthodoxy of the empowered executive persists in reform efforts, however, as in the highly publicized Winter Commission report of an agenda for state and local government reform (National Commission on the State and Local Public Service, 1993).

At the national level, the executive model has been both a focus of advocacy for a strong presidency and a subject of deeper analysis of distinctively American features of separation of powers. In public administration, thinking reaches well beyond dominant polemics in support of presidential power. As at the local and state levels, executive leadership at the national level became orthodoxy to clean up corruption and ineptitude. Presidential power was especially broadly embraced as a practical necessity to cope with growing governmental complexities. The best-known judicial example of that is Chief Justice William Howard Taft's six-to-three majority opinion in *Myers* v. *United States* (1926). Writing some fourteen years after his own presidency, Taft endorsed unrestricted presidential power to remove any officer without constitutionally fixed tenure. While this view could not ultimately withstand scholarly scrutiny and subsequent Supreme Court interpretation, it reinforced administrative orthodoxy for decades thereafter.

Professor Fred Riggs, principal comparativist among presidential scholars, uses *presidential government* not as a term to advocate executive power but to distinguish from parliamentary government a separation of powers in which the executive head is elected for a fixed term and not subject to termination by a no-confidence vote of the legislative branch. Riggs observes that "the United States is the only presidentialist system that has not experienced at least one catastrophic breakdown, followed by a period of military or presidential authoritarianism" (Riggs, 1994, p. 66). This record may be attributed to the existence of public bureaucracy that is neither powerful (it is widely dispersed, mostly at varied local and state levels, with relatively small, fragmented national public services) nor powerless (it represents valued expertise, some professionalism, and practical politics, spread across the country). These are most important realities of America's separation of powers, reflecting the nation's historical experience.

Another significant perspective on separation of powers and American public bureaucracy is provided by John Rohr. In his bicentennial era analysis, *To Run a Constitution: The Legitimacy of the Administrative State* (1986), Rohr observed that public administrators may not properly function as merely obedient tools in a hierarchical system. Rather, they are regularly confronted with conflicting expectations from the three branches, requiring choices about which constitutional master to follow. Ultimately, Rohr argues, the master must be the founding constitutional values, which require morally based decisions. Thus Rohr sees what some others do not: what he calls "*the* public administration," in terms akin to its importance in continental theory and practice, while basing his analysis deeply in American constitutional fundamentals.

FRAMEWORKS OF INTERPRETATION
OF SEPARATION OF POWERS

Given the broad and open-textured constitutional language, statutory and constitutional interpretation necessarily serves as a primary vehicle in the development of separation of powers doctrine. Examples of contemporary theories that guide interpretation are briefly discussed here. Then two sets of recurrent conflicts in congressional and presidential powers are noted.

Theories of Interpretation

Interpretations of statutes, combined with relatively rare judicial review involving constitutional interpretations, are the means by which the judiciary has established its roles within the framework of separation of powers. However, congressional, presidential, and administrative interpretations are likewise important, and examples are restricted here only by space limitations. The focus is on three recent examples. The first is the New Textualism, a resurrection of the old Plain Meaning Rule in statutory interpretation. The second is the doctrine of original intent with respect to the Constitution, only briefly noted as an illustration of executive branch interpretation. The third is the dominant accommodation perspective of coordinate construction. All of these perspectives compete as guides to interpretation in public administration as well as by the judiciary.

The New Textualism. The New Textualism is a revival led by Supreme Court Justice Antonin Scalia of doctrine reaching back to the nineteenth century, when American courts borrowed the theory of statutory interpretation from the English courts. Judges embraced a rule binding courts to the "plain meaning" of a statute unless that meaning was absurd because of a patently unfair or unjust result or because of a result clearly unintended by the legislature. A classic example is the Supreme Court's interpretation of a prohibition against bringing a foreigner into the country "to perform labor or service of any kind" (*Church of the Holy Trinity* v. *United States*, 1892, p. 458). The immigrant employed to perform service in this case was a clergyman. The Court decided that in a "Christian nation," Congress could not have intended the statute to apply.

For another fifty years, the Supreme Court continued to cite the Plain Meaning Rule, but conservative opponents of social legislation commonly embraced a "right, just, and fair exception" doctrine to interpret legislation narrowly or to hold it unconstitutional. The example that gave its name to an era of libertarian judicial activism through use of this exception was *Lochner* v. *New York* (1905), in which the Supreme Court struck down a state statute setting maximum work hours for bakers.

Early in the Lochnerian Era, such critics of conservative judicial activism as Professor Roscoe Pound and Judge Learned Hand urged less "mechanical jurisprudence." Yet such caveats as determined the outcome in the *Holy Trinity* case later came to provide enlarged leeway for judicial interpretation. This approach became firmly established before World War II, when Justice Stanley Reed wrote for the Court that when plain meaning "has led to absurd or futile results, . . . this Court has looked beyond the words to the purpose of the act. Frequently, however, even when the plain meaning did not produce absurd results but merely an unreasonable one 'plainly at variance with the policy of the legislation as a whole' this Court has followed that purpose, rather than the literal words" (*United States* v. *American Trucking Associations, Inc.*, 1940, p. 543). From the time of Reed's explanation of the legal process, dominant theory has been that texts of statutes are important in part as evidence of legislative intent, opposite to earlier doctrine that legislative intent is only important to interpret statutory texts.

This legal process theory was intended to prevent judicial usurpation of legislative authority, but critics soon saw it as affording enlarged opportunities for policymaking by judges. When Justice Scalia was appointed to the Supreme Court in 1986, he brought those perspectives with him, as follows: "Although it is true that the Court in recent times has expressed approval of this doctrine (that legislative history can sometimes overturn plain meaning), that is to my mind an ill advised deviation from venerable principle that if the language of a statute is clear, that language must be given effect—at least in the absence of patent absurdity" (*Immigration and Naturalization Service* v. *Cardoza-Fonseca,* 1987, p. 452).

Justice Scalia says that through his New Textualism he seeks to strengthen separation of powers. He says that he wants to limit temptations of judges to participate in lawmaking and that he seeks to limit the efforts of interest groups and individual legislators to create such temptations by introducing their views into legislative records as evidence of legislative intent—to become later legislative intrusions upon the judiciary. Similar arguments could be made with reference to executive-branch managers who must strive for workable government within a framework of separated powers.

Scalia's efforts to insulate the branches from one another has stimulated renewed debate over old theory of statutory interpretation. However, the New Textualism, like the Plain Meaning Rule, has remained largely honored in the breach. Reasons are many, and they are well known among experienced public administrators. Most notably, in difficult legislation conscious use is regularly made by legislators at all levels of unclear language and expansive records, passing on to administrators and courts the determination of some important meanings. In highly political legislative processes, such compromises allow advocates on conflicting sides to claim some victories, without which much important legislation would fail passage. Also, since legislators cannot unfailingly predict the future, delegation to administrators and judges to interpret statutory language and intent in unforeseen circumstances is broadly accepted as necessary, just as such delegation is in constitutional interpretation.

The Doctrine of Original Intent. A second old theory of interpretation was given renewed life in the Reagan years when Attorney General Edwin Meese embraced the jurisprudence of original intent (or "intention," as he called it) to apply in constitutional review. As explained by Meese, this doctrine has elements of both the Plain Meaning Rule and the legislative intent doctrine in statutory interpretation: "The text of the document and the original intention of those who framed it would be the judicial standard in giving effect to the Constitution" (Meese, 1985, p. 701). The attorney general critiqued Supreme Court decisions, interpreting the coequality doctrine to include executive branch interpretation of the Constitution. Meese quoted Justice John Marshall, that the Constitution limits judicial power as well as executive and legislative power, and he promised that "in the cases we file and those we join as *amicus,* we will endeavor to resurrect the original meaning of constitutional provisions and statutes as the only reliable guide for judgment" (p. 704).

Akin to Justice Scalia's efforts to demarcate boundaries, Meese sought clear separation between Congress and the executive branch. He also opposed independent regulatory commissions, considered by the Reagan administration to be an illegitimate fourth branch of government, despite their long history. Thus he argued that the president should be essentially free to act, subject to electoral success or failure.

Advocacy by Justice Scalia and Attorney General Meese of clear boundaries between branches in the face of the realities of complex interactions is associated with their perspectives on outcomes. These perspectives in turn relate to institutional considerations of these parties' branches and substantive policies of government. Policy outcomes appear to be commonly associated with support of these doctrines. This was also characteristic of key figures in the Lochnerian Era and the New Deal, and it applies to other figures today.

The Accommodation Perspective of Coordinate Construction. A third, nondoctrinaire approach remains dominant. Favorable to shared-authority perspectives, it is an approach of accommodation of coordinate construction. This more open-textured approach to separation of powers is dominant on the U.S. Supreme Court and is characteristic of practice among professionally expert staffers and political leaders both "on the Hill" and "downtown" who regularly search together for reasonableness as a foundation for workable government, attempting to balance separation with realistic checks and balances. Justice Sandra Day O'Connor expressed this generally accepted view, upholding the

Federal Insecticide, Fungicide, and Rodenticide Act (FIFRA) against claims that its mandatory arbitration provisions violated Article III judicial powers. In *Thomas v. Union Carbide Agricultural Products* (1985, p. 587), she wrote that "practical attention to substance rather than doctrinaire reliance on formal categories should inform application of Article III." Reminiscent of Justice Benjamin Nathan Cardozo's perspectives on jurisprudence, O'Connor embraced *purpose* as basic: "Looking beyond form to the substance of what FIFRA accomplishes, we note several aspects of FIFRA that persuade us the arbitration scheme adopted by Congress does not contravene Article III" (473 U.S. 589). Other such perspectives are basic to the well-known case of *Morrison v. Olson* (1988), noted in the next section of this chapter.

Interpretation of Appointment and Removal Powers

The *Myers* case and the *Humphrey's Executor* case, both key decisions on appointment and removal powers, have already been noted as illustrative of enduring conflicts in congressional and presidential relationships. More importantly, examples of conflicts and cooperation among the branches in this set of constitutional issues demonstrates that while searches for boundaries to separate the branches may be useful for momentary political purposes, the system of checks and balances and complexities of contemporary government yields fuzzy sets of understandings at best, and their survival is often temporary.

Concluding a detailed analysis of one such set, Louis Fisher said: "The appointment power operates in a framework of studied ambiguity, its limits established for the most part not by court decisions but by imaginative accommodations between the executive and legislative branches" (1991, p. 51).

The independent counsel case, *Morrison v. Olson* (1988), illustrates the complexity of appointment and removal frameworks. It also illustrates that constitutional meaning on separation of powers, even as defined in such leading cases as *Myers* and *Humphrey's Executor,* is in fact defined by moments in history. In *Morrison,* the Supreme Court in a seven to one decision written by Chief Justice William Rehnquist, Justice Scalia dissenting, upheld unusual appointment and removal provisions for independent prosecutors, as provided for by Congress in the Ethics in Government Act of 1978. In this act, Congress sought to deal with issues that arose during the Watergate scandal: How can an inferior officer defy a president and require his compliance with lawful procedures in independent investigations of alleged wrongdoing? Congress accomplished that by providing for independent counsel appointed by a three-judge panel, and removal only by impeachment or due to physical incapacity or other condition substantially impairing performance.

Both the appointment and removal provisions were challenged as violations of Article II. Opponents argued that the position of independent counsel is not one of an "inferior officer" that can be filled by judicial appointment; rather, they argued, the independent counsel is a principal officer who must be appointed by the president with the advice and consent of the Senate. The chief justice held for the majority that the independent counsel is an inferior position under the Article II provision that "Congress may by law vest the Appointment of such inferior Officers, as they think proper, in the President alone, in the Courts of Law, or in the Heads of Departments" (Sec. 2). Rehnquist's opinion went further, departing from the *Myers* and *Humphrey's Executor* cases. He said that the "analysis contained in our removal cases is designed not to define rigid categories of those officials who may or may not be removed at will by the President, but to ensure that Congress does not interfere with the President's exercise of the 'executive power' and his constitutionally appointed duty to 'take care that the laws be faithfully executed' under Article II" (*Morrison v. Olson*, 1988, pp. 689–690).

Justice Scalia dissented vigorously, arguing that an independent counsel is not an inferior officer but an officer according to the meaning of Article II. He maintained that criminal prosecution is a "quintessentially executive activity" (*Morrison v. Olson*, 1988, p. 706). Thus he found that a deeper issue of separation of powers was involved, arguing that "it is not for us to determine, and we have never presumed to determine, how much of the purely executive powers of government must be within the full control of the President. The Constitution prescribes that they *all* are" (*Morrison v. Olson*, 1988, p. 709). Scalia charged that the majority opinion gave "shoddy treatment" to the *Humphrey's Executor* case, sweeping it "into the dustbin of repudiated constitutional principles" (*Morrison v. Olson*, 1988, p. 725).

The view that Article II, Section 2, Clause 2 of the Constitution—the Appointments Clause—is a strong bulwark against one branch of the government aggrandizing its power at the expense of another was expressed for a unanimous court by Chief Justice Rehnquist in a 1995 decision involving civilian judges on a military appellate panel (*Ryder v. United States*). In this case, two judges were appointed by the General Counsel of the U.S. Department of Transportation to the Coast Guard Court of Military Review (CGCMR). Counsel for an accused enlisted man successfully challenged that this CGCMR composition violated the Constitution's Appointments Clause and the principle of separation of powers. The Court, in short, acted to protect an independent judiciary.

Congressional Investigation, Judicial Power to Compel Evidence, and Executive Privilege

Neither congressional power to investigate nor executive privilege of the president to withhold information are explicitly provided for in the Constitution, but each has been found essential. These implied powers are often in conflict, and no simple boundaries of separation of powers or easy formulas of checks and balances have been found to resolve differences in their interpretation.

Contingencies of moments in history, including practical realities of politics and needs for workable government, are crucial in the search to accommodate the needs of all three branches consistently with constitutional principles. In short, here again separation of powers doctrine, like law generally, moves with historical currents.

Both congressional power to investigate and executive privilege were established in practice in 1792 when the House appointed a committee to inquire into a failed military expedition. The committee was authorized to require testimony and turnover of papers and records. President George Washington, with cabinet consultation, decided to provide papers consistent with the public good, but to "exercise a discretion" with respect to presidential papers (Fisher, 1991, pp. 154–155). This formally courteous beginning, followed by other early precedents, firmly established these implied powers. Congress possesses investigative authority to facilitate its legislative functions, to oversee governmental activities, to protect its institutional integrity, and to inform the public. It may exercise a contempt power to support its authority. In turn, the president may assert executive privilege in matters within the exclusive province of the chief executive, including details of treaties being negotiated, pardons, and removals of executive officers. The judiciary, in its turn, sometimes as final arbiter in conflicts between the other branches, requires evidence for integrity in its legal processes. Thus accommodations by all involved are necessary for the government to function.

In congressional-executive interactions, litigation is relatively uncommon. Yet it is through court cases that many challenging margins of separation of powers are tested. Only two closely related cases are noted here—selected to demonstrate both the important complexities and the exceptional character of really big conflicts. The cases are *United States* v. *Nixon* (1974), involving the Watergate tapes, and *Nixon* v. *Administrator of General Services* (1977), involving presidential papers.

The 1974 *Nixon* case involved a conflict over executive privilege and the judiciary's need to compel production of evidence essential to its performance of duties. Seven employees of the White House and of the Committee for the Re-Election of the President were indicted by a federal grand jury. Presidential recording tapes, established by congressional inquiry to exist but never earlier made public because of Nixon's claim of executive privilege, were relevant to charges against the defendants. The court ordered release of the tapes as evidence, placing the needs of the criminal justice system above the president's claim of privileged communications. Nixon was compelled to comply, and that led to his resignation.

Earlier, congressional efforts to secure the Watergate tapes to assist in an impeachment process had failed. In that congressional process, Nixon's lawyers agreed that executive privilege could not be claimed as a shield from criminal prosecution. However, they asserted that only the president could determine whether information was within the scope of privilege, with the only recourses being impeachment (without disclosure of the information) or defeat through election.

The later *Nixon* presidential papers case, decided seven to two, upheld the statute created after Watergate that gave the government custody of all of Nixon's presidential papers and records, including tape recordings. Theretofore, papers of all presidents had been personal property, although all recent presidents had deeded many or all of their papers to government for administration through the National Archives in compliance with presidential dictates. From Washington's time it was accepted practice that executive privilege survived tenure in office. The Supreme Court agreed with that in the 1977 *Nixon* case, but it nevertheless upheld the presidential papers statute as applied to Nixon, respecting the conclusion by Congress that he was not a trustworthy custodian of papers being screened by archivists according to statute.

In summary, with respect to both congressional investigations and executive privilege, accommodation is essential. At routine working levels of government, accommodation has most generally been voluntary, even collaborative. Increasingly, however, it is forced politically. With growing frequency, it is required legally.

POLITICAL AND INSTITUTIONAL FRAMEWORKS OF ADMINISTRATION

Today, the workability of this form of government is greatly challenged. Coequality of the branches is threatened by decades of executive aggrandizement, reinforced since the late 1960s by increased presidential politicization of the executive branch. Reassertions of congressional power since Watergate add to conflicts. Separation between the branches is increasingly promoted, as in important staff agencies of government, at the expense of shared responsibility and reasonable accommodation.

Two categories of interbranch conflicts and failures in the 1980s and 1990s are examples: annual budget deficits and a national debt projected at six trillion dollars before the year 2000; and fractious interbranch relationships on war powers and conduct of international affairs generally. Both of these examples illustrate that analysis in public law and separation of powers must reach well beyond the study of court cases. They also illustrate the limited capacities of law to correct political problems.

Failed National Government Budgeting

Deficits and debt-driven government have largely dominated national policy considerations since the Reagan Administration's successful push in 1981 to reduce revenues and congressional-presidential failures to cut overall expenditures. In the thirty-five years from 1960 to 1995, the national government went from a budget surplus of $270 million to a *visible* annual deficit of $220.4 billion, not counting more than $100 billion hidden in each of several years by use of surplus Social Security trust funds and other political calculations to keep the real scope of annual deficits invisible. The visible annual deficit peaked in 1992 at $290 billion, then declined slightly in subsequent years. It climbed again in the president's proposed fiscal year 1996 budget, and no congressional-presidential agreement could be reached for that election year until five months before the end of the budget year.

Congresses and presidents have been unable to collaborate politically to deal successfully with these deficits and resulting debt problems. Politicians have feared the consequences of budget-balancing decisions. Thus they have sought to invent ways to escape their clear constitutional responsibilities, creating peculiar legal frameworks that supposedly may compel balanced budgets. Such efforts since the Budget and Impoundment Control Act of 1974, however, have exacerbated separation between Congress and the executive branch and have greatly contributed to failures to resolve budgetary problems collaboratively. The 1974 act and the Gramm-Rudman-Hollings (GRH) Act of 1985 and its 1987 revision illustrate this contemporary aspect of separation of powers, made unworkable by irresponsible politics. A recurrently proposed balanced budget amendment is a more visible example.

The Budget and Impoundment Control Act of 1974 was designed to strengthen congressional budget control following the excesses of Watergate, but its mechanisms undermined the earlier legal framework of distinct presidential-congressional roles that had facilitated budgeting under the separation of powers. Forty-three years earlier, the Budget and Accounting Act of 1921 had successfully balanced presidential responsibility for budget estimates and congressional authority over final appropriations. The two branches functioned more or less together under that formula throughout the subsequent expansion of the American administrative state. By the 1970s, however, the relatively clear assignment and performance of distinct responsibilities began to disintegrate under such pressures as "uncontrollable" entitlements, mounting distrust of politicians and government, and changed politics. The 1974 act was intended to achieve congressional-presidential balance, but it largely accomplished opposite results. Newly created budget committees were quickly transformed into new pressure points for members who failed to get all they wanted from authorization and appropriations committees. Required aggregation in budget resolutions so increased congressional conflicts and needs for concessions to gain passage that responsibility plummeted instead of increasing as had been hoped. Instead of producing enhanced discipline within Congress, accountability declined. This result starkly demonstrates again that law, especially when statutes deliberately ignore well-established knowledge, can go only so far in correcting political irresponsibility.

One positive result of the 1974 act was creation of the Congressional Budget Office (CBO), resulting in enhanced technical capacity and availability of budget analyses that became more trusted than products of the Office of Management and Budget (OMB). But serving within the dispersed-authority framework of Congress, CBO could never achieve the institutional force of OMB's predecessor, the Bureau of the Budget (BOB). Rather, CBO came to have great respect as compared to OMB's lower reputation following its presidential politicization. Each agency became increasingly a symbol of separation between the branches rather than of a unifying institution in service of effective government in the fashion of the former BOB. Starting during this same period, the U.S. General Accounting Office (GAO) nearly became identified not as an agency under oversight of Congress in service of government generally but rather as a "gotcha" tool of Congress, particularly the majority, in a starkly separated system. The GAO's close embrace of Total Quality Management in the late 1980s and early 1990s, identifying Congress as its "customer," added to this image.

The Gramm-Rudman-Hollings Act of 1985 was an acknowledgment of failure of the Budget and Impoundment Control Act of 1974. Yet, in pursuit of an image of seeking balanced budgets while avoiding constitutional responsibility, it carried the same idea even further: creation of a statutory requirement of fixed annual budget targets to force congressional-presidential budgetary accommodation. It failed more visibly than the 1974 act. GRH focused glaring attention on one-year targets, resulting in use by both branches of short-run tactics, such as shifting costs and revenues from year to year. Long-term considerations became lost in interbranch one-upmanship. As noted earlier, in the *Bowsher* case the Supreme Court held unconstitutional those GRH provisions that sought to use GAO to get politicians off the hook of making decisions. Having failed, GRH was revised in 1987 to move the balanced-budget goal to then-distant 1993. In subsequent years, the horizon continued to be moved further into the future.

Proposals of a balanced budget amendment parallel statutory efforts to create a legal framework to force responsible congressional-presidential actions. The questions remain: How successful can statutory or constitutional law be in preventing irresponsible politics? And how necessary to a workable separation of powers is responsible politics? Following discussion of war and treaty powers, these questions are the final focus of this chapter. However, some answers are already clear from recent budgetary struggles. First, separation of powers is not a subject that can be understood by examination of court cases alone. As in most subjects, public law involves far more. Second, government under a rule of law is an American foundation principle, but such transformational rule can be and is undermined by transactional politics in pursuit of irresponsible interests.

War Powers and International Affairs

The American Constitution departed clearly from the British model of exclusive executive war powers and control of foreign affairs. It vested in Congress power to declare war and extensive control over external matters. However, following World War II, the last congressionally declared conflict, the half-century-long Cold War period of the garrison state greatly changed the exercise of war power and the conduct of international affairs. From the Korean War onward, presidents have regularly exercised war powers with scarcely more than congressional consultation, and that sometimes after the fact or minimal. President George Bush did secure congressional authorization for use of troops in the Iraq-Kuwait "Desert Storm" War in 1991, but only at the final minute, declaring presidential authority to act alone. As in the August 1995 U.S. strikes against Serbs in Bosnia—the largest European military action since World War II—presidential decisions have often been based on NATO and United Nations treaties or other grounds interpreted by presidents as not requiring congressional mandates for actions. In lawsuits by congressional members, the judiciary has regularly avoided issues of limits on the president as commander in chief.

Congress sought to reestablish checks and balances through legislative controls imposed by the War Powers Act of 1973 and added provisions in 1980 and 1991. From a legislative perspective, their purpose was to require a joint congressional-presidential judgment for commitment of U.S. troops to hostilities beyond relatively limited actions. The 1973 Act provided for a deadline of sixty to ninety days on presidentially initiated military actions—a period criticized by congressional supporters as too long and by presidential advocates as too restrictive. Another major provision requiring consultation with members of Congress has presented major questions about logistical problems and the extent of exchange required. Provision for congressional use of a concurrent resolution to compel a president to withdraw troops from hostilities has drawn the greatest constitutional challenge. Presidential advisors have argued that executive power to put troops into combat is constitutional and cannot be interfered with by a concurrent resolution. That argument has been based on wording in *Immigration and Naturalization Service* v. *Chadha* (1983), discussed earlier, which says that executive actions can only be controlled by Congress through a bill or joint resolution presented for signature or veto.

Ultimately, congressional authority over spending has remained a most practical means of control over use of military force (Fisher, 1995). Congress regularly places limits on uses of appropriated funds. For example, in its 1991 authorization to use force in the Desert Storm war, Congress approved spending only for actions to drive Iraq out of Kuwait. It did not authorize use of funds to invade or occupy Iraq, accounting in part for how that war was ended (in midcourse, in the views of informed critics, with Saddam Hussein remaining in power amidst long-continuing instability in the region).

Disintegrative Politics and Separation of Powers

The Constitution of the United States seeks to facilitate government under a rule of law. Workability of the American system of separation of powers with checks and balances, however, depends heavily on politics, demonstrating that reliance on law to accomplish such purposes as balanced budgets and fighting wars has limits.

Disintegrative politics often dominates national government today, undermining collaborative checks and balances to facilitate a workable separation of powers. Representatives, senators, and presidents are often driven to compete against one another, even if identified with the same national party, in a system of fragmented, entrepreneurial, demolition politics.

Of several forces that account for this, three are sufficiently well known that they warrant mention here: (1) growing media impacts on elections since 1956, including costs for mass marketing of contrived images and issues; (2) political action committees (PACS), including important ones run by members of Congress, and various deep-pocket sources of financing; and (3) the rise of a for-hire political consulting industry, fueling and living off of entrepreneurial politics as the successors to the old political machines.

While all of these forces affect the political environment in which the system of separation of powers now functions, two other sets of changes in politics have particularly affected the constitutional framework: (1) fragmentation into "electoral parties" and (2) considerable fracturing of the old "iron triangle" of bureaus, congressional committees, and related interest groups.

American political parties have always been fractious, but growing separation of presidential and congressional electoral machinery has increasingly affected candidates' behaviors once elected. Even when a president and congressional majorities are nominally of the same political party, they often owe their elections to competing interests and personal loyalists. The rise in importance of presidential primaries, starting with the 1960 nomination and subsequent election of John F. Kennedy, signaled the beginning of a costly trend. Presidential candidates since then have been compelled to put together their own campaign organizations and financing—"electoral parties"—staffed with personal loyalists and hired guns who later accompany victors into office, to the general exclusion not only of members of the opposite party but of those in their own party who are not in their personal circle of loyalists. The building of coalitions across party lines, as among the cabinet members and other appointees of Presidents Truman, Eisenhower, and Johnson, almost became a forgotten political art to seek a workable separation of powers. Then President Clinton, after his second-term election, again by less than a popular majority, was virtually compelled to restore the practice somewhat by appointment of a former Republican senator as secretary of defense.

Separation of presidential campaign politics has reinforced such preexisting tendencies in congressional, senatorial, and state political activities. Today, these more or less separate campaign organizations compete for financial support and votes, sometimes distancing themselves from other elements of their parties. Yet congressional and senatorial campaign committees function on behalf of efforts to gain or retain party control of Congress. Presidents and leading presidential contenders are sometimes visibly connected with these efforts. PACs seek to exercise influence through support of both individuals and party slates. The 1994 success of PAC action led by Congressman Newt Gingrich resulted in Republican (GOP) takeover of the House for the first time in forty years and Gingrich's elevation to Speaker. That politics continued in the 1996 elections, with continued GOP control in the new 105th Congress.

Such examples demonstrate extremely ragged and contrary dynamics surrounding the old political science doctrine of "responsible party government." Divided government has become the norm, both nationally and in the states. A series of GOP presidents had to work with many years of Democratically controlled Congresses, followed by Clinton's years with Republicans controlling the Hill. Continuing state-level tendencies, thirty-three states had similarly divided governments following the 1996 elections, including such major states as California, Illinois, Massachusetts, Michigan, New York, and Texas. These developments are associated more with transactional politics of narrow interests and factions than with broader party efforts—and they are crucial in defining separation of powers and relevant public law dynamics.

The so-called iron triangle that once strongly linked congressional committees, interest groups, and bureaus contributed enormously to the workability of separation of powers as the administrative state grew during the New Deal and later. Continuity of linkages brought relative stability in interbranch politics and administration. Likewise, Laurence O'Toole has demonstrated that the politics-administration dichotomy is important to the reconciliation of differences among branches (O'Toole, 1987). For several decades it has been fashionable in public administration to push that dichotomy aside. Aspects of the old triangle and career leadership persist, but no longer as major factors in support of stable, cooperative relationships between government's branches. With the rise of distinct presidential campaign organizations that increasingly function as electoral parties, executive branch staffing and control shifted away from reliance at bureau levels on long-term careerists with professional expertise. A new system of executive branch spoils emerged. By Nixon's administration, top bureau officials throughout the executive branch started being displaced by mostly short-term appointees who could pass litmus tests of presidential loyalty. This trend toward partisan presidential control, largely separate and apart from Congress, was sanctioned and accelerated by the Civil Service Reform Act of 1978. By the 1990s, politicization with presidential partisans reached deeply into government, as shown by Paul Light in his book *Thickening Government* (1995; also see Chapter Three of this book). Such staffing by people with limited experience or with other sources of knowledge about substantive policies and Capitol Hill militates against a workable separation of powers. Yet this system of executive branch spoils continues to expand as a dominant feature of national government today.

SUMMARY

Separation of powers with checks and balances was embraced by the framers of the Constitution to create a workable national government while protecting valued liberties and properties. Shared responsibility among the branches is essential to effectiveness of this system. However, both constitutional doctrines of strict separation and disintegrative politics of parties and elections often militate against essential cooperation among branches to achieve reasonably workable government.

Statutory gimmicks and proposals for constitutional "fixes" have been favored in recent years by Congresses and presidents to duck their clear responsibilities to deal with major issues, such as enormous budget deficits and war powers. These political adventures, staged with the high-technology smoke and mirrors of increasingly transactional politics, have produced repeated failures. These efforts have demonstrated that law is only a partial corrective for irresponsible politics. Clearly, the combination of a separation of powers and disintegrative politics is a formula for failure of American government under law. Constitutional government, by contrast, requires the shared discipline of a search for reasonableness in politics, law, and public administration.

Cases Cited

Bowsher v. *Synar*, 478 U.S. 714 (1986).

Church of the Holy Trinity v. *United States*, 143 U.S. 457 (1892).

Humphrey's Executor v. *United States*, 295 U.S. 602 (1935).

Immigration and Naturalization Service v. *Cardoza-Fonseca*, 480 U.S. 421 (1987).

Immigration and Naturalization Service v. *Chadha*, 462 U.S. 919 (1983).

Lochner v. *New York*, 198 U.S. 45 (1905).

Morrison v. *Olson*, 487 U.S. 654 (1988).

Myers v. *United States*, 272 U.S. 52 (1926).

Nixon v. *Administrator of General Services,* 433 U.S. 425 (1977).

Ryder v. *United States,* 132 L.Ed. 2d 136 (1995).

Thomas v. *Union Carbide Agricultural Products,* 473 U.S. 568 (1985).

United States v. *American Trucking Associations, Inc.,* 310 U.S. 534 (1940).

United States v. *Nixon,* 418 U.S. 683 (1974).

Youngstown Steel and Tube Corporation v. *Sawyer,* 343 U.S. 579 (1952).

References

Fisher, L. "The Administrative World of *Chadha* and *Bowsher. Public Administration Review,* 1987, *47,* 213–219.

Fisher, L. *Constitutional Conflicts Between Congress and the President.* Lawrence: University Press of Kansas, 1991.

Fisher, L. *Presidential War Power.* Lawrence: University Press of Kansas, 1995.

Jones, C. O. *The Presidency in a Separated System.* Washington, D.C.: Brookings Institution, 1994.

Jones, C. O. "A Way of Life and Law." *American Political Science Review,* 1995, *89,* 1–9.

Light, P. C. *Thickening Government.* Washington, D.C.: Brookings Institution, 1995.

Meese, E. III. "The Attorney General's View of the Supreme Court: Toward a Jurisprudence of Original Intention." *Public Administration Review,* 1985, *45,* 701–704.

Montesquieu, C.-L. de. *The Spirit of the Laws.* (D. W. Carrithers, ed.) Berkeley: University of California Press, 1978. (Originally published 1748.)

National Commission on the State and Local Public Service. *Hard Truths/Tough Choices: An Agenda for State and Local Reform.* Albany: Rockefeller Institute of Government, State University of New York, 1993.

Newland, C. A. "A Field of Strangers in Search of a Discipline: Separatism of Public Management Research from Public Administration." *Public Administration Review,* 1994, *54,* 486–488.

Newland, C. A. "Managing from the Future in Council-Manager Government." In H. G. Frederickson (ed.), *Ideal and Practice in Council-Manager Government.* Washington, D.C.: International City/County Management Association, 1995.

Newland, C. A. "Professional Public Management, Demolition Politics, and Trust in Government: A Quarter Century's Search." *Public Manager,* 1996, *25,* 3–7.

O'Toole, L. J. Jr. "Doctrines and Developments: Separation of Powers, the Politics-Administration Dichotomy, and Rise of the Administrative State." *Public Administration Review,* 1987, *47,* 17–25.

Riggs, F. W. "Bureaucracy and the Constitution." *Public Administration Review,* 1994, *54,* 65–72.

Rohr, J. A. *To Run a Constitution: The Legitimacy of the Administrative State.* Lawrence: University Press of Kansas, 1986.

CHAPTER NINE

WHO DOES THE WORK?

*Federalism and the Changing
Nature of Intergovernmental Relations*

Laurence J. O'Toole Jr.

American public administration has been both liberated and shackled by its primary intellectual heritage in management. For many decades, the view of many practitioners and scholars has been grounded in how to organize for efficiency and effectiveness rather than how to use the law for worthy public purposes and to operate appropriately within its constraints.

This relative neglect of the law in public administration is, if anything, even more obvious when issues cross governmental lines. Indeed, the very term *intergovernmental relations* reflects an emphasis on getting beyond legal issues and formal allocations of authority and on to the practicalities of accomplishing objectives in the complex American system. The idea has been to avoid being trapped and misled by the ghost of "dual federalism"—the notion that the national government and the states occupy separate and nonoverlapping spheres of action. Most intergovernmental participants know that such a picture omits much of the important substance of intergovernmental performance, says little about the roles and relationships of the eighty thousand local governments in the United States, and in particular neglects the multifarious links among levels and governments in the variegated intergovernmental pattern.

Thus intergovernmental relations has accentuated grants programs, flows of financial resources, and the vertical two-way exercise of influence in the

---

Note: William Douglas Ballard provided research assistance in the preparation of this chapter.

federal-state-local array. This perspective has been both understandable and apropos, especially given the great expansion in intergovernmental aid—in both dollars and numbers of programs—during the twentieth century. The implications of these flows of funds for program adoption, governmental re-organization and modernization, interjurisdictional cooperation, and policy development and change could hardly be lost on administrators. Managing organizations and programs in a context in which policy fields are stretched across governments has been the issue of central importance.

However, even if the emphasis has been fathomable, it has meant that ques-tions of law have too often been ignored by comparison, and this consequence has resulted in underattention to a set of increasingly pressing issues of practice. In the current era of severely constrained public budgets, reductions in flows of intergovernmental funds, resurgent state roles, and experiments in many policy fields, a rethinking of intergovernmental questions is clearly in order.

One approach is to resurrect the hoary notion of dual federalism, encourage the national government to retreat from its involvement in myriad policy sec-tors, and trim even more severely the nation's fiscal commitment. The states and local governments would be left with more formal independence and less practical support. But an imposition of a dual federalism *redux* is unlikely; the multiple influences encouraging cross-jurisdictional interdependence will not disappear, no matter how controversial the results or how radical the budget trimming.

It is, furthermore, important to recognize that the shifted emphasis away from dollars and toward other channels of influence in the system is no mere parti-san theme. The flow of intergovernmental aid from Washington peaked in 1978. And fiscal federalism in the narrow neglects mechanisms of intergovernmental influence that have ascended in importance for years since then. In particular, the complex questions of intergovernmental regulation and preemption of state jurisdiction by national action have become central.

The present era is a period in which the dimension of public law deserves reintroduction into the more fiscally—and managerially—focused field of inter-governmental relations. This redressing of emphases can be important for administrators because of the increasingly insistent impacts on the public man-agement setting of the developments occurring in public law.

This chapter sketches the federal context for public administration and then examines the implications of public law for the traditionally emphasized inter-governmental issue: the grants system. The discussion then shifts to the more recently contentious themes of preemption and mandating, and it considers how developments in public law influence several administrative issues. Finally, selected additional implications of public law for intergovernmental adminis-tration are sketched.

PUBLIC LAW AND PUBLIC ADMINISTRATION: FEDERALISM AS CONTEXT

A fundamental feature of governmental operations in the United States is the constitutionally enshrined principle of federalism: states and nation, formal equals, each guaranteed independent authority and existence, each provided broad but partially distinguishable realms of operation.

The bargain negotiated at the time of the founding of the Constitution created a general distinction between levels, but it also introduced by design several points of potential dispute and renegotiation. The national government was to possess indisputable power to exercise important responsibilities. The states were to be the repository of much of the domestic policymaking initiative. And where the constitution did not speak explicitly, the states were given "reserved powers," with the Tenth Amendment stipulating that the states would be the presumptively authoritative actor when new issues or unanticipated policy questions were forced onto the public agenda.

But matters were not, and are not, so simple. Some constitutional provisions raised questions that would become perennial. The national government was authorized to act for the "general welfare." And state authority was to be superseded on matters affecting interstate commerce. These clauses provided contestable entrée for Washington to address a variety of issues, as conditions and political support would dictate. Much of the nation's history has seen extensions of federal effort and jurisdiction, always justified by the pressing nature of policy issues and the constitutional basis for national expansion.

The result of the long series of resolutions has been a system of federal-state-local relations marked by great complexity, substantial national reach (in both breadth and depth), continuing diversity of effort and approach among the states and localities, and extensive interdependence at all levels of the system. The resulting interpenetration of influence across governments is mediated in an ongoing fashion by the federal courts. In virtually every sector of policy, most of the major programs and initiatives are intergovernmental. Most public administrators in the United States are employed by and owe legal accountability to one government (but see Grodzins, 1960), yet most administrators also help to coordinate programs that operate across governmental units, as people and resources are marshaled to deal with public problems.

Many factors, including the nature of the intergovernmental program instrument, the level and kinds of resources applied, and the public management skill devoted to the effort, influence what happens in practice. So, too, does public law.

PUBLIC LAW AND THE ADMINISTRATION
OF GRANTS PROGRAMS

It has been widely recognized that intergovernmental grants-in-aid have been central elements of the American system. It is less well known that the legal foundation of the grants system affects how the national government has long pursued so many of its goals through such apparently complex instrumentalities.

In the nineteenth century, land grants were offered to the states to promote infrastructure and other development. In-kind assistance by the national government was a significant force in certain other programs (see Elazar, 1962). But there were spheres of separated, divided authority as well; and part of the jurisdictional tension was bolstered by the predominant view, among both politicians and the judiciary, of what public law required in terms of federal-state separation (see Scheiber, 1966). Only in the twentieth century was the cash grant-in-aid adopted as a major channel of assistance. Indeed, early authorities opined that such aid would be an unconstitutional infringement by the national government on the states.

Nonetheless, in the first part of the twentieth century political support began to build for grant-in-aid support. The initiative was contentious. In 1923, the Supreme Court ruled on the issue in a case involving efforts to support state programs for maternal and child health. In *Frothingham* v. *Mellon* (1923) and *Massachusetts* v. *Mellon* (1923), the Court validated grants-in-aid as a constitutionally legitimate tool of national purpose. The Court acknowledged the political difficulty of states' rejecting federal largesse, but concluded that the instrument was noncompulsory.

No judicial proscriptions were placed on the range of possible grant purposes or provisions. In succeeding years, national authorities extended their adoption of grants-in-aid on at least two dimensions. First, many substantive specialties became subject to grant assistance and influence. By the 1970s and continuing to the present, several hundred grants-in-aid had been enacted. The programs varied considerably in matching ratio, funding mechanism, breadth of discretion introduced for states or local governments (narrowly categorical to broad block grants; for a several-year period, virtually unrestricted general revenue sharing was also available), and policy objective.

Second, grants-in-aid ranged greatly in conditions of assistance. The early litigation cleared the way for the national government to attach strings; no limit was specified. In many cases federal conditions became detailed in the extreme, thus creating potent, if indirect, channels of influence, fueling the ire of state and local officials, and necessitating a large investment in monitoring for compliance.

The grant mechanism, then, was legitimized in a fashion that encouraged its use. As the public agenda grew, and as pressure mounted for national initiatives on pressing issues, grants-in-aid catalyzed action while providing deference to the federal principle, thus encouraging more widespread political support for still newer efforts in several fields, including welfare, health, and social services.

Care should be taken, nonetheless, not to exaggerate the strength of the grant mechanism as a vehicle for national influence. The option to cut off funds when grantee governments do not comply with the conditions of assistance is severely limited in practice. One reason is political: interests advantaged by assistance are unlikely to sit idly by as the aid spigot is closed. Another reason has to do with the processes of public law. Appeal routes for recipient governments can involve the federal courts, thus rendering such options cumbersome, expensive, and time-consuming. Such judicial resolution of intergovernmental conflicts on grants-in-aid must be restricted to a few extreme cases—note, for instance, the still-simmering litigation in the south on vestiges of dual-race systems of higher education. After several years and sometimes-heated maneuvering, no funding has ceased, and the possible remedies are still under contest.

Despite these practical limitations, grants programs have been the object of a range of legal challenges. In fact, as noted by George Brown (1981), a litigation boom has enveloped many grants programs as grantors, grantees, and third parties have found access to the courts a feasible and attractive option to resolve disputes. Indeed, some of the nonfiscal developments, like the emergence of broader crosscutting requirements, provides further impetus to continue this trend, which will be discussed in the next section of this chapter.

All in all, then, grants programs themselves, which provide perhaps the most familiar setting for public administrators, have been closely linked to issues of public law from their earliest uses in the twentieth century to the present day. Grants, nevertheless, are hardly the only intergovernmental instrument or source of intergovernmental contest. As mentioned earlier, preemptions and mandates have seen an upsurge and become a focus of public law.

STICKS WITHOUT CARROTS: MANDATES, PREEMPTION, AND REGULATION

Efforts by federal officials to direct, constrain, and impel action on the part of state and local governments have seen a recent upsurge. Several measures demonstrate the point. First, by any measure, the regulatory requirements imposed by the federal government on states and local governments have grown in volume and extensiveness during the last two decades, despite some efforts to trim these. In a study of the regulatory developments, the U.S. Advisory Commission on Intergovernmental Relations has documented these shifts and analyzed their implications (U.S. Advisory Commission on Intergovernmental Relations, 1993).

Second, the reach of federal requirements was extended considerably from the 1970s onward by the increasing reliance on crossover sanctions and cross-cutting mandates. The former penalize states or localities in one field for a failure to act in another; thus, highway funds, for example, are threatened for states failing to raise the drinking age to twenty-one. The latter apply regulatory requirements, in fields like civil rights or environmental protection, to actions across a wide range of programs. These broadly influential rules have fueled litigation in a number of cases. The political antipathy to so-called "unfunded mandates," however, has triggered the passage of the national Unfunded Mandate Control Act of 1995 to block some such actions unless funding is also provided. Further litigation on the provisions of this contentious statute is virtually inevitable. Meanwhile, it is worth noting that most unfunded mandates are imposed by states on their localities. Recently, a number of states have enacted self-imposed limitations (Zimmerman, 1994).

Regulation is closely linked to the subject of partial preemption. Preemption refers to national legislation that establishes federal policy on a subject in such a way as to prevent states or localities from occupying the same policy space with a less stringent position. Partial preemption occurs when national action establishes minimal standards or criteria in some field, with states or localities eligible to enact their own directly crafted and operated programs on the subject, provided that these programs meet the national minimum criteria.

Preemptions have been frequently adopted initiatives in recent years. It is clear from analyses of law at the national level that, as David O'Brien puts it, "during the last two decades, the Congress dramatically increased the number of federal statutes preempting state and local laws" (1993, p. 20). Comprehensive treatments of preemption indicate that most of the activity in this field has developed during the last quarter century, and the national efforts have taken place in multiple fields of policy (U.S. Advisory Commission on Intergovernmental Relations, 1992, p. 9).

The phenomenon is especially noteworthy in regulatory arenas, despite its origins in social services. Litigation challenging the Surface Mining Control and Reclamation Act of 1977 set important precedents. The Supreme Court upheld this law, which relied on partial preemption to ensure that state regulatory efforts on strip mining would meet stringent standards (see *Hodel* v. *Virginia Surface Mining,* 1981, and *Hodel* v. *Indiana,* 1981). In other environmental fields, the pattern has been similar: national legislation establishes policy objectives and minimal requirements for program administration and regulatory stringency. States that obtain national approval can run the program themselves within their boundaries, with oversight from the relevant national agency. For instance, thirty-eight states are authorized to conduct permitting programs under the provisions of the Clean Water Act. Some of these state efforts operate with standards more exacting than those required by national policy; others meet only the federal stipulations. Program administrators operate with some latitude but also need to be mindful of the partial preemption provisions, including the mandatory requirements.

Similar program structures operate for the Clean Air Act Amendments and the Resource Conservation and Recovery Act, which focuses on toxic wastes. From the perspective of policymakers in Washington, partial preemptions leverage national action in an era of constrained resources while also allowing some state initiative. The states, needless to say, sometimes see them as encroachments on legitimate state prerogatives.

It is clear that this kind of approach has been an important vehicle of national influence. Recent years have seen some Congressional efforts to trim, and also increase, preemptions from Washington. The courts themselves have sometimes relieved states from—and sometimes expanded—such policies. As one analyst comments, "the colloquy that takes place between the Congress and the federal courts remains a two-way street, which has run primarily in the direction of expanding the federal government's power over the states" (O'Brien, 1993, p. 20), at least regarding this instrument of policy.

To conclude, nevertheless, that the stream of preemption decisions has headed entirely along one path ignores the full set of recent public law developments of intergovernmental significance. Many cases have indeed emphasized and expanded national jurisdiction, with the Supreme Court upholding preemption via the Supremacy Clause of the Constitution or the idea that Washington possesses dormant-commerce powers to preempt state regulations (O'Brien, 1993, pp. 20–29). But the Court has also expressed concern about the states' possible loss of influence. In *Pacific Gas & Electric* v. *State Energy Commission* (1983), the nuclear power plant moratorium enacted in California was upheld. The Court reasoned that Congress had preempted the safety issues associated with nuclear power, but the economic-regulatory dimension was to remain in state hands.

Furthermore, the preemption issue raises more questions than simply whether and when federal action is justifiable. For instance, how far can nonnational governments be allowed to proceed *beyond* national requirements? In *Wisconsin Public Intervenor* v. *Mortier* (1991), the Court was asked to decide whether a partial preemption precluded localities' developing their own regulations. The case involved a Wisconsin community imposing regulations under the Federal Insecticide, Fungicide, and Rodenticide Act, and the Supreme Court determined that the statute did not preempt such actions. In an interesting twist, this decision was seen in several agricultural states as threatening politically powerful interests: these governments enacted legislation to limit the authority of *local* units on the issue.

Another even less apparent aspect of the preemption question is raised by federal-level policy shifts. When Washington alters its role, states may have to consider how to adjust. For example, when the national government eliminated the Civil Aeronautics Board, a federal agency charged with airline price and route regulation, state attorneys general sought to respond by assuming a consumer protection role (see *Morales* v. *TWA,* 1992).

In short, the pattern is complex: sometimes state discretion is significantly limited by national preemption; at other times states are left to deal with policy questions presented by federal withdrawal or retreat. In the current political climate, with Congress seeking reductions in federal responsibilities, deregulation in several fields, and further limitations in policy agendas, a number of additional questions like these can be expected to develop. Once the preemption "genie" is released from the bottle, the effects with which the states must deal can ramify—ironically enough—through even an eventual diminishment of national presence.

Public law on the subject of the regulatory reach of the national government has developed in still more dimensions. One development that is obvious and central for public administration is direct federal efforts to regulate states and localities (as opposed to partial preemption of state authority to regulate others). The paradigmatic, albeit conflicting, rulings in this domain occurred nearly a decade apart. The Court concluded in the widely publicized *National League of Cities* v. *Usery* (1976) that the national government should respect substantial limitations on its authority to regulate states and localities in the realm of their core responsibilities. These limitations, the Court reasoned, were constitutionally created and practically necessary to maintain the independence of the states and the vigor of the federal system.

However, the Court overruled its own decision later, in *Garcia* v. *San Antonio Metropolitan Transit Authority* (1985), upholding the imposition on a local government of national regulations regarding overtime and minimum-wage requirements. The Court's majority declared that the realistic protection of the independence of states and localities was, practically speaking, the support for their interests that could be mustered through national political institutions. Writing in dissent, Justice O'Connor argued that this kind of purely political protection was likely to be a thin reed indeed (469 U.S. 588). Some scholarly observers agreed and proclaimed the decision a disaster for federalism (Howard, 1985). Certainly, *Garcia* has substantially influenced public administrators at state and local levels. With these governments subject to forms of direct and detailed federal regulation, national influence now extends directly to day-to-day administration at other levels.

But others who have examined the details of the Court's decisions in the years following *Garcia* see considerable evidence of "case-by-case balancing" (Wise and O'Leary, 1992, p. 561). And recent signs suggest that the Court may reestablish some grounds for autonomy from certain forms of federal intervention—note its rejection, in a sharply divided five to four opinion, of the Gun-

Free School Zones Act of 1990 on grounds that regulating the education function even in this fashion cannot be defended on Commerce Clause grounds (*United States* v. *Lopez,* 1995). Indeed, some might consider it ironic that the *Garcia* decision came at the beginning of a decade of resurgent policy activism by the states, a period marked by substantial and frequent subnational initiatives in fields like health, welfare, economic development, and education (see Beam, 1993; Rivlin, 1992).

What is clear is that, from a number of directions, developments in public law have influenced markedly the context, constraints, opportunities, and responsibilities of American public administrators operating in the intergovernmental system. It would be an error, nonetheless, to infer that these developments have now fully fixed the intergovernmental features in which the nation's administrators perform their tasks. The constitutional bargain itself left substantial room for future contestation. It can be expected that public law will continue to influence but not completely stipulate the grounds and results of partially contrasting national, state, and local perspectives in the years ahead. And public administrators will certainly remain in the center of the action.

In fact, the continuing developments in public law often catalyze new challenges and require creative decision making on the part of administrators, rather than settle administration into routine. Some instances of this dynamic are the subject of the next section.

PUBLIC LAW DEVELOPMENTS OF INTEREST TO PUBLIC ADMINISTRATION: SOME INTERGOVERNMENTAL INSTANCES

Beyond preemptions, broadly defined, lie other implications for public administrators in the intergovernmental realm. This general point can be demonstrated through a brief review of some recent instances focused on two subjects of perennial interest to administrators: budget and finance, and personnel. With regard to the former, the analysis here touches on issues that are influenced by public law but not adequately dealt with in the usual fiscal federalism discussion.

Budget and Finance in the Intergovernmental System

Without question, developments in public law have influenced administrators as they seek to acquire and manage financial resources in the intergovernmental system. Federal courts, for instance, have been active in helping to define the options available and constraints operating on states' and localities' economies and, more directly, on their prospects and alternatives for revenue generation. Furthermore, the courts have influenced the intergovernmental apportionment of the costs of public problems and the revenue available from certain sources.

States have been active in seeking to tap revenue possibilities in their jurisdictions, of course, but what constitutes their legitimate domain is not always clear. In particular, the economic shift from manufacturing to services and the expansion of markets to encompass ever-broader territory have raised issues of public law. Can states levy sales taxes, for instance, on purchases from out-of-state-based companies? In particular, can mail order companies be compelled to collect sales tax for the many states in which their customer base resides? The issues raised by this question include considerations of fairness, economic efficiency, state authority, and revenue potential (see Coleman, 1992). In *Quill Corporation* v. *North Dakota* (1992), the Supreme Court ruled out such revenue sources for states, with obvious implications for issues of budgeting and finance.

In a related vein, the Court has become involved in determining under what circumstances a state's power to tax corporations operating within its jurisdiction is limited. The issue arises, in part, because of the complex corporate changes that accompany mergers and acquisitions (see *Allied Signal* v. *Director, Division of Taxation,* 1992).

Also, in a widely cited decision the Court ruled, in *South Carolina* v. *Baker* (1988), that municipal bonds were not constitutionally protected from federal taxation, thus not only opening the door for a potential change in tax status of these financial instruments but also, by implication, challenging state and local tax immunity more broadly. No policy change has followed from this precedent, but the possibility of it dramatically altering the revenue picture for nonnational governments remains quite real.

On the question of the apportionment of costs with potential intergovernmental ramifications, some recent developments have restricted states' authority to protect themselves from negative externalities originating from elsewhere in the intergovernmental system. In two recent cases, for instance, the Court sided against a state's or locality's ability to limit the financial impact of a problem stemming from sources outside its borders. A Michigan county was unsuccessful in blocking the importation of waste from other jurisdictions, including other states, in the interest of preserving landfill capacity for itself (*Fort Gratiot Landfill* v. *Michigan Department of Natural Resources,* 1992). And the state of Alabama tried but was rebuffed in its efforts to limit use of the country's principal waste site at Emelle for very hazardous toxic chemicals by out-of-state companies and the EPA (*Chemical Waste Management* v. *Hunt,* 1992).

A related question, from another direction and emphasizing state resources rather than costs, arises when states try to tax the extraction of their nonrenewable resources when these are being used as commodities nationwide. States' ability to use taxes to derive compensation for the loss of their resource riches was dealt with in cases focusing on oil and gas in Montana and Louisiana (*Commonwealth Edison* v. *Montana,* 1981; *Maryland* v. *Louisiana,* 1981). In the former case, the Court upheld the severance tax instrument for states; in the latter, a "first use" tax imposed by Louisiana on natural gas processed there was deemed unconstitutional.

More well known, perhaps, and also potentially more important for public administrators was the ruling that upheld a federal district court decision ordering local officials to raise property taxes to assist in school desegregation. *Missouri v. Jenkins* (1990) obviously carries major implications for administrators and others who are charged with balancing budgets, predicting revenue streams, and handling other essential tasks of public management. This point holds, despite the Court's revisiting the long-running dispute in 1995 and deeming some expenditure requirements imposed by the district court to be excessive. The power of the courts to compel such revenue raising may appear both as a source of leverage to administrators in need of funding for pressing program needs and as an intrusion into state and local budget priority setting. (For an analysis of the implications of this decision for public administrators, see O'Leary and Wise, 1991.)

Of course, additional influences on state or local spending priorities stem from the *Garcia* decision, already discussed, since this determination now influences wage levels and regulatory requirements in thousands of governments. Indeed, *Garcia* shows that public law can simultaneously influence central administrative issues like intergovernmental finances and personnel.

Personnel Issues in the Intergovernmental System

It is obvious from *Garcia* that some of the nuts-and-bolts issues of personnel management can be affected by intergovernmentally directed public law developments. The intent and some of the results of such intervention by federal courts can help to further important policy objectives. Nevertheless, judicializing the state and local administrative environment can reduce the opportunity for easy and informal collaboration in the intergovernmental system (see O'Leary and Wise, 1991).

If the nuts-and-bolts issues of personnel management in the federal array have become judicialized—and this development poses potential barriers to cooperative efforts—the tendency is similar with other interventions that seek to influence some of the more contentious aspects of human resources in government. Thus, for instance, decisions like *Rutan v. Republican Party of Illinois* (1990), which limited political leaders in state or local government in their powers to make personnel decisions based partly on partisan criteria, are likely both to protect administration against certain forms of abuse and to restrict the opportunities for leaders to deal expeditiously with their agendas. The ruling may also stimulate litigation that could ultimately impede efficient and timely public management in state and local governments. Similarly, but on a very different kind of issue, *Martin v. Wilkes* (1989) has triggered new rounds of lawsuits against state and local governments by racial majorities interested in challenging Affirmative Action plans because of alleged discrimination.

As personnel management becomes judicialized and politicized, administrators at all levels are likely to find they have to juggle this newer set of demands with the more instrumentally oriented requirements of "standard" program management.

CONCLUSION: ACCOUNTABILITY, RESPONSIBILITY, AND ADMINISTRATIVE CHALLENGES

The practical world of intergovernmental management is an increasingly challenging setting for American public administrators. Even if one were to leave aside the developments of public law, the current era of strained budgets, programmatic uncertainties stemming from interdependence across governments, large policy agendas, and fragmentedly discordant politics would render the administrative task difficult at all levels. When one adds to this mix the impact of public law, the picture becomes even more complex.

No longer can practitioners afford to ignore, if they ever could, the public law dimension in intergovernmental administration. Heightened concerns about administrative accountability nowadays surely mean growing attention to the requisites of public law. And in the links among the American governments administrators face some of their most interesting and intricate demands. Grants-in-aid and the old staples of fiscal federalism may be constitutionally valid instruments of national (and state) initiative, but many of the most central issues for administrators involve more tendentious matters: What does the law permit, and how does it constrain, when partial preemptions and mandates comprise sizable parts of the administrative context? How can administrators at multiple levels work together responsibly and effectively when such regulatory measures are a principal means of intended influence, and the cross-pressures of the intergovernmental system are not so easily assuaged by the balm of financial assistance? And how can administrators make sound decisions and operate effectively in contexts that are now more litigious and more prone to detailed constraint by the complex, intergovernmentally applied reach of the federal courts on issues as "managerial" as budgeting or personnel?

These issues, and more, compel administrators operating in intergovernmental realms to find ways of integrating the imperatives of "good management" with the important and increasingly intricate obligations of the law. Shifts in perspective from authoritative bodies like the Supreme Court are inevitable. Indeed, these shifts constitute a significant source of the uncertainty that administrators must manage in the years ahead. But one thing is certain: administrators of any government will be able to achieve their objectives only if they can develop productive and responsible links with counterparts from other units. How to do so while also being true to their obligations as guardians of the public interest within their own jurisdiction and accountable to the standards of the law is a central challenge for the future.

Cases Cited

Allied Signal v. *Director, Division of Taxation,* 119 L.Ed. 2d 533 (1992).

Chemical Waste Management v. *Hunt,* 119 L.Ed. 2d 121 (1992).

Commonwealth Edison v. *Montana,* 453 U.S. 609 (1981).

Fort Gratiot Landfill v. *Michigan Department of Natural Resources,* 119 L.Ed. 2d 139 (1992).

Frothingham v. *Mellon,* 262 U.S. 447 (1923).

Garcia v. *San Antonio Metropolitan Transit Authority,* 469 U.S. 528 (1985).

Hodel v. *Indiana,* 452 U.S. 314 (1981).

Hodel v. *Virginia Surface Mining,* 452 U.S. 264 (1981).

Martin v. *Wilkes,* 492 U.S. 932 (1989).

Maryland v. *Louisiana,* 451 U.S. 725 (1981).

Massachusetts v. *Mellon,* 262 U.S. 447 (1923).

Missouri v. *Jenkins,* 485 U.S. 495 (1990).

Morales v. *TWA,* 119 L.Ed. 157 (1992).

National League of Cities v. *Usery,* 426 U.S. 833 (1976).

Pacific Gas & Electric Company v. *State Energy Commission,* 461 U.S. 190 (1983).

Quill Corporation v. *North Dakota,* 119 L.Ed. 2d 91 (1992).

Rutan v. *Republican Party of Illinois,* 110 S.Ct. 2729 (1990).

South Carolina v. *Baker,* 486 U.S. 1062 (1988).

United States v. *Lopez,* case no. 93–1260, Apr. 26, 1995.

Wisconsin Public Intervenor v. *Mortier,* 115 L.Ed. 2d 532 (1991).

References

Beam, D. R. "Reinventing Federalism: State-Local Government Roles in the New Economic Order." In L. J. O'Toole Jr. (ed.), *American Intergovernmental Relations.* (2nd ed.) Washington, D.C.: Congressional Quarterly Books, 1993.

Brown, G. D. "The Courts and Grant Reform: A Time for Action." *Intergovernmental Perspective,* 1981, *7,* 6–14.

Coleman, H. A. "Taxation of Interstate Mail-Order Sales." *Intergovernmental Perspective,* 1992, *18,* 9–13.

Elazar, D. J. *The American Partnership: Intergovernmental Cooperation in the Nineteenth-Century United States.* Chicago: University of Chicago Press, 1962.

Grodzins, M. "The Federal System." In *Goals for Americans.* Report of the President's Commission on National Goals, the American Assembly. Upper Saddle River, N.J.: Prentice Hall, 1960.

Howard, A.E.D. "*Garcia:* Federalism's Principles Forgotten." *Intergovernmental Perspective,* 1985, *11,* 12–14.

O'Brien, D. M. "The Rehnquist Court and Federal Preemption: In Search of a Theory." *Publius,* 1993, *23,* 15–31.

O'Leary, R., and Wise, C. "Public Managers, Judges and Legislators: Redefining the 'New Partnership.'" *Public Administration Review,* 1991, *51,* 316–327.

Rivlin, A. M. *Reviving the American Dream: The Economy, the States, and the Federal Government.* Washington, D.C.: Brookings Institution, 1992.

Scheiber, H. N. *The Conditions of American Federalism: A Historian's View.* Study submitted by the Subcommittee on Intergovernmental Relations pursuant to S. Res. 205, 89th Congress, to the Committee on Governmental Operations, U.S. Senate. Washington, D.C.: U.S. Government Printing Office, 1966.

U.S. Advisory Commission on Intergovernmental Relations. *Federal Statutory Preemption of State and Local Authority: History, Inventory, and Issues.* Washington, D.C.: U.S. Advisory Commission on Intergovernmental Relations, 1992.

U.S. Advisory Commission on Intergovernmental Relations. *Federal Regulation of State and Local Governments: The Mixed Record of the 1980s.* Washington, D.C.: U.S. Advisory Commission on Intergovernmental Relations, 1993.

Wise, C., and O'Leary, R. "Is Federalism Dead or Alive in the Supreme Court? Implications for Public Administrators." *Public Administration Review,* 1992, *52,* 559–572.

Zimmerman, J. F. "State Mandate Relief: A Quick Look." *Intergovernmental Perspective,* 1994, *20,* 28–30.

CHAPTER TEN

Local Implementation of Federal and State Programs

Preemption, Home Rule, and Federalism

Beverly A. Cigler

Federalism, the major organizing principle of American government, is subject to interpretation—about the founders' and Congress's intent, administrative agency practice, the consequential power of various levels of governments, and the courts' role in protecting the system. It has been changed dramatically by political realities from how it was originally devised. A classic case of "where you stand is where you sit," federalism's meaning is dependent on who is speaking. In the increasingly complex, interdependent, and layered system of American governance, the national government's power has expanded while subnational (state and local) governments seek more discretionary authority. The courts have attempted to reconcile the basic principles of federalism with the actions of the various levels of government.

The constitutional design of the federal system, the roles of subnational governments at the national level, the intersection of national and local interests at the state level, and the unique nature of state-local relations are important to understanding federalism. This chapter reviews the following:

1. The trend toward expansionary national power

2. The differing constitutional roles of states and local governments

---

Note: This chapter was developed in part from research supported by a grant from the U.S. Department of Agriculture, National Research Initiative (NRICCP Project No. 93–337401–9088).

3. The court protections of federalism and the trends in state-local relations

4. The nonjudicial trends affecting federalism

EXPANSIONARY NATIONAL POWER

Through its enumerated powers, Congress may preempt state laws and administrative regulations (including local ordinances), that is, it may announce one uniform law to be followed throughout the nation. Congress also grants agencies powers to promulgate preemptive laws, either at the time of agency creation or later. Preemption arises from the Supremacy Clause of Article VI of the U.S. Constitution. Many state actions also affect interstate commerce within the broad meaning of the Commerce Clause; preemption is most often exercised by Congress in the context of its general authority to regulate interstate commerce.

Questions about supremacy are generally not about whether Congress can preempt state laws, but about whether it should do so. In interpreting the Supremacy Clause, the courts have generally defined national powers—that is, those of Congress and executive branch agencies—to be expansive or elastic. Courts find that national law preempts state (and local) law in three ways:

1. Statutory language can expressly preempt state law based on an explicit expression of congressional intent.

2. Courts can interpret the history, structure, and purpose of a congressional statute to imply preemption. If the courts find that a statute devises a pervasive regulatory scheme such that Congress "occupies the field," state law in the field is preempted and states must respond solely to the commands of Congress, not to their voters. Implied preemptions can nullify compatible or incompatible state laws, with "judicial federalism" leading to costly litigation.

3. If Congress has not expressly or implicitly preempted state laws, they are preempted to the extent that they conflict with national law. Such conflict exists whenever compliance with both laws is impossible and when the state law acts as an obstacle to accomplishing and executing national purposes and objectives.

Total (or full) preemptions of state (and local) laws give the national government complete regulatory responsibility for a function. Civil or criminal penalties for failure of states to enact conforming laws may ensue. Supremacy was meant as a technique for conflict resolution when a state and the national government each have valid laws that conflict, but full preemption can deprive states of power to act at all in some areas (that is, preemption strips the state's jurisdiction for lawmaking).

With partial preemptions, the national government sets minimum national standards (floor preemptions) and allows states to continue to exercise authority if they enforce standards that are at least as high as the national standards. Subnational governments may wish to impose stricter standards that supplement national law without prohibiting it. An exception is the Clean Air Act's limit on state authority to enact stricter regulation on mobile sources of air pollution, because the automobile industry serves a national market and could not respond to fifty-one different standards. Enforcement plans are approved by the appropriate national agencies, such as the Environmental Protection Agency (EPA).

The areas of environmental protection, natural resources, and health and safety are especially characterized by partial preemption statutes (such as air and water laws) by an activist Congress. These are justified by the Supremacy and Commerce Clauses, but also by congressional spending powers and the Necessary and Proper Clause (Art. I, Sec. 8, Cl. 18).

In environmental cases, the preemption question is especially delicate because of the interplay of national and local needs for environmental protection and the frequent intersection of those needs at the state level. Congress fashions broad environmental statutes meant to cover the nation as a whole, providing uniformity and consistency. Effective regulation of a specific environmentally degrading project, it can be argued, is dependent on state and local uniqueness—in history, culture, and geography—which is defeated by uniformity. The courts attempt to balance the conflict between the national interest and the police power traditionally retained by states (and usually delegated to local governments), including the power to regulate public health and safety.

The U.S. Advisory Commission on Intergovernmental Relations (ACIR) (1955, 1984, 1988) has provided national justifications for preemption:

- Conflicting state policies create a burden for interstate commerce.
- A state's policies may cause problems for other states.
- Pressing needs (such as for international security or trade issues) sometimes require one national policy.
- Unequal resources exist across the states for implementing policy.

Zimmerman (1991, 1992, 1995) has developed extensive typologies of the various federal preemption policies and the conditions under which they occur. He provides details on fourteen types of total federal preemptions and eight types of partial federal preemptions. There has been a dramatic increase in the number, scope, and types of federal preemptions over the last twenty-five years

(U.S. Advisory Commission on Intergovernmental Relations, 1984, 1996; Derthick, 1992).

A draft U.S. ACIR report, *The Role of Federal Mandates in Intergovernmental Relations* (1996), highlights the many common issues that trouble national-state-local relations. These include detailed procedural requirements, spiraling costs, congressional failure to understand state and local governments' public accountability, lawsuits by individuals against state and local governments to enforce national laws, small local governments' inability to meet standards and timetables, and a lack of coordinated policy with no single national agency empowered to make binding decisions about requirements.

The states have greatly expanded their regulatory roles since the 1980s and have been lauded for innovation. Many preemptions are now viewed as obstacles in a wide variety of areas in which the states have taken action, such as environmental protection, workplace safety, nuclear power, labor law, employment discrimination, and securities. With increasing sophistication, corporations have manipulated the preemption doctrine by raising questions of so-called interfield conflict. Is the aim consistency or to weaken laws?

When the contemporary broad-based nature of preemption crosses policy areas traditionally handled by the states, financial costs are but one issue; threats to self government and choice may be an even greater concern. The various arguments are difficult to assess, given the sparse data on actual costs incurred by subnational governments and the effects of preemptions on worthwhile national goals (Ray and Conlan, 1996; Price Waterhouse, 1993a, 1993b; Ohio Municipal League, 1992; U.S. Senate, 1994).

In a study of state efforts to enforce federally enacted Occupational Safety and Health Administration standards, Frank Thompson and Michael Scicchiatano (1985) showed how shared enforcement by the national and state governments helps alleviate some of the problems caused by complete preemption. Environmentalists generally argue for a system in which the states and the national government work in partnership for the development and enforcement of regulations.

Among the most criticized preemptions are national and state environmental laws, which rely on local implementation by municipalities, counties, special districts, and regional organizations. National laws regulating drinking water and wastewater and national and state laws regulating solid waste management and recycling tend to have the greatest financial impact on local governments (Price Waterhouse, 1993a, 1993b; Ohio Municipal League, 1992).

Is preemption a drift away from the principles of federalism, that is, a shift away from a balancing of competing state and national interests and toward a predominance of national interests? Preemption critics claim that the Supremacy Clause must be joined with the Tenth Amendment to ensure that neither the states nor the national government dominates. The issues are all the more pressing today for subnational governments, given the importance of fiscal federalism (Cigler, 1993a), including the use of the spending power to attach conditions-of-aid to federal grants, with preemptive effects.

Does preemption erode a goal of federalism: the enabling of state and local regulatory agencies to serve as laboratories for innovation (which is defeated by uniformity)? A regulatory floor below which subnational governments cannot set their laws works well when dealing with solely in-state pollution and with environmental problems for which state violations can be quantitatively measured. A violation of the Clean Water Act, for example, occurs when a given percentage of pollutants exist in a given quantity of water. The act allows states the freedom to deal with their unique problems while ensuring that no state can drop its standards in order to attract business. If a state wants to be recognized as a leader in the environmental field, it has incentive to go beyond minimum national standards.

There are some environmental problems, however, for which quantitative assessments are not always possible, such as the use of environmental or "green" claims in the marketing of products. Clearly defined national standards can protect against deception by manufacturers more efficiently than states' relatively ambiguous deceptive advertising laws. Differing state standards would make it difficult for manufacturers to market nationwide.

The siting of hazardous waste disposal facilities and the rise of the "not in my backyard" (NIMBY) movement illustrate some key dilemmas associated with preemption, as well as alternatives to reliance on the courts (Rabe, 1994). NIMBYs associated with the siting of locally unwanted land uses (LULUs) threaten the nation's health and safety by interfering with the safe disposal of hazardous waste.

NIMBYism symbolizes a growing decline in public trust. From a local perspective, the benefits of hazardous waste disposal facilities are shared nationwide but the costs are borne by the few in the proximity of a facility, often the least affluent. Under the Resource Conservation and Recovery Act (RCRA), preemption is involved if a local government sets overly stringent site selection standards for hazardous waste disposal. Congress's goal under RCRA of minimizing the threat of hazardous waste disposal to human health and the environment is frustrated under the third category of the preemption doctrine. Ironically, RCRA expressly authorizes the use of more stringent regulation by state and local government, but the courts have used preemption to protect the program from those same standards.

Legal remedies represent only a "stick" to demand local compliance. What has evolved is a greater use of "carrots," or incentives, to induce political behavior such as community compliance to RCRA's mandates. Alternative dispute resolution techniques and financial incentives for waste receiving communities are examples. Increased communication, public participation, and negotiations between developers and the public are other alternatives (John, 1994).

Conflicts between the national and subnational governments regarding field preemption are occurring more frequently than in the past and will continue to increase. Citizen and interest group local activism at all stages of the policy process—from problem definition and agenda setting to formulation to implementation—has also increased (Cigler, 1996a). Since the late 1970s, local regulations have included the expression of community sentiments regarding such issues as nuclear weapons production, apartheid, and an array of issues related to siting LULUs. In addition, few laws at any level are designed to serve a single purpose. Another preemption issue is whether laws are worded in broad terms to evade preemption.

Solid waste management, mandated at the local level, offers additional lessons about preemption. The *City of Philadelphia* v. *New Jersey* (1978) and *Carbone* v. *Town of Clarkstown, New York* (1994) decisions forbade state and local governments from engaging in any activities that place an undue burden on interstate commerce (such as using different fees on in-state and out-of-state solid waste). *Carbone* specifically struck down waste flow control at the local level.

Pennsylvania has planned responsibly for its own waste disposal needs by requiring all of its sixty-seven counties to adopt municipal waste plans. Due in large part to its adequate landfill capacity, compared to states that did not plan well, Pennsylvania has become the largest importer of out-of-state waste, with a waste management industry employing 7,800 individuals and generating more than $1 billion per year. Trash imports come from twenty-two other states and the District of Columbia, and account for nearly 40 percent of the waste disposed of in Pennsylvania. Local landfills are filling rapidly.

Much of Pennsylvania's imported trash comes from New York and New Jersey (15 percent of New York's municipal solid waste is sent to Pennsylvania). In 1996 it was announced that Staten Island's Fresh Kills landfill, the world's largest, will close in the year 2001. This announcement prompted New York City's mayor to suggest increased shipment to landfills in other states, including Pennsylvania. Despite the pleas of Pennsylvania's (and Ohio's) legislators and governors, Congress, for the sixth time, failed to pass a bipartisan interstate waste control bill in September 1996. Without such legislation, trash importing states do not have the authority to limit how much out-of-state trash flows in. Integrated solid waste management planning, with counties in the lead, is jeopardized.

STATES AND THE CONSTITUTION

Understanding preemption requires a grasp of the various interpretations of the original conception of federalism and of the linkage between preemption and the Constitution. Much of the formal language of federalism treats the states as sovereign, with the national-state relationship resulting from a compact of the states. The Tenth Amendment, it is argued, denotes a separate sphere of state authority, that is, powers retained by the states beyond those enumerated for the national government. Until recently, court decisions on federalism were preoccupied with attempting to sort out so-called traditional areas of state powers.

If states and the national government possess dual sovereignty, federalism is horizontal in nature. Elazar (1977) maintains that federalism is "noncentralization" and not "decentralization" and that the national-state relationship is not vertical in any way. To him, decentralization is a misnomer in that a hierarchy is implied for a system in which there is no hierarchy. Any erosion of state sovereignty threatens federalism.

Elazar (1984) also describes the states as distinct civil societies and makes a persuasive case that the formal role of states in terms of political, economic, and cultural identity has important functional consequences for the political system that must be protected. Normative arguments for a heightened state role in the political system are often made by associations of state officials. Loosely defined terms such as *decentralization* and *devolution* symbolize the effort to stop the perceived erosion of the Tenth Amendment. An array of values associated with state government are mentioned: checking abuses of national power, ensuring adequate citizen participation, representing diverse groups in policy deliberation, maintaining political responsiveness, and developing innovative policy and regulatory approaches.

Public choice theorists (Ostrom, 1991) complement such arguments by pointing to small government size and multiple power centers for promoting these values, as well as to achieving service delivery and promoting a sense of community, although such arguments apply more to the "creatures of the states" (Ostrom, Bish, and Ostrom, 1988). Similarly, Kincaid (1991) argues that interstate competition constrains taxation, spending, and administrative costs, and is thus a vehicle for enhancing political system accountability. The sparse empirical evidence is harsh to inconclusive in buttressing those arguments (see, for example, Lyons and Lowery, 1989).

The genius of American federalism was praised by Tocqueville ([1835] 1966) as the striking of a balance between the national and state governments, which derived sovereignty directly from the people. Extensive constitutional procedural safeguards to define the boundaries of state and national sovereignty were not necessary, he explained, because coexistence was assumed. The judicial branch was expected to restrain the national government from eroding the principles of federalism.

Beer (1978, 1993) argues that the federal structure was devised as a compact of the people, not a compact of the states. Blind deference is not to be given to states' rights; instead, federalism exists to protect the people. States are not sovereign in the sense of being the final political authority. It follows that the national government may have elasticity in its preemptive powers despite the

Tenth Amendment. And the Fourteenth Amendment serves as an umbrella protection for individual rights.

The formal structures of the American states clearly have constitutional protection, such as state boundaries, territorial integrity, and authority to make laws. The states' special role in the governance system is to prevent national tyranny by dispersing power. In this view, protecting the states as states is not the end; the states are a means to preserving individual liberty. Liberty may be enhanced through mechanisms that promote democratic self governance.

LOCAL GOVERNMENT IN LAW

It is local government, with its daily face-to-face interaction with citizens, that most characterizes the *potential* for effective democratic self governance. Theoretically, local governments encompass the values cited as necessary for protecting federalism. Local governments, however, are not mentioned in the Constitution and, unlike the states, have no constitutional protection for their formal structure. Local law can be preempted by two other layers of government.

State superiority over municipalities is not questioned. Formally, the state-local relationship is unitary and hierarchical (that is, vertical). Local governments—whether general purpose towns, boroughs, townships, cities, or counties—are creatures of the states and treated legally as municipal corporations. The Local Government Commission in Pennsylvania estimates that more than eight hundred state mandates are imposed upon that state's governmental units. These include an array of procedural requirements (such as fiscal, personnel, reporting, record keeping, performance, operations, and planning) across government functions (such as operations and administration, finance, public facilities, taxation, and all policy areas) and government types.

County governments are usually granted weaker authority by states and have less autonomy than municipalities. Historically, counties have existed primarily as administrative arms of the state for implementing state and national programs. Today, this often has debilitating impacts on counties, the major human service providers in the governance system, and the governments increasingly being turned to for regional problem solving (Cigler, 1995a, 1996b).

In granting home rule powers, states curb their own superiority by providing for some limited municipal (including county) immunity from state control. Judge John F. Dillon's pronouncement in *City of Clinton* v. *Cedar Rapids and Missouri Railroad Company* (1868) that local governments are creatures of the state still dominates state superiority under all forms of municipal home rule, however. Perhaps more important, only a small number of communities eligible for structural home rule, especially counties, have sought it (Cigler, 1995a).

Unlike claims of dual sovereignty for national-state relations, home rule makes no claims about separate spheres of state and local authority. Home rule is, instead, an umbrella of policies and understandings between a state and its local governments. States have legislative superiority in sharing power with their local governments over matters of state concern, either by prohibiting conflict with state laws explicitly (in constitutional and charter provisions) or by using prohibitive language so that municipal exercise of authority is not inconsistent with state laws. Historically, courts have usually agreed that municipal regulations more restrictive than state regulations are not in conflict with a state provision.

Local governments establish considerable autonomy through allocation by the state of the power of initiation and the power of immunity. Shared power and administration in the state-local relationship promotes values such as liberty and can inhibit the concentration of power. Shared power arrangements promote citizen participation in the governance process and may enhance service delivery (Zimmerman, 1995).

President James Madison's concerns about the dangers of majority abuse of government by factions, however, are important to state-local relations. Potential municipal abuse of individual liberties must be guarded against. The proper and specific roles for state legislatures and the courts have not been determined, but the "solution" is generally for constitutional provisions that specify authority, along with general laws regarding state-local relations.

Regulatory Freedom

Local governments possess substantial power in the regulatory arena. They are the key public service providers in the governance system. They make significant decisions affecting life (such as the operation of police, fire, sanitation, public health, and water and sewer systems) and lifestyle and property (such as decisions about planning, housing, zoning, land use, taxation, schools, and libraries). Counties are the major human service providers, implementing state and local programs. Mixed with the great diversity of local governments—in type, function, size, wealth, and demographics (age, race, income, and class)—is interjurisdictional competition that leaves a pattern of fiscal disparities in service delivery and social inequities across metropolitan areas and between rural and urban places.

Traditionally, the federal courts have not played a major role in challenging local regulatory autonomy, despite interlocal inequities in wealth (which are often extended by exclusionary or snob zoning policies). Significant examples include the following:

- *San Antonio Independent School District* v. *Rodriguez* (1973), which upheld the traditional school finance system in Texas

- *Village of Belle Terre* v. *Boraas* (1974), which agreed that local government's zoning authority includes power to zone in order to maintain a community's character

- *Warth* v. *Seldin* (1975), in which nonresidents seeking to challenge exclusionary local zoning policies lacked standing

- *Village of Arlington Heights* v. *Metropolitan Housing Development Corporation* (1977), which upheld a village's power to prohibit multifamily housing

Elsewhere, I have reviewed the legal reasoning for these decisions (Cigler, 1979), which clearly spared the states tremendous political and financial burdens by not addressing local fiscal disparities or their implications for differential local spending.

More recently, judicial activism at the state level regarding local fiscal disparities has led to court orders regarding prison overcrowding, and court takeovers of such areas as child welfare services at the county level. After many years of favoring local autonomy in cases of school finance inequities, recent state court decisions in Montana, Kentucky, and Texas have invalidated local school financing systems. Kentucky revamped its entire system of education due to the decision. School financing lawsuits are pending in a number of other states.

A similar narrowing of local autonomy has occurred through recent state court cases involving charges of exclusionary zoning. Courts in California, New York, New Jersey, and Pennsylvania, for example, have dealt with differences in interlocal wealth by linking housing policies to the regional general welfare concept. Fair share affordable housing is being promoted in some states.

School finance and exclusionary zoning cases highlight the call for a greater state role and increased supervision of local governments, as well as a need for more local accountability in projecting "reasonableness" into policies regarding lifestyle issues. This demonstrates the intersection of law with social, economic, political, and demographic factors.

There has been an increase in state assertion in the land use policy and growth management arena (Caves, 1992; Kelly, 1993). The classic challenge argues that growth management policy violates the "Taking" Clause (or the Due Process Clause) of the Fifth Amendment or the Fourteenth Amendment (or similar clauses in state constitutions). Minorities have also argued violation of national and state Equal Protection Clauses. Landowners, in general, are increasingly likely to challenge "takings" (Cigler, 1979). A five-to-four U.S. Supreme Court decision on property development in Oregon, *Dolan* v. *City of Tigard* (1994), held that when a local government places conditions on property development, there must be a "rough proportionality" between the impacts of the development and the extent of alleviation provided by the conditions. The decision has fueled anger and fear regarding the County Supremacy Movement, also known as the Wise Use or Property Rights Movement.

Fiscal Constraints

The most significant constraint on municipal power is in fiscal matters, regardless of formal home rule status (Cigler, 1996b). Preemption is the most common form of state control over municipal taxing power, that is, state legislatures often deny their municipalities the power either to impose a particular tax or to impose a tax on a particular class of taxpayers. This is little different from an express denial of municipal taxing power.

Extensive state legislative limits on revenue raising and expenditure powers, along with tightly earmarked limits on revenue flexibility, are usually more restrictive than state restraints on local regulatory power. Rigid constitutional limits on the power to tax or borrow, and upon the sources of revenue, burden local governments strapped with growing responsibilities, unfunded mandates, and dwindling intergovernmental aid. Counties are especially hard hit since they are most reliant on the property tax for revenue generation (Cigler, 1995a, 1995b) and have growing regional roles (in solid waste management, transportation, land use, parks and recreation, air and water planning, physical planning, natural resources, the gamut of human services problems, and so forth).

Local taxing and borrowing policies could have disastrous effects on state interests; protection of taxpayers and bondholders against local government abuses is necessary. Special interests generally weaken attempts at uniform state legislation that would provide adequate protection, however. Still, local autonomy rests on fiscal flexibility. Local revenue diversification is the major focus of reform, primarily through loosening rigid restraints on levying property taxes and borrowing and increasing the types of tax and user fee options available to local governments, especially counties (Cigler, 1996b). Popular referenda on fiscal matters, rather than reliance on constitutional or legislative restraint, has also increased, but the drawback is that voters are often unwilling to pay taxes for necessary services.

Protecting Local Governments from the States

States and local governments do not always stand together in opposing expansive national government. A 1996 Pennsylvania example illustrates this point and shows the intersection of national law with local autonomy. Chester, Pennsylvania, a declining factory town on the Delaware River just south of Philadelphia, has suffered serious pollution from its history of steel and heavy manufacturing. To create more jobs, the city began to accept waste facilities that its wealthy neighboring communities rejected. Eight of these facilities are in the city and adjoining Chester Township already, and five have received permits from the state's environmental agency in the last decade.

Chester also treats all of the county's solid waste and most of its raw sewage, and it accounts for most of the county's air pollution complaints. The population of Chester is mostly black; the rest of the county is overwhelmingly white. Chester has the state's highest infant mortality rate and highest death rate from malignancies. Kidney, liver, and respiratory disease risks from pollution are very high, as is the exposure of children to lead.

In early 1996, Pennsylvania issued a permit for a new waste facility in a mainly black part of Chester that has several such facilities already. A citizens' group and several individuals filed a lawsuit against the state's Department of Environmental Protection (DEP) on May 28, 1996. *Chester Residents Concerned for Quality Living* v. *Seif* (1996) argued that the new permit violates Title VI of the Civil Rights Act, which forbids discriminatory behavior by any agency receiving federal funds. The U.S. Justice Department filed a brief in support of the plaintiffs, claiming that Pennsylvania's DEP may have violated both Title VI and EPA regulations. A successful suit will force Pennsylvania to rescind the most recent permit and require a rewriting of regulations to ensure nondiscrimination. The U.S. District Court for the Eastern District of Pennsylvania ruled on November 5, 1996, that no intentional discrimination had been alleged, as required to file such a suit, and that grievances should have been pursued under the EPA's established administrative process. Chester Residents Concerned for Quality Living plans to appeal the decision; the EPA, which had joined the action on behalf of the citizens group in August 1996, has not indicated whether it will appeal.

The state claims that its permits are awarded on a race-neutral basis, placing blame on Chester's zoning plan. Does a state bear a legal and moral responsibility to ensure that its poor communities do not turn themselves into toxic dumps in economic desperation? Pennsylvania has developed a number of initiatives to help Chester. In 1995, an interagency initiative was established to pool resources and coordinate actions to deal with Chester's environmental and local health concerns. Interagency meetings have resulted in three breakout groups, for addressing health, quality of life, and land use issues. By late 1996, the three interagency groups were discussing the possibility of forming a nonprofit organization to guide local efforts. In addition, a group of local industries has organized to identify ways that the business community might help. A governor's cabinet committee reported in October 1996 on several proposals to help the city deal with many of its environmental, education, and economic challenges. The committee represents a wide variety of state agencies: environmental; community and economic development; health, labor, and industry; public welfare; transportation; state police; corrections; and general services.

TRENDS IN JUDICIAL PROTECTION OF FEDERALISM

The Supreme Court has not developed a stable constitutional doctrine about the roles of Congress and the courts in protecting federalism. The five-to-four majority in *National League of Cities* v. *Usery* (1976) held that Congress's attempt to force state and local governments to comply with the national Fair Labor Standards Act violated the principles of federalism but the judicial test for striking a balance between state and national power was unclear. In the years following the settlement of that case, no other national statutes were found to be unconstitutional on federalism grounds. National strip-mining regulations, which involved restoration of local lands, were upheld in the name of interstate environmental concerns (*Hodel* v. *Virginia Surface Mining and Reclamation Association,* 1981). Energy policies that forced specific approaches to state rate making, the application of age discrimination laws to state employees, and the application of national collective bargaining rules to a state-owned commuter railroad were all upheld. On the other hand, since the mid-1980s specific court decisions in such industries as trucking and telecommunications have favored the states or kept preemption narrowly drawn (Zimmerman 1991; Teske, Mintrom, and Best, 1993).

Assessing Political Safeguards for States as States

Some argue that the Constitution's three structures—national power, federalism, and judicial review—fit together well within a Madisonian theme (Wechsler, 1954). Because the interests of "states as states" are represented in the national political process, it is not necessary to use the courts and judicial review to protect or enhance the states' interests against assertions of national legislative power.

This was the premise of *Garcia* v. *San Antonio Metropolitan Transit Authority* (1985), the major decision of the modern Court addressing federalism. *Garcia* was upheld in a unanimous decision in *South Carolina* v. *Baker* (1988), a decision widely interpreted as signaling the demise of constitutionally protected intergovernmental tax immunity. *South Dakota* v. *Dole* (1987) validated a conditional spending requirement attached to a national grant but concluded that there are no implied conditions on Congress's spending power.

National power reaches far beyond Congress. *Missouri* v. *Jenkins* (1990) upheld a U.S. District Court's order that a school district double its tax levy (even though the district had no authority to do so under Missouri's constitution) to fund a court-ordered school integration plan. Choosing to usurp state power, the judiciary overlooked other remedies such as granting interdistrict relief (Freilich and Richardson, 1994) that would have sought a regional solution to a regional problem.

These cases took a structural view of federalism, maintaining that states have significant influence in Congress to protect their interests and do not need courts to enforce Tenth Amendment limitations on the national commerce power. The political safeguards of federalism are found in the Constitution itself: state selection of presidential electors, state drawing of congressional districts, state control of electoral qualifications, and equal state representation in the Senate. State influence in the legislative process comes also from grants to states (which boost their budgets) and state exemption from some federally imposed obligations.

The effects of many of the so-called political safeguards are relatively insignificant today. Having two senators from each state appears to advantage small states the most, for example. From the states' perspective, *Garcia* and other decisions that dismiss Tenth Amendment and federalism objections are insensitive to the reality that states today must behave more like interest groups than sovereign entities when dealing with Congress (Cigler, 1995b).

Formal constitutional amendments, legislation, and court decisions (such as the Seventeenth Amendment, voting rights legislation, and reapportionment decisions) limit the representation of states as states in the national political process. Critics would argue, however, that such factors guarantee liberty for individuals (Rivlin, 1992). Other developments, such as a national two-party system, the nationalization of campaign finance, and the rise of national primaries for selecting nominees for public office, further reduce the political power of states (Howard, 1986). Private interest group power in the legislative process, including interests that cross state lines, erodes the ability of the states to pursue their interests. The national media are a major influence in shaping the political agenda. Budget-driven and deficit-driven federalism, the growing attachment of conditions-of-aid to grant applications, increasing preemption and unfunded mandates, and the loss of an information infrastructure to study federalism issues (such as demise of the U.S. ACIR) adversely affect the states and lessen their influence in Congress.

The deference to state interests that the framers took for granted and the safeguards established in the Constitution to preserve the integrity of the states are less relevant than in the past (Lee, 1988; Pittenger, 1992). The nationalization of the economy, in turn, has led the Supreme Court to abandon its pre–New Deal efforts to limit congressional power in the name of federalism (Walker, 1995). One by one, areas of "traditional state powers" have been erased, with Congress now likely to intrude on any issue. Opportunistic behavior by private interest groups seeking to avoid fifty-one sets of regulations spawns more congressional action than do state interests (McCray, 1993).

An erosion of state interest representation (Cigler, 1995b) demands a reassessment of the role of judicial review, according to this argument. If the interests of states are not protected in the national political process to the degree the framers thought appropriate, perhaps the courts should assume a role not held initially. Judicial review was designed to deal with situations in which the interests that constitutional principles are designed to protect are not adequately represented in the political process (Ely, 1980). The importance of court intervention to protect individual rights is widely acknowledged; should the same principle be used to protect state interests in order to ensure the fairness of what John Hart Ely calls the political marketplace?

Is state sovereignty a viable concept today? Is federalism still a system for structuring relationships between sovereigns, or is it a procedural framework that relates to the political process? How much power do states exercise in Congress today? What protects local governments at the national or the state level? What should protect citizens from the excesses of government at any level? Issues of federalism present a constitutional struggle because of the difficulty of developing a workable balancing test to determine whether Congress has gone too far or to determine how great the national interest is compared to the adverse impacts on states (and local governments).

In addition, recent congressional decisions to devolve more program responsibilities to the states raise a variety of questions about state-local relations. How can local governments be better represented at the national level to have input into their roles in the devolution process? Will governors increase their powers in contrast to state legislators? How will an increase in gubernatorial power affect state-local relations? Will or should governors develop partnership councils with local and other officials to develop plans for the devolution of responsibilities symbolized by more block grants to the states? If most problems are regional in nature, will political decision makers and the courts seek regional solutions?

Case-by-Case Protection of Federalism

Despite *Garcia, Dole,* and *Baker,* the Supreme Court appears to be patrolling the boundaries of the Supremacy Clause and of the Tenth Amendment. Those who have called for a restoration of federalism have hailed a series of 1990s Supreme Court decisions. The cases have dealt less with areas for national action and more with the manner (that is, the scope and mode) of congressional action.

Gregory v. *Ashcroft* (1991) held that a Missouri state constitutional provision mandating all judges to retire at age seventy is not in violation of Congress' Age Discrimination in Employment Act, thus indicating that overlapping spheres of authority exist between the national and state and local governments. If Congress seeks to displace state law, it must be unambiguous in its intent.

A 1992 Commerce Clause case, *New York* v. *United States,* tried to articulate a judicially enforceable limitation on congressional power to regulate the activities of state governments. The decision, which invalidated national law requiring states to dispose of low-level radioactive waste, suggests that Congress lacks the power to regulate certain subjects and that federalism requires Congress to remain accountable to state voters without entangling state government in its regulatory processes. Freilich and Richardson (1994) argue that the Court's ruling in another case, *Cipollone* v. *Liggett Group, Inc.* (1992), which reiterated a well-established presumption against implied preemption of traditional state powers, can be combined with the Court's posture in *Dole* (regarding no implied conditions on Congress's spending power) to argue that there never should be implied preemption of state authority.

In *United States* v. *Lopez* (1995), the Supreme Court, in a five-to-four decision, affirmed a lower-court decision to strike down the Gun-Free Schools Act of 1990 (PL 101–647/104 Stat 4844/18 USC 921), deciding that Congress exceeded its constitutional authority when it passed the law. The Court majority refused to equate congressional authority under the Commerce Clause to a general police power of the type retained by the states. In March 1996, the Supreme Court ruled in another five-to-four decision (*Seminole Tribe of Florida* v. *State of Florida*) that the Eleventh Amendment prevents Congress from subjecting states to suits in federal court under most federal laws. This Commerce Clause ruling came in a case that restricts federal court oversight of Indian casinos, but it has far-reaching significance because it struck down part of a 1988 federal statute that let Indian tribes sue states in federal court over impasses on negotiating agreements for gambling on tribal lands.

Incrementally, case by case, this series of decisions allows state and local diversity while protecting national interests. The complexities and interdependencies of modern governance may not lend themselves to a strict separating out of spheres of sovereignty, however. The Tenth Amendment may come to represent a bundle of rights for the states similar to incorporation of the Bill of Rights into the Fourteenth Amendment. Freilich and Richardson (1994) compare the notion that the Tenth Amendment should be understood as an umbrella of policies and understandings about home rule in the state-local relationship.

NONJUDICIAL TRENDS

If federalism is not meant simply to pay respects to the states but to protect the people, there is much to argue regarding decentralization (or noncentralization) as a way to prevent national tyranny through diffusion of powers. Whatever the Court's intellectual commitment to the principles of federalism, conflicting regulations in the governance system demand a resolution. If courts give consideration to the values underlying federalism only if they are formally incorporated into the decision-making process, political strategies pursued by state and local officials can push Congress toward the exercise of greater responsibility in its intention with regard to preemption. Clear statement of rules of statutory construction may help ameliorate the negative effects of preemption.

State and local officials complain that the burdens of preemption and unfunded mandates allow Congress to receive political benefits for imposing regulations without having to bear the political costs of raising taxes. On October 27, 1993, those officials sponsored Unfunded Mandates Day, which led in part to the Unfunded Mandates Reform Act of 1995 (PL 104–4), an attempt to restore balance to intergovernmental fiscal relations with provisions relating to information, accountability, and consultation for new national mandates.

The draft U.S. ACIR report, *The Role of Federal Mandates in Intergovernmental Relations* (1996), called for nullification of some existing preemptions and mandates—for labor, the environment, and disability protections. The report was never published due to intense opposition from environmental groups, the Clinton Administration, and others. The opposition to the unpublished report indicates the difficulties of balancing national interest and state and local autonomy.

Fueled by the 1992 Supreme Court ruling in *New York* v. *United States,* the Alabama state legislature that year was the first to pass a binding joint resolution that requires the state's congressional delegation to attend a joint session of the legislature to account for federal mandates. Tenth Amendment resolutions have passed in other states.

Increased informal consultation between the federal government and states (or between states and their local governments) before exercising preemption powers may yield some alternatives for implementing mandated goals. Some states (such as Florida and Connecticut) provide cost estimates of legislation for local governments and several require reimbursement for mandates (such as California, Michigan, Tennessee, Colorado, and Massachusetts) or passage by a supermajority without funding (such as Florida and Louisiana). Is it good policy for states to require localities to spend funds for implementing programs without also providing them with the authority to generate additional revenues? How responsible are states in monitoring programs and using sunset and sunshine provisions in laws?

More funding to implement national or state mandates and greater flexibility for small governments in meeting regulations was provided for in the mid-1996 revisions of the Safe Drinking Water Act, which included greater flexibility, less monitoring and record keeping, and loans to small governments. Careful public participation requirements written into legislation improve policies and avoid preemptions later. Reasonable procedures for benefit-cost analyses and risk assessments, along with sounder evaluation of the effects of preemption, are other trends.

A 1996 Council of State Governments report, *Restoring Balance to the American Federal System,* analyzes several proposals, including a federal statute or federalism amendment to limit the national government's fiscal and regulatory overreach by enhancing the political safeguards of federalism, a national reconsideration amendment to require Congress to reconsider laws or regulations that a supermajority of states disapprove, and an amendment to allow states to propose specific constitutional amendments without first having to convene a constitutional convention.

The proposals were initially discussed at a States' Federalism Summit held in Cincinnati, Ohio, in October 1995, organized by five leading organizations that represent state governments. The national government was acknowledged as having enumerated powers to provide for the national defense, to conduct foreign policy, and to ensure the civil and constitutional rights of citizens. No local government organizations were included, and no proposals relating to state-local relations were made.

The values that are espoused for decentralization and devolution to the state level are the values, it can be argued, best represented at the local level, where officials have daily face-to-face contact with their constituencies. Local governments are also the smallest units for representation. Most local governments, however, lack the legal, political, fiscal, and managerial capacity either to meet state and national preemptions or to fulfill their potential for promoting democratic self governance.

Elsewhere, I have put forth a partial agenda for reinventing state relations across four categories of interaction:

1. State mandates

2. State capacity building and technical assistance to local governments

3. Provision of incentives to induce positive local activities (such as cooperative service delivery and acceptance of low level radioactive wastes)

4. Restructuring local governance systems (such as by shifting some responsibilities from municipalities to counties or by promoting tax base sharing)

Among the most promising reforms are those in the fourth category, especially those tied to revenue diversification schemes (Cigler, 1993a, 1993b, 1996a). Giving counties greater authority over land use planning, over zoning and growth management, and for devising regionwide service delivery systems (such as requiring intergovernmental agreements as a condition for providing extraterritorial services, and establishing joint utility systems) is growing in interest and use. Pinellas County, Florida, is a good example; municipal plans must be consistent with the county's comprehensive plan, with final authority on consistency resting with the county commission.

Another trend is toward state financing of selected local functions. Should there be state funding and administration of the lower courts, for example? Do trial court systems that rely on the disparate fiscal capacities of a state's different counties create inherently unequal systems of justice that can be overcome only by state takeover of funding? If counties are constitutionally inferior to the courts (a coequal branch with a state legislature), then state financing and administration may be the only remedy to inequalities. Should judges or voters decide?

One reaction to recent state court activism is an increase in legislative action to counter the court decisions. The County Supremacy Movement (or so-called Wise Use Movement or Property Rights Movement), based on Fifth Amendment "takings" arguments, has placed property rights bills on the dockets of dozens of state legislatures. Such legislation would put in place procedures for compensating landowners for lost property caused by government activities. This would likely overburden state and local finances.

CONCLUSION

In a mobile society, the economy is integrated across jurisdictional boundaries, whether state or local. People, goods, services, and capital cross state and local borders. Geographic boundaries are less important than economic boundaries that are regional. Current thinking about federalism overlooks the growing regionalism across metropolitan America (Downs, 1996). Most local problems are regional—water and air pollution, landfills, uses of green technology, industrial site reuse, economic development, mine reclamation, flood control, crimes and drug use, teenage pregnancies, hazardous wastes, siting of LULUs, and so forth.

Citizens of states and localities are regional and national citizens, too. The push for decentralization (or noncentralization) and devolution to the states may actually weaken the states. National intervention could be justified on behalf of local governments, as in the Chester toxic pollutant example. As more program responsibilities devolve to the states and local governments (such as more block grants), the demand for greater state flexibility will increase, but so will the complaints about fifty or fifty-one different standards. Spillover effects of state actions will have to be ameliorated, most likely through concern for redistributive policies (Peterson, 1995). Will congressional distrust of state flexibility lead to a new round of mandates to protect state block grant programs? How prescriptive will state laws be in monitoring the administration of new block grants at the local level? Will new mandates to protect against arbitrary actions by county caseworkers increase demands for enlarged flexibility to respond to individual families? Will some human service providers—highly rated county nursing homes, medical laboratories, or day care centers—seek special protections as newcomer providers fight for equal status? Will states increase their oversight and supervisory responsibilities effectively, or generate unnecessary rules, monitoring, and reporting requirements—which will anger local officials?

Devolution is generally mentioned as a shift in responsibility from the national government to the states. This overlooks the important shift from states to local governments of key implementation responsibilities. For medical care and welfare reform policies, for example, the question is not whether there will be significant changes in state-local relations, but how and by whom. Devolution and decentralization may actually strengthen the already growing role of counties in the governance system as some municipal functions shift to counties. For example, exclusionary zoning and haphazard land use and growth management policies may be ameliorated by giving counties greater planning and zoning powers. Spending, taxing, and regulatory policies across the myriad of diverse local governments will yield substantial policy spillovers and negative externalities and inequities in the delivery of basic services. Even if they remain at the municipal level, service delivery and fiscal disparities can be lessened by empowering counties with increased authority to require municipal service delivery plans.

The emerging global economy also suggests that current thinking about American national-state-local relations may be outdated as subnational governments become more aggressive in the world economy. Trade agreements such as the North American Free Trade Agreement (NAFTA) and the General Agreement on Tariffs and Trade (GATT) can challenge state laws; regulations regarding product quality, for example, may face global preemption. One early GATT decision found that state tax breaks for local beer and wine industries discriminated against Canadian beer and wine imports, thus violating international trade law.

The national government is increasing its role outside the courts as convener, mediator, and facilitator in the political system in order to forge better working relationships among the various levels of government and with other sectors. National, state, and local governments, in general, are becoming more adept at facilitating partnerships—in health, education, welfare, transportation, jobs training, and so forth.

If federalism is about states as states, the significant gaps in political safeguards for the states at the national level will grow ever more problematic as the governance system shifts greater responsibilities to the states. Local governments lack formal political safeguards at the congressional level, and they are too often treated as "just another special interest" and bypassed in discussions of how to make federalism work. They are also treated as special interests in state legislatures (Cigler, 1995b).

The indeterminate status of local authority—in terms of state delegation and oversight, judicial decisions, and differences in managerial, fiscal, administrative, and legal capacity—remains. This reality collides with interjurisdictional conflicts within regions and rapidly changing economic, social, political, and technological factors in the globalizing economy. Can devolution work if the general pattern of state delegation remains unchanged: substantial service delivery and fiscal responsibility to local governments, but little fiscal flexibility? Should states assume a greater role in financing local services in which there are inequalities across jurisdictions, such as in school financing? Should states offer even broader delegation of authority to their local governments through revenue flexibility for the financing of other services? Can effective service delivery and policymaking responsibilities continue to overlook the regional nature of problems? Can the regional general welfare concept used by state courts to resolve conflicts within metropolitan areas—especially in the area of land use—be used by political bodies to enact laws to protect those excluded by exclusionary zoning practices?

If federalism is about protecting individual liberty, should states (or the national government) take a greater role in ameliorating the negative effects of the significant delegation of administrative and regulatory authority to local governments in such areas as land use planning and regulation? Should states provide inducements to county governments, which are regional, to assume greater responsibilities in the governance system? Can individual liberty and local autonomy be balanced while supporting national, regional, and state interests?

A well-functioning and effective federal system must take into account the necessity of consequential power at all levels of government—national, state, and local. In devising relationships among all three levels of government in the protection of liberty for citizens, local governments—those closest to the people—have been relatively neglected by political institutions at the national and state levels, and in constitutional jurisprudence. On the other hand, the value most associated with local autonomy—popular participation—is beset with a set of counter outcomes that can sometimes erode the protection of liberty through race and class separation. National and state preemption, local home rule, and federalism itself continue to face a balancing test about checking power, promoting diversity, and ensuring accountability—challenges that will continue to be played out in the courts and in the political marketplace.

Cases Cited

Carbone v. *Town of Clarkstown, New York,* 511 U.S. 383 (1994).

Chester Residents Concerned for Quality Living v. *Seif,* U.S. District Court for the Eastern District of Pennsylvania, Docket 96–3960, Lexis 16475 (1996).

Cipollone v. *Liggett Group, Inc.*, 505 U.S. 504 (1992).

City of Clinton v. *Cedar Rapids and Missouri Railroad Company*, 24 Iowa 455 (1868).

City of Philadelphia v. *New Jersey*, 437 U.S. 617 (1978).

Dolan v. *City of Tigard*, 114 S. Ct. 2481 (1994).

Garcia v. *San Antonio Metropolitan Transit Authority*, 469 U.S. 528 (1985).

Gregory v. *Ashcroft*, 501 U.S. 452 (1991).

Hodel v. *Virginia Surface Mining and Reclamation Association*, 452 U.S. 264 (1981).

Missouri v. *Jenkins*, 495 U.S. 33 (1990).

National League of Cities v. *Usery*, 426 U.S. 833 (1976).

New York v. *United States*, 505 U.S. 144 (1992).

San Antonio Independent School District v. *Rodriguez*, 411 U.S. 1 (1973).

Seminole Tribe of Florida v. *State of Florida*, 116. S.Ct. 114 (1996).

South Carolina v. *Baker*, 485 U.S. 505 (1988).

South Dakota v. *Dole*, 483 U.S. 203 (1987).

United States v. *Lopez*, 131 L.Ed. 2d 626 (1995).

Village of Arlington Heights v. *Metropolitan Housing Development Corporation*, 429 U.S. 252 (1977).

Village of Belle Terre v. *Boraas* 416 U.S. 1 (1974).

Warth v. *Seldin*, 422 U.S. 490 (1975).

References

Beer, S. H. "Federalism, Nationalism, and Democracy in America." *American Political Science Review*, 1978, *72*, 9–21.

Beer, S. H. *To Make a Nation: The Rediscovery of American Federalism.* Cambridge, Mass.: Belknap Press, 1993.

Caves, R. W. *Land Use Planning: The Ballot Box Revolution.* Thousand Oaks, Calif.: Sage, 1992.

Cigler, B. A. "Local Growth Management: Changing Assumptions About Land? *Urban Interest*, *1*(2), 1979, 52–58.

Cigler, B. A. "Challenges Facing Fiscal Federalism in the 1990s." *PS: Political Science and Politics*, 1993a, *26*, 181–186.

Cigler, B. A. "State-Local Relations: A Need for Reinvention?" *Intergovernmental Perspective*, 1993b, *19*, 15–18.

Cigler, B. A. "County Governance in the 1990s." *State and Local Government Review*, 1995a, *27*(1), 55–70.

Cigler, B. A. "Just Another Special Interest: The Intergovernmental Lobby." In A. J. Cigler and B. Loomis (eds.), *Interest Group Politics.* (4th ed.) Washington, D.C.: Congressional Quarterly Press, 1995b.

Cigler, B. A. "Adjusting to Changing Expectations at the Local Level." In J. Perry (ed.), *Handbook of Public Administration.* (2nd ed.) San Francisco: Jossey-Bass, 1996a.

Cigler, B. A. "Revenue Diversification Among American Counties." In D. C. Menzel (ed.), *The American County: Frontiers of Knowledge.* Tuscaloosa: University of Alabama Press, 1996b.

Council of State Governments. *Restoring Balance to the American Federal System.* Lexington, Ky.: Council of State Governments, 1996.

Derthick, M. "Federal Government Mandates: Why the States Are Complaining." *Brookings Review,* 1992, *10*(4), 50–53.

Downs, A. *The Devolution Revolution: Why Congress Is Shifting a Lot of Power to the Wrong Levels.* Washington, D.C.: Brookings Institution, 1996.

Elazar, D. J. *Exploring Federalism.* Tuscaloosa: University of Alabama Press, 1977.

Elazar, D. J. *American Federalism: A View from the States.* (3rd ed.) Old Tappan, N.J.: Macmillan, 1984.

Ely, J. H. *Democracy and Mistrust: A Theory of Judicial Review.* Cambridge, Mass.: Harvard University Press, 1980.

Freilich, R. H., and Richardson, D. G. "Returning to a General Theory of Federalism: Framing a New Tenth Amendment United States Supreme Court Case." *Urban Lawyer,* 1994, *26,* 215–234.

Howard, A.E.D. "Garcia: Of Federalism and Constitutional Values." *Publius,* 1986, *16,* 17–31.

John, D. *Civic Environmentalism.* Washington, D.C.: Congressional Quarterly Press, 1994.

Kelly, E. D. *Managing Community Growth: Policies, Techniques, and Impacts.* New York: Praeger, 1993.

Kincaid, J. "The Competitive Challenge to Cooperative Federalism: A Theory of Federal Democracy." In D. A. Kenyon and J. Kincaid (eds.), *Competition Among States and Local Governments: Efficiency and Equity in American Federalism.* Washington, D.C.: Urban Institute, 1991.

Lee, C. F. "The Political Safeguards of Federalism: Congressional Responses to Supreme Court Decisions on State and Local Liability." *Urban Lawyer,* 1988, *20,* 301–340.

Lyons, W. E., and Lowery, D. "Governmental Fragmentation Versus Consolidation: Five Public-Choice Myths About How to Create Informed, Involved, and Happy Citizens." *Public Administration Review,* 1989, *49,* 533–543.

McCray, S. B. "Federal Preemption of State Regulation of Insurance: End of a Two-Hundred–Year Era? *Publius,* 1993, *23,* 33–47.

Ohio Municipal League. *Ohio Metropolitan Area Cost Report for Environmental Compliance.* Columbus: Ohio Municipal League, Sept. 15, 1992.

Ostrom, V. *The Meaning of American Federalism: Constituting a Self-Governing Society.* San Francisco: ICS Press, 1991.

Ostrom, V., Bish, R., and Ostrom, E. *Local Government in the United States.* San Francisco: ICS Press, 1988.

Peterson, P. E. *The Price of Federalism.* Washington, D.C.: Brookings Institution, 1995.

Pittenger, J. C. "Garcia and the Political Safeguards of Federalism: Is There a Better Solution to the Conundrum of the Tenth Amendment?" *Publius,* 1992, *22,* 1–19.

Price Waterhouse. *The Burden of Unfunded Mandates: A Survey of the Impact of Unfunded Mandates on America's Counties.* New York: Price Waterhouse, Oct. 26, 1993a.

Price Waterhouse. *Impact of Unfunded Federal Mandates on U.S. Cities: A 314–City Survey.* New York: Price Waterhouse, Oct. 26, 1993b.

Rabe, B. G. *Beyond NIMBY: Hazardous Waste Siting in Canada and the United States.* Washington, D.C.: Brookings Institution, 1994.

Ray, M. R., and Conlan, T. J. "At What Price? Costs of Federal Mandates Since the 1980s." *State and Local Government Review,* 1996, *28,* 7–16.

Rivlin, A. M. *Reviving the American Dream: The Economy, the States, and the Federal Government.* Washington, D.C.: Brookings Institution, 1992.

Teske, P., Mintrom, M., and Best, S. "Federal Preemption and State Regulation of Transportation and Telecommunications." *Publius,* 1993, *23*(4), 71–85.

Thompson, F. J., and Scicchiatano, M. J. "State Enforcement of Federal Regulatory Policy: The Lessons of OSHA." *Policy Studies Journal,* 1985, *13,* 591–598.

Tocqueville, A. de. *Democracy in America.* (G. Lawrence, trans.; J. P. Mayer, ed.). New York: Doubleday, 1966. (Originally published 1835.)

U.S. Advisory Commission on Intergovernmental Relations. *A Report to the President for Transmittal to Congress.* Washington, D.C.: U.S. Government Printing Office, 1955.

U.S. Advisory Commission on Intergovernmental Relations. *Regulatory Federalism: Policy, Process, Impact and Reform.* Washington, D.C.: U.S. Government Printing Office, 1984.

U.S. Advisory Commission on Intergovernmental Relations. "Federal Preemption of State and Local Authority." *Intergovernmental Perspective,* 1988, *14,* 23–25.

U.S. Advisory Commission on Intergovernmental Relations. *The Role of Federal Mandates in Intergovernmental Relations.* Unpublished draft report. Washington, D.C.: Advisory Commission on Intergovernmental Relations, 1996.

U.S. Senate, Committee on Environment and Public Works. *Staff Report: Analysis of the Unfunded Mandates Surveys Conducted by the U.S. Conference of Mayors and the National Association of Counties.* Washington, D.C.: Senate Committee on Environment and Public Works, June 14, 1994.

Walker, D. B. *The Rebirth of Federalism: Slouching Toward Washington.* Chatham, N.J.: Chatham House, 1995.

Wechsler, H. "The Political Safeguards of Federalism: The Role of the States in the Composition and Selection of the National Government." *Columbia Law Review,* 1954, *54,* 543–560.

Zimmerman, J. F. *Federal Preemption: The Silent Revolution.* Ames: Iowa State University Press, 1991.

Zimmerman, J. F. *Contemporary American Federalism.* New York: Praeger, 1992.

Zimmerman, J. F. *State-Local Relations: A Partnership Approach.* (2nd ed.) New York: Praeger, 1995.

PART FOUR

ADMINISTRATIVE LAW AND TODAY'S STREET-LEVEL CHALLENGES

Part Four goes beyond the preceding analyses of general legal authorities and techniques of interpretation to address more specific elements of administrative law. Thus it examines the devices used by presidents and governors to mandate actions, such as executive orders and proclamations; the relationships between statutes and ordinances at local levels; the operation of rulemaking processes, including contemporary attempts to introduce negotiated rulemaking; and the essential elements of administrative adjudication and their relationships to effective management practices.

In Chapter Eleven, Jennifer A. Utter and Phillip J. Cooper explore an often overlooked set of legal devices that chief executives have used to accomplish their purposes without depending on legislative enactments or rulemaking by administrative agencies. The emphasis in this chapter is on the use of executive orders and proclamations, but the authors also explain that these tools are part of a larger set of mechanisms that include legislative signing statements, memoranda, and national security directives. Few Americans, even many otherwise-knowledgeable public managers, have any idea that these devices even exist, much less how important and pervasive they are, covering as they do everything from regulatory oversight to the means used to address the Haitian refugee crisis of the early 1990s. In an era when the president is being advised to avoid the quagmire of Congress and the labyrinth of Washington administrative rulemaking, the use of executive orders has been growing.

The authors point out as well that governors in various states have come to see advantages in direct action as well, led most visibly in recent years by California's Governor Pete Wilson, whose orders on illegal immigrants and affirmative action garnered national publicity.

After the explanation of these tools of executive direct action, most of Chapter Eleven consists of an extended demonstration of how they are employed, based on an analysis of the Clinton administration. The analysis demonstrates that executive orders and proclamations are not limited to foreign policy but apply across a wide range of domestic policies and institutions. They reach into most of the aspects of contemporary public administration affected by statutes or regulations.

David L. Corliss, in Chapter Twelve, focuses on local public administration and law, addressing the relationships among ordinances, rules, and statutes. While ordinances are far more numerous than any other kind of legal authority in the United States, they are among the least understood. Almost nothing in public administration literature seeks seriously to explain what ordinances are, how they are developed, and how they can be improved.

In this chapter, Corliss, an experienced city attorney who also holds a Master of Public Administration degree, explains how local governing bodies, department heads, city attorneys, and citizens' groups interrelate in the real-world laboratories of constitutional democracy. Using a variety of examples, from land use planning to the regulation of adult entertainment businesses, Corliss presents both an anatomy and a physiology of ordinances.

In the process of explaining the processes for developing, enacting, and implementing ordinances, Corliss analyzes legal constraints, managers' concerns, and essential political considerations, all of which combine to produce the ordinances that local administrators must implement. Recognition of the practical interrelationships among these forces is all the more important in this era of federal preemption, unfunded mandates, and an emerging array of legal constraints in areas where local governments were formerly able to regulate with more latitude.

Another of the little understood but pervasive fields of today's public law and administration is rulemaking. In Chapter Thirteen, Cornelius M. Kerwin discusses not merely the concepts of rules and rulemaking, but also contemporary developments in what has been one of the most rapidly changing areas of administrative law.

At this time when many in the legal community, as well as administrative reformers, are calling for less confrontation and the creation of alternatives by which conflict can be managed, it is no surprise that more inclusive approaches to rulemaking have been undertaken. A principal approach, popularly termed *negotiated rulemaking*, Kerwin explains, is intended to bring stakeholders together at early stages of policy development. Purposes are both to improve the rules that are produced by administrative agencies and to reduce the likelihood of endless legal challenges once those regulations are issued. Kerwin explains that those outcomes should in turn result in enhanced implementation and improved, long-term compliance.

While the general idea is one of simplification and conflict mitigation, Kerwin explains that negotiated rulemaking is itself a complex process that requires administrators to master new techniques. Partly because of that, and because essential conditions are often not present, uses of negotiated rulemaking have been limited and cannot be expected to displace more standard rulemaking. Kerwin therefore urges public administrators both to explore opportunities for negotiated rulemaking and to consider ways to make more traditional practices work more effectively.

Turning to another fundamental administrative law process, Hal G. Rainey explains in Chapter Fourteen that the use of proper administrative adjudication techniques is not only good law but good management as well. Rainey addresses the fact that a general attack on the due process revolution of the 1960s and early 1970s has recently been led by managers as well as by conservative jurists. Waving banners of efficiency, responsiveness, and accountability, critics assert that so many due process requirements have been piled onto administrative decision making that it has, for example, become extraordinarily difficult to discipline employees and bring abusers of various social welfare programs to justice.

Rainey observes that the U.S. Supreme Court has been relatively consistently leading lower courts away from demanding increased due process protections either in personnel management or for benefit claimants and regulated parties. Indeed, he explains, where human resource management is the focus, the Supreme Court has issued a number of relatively extreme rulings that insist that judges recognize the needs of managers to operate their organizations and permit them to control or terminate recalcitrant employees without excessive procedural burdens, at least from a constitutional rights viewpoint.

In addition to this analytic argument, Rainey demonstrates that due process is an important aspect of good management. He explores organizational justice literature from the field of organizational behavior that is largely ignored in courts' opinions. In this literature, there is strong empirical evidence that managers ought to be concerned about providing notice, opportunities to respond, fair decision makers, and nonarbitrary decision processes, whether or not such processes are required by courts, because employees who feel that they enjoy those protections and that they work within an organization that demonstrates a commitment to the kind of fundamental fairness ensured by due process are more productive and loyal. Strong organizational protections for due process, in short, lead to a more positive organizational culture and success, and therefore leading firms practice such informed management.

CHAPTER ELEVEN

Executive Direct Administration

The Importance to Public Administration of Executive Orders and Proclamations

Jennifer A. Utter

Phillip J. Cooper

O n February 21, 1995, the United States and other parties entered into a preliminary agreement providing more than $20 billion in foreign aid to Mexico. What is particularly noteworthy about this event, aside from the sheer magnitude of the assistance, is the twist of events played out between President Bill Clinton and Congress that culminated in Clinton's use of executive orders to mandate the policy.

The economic conditions in Mexico had been worsening for quite some time, following deliberate inflation of the peso to provide support for the party in power as it neared what seemed likely to be a hotly contested election. After the election, the price had to be paid, which meant a near free fall in the Mexican economy. President Clinton asked Congress for legislative action to address the weakening peso. After nearly two weeks of congressional debate, and with the negotiators still unable to draft consensus legislation to bring to the floor, Clinton abandoned his original proposal and announced an alternative plan to provide to Mexico by executive action $20 billion from the U.S. Treasury's Exchange Stabilization Fund in support of a broad fiscal recovery plan. Later that evening, in a speech given at the National Governor's Association Conference, the president stated, "Rather than face further delay, I met with the congressional leadership this morning and told them that I will act under my executive authority. . . . The leadership advised me that while they believe Congress will—or at least, might well eventually—act, it will not do so immediately. And therefore, it will not do so in time" (Clinton, 1995a).

Such a broad use of direct executive authority is not uncommon for the Clinton administration. Following his inauguration in January 1993, Clinton issued dozens of executive orders, memoranda, and presidential proclamations that had wide-ranging policy and fiscal impact. The president's frustration with Congress and his willingness to go it alone, as exemplified in the Mexico events, have been continuing themes in his administration. The Clinton administration has, from its beginning, seen executive orders as an important tool for "creating a government that works better and costs less" (Gore, 1993), the clarion call of the administration's effort to reinvent government. But in making the decision to use the tools of direct presidential action—executive orders, proclamations, presidential memoranda, and national security directives—Clinton was actually following a practice common to modern chief executives.

Indeed, governors have come to see their own opportunities to use these devices. Thus California Governor Pete Wilson used the issuance of an executive order banning most affirmative action programs in state organizations not only as a major policy push but also as a way to fuel his ultimately unsuccessful bid for the Republican presidential nomination in 1996. Other governors had used such devices in less visible but nevertheless important ways in the past. Former New York Governor Mario Cuomo, for example, employed executive orders to ban sexual harassment in state agencies well before the U.S. Supreme Court held that harassment was a violation of Title VII of the Civil Rights Act of 1964 (*Meritor Savings Bank* v. *Vinson,* 1986). He also used an executive order to overhaul important elements of administrative procedure in the state, including redefining the requirements of due process in state proceedings. Even some mayors have been tempted to use executive orders or proclamations as the basis for quick action. For example, former New York mayor Ed Koch issued an order requiring protective detention of homeless persons who would not go to shelters on extremely cold winter nights (an order later struck down on constitutional grounds).

While President Clinton's actions and those of other contemporary chief executives may not have been altogether novel, they are important and carry consequences. Not only did Clinton circumvent the democratic process, but his "'end run' around Congress" (Congressional Press Release No. 1701, February 1995) infuriated some of its members. On the other hand, it also allowed Congress to avoid responsibility for a serious policy decision. (There was an almost audible sigh of relief from congressional leaders who were delighted that they had been saved a vote on the issue but quietly pleased with the actual policy decision.) Moreover, expansive interpretations of existing policies to support sweeping new initiatives can be troubling. For instance, the U.S. Treasury's Exchange Stabilization Fund was intended to manage the value of the dollar. It was never intended to provide foreign assistance or guarantee the strength of other economies.

In any event, it is clear that the use of these tools of direct executive action has been increasing in frequency, scope, and impact. It is equally obvious that few Americans, and even relatively few experienced public administrators, truly understand the nature and use of orders, proclamations, and the like. This chapter describes these tools. It then uses the experience of the Clinton administration to place the use of these tools in context and to demonstrate how and why they are employed.

TOOLS OF THE CHIEF EXECUTIVE

The president and state governors inherit legacies from their predecessors that include a host of executive orders, proclamations, memoranda, legislative signing statements, and national security directives. In Clinton's case, that meant that he inherited a history of 12,834 executive orders, more than 6,000 presidential proclamations, and unknown numbers of national security directives and presidential memoranda. In truth, it is not even known how many executive orders really existed historically, since the numbers that are now used to designate them were derived by taking the numbers in use during the 1940s and numbering backwards in time (Office of the Federal Register, 1990; U.S. House of Representatives, 1957). In any case, the legacy that greets the new chief executive remains in force unless and until these presidential declarations are superseded, modified, or rescinded by new presidential action, or until they are struck down by legislation or judicial rulings. Although the bulk of this chapter focuses on executive orders and what one modern president did with them, it is important to know something about each of these presidential power tools and the ways they can be used.

Executive Orders

In light of the legacy of executive orders, and given how easy they are to use, it is no surprise that their issuance has been one of the first actions of many new administrations. Executive orders are directives issued to government officials that instruct them to take action, change their agency's behavior, or stop some ongoing activity. As long as these orders are issued in an area in which the president has the power to act, and as long as they do not violate either existing statutes or the Constitution, they are valid and carry the force of law (see *Armstrong* v. *United States*, 1871; *Jenkins* v. *Collard*, 1893; *American Pilots' Association* v. *Gracey*, 1986; *Farkas* v. *Texas Instruments*, 1967; and *Farmer* v. *Philadelphia Electric Company*, 1964). There are effectively no procedural requirements, because the only guidelines that exist are themselves contained in an executive order (E.O. 11030, 1962). Indeed, some orders are classified and therefore not public. What is classified and the processes to be used are also governed by executive order (see, for example, Clinton's E.O. 12937 and Ronald Reagan's E.O. 12356). Most orders, however, must be published in the *Federal Register.*

The most important question concerns where the president, or the governor in the states, finds the authority to support an order. Many chief executives have relied primarily on statutes as the basis for the issuance of orders (see Cooper, 1986). Indeed, Congress has often enacted legislation that instructs the president to issue an executive order to set in motion a program of action if a particular set of events occurs, such as when a trading partner violates a treaty. Since the years of Jimmy Carter, however, presidents have increasingly issued orders based on nothing more than a general reference to the powers vested in the president by the Constitution and laws of the United States. The theory is that the president is merely exercising the Article II executive powers by managing the operation of the executive branch. (Governors make similar arguments about state constitutions.) Presidents Reagan and Clinton have used this kind of broad claim to support their efforts to significantly change regulatory processes and to "reinvent" government (Kerwin, 1995).

When the president is acting with respect to foreign policy, such as in the orders concerning Haitian refugees issued by the George Bush administration and renewed by Clinton, the courts tend to grant considerable deference to claims of presidential authority (see *Sale* v. *Haitian Centers Council,* 1993). They have even allowed chief executives to use other presidentially adopted policies to support their claims. Thus the Supreme Court upheld the executive agreement reached during the Carter administration to end the Iran hostage crisis, and the executive orders used to implement it during the Reagan administration, even though no treaty was offered for ratification by the Senate (*Dames and Moore* v. *Reagan,* 1981). As the Iran hostage case suggests, the courts have been even more solicitous of executive claims in cases of national security emergency. Indeed, Presidents Woodrow Wilson and Franklin Roosevelt issued literally hundreds of orders during wartime. Some of these orders were broad in reach and carried serious consequences; for example, Roosevelt's Executive Order 9066, upheld by the Supreme Court in *Korematsu* v. *United States* (1943), was the basis for the exclusion of Asian Americans from their homes and their incarceration in concentration camps (euphemistically called relocation centers).

In practice, legislatures may ratify executive orders after the fact, which is what has often happened in times of war or other emergency. Indeed, the Court has even read inaction by the legislature as "acquiescence" to a particular order (*Dames and Moore* v. *Reagan,* 1981). However, when tension has existed between the executive and Congress, some presidents have encountered difficulties, even in critical situations. There is the famous case of President Harry Truman's seizure by executive order of the nation's steel mills during a labor dispute that flared while the United States was engaged in hostilities in Korea

(*Youngstown Sheet and Tube* v. *Sawyer,* 1952). While President Richard Nixon was able to use his Executive Order 11615 and a related proclamation to impose a wage and price freeze during the economic crisis of the early 1970s, Jimmy Carter was not successful in his effort to mandate an oil import fee in the face of dramatic economic impacts from the Arab oil boycott (*Independent Gasoline Markets Council* v. *Duncan,* 1980).

Of course, more than one president before Bill Clinton used executive orders to get around the legislature. One of the best known examples was Lyndon Johnson's reliance on an executive order to implement affirmative action in federal government contracting when he could not get that policy out of Congress during debate over civil rights legislation (E.O. 11246, 1965). There is a certain irony in the fact that California's Governor Wilson did exactly the same thing thirty years later with his state legislative order prohibiting affirmative action. President Reagan tried a similar tactic with his orders imposing a stranglehold on regulatory agencies (E.O. 12291, 12498). While the orders imposed many burdensome requirements on agencies that were required by statute to issue rules, the situation was rendered completely untenable because the Office of Management and Budget (OMB) was, under the guise of regulatory review, blocking policies with which the White House disagreed but that had been mandated by Congress. A federal district court warned the administration that such efforts to frustrate the law would not be tolerated (*Environmental Defense Fund* v. *Thomas,* 1986).

In a new twist on the theme of executive orders as mechanisms to circumvent Congress, White House officials reported to National Public Radio reporters on July 31, 1996, that while President Clinton had decided to sign legislation mandating dramatic changes in welfare, he could later use executive orders to attack what he saw as defective provisions in the legislation. In this situation, the president was not reacting to refusal to pass legislation but serving notice, however indirectly, that the process of policy development was far from over, notwithstanding the fact that Congress had adopted legislation that Clinton felt obliged to sign in the face of a pending election.

Proclamations

It is a dramatic understatement when a president says that executive orders are merely internal pronouncements, because they often direct agencies to take actions that affect thousands of people. Even so, there is a technical distinction by which the executive order is the tool to use for pronouncements inside government while the presidential proclamation is the device to be employed in mandating policy outside of government. Legally, no distinction exists between the two in terms of their binding effect (*Wolsey* v. *Chapman,* 1879).

Like executive orders, proclamations have been used since the earliest days of the republic, dating back to the Neutrality Proclamation issued by President George Washington. Most proclamations are ignored because they are only symbolic statements of recognition or celebration. Others, particularly those supported by statute, may carry the force of law, and criminal prosecutions have been brought against citizens using a proclamation as the basis (see *United States* v. *Wayte,* 1983).

Proclamations are often issued in conjunction with executive orders (see Ford's E.O. 11947 and Proclamation 4483 on the Vietnam amnesty program) or national security directives. Proclamations are clearly more subject to legal attack than executive orders because they directly affect people's liberty or property while executive orders do so in a much more indirect fashion. If the proclamation is not related to a significant national security or foreign policy issue, the White House normally must find a statute that can be interpreted to support the pronouncement.

National Security Directives

A less visible but very important device for presidential direct action is the national security directive (NSD). Dating back to the Truman administration, the NSD grew out of memoranda known as National Security Council Policy Papers, which were prepared for the president by the National Security Council. As these papers were approved, they became known as national security directives, though the name has changed over the years with new administrations (under Reagan they were known as national security directives, but under Bush they were known as national security decision directives, and under Clinton, as presidential decision directives).

The Nixon administration developed a fondness for this device, because unlike executive orders the White house is not legally required to disclose that an NSD exists, let alone what its contents might be. To this day, even Congress does not know how many NSDs have been issued by which administrations. Congressional investigators have estimated from the evidence they could locate that more than a thousand NSDs were issued from 1961 to 1988 and that President Reagan alone issued nearly three hundred of them in his first seven years in office (U.S. House of Representatives, 1988).

Even members of Congress agree that a device like the NSD is necessary, but there are two difficulties. First, concern is great that there is no mechanism, and no willingness in most administrations, for even the most limited disclosure of NSDs to Congress. Second, and in many respects more controversial, is the fact that since at least the Reagan administration it has become clear that NSDs have had important impacts on domestic matters and not just on foreign or military affairs. In fact, the General Accounting Office found that during the Reagan years there were as many NSDs that had domestic impacts as those that had military impacts, and there were more that had domestic impacts than had foreign policy impacts (statement of Frank C. Conahan, assistant comptroller general, National Security and International Affairs Division, General Accounting

Office, in U.S. House of Representatives, 1988, pp. 80–83). For the present, it is important to know that such a device as the NSD exists and that it is sometimes used in conjunction with executive orders. An example was when the Reagan administration used Executive Order 12333 as the basis for NSDs authorizing various actions in support of the increased effort at drug interdiction. Another example involved the use of Executive Order 12356, on security classification, as the basis for an NSD that imposed confidentiality, personal disclosure, and other restrictions on domestic civil servants without security clearances.

Presidential Memoranda

Another tool has become increasingly popular. The presidential memorandum is a relatively ambiguous device, and that is why it is attractive. Originally, presidential memoranda were used to announce findings required by statute, such as when the president was required to issue a finding that a trading partner was in violation of an agreement. However, like other presidential tools, it has taken on a life of its own over the years. Technically, a memorandum is not exactly an executive order, and it is not entirely clear what obligations the White House has to disclose such documents. In fact, when the Clinton White House issued its guidance to the secretary of the Department of Health and Human Services (HHS) requesting a change in regulations that would eliminate the so-called gag rule on abortion counseling, it authorized HHS to publish the memorandum. The implication, of course, was that not all such memoranda are to be published. In addition, no particular process is required to issue a presidential memorandum. It is not surprising, therefore, that the National Performance Review suggested to President Clinton that he should use directives and memoranda to effect major change in the executive branch (Gore, 1993).

Memoranda can be important in at least three ways. First, they may be issued with the intention that they are executive orders in another form. Thus, although President Bush issued his moratorium on rulemaking (directing agencies to stop all rulemaking for a period) as a memorandum, there was no doubt that it was intended as an order (Bush, 1992). Second, memoranda may be issued along with executive orders, substantially altering the apparent contents of the orders such that public attention falls on what appears to be limited executive orders when in fact the memoranda may expand them considerably. An example occurred when the Reagan administration issued what appeared to be a relatively innocuous order on regulatory planning and development (E.O. 12498) that contained references to things like pre-rulemaking activity. However, in the memorandum issued at the same time as the order, it was clear that the term *pre-rulemaking activity* was defined to mean that OMB could prevent agencies from expending funds to do a study to determine whether a rulemaking process was necessary (Reagan, 1985; OMB Watch, 1985a, 1985b). Third, the murky status of memoranda provides a way to make clear what the White

House wants done without the White House actually having to take responsibility for mandating an action by executive order.

Interestingly, there seems to be a lack of clarity on behalf of the Clinton administration and on the part of President Clinton himself—who is an attorney and was a professor of constitutional law—on the distinctions between tools. For instance, in a speech given at Carlmont High School in Belmont, California, on October 22, 1994, President Clinton repeatedly referred to the "executive order" that he was about to sign to direct the secretary of education to withhold funding from states that do not comply with a zero tolerance policy for guns (Clinton, 1994). The "executive order" that Clinton spoke of was actually a presidential memorandum to the secretary of education on the implementation of safe schools legislation, specifically the Gun-Free Schools Act of 1994 and the Safe and Drug-Free Schools and Community Act. The confusion also seems to exist within Congress. On January 22, 1993, two days after taking office, President Clinton issued a series of four presidential memoranda, all aimed at issues of reproductive health. Three days later, on January 25, Representative Pat Schroeder spoke on the floor of the House about "the incredible historic significance of the *executive orders* signed by President Clinton" ("Historic Executive Orders Signed," 1993, p. H187, italics added).

Whatever they are called, these tools of presidential direct action are clearly important. They affect everything from the structure and operation of the federal civil service to controls on regulations issued by health and environmental agencies. They are often legally binding, are generally poorly understood, and are sometimes simply out of sight. They are increasingly popular with presidents (and governors) frustrated by legislative gridlock or what they regard as recalcitrant bureaucracies in the executive branch. No serious public manager can afford to be ignorant of their nature, existence, or importance. These actions at the White House affect all levels of government and even the relationships between the public sector and not-for-profit organizations, because they affect not only policies that the federal government administers directly but also the manner in which federal funds flow to the state and local levels. Of course, many of those intergovernmental programs are actually implemented through contracts with not-for-profits.

THE CLINTON EXAMPLE: EXECUTIVE TOOLS, POLITICAL TACTICS, AND ADMINISTRATIVE REALITIES

One way to understand how and why executive orders, and their relatives, are used is to examine how a contemporary president has employed them. What follows is a description of the Clinton administration's use of the executive order through its first three years.

The First One Hundred Days: Making Good on the Campaign

A president enjoying the "honeymoon" of his first one hundred days in office has an opportunity to take advantage of a wave of energy created during the campaign. During these early days, the president usually enjoys favorable support from the press and possesses the most presidential capital (Sullivan, 1991). This is a time when White House watchers pay close attention, hoping to observe tangible efforts of a newly elected president to deliver on promises made during the campaign. President Clinton made several uses of the tools available to him during this time to set in place rapidly many new policies.

Immediately upon taking office on January 20, 1993, President Clinton's first official act was to sign Executive Order 12832, which established a new ethics policy for executive branch appointees. This order required every new senior appointee to sign and be contractually committed to the policies as a condition of employment. There was a certain irony in the fact that the president who moved to cut red tape and eliminate duplicative rules added more requirements for prospective appointees beyond the complexities of the Ethics in Government Act. In so doing, Clinton erected a significant barrier to his own appointment process, the results of which are well known. More important, however, that order marked the beginning of a trend for President Clinton in his propensity to use tools of presidential direct action.

During his first hundred days (from January 20 through April 29, 1993), President Clinton signed more than a dozen executive orders, twelve published memoranda, and twenty-eight proclamations, many of which can be directly linked to key issues raised during the campaign. One such issue was Clinton's economic plan. By Executive Order 12835, he established the first of several new advisory bodies—the National Economic Council—to coordinate economic policy, advise the president, and monitor implementation. All executive departments and agencies were directed to cooperate with the new council.

Two days after taking office, Clinton issued four memoranda on the issue of reproductive health, another key issue in the campaign. Three of these memoranda were addressed to the secretary of health and human services. The first was a directive to the secretary concerning the importation into the United States of RU-486, also known as the abortion pill. In addition, the secretary was directed to proceed promptly on initiatives to promote the testing, licensing, and manufacturing of RU-486 in the United States. A second memorandum, mentioned previously, to the secretary of HHS was a directive to proceed "as soon as possible" with the suspension of the Title X Gag Rule through rulemaking proceedings. The third memorandum directed the secretary to lift HHS's moratorium on federal funding of research involving the transplantation of fetal tissue from induced abortions. The final memorandum issued on this day was addressed to the secretary of defense, directing that he reverse the ban immediately and permit abortion services to be provided in military hospitals as long as that they were not paid for by Department of Defense funds.

Another key issue raised during the campaign was the size and cost of the federal bureaucracy. *Reinventing government* (taken from Osborne and Gaebler's 1992 book of that title) was the buzzword of the day. President Clinton quickly issued three executive orders and three memoranda all aimed at achieving a more efficient and effective government. He ordered the elimination of 100,000 federal positions (E.O. 12839) over the next three years, the elimination of at least one-third of the advisory committees subject to the Federal Advisory Committee Act by the end of fiscal year 1993 (E.O. 12838), and the reduction of administrative costs by all executive departments and agencies. He also issued to all heads of executive departments and agencies three memoranda restricting the use of government vehicles and reducing the size of the federal government motor pool by half by the end of fiscal year 1993, limiting the use of federal aircraft, and eliminating the existence of below-cost meals at executive dining facilities.

This effort at reinventing government was, of course, to become a continuing theme of the administration. Although the next steps came in September 1993, after the first one hundred days, the use of presidential direct action to attempt a radical redesign of the executive branch had a kind of self-perpetuating quality to it. President Clinton charged Vice President Al Gore with taking the leadership of a project called the National Performance Review (NPR), designed to assess the task of reinventing government and to accept responsibility for its implementation. It should probably have come as no surprise to anyone that when the report of the NPR, entitled *From Red Tape to Results: Creating a Government That Works Better and Costs Less* (Gore, 1993) was issued, it specifically and repeatedly called upon the president to make the changes suggested in the report through presidential directives rather than by the more difficult mechanisms of administrative rulemaking or legislation.

The way President Clinton responded to promises made to gay and lesbian voters during the campaign resulted in the loss of political capital for his administration during the first one hundred days. The reference, of course, is to Clinton's memorandum to the secretary of defense issued on January 29, 1993, requesting a draft executive order to end discrimination in the military. Gays in the military became the focus of a great deal of press coverage during the first month of the Clinton administration, diverting attention away from the much heralded economic plan.

Other activities during the first one hundred days included changes in federal procurement policies (formally known as acquisitions policies). Agencies were directed to purchase energy-efficient computer equipment (E.O. 12845), to adopt policies to exceed the alternative fuel purchase requirements established by the Energy Policy Act of 1992 (E.O. 12844), and to substantially reduce the procurement of ozone depleting substances (E.O. 12843). Aside from a number of procurement changes, these orders also marked the beginning of a number of subsequent actions taken by Clinton designed to shore up the administration's bona fides on environmental issues even as the administration was moving to take a less aggressive posture on environmental enforcement than had been anticipated by supporters.

The remaining memoranda and orders employed during the first one hundred days largely involved foreign policy issues. President Clinton directed the acting administrator of the Agency for International Development (AID) to remove all conditions on AID grants to nongovernmental organizations that were not explicitly mandated by law, authorized a loan to be extended to the People's Republic of China, designated the International Development Law Institute as a public international organization entitled to all the benefits of such organizations (E.O. 12842), and extended the United States' relationship with EURATOM, the European Atomic Energy Community (E.O. 12840).

The vast majority of the twenty-eight proclamations issued during Clinton's first one hundred days in office were consistent with the usual hortatory nature of proclamations. Twenty-five of the proclamations involved such issues as the recognition of the deaths of former U.S. Supreme Court Justice Thurgood Marshall (Proclamation 6526) and Cesar Chavez (Proclamation 6552), as well as many designations of days, weeks, and months of recognition. For instance, March 1993 was designated as Irish-American Heritage Month (Proclamation 6533), American Red Cross Month (Proclamation 6535), and Women's History Month (Proclamation 6537).

There were three notable exceptions to the hortatory nature of Clinton's presidential proclamations. The first, Proclamation 6534, was a revocation of Proclamation 6491 issued on October 14, 1992. Proclamation 6491 allowed payment of less than locally prevailing wages during recovery from Hurricanes Andrew and Iniki. The second, Proclamation 6543, extended special rules of origin applicable to certain textile articles woven or knitted in Canada. The third, Proclamation 6544, modified both the duty-free treatment under the Andean Trade Preference Act and the Generalized System of Preferences. These proclamations are in the tradition of the use of proclamations as devices to be employed in international trade policy.

The First Year: Settling In and Setting the Agenda

What remained of the first year of the Clinton administration beyond the first one hundred days was largely a continuation of several of the policy stances taken during the campaign. Many of the orders and memoranda issued during that year were measures designed to implement aspects of the NPR and the North American Free Trade Agreement (NAFTA), as well as to engage in the establishment and implementation of foreign policy. What was absent, however, and what makes the remainder of the first term distinct from the first one hundred days, were the overt political actions to repay campaign favors and reverse Republican policies left from previous administrations (that is, gays in the military and issues surrounding reproductive health).

Several orders and memoranda were issued to implement recommendations made in the NPR process. On September 11, 1993, each department and agency was directed to submit a streamlining plan to the OMB to achieve the NPR's recommendation to reduce the federal civilian workforce by 250,000 by the end of fiscal year 1999. Shortly thereafter Clinton issued a memorandum directing each agency to identify at least one rulemaking process in which it intended to use negotiated rulemaking as set forth in Executive Order 12866 on Regulatory Planning and Review. Moreover, each agency was directed to eliminate at least one-half of all internal government regulations (E.O. 12861), and to eliminate the promulgation of unfunded mandates not required by statute and streamline its process for issuing waivers to mandates (E.O. 12875).

Management reform within the executive branch was to be undertaken as directed by the NPR. Executive Order 12861 required agencies to eliminate at least half of the existing internal management regulations within three years. Each agency was to establish an "environmental executive" to work on effective waste prevention and recycling (E.O. 12873). Each agency was directed to identify its customers, survey them, establish customer service benchmarks, and establish customer service plans (E.O. 12862). In addition, a National Partnership Council was established to foster goals on labor-management partnerships set forth by the NPR (E.O. 12871).

Federal procurement policies did not escape scrutiny by the NPR, and President Clinton directed that an electronic commerce system be established to streamline the procurement process. In addition, agencies were no longer to apply price differentials between American products and those from the European Community (E.O. 12849).

The effort to implement NAFTA was another significant area of activity and use of presidential tools by the Clinton administration. On January 1, 1994, a determination was made that the Interstate Commerce Commission could grant Mexican motor carriers authority to transport passengers on tour buses between the United States and Mexico. In addition, Executive Order 12889 was issued to support the implementation of NAFTA within the executive branch, establishing the U.S. Section of the NAFTA Secretariat within the Department of Commerce. This order also granted a waiver to eligible Mexican and Canadian products with respect to federal government procurement, and waived the procedures of notification of patent owners whenever a product is used or manufactured by or for the federal government.

As an aside, it appeared within Executive Order 12889 that the Clinton administration unilaterally determined that "remuneration," as it appeared in

NAFTA, was to mean "reasonable and entire compensation." It appeared likely that the administration intended to use direct statements in orders rather than other administrative law tools to interpret and implement the agreements. Such interpretations would ordinarily have come in administrative rules.

During the first year of the Clinton administration, several new boards, commissions, and councils were established. By executive order Clinton created the President's Council on Sustainable Development (E.O. 12852), the Domestic Policy Council (E.O. 12859), the President's Foreign Intelligence Advisory Board (E.O. 12863), the United States Advisory Council on the National Information Infrastructure (E.O. 12864), the Trade Promotion Coordinating Committee (E.O. 12870), an emergency board to investigate the dispute between the Long Island Rail Road and members of the United Transportation Union (E.O. 12874), the Bipartisan Commission on Entitlement Reform, the National Science Technology Council (E.O. 12881), the President's Committee of Advisors on Science and Technology (E.O. 12882), the Advisory Committee on Human Radiation Experiments (E.O. 12891), the President's Community Enterprise Board to assist in implementation of empowerment zone legislation, and the President's Board of Advisors on Historically Black Colleges and Universities (E.O. 12876). The president also specifically continued at least twelve other previously established federal advisory committees (E.O. 12869). Why most new councils, boards, and committees were established by executive order while others, such as the President's Community Enterprise Board, were established by presidential memorandum is unclear.

Other important domestic policy actions taken by Clinton in the first year included efforts to control federal spending. By Executive Order 12858, Clinton ordered the establishment of a Deficit Reduction Fund to be kept in a separate account in the Treasury Department. All spending reductions achieved by the Omnibus Budget Reconciliation Act of 1993 were to be deposited into this account to be used exclusively to redeem maturing debt obligations held by foreign governments. Clearly this was an example of a use of the executive order as a legal tool for an obvious political purpose. It was specifically a counter to Republican charges that the White House was merely shifting spending rather than seeking to address the deficit. In addition, Clinton issued an order (E.O. 12857) that created a number of direct spending targets to be implemented by the director of the OMB to create a mechanism for monitoring the costs of direct spending programs.

Furthermore, three important domestic policy areas were enhanced by executive order. First, Executive Order 12880 established the National Drug Control Program under the director of the Office of National Drug Control Policy for the express purpose of implementing the National Drug Control Strategy. Second, Executive Order 12892 called for agency heads to engage in leadership and coordination of fair housing in federal programs and affirmatively to further fair housing across the executive branch (E.O. 12892). Third, Executive Order 12848 promoted federal efforts to break the cycle of homelessness in America. Clearly these three orders were efforts to address both symbolic and substantive issues. They addressed growing anxiety about attention to deficit issues in the absence of progress on traditional Democratic social service programs. There was also frustration in the civil rights community about whether more market-oriented strategies for housing policy change would be pursued to the detriment of fair housing enforcement.

Last, presidential power tools were used by President Clinton in foreign policy. By memorandum Clinton provided assistance to a number of refugees, including those from Africa in general and those from Mozambique and Haiti. Foreign sanctions were levied against Serbia and Montenegro in a memorandum to the secretary of state, and property located within the Federal Republic of Yugoslavia was blocked by Executive Order 12846. Similarly, Haitian property interests were blocked by Executive Orders 12853 and 12872. Clinton followed his predecessor, President Bush, in the use of sweeping orders to address the Haitian situation, and these actions were later upheld by the U.S. Supreme Court (*Sale* v. *Haitian Centers Council,* 1993).

In addition, many trade actions were taken through executive order. The conditions for most-favored-nation status for the People's Republic of China were issued through Executive Order 12850, and actions were taken to prohibit transactions involving the supply of arms to the Angolan rebel group UNITA, or to any part of Angola for that matter (E.O. 12865).

Proclamations issued during the first year totaled more than one hundred. Again, the vast majority of these tools were hortatory in nature, but there were exceptions. Proclamation 6569 suspended the entry of immigrant and nonimmigrant people who were impeding the negotiations seeking to return constitutional rule to Haiti. Similarly, Proclamation 6574 suspended entry of those persons impeding the transition to democracy in Zaire, and Proclamation 6636 was issued with respect to democratization in Nigeria. Proclamation 6577 was an agreement on trade relations between the United States and Romania. Proclamation 6579 implemented an accelerated tariff schedule of duty elimination under the U.S.–Canada Free Trade Agreement. Proclamation 6585 designated Peru as a beneficiary country under the Andean Trade Preference Act, and Proclamation 6641 addressed the implementation of NAFTA. Other proclamations (6575, 6599, and 6635) were issued to amend the Generalized System of Preferences, the normal means for making such changes.

The Second Year: Approaching Midterm Elections

During his second year in office, President Clinton issued more than fifty orders, dozens of published memoranda, and more than one hundred proclamations. Much like the previous year, Clinton used the tools to address both domestic and foreign policy issues on a variety of topics. However, implementation of NAFTA and NPR continued to dominate the use of presidential tools. Still more commissions, boards, and committees were established.

As chief executive, the president must address the concerns of federal employees, a sensitive matter in the context of the effort to reinvent government. Several such issues surfaced during Clinton's second year in office that received his attention. The first were amendments to civil service rules regarding political activity (E.O. 12896) and to Civil Service Rule VI (E.O. 12940). Issued on the same day was another order establishing a policy on the garnishment of federal employees' pay (E.O. 12897). A memorandum was distributed to all heads of executive departments and agencies, directing them to take actions to expand family-friendly work arrangements in the executive branch; and adjustments to rates of pay and allowances were made by Executive Order 12944.

President Clinton issued directives in response to several newsworthy events around the country. On April 23, 1994, Clinton ordered that all government departments and agencies were to close on April 27 in recognition of former President Nixon's death (E.O. 12910). To help alleviate some of the burden on executive branch employees struck by natural disasters, on July 15, 1994, Clinton issued a memorandum to allow excused absences for employees affected by Tropical Storm Alberto.

In his role as commander in chief of the armed forces, Clinton issued several directives regarding operation of the military. Executive orders were issued to designate the order of succession of officers to act as secretary of the army (E.O. 12908) and of the air force (E.O. 12909). Clinton ordered the selective reserve of the armed forces to active duty to assist in restoring constitutional government in Haiti (E.O. 12927), and he amended (in E.O. 12935) a previously issued order (E.O. 11157) that defined field duty. Also, as a matter of routine administration, amendments to the Manual for Courts-Martial, United States, were made by Executive Order 12936. All of these orders are standard type actions taken by presidents. They are typical and routinely issued by administrations over the years.

Implementing the NPR and NAFTA remained key targets of presidential tools. Items relating to the NPR implemented during Clinton's second year in office included several actions to improve federal infrastructure and the seismic safety of federally owned or leased buildings (E.O. 12941). Principles were established to govern federal infrastructure investments (E.O. 12893) and to improve energy efficiency and water conservation at existing federal facilities (E.O. 12902). Moreover, a memorandum was issued directing executive departments and agencies to advance environmentally and economically beneficial landscaping on federal grounds, again to increase energy efficiency and water conservation.

In keeping with recommendations made by the NPR, Clinton worked to advance many social policy issues through the use of reformed government procurement policies (E.O. 12931). He promoted federal procurement with small businesses owned and controlled by socially and economically disadvantaged individuals, as well as historically black colleges and universities and other minority institutions (E.O. 12928). In addition, in an attempt to appease labor unions, Clinton ordered that qualified workers under certain government contracts were not to be displaced even if the contracts were awarded to different firms in subsequent bids (E.O. 12933). A year later, Clinton continued in this direction, favorable to labor, in his very controversial "striker replacement" order.

The North American Free Trade Agreement and related side agreements were the focus of many executive actions taken by the White House. By executive order, Clinton ordered American participation in the Commission for Environmental Cooperation, the Commission for Labor Cooperation, the Border Environmental Cooperation Commission, and the North American Bank, pursuant to provisions within NAFTA (E.O. 12904). He then supported implementation of each commission's recommendations (E.O. 12915 and 12916).

Many other key domestic policy issues were addressed by unilateral executive action. Federal environmental policy was one such area. Early in 1994, Clinton issued an order for federal action to address environmental justice in minority and low-income populations (E.O. 12898). While not widely noticed, the effort to address "environmental equity," as the issue was termed, was a complex effort at political compromise. Critics insisted that communities populated by African Americans and Hispanics have often born the brunt of historically poor environmental practices and that they are now used for siting of disposal facilities or otherwise employed as safety valves for middle class not-in-my-backyard tensions. Without seeking legislative action, the administration created a unit within the Environmental Protection Agency to attack this problem, addressing a challenge from traditional Democratic allies without significantly altering its overall strategy in the environmental arena, thereby avoiding challenges from "New Democrats." Moreover, Clinton established a Trade and Environment Policy Advisory Committee to help in these areas (E.O. 12905).

Education was also toward the top of Clinton's agenda. Providing safe schools and educational excellence for Hispanic Americans in particular were the subjects of executive action (E.O. 12900). However, not only education of the nation's youth but also education of the American public about opportunities was a priority for Clinton. He directed agencies to engage in efforts to educate the public and assist states and localities in the implementation of the National Voter Registration Act (the so-called Motor Voter law). On March 9, 1994, he directed agencies by memorandum to inform employees and the public about the Earned-Income Tax Credit that was being underutilized by eligible taxpayers.

The administration has repeatedly argued that education and information go hand in hand in this technological age. Access by educational institutions, and the general public, to government information was addressed by Clinton. In April 1994, he called for the establishment of the National Spatial Data Infrastructure for the coordination of geographic data acquisition and access (E.O. 12906). Later, in November, Clinton ordered the declassification of selected records within the National Archives of the United States and had the declassification process streamlined (E.O. 12937).

Domestic policy issues were not the only targets of Clinton's actions, however. The United States became involved in many developments around the world in 1994. Restoring government in Haiti, providing refugee assistance to many displaced persons, and assisting the Newly Independent States of the former Soviet Union captured the attention of the Clinton administration. Blocking the property of Haitian nationals (E.O. 12922) and prohibiting transactions with Haiti (E.O. 12920) as well as Rwanda (E.O. 12918) and Bosnia (E.O. 12934) were addressed.

As in his first year, efforts were made by Clinton to address the state of the economy and trade priorities. In early March 1994, the Clinton administration identified several priorities for trade expansion (E.O. 12901), including lifting the embargo against Vietnam, while continuing many other export control regulations (E.O. 12923 and 12924). Another target for Clinton's trade priorities was China. In a memo to the U.S. trade representative, Clinton determined under Section 406 of the Trade Act of 1974 that American honey producers, who were competing with honey imported from the People's Republic of China, did not warrant protection but imports would be monitored. These findings were vehicles for sending messages to a difficult negotiating partner.

Of the more than one hundred proclamations issued by President Clinton in his second year in office, only eleven were nonhortatory. Five of those were related to the Generalized System of Preferences (Proclamations 6650, 6655, 6676, 6704, and 6714). With one exception, those remaining dealt largely with foreign policy, immigration, or trade. Proclamation 6662 transferred the functions carried out by another agency under the Domestic Volunteer Services Act of 1973 to the Corporation for National and Community Service within the executive branch. Proclamation 6685 restricted immigration for persons impeding negotiations in Haiti, 6730 dealt similarly with the transition to democracy in Liberia, and 6749 fully implemented immigration measures in conjunction with United Nations Security Council Resolution 942. Finally, proclamations were used to place into full force and effect the Compact of Free Association with the Republic of Palau (Proclamation 6726) and to impose tariff rate quotas on certain wheat imports (Proclamation 6740).

It should be noted that the vast majority of proclamations issued by the president are at the request of Congress, either through legislation itself or by joint resolution. For instance, the designation of October 1994 as Country Music Month (Proclamation 6742) was requested by Congress in Public Law 103–107.

Designating 1994 also as the Year of Gospel Music (Proclamation 6752) was requested by Senate Joint Resolution 157.

Staying the Course: Toward Reelection and Beyond

The third year of Clinton's first term, 1995, was designated the Year of the Grandparent (Proclamation 6766), as requested by Public Law 103–368. It appears that in that year President Clinton's propensity to use presidential tools for political purposes was not at all curbed by the results of the midterm elections. The rate at which President Clinton issued orders was not constrained, nor was the range of topics addressed narrowed. As in previous years, the president used presidential tools to address matters of executive branch administration as well as key domestic and foreign policy issues.

In 1995, the United States was deeply affected by a number of catastrophic events. Massive flooding in California and the Oklahoma City bombing touched the lives of federal employees in highly destructive ways. By presidential memoranda Clinton permitted excused absences of employees affected by the flooding and the bombing, established a scholarship fund for the children left behind by the Oklahoma City tragedy, and issued directives to upgrade security at remaining federal facilities. In addition, Clinton actively promoted campaigns to raise funds for needy charities and for the purchase of U.S. Savings Bonds.

The White House acted as if the dramatic changes in Congress required even more dramatic direct presidential action, the best examples of which are probably the Mexican bailout and the striker replacement order (E.O. 12954). Congress had failed to pass a bill to protect labor unions from decisions by employers to hire permanent workers to replace striking employees. Having moved in a far more conservative direction on the economy than many of his earlier supporters had anticipated, Clinton was under pressure to prove his bona fides as a Democrat with one of the party's strongest constituencies. The order, entitled "Ensuring the Economical and Efficient Administration and Completion of Federal Government Contracts," states that "to ensure the economical and efficient administration and completion of Federal Government contracts, contracting agencies shall not contract with employers that permanently replace lawfully striking employees" (Clinton, 1995b). Legal and political challenges were immediately launched against the order (Krupin, 1995; U.S. House of Representatives, 1995).

The first several months of Clinton's third year were a time when the White House revisited and reinforced previous policies. The president issued several memoranda concerning NPR topics to heads of executive departments and agencies. Two of these memoranda were on regulatory reform and again directed the executive agencies to engage in negotiated rulemaking. Other memoranda revisited customer service in the federal government and unfunded mandates.

Key domestic policy issues, both new and old, were also addressed by Clinton. Information technology, the release of certain environmentally useful imagery acquired by space-based national intelligence reconnaissance systems (E.O. 12951), and access to other classified information (E.O. 12958 and 12968) continued to be addressed. In keeping with his administration's increased openness concerning selected government information, Clinton issued an order concerning federal acquisition and community right-to-know (E.O. 12969). Classification orders have been issued by presidents for the past fifty years, but they have been particularly significant during the Carter, Reagan, and Clinton years. Carter used a participatory process to produce an order calling for significant release, an action that the Reagan White House trumped in E.O. 12356, which moved dramatically in the opposite direction (U.S. House of Representatives, 1982). Clinton moved back toward the Carter approach and went even further in some respects.

Other social policies centered around the family, civil liberties, and the promotion of minority interests. Clinton ordered the federal government to assist in ensuring the payment of child support (E.O. 12953) and to engage in activities that promoted the role of the father. This executive order called for dramatic action, including the use of governmental data, to pursue child support by government employees.

Clinton also issued a memorandum to the secretary of education and the attorney general about religious expression in public schools and directed them to work towards clarifying a number of misconceptions Americans have about their rights. This order was another significant political statement, but one that sought to address pressures from the political right as the 1996 elections neared. The administration intervened in the Justice Department's position on a major legal battle over gifts to religious institutions by persons in bankruptcy proceedings. Clinton took a dramatic turn toward changing traditional Democratic support for a strong separation of church and state. The White House was using the memorandum and other statements to position itself to the right of that traditional posture.

Last, following the U.S. Supreme Court attack on affirmative action in America in *Adarand Constructors, Inc.* v. *Pena* (1995), President Clinton reaffirmed the use of affirmative action policies in the executive branch and directed each agency to evaluate its current policies.

Remaining actions taken by Clinton during the closing years of his first term revolved around foreign policy. As in previous years, Clinton issued orders prohibiting certain transactions with a number of parties, including those who threaten to disrupt the Middle East peace process (E.O. 12947), those who wish to engage in the development of Iranian petroleum resources (E.O. 12957), and Iran (E.O. 12959). Other orders established policies for foreign intelligence physical searches (E.O. 12949), continued cooperation with EURATOM (E.O. 12955), the Israel–United States Binational Industrial Research and Development Foundation (E.O. 12956), the Commission on United States–Pacific Trade and Investment Policy (E.O. 12964), and foreign disaster assistance (E.O. 12966). Using memoranda, Clinton provided assistance to the newly independent states of the former Soviet Union and directed additional federal actions to deter illegal immigration.

President Clinton issued more than forty proclamations during his third year, only four of which did not conform to the usual hortatory nature of proclamations. Three of these were further amendments to the Generalized System of Preferences (Proclamations 6767, 6778, and 6813). The fourth implemented parts of the trade agreements resulting from the Uruguay Round (Proclamation 6780).

CONCLUSION

In sum, from its first moment in office the Clinton administration employed the tools of presidential direct action to achieve its political, administrative, and policy goals. Most political observers enjoy the irony of politics, and that quality is certainly present with respect to the use of direct presidential action. The Carter administration focused on legislation, much of it deregulation legislation, to achieve its goals. The Reagan White House, best known for attacking bureaucracy, often used administrative means, particularly administrative deregulation through rulemaking and policy statements, to move toward its goals. The Clinton administration, which called for national conversations and enhanced democratic processes to achieve policy goals, has chosen to use executive orders, memoranda, and proclamations to pursue a number of its most important objectives and to address a number of its thorniest political problems.

The important lesson is that administrators need to understand the nature and uses of these executive branch tools and need to pay attention to their application. These tools are no less important than statutes, rules, or judicial decisions in shaping the legal environment of public management. It is also important to understand that the term *executive order* is often used, rightly or wrongly, to refer not merely to the technical device properly called an executive order but to an entire family of instruments of presidential direct action, including orders, proclamations, memoranda, and national security directives, which are often interrelated. What may seem like merely internal and technical orders and memoranda may have dramatic consequences throughout the nation. What may appear to be national-security-related directives may have just as much impact domestically as they do outside the borders of the United States. What may seem to be an inside-the-beltway phenomenon affects all levels of government through the ability of the White House to shape intergovernmental administration.

Cases Cited

Adarand Constructors, Inc. v. *Pena*, 132 L.Ed.2d 158 (1995).

Amalgamated Meat Cutters and Butcher Workmen of North America v. *Connally*, 337 F.Supp. 737 (D.D.C., 1971).

American Pilots' Association v. *Gracey*, 631 F.Supp. 828 (D.D.C., 1986).

Armstrong v. *United States*, 80 U.S. (13 Wall.) 154 (1871).

Dames and Moore v. *Reagan*, 453 U.S. 654 (1981).

Environmental Defense Fund v. *Thomas*, 627 F.Supp. 556 (1986).

Farkas v. *Texas Instruments*, 372 F.2d 629 (5th Cir., 1967).

Farmer v. *Philadelphia Electric Company*, 329 F.2d 3 (3rd Cir., 1964).

Fullilove v. *Klutznick*, 448 U.S. 448 (1980).

Independent Gasoline Markets Council v. *Duncan*, 492 F.Supp. 614 (D.D.C., 1980).

Jenkins v. *Collard*, 145 U.S. 546 (1893).

Korematsu v. *United States*, 319 U.S. 432 (1943).

Meritor Savings Bank v. *Vinson*, 477 U.S. 57 (1986).

Rust v. *Sullivan*, 500 U.S. 173 (1991).

Sale v. *Haitian Centers Council*, 125 L.Ed.2d 128 (1993).

United States v. *Wayte*, 710 F.2d 1385 (9th Cir., 1983).

Wolsey v. *Chapman*, 101 U.S. 755 (1879).

Youngstown Sheet and Tube v. *Sawyer*, 343 U.S. 579 (1952).

References

Bush, G. "Memorandum for Certain Department and Agency Heads on the Subject of Reducing the Burden of Government Regulations," 1992.

Campbell, C. *Managing the Presidency.* Pittsburgh: University of Pittsburgh, 1986.

Clinton, W. J. "Remarks to the Students at Carlmont High School in Belmont, California." *Weekly Compilation of Presidential Documents,* 1994, *30*, 2115.

Clinton, W. J. "Remarks to the National Governors' Association Conference." *Weekly Compilation of Presidential Documents,* 1995a, *31*, 151.

Clinton, W. J. "Ensuring the Economical and Efficient Administration and Completion of Federal Government Contracts." *Weekly Compilation of Presidential Documents,* 1995b, *31*, 382.

Cooper, P. J. "By Order of the President: Administration by Executive Order and Proclamation." *Administration and Society,* 1986, *18*, 233–262.

Gore, A. Jr. *From Red Tape to Results: Creating a Government That Works Better and Costs Less.* Report of the National Performance Review. Washington, D.C.: U.S. Government Printing Office, 1993.

"Historic Executive Orders Signed by President Clinton." *Congressional Record*, 1993, *139*, H187.

Kerwin, C. M. *Rulemaking: How Government Agencies Write Law and Make Policy.* Washington, D.C.: Congressional Quarterly Press, 1995.

Krupin, J. "Sidestepping Congress." *National Law Journal*, 1995, *17*, A21.

Office of the Federal Register. *Codification of Presidential Proclamations and Executive Orders, April 13, 1945–January 20, 1989.* Washington, D.C.: U.S. Government Printing Office, 1990.

OMB Watch. "The Administration's Regulatory Program, 1985." *OMB Watch Bulletin*, Jan. 10, 1985a.

OMB Watch. "The Administration's 1985 Regulatory Program: What It Means for You." *OMB Watch Bulletin*, Jan. 24, 1985b.

Osborne, D., and Gaebler, T. *Reinventing Government: How the Entrepreneurial Spirit Is Transforming the Public Sector from Schoolhouse to Statehouse, City Hall to the Pentagon.* Reading, Mass.: Addison Wesley Longman, 1992.

Reagan, R. "Development of Administration's Regulatory Program." Memorandum for the Heads of Executive Departments and Agencies, Jan. 4, 1985.

Sullivan, T. "The 'Bank Account' Presidency: A New Measure and Evidence on the Temporal Path of Presidential Influence." *American Journal of Political Science*, 1991, *35*, 686–723.

U.S. House of Representatives, Committee on Economic and Educational Opportunities. "Nullifying an Executive Order That Prohibits Federal Contracts with Companies That Hire Permanent Replacements for Striking Employees." 104th Cong., 1st Sess., 1995.

U.S. House of Representatives, Committee on Governmental Operations. "Executive Orders and Proclamations: A Study of a Use of Presidential Power." 85th Cong., 1st Sess., 1957.

U.S. House of Representatives, Hearing Before the Committee on Government Operations. "Executive Order on Security Classification." 97th Cong., 2nd Sess., 1982.

CHAPTER TWELVE

Ordinances, Statutes, and Democratic Discipline

A Local Perspective on Drafting Laws

David L. Corliss

Laws exist for a purpose. Individuals or groups who wield power in a community (whether they are duly elected officials, machine politicians, citizens in a referendum, or some other source of authority) decide to enforce some code of conduct for others and possibly for themselves. Laws reflect these choices of those in power to require, authorize, or prohibit conduct. Paying taxes, limiting mergers and acquisitions of companies, prohibiting murder or theft, spending public funds on some goods and not on others, limiting certain medical procedures, such as abortion, and requiring vehicles to come to a complete stop at Main and Elm all reflect choices of those in power to affect individual or group conduct.

The desire of those in power to affect certain conduct is as old as the Ten Commandments and the Code of Hammurabi. As societies and communities have changed and evolved, the repositories of power have also changed. Democracies of various forms and functions have wielded power in the name of the people. The laws written in democracies have been promulgated in the name of the people and for the benefit of the people. The advent of a professional cadre of public administrators to aid the endeavors of democracies has also grown and flourished.

The task of most public administrators at all levels of government in constitutionally democratic states is to do the reasonable will of the public and their elected officials as set forth in duly adopted laws. However, many public administrators are also involved in drafting the laws to be debated, amended, and eventually adopted by elected officials. The process of drafting statutes, rules, and ordinances is one of the several areas in which attorneys and administrators are important partners. The practice of drafting laws is taught in law schools, the routes of legislation are studied, and most legislative bodies have at their disposal attorneys skilled in drafting laws. To be sure, many of those who challenge new laws mobilize such legal resources as well.

At the local government level, the drafting of laws follows a path roughly analogous to the path followed at the federal and state levels. Most general government municipalities (in contrast to special purpose districts such as water or sewer districts) have authority to adopt ordinances. Ordinances are laws with legal implications similar to statutes adopted at the state and federal level. The authority to enact municipal ordinances comes from state governments and differs in degree and kind for each state. Some municipalities, notably cities, have authority from state constitutions or statutes to adopt ordinances on any subject of local affairs not preempted by state or federal statutes. Thus, in some fields the U.S. Constitution or a state constitution authorizes the national or state government to dominate policymaking, but where the national and state governments elect not to take action, they may authorize local governments to lead the way. These cities have strong "home rule" powers to legislate on local matters. Other states reign in the authority of municipalities more tightly, limiting their self determination powers to only those areas specifically prescribed by state law.

Regardless of home rule powers, no ordinance can conflict with state statutes or occupy areas of the law that have been preempted by state statutes. Much litigation occurs to determine whether such conflicts are present in given situations. Of course, no locally adopted ordinances can conflict with federal law because Article VI, Section 2 (the Supremacy Clause) of the U.S. Constitution establishes federal law as the supreme law of the land in those fields where federal authority exists.

Many citizens think of ordinances as mere local bylaws or rules and fail to appreciate their standing as laws. It is not an uncommon necessity to advise citizens that an ordinance with which they disagree is not a suggestion but the law and must be followed.

This chapter examines the well-worn path of drafting laws, not at the state or federal level—although some of the same considerations are applicable—but at the local government level. How are the choices made by those in power at the local government level carried out in the local legislation called ordinances?

PURPOSE OF THE LAW: WHICH DRAGON IS TO BE SLAIN?

As noted earlier, and consistent with the perspectives of analytical jurisprudence, laws reflect the choices made by those in power to affect some conduct on the part of individuals or groups. This definition applies to local government laws as well as those at the state and federal levels. A local governing body (whether it is called a commission, council, or legislature) determines that the best interests of the public are served by adopting an ordinance that authorizes, prescribes, or prohibits a particular conduct. Most local laws attempt to prohibit something from occurring.

In drafting an ordinance, a first task for both the public administrator and the attorney is to consider the rumblings and rhetoric surrounding the matter, and especially to understand the concerns and expressions of elected officials, and then to chart a reasonable course for enactment. Most elected officials talk in terms of the "results" of adopting or repealing a law—for example, "This law will stop crime," or "This proposed law will curb teenage pregnancies." Seldom do elected officials speak of the details of laws or the legislative process. One is reminded of the dying pharaoh in the movie *The Ten Commandants* uttering another command on his deathbed: "So it is written, so it shall be done." The faithful scribe is left to fill in the necessary details to accomplish the will of the pharaoh.

To accomplish the will of elected officials, administrators and attorneys must first seek to determine the purpose and intent of the proposed law. What does the governing body really want to accomplish? What conduct or activity is to be prohibited or prescribed? Laws may have multiple purposes. The purposes behind an impact fee ordinance may be to raise revenue for public infrastructure and to slow development in a community. Laws may have primary and secondary purposes. Regulatory requirements that affect health services workers may undoubtedly seek to ensure quality health care, but they may operate so as to increase or decrease the supplies of particular caregivers and the hours, locations, and other conditions of their availability. Whatever the nature and mix of purposes, the drafters of laws must understand the purpose or purposes sought by elected officials—and the system relationships that affect objectives. By keeping the purpose and context of a law in mind and using it as a constant guide in the necessary decision making that constitutes the details of drafting laws, the drafter will know which dragon is to be slain. Without such understanding, the necessary choices in the drafting process are frequently ill considered.

THE RESEARCH HUNT: KNOWING
WHEN ANALYSIS BECOMES PARALYSIS

Consider the following example. After receiving several phone calls, reading letters to the editor, and hearing an anecdote by a prominent citizen, a majority of a local governing body decides to adopt an ordinance prohibiting the practice of "cruising" the community's Main Street. The dragon this governing body wishes to slay is the recurrent adolescent-and-twenty-something phenomenon of repeatedly driving clusters of automobiles up and down Main Street while participating in some combination of crude mating rituals, teenager show-and-tell, and midsummer boredom. This repetitive driving is causing gridlock on Main Street, irritating other would-be drivers and Main Street merchants, and perhaps endangering the public because emergency vehicles are impeded from crossing town. The police chief indicates that no violation of law can be found in this congregant behavior of youth, so the law must be changed, and it must be done quickly before more harm by cruisers occurs.

The drafter of a proposed law is always faced with the practical problem of finding time to prepare it adequately. The dilemma faced is often the choice between getting it *right* and getting it *right now.* With any proposed law of significance, it is important to understand the time needed to do adequate research. Legislative bodies do not want to be slowed down by the problems of time-consuming drafting. Whether the legislature is Congress or a city council, elected officials commonly want to see their legislative desires quickly and effectively placed into written word, debated, amended, and adopted.

One challenge for a drafter, then, is to acquire timely knowledge of both the technical and the general issues presented by a proposed ordinance. Which other communities have adopted similar ordinances? Which other jurisdictions have court decisions that speak to the legal issues raised by this proposed law?

It is especially essential to consider externalities, and possible unintended consequences. Among the least understood perils for administrators is what unanticipated matters may arise out of the definitions in a new ordinance. Thus, for example, a city council that adopts restrictions on trucks might find itself besieged by angry local pick-up truck owners when the council's original intention had been to regulate commercial freight haulers.

A fundamental task is to manage research in the drafting of an ordinance. As noted, the initial questions are easy: What other jurisdictions have similar laws, and are challenges to those laws pending? But deep probing is essential to discern some hard issues. For example, Boston adopted a requirement that at least half of all employees on city construction projects had to be Boston residents, and that law was upheld against a charge that it violated constitutional restrictions on interstate commerce (*White v. Massachusetts Council of Construction Employers,* 1983). When Camden, New Jersey, modeled its own ordinance on the Boston law, the city was surprised to find that although the law survived a challenge on the grounds of the Commerce Clause (Article III, Section 8, Clause 3), it fell because it was held to violate the Privileges and Immunities Clause (Article IV, Section 2, Clause 1) by interfering with the ability of would-be employees to travel in order to obtain employment (*United Building and Construction Trades Council v. Camden,* 1984). Another example occurred after the U.S. Supreme Court struck down attempts by New Jersey to block the City of Philadelphia from hauling solid waste to New Jersey landfills (*Philadelphia* v. *New Jersey,* 1978). A Michigan county decided to try a new strategy. It thought that by taking advantage of an option under the state's new solid waste law it could prohibit importation of solid waste from other counties as well as from other states and thereby avoid the charge that it was interfering with interstate commerce while simultaneously making its solid waste disposal policy more rational. The Supreme Court disagreed (*Fort Gratiot Sanitary Landfill* v. *Michigan Department of Natural Resources,* 1992). The moral is that careful research reveals not merely what another jurisdiction tried but what happened when the next generation of ordinances, developed on the earlier history, was tested.

The city attorney and council need to involve relevant groups while drafting the law, such as regulatory or law enforcement personnel who will enforce the new ordinance. But in designing the process the city and its attorney must decide what form their participation should take and how much time to take to review and discuss the draft.

All of these issues must be addressed in order to draft an effective law, yet time is of the essence. The experienced drafter of laws will maintain a checklist of drafting issues during the legislative process. No map will advise the drafter when the research and drafting tasks are complete. However, the items discussed in this chapter can serve as a general outline for a checklist of drafting issues.

INITIAL QUESTIONS: AUTHORITY, PREEMPTION, AND CONFLICT

Every ordinance must get past several initial questions. Given that the city council has general authority to issue ordinances, what is the authority for the proposed law? Is the subject completely or partially preempted by state or federal law? That is, if the federal or state government has legislated in the target subject area, do their statutes leave room for local governments to act as well or does the proposed ordinance actually conflict with a state or federal law? These are initial questions on any checklist for drafting an ordinance. Without adequate answers, the proposal fails. But careful drafting scores wins, sometimes at the cost of litigation. For example, one small Wisconsin community took advantage of gaps between the federal and state governments' actions under the federal Insecticide, Fungicide and Rodenticide Act. The Environmental Protection Agency had not adopted regulations concerning the spraying of insecticides in populated areas and neither had state authorities. The federal law did not clearly authorize or prohibit action by local governments. Frustrated by the lack of protection for its residents from over-spraying and misapplications of agricultural chemicals, the Wisconsin town simply adopted its own regulations restricting spraying. Although state officials joined agricultural interests in challenging the ordinance, no one, including the U.S. Supreme Court could find that either Congress or the state had preempted regulation of chemical spraying (*Wisconsin Public Intervenors* v. *Mortier,* 1991).

All laws must have organic authority. Federal statutes rely on grants of authority in the U.S. Constitution. State constitutions and laws come from the plenary authority of sovereign states and must not conflict with federal statutes or the Constitution. Local laws must have authority from state law, either constitutional or statutory. In fact, increasingly, federal or state laws may even mandate the development of ordinances or their equivalent. For example, the federal Right-to-Know statute requires local governments to take a variety of actions, from ensuring reporting about pollution sources in the community to developing emergency evacuation procedures.

INVOLVING THE STAKEHOLDERS
IN WRITING THE ORDINANCE

Experience shows that one of the most effective ways to kill a law, particularly at the local level, is for major stakeholders to be able to argue that they were not consulted during the drafting. At the state and federal levels, professional lobbyists represent the interests of major stakeholders, but the situation is more ambiguous at the local level. Some affected groups may be aware of a developing ordinance, but many may not. Some citizens may distrust government, and many others do not closely follow its agendas. When a new law greets them by surprise, the results can be disastrous. An aggrieved stakeholder who can complain of being left out of deliberations may not directly assault the proposed law but nonetheless may pick apart an existing agreement from the periphery and demand deferral for further study. Time and again, such action may doom existing or future agreement.

Because of such realities, governing bodies increasingly expect their administrative staffs to seek citizen participation as an essential part of decision-making processes. In short, at the local level, participatory democracy is not abstract theory. Affected individuals, businesses, and groups of all sorts expect to be invited to join in the choices made in drafting a law that may affect their lives, neighborhoods, and businesses. Failure to put participatory theory into practice is an invitation to disaster.

Consider a typical example. An amendment to a city's zoning code has a slight impact on the required landscaping for certain industries in town. The ordinance was drafted without input from the owners of the industries, who now complain to their elected officials that they feel left out of the process. The industries doubt the city staff's claim that only a few more trees and shrubs will have to be installed if an industrial plant expands. Their lack of participation in the drafting and initial consideration of the law leaves these stakeholders questioning the proposed law and disheartened with the process. The governing body questions whether alienating the owners of local industries is worth the public benefit of more landscaping. No one has a good feeling about either killing the ordinance or adopting it.

In addition to involving outside stakeholders, an attorney drafting a local government ordinance must also attempt to involve relevant parties within the local government itself. Often administrators in the organization, other than those who may have initiated a request for an ordinance, will be affected by the law and should become involved in drafting. In many cases, these administrators are helpful in pointing out problems in an initial draft, noting how a certain definition is inconsistent with current practices and indicating potential unintended consequences of certain terms or phrases in the proposal. Such coordinated efforts can also help to buffer possible tensions between political forces in the community and city staff (Nalbandian, 1991). How will the law work in relation to the existing duties of administrators in the organization? Who will enforce the new law? Many administrators will view a new ordinance as an "unfunded mandate," an addition to their already burdened job descriptions. It is one thing to adopt a new law, but quite another actually to implement its requirements or prohibitions. In a more positive vein, participation allows relevant departments to plan for implementation in advance, reducing lag time between enactment and action.

FUTURE READERS: MAY A JUDGE GRADE YOUR WORK?

Fortunately, most laws are not challenged in court. Indeed, most ordinances adopted by municipalities are never read by a judge who must ponder its meaning. The same is likely true for federal and state statutes. Unfortunately, litigation and challenges to the express will of elected officials are a fact of life. The drafters of a proposed law must always be cognizant of the possibility of judicial review of their work.

Consider an example. In response to inquiries that a "girlie bar" is coming to their community, a county commission seeks to prohibit nude dancing in their county. The county counselor is tasked with the responsibility of drafting this law for prompt commission consideration. The prospective bar operator threatens litigation if the county proceeds with adoption of a law that he claims will infringe on his First Amendment rights to express himself through the forum of nude dancing. Knowing that the new law is likely to face legal challenges in court, the drafter must pay keen attention to precedents such as *Barnes* v. *Glen Theater, Inc.* (1991) and *Schad* v. *Mount Ephraim* (1981) and ensure that the adoption of the new law is accompanied by ample findings from the commission that provide a sufficient rationale for adoption. Staff summaries of the proposed law will be similar to legal briefs, setting out the clear authority for the law, showing how its provisions can be distinguished from laws that have been challenged successfully, and providing examples of court decisions upholding the proposed provisions.

POSITIVE PLAGIARISM: USING RESULTS FROM THE LABORATORIES OF DEMOCRACY

"It is one of the happy incidents of the federal system that a single courageous state may, if its citizens choose, serve as a laboratory; and try novel social and economic experiments without risk to the rest of the country" (*New State Ice Company* v. *Liebmann*, 1932, p. 311, Judge Louis Brandeis, dissenting). Few laws are new to this world. This is particularly true at the local level. Traffic prohibitions, zoning restrictions, and laws for licensing taverns and beer halls, keeping dogs from running at large, and prohibiting certain electrical wires from exposure are common problems nearly everywhere.

It is a common practice to borrow from other jurisdictions that have passed laws that one's community wishes to adopt. For example, if a city wants to regulate telecommunications towers, it is useful to look at what a few other cities have successfully adopted as regulations. In a city where graffiti is a plague and where elected officials want to require private property owners to remove it swiftly from their property it is useful to know that other cities and national crime prevention groups have relevant ordinances and model language. The functions and policy concerns of municipalities are strikingly similar even if their geography, climate, and economics make them visibly different.

One observation about these laboratories of democracy is that some communities and states fail to share their test results with great regularity or technical precision. Some jurisdictions try to reinvent the wheel even though the patent holder and expert lives right down the river. Fortunately, many communities do in fact frequently discuss and share their legislative experiences. The track records of many important ordinances bear witness to sharing among communities.

Unfortunately, borrowing ordinances from other jurisdictions often presents pitfalls. Wholesale adoption of what another community has adopted can cause problems for the unaware. Success in one jurisdiction does not automatically make a law a perfect candidate for adoption in another place. Does the adopting state or municipality have the same authority to adopt the law as the government from which it is being adopted? How does a law from one jurisdiction work with the case law of the foreign jurisdiction? Will an ordinance from one city work in another city that has a different form of government and is governed by different state laws because of its size or classification? Has the case law that supported an ordinance when it was adopted several years earlier in the originating community significantly changed over time? For example, a city ordinance prohibiting concealed weapons may be preempted in another state that has a law limiting city authority on that subject. Court decisions in one jurisdiction may favor the authority of government to provide certain public incentives to private industries while court decisions in another jurisdiction consider such an incentive to be a violation of the common law doctrine requiring public funds to be spent only for public purposes.

The change issue is also important. For example, most communities would have agreed with Tigard, Oregon, that it was permissible to require greenways and other development requirements in land use decisions, but the Supreme Court used this case to announce that many kinds of property development requirements imposed by local governments may perhaps be classified not as regulations of land use but as regulatory takings of property for which compensation must be paid (*Dolan* v. *City of Tigard*, 1994). Any community that modeled its land use ordinances on those requirements existing before 1994 would have to take another look.

In sum, borrowing from other jurisdictions is a common form of legislative research and drafting, but it must be performed with caution and care. The successful use of a particular law in one jurisdiction is a helpful indication that it may be valuable elsewhere, but it is not a sure answer.

BASIC BUILDING BLOCKS FOR A LAW

It is somewhat dangerous to generalize about the exact components of ordinances. Generalization—attempts to compress all elements of law drafting into a few simple phrases—may lead to slipshod work. With this warning in mind, it is nonetheless important to consider the most frequently observed elements of a law. Indeed, consider that every law shares these elements, whether explicit or implied; that those laws that succeed in achieving the intentions of their creators must have them; and that other laws that fail and endure the ignominy of recurrent judicial interpretation and legislative amendment have often failed in some or all of these essentials. The elements discussed here constitute a helpful checklist for drafters of ordinances to ensure that the essentials have been covered. Also, those public administrators who must implement laws can use their awareness of these elements to understand not only the drafting process but also the techniques of interpretation of ordinances.

Purpose and Intent

Every law has a purpose and intent. Much has been written about legislative intent and the attempt to glean the meaning of the legislators who parented a particular statute or ordinance. Many laws do not clearly set out the findings or purposes of the legislative body. Generally, laws that are controversial and likely to be subject to judicial challenge are most likely to have a findings or purpose section, if wisely drawn. That portion of an ordinance guides those charged with defending a law in setting out its legislative rationale.

Local ordinances or resolutions frequently contain language (sometimes called recitals) that lays out the background and reasoning behind the particular law. Recitals and findings are valuable to subsequent legislators, who can be reminded quickly of the legislative history of a bill or draft ordinance that is up for consideration. As noted before, recitals and findings can also point to the legislative intent behind a law, thus providing valuable insight for judicial review.

The earlier example of a nude dancing ordinance illustrates the importance of care in stating intent. Many communities have sought to regulate establishments that allow nude dancing, but courts have interpreted the First Amendment as providing protection of these activities as expressive conduct. Yet a community may regulate these establishments, not on the basis of nude dancing but because of harmful secondary effects in the community. The expressed intent of the governing body is thus an important element in the constitutionality of an ordinance. A community adopting such an ordinance needs to have clear recitals or findings that indicate that the rationale is not regulating nude dancing but instead regulating the harmful secondary effects.

Definitions

Almost every law of any substance includes a definition provision that provides the keys to understanding the terms of the law. What is a disability under the Americans with Disabilities Act? See the definition of disability set out in the law. Do the ordinance provisions that prohibit the parking of motor vehicles on certain streets also prohibit motorcycles? The answer is likely found in the ordinance's definition of motor vehicles.

The drafter must ensure that definitions are consistent throughout the ordinance and not in conflict with other laws. Obviously, not every word or term in an ordinance needs to be defined. A helpful rule to follow is that if a term is key to the primary prohibition or process that is the essential part of the law or if it describes the persons or things to be governed, that term should be defined. Also, words and terms that have a special meaning in the law need to have that particular meaning amplified and clarified. A law with ample and thorough definitions helps administrators in implementation and resists litigation. Indeed, ordinances that are struck down by courts often meet that fate precisely because they are found to be vague or overbroad. Vagueness means that a reasonable person cannot be expected to be able to read the law and know whether his or her conduct is lawful. An ordinance may be overturned as overbroad if it sweeps too widely, exceeding in impact the original justification for the law. The classic examples of such problems arise in regulation of adult businesses or sign ordinances. It is not uncommon to see amendments to ordinances primarily reflecting the need to add additional definitions to an existing law because questions have arisen regarding the definition provisions of the ordinance.

A Process, Prohibition, or Prescription

As a general rule, a single law contains a primary process, prohibition, or prescription that is the goal of the legislative body and the drafter. Title VII of the Civil Rights Act of 1964 seeks to prohibit discrimination in employment. The Internal Revenue Service Code seeks to prescribe the process for the payment of federal income taxes. A local government's animal control ordinance seeks to prohibit certain animal conduct in a community. The purposes, findings, definitions, penalties, and enforcement provisions all point to this key process, prohibition, or prescription of an ordinance. This essential element is really just the conventional translation of the law; it is what a layperson would say the law does.

Enforcement and Penalty Issues

Most laws also have enforcement and penalty provisions that reflect the desire of the legislature for the law to have consequences. This element is necessary in most laws and is essential in criminal laws or others that seek to regulate conduct (such as antidiscrimination laws). For one thing, such provisions help block general attacks claiming arbitrary and capricious behavior. They have the added benefit, as long as they are well drafted, of avoiding the feeling that council has merely passed the political buck to city departments, leaving the city employees to face the wrath of local citizens. There is also a more positive dimension in that clear enforcement and penalty provisions aid city staff who must perform inspections or address permit violations. Implementation is thereby improved.

IN MODEST PRAISE OF LENGTHY LAWS

A constant drumbeat is sounded against lengthy laws, with the frequent refrain that the volumes of statutes and the shelves of regulations make the law unapproachable and unknowable. As with many conventional thoughts, this observation conveys important wisdom. The popular publication *The Death of Common Sense,* by Philip K. Howard (1994), contains a sharp rebuke to the practice of adopting lengthy laws and regulations. Howard explains that such laws harm democratic institutions because citizens cannot possibly understand the overly complex and drawn out laws that affect their lives.

Yet a properly drafted law on any subject of even moderate complexity necessarily needs adequate definitions to cover its key terms; clear procedures, prohibitions, and prescriptions; and some attention to enforcement and penalty issues. Thus while calls for plain-language ordinances recur, there is always tension between that goal and the need to ensure precision and technical accuracy. That need is particularly true in technically complex fields such as health and environmental regulation.

Consider, for example, a simple municipal law commonly found in most communities—the weed ordinance. Cut to the vernacular, these laws state: "Keep your weeds cut or the government will cut them for you and send you the bill." This is a simple public concept that most citizens take for granted as a given fact of life in urban and suburban communities. Implementation of such an uncomplicated policy should be simple and short. However, even this widespread policy requires attention to all key elements of a workable law, making the ordinance longer than might commonly be expected. The purposes of the weed ordinance need to be expressed to avoid claims that height limits on grass and weeds were arbitrarily established without a clear public purpose. What is a weed? Is tall grass that has gone to seed included? What is excessive growth of weeds? Clear definitions must be established in the ordinance to ensure fair enforcement. Due process requires notification of property owners before government can cut excessive weeds and bill the property owner. Thus the ordinance must contain appropriate notice procedures. Staff members who investigate and enforce the law need clear legal authority to enter private property and measure the nefarious weeds, requiring that these procedures be set out in the ordinance. The law must contain a penalty provision and directions for billing property owners. It must also contain an appeal process for property owners aggrieved by decisions of staff in enforcing the law. All of these issues, and several others, must be addressed in an ordinance to cut weeds and grass that grow too high.

This weed example illustrates why the complaint that laws are too lengthy and complex finds support. However, there is also reason to respect lengthy laws: in the terms of public administration, their length is likely the result of attention to necessary elements to make laws work economically, efficiently, and effectively to accomplish intended purposes.

Considering the number and length of laws, it is easy to wonder whether legislators ever find time actually to read the varied laws that they consider and enact. Most legislators, including those at the state and local levels, rely on staff summaries of legislation to understand the meanings of their votes. Those staff summaries must be unbiased and complete but not so exhaustive as to defeat their purpose as brief abstracts of proposed laws. These important summaries typically go beyond the audience of legislators to include the media and the public, who seldom ever see the actual legal document of a statute or ordinance.

CONCLUSION

The American philosopher, poet, and political scientist T. V. Smith, a teacher who served in Congress, was an enduring optimist about constitutional democracy. But he understood its limits, writing that "there are billions of things that may be felt, millions of things that may be thought, thousands of things that may be said, hundreds of things that may be done, dozens alone of which may be done collectively" (Smith, 1942, p. 8). Even then, he said, such accomplishment requires "discipline for democracy," which is the title of a book he wrote to sustain faith during battles against Nazism during the darkest days of World War II. The words of this practical political philosopher are a worthy reminder to public administrators and attorneys as they seek to build better communities through the drafting and adoption of new laws. Seldom does a new law solve all problems. It may even create new issues and challenges for the city, state, or nation. However, carefully disciplined drafting goes far toward the ultimate success of legislation. It gives informed attention to the practical nuts and bolts that underpin reasonableness in public policy and its implementation. That, after all, is the ultimate test of the successful drafting of laws in service of constitutional democracy.

Cases Cited

Barnes v. *Glen Theater, Inc.,* 501 U.S. 560 (1991).

Dolan v. *City of Tigard,* 512 U.S. 374 (1994).

Fort Gratiot Sanitary Landfill v. *Michigan Department of Natural Resources,* 504 U.S. 353 (1992).

New State Ice Company v. *Liebmann,* 285 U.S. 262 (1932).

Philadelphia v. *New Jersey,* 437 U.S. 617 (1978).

Schad v. *Mount Ephraim,* 452 U.S. 61 (1981).

United Building and Construction Trades Council v. *Camden,* 465 U.S. 208 (1984).

White v. *Massachusetts Council of Construction Employers,* 460 U.S. 204 (1983).

Wisconsin Public Intervenors v. *Mortier,* 501 U.S. 597 (1991).

References

Howard, P. K. *The Death of Common Sense: How Law Is Suffocating America.* New York: Random House, 1994.

Nalbandian, J. *Professionalism in Local Government: Transformation in the Roles, Responsibilities, and Values of City Managers.* San Francisco: Jossey-Bass, 1991.

Smith, T. V. *Discipline for Democracy.* Chapel Hill: University of North Carolina Press, 1942.

CHAPTER THIRTEEN

Negotiated Rulemaking

Cornelius M. Kerwin

Negotiated rulemaking—frequently termed *regulatory negotiation,* or *reg neg*—is a significant reform of one of the oldest and most important legal instrumentalities of American government. The search for better rulemaking is very old and has taken many different paths. Legislative veto, review by the Office of Management and Budget, paperwork reduction, flexibility for small businesses, moratoria, cost-benefit analysis, plain English, risk assessment, and subsidized public participation are among the other ideas that have been put forward to improve either the process or results of rulemaking. Negotiated rulemaking is distinctive, however. It promises to accommodate all of these ideas, and more, in the context of a fundamentally different overall approach to the task of developing regulations. This chapter examines the origins of negotiated rulemaking, the arguments of its proponents, and what is known about the experiences of national government agencies and affected parties when the technique has been used.

It is useful at the outset of this effort to review reasons why so much time and effort have been directed at the reform of rulemaking. No process under the stewardship of national government managers has received more attention from Congress, the president, or the courts than rulemaking. In lavishing on it their many and varied ideas for refinement and reform, all three branches acknowledge that, relative to basic constitutional principles, rulemaking is the most important function performed by administrative agencies. Elsewhere I have detailed the reasons that rulemaking occupies this status (Kerwin, 1994).

Rulemaking is delegated lawmaking, and legislative power is the cornerstone of the Constitution. Rulemaking provides the specific articulations of rights, obligations, and procedural details needed to operate public programs. Thus it carries profound implications for the integrity of constitutional democracy and the success of public management. Reforms, such as negotiated rulemaking, that propose to alter significantly the conduct of this critical process deserve serious scrutiny by public managers.

It is important to remember that negotiated rulemaking is more than a method of developing regulations; it is a product of a distinctive philosophy of governmental decision making. Alternatives to conventional methods of conducting legislative, executive, and judicial functions have long been advocated by a variety of reformers. Negotiated rulemaking is a prominent example of proposals directed at the legislative responsibilities of administrative agencies. There are other proposals that will be considered briefly in this chapter. Recently reformers have suggested that cooperative partnerships between regulators and regulated and a customer orientation to the delivery of public services of all sorts have been employed as means to improve the executive function of government agencies. Alternative dispute resolution, a major movement affecting the entire legal system and the subject of Chapter Thirty in this book, has been recommended for every agency with significant judicial responsibilities. Negotiated rulemaking is properly viewed as an element in a much larger effort to greatly increase the use of consensual processes in public discourse and decision making.

A BRIEF HISTORY

Conventional wisdom and several studies fix the origins of negotiated rulemaking during John Dunlop's term as secretary of labor (Perritt, 1987, p. 871). A leader in American labor relations, Dunlop advocated the use of collective bargaining techniques for the development of regulations, which had become notoriously difficult and contentious in his department. However, the use of negotiation in rulemaking long predates Secretary Dunlop's proposal that its use become an explicit policy. The first systematic study of rulemaking across the federal government (Kerwin, 1994) confirms that consultations between responsible agencies and external parties has been common from as early as the beginning of the twentieth century, and in some instances the express purpose of these communications has been the development of consensus. It is nevertheless true that Dunlop's urgings contributed to a broader discussion of the feasibility and advisability of using negotiation in the writing of rules.

The Administrative Conference of the United States, a recent victim of budget cuts, commissioned a 1982 study of negotiated rulemaking by Phillip Harter, who has since become a leading theoretician, advocate, and practitioner of the technique. Harter's study led to formal recommendations by the conference endorsing the use of negotiated rulemaking and setting standards for its use (Administrative Conference of the United States, 1982, 1985). The conference's recommendation became the basis for a legislative proposal that was eventually adopted by Congress in the Negotiated Rulemaking Act of 1990. The act encourages but does not mandate the use of reg neg, and it establishes requirements that those using the technique must meet. President Bill Clinton pushed the concept further, early in his first term, when he called on all agencies to use negotiated rulemaking in the development of at least one regulation. Thus he deviated from his predecessors, Presidents Ronald Reagan and George Bush, who had cast cold eyes on anything that might make the issuance of regulation easier.

FAILURES OF CONVENTIONAL RULEMAKING

Negotiated rulemaking has attracted a great deal of attention because it promises to eliminate some of the most troublesome aspects of conventional rulemaking. But even its most ardent admirers stop well short of declaring it a panacea. No single reform, and perhaps no combination of reforms that have been offered to date, could fix the many problems critics had found with conventional rulemaking by the time this new technique was being widely discussed and seriously debated. The perceived problems of rulemaking reflect discontents with the larger political system, including those features that necessitate rulemaking in the first place. This leads some people to reject its claims to legitimacy and to question the need for it, despite the fact that its use began at the dawn of the republic (Schoenbrod, 1993). Those willing to accept its existence take strong issue with the way it is conducted and the results it produces.

Conventional rulemaking remains identified with provisions of the Administrative Procedure Act (APA), which are now more than fifty years old. Informal, or "notice and comment," rulemaking, is outlined in Section 553 of the APA. To comply with these provisions, an agency publishes a notice of proposed rulemaking and invites interested parties to submit written comments on the draft. The agency considers the comments in formulating a final rule, also published with an effective date in the *Federal Register*. This formula for rulemaking appears relatively easy and flexible for the agencies. But it grants few prerogatives to those who wish to participate and even fewer directions to agencies on the types of issues they are to consider when writing rules and on how such issues are to be handled. Over time, demands for greater access to agency decision making, combined with insistence that certain classes of issues be afforded special treatment, led to serial additions to the basic APA design. Through general statutes directed at all rulemaking—such as the National Environmental Policy Act and the Paperwork Reduction Act, through provisions in agency or program-specific statutes and presidential executive orders about different types of mandatory public participation, and through initiatives from the agencies themselves—rulemaking changed. As it became more complex procedurally, agency discretion declined apace.

Ironically, as the body of reform designed to improve rulemaking grew, so did criticism of the process (Susskind and McMahon, 1985). The indictments are many and admittedly mutually inconsistent. Some critics argue that too much rulemaking occurs, resulting in a choking of freedom and innovation. According to others there is too little rulemaking, resulting in inadequate protection of public health, safety, and general well-being. Rulemaking occurs too quickly for some, leading to what they think are ill-considered results, and too slowly for others, ensuring, in their eyes, obsolete results. Some critics claim that national agencies continue to exercise inappropriate and sometimes unconstitutional amounts of discretion when writing rules, leading to distortions of the democratic process. Others see agencies as so hamstrung by procedural requirements and cowed by gathering political pressure that they fail to exercise the discretion they were expressly created to use (McGarrity, 1992, p. 1385).

But these are general complaints about rulemaking, and their implications stretch well beyond the procedural dimension. The criticisms more directly tied to the rise of negotiated rulemaking deal with process itself. To these critics, conventional rulemaking procedures distort information and are intrinsically biased in favor of organized, well-resourced, and entrenched interests. Written information submitted by affected interests or coalitions of affected interests in response to a notice of proposed rulemaking in the *Federal Register* has been unilateral. Many subsequent procedural reforms, such as longer periods of public comment, disclosures of information, diversified means of information dissemination, public hearings, and even cross-examination do not penetrate to the core of these problems. Unless the parties involved devote considerable time and effort to review material submitted by others, their submissions are uninformed by alternative positions, and these different points of view go unanswered.

Conventional rulemaking encourages parties to present their views in largely adversarial, selective, and frequently extreme terms. An adversarial stance is assumed because parties focus the bulk of their energies on those parts of the proposed rule that threaten their interests (Harter, 1982). The information presented is selective because the purpose of the comment is to support a partisan position rather than to present a balanced, objective appraisal of what would best serve the public interest. The negative effects of selectivity in the presentation of information are exacerbated by a process that frustrates direct challenges or answers by those with different or opposing points of view. Extreme positions are frequently adopted because commenters know that contending points of view will be presented but they cannot predict their content with precision or certainty. In assuming an extreme point of view, parties expect agency personnel to seek a compromise that accommodates contending positions, and they hope for a more favorable result than they might achieve if they started with a more moderate, reasonable proposal (Harter, 1982, p. 19). Also, in a litigation-rich atmosphere such as that surrounding rulemaking, extreme positions establish starting points for bargaining should a lawsuit result in judicially supervised negotiations between parties and the agency (O'Leary, 1993, pp. 153–157).

Participation in conventional rulemaking is considered less than optimal for many of the same reasons that information quality is deemed flawed. Participation is potentially misdirected and always disproportionate. Failing to learn the positions taken by other parties, and their rationales, does not allow for the development and communication of a truly informed position. Of greater practical importance is that a given interest's influence is likely to be diminished because participants are deprived of the opportunity to consider the best arguments put forward by others. Participation is disproportionate because resources and sophistication determine its quality and impacts. Well-defined interests with economic power and technical sophistication are greatly advantaged in a rulemaking process that places high value on the quality and utility of information submitted. Broad-based interests with little access to technical information usually find themselves without the currency that is required for effective participation in rulemaking.

Shortcomings in information and participation in rulemaking contribute to subsequent problems in compliance and enforcement. Perceived flaws in the technical content of rules and participation that either appear unfair or promote no sense of ownership of the final rule damage credibility and legitimacy. These in turn damage compliance. Conventional rulemaking fails to educate the affected communities about the purpose and content of the rule and thus fails to prepare them for the often complex task of compliance (Kerwin, 1994). The failure of rulemaking in preparation for compliance leads directly to difficulties for the agency when the time comes to enforce the rule in an environment beset by ignorance, hostility, or both.

ELEMENTS OF NEGOTIATED RULEMAKING

To understand why the supporters of negotiated rulemaking believe it will improve upon more conventional processes, it is useful to review how the technique is expected to work. Except when otherwise noted, the following general description is drawn from Phillip Harter's work (1982), the Administrative Conference Recommendation (1982, 1985), and the Negotiated Rulemaking Act of 1990.

Selecting Rules and a Committee

Negotiated rulemaking begins with the agency's selection of a rule as a candidate for reg neg. Ideally, selection is based on criteria established in the scholarly and practitioner literature, included in part in the Administrative Conference Recommendation and the 1990 act. The act also requires the agency to issue a notice in the *Federal Register* regarding its intent to conduct a negotiated rulemaking and inviting interested parties to request membership on the negotiating committee. The notice is commonly supplemented with informal contacts between the agency and affected parties. This is a critical stage in the process because the breadth and quality of participation by the public is central to the maintenance of legitimacy and the quality of the ultimate product (Robinson, 1991, p. 129). The *Federal Register* notice also contains a "charter" for the negotiating committee, outlining its purpose and objectives and setting a date on which the committee will cease to function.

When membership is determined, the committee is convened, and it begins its work with the assistance of a professional facilitator—another crucial feature of the reg neg process. Hired and paid by the agency, the facilitator is usually an experienced professional mediator who is to maintain strict objectivity while moving the group to consensus. With the assistance of the facilitator, the committee establishes a set of protocols for its work, including an operational definition of consensus and a commitment on the part of the members to support a consensual result. Critical here is the status of the agency representatives, because they are participants in every sense of the word and are expected to have the authority to bind the agency to accept a negotiated result.

The negotiating committee may proceed with its work in varied ways once the operating protocols have been established. In the end, however, the committee will either succeed, succeed in part, or fail to reach consensus. When an agency seeks to adopt a consensus report as rules, it must still comply with the notice and comment provisions of the Administrative Procedure Act. This is the result that participants in reg neg ostensibly seek, but failed reg negs also have potential value.

According to the theoretical literature and governmental policy, to be selected for development using negotiation a rulemaking project should display certain characteristics. First, no attempt should be made to negotiate in a situation in which fundamental values are in opposition. If, for example, parties challenge the legal authority of the agency to write a given rule, it makes little sense to try to negotiate details that will be rejected as illegitimate per se. Those who have written from a base of experience with reg neg posit a number of other criteria worthy of mention. The issues in question should be sufficiently well defined to make it possible to assemble an effective working committee. That means that the necessary technical information needed to fashion the rule should be at hand or able to be developed with a reasonable expenditure of effort and that those affected by the rule should be known and encouraged to participate. This point raises a perennial dilemma for the administrative process. Some classes of interests, while identifiable, are insufficiently organized, resourced, or sophisticated to answer a general call for participation. In such cases the agency must decide how to reach these interests, explain the importance of the rule, and perhaps subsidize or otherwise support their involvement in the negotiation.

There are also criteria for the number of affected interests, the certainty of decision making, and the role of the government agency undertaking the development of the rule in question. Limits on the number of parties that can participate in a negotiation are necessary, because having too many participants renders the proceedings unmanageable. Harter suggests that a wise outer limit is twenty, but somewhat larger groups have successfully reached consensus. Certainty in decision making means a deadline and the knowledge that the agency will issue a rule whether or not the negotiation succeeds. Without these levers, those wishing simply to delay or avoid the rule and the costs it imposes can manipulate the negotiations and extend them indefinitely.

The role of the agency is complex. On the one hand, it cannot agree to accept every result a negotiating committee achieves, because it has the responsibility to carry out the law. On the other hand, no participant of substance will agree to make the investment a reg neg requires without the expectation that the agency will accept what is produced. This dilemma is more apparent than real. Selecting knowledgeable officials who have ready access to superiors and who are willing and able to use that access prevents negotiations from proceeding to a conclusion that the responsible agency cannot accept. Of course, the same approach needs to be taken by the nonagency participants in the negotiation. Delegation of authority issues are not confined to the public sector.

Process Innovations

Once these criteria are met and an issue appears to be a solid candidate for negotiated rulemaking, what is it about the process itself that promises a better result than the conventional alternative? Proponents offer a number of clear and attractive advantages that negotiated rulemaking enjoys. First, information flows to the decision-making process more freely and completely, and is treated more critically, in a negotiated rulemaking process than in a conventional, adversarial proceeding (Susskind and McMahon, 1985). Participants are charged with developing a proposed rule rather than commenting on someone else's proposal and preserving options for subsequent litigation. To influence the course of a rule that they have usually agreed in advance to support, their only currency is the information at their disposal and the persuasive strength of their arguments. The information and arguments presented are subjected to full discussion and the strongest challenges opponents can mount during the development of the proposal rather than in front of a judge presiding in a lawsuit.

Participation in negotiated rulemaking is vastly different, at least in intent and design, from what occurs in conventional rulemaking. Members of the negotiating committee are coproducers of the rule rather than distant critics or privileged insiders. Unidimensional participation through written comment or some other form of limited input that characterizes conventional rulemaking is transformed into a cooperative effort to draft actual rule language and develop basic supporting materials. Also, participation is better informed due to the sharing of high quality information.

As noted earlier, quality information and limited participation conspire to undercut compliance and complicate enforcement. Good quality information and participation that lead to acceptance of a rule and full knowledge of its contents among all those affected by it can immeasurably facilitate compliance and enforcement. If all who are supposed to be involved do in fact participate, completing the regulatory negotiation fully aware of their rights and obligations and accepting the results as legitimate, much of the compliance and enforcement problem goes away (Harter, 1982).

EXPERIENCE TO DATE

Negotiated rulemaking has been used by many agencies of the federal government (Pritzker and Dalton, 1990, ch. 10). However, the number of rules developed using reg neg remains a tiny fraction of the overall number of rules issued by government. Still, it is also true that the technique has been applied in a number of highly visible and controversial areas ranging from the amount of time airline crews can work to asbestos contamination of public schools. Nothing approaching a systematic study of negotiated rulemaking across the government has yet been attempted. Anecdotal reports and one empirical study of the use of negotiated rulemaking in the development of a number of rules by the Environmental Protection Agency (EPA) (Kerwin and Langbein, 1995) are available and provide valuable insights into the operational strengths and weakness of this method, certain aspects of its actual performance, and questions that remain about its value (also see Funk, 1987).

The available summary reports on attempted reg negs indicate that a majority of those attempted have concluded successfully. Most have either resulted in a consensus that became the proposed rule, or generated information that served as a basis for a rule that was eventually issued by the agency. Most of these reports contain little information about how a given rule was selected as a candidate for negotiated rulemaking. The results of the EPA study suggest that the desire to avoid litigation and delay in the implementation of important program elements were important factors in the selection of reg neg projects (Kerwin and Langbein, 1995, p. 7). With regard to the representation of interests, there is no evidence to suggest that exclusion of affected parties has been a significant problem. The EPA study indicates, however, that agencies may have to engage in extensive outreach to alert such interests and support the participation of some with limited resources. As always, there is a nagging concern that interests that have no organized representation in the form of a group or institution are ignored and have no public voice with which to protest. In this respect, negotiated rulemaking is no different from many governmental decision-making processes.

Information on the development of protocols for the negotiating committee is not available for all cases. The EPA study found that protocols were routinely developed and dealt with deadlines, the definition of consensus, communication with the press and other outside groups, behavior during negotiations, and commitments to support consensus agreements during the postnegotiation period. Facilitators, or "conveners," are commonly used. In most instances they are independent consultants, but in a few cases agency personnel are used in this capacity. The EPA study found that convenors performed a number of functions during the course of the negotiations, and evaluation indicates that they were generally viewed as contributing to consensus. Such personnel commonly assist in setting the protocols and ground rules for negotiations, provide basic training in the negotiation, set agenda, facilitate discussions, keep track of resolved and unresolved issues, and suggest ideas that may break impasses. The assessments of the performance of these facilitators vary somewhat, but the most common responses regarding their competence and objectivity have been positive. When criticisms are voiced, they vary considerably. For example, some may find the facilitator too passive; others may find the facilitator too intrusive or likely to defer to a particular type of participant, such as the sponsoring agency.

NEGOTIATING COMMITTEE OPERATIONS

Reports on the conduct of negotiations reveal a number of interesting features of the process. It is common for negotiating committees to reassemble into smaller work groups, normally organized around discrete technical issues (Perritt, 1986). Like-minded participants also form working coalitions, or caucuses, and attempt to reach consensus among themselves in order to present a strong bargaining position in the larger committee (Kerwin and Langbein, 1995). The charge of negotiation committees differs among agencies. In some, the negotiation committees continue their work through the publication of the final rule in the *Federal Register*. In the case of the EPA, the negotiating committee worked to produce the basis of proposed rules only. While the EPA participants generally remained involved in the development of final rules, that involvement was through bilateral communications with the agency rather than in full or partial committee meetings.

Beyond these basic observations about the mechanics of negotiation, one observation runs consistently throughout both the anecdotal reports and the EPA findings. Participation in a negotiated rulemaking is exceedingly demanding (National Institute of Dispute Resolution, 1986). The negotiation sessions are lengthy, difficult, and at times stressful. Some of the reported stress is attributed to the balance that participants must sometimes strike between the interests of the organization they represent and loyalty to the negotiating committee and process. The EPA study indicates that the pressures of membership on the negotiating committee can be substantial. When their organizations' delegations of authority are unclear to committee members, they are usually caused to communicate frequently with their superiors. In such circumstances, the work and stress increase. The preparation required to participate effectively can also be arduous, especially for those who come to the process without ready access to or familiarity with the full range of technical information relevant to the rule. Evidence indicates that obtaining the necessary information is an issue for many participants, and to get it they must rely on multiple sources (Kerwin and Langbein, pp. 20–22). For persons representing small organizations or firms, the demands can be especially burdensome because the reg neg is not the only matter with which they are concerned, and it must be managed in addition to their normal responsibilities. Here it is evident that the inequities that afflict conventional rulemaking cannot be entirely eliminated in negotiated rulemaking, although some reports indicate that considerable leveling of playing fields does occur (Susskind and McMahon, 1985). Large, wealthy, and sophisticated organizations enjoy the advantages of time and expertise, frequently assigning multiple specialists to a single negotiation. Relying on the sponsoring agency to help those who are disadvantaged to overcome disparities in resources and the asymmetries in information they create may be unrealistic. Participating agencies may face many of the same resource constraints that participants from smaller organizations confront.

QUALITY OF RESULTS

Evaluations of the quality of rules produced through negotiated rulemaking are very limited. The results of reg negs are infrequently litigated (Kerwin and Langbein, 1995, p. 34), which cannot be said for major rules developed by many of the same agencies using conventional techniques. There are, however, serious scholarly critiques of the legitimacy of negotiated rulemaking and the legality of some of its results. No systematic information exists regarding the compliance and enforcement dimensions of negotiated rules.

The EPA study indicates high levels of satisfaction among those who participated in those reg negs. Participants rate the resulting rules highly with regard to technical content, supporting information, ease of compliance, and ability to survive legal challenge. Participants are also very positive about their personal experiences during the negotiated rulemaking. They appear to value most highly what they learned during the process about the technical issues associated with the rule, the positions of other parties, and the task confronting the agency when it sets out to develop a rule.

CONCLUSION

In his seminal article devoted to negotiated rulemaking published more than a decade ago in the *Georgetown Law Journal,* Phillip Harter concluded that its widespread use was "worth a try" (Harter, 1982). Nothing that has occurred since then would cause one to challenge this modest recommendation, or to conclude that reg neg alone has or will revolutionize rulemaking. The use of fully realized negotiated rulemaking has been infrequent. Relatively low levels of use will probably continue, due in large part to the costs associated with the technique. However, it would be unfair to conclude that its impact has been negligible or is limited solely to the cases in which it has been fully applied.

Negotiated rulemaking has clearly contributed to the government-wide movement that seeks consensual means for resolving disputes. One would be hard-pressed to find a major regulation currently under development in which there is conflict that is proceeding without some type of negotiation. Certainly the historical concern that agencies would cede authority to pursue reasonable compromise has faded. Granted, major policy initiatives such as the National Performance Review deserve considerable credit, if that is the right word, for putting agencies in a mood to negotiate. But experiences with reg neg have also eased the path by demonstrating that becoming a party to negotiation does not automatically require that an agency suspend stewardship of the public interest. Negotiated rulemakings may never number in the hundreds per year for the simple reason that those involved in the public policy process have found other, less expensive ways to put to work the sound fundamental ideas of this approach.

References

Administrative Conference of the United States. "Administrative Conference Recommendation 82–4." In *Procedures for Negotiating Proposed Regulations.* Washington, D.C.: Administrative Conference of the United States, 1982 and 1985.

Funk, W. "When Smoke Gets in Your Eyes: Reg Neg and the Public Interest—EPA's Woodstove Standards." *Environmental Law*, 1987, *18*, 55–98.

Harter, P. "Negotiating Regulations: A Cure for the Malaise." *Georgetown Law Journal*, 1982, *71*, 1–113.

Kerwin, C. M. *Rulemaking: How Government Agencies Write Law and Make Policy.* Washington, D.C.: Congressional Quarterly Press, 1994.

Kerwin, C. M., and Langbein, L. *An Evaluation of Negotiated Rulemaking at the Environmental Protection Agency, Phase 1.* Washington, D.C.: Administrative Conference of the United States, 1995.

McGarrity, T. "Some Thoughts on Deossifying Rulemaking." *Duke Law Review*, 1992, *41*, 1385–1462.

National Institute of Dispute Resolution. "Regulatory Negotiation: Four Perspectives." *DR Forum*, Jan. 1986, p. 859.

O'Leary, R. *Environmental Change: Federal Courts and the EPA.* Philadelphia: Temple University Press, 1993.

Perritt, H. "Negotiated Rulemaking Before Federal Agencies: Evaluation of Recommendations of the Administrative Conference." *Georgetown Law Journal*, 1986, *74*, 1625–1692.

Perritt, H. "Administrative ADR: Development of Negotiated Rulemaking and Other Processes." *Pepperdine Law Review*, 1987, *14*, 863–920.

Pritzker, D., and Dalton, D. *Negotiated Rulemaking Sourcebook.* Washington, D.C.: Administrative Conference of the United States, 1990.

Robinson, G. *American Bureaucracy: Public Choice and Public Law.* Ann Arbor: University of Michigan Press, 1991.

Schoenbrod, D. *Power Without Responsibility: How Congress Abuses the People Through Delegation.* New Haven, Conn.: Yale University Press, 1993.

Susskind, L. E., and McMahon, G. "The Theory and Practice of Negotiated Rulemaking." *Yale Journal of Regulation*, 1985, pp. 133–165.

CHAPTER FOURTEEN

The "How Much Process Is Due?" Debate

Legal and Managerial Perspectives

Hal G. Rainey

Thorate his chapter brings together two perspectives on the subject of the due process rights of public employees—rights that arise in administrative adjudications both formal or informal. Legal scholars have developed an elaborate literature on these rights, and courts have rendered numerous decisions and opinions on them. However, what is generally less well known is that researchers in organizational behavior and psychology have produced a related body of evidence and insights on justice in work organizations. This research often focuses on procedural justice—the processes that organizations follow to provide fair and just treatment of employees, which is very much at the heart of the discussion of due process. Examination of the two bodies of work together raises interesting issues and ideas not only from the standpoint of employee rights but also as an important dimension of public management.

In a review of the literature on the legal dimension of employees' rights, this chapter generally accepts Cooper's depiction of the courts' development of due process rights for public employees (the court cases he analyzed are reviewed in Chapters Fifteen and Seventeen of this book). Cooper (1994) indicates that the courts, which for many years had been expanding due process protections, have more recently moved toward restricting employees' rights by such means as increasing the burden on an employee to show precisely defined damage to a specifically protected liberty or property right, for example, in a disciplinary action against him or her. Second, courts have adopted a "balancing test" formulation for use in decisions about due process for employees, rather than a more rights-based approach. Under these tests, when employees bring challenges on due process grounds, courts consider the costs to the organization of providing various degrees and types of due process balanced against the degree of damage or deprivation to the employee that results from the organization's action (*Cleveland Board of Education* v. *Loudermill*, 1985; *Connick* v. *Myers*, 1983; *Mathews* v. *Eldridge*, 1976; *Arnett* v. *Kennedy*, 1974). These developments suggest that the courts assume that due process is inherently costly to an organization and that they have been seeking to lower those costs by supporting greater managerial control over employees. These assumptions are examined here.

The chapter then turns to behavioral research on justice in organizations and points out that behavioral organizational justice results in important benefits for management and for those who work in organizations in all capacities. This research suggests that neither legal decision makers nor managers should assume that due process in organizations, involving such procedures as notice requirements and hearings, constitutes just a deadweight loss. Rather, well-designed provisions for due process and assurance of fair treatment can and should be part of an effective organizational strategy and indeed of an organization's culture.

THE LEGAL PERSPECTIVE

The elaborate development of the concept of due process includes a literature and body of law on administrative due process in general (Mashaw, 1985). Requirements are based on the Fifth and Fourteenth Amendments to the U.S. Constitution, which provide that no person can be deprived by government of life, liberty, or property without due process of law. In addition, many legal decisions and extensive scholarship have concentrated specifically on due process for government employees (Lewicki, 1988; Rosenbloom, 1988). The discussion of due process developed following World War II, during the abuses of the anti-Communist witch-hunt that drove thousands of public servants from government in a most arbitrary and capricious fashion. The discussion grew during the 1960s and early 1970s as the number of public servants, particularly state and local workers, grew dramatically. The bodies of literature and case law are richly interrelated, but they are also distinct in important ways.

Internal and External Due Process

This chapter employs a distinction between external and internal due process. External due process concerns the rules and procedures that an agency follows in its outside dealings and emphasizes the ways that these rules and procedures affect the due process rights of external parties. Generally speaking, the relevant situations are those in which agencies respond to claims by people or organizations for benefits or services or handle cases in which regulatory actions are taken against a business. Obviously, administrative law and public administration treat as fundamental topics the proper and effective constraints on administrative authority, the rights of persons facing agency action in relation to that authority, and what is just and fair in agencies' relations with people. Indeed, the watchword for due process in administrative actions is fundamental fairness. However, even when agencies take internal action, they must be alert to the institutional accountability mechanisms mandated by external political and legal actors, from legislatures to courts.

Internal due process pertains to decisions made, the procedures for reaching them, and the ways in which managers operate within the organization. Here the primary emphasis is on due process as it affects employees. The decisions are those that are made with respect to a particular employee and that therefore have the character of adjudications, as compared to general policies that affect all personnel. Notwithstanding the requirements of due process, some agencies have established careful review processes for such actions as a manager's decision to fire or discipline a person, while other agencies approach such matters far more loosely.

Walters (1994) reports a situation in which administrators in one state should have been on clear notice that the Supreme Court had ruled that a public agency must provide a hearing before taking significant disciplinary action against an employee. Even though the rulings had been widely publicized around the country, many administrators continued regularly to discharge employees without providing a hearing. The dismissals were often appealed to state personnel boards and ultimately overturned. Walters quotes a personnel board representative who complained about the incompetence of the managers and said that many of the employees deserved to be fired and that the managers had ignored the obvious requirement for a hearing.

It is ironic, though not surprising, to find that the same administrators who would never think of taking a significantly punitive action against a person or organization that is an external client of the agency without a hearing would undertake to dismiss employees without the process of a hearing. What the Constitution requires of agencies and officials is, at root, that they have the same concern for fundamental fairness and rudimentary protections for due process in their treatment of both clients and employees.

Employees differ from clients or others in their relations to a government agency, however, although it is not always easy to express these differences precisely. With varying degrees of formality and elaboration, employment involves a contract between employer and employee. The relationship inherently implies an agreement by the employee to cooperate reasonably with the organization's objectives and procedures. Indeed, where collective bargaining agreements exist, they often specify working relationships as well as the kind of process that is due, when it is due, and under what circumstances (see Chapters Sixteen and Thirty of this book). These agreements create relationships unlike those between agencies and clients.

In various ways, one can draw analogies between agency-employee relations and agency-client relations in that agencies must act lawfully—meaning in accord with due process—in each case. But such analogies are often strained, as the distinction between employees and outside parties illustrates. An outside person or organization that decides not to apply for the services of an agency or comply with rules, for whatever reasons, may inconvenience the agency in various ways, but often the individual or organization inconveniences herself or itself more. An employee absent from work for unacceptable reasons violates the contract with the agency and disrupts its operations and ability to serve clients and meet other objectives. Consider the difference between a person who tells a Social Security employee that she does not want to apply for her benefits because she does not feel like taking the time, and the employee of the agency who tells an applicant that he will not accept her application for Social Security benefits for the same reason. The applicant has that option, but the official does not.

One can understand, however, the problems that justices and other decision makers face in deciding the extent of an agency's claims on employees (Dwoskin, 1978). And of course these legal limits may not be the same as the special ethical obligations of governments toward employees, which are in turn more stringent than those of nongovernmental employers—that is, should governments be model employers? One can argue that, quite apart from the technical legal obligations, governments need to represent the highest values and aspirations of the nation in how they treat employees. Since government employers represent the authority of the state, a potentially monopolistic and powerful authority, exclusion from public employment by being rejected as an applicant, disciplined as an employee, or terminated are in several respects more severe sanctions when imposed by government than when carried out by a private employer. Exclusion from government employment is tantamount to being told that one is unfit for public service. By the same token, the Supreme Court has determined that government has special interests on behalf of all citizens with respect to the qualifications and performance of public employees and that it has concomitant special needs in connection with their supervision (*O'Connor v. Ortega*, 1987). Thus, for example, the Court has permitted drug testing for some public employees that would be unconstitutional if required of private citizens (*National Treasury Employees Union v. Von Raab*, 1989).

Further legal complications arise in relation to such issues as liberty and property rights in employment. Since the Fifth and Fourteenth Amendments restrict the authority of government to deprive people of life, liberty, or property without due process of law, it is important to consider just what interests are protected. When does a government employee have a property right to his or her job? Since a contract exists between employee and employer, it would seem that to take away the job that one possesses under this contract is like taking away a piece of property one had exchanged under contract. However, there is no basic right to public employment and there is usually considerable debate over just how much a particular employee is entitled to expect his or her position to be treated as a property interest. The courts have tended to look at the provisions of the contract, or such other sources as job-related statutes, to determine the extent of the property interest (Cooper, 1988). If, as part of a tenure arrangement, an agency tells employees that they cannot be fired except for certain specific causes, such as illegal or unethical behaviors, this becomes part of the contract and helps to define the property interests in the job. An abundance of research has shown that government organizations tend to have more extensive formal, written rules and provisions for employment, which reflects the stronger tendencies for such provisions in civil service systems (Rainey, Facer, and Bozeman, 1995). After all, these systems were created both to protect workers from abusive political machines and to protect the civil service as a system from those same machines, in the public interest. This suggests that government employment, as compared to employment in the private sector, may now involve more ways in which employees can claim property rights in their jobs (although the reverse was true until the 1960s).

There are continuing discussions about the similarities and differences between public and private sector employees. It has been argued that courts have eroded the principle of "employment at will" (work at the pleasure of the employer) by implying rights in employment even for private sector employees (Bockanic and Forbes, 1986; Lopatka, 1984). This erosion of the so-called at-will doctrine seems to make private sector employment look more like public employment. However, erosion of a distinction does not erase it. While observers might see areas of convergence, the law retains distinctions. Indeed, recent surveys show that managers in government are vastly more likely than their counterparts in the private sector to say that rules and procedures constrain their authority to fire poor performers (Rainey, Facer, and Bozeman, 1995). In part, that tendency has something to do with the lack of awareness by both public managers and many public administration academicians that courts have been moving rather dramatically away from the expansion of public employee protections, which had been the direction prior to the late 1970s, the 1980s, and particularly the 1990s (see *Waters* v. *Churchill*, 1994; *Connick* v. *Myers*, 1983; Cooper, 1994); and in part it is based on the fact that statutes and collective bargaining agreements have added constraints even as judges have moved away from mandating them on constitutional grounds. Even so, the Due

Process Clause applies to governments and not to the private sector, and the processes of human resources management must be conducted accordingly.

Due Process, Substantive Employee Rights, and Organizational Justice

Further complications arise in relation to employees' substantive constitutional rights as citizens, such as freedom of assembly and freedom of expression, and the degree to which a government employer can restrict those rights out of its concern for efficiency and effectiveness. Consider the case of *Bennett* v. *Thomson* (1976), in which a politically appointed, executive-level agency administrator who, having been asked a direct question about his own views, stated in a public meeting that he sharply disagreed with a decision by the governor to allow construction of a pulp mill that posed threats of environmental damage. The public employee was fired, and the courts upheld the dismissal against his claim that the termination violated his right to freedom of expression. Of course the key here was that he was a politically appointed policymaker and not a rank-and-file civil servant. Cooper also describes various cases in which employees were fired after criticizing the organization in which they were employed or its officials and subsequently appealed for reinstatement (Cooper, 1994, pp. 92–97).

Two important points are of interest here. First, there are differences between substantive legal protections afforded to employees that derive from the Bill of Rights, which are applied to the state and local governments through the Due Process Clause of the Fourteenth Amendment, and what is commonly called procedural due process, also protected by the Fourteenth Amendment (and by the Fifth Amendment for federal government agencies). For the most part, the discussion in this chapter focuses on procedural due process. However, the concept of organizational justice is much broader and addresses both process and substance. Still, even in law the relationships between substantive and procedural protections remain close.

A tendency in recent years has been to return to the so-called right-privilege dichotomy. For a long time public employees retained certain relatively inviolable rights, such as the constitutionally protected right of freedom of expression, that could not be restricted without a compelling interest (Cooper, 1994). The return to the long-rejected privilege concept means that when people accept public employment, many of their rights become privileges that can be revoked or diminished as a condition of employment (see *Rutan* v. *Republican Party of Illinois*, 1990, p. 80, Judge Antonin Scalia, dissenting; *Cleveland Board of Education* v. *Loudermill*, 1985, p. 536, Judge William Rehnquist, dissenting). Early in the history of the nation the courts leaned toward the privilege side of the dichotomy (see *McAuliffe* v. *Mayor of New Bedford*, 1892). In the wake of McCarthy-era abuses of government employees and in light of the growing numbers of citizens who would in effect be asked to forfeit their rights to serve the public, however, the courts rejected this dichotomy (*Keyishian* v. *Board of Regents,* 1967). In its place, the Supreme Court presented the doctrine of unconstitutional conditions, which holds that neither public jobs nor governmental benefits may be conditioned on the surrender of constitutional rights.

In particular, as government expanded with the New Deal and Great Society initiatives, and with the burgeoning growth of communities demanding a wide range of public services after World War II, litigation based on due process claims increased greatly. Mashaw (1985, pp. 6–9) points out that the Due Process Clauses are vague and ambiguous. This is one of the factors that gives due process an extensive domain that reaches into a long list of government policy and program areas—seemingly into any matter in which the procedures and activities of government agencies significantly impinge on the liberty or property of clients, citizens, or employees.

According to Mashaw's account, the explosion of due process activity during the 1960s and part of the 1970s produced ironies. Critics attacked the developments as having been both overly intrusive and underprotective at the same time (Mashaw, 1985, pp. 32–36). They argued that increased due process demands intruded extensively into administrative activities in ways that were often excessively costly, seemingly trivial, and apparently irrelevant to the problems at hand. Other critics charged that, in spite of the costs and intrusions on administrative operations, the due process mandates did not alone ensure protection of basic rights. Both sets of concerns had to be addressed simultaneously.

Some of these problems appear to have developed because of what seemed to be a flood of litigation and others because of responses to that litigation. That impression caused many administrators to approve the Burger Court's move toward the restoration of the right-privilege dichotomy. Thus, from the late 1970s through the mid-1990s, when an employee claimed that he or she was deprived of his or her job without due process, the Court was more likely than before to require the person to show that a property right had been violated. In the case of *Board of Regents* v. *Roth* (1972), for example, a college professor who had been fired brought suit claiming that he had been terminated without a hearing for criticizing the university. He claimed that he had a right under the Fourteenth Amendment not to have his freedom of expression restricted and a further right to due process—a hearing on his dismissal. There was an ironic response to the *Roth* ruling. The opinion was taken by some people who had not been reading earlier decisions to mark an expansion of due process protections, but the actual holding and disposition in the case really marked the beginning of a move in the other direction.

The Supreme Court moved toward recasting the Fourteenth Amendment rights as privileges when it upheld the firing on grounds that Roth had not demonstrated the loss of a liberty or property right that entitled him to a hearing. This moved the concept of rights in the direction of privileges because the

Court indicated stringent requirements that Roth had to meet or he would enjoy no protection at all. To claim a deprivation of a liberty right, he had to show that the university had damaged and stigmatized him. Concerning property rights, the Court said that such rights do not come directly from the Constitution but are created by state law, rules, or contracts. For someone like Roth, they said, these property rights were defined by the conditions of his employment, and he had not shown that the university, in employing him, had extended to him the rights he claimed. Thus rights became more susceptible to definition by employing organizations (or other sources such as statutes) and hence more like privileges that those organizations could bestow or withhold.

Cooper points out that legal scholars have criticized *Roth* and similar rulings on the grounds that they tend to make rights manipulable. One can indeed complain that the Court acknowledged that a person might have freedom of speech and related due process rights severely restricted by an organization, but the person faced the burden of showing that the organization somehow promised to extend those rights. Critics have complained that the Court indicated that it is not fundamental fairness that must govern the organization's treatment of employees and that the decision would allow wrong decisions and severe harm to employees unless they could show that they were somehow vested with rights by agreement with the organization or by other sources such as state law.

Moreover, the use of balancing tests to determine when, whether, and how much process is due (see *Waters* v. *Churchill,* 1994; *Cleveland Board of Education* v. *Loudermill,* 1985; *Connick* v. *Myers,* 1983) has tended to make employee claims look more like requests to enjoy privileges rather than the assertion of protected rights (Cooper, 1994). Such balancing tests have been extended to all areas of civil due process litigation, in both the internal and external senses described earlier (Mashaw, 1985, pp. 46–47). Under this formulation, in considering a due process claim the Court takes into consideration the government's interest in expedient procedures and lower costs, the magnitude of the interest of the private parties, and the possible contribution of various procedures that might be required to reach an accurate, factual finding in the dispute (*Mathews* v. *Eldridge,* 1976, p. 335). In employee relations and with respect to substantive claims to rights like free speech, the Court also employs a balancing test, this time to determine whether the interests of the employer outweigh the interests of the employee in those rights (*Waters* v. *Churchill,* 1994; *Connick* v. *Myers,* 1983).

The return to the privilege approach and the tendency to use ad hoc balancing tests create management as well as legal difficulties. They tend to assume the primacy of a "Theory X" management orientation. This assumption refers to Douglas McGregor's now-classic distinction between Theory X management, which assumes that employees are lazy and in need of direction and hierarchical control, and a Theory Y approach that assumes that employees have the capacity for self motivation and self direction (McGregor, 1960). The pessimistic view is that managers should impose strict controls and directions on employ-ees, while the optimistic theory implies the value of more employee self direc-tion and participation in important decisions. The literature on management and organizational behavior has generally accepted Theory Y assumptions, but courts generally have not turned to this literature that suggests the value of enhancing rather than restricting certain aspects of due process for employees.

ORGANIZATIONAL JUSTICE IN MANAGEMENT AND BEHAVIOR LITERATURE

In this second body of literature, the predominance of optimistic, Theory Y assumptions leads to an emphasis on decentralized, participative management. Building on conclusions of the human relations movement, long-term trends were in that direction, as exemplified in the research on organizational justice within the field of organizational behavior. That field, sometimes referred to as industrial and organizational psychology, grew out of the fields of industrial psychology and related fields such as social psychology. Researchers in this area study the behavior and psychology of people in work settings. They ana-lyze such topics as motivation, incentives, leadership, work satisfaction, and group processes in the workplace. In the last several decades, research on moti-vation and related topics has produced an extensive body of work on organi-zational justice. This research has emphasized procedures for providing justice, making the evidence produced quite relevant to the due process debate. Sim-ply put, this research finds that justice in organizations is a positive force (Greenberg, 1996; Sheppard, Lewicki, and Minton, 1992; Murnighan, 1993). Providing justice in the distribution of outcomes and in the procedures for dis-tributing those outcomes, and for making other decisions, has beneficial effects on important organizational dimensions. These research results suggest that legal decision makers considering due process in organizations should not assume that due process is inherently costly and burdensome to the organiza-tion. One can argue, as some organizational behavior researchers do (Shep-pard, Lewicki, and Minton, 1992; Lawler, Mohrman, and Ledford, 1995), that well-developed procedures for justice in organizations contribute to productive management. Such procedures can play an essential role in the strategy and culture of effective organizations.

This difference between the trends in the courts and the developments in behavioral research resembles a similar conflict between approaches to man-agement implicit in much civil service reform activity, on the one hand, and the contemporary literature on organizations and management, on the other. Civil service reforms in the United States and some other countries have often emphasized the enhancement of managerial controls, especially in such matters as pay, termination, assignments, and discipline. Among other objectives, the Civil Service Reform Act of 1978 sought to streamline procedures for firing employees and to tighten connections between pay and performance by giving managers more authority to base pay raises on performance ratings. In subsequent years, governments around the United States and in other nations undertook pay-for-performance programs, usually to little avail (Ingraham, 1993; Kellough and Lu, 1993). In a recent example of this trend, the governor of Georgia proposed legislation in 1996 that would phase out civil service and merit system protections for state employees, and the state legislature has passed the measure (see Chapter Twenty of this book). Implicit in these trends is the assumption that public sector management will be improved by tightening managerial control and streamlining procedures for carrying out disciplinary or compensation decisions.

This recent tendency in public sector reform runs counter to a continuing, powerful orientation to the contrary in management literature (Lawler, Mohrman, and Ledford, 1995; Hersey and Blanchard, 1992). As noted earlier, for more than half a century there has been increasing emphasis in management thought on the effectiveness of more flexible, humane management techniques and structures that emphasize such intrinsic incentives as interesting work, a sense of membership in a desirable and supportive group, and a sense of growth, development, responsibility, and participation in important decisions. The fairly standard position in this literature treats classic models of organization, which emphasize strong chains of command, hierarchical control, precise job descriptions, and strict rules, as too inflexible for the complexities and challenges that contemporary organizations face (see, for example, Daft, 1995). In addition, management pundits condemn such modes of organization as too stifling to motivate employees, especially the highly professionalized and educated people who work in many contemporary organizations. If anything, these themes have reached a crescendo in recent years, with writers on organizations and management pouring out books on team-based management, transformational and visionary leadership, and seamless organizations (Rainey, 1996). Major topics in management writing and practice—such as strategic management, organizational culture, and total quality management—incorporate many of these themes. Writers and practitioners advocate teamwork, participation, and motivation through shared values and a sense of shared mission and vision, as opposed to more narrowly self-interested concentration on material rewards.

Certainly there are problems in assessing the value of these prescriptions and the extent of their valid use in organizations. However sincere in principle are the scholars and experts who claim that these approaches support productive management, in practice these approaches may have mainly produced abundant hypocrisy and torrential psychobabble. The *Dilbert* cartoon strip that came into prominence in the mid-1990s quickly achieved wide popularity by aggressively mocking the oblique doubletalk that these management themes have engendered in business firms. Rather than depicting work organizations as positive examples of these values, the strip depicts them as havens for incompetent, selfish, manipulative managers (Levy, 1996). In addition, the recent "downsizing" strategies adopted by many organizations have made even more glaring the incongruity of the corporate executives who talk about teamwork and shared mission as they draw millions of dollars in total compensation and abruptly lay off employees with long service in their firms. Trends that sweep business often sweep government a little later, and government employees now complain of "flavor of the month" management or "management by best-seller" as the executives in their agencies embrace a succession of gurus who advise on visioning, reinventing, reengineering, managing quality, or some other pattern of salvation.

Even widespread abuse of principles in contemporary management thought does not invalidate those principles, however. Many of them developed out of careful observation of successful firms (see, for example, Burns and Stalker, 1961; Peters and Waterman, 1982; Lawler, Mohrman, and Ledford, 1995). Clear examples and considerable evidence demonstrates that serious, well-designed applications of the high-involvement management described earlier are commonly supportive of effective organizations.

The contrast between the orientation in the courts and organizational management thought is similar to contrasts between civil service reforms and these same trends. Judges have many justifications for staying out of an agency's dealings with its employees, such as a conservatism about the extent of their legitimate authority and a reasonable concern for effective management of their own resources. In the balancing test formulation, however, the justices of the U.S. Supreme Court have explicitly stated an intention to consider the costs to the organization of due process requirements. However, assessing costs to both parties to a dispute is a problem inherent in the balancing tests for both internal and external applications (Mashaw, 1985, p. 47), because the costs are typically hard to specify and measure. As suggested earlier, however, the balancing test appears to assume that due process requirements tend to be costly and burdensome to the organization. In the very imprecise process of assessing those costs, the evidence from research on organizational justice needs to be taken into account. That evidence suggests that due process for people in organizations can have benefits for organizational effectiveness and that these benefits can outweigh the costs.

Research on Organizational Justice

Researchers on justice in organizations have developed a distinction between distributive justice and procedural justice that has similarities to the distinction that legal scholars make between substantive and procedural due process.

Distributive justice concerns the degree of justice in the distribution of outcomes in the organization. For example, if two employees both make the same contributions to the organization during a year and they both receive the same pay raise at the end of that year, most people would regard that distribution as fair and just. Procedural justice concerns whether the procedures used in distributing the outcomes is just. The two employees who got the same raise may regard the raises as just but not the procedures used in awarding the raises. If a superior awarded the raises based on his unaccountable, subjective decision and gave no raise to a coworker whom the two employees regarded as equally deserving, they might regard the process as unjust. Mashaw (1985, p. 5) points out that the concepts of substantive and procedural due process overlap, and so do the concepts of procedural and distributive justice. Concepts can be overlapping and still refer to useful distinctions, however. Researchers have shown that the distinction between procedural and distributive justice is useful in analyzing different aspects of organizational justice and predicting different outcomes from it. Similarly, while from an employee point of view substantive and procedural due process may come together, they are in fact legally distinct.

Greenberg (1996) describes the topic of organizational justice as having begun with an emphasis on distributive justice and moved toward an emphasis on procedural justice, especially as perceived by the subjects of the procedures. He cites the equity theory of work motivation as one of the early developments on the topic of organizational justice. Adams (1965) developed equity theory, drawing on theories of social comparison processes and theories of cognitive balance and cognitive consistency from social psychology. Theories of social comparison processes are concerned with how people use other people as references in assessing themselves. Theories of cognitive consistency are concerned with how people try to maintain consistency and balance among such cognitive factors as their beliefs and values. Researchers on cognitive dissonance have analyzed, among other matters, how people respond to evidence of the dissonance or inconsistency of their beliefs and values, such as evidence that they made bad decisions about purchasing an item, which threatens their images of themselves as rational, informed decision makers. People find that such dissonance is unpleasant and they take steps to reduce or avoid it.

Adams's equity theory long ago posited that people in organizations experience discomfort when they feel they are being underrewarded or overrewarded in comparison to other members of the organization that they choose as referents. According to the theory, people place a value on just and equitable treatment for themselves and others. They assess the level of equity in their organization by comparing themselves to others who are regarded as appropriate referents. They observe the levels of outcomes or rewards that they receive from the organization in relation to the levels of their contributions and inputs. They compare this balance between rewards and contributions to that of a referent person or persons. If people perceive themselves as underrewarded in comparison to another person, they experience inequity and seek to avoid that sense of wrong. For example, workers may speed up their work when they feel overpaid and slow down if they feel underpaid.

More important, equity in organizations and in human life is obviously a significant factor, regardless of whether all the propositions in Adams's particular theory have been proved—that is, whether or not people actually speed up work when overpaid on an hourly basis, and other specific propositions. The general significance of equity theory is that it makes the point that equity (just treatment) in organizations is important. It can influence motivation, job satisfaction, and the attitudes of employees toward the organization and each other. This simple proposition made equity theory one of the seminal influences on the work of Greenberg (1996) and others who have carried on the research on organizational justice.

As Greenberg also says, however, equity theory concentrates mainly on distributive justice, and much of the recent research on organizational justice has analyzed procedural justice, especially in the sense of the perception of it by recipients of the treatment. Researchers in social psychology have often found that people were more likely to feel that they had received fair treatment when they had some control over the process, such as a voice in it, especially in the form of opportunities to influence the information that was communicated and the evidence that was used in the proceeding. Procedures providing a person with some influence or voice made the person feel that both the procedures and the results were fairer. In effect, these researchers found confirmation of the principles expressed in a statement by an Egyptian of the Sixth Dynasty, circa 2300–2150 B.C., quoted by Mashaw (1985, p. vii): "Not all one pleads for can be granted, but a good hearing soothes the heart."

Researchers in the field of organizational behavior have found evidence that procedural justice in organizations has beneficial effects for individuals who receive it and for their organizations in general. Alexander and Ruderman (1987), for example, found that people with more positive perceptions of procedural justice in their organizations evidenced greater trust in management, gave higher evaluations of their superiors, and indicated greater job satisfaction. They also showed less intention to turn over (to quit the organization). Greenberg (1996, pp. 32–33) reports similar findings. These organizational behavior researchers have explored several different theories, dimensions, and typologies of organizational justice and have developed prescriptive models that offer guidance to achieve it (Sheppard, Lewicki, and Minton, 1992).

There are many additional dimensions and issues in the research and theory of organizational justice, but the conclusions reviewed above and the discussions to this point support two general propositions. First, effective and efficient organization and management are not necessarily enhanced through increasing the hierarchical controls that superiors have over subordinates, especially if powers are exercised in relatively unaccountable and arbitrary ways. Heavy emphasis on such conditions can actually damage organizational effectiveness. Second, organizational procedures that provide and demonstrate fair treatment for employees can be highly beneficial as part of the culture and strategy of an efficient, effective organization.

Judges and other decision makers need to take these propositions seriously into account in their considerations of internal due process issues of the sort presented by employees. In a balancing test considering costs to organizations and costs to plaintiffs, all concerned should avoid assumptions that due process imposes deadweight costs and represents only a burden. Rather, an organization can gain net benefits from the practice of just and fair procedures and from having a reputation for that kind of management.

One of the common complaints among public managers is not an attack against due process for employees in personnel actions but a concern about excessive procedural constraints that seemingly provide elaborate protections for flagrantly bad employees. These procedures, they complain, make it extremely costly and time-consuming for a manager to deal with an employee who is simultaneously stubborn and unproductive. As mentioned earlier, surveys of public and private managers in a wide variety of organizational settings show that government managers are vastly more likely than private sector managers to report that rules governing terminations in their organizations make it difficult to remove a poorly performing employee (Rainey, Facer, and Bozeman, 1995). One implication of the public managers' complaints is that complex due process requirements for public employees actually produce a sense of organizational injustice that the equity theory described earlier would predict. The good performers must watch as the bad performers evade accountability for their poor performance while receiving rewards equal to those of the good performers.

TOWARD ORGANIZATIONAL JUSTICE: GOOD MANAGEMENT AND GOOD LAW

The complications described in this chapter strain the connection between organizational justice, organizational costs and performance, and legal issues of due process. The evidence of the beneficial influences of organizational justice is convincing. As this chapter has indicated, a fairly strong agreement exists among management experts and scholars that supports the value to an organization of positive attitudes on the part of members, including trust, commitment, satisfaction, and other perceptions that can be enhanced by organizational fairness. Research also supports the value of a well-developed organizational culture and strategy, designed with as comprehensive an approach to major organizational dimensions as possible, including justice for employees. Among many examples of the justification for this perspective is the fact that while evidence about the relation of work satisfaction to productivity is mixed, evidence of a relationship between work satisfaction and other important—and expensive—responses, such as absenteeism, sabotage, and turnover, is stronger. Greenberg's findings (1996) about the role of justice in, for example, reducing theft should be adequate to convince managers that the results can be well worth the effort to enhance organizational justice through such devices as the effective use of due process concepts of notice, fair hearing, reasoned decisions, and a fair decision maker.

Complaints about excessive rules and protections for public employees have been matters of debate for years. Many experts take the position that the problems that public managers encounter in dealing with the rules and procedures that protect public employees are matters of the managers' own making (Walters, 1994). They say that managers blame the procedures for their own inadequate mastery and use of them and that complications often could be avoided if managers would simply carry out the procedures properly and perform well as managers in the first place. Similarly, where court cases go well beyond issues of procedures for terminations and discipline and raise questions about substantive rights, the complaints are not in truth about procedural due process. In such instances, it is nevertheless important to avoid compounding difficulties by making procedural errors.

In sum, the research and theory on justice in organizations offer no simple formula for use in balancing tests or for determining precisely how much process is due to public employees in any particular setting. They do, however, provide considerable evidence that procedural justice, and its legal analogue in due process protections, can benefit an organization in practical ways. There are many reasons for courts to discourage wasteful, unnecessary litigation over due process rights, to manage their own workload carefully, to make sound decisions about the extent of their authority, and to consider the costs and burdens that due process requirements impose. If balancing tests are to be used that involve considerations of costs to agencies, however, a sophisticated assessment of those costs would also recognize the benefits to organizations that come with organizational justice. Recognizing the basic dignity of employees and providing reasonableness and fairness through due process protections, rather than simply burdening an organization, should be part of an effective strategy for the organization's success.

Cases Cited

Arnett v. Kennedy, 416 U.S. 134 (1974).

Bennett v. Thomson, 363 A.2d 187 (N.H., 1976).

Board of Regents v. Roth, 408 U.S. 564 (1972).

Cleveland Board of Education v. *Loudermill,* 470 U.S. 532 (1985).

Connick v. *Myers,* 461 U.S. 138 (1983).

Keyishian v. *Board of Regents,* 385 U.S. 589 (1967).

Mathews v. *Eldridge,* 424 U.S. 319 (1976).

McAuliffe v. *Mayor of New Bedford,* 29 N.E. 517 (Mass., 1892).

National Treasury Employees Union v. *Von Raab,* 489 U.S. 532 (1989).

O'Connor v. *Ortega,* 480 U.S. 709 (1987).

Rutan v. *Republican Party of Illinois,* 497 U.S. 62 (1990).

Waters v. *Churchill,* 511 U.S. 661 (1994).

References

Adams, J. S. "Inequity in Social Exchange." In L. Berkowitz (ed.). *Advances in Experimental and Social Psychology.* Orlando, Fla.: Academic Press, 1965.

Alexander, S., and Ruderman, M. "The Role of Procedural and Distributive Justice in Organizational Behavior." *Social Justice Research,* 1987, *1,* 177–198.

Bockanic, W. N., and Forbes, J. B. "The Erosion of Employment At-Will: Managerial Implications." *SAM Advanced Management Journal,* 1986, *51,* 16–21.

Burns, T., and Stalker, G. M. *The Management of Innovation.* London: Tavistock, 1961.

Cooper, P. J. *Public Law and Public Administration.* (2nd ed.) Upper Saddle River, N.J.: Prentice Hall, 1988.

Cooper, P. J. "Reinvention and Employee Rights: The Role of the Courts." In P. W. Ingraham and B. S. Romzek (eds.), *New Paradigms for Government: Issues for the Changing Public Service.* San Francisco: Jossey-Bass, 1994.

Daft, R. L. *Organization Theory and Design.* (5th ed.) St. Paul, Minn.: West, 1995.

Dwoskin, R. P. *Rights of Public Employees.* Chicago: American Library Association, 1978.

Greenberg, J. *The Quest for Justice on the Job.* Thousands Oaks, Calif.: Sage, 1996.

Hersey, P., and Blanchard, K. H. *Management of Organizational Behavior.* (6th ed.) Upper Saddle River, N.J.: Prentice Hall, 1992.

Ingraham, P. W. "Of Pigs in Pokes and Policy Diffusion: Another Look at Pay-for-Performance." *Public Adminsitration Review,* 1993, *53,* 348–356.

Kellough, J. E., and Lu, H. "The Paradox of Merit Pay in the Public Sector." *Review of Public Personnel Administration,* 1993, *13,* 45–64.

Lawler, E. E. III, Mohrman, S. A., and Ledford, G. E. Jr . *Creating High Performance Organizations: Survey of Practices and Results of Employee Involvement and TQM in Fortune 1000 Companies.* San Francisco: Jossey-Bass, 1995.

Levy, S. "Working in Dilbert's World." *Newsweek,* Aug. 12, 1996, pp. 52–57.

Lewicki, R. J. "The Public Face of Justice: Ineffective Management of Organizational Justice Problem." In J. Greenberg and R. J. Bies (eds.), *Communicating Fairness in*

Organizations. Symposium presented at the Academy of Management, Anaheim, Calif., 1988.

Lopatka, K. T. "The Emerging Law of Wrongful Discharge." *Business Lawyer,* 1984, *40,* 1–32.

Mashaw, J. L. *Due Process in the Administrative State.* New Haven, Conn.: Yale University Press, 1985.

McGregor, D. *The Human Side of Enterprise.* New York: McGraw-Hill, 1960.

Murnighan, J. K. *Social Psychology in Organizations: Advances in Theory and Research.* Upper Saddle River, N.J.: Prentice Hall, 1993.

Peters, T. J., and Waterman, R. H. *In Search of Excellence: Lessons from America's Best-Run Companies.* New York: HarperCollins, 1982.

Rainey, H. G. "Developing an Effective Organizational Culture." In J. L. Perry (ed.), *Handbook of Public Administration.* (2nd ed.) San Francisco: Jossey-Bass, 1996.

Rainey, H. G. *Understanding and Managing Public Organizations.* (2nd ed.) San Francisco: Jossey-Bass, 1997.

Rainey, H. G., Facer, R., and Bozeman, B. "Repeated Findings of Sharp Differences Between Public and Private Managers' Perceptions of Personnel Rules." Paper presented at the Annual Meeting of the American Political Science Association, Chicago, Aug. 31–Sept. 3, 1995.

Rosenbloom, D. H. "The Public Employment Relationship and the Supreme Court in the 1980s." *Review of Public Personnel Administration,* 1988, *8,* 49–65.

Sheppard, B. H., Lewicki, R. J., and Minton, J. W. *Organizational Justice: The Search for Fairness in the Workplace.* San Francisco: The New Lexington Press, 1992.

Walters, J. "Booting Out Bad Bureaucrats." *Governing,* 1994, *7,* 34–39.

PART FIVE

CIVIL SERVANTS, SUPERVISORS, AND CHANGING LAW

Probably no area of public management has experienced more dynamic changes in the relationship between law and administration than human resources management and personnel, the subjects of the chapters in Part Five. This section addresses a wide range of issues related to these areas, including such topics as the constitutional free speech rights of public servants; labor relations authorities, techniques, and conflict resolution; privacy and integrity protection processes for public employees; questions of race and gender in modern administration; and even how such issues come together in the reconceptualization of public personnel systems.

At the broad constitutional level, one of the most revealing aspects of law and human resources management has been the changing nature of First Amendment freedoms enjoyed by public employees and the limits that government employers may place on these freedoms. David M. O'Brien addresses many of these questions in Chapter Fifteen. He points out that the challenge is to reconcile public employees' expectations that they should be able to enjoy the same freedoms of speech, press, and association as other citizens with governments' interests in maintaining responsible and productive workforces.

The challenge is to reconcile the needs and expectations of increasingly diverse public employees while also maintaining controls that are intended to limit systems of political spoils and ensure professional expertise in public service. Thus limitations on partisan political activities continue to be of real concern, whether those activities involve high-level employees at the U.S. Commerce Department, who become deeply engaged in campaign finance activities (as in the Clinton Administration), or the desire by local government employees to take active roles in local political representation. As O'Brien points out, such issues have been more or less continuously in play for years, with the most recent round coming in the 1993 passage of the Federal Employees Political Activities Act.

Even in matters that might be labeled pure speech, the debate continues over how to reconcile competing interests. Thus O'Brien explains the evolution of Supreme Court interpretations of when a public employee's free speech ends and the authority of the manager to control agency operations takes priority. O'Brien points out that, contrary to many common assumptions among administrators, the Court's rulings have moved in the direction of recognizing the necessary interests of managers.

While constitutional provisions are basic, Norma M. Riccucci points to the importance of understanding that most disputes in labor relations are about statutory or contractual rights and processes. These, she observes in Chapter Sixteen, are resolved by varied processes. It is the challenge of operating simultaneously within several frameworks that characterizes dispute resolution. In particular, Riccucci highlights issues associated with negotiated grievance procedures that in some circumstances supplant civil service rules and processes.

Riccucci examines the uses of arbitration and some of its associated uncertainties. What is assumed to be a process designed to reach a final decision may not in fact be final. Uncertainties can arise because of varied rules about just how binding arbitration is in different contexts. They may arise in cases with mixed questions, only some of which are subject to arbitration. Or they may occur because of the process of judicial review of arbitrators' decisions. In the end, Riccucci finds needs for streamlining and clarification, not only in the managers' interest but also to benefit employees.

N. Joseph Cayer (Chapter Seventeen) examines rights to privacy in contexts of integrity testing of public employees. With respect to privacy rights, he examines searches and seizures, polygraph testing, and the use of data gathered through medical examinations.

Cayer deals with a set of ongoing tensions between what may appear as reasonable but contrary arguments presented by both employers and employees. In working out these close conflicts in actual cases, Cayer reports that much depends on the particular types of employees as well as on the purposes and nature of testing. It is one thing to require drug testing of an airplane pilot or other transportation employee, but it may be quite another to require blanket testing of all employees in an agency not assigned to inherently sensitive or dangerous activities.

In the case of medical testing, Cayer points out, public sector employers must take care not to discriminate on the basis of physical condition in violation of the Americans with Disabilities Act. Yet it is necessary to protect obviously legitimate interests of employers in knowing the health conditions of employees. Cayer points out that, ironically, private sector employees retain more protections against the use and abuse of polygraph testing by their employers than do government workers. He provides a useful explanation of the uses as well as the limitations of polygraphs and psychological screening of employees. He points out that public service is a long way from resolution with respect to these screening and testing issues, and he warns that it will take considerable time for the law, as well the policies, in these areas to evolve.

If any certainty characterizes today's public sector workforce it is that those who make up the public service sector are far more diverse than ever before. At the same time, there is considerable reason to believe that much more needs to be done if the public sector workforce is, as President Clinton has put it, to look like America. Conversely, opposition has grown to some affirmative action strategies employed in support of that goal. Maxine Kurtz, a long-time practitioner of public personnel law and administration, addresses those tensions in Chapter Eighteen.

Kurtz explores the debates over affirmative action in a broad, applied compass, paying heed that the contemporary version of the argument is quite different from the argument during the early years of affirmative action. Having reviewed the many dimensions of the problem, Kurtz seeks to give guidance to public managers about the various forms and approaches to affirmative action— those that are permissible and those that are perhaps no longer acceptable tools for enhancing diversity, lest they subject their users to charges of reverse discrimination that the courts might support.

Clearly one of the most important changes in public sector workforce profiles in the past twenty-five years is the rise in the number of women in key positions throughout government. In Chapter Nineteen, Mary E. Guy and Stacey Simpson Calvert address in depth the key issues presented by this important change.

Guy and Calvert lay out in practical detail the legal framework constructed to open the public sector to women and to prohibit gender discrimination. It is a framework made up of virtually all of the policy tools addressed earlier, from statutes to regulations to executive orders to judicial precedents. It covers everything from outright gender barriers to employment to equal pay issues and sexual harassment problems. While the basic need to protect women from workplace discrimination is not a topic of debate, the more specific issues of affirmative action, veterans preference, and reproductive safety certainly are. Chapter Nineteen addresses all of these concerns and more.

Guy and Calvert anchor their assessment of progress to date and of the problems that remain to be adequately addressed by focusing first on confronting assumptions about the employment of men and women. Like Cayer, they recognize that, because of the fundamental nature of the issues at play in this field, change tends to be evolutionary rather than revolutionary. Still, they argue for more effective mechanisms by which women and their employers can move toward gender equality and not make women's rights dependent upon the whims of shifting public opinion and excruciatingly slow social change.

In Chapter Twenty, Lloyd G. Nigro moves beyond the individual areas of public sector human resources management addressed previously to provide an example of fundamental change in the public service arena. He uses the case of Georgia's efforts to abandon civil service as it has been structured and to move toward a decentralized, at-will type of employment. In such a system, centralized civil service offices are transformed from regulatory bodies into consulting groups used to assist individual agencies and managers in addressing human resources management challenges. To some extent, Nigro finds at the root of this radical move a tendency to dichotomize between public-law-based principles of civil service and assumptions that effective human resources management is blocked by the same public law premises.

In the end, however, serious questions are raised about the abandonment of merit principles buttressed by public law in a rush to achieve responsiveness. Dangers are posed by the Georgia strategy. Nigro recalls former days when the key value in public sector management was responsiveness to political bosses without regard to merit. Indeed, he explores what is missing in the kind of approach used by Georgia and the institutional and management problems that approach is likely to entail. In so doing, Nigro provides the counterbalance in the area of human resources management that Moe insisted on in Chapter Three as necessary in public administration. The tendency to jump quickly away from public law perspectives can bring with it a variety of serious costs for managers and for the public they serve.

CHAPTER FIFTEEN

The First Amendment and the Public Sector

David M. O'Brien

The tensions between politics and administration are deeply rooted in the history of the federal government and public administration. Those tensions have been exacerbated by growth in the size of government as well as by new claims by public employees to the protection of the First Amendment. The First Amendment guarantees the freedoms of speech and the press as well as the freedoms of association and to engage in political activities (*Sweezy* v. *New Hampshire*, 1957; *National Association for the Advancement of Colored People* v. *Alabama*, 1958). Those guarantees have also been interpreted to apply against state and local governments no less than the federal government (*Gitlow* v. *New York*, 1925; *Near* v. *Minnesota*, 1931). The First Amendment rights of public employees, however, are limited and circumscribed by legislation and rulings of the Supreme Court (O'Brien, 1995).

In general, both Congress and the Supreme Court have attempted to accommodate public employees' interests in free speech and association with governmental interests in an efficient and productive workforce. To be sure, the reconciliation of these competing interests has not been easy and the lines of accommodation have shifted as well as become more complex. Although Congress and the Court have considerably broadened public employees' freedoms of speech and association since the end of World War II, public employees still remain subject to numerous prohibitions and restrictions.

POLITICAL EXPRESSION AND ACTIVITIES

Throughout much of the nineteenth century, the federal government was dominated by a political spoils system. Federal employment was viewed as a reward for partisan loyalty. With the passage of the Pendleton Act in 1883, however, Congress moved in the direction of creating a merit-based system of federal employment. Subsequently, in 1907 President Theodore Roosevelt amended civil service rules to provide that employees covered by the rules could take no "active part" in political campaigns. Three decades later, the expansion of the government under President Franklin D. Roosevelt's New Deal programs and growing concerns about politicians' manipulation of civil service employees moved Congress to revisit the issue of banning partisan activities by federal employees. In 1939, Democratic Senator Carl Hatch from New Mexico succeeded in pushing through Congress the first "Hatch Act," officially titled "An Act to Prevent Pernicious Political Activities."

One of the most controversial Hatch Act provisions was that "no officer or employee in the executive branch of the Federal Government, or any agency or department thereof, shall take part in political management or political campaigns. All such persons shall retain the right to vote as they may choose and to express their opinions on all political subjects" (53 U.S. Statutes 1147 [1939]). This and other provisions of the Hatch Act were extended in 1940 to state and local employees whose programs were funded by the federal government (54 U.S. Statutes 767 [1940]). Public employees could still register and vote in elections, attend political conventions and rallies, and participate in nonpartisan activities, for example. But they were barred from holding office in political parties, soliciting funds for candidates, and managing political campaigns, among many other political activities ("Federal Employees' Political Activities," 1993).

Twice the U.S. Supreme Court has ruled on First Amendment challenges to the constitutionality of the Hatch Act. Both times the Court upheld the act's restrictions on employees' political expression. The constitutionality of the Hatch Act was first challenged in *United Public Workers of America* v. *Mitchell* (1947). George Poole, a skilled laborer at the Federal Mint, was a ward committeeman in the Democratic Party and actively participated on election days as a worker at the polls. Following the passage of the Hatch Act, the Civil Service Commission ordered Poole's dismissal for engaging in the activities of managing and participating in political campaigns. Poole and the United Public Workers of America challenged the constitutionality of the Hatch Act's prohibitions against public employees' engaging in such activities on the grounds that these prohibitions violated the First Amendment and were too sweeping and unrelated to the effective performance of public employees.

With two justices not participating in the decision, the Supreme Court split four to three on upholding the provisions of the Hatch Act. Writing for the majority, Justice Stanley Reed construed Congress's purpose in passing the act to be the promotion of "efficiency and integrity in the public service" and deemed the act's prohibitions on public employees a legitimate means to such an end. Although it conceded that the law infringed on public employees' First Amendment freedoms, the Court nevertheless applied a balancing test, weighing those freedoms against a "congressional enactment to protect a democratic society against the supposed evil of political partisanship by classified employees of Government" (*United Public Workers of America* v. *Mitchell*, 1947, p. 96). Congress had concluded that "the principle of required political neutrality for classified public servants was a sound element for efficiency" (p. 97), and basically the Court's majority deferred to Congress on the matter, for as Justice Reed observed, "another Congress may determine that on the whole, limitations on active political management by Federal personnel are unwise" (p. 99).

In *Mitchell*, Justices William O. Douglas, Wiley Rutledge, and Hugo L. Black dissented. The latter justice, who championed an "absolutist" approach to the First Amendment, argued that the Hatch Act was unconstitutional on its face and far too sweeping in its prohibitions. The Hatch Act, in his words, "muzzles several million citizens" and poses a threat to popular government by limiting the "political participation and interest of such a large segment of its citizens" (p. 111).

A quarter of a century later, a second constitutional challenge to the Hatch Act reached the Court. In *United States Civil Service Commission* v. *National Association of Letter Carriers* (1973), six federal employees, a union, and several Democratic and Republican committees again raised First Amendment objections to the act. This time a federal district court invalidated the Hatch Act's prohibitions against federal employees taking an active part in political management and campaigns as "vague and overbroad, and therefore unconstitutional and unenforceable" (p. 553). But in another divided decision the Supreme Court reversed that ruling and upheld the constitutionality of the Hatch Act.

Writing for the majority in *Letter Carriers*, Justice Byron White reaffirmed the underlying policy that "it is in the best interest of the Court, indeed essential, that Federal service should depend upon meritorious performance rather than political service" (p. 557). As in *Mitchell*, the Court's majority in *Letter Carriers* was unwilling to second-guess Congress, noting that "perhaps Congress at some time will come to a different view of the realities of political life and Government service" (p. 567).

By contrast, dissenting Justice Douglas, joined by Justices William J. Brennan Jr. and Thurgood Marshall, sharply criticized the Court's majority and Congress for imposing such vague and sweeping prohibitions on federal employees.

The impact of the Hatch Act on federal employees, according to Justice Douglas, was "self-imposed censorship imposed on many nervous people who live on narrow economic margins" (p. 600).

Subsequently, Congress did lift some restrictions and extend broader protection for public employees' political expression and activities. The Federal Election Campaign Act of 1974, for instance, eliminated most restrictions on the political activities of state and local government employees. When Congress enacted the Civil Service Reform Act of 1978, reorganizing the Civil Service Commission as the Office of Personnel Management and the Merit Systems Protection Board (MSPB), authority to enforce the Hatch Act was given to the MSPB's Office of Special Counsel. And in 1989 Congress passed the Whistleblower Protection Act, giving greater protection to federal employees who speak out about government waste and abuse, and establishing the Office of Special Counsel as an independent federal agency.

Still, the Hatch Act's prohibitions on federal employees' political activities remained contentious. Those challenging the act's restrictions argued that its provisions created confusion and inconsistencies that required drawing a "bright line" between the activities permitted and those prohibited. In addition, reformers contended that federal employees have a right to participate in the political process free from reprisal and penalties. Opponents of proposed reforms, however, maintained that the Hatch Act successfully insulated federal workers from political exploitations and pressures to please superiors by allowing them to become more active in partisan politics. In 1976, Republican President Gerald R. Ford vetoed legislation that would have repealed many of the Hatch Act's barriers to federal employees' participation in campaigns and other political activities. And in 1990 Republican President George Bush vetoed the Hatch Act Reform Amendments of that year because he thought they would result in pressures on federal employees to participate in partisan political activity.

A compromise was finally reached when Democratic President Bill Clinton signed into law the Hatch Act Reform Amendments of 1993, otherwise known as the Federal Employees Political Activities Act. Under that act, federal employees may on their own time manage political campaigns, raise funds, and hold positions in political parties. They are still barred from running for partisan political office, from wearing political campaign buttons, and from distributing campaign literature in the workplace.

Other restrictions on employees in law enforcement and those involved with national security matters also remain in force. The Central Intelligence Agency (CIA) thus requires agents to sign a "secrecy agreement" and to submit, both while they are employed and after they leave the CIA's service, any writing, whether fiction or nonfiction, for prepublication review by the agency. Over First Amendment objections, the CIA's "secrecy agreement" was upheld as a contractual condition of employment in *Snepp* v. *United States* (1980). However, if a public employee publishes confidential material bearing on the national security, any government attempt at censorship or suppression of the publication bears "a heavy presumption against its constitutional validity" under the First Amendment (*New York Times Company* v. *United States,* 1971; O'Brien, 1981).

Whereas the challenges to the Hatch Act presented the Court with the issue of whether governmental restrictions and prohibitions on federal employees' political expression and activities violate the First Amendment, the Court also confronted the reverse issue of whether, under the First Amendment, public employees may be compelled to make contributions in the form of mandatory fees in lieu of union dues that support political activities. While craft-oriented unions in such activities as postal service, fire fighting, police, and public works grew in political importance in the public sector during the first quarter of the twentieth century, broader-based public sector unions did not become important until the period between the 1930s and 1960s. Even then, forms of public sector collective bargaining did not generally emerge until the late 1950s and the 1960s. Since 1962, public sector unions have rapidly increased in size and influence. Their membership increased more than 175 percent between 1962 and 1982, to 2.8 million workers, and by the 1990s public sector unions constituted 40 percent of all union membership, whereas the percentage of private union members dropped from 94 percent to 60 percent of total union membership (Troy, 1994).

Some public employees object to public sector unions and, in particular, resist paying mandatory fees that are used to support political candidates and activities. They argue that such fees are coercive to nonunion public employees and violate their First Amendment rights, because public employee unions attempt to influence governmental policymaking and their activities are therefore inherently political. These were the claims that the Court faced in *Abood* v. *Detroit Board of Education* (1977).

Abood stemmed from Michigan's enactment of legislation authorizing union representation for state and local government employees, including the creation of "agency shop" arrangements under which every employee represented by a union, even if not a member of the union, had to pay as a condition of employment a service fee equal in amount to the union dues. When the Detroit Federation of Teachers was certified under the law as the exclusive union representative for teachers employed in Detroit public schools, several teachers filed a lawsuit contending that the required fees violated their First Amendment freedoms of expression and association because some fees financed political activities that they opposed.

In *Abood,* the Court agreed that "the fact that the [teachers who are objecting to union fees and the union's political activities] are compelled to make, rather than prohibited from making, contributions for political purposes works no less an infringement of their constitutional rights" (*Abood* v. *Detroit Board of Education*, 1977, p. 234). Writing for the Court, Justice Potter Stewart affirmed that public sector unions, no less than unions in the private sector, may spend money for the expression of political views and on behalf of political candidates; indeed, the First Amendment's guarantee of freedom of association protects such activities. However, in recognition of the First Amendment rights of public employees who object to the fees and political activities of public sector unions, Justice Stewart held that "the Constitution requires only that such expenditures be financed from charges, dues, or assessments paid by employees who do not object to advancing those ideas and who are not coerced into doing so against their will by the threat of loss of government employment" (pp. 235–236). As a result, public sector unions may collect agency fees from nonmember employees they represent to cover the cost of only three activities: collective bargaining, contract administration, and grievance proceedings (*Communications Workers of America* v. *Beck*, 1988).

STATE AND LOCAL EMPLOYEES AND POLITICAL PATRONAGE

The federal Hatch Act promoted the merit principle and curbed political spoils systems in state and local governments as well as in the federal government. As political scientist James Fesler put it, "much of the improvement that had occurred in state and local administrative capacities is attributable to federal government pressure, rather than to initiatives for self-improvement" (Fesler, 1967, p. 586). While many of the restrictions on the political activities of state and local employees were eliminated with the Federal Election Campaign Act of 1974, some remain. The three principal restrictions are that state and local employees working in federally funded programs may not (1) coerce or be coerced to contribute to political parties or candidates, (2) use their authority or influence to interfere with elections, and (3) become candidates for partisan political office (U.S. Merit Systems Protection Board, 1988).

The overwhelming majority of the states also now have in place laws known as "Little Hatch Acts" that enforce merit principles and restrict state and local employees' political activities. No single model or code appears to have been followed in the state and local regulations (Council of State Governments, 1992). For example, while forty-one states permit employees to participate in political campaigns while off duty, thirty-four states allow their employees to become candidates in partisan elections (Pearson and Castle, 1991).

In addition, in a series of highly controversial rulings beginning in the mid-1970s the Supreme Court struck down political patronage systems as a violation of the First Amendment rights of public employees. First, in *Elrod* v. *Burns* (1976) the Court, by a vote of six to three, with Justice John Paul Stevens not participating, struck down the practice of patronage dismissals as an unconstitutional restriction on city employees' First Amendment freedoms. In this case, the Court concluded that a newly elected Democratic sheriff could not constitutionally engage in the patronage practice of replacing certain office staff with members of his own party "when the existing employees lack or fail to obtain requisite support from, or fail to affiliate with, that party" (p. 351). In the majority's view, such patronage practices infringe on and impermissibly limit public employees' First Amendment freedoms of expression and association.

Four years later, in *Branti* v. *Finkel* (1980), with the justices again splitting six to three and with Justices Stewart, Lewis F. Powell Jr., and William H. Rehnquist dissenting, the Court held that the First Amendment protects district attorneys from being discharged for expressing their political views. Here, a newly appointed public defender who belonged to the Democratic Party discharged several assistant public defenders because they did not have the support of the Democratic Party. As in *Elrod,* the Court ruled that the First Amendment forbids government officials from discharging or threatening to discharge public employees solely because they are not supporters of the political party in power, unless party affiliation is an appropriate requirement for the position involved.

The controversy and struggle within the Court over the permissibility of political patronage continued in *Rutan* v. *Republican Party of Illinois* (1990). In that case, Justice Brennan pulled together a bare majority for extending *Elrod* and *Branti* and sharply limiting political patronage in the hiring, promoting, and transferring of most public employees in state and local government. The case arose a decade earlier, when in 1980 Illinois's Republican Governor James Thompson issued an executive order freezing all hiring of state employees and placing virtually all of the state's 62,000 civil service positions under the jurisdiction of his personnel office. Cynthia Rutan and several other public employees who had never supported the Republican party were subsequently denied promotions. Rutan sued on the ground that her promotion was denied simply for partisan reasons in violation of her First Amendment rights to freedom of speech and association.

Writing for a bare majority, Justice Brennan observed that "employees who do not compromise their beliefs stand to lose the considerable increases in pay and job satisfaction attendant to promotions, the hours and maintenance expenses that are consumed by long daily commutes, and even their jobs if they are not rehired after a 'temporary' layoff. These are significant penalties and are imposed for the exercise of rights guaranteed by the First Amendment. Unless these patronage practices are narrowly tailored to further vital governmental interests, we must conclude that they impermissibly encroach on First Amendment freedoms" (p. 74).

By contrast, the four dissenters thought otherwise. In a rather biting dissent, joined by Chief Justice Rehnquist and Justices Sandra Day O'Connor and Anthony M. Kennedy, Justice Antonin Scalia countered that the merit principle for government employment is probably the most favored in modern America, having been widely adopted by civil-service legislation at both the state and federal levels. But there is another point of view. . . . Patronage stabilizes political parties and prevents excessive political fragmentation—both of which are results in which States have a strong governmental interest. Party strength requires the efforts of the rank-and-file, especially in "the dull periods between elections," to perform such tasks as organizing precincts, registering new voters, and providing constituent services [pp. 93, 104].

Lamenting the decline of a strong two-party system since the end of World War II, Justice Scalia concluded that political patronage was not "a significant impairment of free speech or free association" and that "the desirability of patronage is a policy question to be decided by the people's representatives" (497 U.S. 62 at 110).

FREEDOM OF SPEECH IN THE PUBLIC WORKPLACE

Though it has upheld the Hatch Act's restrictions on federal employees' political expression and activities over First Amendment objections, the Supreme Court after World War II has generally moved in the direction of giving greater protection to public employees' claims of free speech. During the nineteenth century and the first half of the twentieth century, the courts generally maintained that constitutional rights could be suspended as terms and conditions of public employment. The classical view was expressed by Justice Oliver Wendell Holmes, writing for the Supreme Court of Massachusetts in *McAuliff* v. *Mayor of New Bedford* (1892), who stated that a public employee "may have a constitutional right to talk politics, but he has no constitutional right to be a policeman" (p. 517). That view was reiterated by the Supreme Court in *Adler* v. *Board of Education* (1952), which upheld New York's Feinberg law, barring from employment in public schools any person who advocated the overthrow of the government or who belonged to an organization deemed to teach and advocate the overthrow of the government.

Not until the 1960s did the Court begin expanding the First Amendment's protection for public employees, when it first struck down "loyalty oath" requirements as too vague or overly broad (*Shelton* v. *Tucker*, 1960; *Cramp* v. *Board of Public Instruction*, 1961; *Baggett* v. *Bullitt*, 1964; and Emerson, 1970). Then, in *Keyishian* v. *Board of Regents* (1967), the Court overturned *Adler* and ruled that New York's Feinberg law was unconstitutionally vague and overbroad. Writing for the majority, Justice Brennan further held that public employers may neither deny persons employment because of the exercise of their First Amendment rights nor condition their employment on the sacrifice of those freedoms. Basically, *Keyishian* discarded the distinction between the "rights" and "privileges" of public employees in ruling that the government may not impose "unconstitutional conditions" on public employment.

After *Keyishian,* however, the Court was confronted with the problem of how to accommodate the government's interest, as an employer, in providing effective public services with public employees' free speech claims. As a result, the following year the Court crafted a "balancing test" in *Pickering* v. *Board of Education of Township High School District* (1968). In *Pickering,* a public school teacher was dismissed for writing a letter to a newspaper criticizing the local school board's handling of a bond proposal and its appropriations for educational and athletic programs. The Court held that the teacher could not be dismissed for exercising the First Amendment right to free speech without a showing that the teacher had knowingly or recklessly made false statements.

In handing down its decision in *Pickering,* the Court set forth a "balancing test," requiring the weighing of the interests of public employees, as citizens, in commenting on "matters of public concern" against the government employer's interest in the efficient delivery of public services. That test must be applied on a case-by-case basis, taking into consideration the parties' working relationship, the content and context of the employee's speech, and the effect on the employer, among other factors. In short, while public employees do not forfeit their First Amendment right to free speech as a condition of employment, they remain subject to restrictions deemed necessary to accommodate the government's interests in efficient productivity.

The Court has stood by the reasoning in *Pickering* and brought it to bear on the controversy stemming from Congress's inclusion of federal employees in a ban on receiving honoraria enacted in the Ethics Reform Act of 1989. Under provisions of that law, federal employees were barred from receiving honoraria for giving speeches and publishing articles and books, even when those speeches and writings were completely unrelated to their work. The ban was immediately challenged, and a federal court struck down the provisions as applied to federal employees on the grounds that the ban infringed on their First Amendment rights to freedom of speech and press. On appeal to the Supreme Court, a majority of the justices agreed with the lower court's ruling. Writing for the Court in *United States* v. *National Treasury Employees Union* (1995), Justice Stevens explained:

> Even though respondents work for the Government, they have not relinquished "the First Amendment rights they would otherwise enjoy as citizens to comment on matters of public interest" (*Pickering v. Board of Ed. of Township High School Dist.,* 1968). They seek compensation for their expressive activities in their capacity as citizens, not as Government employees. . . . With few exceptions, the content of respondents' messages has nothing to do with their jobs and does not even arguably have any adverse impact on the efficiency of the offices in which they work. They do not address audiences composed of co-workers or supervisors;

instead, they write or speak for segments of the general public. Neither the character of the authors, the subject matter of their expression, the effect of the content of their expression on their official duties, nor the kind of audiences they address has any relevance to their employment [p. 978].

Justice Stevens added, "The large-scale disincentive to Government employees' expression also imposes a significant burden on the public's right to read and hear what the employees would otherwise have written and said." And he concluded that "the honoraria ban imposes the kind of burden that abridges speech under the First Amendment" (pp. 981–982). By contrast, Chief Justice Rehnquist, joined by Justices Scalia and Clarence Thomas, dissented because the Court's majority, in the words of the chief justice, "understates the weight which should be accorded to the governmental justifications for the honoraria ban and overstates the amount of speech which actually will be deterred" (p. 994).

Although *Keyishian*, *Pickering*, and *National Treasury Employees Union* significantly expanded the scope of First Amendment protection for public employees' exercise of free speech, those decisions did not reach the question of constitutional protection for public employees' free speech in the workplace, when they speak as employees, not as citizens. The issue was first addressed in *Connick* v. *Myers* (1983). In this case the Court ruled that public employees' work-related speech is covered by the First Amendment only if it embraces a matter of public concern and does not disrupt the workplace.

The facts surrounding *Connick* v. *Myers* are important to consider. In 1980, Sheila Myers, an assistant district attorney, was told by Harry Connick, the district attorney, that she was going to be transferred to a different section. When Myers objected and criticized office policies, she was told that her supervisors did not share her view. In response, Myers circulated a questionnaire to coworkers to find out whether they agreed with her. When a supervisor found out about the questionnaire, he telephoned Connick and told him that Myers was "instigating a mini-insurrection," whereupon Connick promptly fired Myers for refusing the transfer and for insubordination.

Myers sued, contending that the termination violated her First Amendment right of free speech. A federal district court, and an appellate court, agreed that her termination was prompted by the questionnaire, that the questionnaire raised matters of public concern and did not substantially interfere with the operation of the office. The questionnaire was therefore constitutionally protected speech and Myers had been improperly dismissed (*Myers* v. *Connick*, 1981). The Supreme Court, however, reversed the decision upon concluding that the questionnaire "touched upon matters of public concern in only the most limited sense" and was more "accurately characterized as an employee grievance concerning internal office policy." Drawing on *Pickering*, Justice White's opinion for a bare majority emphasized that the First Amendment's protection for public employees in the workplace comes into play only when an employee's speech involves a matter of public concern, as determined by the "content, form, and context" of the speech. Applying that test to Myers's questionnaire, Justice White deemed that only one question on it, pertaining to pressure on employees to participate in political campaigns, raised a matter of public concern. The remaining questions were characterized by Justice White as merely expressions of personal grievances, "an attempt to turn that displeasure into a cause celebre," and he deferred to the government's claim that the questions were disruptive (*Connick* v. *Myers,* 1983, pp. 147–148).

The four dissenters—Justices Brennan, Marshall, Stevens, and Harry A. Blackmun—took a very different view of both the facts and the First Amendment's protection of public employees' speech in the workplace. Writing for the dissenters, Justice Brennan countered that Myers's questions about office morale and workers' performance involved matters of public concern. Moreover, he contended that once a matter of public concern has been identified, public employers should be required to justify their disciplinary actions by showing that an employee's speech was actually disruptive. In other words, courts should not simply defer to the government's characterization of speech as disruptive to the workplace.

The four dissenters in *Connick* v. *Myers* were subsequently joined by Justice Powell in *Rankin* v. *McPherson* (1987), and they prevailed in that five-to-four decision recognizing the First Amendment's protection for public employees' workplace speech. In that case, the five justices agreed that a clerical worker in a Texas county constable's office could not be fired for remarking during a private conversation, after criticizing the White House's proposed welfare cuts and hearing of the 1981 assassination attempt on President Ronald Reagan, "If they go for him again, I hope they get him." Writing for the Court, Justice Marshall reaffirmed the need to balance the First Amendment rights of public employees against the government's interests in a productive workforce. The clerical worker's remark, in Marshall's view, touched on a matter of public concern and, because there was no evidence that it interfered with the functioning of the office, received First Amendment protection. However, the four dissenting justices sharply disagreed. Justice Scalia, joined by Chief Justice Rehnquist and Justices O'Connor and White, countered flatly that such speech conveys no public concerns entitled to First Amendment protection and would have affirmed the employee's dismissal.

Connick and *Rankin* are worth contrasting. Both were decided by bare majorities that advanced rival views of the weight that should be given to public employees' free speech claims and of the contexts for those claims. Although public employers may not condition employment on the surrender of employees' First Amendment freedoms, they may significantly regulate, restrict, and discipline employees' work-related speech. Public employees who challenge adverse employment decisions on First Amendment grounds must prove not only that their speech merits protection because it addresses a matter of public concern and was not disruptive, but also that their speech caused their dismissal or their employer's other disciplinary actions (*Mount Healthy City School District Board of Education v. Doyle,* 1976).

Public employees thus face a number of obstacles to successfully establishing their claims to First Amendment protection for work-related speech. They must do so, moreover, on a case-by-case basis. Furthermore, lower federal courts frequently conclude, as the majority did in *Connick,* that the speech in question was merely personal and that because it is not deemed to raise a matter of public concern, it consequently receives no protection. Even when courts find that public employees' speech touches on matters of public concern, they often defer to the government's contention that the speech was or might prove disruptive, and deny First Amendment protection (Massaro, 1987).

Finally, in an important ruling, though not expanding First Amendment protection for public employees per se, the Court gave greater procedural protection to public employees who object on First Amendment grounds to their dismissals or disciplining. In *Waters v. Churchill* (1994) the Court ruled for the first time that the First Amendment confers a procedural guarantee requiring employers to conduct some kind of investigation into the basis for disciplining or firing employees for speech deemed to be insubordinate. Cheryl Churchill was fired from her position as a nurse in a city hospital after administrators were told by other nurses that she had criticized the obstetrics department and denigrated her supervisors. Churchill claimed that she was simply raising concerns about patient care and staff shortages.

Writing for the majority in *Waters,* Justice O'Connor reaffirmed that "the extra power the government has in this area comes from the nature of the government's mission as an employer. When someone who is paid a salary so that she will contribute to an agency's effective operation begins to do or say things that detract from the agency's effective operation, the government employer must have some power to restrain her" (p. 699). Only dissenting Justices Blackmun and Stevens thought otherwise. They argued that Justice O'Connor "underestimated the importance of freedom of speech for the more than 18 million civilian employees in this country's federal, state, and local governments, and subordinated that freedom to an abstract interest in bureaucratic efficiency" (p. 713).

Justice O'Connor's opinion for the Court nonetheless proceeded to hold that government employers who discipline or fire employees for their speech "must tread with a certain amount of care" and conduct an investigation into the basis for their action. The First Amendment, according to Justice O'Connor, contains a procedural safeguard against the erroneous punishment of protected speech, though that safeguard depends on each case and on the consideration of its costs versus the risks posed for employees' free speech. Declining to lay down precise procedural guidelines, Justice O'Connor concluded that no specific kind of investigation must be conducted or is constitutionally required. "Many different courses of action will necessarily be reasonable" (p. 701), the justice reasoned, depending on a case-by-case analysis. In so holding, Justice O'Connor picked up the votes of Justices Blackmun and Stevens but lost those of Justices Scalia, Thomas, and Kennedy. In a separate opinion joined by the latter two justices, Justice Scalia countered that the First Amendment imposed no such procedural requirement, and he sharply attacked Justice O'Connor's analysis as unprecedented, ambiguous, and certain to burden both government employers and the courts with litigation brought by public employees.

SUMMARY

Employees in the public sector sacrifice some of their freedoms under the First Amendment. Under the federal Hatch Act and similar state and local laws, public employees' political expression and activities are limited and restricted. At the same time, their freedom of association, including the right to organize and to join public sector unions, has been recognized. Public sector unions may engage in political expression and activities, while nonmember employees represented by public sector unions may not be required to pay fees that support the political activities of these unions. The Supreme Court has ruled that the First Amendment protects most public employees from political patronage in hiring, firing, and promotion decisions. The Court has also established that First Amendment freedoms may not be forfeited as a condition of employment in the public sector and that public employees enjoy protections for their speech in the workplace, though the government may restrict and punish work-related speech that does not address matters of public concern and that is disruptive.

Cases Cited

Abood v. *Detroit Board of Education,* 431 U.S. 209 (1977).

Adler v. *Board of Education,* 342 U.S. 485 (1952).

Baggett v. *Bullitt,* 377 U.S. 360 (1964).

Branti v. *Finkel,* 445 U.S. 507 (1980).

Communications Workers of America v. *Beck,* 487 U.S. 735 (1988).

Connick v. *Myers,* 461 U.S. 138 (1983).

Cramp v. *Board of Public Instruction,* 368 U.S. 278 (1961).

Elrod v. *Burns,* 427 U.S. 347 (1976).

Gitlow v. New York, 268 U.S. 652 (1925).

Keyishian v. Board of Regents, 385 U.S. 589 (1967).

McAuliff v. Mayor of New Bedford, 29 N.E. 517 (1892).

Mount Healthy City School District Board of Education v. Doyle, 429 U.S. 274 (1976).

Myers v. Connick, 507 F. Supp. 752 (1981).

National Association for the Advancement of Colored People v. Alabama, 357 U.S. 449 (1958).

Near v. Minnesota, 283 U.S. 697 (1931).

New York Times Company v. United States, 403 U.S. 670 (1971).

Pickering v. Board of Education of Township High School District, 391 U.S. 563 (1968).

Rankin v. McPherson, 483 U.S. 378 (1987).

Rutan v. Republican Party of Illinois, 497 U.S. 62 (1990).

Shelton v. Tucker, 364 U.S. 479 (1960).

Snepp v. United States, 444 U.S. 507 (1980).

Sweezy v. New Hampshire, 354 U.S. 234 (1957).

United Public Workers of American v. Mitchell, 330 U.S. 75 (1947).

United States Civil Service Commission v. National Association of Letter Carriers, 413 U.S. 548 (1973).

United States v. National Treasury Employees Union, 130 L.Ed.2d 964 (1995).

Waters v. Churchill, 128 L.Ed.2d 686 (1994).

References

Council of State Governments. *The Book of the States.* Lexington, Ky.: Council of State Governments, 1992.

Emerson, T. I. *The System of Freedom of Expression.* New York: Random House, 1970.

"Federal Employees' Political Activities." *Congressional Digest,* Aug.-Sept. 1993, pp. 195–224.

Fesler, J. *The Fifty States and Their Local Governments.* New York: Knopf, 1967.

Massaro, T. M. "Significant Silences: Freedom of Speech in the Public Sector Workplace." *Southern California Law Review,* 1987, *61,* 3–77.

O'Brien, D. M. *The Public's Right to Know: The Supreme Court and the First Amendment.* New York: Praeger, 1981.

O'Brien, D. M. *Constitutional Law and Politics.* Vol. 2: *Civil Rights and Civil Liberties.* (2nd ed.) New York: Norton, 1995.

Pearson, W. D., and Castle, D. S. "Liberalizing Restrictions on Political Activities of State Employees: Perceptions of High-Level State Employees." *American Review of Public Administration,* 1991, *21,* 91–104.

Troy, L. *The New Unionism in the New Society: Public Sector Unions in the Redistributive State.* Fairfax, Va.: George Mason University Press, 1994.

U.S. Merit Systems Protection Board, Office of Special Council. *Political Activity and the State and Local Employee.* Washington, D.C.: U.S. Government Printing Office, 1988.

CHAPTER SIXTEEN

Constitutions, Statutes, Regulations, and Labor Relations

Dispute Resolution in a Complex Authority Mix

Norma M. Riccucci

By its nature, labor-management relations is a highly regulated, conflictual field of public administration. Moreover, there is no unified, consistent system of labor relations in the public sector (Kearney, 1992). The U.S. Postal Service conducts labor-management relations under the Postal Reorganization Act, which incorporates most of the provisions of the National Labor Relations Act, which covers private sector employees. Another statute and separate rules and orders govern most other labor issues for federal government employees. Each state, in turn, enacts its own labor law to cover state and local government employees. This complexity presents a challenge to the management or study of any aspect of labor relations, but especially dispute resolution, in which greatly varied means and sources of settlement are used.

This chapter begins with a discussion of various forums through which employee disputes can be resolved. Its primary focus is on dispute resolution under negotiated grievance procedures. In particular, it examines complexities in the national government for filing appeals to arbitrated awards that result from grievances initially filed through contractual grievance provisions. The chapter concludes with a discussion of the implications of this complex authority mix for employers as well as employees.

CONCEPTS AND ISSUES

Disputes arise over a host of issues in the labor relations setting. One set of issues commonly emerges during collective bargaining. For example, when labor and management cannot reach an agreement, for instance, over wages or terms and conditions of employment (such as sick leave, vacation time, or overtime pay), an impasse is declared. To resolve such an impasse, a third party (such as a mediator, fact finder, or arbitrator) may be called in. Other types of disputes may also arise at the bargaining table. For example, if labor or management believes that the other party is not negotiating fairly, either party can file an unfair labor practice (ULP) complaint with the labor-relations oversight agency in that jurisdiction.

Disputes can also arise over representational issues. These disputes take many forms, including a union's petition for exclusive recognition, unit clarification, or decertification. These disputes can be resolved in a several ways, including through ULP or representation proceedings (Rosenbloom, 1988–1989).

Another type of dispute that commonly arises during contract administration involves conflicts over contract rights. For example, if a union perceives that management is misinterpreting or making a unilateral change to the contract, the union may file a ULP charge (Riccucci and Ban, 1989). Other disputes during contract administration surface as grievances. For instance, if an employee believes that the organization is abridging the contract in regard to use of vacation leave, the employee can file a grievance. There are several, sometimes conflicting, ways in which the grievance can then be resolved. It is the resolution of grievances over rights that is the subject of this chapter.

A COMPLEX AUTHORITY MIX

Several forums are available for resolving grievances. Perhaps the most familiar is the negotiated or contractual grievance procedure. Since such procedures are negotiated between a union and an employer, they may vary from contract to contract. In general, however, a contract delineates a series of commonly used steps for grievance resolution, with the final step usually being binding arbitration. At the last stage, a neutral third party, agreed upon by both labor and management, is called upon to resolve the dispute or grievance. Grievance arbitrators can be selected from lists provided by a relevant state agency, the American Arbitration Association, or the Federal Mediation and Conciliation Service (Rosenbloom and Shafritz, 1985).

Another way to resolve grievances is through civil service procedures, which are established via statute or unilaterally by the governing body (that is, management).

Negotiated grievance procedures can supplant civil service grievance procedures in some cases, but the two often coexist. While this creates overlap and duplication from a managerial efficiency standpoint, it also provides the griev-ing employee with multiple access points (Kearney, 1992). For example, under the Civil Service Reform Act of 1978 (CSRA), at the federal level of government, disputes can in some cases be processed either through negotiated grievance procedures, agency grievance procedures, or through a number of federal agen-cies, including the Merit Systems Protection Board (MSPB), the Office of Spe-cial Counsel (OSC), the Federal Labor Relations Authority (FLRA), the Office of Personnel Management, the Equal Employment Opportunity Commission (EEOC), and even the Department of Labor (Feder, 1989; Moore, 1990). Even within one federal agency, a single dispute can mutate into multiple claims. As Feder (1989, p. 268) points out, "even within the same . . . agency, disputes aris-ing out of the same fact situation may be pending in as many as four different forums. Within the FLRA, a dispute may be pending as a negotiability appeal, an unfair labor practice (ULP), an impasse before the Federal Service Impasses Panel (FSIP), and a grievance subject to arbitration and FLRA review."

Table 16.1 lists the various forums within the national government through which grievances can be processed.

While the availability of different paths for grievance resolution may be favorable to the grieving employee, it represents costly duplication and over-lap for American taxpayers. Additional costs present themselves if the griev-ing employee or the union representing the employee appeals a decision issued by one body to a higher-level authority. For example, federal employ-ees or unions that are not satisfied with the disposition of an arbitrator are often ready and willing to appeal that disposition to a labor relations agency (such as the FLRA for federal employees), to other administrative agencies (such as the MSPB) or to the courts (Frazier, 1986). In fact, appealing arbi-trated awards is very common in the federal government (Frazier, 1986, p. 74), despite the presumption that an arbitrator's award is final, binding, and re-viewable only by an administrative agency or the courts under very limited circumstances. This presumption emanates from case law in a series of pri-vate sector lawsuits involving challenges to arbitrated grievance awards as well as to the statutes and case law governing labor relations for federal employees. The next section provides a closer look at the finality of arbitra-tion awards, further illustrating the complexity of dispute resolution in the public sector.

HOW FINAL IS BINDING ARBITRATION?

In the private sector, the legal tradition is that judges do not supplant arbitra-tors' decisions in the absence of fraud, misconduct, or conflicts of the award with established public policy (Kearney, 1992; Moore, 1990). This practice stems from several U.S. Supreme Court rulings (see *Textile Workers Union* v. *Lincoln*

Table 16.1. Administrative Forums for Dispute Resolution in the U.S. Government.

Type/Nature of Dispute	Administrative Forum
Appealable actions—include adverse actions (such as removal or reduction in grade), performance-related actions, within-grade increase denial, reduction-in-force action, and retirement-related action	• MSPB • Negotiated grievance procedure
EEO violations	• Agency EEO complaint procedure • MSPB • Negotiated grievance procedure
Mixed cases—involve an EEO violation and an appealable action	• Agency EEO complaint procedure • MSPB • Negotiated grievance procedure
Prohibited personnel practices—include reprisal for whistle-blowing, influencing someone to withdraw from job competition, and coercing an employee into political activity	• OSC of the MSPB • Negotiated grievance procedure
Unfair labor practices	• FLRA • Negotiated grievance procedure
Actions reviewable by OPM—include actions pertaining to position classification, life and health insurance, and examination ratings	• OPM
Other actions—include suspensions from work for less than fourteen days, challenges to performance appraisals, job transfers, or reassignments	

Source: Adapted from Moore, 1990.

Mills, 1957, and the "Steelworkers' Trilogy"—*United Steelworkers of America* v. *Warrior and Gulf Navigation Company,* 1960, *United Steelworkers of America* v. *Enterprise Wheel and Car Corporation,* 1960, and *United Steelworkers of America* v. *American Manufacturing Company,* 1960) that have held that arbitration is final, binding, and exempt from court review (Edwards, Clark, and Craver, 1979; Kearney, 1992; Rosenbloom, 1988–1989).

In yet another realm, the courts have been willing to review arbitrated decisions when statutory or constitutional rights are involved. For example, in *Alexander* v. *Gardner-Denver* (1974), a unanimous U.S. Supreme Court ruled that even if a grieving employee exhausts administrative remedies through binding arbitration, the grievant is not precluded from seeking a trial de novo under Title VII of the Civil Rights Act of 1964 as amended (Levine, 1985). In a later ruling, *Barrentine* v. *Arkansas-Best Freight System, Inc.* (1981), the Supreme Court held that employees who lost in grievance arbitration could pursue de novo claims under the Fair Labor Standards Act.

In the public sector, the concept of finality of arbitration awards varies among jurisdictions. For example, some state courts (such as Wisconsin and Minnesota) have ruled that arbitration awards are final, binding, and not reviewable by the courts. Other state courts (such as New York), however, have held just the opposite (Kearney, 1992). At the federal level, by statute only certain cases can be appealed to the courts, and in some instances directly (that is, without first appealing to the FLRA). Title VII of the CSRA, which is generally referred to as the Federal Service Labor-Management Relations Statute, allows for most arbitrated awards to be appealed to the FLRA, but in some cases the FLRA decision is final and not subject to judicial review. The statutory law governing federal employees prescribes which types of claims can be appealed to the courts.

It should be further noted, however, that the courts have issued rulings expanding public employees' access to the federal courts for review of certain arbitrated awards. For example, *Gardner-Denver* was extended to the public sector in 1984 by the Supreme Court's ruling in *McDonald* v. *City of West Branch, Mich.*, which arose under Section 1983 of the Civil Rights Act of 1871 (Carmell and Westerkamp, 1986). *McDonald* involved a claim by a police officer who was discharged for exercising his First Amendment rights of speech, freedom of association, and freedom to petition the government for redress of grievances (see also *Griffith* v. *FLRA*, 1988).

In sum, in the private sector the courts are reluctant to review arbitrated awards unless the legal rights of employees have been violated, the award violates public policy, or the arbitrator's conduct is called into question. This is also the case for nonfederal public employees in some jurisdictions. But for federal employees, the right to appeal arbitration awards is more complicated, given that the labor statute expressly limits the types of cases that can be appealed to the courts. Moreover, just as with initiating a grievance, in some cases, multiple avenues for appealing the award are available. The following section examines these issues.

THE REVIEW OF ARBITRATED AWARDS IN THE FEDERAL SECTOR

As discussed earlier, a federal employee has several forums through which to process a dispute. One of these is the contractual grievance procedure, which provides for binding arbitration as a final step. Despite the fact that an arbitrator's award is commonly considered binding and presumed to be final, it is nonetheless subject to review. (If no appeal or exception to the award is filed with the FLRA within thirty days, the arbitrator's award is final and binding.) In some cases, the arbitration award is appealable directly to the courts. However, in most cases an appeal would be made to the FLRA, which by statute can set aside or modify an award only if the arbitrator's award is "contrary to any law, rule or regulation" or is based on "other grounds similar to those applied by Federal courts in private sector labor-management relations" (Federal Service Labor-Management Relations Statute, 5 U.S.C. 7101–7135, 1982, and Supp. III, 1985, sec. 7122a; see also Hardiman, 1990, pp. 332–337).

While the FLRA award is final and binding in most instances, FLRA rulings can be appealed to the courts in five circumstances: (1) when a dispute involves a ULP, (2) when an alleged violation of the Constitution is involved, (3) when a question exists as to whether the FLRA acted in excess of its statutory powers or jurisdiction, (4) when a case involves an EEO violation, or (5) when a case is mixed. The latter two situations are discussed in more detail here, as are the appeals of arbitrated awards that can completely bypass the FLRA.

Alternative Paths of Resolution

An appeal of an arbitration award is usually directed to the FLRA. There are, however, three exceptions. One is when the case involves either a performance-based action or an adverse action. The former is defined by law as a reduction in grade or a removal based upon unacceptable performance, and the latter is defined as a removal based on conduct, reduction in grade, or suspension of more than fourteen days. There are five major categories of appealable actions, of which performance-based and adverse actions are two. The others are denial of a within-grade increase, reduction-in-force (RIF), and retirement-related action. In performance-based or adverse action cases, the FLRA is barred by law from reviewing the arbitrator's decision. These cases are appealable only to the U.S. Court of Appeals for the Federal Circuit, which was created in 1982 to provide a single federal forum in which appeals to certain subject matters, such as MSPB employment actions, could be considered.

An employee or a union representing the employee can also bypass the FLRA in appealing an arbitrator's award if the case involves an EEO violation (such as racial or sexual discrimination or harassment). In such cases, the employee or union can appeal the case to either the FLRA or the EEOC, or file suit in a federal district court (for greater detail, see Moore, 1990, pp. 37–38). If the employee or union first chooses the FLRA or the EEOC, the decision is ultimately appealable to the courts.

Finally, the FLRA can be bypassed—or its decision can be reviewed by the courts—if the case is mixed. A mixed case involves an EEO complaint *and* an appealable action (such as when an employee is removed from a job allegedly because of gender). The complainant in such a case can commence the grievance through the negotiated grievance process (providing that the negotiated agreement does not explicitly exclude EEO, appealable actions, or mixed cases from coverage), the MSPB appeals process, or the EEO complaints process of the employing agency. However, regardless of the initial forum selected, the MSPB represents one of the administrative forums for the case (Moore, 1990). For example, if the grievant chooses the agency EEO complaint process and is not satisfied with the outcome, the employee or union would first appeal not to the EEOC but to the MSPB. The grievant would appeal to the EEOC or the courts after MSPB issuance of a decision. Of course, the grievant can also bypass the MSPB and appeal directly to a federal district court, depending on the circumstances.

If the employee in a mixed case chooses the negotiated grievance procedure route and wishes to appeal the arbitrator's award, the employee can file suit in federal district court (compare *Johnson* v. *Peterson*, 1993, with *AFGE* v. *Reno*, 1993), appeal to the MSPB, or file an exception with the FLRA, providing the arbitrated award does not involve an adverse or performance-based action. It may be recalled that by law these types of actions cannot be appealed to the FLRA. However, arbitration awards involving an EEO complaint and one of the other appealable actions such as an RIF may be appealed to the FLRA.

If the employee appeals the award to the MSPB and is not satisfied with the outcome, a further appeal may be taken to the EEOC—a decision by which is ultimately appealable to the courts—or directly to a federal district court. Initially, some confusion existed as to whether mixed cases would be appealed directly to the U.S. Court of Appeals for the Federal Circuit—which is where MSPB decisions must be appealed—or to a federal district court—which is where EEO decisions are appealed. As Moore (1990, p. 53) states, however, a body of case law now indicates that the federal district court is the proper forum for a mixed case.

If the employee files an exception to the arbitrator's award with the FLRA and is not satisfied with the FLRA's ruling, the employee can appeal to a federal district court or the MSPB. If the employee selects the MSPB and is not satisfied with the ruling, the decision is appealable to a federal district court or the EEOC. The EEOC decision is ultimately appealable to the courts.

Figure 16.1 provides a summary of the avenues for appealing a mixed case that has been commenced through the negotiated grievance procedure.

Appeals to Arbitration Awards

This chapter is less interested in the actual disposition of disputes than it is in the avenues for dispute resolution. As such, it does not look at the substantive decisions issued at any stage in the process. Rather, it provides information on the number of appeals or exceptions filed only to arbitrated awards. These data do not reflect the total number of cases that go through the appeals process outlined in Table 16.1. Given this chapter's interest in dispute resolution in a labor

Figure 16.1. Avenues for Appealing a Mixed Case Commenced Through the Negotiated Grievance Procedure.

Arbitration Award Issued → Exceptions Filed

Exceptions Filed → Courts

Exceptions Filed → MSPB → EEOC → Courts

MSPB → Courts

Exceptions Filed → FLRA[a] → MSPB → EEOC → Courts

MSPB → Courts

FLRA[a] → Courts

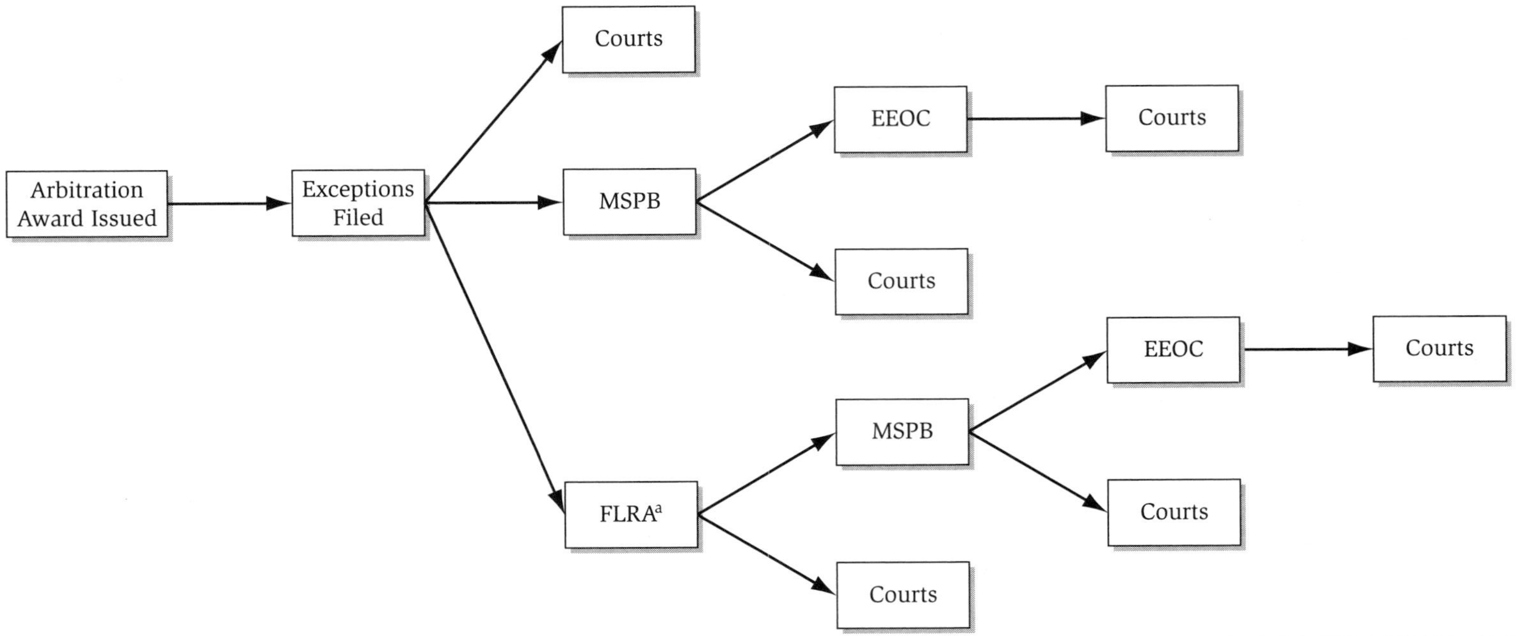

Note: The employee has the further option of appealing the decision directly to the EEOC if the grievance does not go to final arbitration but, rather, the "final decision" is made by the *agency* at the end of the process. Also, the negotiated grievance process can be used unless the collective bargaining contract explicitly excludes EEO, appealable actions, or mixed cases from coverage by the negotiated grievance procedure.

[a] Exceptions can be filed with the FLRA if the grievance does not involve adverse or performance-based actions.

relations setting, it focuses solely on cases that commence through the negotiated grievance procedure.

As Table 16.2 shows, notwithstanding the limited grounds for appeal, 927 appeals, or "exceptions," to arbitration awards were filed with the FLRA between January 1990 and the end of December 1994. This represents almost a third of the total (3,000) awards issued during this period (Labor Agreement Information Retrieval Service, telephone interview, Sept. 14, 1995). In addition, 22 FLRA decisions on arbitrated awards were appealed to the courts, which represents about 2.5 percent of the total decisions issued by the FLRA.

Table 16.2 also provides information on the number of appeals filed in mixed cases. Only totals are presented here, because for a variety of reasons it is impossible to track mixed cases through the entire appeals process presented in Figure 16.1. For one thing, the administrative agencies do not maintain data on the forum from which the appeal is made. For example, as Table 16.2 shows, thirty-three mixed cases were appealed to the MSPB, but the MSPB does not keep data on whether the appeals are made directly from the arbitrated award or have first been acted upon by the FLRA. The same holds true for the EEOC. It should further be noted that the FLRA does not even maintain data on certain categories of appeals, mixed cases being one of them.

Such limitations in how administrative agencies collect and maintain data make it difficult to assess appeals to arbitrated awards. It cannot be definitively concluded, for example, that only small numbers of mixed cases are appealed to administrative bodies or to the courts because it is impossible to determine how many of the total number of awards (3,000) are mixed cases. Moreover, it is impossible to determine whether employees involved in a mixed case had initially pursued another venue for dispute resolution (such as the agency EEO complaints procedure) rather than the negotiated grievance procedure.

It should further be stressed that these data reflect only those disputes processed through the negotiated grievance procedure. The EEOC, for example, receives thousands of complaints from federal employees per year. In fiscal year 1993, for example, 22,327 complaints were filed by federal employees (U.S. Equal Employment Opportunity Commission, 1993). However, because of staffing shortages, the EEOC cannot provide data on the percentage of mixed cases in the total. In short, the actual extent to which the various appeals processes are accessed for mixed cases cannot be definitively measured.

Limitations of available data further illustrate the complexities and arcane nature of the dispute resolution process over grievances, particularly for those complaints initially pursued through the negotiated grievance route. As is discussed in further detail in the following section, at the time of this writing a bill is before Congress to streamline the appeals process at least for mixed cases.

Table 16.2. Dispute Resolution Actions Around Grievances for Federal Employees, 1990–1994.

Dispute Resolution Action	Number
Arbitration awards issued	3,000[a]
Appeals/exceptions to arbitrated awards filed with FLRA	927
FLRA decisions appealed to the courts	22
Mixed cases appealed to the FLRA	N.A.[b]
Mixed cases appealed to the MSPB[c]	33
Mixed cases appealed to the EEOC[d]	1,030
Mixed cases appealed to the courts[e]	23

[a]The Labor Agreement Information Retrieval Service, which maintains these data, was not able to provide a breakdown on the substantive nature of these awards. For example, it could not provide data on the percentage of mixed cases among these 3,000.

[b]Not available. The FLRA does not maintain data on mixed cases.

[c]Data available only for 1991–1994.

[d]These include mixed case appeals to arbitrated awards, but the preponderance of these appeals, while commenced through the negotiated grievance procedure, had "final decisions" issued by the agency and not by an arbitrator. The EEOC could only provide data in this fashion.

[e]These cases include appeals of district court decisions to the appellate courts. Also, the preponderance of these cases involve the appealing of arbitrated awards directly to the courts.

CHALLENGES POSED BY A COMPLEX AUTHORITY MIX

The Civil Service Reform Act of 1978 was supposedly intended to improve the efficiency of federal government operations by instituting structural and procedural reforms in the federal bureaucracy. At the same time, the interests of federal employees were not be to compromised (Ingraham and Ban, 1984; Shafritz, Riccucci, Rosenbloom, and Hyde, 1992). But many provisions of the reform act have not been successful in terms of such promises (Ingraham and Rosenbloom, 1988–1989). One failure is the dispute resolution process.

From the government's standpoint, the system for dispute resolution is cumbersome and inefficient. Indeed, the process is so Byzantine that it is virtually impossible to collect meaningful statistics to study its use and operation. Many have argued that the system is wasteful, duplicative, costly, and confusing (Feder, 1989, p. 269). Further, if one were to factor in the time involved in the appeals process, the cost of maintaining the overlapping forums would be found to be staggering. In illustrating the costs of the process, Feder looks at the fiscal year 1988 budgets of the FLRA, the MSPB, and the OSC, which total almost $50 million.

From labor's standpoint, the purpose of dispute resolution procedures has never been to promote managerial efficiency. As Sulzner (1997, p. 163) states:

"The grievance/arbitration process was not originally designed or incorporated to enhance the efficiency of an organization. That end may be a by-product, but the grievance/arbitration system was implemented at worksites as a form of industrial justice to guarantee due process for handling employee discipline and other operational problems."

Notwithstanding such hopes, although employees are afforded multiple access points to dispute resolution, their interests may not be protected. The complexity of the appeals process creates costs and time delays that do not serve the best interests of the grievant. Further, the conflicting administrative regulations, as well as the civil procedures in court, especially those involving mixed cases, create confusion and difficulties for the grievant and for unions in selecting the appropriate forum for resolving the dispute. In short, unions, like management, are frustrated and dissatisfied with the process, seeing it as too time-consuming, unpredictable, and costly.

Some critics have called for streamlining the process by cutting the dispute resolution functions of various agencies (such as the FLRA, the MSPB, the EEOC, and the OSC) and creating a single agency or board for processing disputes in the federal government (Feder, 1989). Others have called for these same executive branch agencies to work with Congress to reform the process that governs mixed cases (Levinson, 1986). Indeed, as of 1996, Congress was considering a bill that would streamline the process for mixed cases. Specifically, it would eliminate the unit of the EEOC that processes mixed cases. If passed, the bill would require all mixed cases to be processed only through the MSPB. It should be noted that these efforts are not to be confused with the Federal Employee Fairness Act of 1995 (H.R. 2133), which amends Title VII of the Civil Rights Act of 1964 and the Age Discrimination in Employment Act of 1967 to improve the effectiveness of administrative review of employment discrimination claims made by federal employees under these two statutes. The Fairness Act does not address the processing of mixed cases.

CONCLUSIONS

Based on the analysis presented in this chapter, it would seem that certain reforms to the dispute resolution process as it currently operates in the federal government are warranted. One would hope, however, that such reforms would be balanced with workers' desires and guarantees of due process and industrial fairness and equity.

It should also be stressed that the focus of this chapter was exclusively on the dispute resolution process as it applies to federal employees. Coverage of state and local government employees was deliberately omitted because, as noted at the beginning of the chapter, each state has its own set of statutes, regulations, and case law governing the operation of dispute resolution processes. Thus no central database or information bank exists to track dispute resolution practices or outcomes in the fifty states. Nonetheless, it should be noted that the systems are no less complex at the state and local levels of government (Deitsch and Dilts, 1990). Multiple bargaining units, variation of work rules, and bodies of distinct administrative law in each state create problems for management as well as for labor in the processing and resolution of disputes. In short, at every level of government, a complex authority mix surrounds dispute resolution, posing challenges for employers, unions, and employees.

Cases Cited

AFGE v. *Reno,* 992 F.2d 331 (D.C. Cir., 1993).

Alexander v. *Gardner-Denver,* 415 U.S. 36 (1974).

Barrentine v. *Arkansas-Best Freight System, Inc.,* 450 U.S. 728 (1981).

Griffith v. *FLRA,* 842 F.2d 487 (D.C. Cir., 1988).

Johnson v. *Peterson,* 996 F.2d 397 (D.C. Cir., 1993).

McDonald v. *City of West Branch, Mich.,* 466 U.S. 284 (1984).

Textile Workers Union v. *Lincoln Mills,* 355 U.S. 448 (1957).

United Steelworkers of America v. *American Manufacturing Company,* 363 U.S. 564 (1960).

United Steelworkers of America v. *Enterprise Wheel and Car Corporation,* 363 U.S. 593 (1960).

United Steelworkers of America v. *Warrior and Gulf Navigation Company,* 363 U.S. 574 (1960).

References

Carmell, L. A., and Westerkamp, P. "Arbitration of EEO Claims a Decade After *Gardner-Denver.*" *Employee Relations Law Journal,* 1986, *12,* 80–97.

Deitsch, C. R., and Dilts, D. A. *The Arbitration of Rights Disputes in the Public Sector.* Westport, Conn.: Quorum/Greenwood, 1990.

Edwards, H. T., Clark, R. T. Jr., and Craver, C. B. *Labor Relations Law in the Public Sector.* (2nd ed.) New York: Bobbs-Merrill, 1979.

Feder, D. L. "'Pick a Forum—Any Forum': A Proposal for a Federal Dispute Resolution Board." *Labor Law Journal,* 1989, *40*(5), 268–280.

Frazier, H. B. III. "Arbitration in the Federal Sector." *Arbitration Journal,* 1986, *41*(1), 70–76.

Hardiman, J. P. "Arbitration of Grievances in the Federal Sector." In E. M. Bussey (ed.), *Federal Civil Service Law and Procedures: A Basic Guide.* (2nd ed.) Washington, D.C.: Bureau of National Affairs, 1990.

Ingraham, P. W., and Ban, C. (eds). *Legislating Bureaucratic Change: The Civil Service Reform Act of 1978.* Albany: State University of New York Press, 1984.

Ingraham, P. W., and Rosenbloom, D. H. "Symposium on the Civil Service Reform Act of 1978." *Policy Studies Journal,* 1988–1989, *17*(2), 311–447.

Kearney, R. C. *Labor Relations in the Public Sector.* (2nd ed.) New York: Dekker, 1992.

Levine, M. J. "Judicial Review of Arbitration Awards: Criticisms and Remedies." *Employee Relations Law Journal,* 1985, *10,* 669–683.

Levinson, D. R. "Federal Personnel Law and the Mixed Case." *Labor Law Journal,* 1986, *37*(12), 811–816.

Moore, C. D. "Where and How to Challenge an Agency Action." In E. M. Bussey (ed.), *Federal Civil Service Law and Procedures: A Basic Guide.* (2nd ed.) Washington, D.C.: Bureau of National Affairs, 1990.

Riccucci, N. M., and Ban, C. "The Unfair Labor Practice Process as a Dispute-Resolution Technique in the Public Sector: The Case of New York State." *Review of Public Personnel Administration,* 1989, *9*(2), 51–67.

Rosenbloom, D. H. "The Federal Labor Relations Authority." *Policy Studies Journal,* 1988–1989, *17*(2), 370–389.

Rosenbloom, D. H., and Shafritz, J. M. *Essentials of Labor Relations.* Upper Saddle River, N.J.: Prentice Hall, 1985.

Shafritz, J. M., Riccucci, N. M., Rosenbloom, D. H., and Hyde, A. C. *Personnel Management in Government.* (2nd ed.) New York: Dekker, 1992.

Sulzner, G. "New Roles, New Strategies: Reinventing the Public Union." In C. Ban and N. M. Riccucci (eds.), *Public Personnel Management: Current Concerns, Future Challenges.* (2nd ed.) Reading, Mass.: Addison Wesley Longman, 1997.

U.S. Equal Employment Opportunity Commission. *Federal Sector Report on EEO Complaints and Appeals.* Washington, D.C.: U.S. Equal Employment Opportunity Commission, 1993.

CHAPTER SEVENTEEN

Privacy and Integrity Testing for Public Employees

Searches, Drug Testing, Polygraphs, and Medical Examinations

N. Joseph Cayer

U.S. citizens take privacy for granted, although the Constitution provides no explicit mention of any right to privacy. The courts and public policymaking bodies have engaged in debate over whether there is such a right to privacy. Over time, a body of laws and judicial decisions has emerged that stakes out some privacy rights. In employment, these rights emanate from common law, constitutional provisions, statutes, and rules and regulations (Baird, Kadue, and Sulzer, 1995; O'Neil, 1993; Rosenbloom and Carroll, 1995; Sovereign, 1989). Common law foundations apply primarily to the private sector, and constitutional provisions apply only to government employees. Statutes and administrative rules and regulations apply to both sectors.

CURRENT STATUS AND CONCERNS

In public employment, tension arises between employees' interest in being free from intrusion into private matters and the employer's interest in serving the public. The employee's interest may be categorized as a confidentiality interest or an autonomy interest (*Whalen* v. *Roe,* 1977). The confidentiality interest refers to freedom from intrusion into personal matters and the autonomy interest concerns freedom over basic issues such as decisions regarding lifestyle, family planning, and religious beliefs. The confidentiality interest is more likely than the autonomy interest to come into conflict with the interests of the employer and thus serves as the basis for most of the analysis in this chapter. The employer's interests involve issues such as ensuring a competent and ethical workforce, ensuring the safety of the public being served, protecting employer property, and being able to implement a policy (for example, drug interdiction). Generally the courts have used a balancing strategy in reconciling the interests of employee and employer, thus determining whether intrusion into employee privacy is permissible (*Waters* v. *Churchill,* 1994).

Challenges to privacy for public employees emerge in testing potential and current employees for appropriateness for employment, in searches of employee offices and desks, and in drug or other substance testing, polygraphs, and medical testing. The law of privacy and integrity testing stems from several constitutional provisions, federal statutes, and state and local government policies. The Fourth, Fifth, and Fourteenth Amendments to the U.S. Constitution serve as the basis for most employee privacy rights involving confidentiality. The Fourth Amendment prohibits unreasonable searches and seizures while the Fifth Amendment prohibits compelling self incrimination. The Due Process Clauses of the Fifth and Fourteenth amendments have been used to protect individuals from being deprived of property or liberty. While the Fifth Amendment applies to the national government, the Fourteenth applies to state and local governments. Various federal laws have been passed to clarify the rights of employees, and many state constitutions and state and local statutes and ordinances also provide protections to their public employees beyond those established by the U.S. Constitution and national law.

Typically, employees must sue to ensure their privacy rights, although it has been difficult to do so until recent decades. Prior to 1972, the privilege doctrine governed much of public employment (Rosenbloom and Carroll, 1995). The privilege doctrine held that public employment was a privilege and that conditions imposed on such employment were not subject to the restrictions emanating from constitutional rights. Thus due process was not required in denying employment or in taking other actions against a public employee. In *Board of Regents* v. *Roth* (1972), the U.S. Supreme Court rejected the traditional view of public employment as a privilege and extended due process rights to the employment relationship in the public sector (Jaegal and Cayer, 1991). Since that time, privacy rights have been established and refined through judicial decisions. The courts also make distinctions between the privacy rights of applicants for employment and the rights of those already employed. For example, applicants may be required to submit to drug tests, but those already employed may be required to do so only under limited circumstances.

Some policies allow employees to waive their rights in certain instances. Additionally, sovereign immunity has been used as a basis for exempting governments from litigation, although the trend has been for governments to voluntarily waive that immunity.

SITUATIONS THAT CHALLENGE PRIVACY RIGHTS

Several situations lead to intrusion into the privacy of public employees or applicants. The following discussion focuses on several areas: drug and alcohol testing, medical exams, polygraphs, and some general areas of concern.

Drug and Alcohol Testing

In recent years, employers instituted tests for drug and alcohol use in response to the pervasiveness of substance abuse problems and because of some related legitimate interests of employers (Stevenson and Williamson, 1995). Generally, employers justify drug and alcohol testing as necessary to ensure the safety of employees and the workplace, to protect sensitive information, and to facilitate employee compatibility with the specific function of the position (for example, interdiction of drugs). Employee challenges to substance testing arise from the Fourth Amendment prohibition against unreasonable searches and seizures and from the Fifth and Fourteenth Amendment due process requirements. The constitutionality of testing depends on the reasonableness of the testing, the privacy expectations of employees, and the circumstances. The due process rights of public employees provide limits on the substance testing process (Riccucci, 1990; Thompson, Riccucci, and Ban, 1991).

The legality of testing also depends, to some extent, on who is being tested. Thus applicants for public service jobs are subject to more testing than those already employed. Public safety and transportation employees usually are more likely to be subject to testing than most other public employees. The Omnibus Transportation Employee Testing Act of 1991 requires testing of those in safety-sensitive employment. Among public agencies, those employees often are in mass transit systems. The U.S. Transportation Department has issued regulations that provide for testing programs. Similarly, military employees and those handling hazardous materials are more likely than most others to undergo testing.

Due process rights arise from the Fifth and Fourteenth Amendments, and much litigation helps to clarify the role of due process in substance testing programs. Additionally, Executive Order 12564 (1986), the Drug Free Workplace Act of 1988, and various state and local policies govern drug and alcohol testing. Executive Order 12564 prohibits drug use on and off duty for national government employees, and it requires agencies to develop procedures for random testing of employees in sensitive positions and to test all employees suspected of impairment. The Drug Free Workplace Act requires contractors with the national government and recipients of federal grants to provide for drug-free workplaces. State and local policies often mirror national policy, but frequently they go even further with respect to definitions, testing, and penalties. Some policies, however, may be more strict in providing protection of the privacy of employees.

Suspicion-Based and Post-Accident Testing. Drug testing based on reasonable suspicion meets the Supreme Court's constitutional test. Constitutional issues emerge because the Court, in *National Treasury Employee's Union* v. *Von Raab* (1989), ruled that a urinalysis test constitutes search and seizure subject to Fourth Amendment safeguards. In *O'Connor* v. *Ortega* (1987), the Court had established the foundation for the reasonableness of warrantless searches based on the scope of the search, the way it was conducted, the place, and the justification for the search. This case involved the search of an employee's office upon complaints of sexual harassment against him. The Von Raab case held that searches must be reasonable, thus implying probable cause or the use of a search warrant. Probable cause can take many forms. Employees may be observed using illegal substances, or their behavior may be consistent with drug-use behavior. If an employee is arrested off the job for drug use, that constitutes probable cause as well in most instances. *Skinner* v. *Railway Labor Executives Association,* also decided in 1989, further clarified the situation by affirming the constitutionality of reasonable suspicion-based drug testing and post-accident testing for railway employees.

The decisions affirming use of suspicion-based drug testing rest on several considerations. The public safety and the safety of other employees and the workplace play major roles in the Court's reasoning in many of these cases. The Court also uses access to sensitive information and national security concerns as justification for testing. The questions of how invasive the test is and whether it is part of a regularly scheduled medical exam also play a role in these decisions.

Post-accident testing has been accepted as reasonable and Constitutional by the Court as well (*Skinner* v. *Railway Labor Executives Association,* 1989). In the transportation industry, safety interests and compelling government interest in discerning the causes of accidents justify use of drug and alcohol testing. Additionally, the courts recognize that requiring a search warrant could lead to a time lapse during which the substance could be eliminated from the bloodstream. The courts also indicate that employees have a reduced expectation of privacy in employment in which public safety is a major concern.

Although reasonable suspicion justifies a search, it must meet due process standards. Employees subject to drug tests have the right to know the results and to challenge those results and to have a pre-termination hearing (*Fraternal Order of Police, Lodge No. 5* v. *Tucker,* 1989).

Random Testing. Random testing for prohibited substances presents the most troublesome situations for public employers in meeting constitutional requirements. Generally the courts allow random testing in situations of great safety concerns and supplement the justification with the idea that employees in such situations have reduced expectations of privacy (*Rushton* v. *Nebraska Public Power District,* 1988).

The courts also permit random testing in heavily regulated activities or where administrative search was appropriately based on safety or other issues. In a private sector case involving very close state regulation, the court permitted random tests for jockeys as necessary for regulators to carry out administrative responsibilities (*Shoemaker* v. *Handel,* 1986). Random testing of police officers (*Policeman's Benevolent Association of New Jersey Local 318* v. *Township of Washington,* 1988, 1989) and U.S. Justice Department employees with access to sensitive information (*Harmon* v. *Thornburgh,* 1989, 1990) met constitutional conditions. At the state and local levels, many cases have produced similar results, with the courts permitting random testing when safety, security, and law enforcement are at stake. The courts generally do not permit general testing unless a necessity is established in terms of safety, administrative need, or maintenance of sensitive information (*American Postal Workers* v. *United States Postal Service,* 1989).

Because of the many issues associated with drug testing, the U.S. Department of Health and Human Services issued "Mandatory Guidelines for Federal Workforce Drug Testing Programs" (1988). This manual prescribes procedures and standards and identifies certified laboratories for testing and analysis of substances. The chain of custody of samples represents just one major concern with the accuracy of testing. Contamination of samples and opportunities for tainting of samples can invalidate tests. Guidelines also relate to the due process rights of the employee.

Medical Testing

Many employers use medical tests other than drug tests. These tests frequently apply to applicants for positions and thus are preemployment exams; however, some employers require such tests for employees on a periodic basis. Generally, under the Americans with Disabilities Act, employers may not use general medical exams for preemployment screening. However, once the screening process is completed and an offer is made, a preemployment physical may be a condition of employment. In such cases, the exam must relate to ability to perform the job.

In recent years, the cost of health care stimulated many employers to use genetic testing and testing for the HIV virus. Under pressure from their insurance companies and based on fears of spread of disease, especially AIDS, many employers instituted such exams. Public policy and litigation resulted in more restricted use of these tests (Falco and Cikins, 1989; Strama, 1993). The rights of potential and current employees counterbalance the interest of the employers in such situations (Nelkin and Tancredi, 1989). Genetic testing has progressed to the point that it can be used to identify individuals as susceptible to the development of particular diseases and to identify potential behavioral patterns. The HIV virus almost always leads to development of AIDS, which is a very expensive disease to treat. Employers interested in containing health care costs find testing for costly diseases tempting. The fear and ignorance surrounding the transmission of AIDS also cause employers to limit employment of those who are HIV positive.

Because people with AIDS are protected from discrimination under the Americans with Disabilities Act, employers now generally may not test for the HIV virus. Lower court decisions permit testing for the HIV virus in cases where protection of the public from transmission of AIDS is an issue (*Anonymous Fireman* v. *City of Willoughby,* 1991), but they do not permit testing in other situations (*Glover* v. *Eastern Nebraska Community Office of Retardation,* 1989). Eventually, this issue will reach the U.S. Supreme Court.

Genetic testing has not achieved the visibility of some other testing in public employment, but it has stimulated some states to develop policies affecting it (Cozzetto and Pedeliski, 1996). Several states (California, Iowa, Louisiana, New Hampshire, Oregon, Rhode Island, and Wisconsin) prohibit or restrict employers from using genetic testing based on the concern that such tests will be used to discriminate against individuals. A bill has been introduced into Congress to protect the genetic privacy of all individuals.

Polygraph and Psychological Tests

Employers sometimes use polygraph and personality tests for selection of employees or when employee misconduct is suspected. Federal law prohibits the use of polygraph exams in private sector employment settings through the Federal Employee Polygraph Protection Act of 1988. The act specifically exempts the public sector, but many of the concerns that led to its passage influence the courts in examining the issue for public employees. Twenty-seven states and the District of Columbia either prohibit or restrict the use of polygraphs as tools of employment. In addition to prohibition, state policy typically requires licensing of polygraph examiners, regulates the questions used, limits the scope and context of the tests, and requires protection of confidentiality of the results.

Bans and restrictions on the use of polygraph exams stem from concerns with both their validity and their intrusion on privacy. Because of problems with their validity, polygraph exams generally are not acceptable as evidence in court. In limiting the use of polygraphs in employment situations, the courts have noted their exclusion as legal evidence.

While employers defend polygraph and psychological exams as important instruments to determine honesty and ferret out misconduct, the courts have balanced those values with the rights of employees to privacy. Thus, in evaluating the use of polygraphs in public employment, the courts rely on the intrusiveness of the exams and the involuntary nature of responses to limit their application. Additionally, of course, job relatedness must be demonstrated by the employer. Polygraph exams meet the job relatedness standard if they are tailored to the needs of the job. The courts also focus on the scope of the questions, the purpose, and the use of the information acquired through the exams to inform their decisions.

Polygraphs may be used in the interest of the employer in creating a drug-free environment. Thus, in *Hester* v. *City of Milledgeville* (1985), a circuit court affirmed the right of the employer to use polygraphs in investigating drug use in a fire department. The court concluded that the use of the polygraph was job related and that no evidence showed that the information would be used for any other purpose, such as embarrassing the employees. Courts do carefully scrutinize the questions used, however, as evidenced in circuit court reasoning in *Thorne* v. *City of El Segundo* (1983, 1984). In this case (which the U.S. Supreme Court let stand through denial of certiorari), questions regarding an applicant's sexual relations with a member of the police department with which she was seeking employment were found to be too intrusive to be constitutionally acceptable. The court could find no compelling state interest in the information and noted that it was shared with members of the police command.

Psychological or personality tests have become popular among many employers for making judgments about integrity, motivation, reliability, and behavior tendencies of potential employees or potential promotees. For example, the Minnesota Multiphasic Personality Inventory promises to demonstrate tendencies toward violence, hostility, addiction, and tolerance, as well as attitudes toward authority and work. Similarly, the Myers-Briggs Type Indicator purportedly measures sixteen personality types. Employers using these tests hope to select individuals who are "compatible" with an organization's culture. By identifying those who may tend toward hostility, addiction, intolerance, and so forth, the employer may also expect to avoid problems in the organization.

These tests, however, may rely on questions that are intrusive and that are not directly job related. The challenge for the employer is to demonstrate the need to know the information in order to ensure selection on the basis of job relevance. Psychological exams usually are classified as medical exams and thus fall under the same rules as medical exams; this means that they cannot be used in the initial screening process but only as a final condition of an offer of employment. The situations in which such evaluations may be used are limited as well. For example, psychiatric evaluation may be required in cases involving potential jeopardy to the welfare of students, but otherwise they may be prohibited (*Daury* v. *Smith*, 1988).

General Areas

Public policy and litigation address several other aspects of employer interest that sometimes conflict with the privacy rights of employees. For example, preemployment inquiries cover many areas of information of interest to the employer. Policy addresses what information may be obtained and what information about an individual may be released. Generally, employers may request a broad range of information, but they are narrowly restricted in what they can release. As a rule, courts have indicated that applying for a position implies a decision to disclose information that is relevant to the job. The Federal Privacy Act limits federal agencies to collecting only that information that is relevant and necessary for the task at hand, in this case, employment. For example, questions about one's criminal record would be relevant for someone pursuing a law enforcement position but may not be relevant for a maintenance job. Equal employment opportunity policy also limits what might be asked of applicants as a way of protecting against discriminatory selection processes. Additionally, the Americans with Disabilities Act prohibits asking about disabilities or medical conditions except under certain circumstances.

Because of the costs of health care benefits, many employers have an interest in the personal habits of current and potential employees. Thus they may want to know whether individuals smoke, drink alcohol, or use illegal drugs. Generally such inquiries are not permissible, but some jurisdictions have instituted policies requiring employees in police and fire departments to quit smoking within a prescribed time or lose their jobs, based on the need for healthy employees to perform the duties of those positions. In order to implement such policies, the employer would need to seek information regarding the prohibited activities. If the employer can demonstrate job relatedness to policies prohibiting even off-work smoking, courts seem to find such policies permissible (*Grusendorf* v. *Oklahoma City,* 1987), but not when relevance to job performance is not shown (*Kurtz* v. *City of North Miami,* 1993).

Financial privacy affects questions about credit ratings and other personal financial records. Questions regarding personal financial matters meet the constitutional tests if they are related to job performance. Thus applicants for positions handling money or in which embezzlement or other corruption may be possible often must provide personal financial information. If credit checks are used, the applicant must be informed of their use.

Employers often have interests in the lifestyles of employees and potential employees. The courts have long held that the privacy of such information is protected (*Loving* v. *Virginia,* 1967; *Skinner* v. *Oklahoma,* 1942). Homosexual activity generates much emotional fervor, and policies still reflect that reaction. Thus many jurisdictions have policies that either protect gays and lesbians from discrimination because of their sexual orientation or prohibit gays and lesbians from employment. The courts are considering that issue regularly in contemporary society. In *Romer* v. *Evans* (1996), the Supreme Court invalidated Colorado's Amendment 2, which would have prohibited Colorado jurisdictions from adopting policies that prevent discrimination based on sexual orientation. Complicating the matter is that homosexual activity is still illegal in most states; thus cases sometimes turn on whether privacy extends to illegal activity (*Bowers* v. *Hardwick,* 1986).

All of these issues involve balancing the rights of the individual applicant or employee and the interests of government. Judicial decisions turn on the need to know an individual's reputation, impact on the morale of other employees, and ability to perform. Establishing relevance to the job challenges employers.

USE OF INFORMATION

Once an employer acquires information about applicants and employees, different privacy concerns arise. Employers may use information about applicants in making hiring decisions; therefore, the information may be passed on to anyone involved in deciding who is to be employed. The information usually may not be disclosed to anyone else, however. Confidentiality becomes increasingly difficult as the number of people involved in the hiring decision increases.

Many public policies govern access to information held by government. Primary among national government policies are the Freedom of Information Act (FOIA) and the Federal Privacy Act of 1974. FOIA requires agencies of the federal government to release information to anyone requesting it, although some information is exempted. Of relevance to this discussion, FOIA exempts personnel records, medical records, and other information, the release of which would lead to an unwarranted intrusion into personal privacy. The Federal Privacy Act governs what can be released and under what conditions release is permissible. Legislation in many states provides similar policies. For the most part, information may be released within the agency and on a need-to-know basis. For example, information that a military person tested positive for HIV can be released to the command so that proper actions can be taken to protect the individual and other personnel (*Plowman* v. *Department of the Army,* 1988). The employer may release information from psychological tests to consulting psychiatrists to help determine fitness for employment (*Redmond* v. *City of Overland Park,* 1987). Employers may release general statements regarding personnel actions, but usually they may not discuss specific reasons for any actions.

What an employer or former employer says when reference checks are made sometimes generates problems. For the most part, reference responses may contain information that is true, complete, and without malice. Most employers tend to limit the information they will release to acknowledgment that the individual was employed, what the period of employment was, and salary level. Litigation over evaluative information has frightened many from releasing such information. Nonetheless, the courts generally have affirmed the right of the employer to provide accurate information as long as it is complete and the employer is not releasing it with malicious intent. Concern over liability of references has led to adoption of reference immunity laws in some jurisdictions.

In Florida and Maine, for example, the law provides that employers who furnish information about former employee performance are presumed to be acting in good faith unless demonstrated otherwise and thus are immune from liability for disclosures.

Information obtained through testing for alcohol and drugs may have many implications for the employer. Depending on the circumstances, a positive test for the substances may lead to termination; however, such cases generally are limited to those involving serious threats to safety or jeopardy to the ability of the employee to carry out responsibilities. For example, a drug task force police officer could not be very effective if found to be using illegal drugs.

More likely, courts will require the employer to take actions to help individual employees who have substance abuse problems. The employer may be required to offer counseling and rehabilitation support before disciplining an individual. If the employee does not take advantage of the assistance available, he or she may then be terminated. Many employers have employee assistance programs (EAPs) to which employees may be referred. EAPs help individuals deal with many problems that may affect job performance. Unless the employer has direct evidence of the use of illegal substances, referral to the EAP or other counseling can be awkward, and the employer may be limited to recommending use of the EAP to deal with whatever is bothering the employee. If direct evidence exists, the employee may be required to seek assistance as a condition of continued employment.

CONCLUSION

To say that employees have certain rights to privacy does not automatically translate into employees enjoying those rights (Fine, Reeves, and Harney, 1996). Clearly, public employers have interests in curbing some of the privacy of employees. Thus actual enjoyment of the rights of employees often requires proactive efforts by an individual employee. Litigation provides a way of defining and ensuring exercise of the rights accorded by the Constitution, statutes, rules and regulations, and court decisions. Where collective bargaining exists, negotiated agreements may also specify rights and spell out procedures for enforcing them. For example, drug testing may be addressed in a labor agreement.

The law on privacy and integrity testing evolves slowly. Courts face continued challenges to policy developed by employers that intrudes on the privacy of public employees. While some areas of concern have been fairly settled (for example, drug and alcohol testing), others such as the privacy rights of homosexuals or the requirement for HIV testing are still emerging areas of the law. Decisions in the lower federal courts and in the states reflect a wide variety of perspectives on many issues. The U.S. Supreme Court has demonstrated little enthusiasm for entering the fray on many of these issues, but over time it will surely do so.

Cases Cited

American Postal Workers v. *United States Postal Service,* 830 F.2d 294 (D.C. Cir., 1987).

Anonymous Fireman v. *City of Willoughby,* 779 F.Supp. 402 (N.D. Ohio, 1991).

Board of Regents v. *Roth,* 408 U.S. 564 (1972).

Bowers v. *Hardwick,* 478 U.S. 186 (1986).

Daury v. *Smith,* 842 F.2d 98 (1st Cir., 1988).

Fraternal Order of Police, Lodge No. 5 v. *Tucker,* 868 F.2d 74 (3d Cir., 1989).

Glover v. *Eastern Nebraska Community Office of Retardation,* 867 F.2d 461 (1989).

Grusendorf v. *Oklahoma City,* 816 F.2d 539 (10th Cir., 1987).

Harmon v. *Thornburgh,* 878 F.2d 484 (D.C. Cir., 1989), cert. denied, 493 U.S. 1056 (1990).

Hester v. *City of Milledgeville,* 777 F.2d 1492 (11th Cir., 1985).

Kurtz v. *City of North Miami,* 625 So.2d 899 (Fla. Ct. App., 1993).

Loving v. *Virginia,* 388 U.S. 1 (1967).

National Treasury Employees Union v. *Von Raab,* 489 U.S. 656 (1989).

O'Connor v. *Ortega,* 480 U.S. 709 (1987).

Plowman v. *Department of the Army,* 698 F.Supp. 627 (E.D.Va., 1988).

Policeman's Benevolent Association of New Jersey Local 318 v. *Township of Washington,* 850 F.2d 133 (3d Cir., 1988), cert. denied, 490 U.S. 1004 (1989).

Redmond v. *City of Overland Park,* 672 F.Supp. 473 (D.Kan., 1987).

Romer v. *Evans,* 116 S.Ct. 1620 (1996).

Rushton v. *Nebraska Public Power District,* 844 R.2d 562 (8th Cir., 1988).

Shoemaker v. *Handel,* 619 F.Supp. 1089, aff'd, 795 F.2d 1136 (3d Cir.), cert. denied, 479 U.S. 986 (1986).

Skinner v. *Oklahoma,* 316 U.S. 535 (1942).

Skinner v. *Railway Labor Executives Association,* 489 U.S. 602 (1989).

Thorne v. *City of El Segundo,* 726 F.2d 456 (9th Cir., 1983), cert. denied, 469 U.S. 979 (1984).

Waters v. *Churchill,* 114 S.Ct. 1878 (1994).

Whalen v. *Roe,* 429 U.S. 589 (1977).

References

Baird, J., Kadue, D. D., and Sulzer, K. D. *Public Employee Privacy: A Legal and Practical Guide to Issues Affecting the Workplace.* Chicago: American Bar Association, 1995.

Cozzetto, D. A., and Pedeliski, T. B. "Privacy and the Workplace." *Review of Public Personnel Administration,* 1996, *16*(2), 21–31.

Falco, M., and Cikins, W. I. (eds.). *Toward a National Policy on Drug and AIDS Testing.* Washington, D.C.: Brookings Institution, 1989.

Fine, C. R., Reeves, T. Z., and Harney, G. P. "Employee Drug Testing: Are Cities Complying with the Courts?" *Public Administration Review,* 1996, *56*(1), 31–37.

Jaegal, D., and Cayer, N. J. "Public Personnel Administration by Lawsuit: The Impact of Supreme Court Decisions on Public Employee Litigation." *Public Administration Review,* 1991, *51*(3), 211–221.

Nelkin, D., and Tancredi, L. *Dangerous Diagnostics.* New York: Basic Books, 1989.

O'Neil, R. M. *The Rights of Public Employees.* (2nd ed.) Carbondale: Southern Illinois University Press, 1993.

Riccucci, N. M. "Drug Testing in the Public Sector: A Legal Analysis." *American Review of Public Administration,* 1990, *20*(2), 95–106.

Rosenbloom, D. H., and Carroll, J. D. "Public Personnel Administration and Law." In J. Rabin, T. Vocino, W. B. Hildreth, and G. J. Miller (eds.), *Handbook of Public Personnel Administration.* New York: Dekker, 1995.

Sovereign, K. L. *Personnel Law.* (2nd ed.) Upper Saddle River, N.J.: Prentice Hall, 1989.

Stevenson, J. G., and Williamson, R. "Testing for Drugs: Bathrooms or Barbershops?" *Public Personnel Management,* 1995, *24*(4), 467–474.

Strama, B. T. (ed.). *AIDS and Governmental Liability: State and Local Government Guide to Legislation, Legal Issues, and Liability.* Chicago: American Bar Association, 1993.

Thompson, F. J., Riccucci, N. M., and Ban, C. "Biological Testing and Personnel Policy: Drugs and the Federal Workplace." In C. Ban and N. M. Riccucci (eds.), *Public Personnel Management: Current Concerns—Future Challenges.* Reading, Mass.: Addison Wesley Longman, 1991.

U.S. Department of Health and Human Services. "Mandatory Guidelines for Federal Workforce Drug Testing Programs." *Federal Register,* 1988, *53*, 11970–11989.

CHAPTER EIGHTEEN

The Raging Debate over Equality

Nondiscrimination, Affirmative Action,
and the Civil Rights Act

Maxine Kurtz

The current debate over civil rights in the economic field has been emotional, intense, and frequently personal. The subject is a classic example of legislative, executive, and court actions responding to the political environment of the times, and of the impacts of the subsequent time lags in responding to changed conditions.

Economic issues substantially replaced legal issues (such as the right to vote) in the civil rights movement during the 1960s. Minorities found that inadequate education, high unemployment and underemployment, and inability to compete in the marketplace combined to block full integration into mainstream society. Access to the ballot was not enough to overcome these barriers. Events ranging from widespread urban riots to the Washington, D.C., rally at which Martin Luther King delivered the famous "I Have a Dream" speech dramatically brought these problems to the attention of "the establishment." Many people also perceived the assassinations of President John F. Kennedy in 1963 and Robert Kennedy and Martin Luther King in 1968 to be backlash against the civil rights positions espoused by these leaders. Contemporary equal employment/affirmative action programs were born during those troubled times.

The Civil Rights Act of 1964 prohibited private employers from discriminating against applicants and employees on grounds of race, color, national origin, religion, or gender. Executive Order 11246, issued the next year, required large organizations receiving federal funds to make reasonable efforts to have their workforces represent the racial mix of the qualified labor force in their recruitment areas. From these modest beginnings, statutes, executive orders, regulations, and court decisions proliferated. Affirmative action requirements for organizations and agencies are diverse, ranging from the Federal Communication Commission's minority preferences in sales of certain broadcast channels, to the Immigration Reform and Control Act of 1986's prohibitions on discrimination by employers on the basis of national origin or citizenship (General Accounting Office, 1990).

THE RAGING DEBATE: ROUND ONE

The first round of the current debate over nondiscrimination and affirmative action occurred from 1989 to 1991 and could have been billed as the Supreme Court versus Congress. In 1989, a divided court reversed years of precedent with respect to the meaning of civil rights statutes, only to be reversed in turn by the Civil Rights Act of 1991. Congress stated that one of the objectives of the 1991 statute was "to respond to recent decisions of the Supreme Court by expanding the scope of relevant civil rights statutes in order to provide adequate protection to victims of discrimination" [PL 102–166, 105 Stat. 1076]. A brief tabulation of the actions and reactions demonstrates the turmoil of the times.

Proof of Disparate Impact

After *Griggs* v. *Duke Power Company* (1971), the common way of proving disparate impact was to compare test results or appointment rates to the racial composition of the labor force. In *Wards Cove Packing Company* v. *Antonio* (1989), Native Americans working in Alaskan fish canneries brought a suit alleging that they were being discriminated against, and they used the common statistical proof in an effort to establish their case. The Supreme Court ruled against the plaintiffs, however, stating that they also had to show which part of the selection process was discriminatory and prove that the employer had no business necessity for using that part.

An outraged Congress found in the Civil Rights Act of 1991 that "the decision of the Supreme Court in *Wards Cove Packing Company* v. *Antonio* has weakened the scope and effectiveness of Federal civil rights protections against unlawful discrimination in employment" [105 Stat. 1071, 2(2)]. The act provided that the plaintiff should show, if possible, which selection technique was discriminatory; otherwise, the case could be filed against the group of techniques. In addition, the act returned the burden of proof of business necessity to the employer.

The "But For" Test

Price Waterhouse v. *Hopkins* (1989) dealt with Price Waterhouse's refusal to promote a female associate to partnership status. Management's reasons had to do in part with the plaintiff's femininity (such as her wearing of jewelry and makeup). The Court ruled that an employer would not be considered to have discriminated if the same result would have been reached for nondiscriminatory reasons. Congress responded by including in the 1991 Civil Rights Act a provision that any reliance on discrimination is illegal.

Reopening Consent Decrees

In *Martin* v. *Wilkes* (1989), a group of white firefighters challenged a ten-year-old consent decree that mandated a quota system for promotion of minorities until a specified percentage was reached. The Supreme Court held that the opponents to a consent decree do not have to intervene to protect their rights. The parties to the decree had to join possible opponents as parties. Accordingly, the white firefighters could reopen the litigation.

Congress responded by barring such intervention under three circumstances: (1) prior to the entry of judgment, the persons must have had notice from any source that a judgment or order might affect their interests, and they must have had a reasonable opportunity to object to the judgment or order; (2) the interests of such persons must have been adequately represented by another person who challenged the order; or (3) the court that entered the judgment or order must have determined that reasonable efforts were made to give notice to the interested parties, consistent with due process.

When Challenges Can Be Filed

The Civil Rights Act of 1964 provided that charges of discrimination had to be filed within 180 days after the discriminatory event occurred. In *Lorance* v. *AT&T Technologies* (1989), an employer and union modified a seniority system in a way that would deprive women of certain future benefits. In trying to bring the case to court, the women were trapped in a catch–22 situation. If they brought the case during the 180 days after the date of the amendment to the union contract, they could not show that they had been harmed; if they waited until they would have been entitled to the benefits, the 180–day limit would have expired. The Supreme Court ruled that the 180–day limit applied to the date of the amendment to the union contract. Congress responded with a provision that the 180–day limit would apply either to the date of the amendment or to the date when the amendment adversely affected the plaintiff.

Employment Rights Contract Rights Protected by Section 1981

Section 1981, passed in 1866, is a post-Civil War era civil rights statute that provided for minorities to have the same powers to make and enforce contracts as white people do. In *Patterson* v. *McLean Credit Union,* the last of the 1989 series of cases, the Supreme Court held that what transpired after a contract had been made was not part of the making or enforcing of an employment contract. More specifically, promotion was not covered unless it would result in a new employment contract.

This ruling had a dramatic impact on civil rights litigation. The National Association for the Advancement of Colored People Defense Fund (Bureau of National Affairs, 1989) reported that within four and a half months after the decision, ninety-six cases filed in lower federal courts had been dismissed because of the *Patterson* ruling. Congress reversed that ruling in the Civil Rights Act of 1991 by providing that the term "make and enforce contracts" includes "the making, performance, modification, and termination of contracts, and the enjoyment of all benefits, privileges, terms and conditions of the contractual relationship" [105 Stat. 1071, sec. 101(b)].

Other Issues

From a political standpoint, round one debates related to the sections of laws dealing with damages and with quotas, pitting employer groups against civil rights organizations. President George Bush vetoed the proposed Civil Rights Act of 1990 over these issues.

In the 1991 act, compromises capped the damages that could be awarded, depending on employer size, and public sector employers were excluded from punitive damages. Section 111 of the Civil Rights Act of 1991 dealt with quotas in these terms: "Nothing in the amendments made by this Act shall be construed . . . to require, encourage, or permit an employer to adopt hiring or promotion quotas on the basis of race, color, religion, sex, or national origin, and the use of such quotas shall be deemed to be an unlawful employment practice under such title. . . ." An exception is made for practices allowed by U.S. Supreme Court decisions or, in the absence of decisions, by employment discrimination laws. These situations usually involve remedies for prior proven cases of discrimination. There was, however, a continuing area of uncertainty with regard to voluntary affirmative action programs implemented in agencies for which there was no proven prior case of discrimination but for which an arguable case could be made that a pattern of discrimination was present (*Johnson* v. *Santa Clara Department of Transportation*, 1987).

THE RAGING DEBATE: ROUND TWO

Round two might be termed a free-for-all, involving all levels of government and all elements of society.

By mid-1995, public debate focused on what were thought to be affirmative action and nondiscrimination requirements, with particular emphasis on perceived adverse effects on white, Anglo-Saxon, Protestant males who were not Vietnam veterans, not disabled, and not forty years of age or older. Media coverage was too widespread to document, and commentators across the political spectrum, from Rush Limbaugh to Jesse Jackson, fueled the debate. Various polls documented the increasing public doubt about the fairness of affirmative action, including a 1994 poll showing that "for the first time in eight years a majority of whites agree with the idea 'We have gone too far in pushing equal rights in this country'" (Lacago, 1995, p. 39). The next month, *Time* noted that "the latest *Los Angeles Times* poll shows the number who believe affirmative action programs 'go too far' is up to 39 percent, from 24 percent in 1991" (Birnbaum, 1995, p. 36).

In the first half of 1995, all branches of the federal government undertook reexaminations of nondiscrimination and affirmative action programs. In the Senate, a report known as the Dole Report, prepared by the Congressional Research Service for majority leader Robert Dole, identified approximately 160 federal programs requiring affirmative action (Congressional Research Service, 1995). The Committee on Economic and Educational Opportunities of the U.S. House of Representatives held hearings to examine affirmative action. President Bill Clinton directed the attorney general's office to review the workability of the government's affirmative action programs (Patrick, 1995). The U.S. Supreme Court decided *Adarand Constructors, Inc.* v. *Pena* (1995), reversing recent decisions that relaxed standards for determining the constitutionality of federal affirmative action programs using "benign" racial classifications. Governor Pete Wilson of California issued an executive order terminating all of the state's affirmative action programs (Wilson, 1995). Other states reportedly have similar actions under consideration (Bureau of National Affairs, 1995).

What the Argument Is All About

The debate over affirmative action has frequently been acrimonious, emotional, and productive of more heat than light. Columnist Clarence Page (1995) summarized the reason in these terms:

> We have little argument over what good or harm it [affirmative action] does largely because there is so little agreement over what it is.
>
> Is it an anti-poverty program? Or is it an equal-opportunity program? Is it a diversity program to create enrollments and payrolls that look like America and produce more role models? Or is it a reparations program, suitable only to native-born blacks and other groups who can claim specific historic grievances?
>
> Perhaps it is a remedial program, intended to make up for specific discrimination at specific companies, universities or municipal departments.
>
> In fact, affirmative action can be any or all of these things. That's why so many of whose who argue the topic simply are not talking about the same thing.

The thesis of this quotation is supported by the findings of a 1995 survey in which 56 percent of municipal executives could not identify which one of three definitions of affirmative action was legally correct (Pace and Smith, 1995). In light of the confusion over definitions, the following meanings are assigned to the terms used in this chapter.

Nondiscrimination. The term *nondiscrimination* is derived from the U.S. Constitution, Amendment XIV, Section 1, which reads in part: "nor shall any State deprive any person of life, liberty, or property, without due process of law; nor deny to any person within its jurisdiction the equal protection of the laws." Amendment V reads in part: "No person shall . . . be deprived of life, liberty or property, without due process of law." The parallel wording of these two amendments led the U.S. Supreme Court to extend limitations on the states to apply to the federal government as well (*Adarand Constructors, Inc.* v. *Pena,* 1995).

The Civil Rights Act of 1964 prohibits discrimination against employees and applicants for employment on the basis of race, color, national origin, religion, or gender. It also prohibits discrimination in housing, education, and public accommodations. Other statutes prohibit discrimination based on age or disability. In civil rights jargon, persons falling within the enumerated categories are members of "protected groups."

A person has been discriminated against when all of the following conditions exist:

1. The person has been harmed by some action of the employer or the union.

2. The action was based on the person's race, color, national origin, religion, gender, age, or disability.

3. The person has been treated differently from other persons who are similarly situated but do not have the same race, color, national origin, religion, gender, age, or disability.

4. No valid business-related reason exists for the difference in treatment.

This relatively simple definition gave rise to several issues in the real world, including disparate treatment versus disparate impact, mixed-motive actions, and "benign" versus "invidious" classifications. Special considerations with respect to gender and disabilities are discussed in later chapters.

Disparate Treatment Versus Disparate Impact. Disparate treatment requires both knowledge by the employer of the discriminatory act and intent of the employer to discriminate, either actual or implied. The question of whether or not an organization or its chief executives are responsible for discrimination by subordinate supervisors is frequently an issue. The answer is, it depends. Each set of circumstances is weighed on its own facts (*Texas Department of Community Affairs* v. *Burdine,* 1981).

The classic definition of disparate impact is an action that is neutral on its face but that has an adverse effect on one or more members of a protected group. For the most part, this type of discrimination is found in recruitment and testing (*Griggs* v. *Duke Power Company*, 1971). The Uniform Guidelines on Employee Selection Procedures (Equal Employment Opportunity Coordinating Council, 1995) have extended provisions identifying what constitutes disparate impact. No intent to discriminate is required.

An argument has raged over whether or not "institutional racism" is covered by constitutional and statutory provisions on civil rights. For instance, current stereotypes based on the fact that blacks were slaves in the 1700s and 1800s are claimed to be harmful to all blacks today. Beginning with the Omnibus Crime Control and Safe Streets Act of 1968, Congress determined that membership in a protected group is automatically evidence of being a victim of discrimination (through a requirement for affirmative action programs with no showing of individually identifiable victims or perpetrators). At this time, the validity of this determination has not been finally determined, but the tide is starting to run against it.

Mixed Motive. In many recent examples of alleged discrimination, the question was, How much discrimination is acceptable? In these cases the test appears to have been whether or not race was the determining consideration (*Regents of the University of California* v. *Bakke*, 1978).

Types of Racial Classifications. For a time, the U.S. Supreme Court divided racial classifications in federal statutes between those that were "benign" and those that were "invidious." A benign classification was one determined by Congress to be designed to aid members of protected groups; all others were "invidious" and presumptively illegal. On the basis of deference to coequal branches of government, the divided Supreme Court sustained statutes when Congress determined that the racial classification was needed for a benign purpose (*Fullilove* v. *Klutznick*, 1980; *Metro Broadcasting* v. *FCC*, 1990). This distinction was blurred in the *Adarand* case (1995).

Affirmative Action

If disparate treatment occurred, victims could receive injunctive relief, reinstatement with full benefits, front pay, back pay, damages for pain and suffering, punitive damages, exemplary damages (against private employers), and attorney's fees.

If disparate impact occurred, the remedies tended to relate to groups of people. Not only could the individual or individuals who brought the suit receive the promotion or appointment being sought, but if the Court found that the discrimination was "egregious," it could also establish quotas to overcome the effects of past discrimination. This is sometimes called "judicially imposed affirmative action."

A subsequent development was the decision by some employers to institute affirmative action programs without going through a court case to establish that they had discriminated. In these instances, the employer admitted that past discrimination had occurred and fashioned its own remedy to overcome the effects of that past action and to prevent future recurrences. Again, there were one or more identifiable victims.

The last form of affirmative action was a remedy without a specific victim. The Equal Employment Opportunity Commission (EEOC) issued interpretive guidelines in 1979, holding that such plans would not be considered reverse discrimination (Equal Employment Opportunity Commission, 1979). The employer or educational institution or whatever organization was involved could decide to institute affirmative action measures to provide role models, to encourage diversity, to "level the playing field" by contracting set-asides for minority- or woman-owned businesses, or simply to qualify for federal grants. (See, for instance, the action of the California Board of Regents to terminate affirmative action programs in the state's universities unless such programs were required for federal grants. Section 2 of the board's resolution, adopted July 20, 1995, prohibited use of race, religion, sex, color, ethnicity, or national origin as criteria for admission; and Section 6 provided that "nothing in Section 2 shall prohibit any action which is strictly necessary to establish or maintain eligibility for any federal or state program, where ineligibility would result in a loss of federal or state funds to the University." A parallel resolution relating to employment and contracting was adopted on the same date.)

The Current Situation: An Evaluation of Affirmative Action

The debate over the effect of affirmative action is based in large measure on anecdotal evidence. Those who support it cite examples of individuals who benefited from programs designed to help members of protected groups, such as U.S. Supreme Court Justice Clarence Thomas. Similarly, those opposed cite abuses such as contractor set-asides being awarded to a minority-owned construction firm that does in excess of $1,000,000 of business annually.

Census data indicate that economic improvements have been made by blacks and Hispanics; data do not indicate how much of the improvement is due to affirmative action. The same challenge can be made to the following passage from testimony at the 1995 Congressional hearings on affirmative action: "This is simply to say that while meaningful progress has been made in eliminating discriminatory barriers to employment, education, and other economic opportunities, some barriers, and the effects of previous barriers remain. African Americans and Hispanics continue to lag far behind whites in rate of employment, income and education level. The unemployment rate for African Americans was more than twice that of whites in 1993, while the median income of African Americans was barely more than one-half that of whites. Hispanics fare only modestly better in each category" (Patrick, 1995, p. 46). Patrick adds, "In 1993, less than 3 percent of college graduates were unemployed, but whereas 22.6 percent of whites had college degrees, only 12.2 percent of African Americans and 9.0 percent of Hispanics did" (p. 47). Granting that these and similar data probably are accurate, there is no indication of how affirmative action would improve these statistics or how past programs have affected these current statistics.

In his statement at the Congressional hearings, Professor Loury (1995) observed the following:

> While substantial differences in income exist between various ethnic groups and while discrimination against women and various minority groups in employment has been and continues to be a matter of concern, there is no sound social-scientific basis for concluding that the existing economic differences have been caused by or reflect the extent of, employment discrimination against various groups. Gross statistical disparities are inadequate to identify the presence of discrimination because individuals differ in many ways likely to affect their earnings capacities which are not adequately measured when group outcomes are compared. Moreover, based on my review of the statistical evidence, there is no basis for the assertion that affirmative action policies have had anything but a marginal effect on these differences [p. 108].

Some members of minority groups claim that they "made good" on their own and that affirmative action programs diminish their achievements in the eyes of others (Loury, 1995). Others worry about affirmative action as a symbol and suggest that termination or limitation of affirmative action programs would be perceived as a rejection by the hostile majority white population of the legitimate aspirations of persons of color. (See, for example, the survey titled "Affirmative Action: A Symbol Under Siege," 1995). Neither of these issues is quantifiable except perhaps through opinion polling.

In summary, despite President Clinton's statement that "affirmative action is an effort to open the doors of education, employment and business development opportunities to qualified individuals who happen to be members of groups that have experienced long-standing and persistent discrimination" (Clinton, 1995b, p. 5) there is little consensus on the goals and objectives of affirmative action programs.

There also appears to be no concrete quantitative evidence by which the effects of affirmative action can be measured if the question is, What difference did the aggregate of programs make? Put differently, What would have been the effect on these figures if affirmative action programs had not existed? Absent an answer to these questions, the debate rages in a near-vacuum of evidence.

The EEOC in 1996 instituted a new system for classifying and handling cases. Class A cases are those that clearly involve discrimination and warrant a detailed and extended investigation. Class C cases clearly lack merit and receive a summary investigation at best. Class B cases are awaiting classification as either A or C. This approach is expected to expedite the handling of the case load.

A GUIDE FOR PUBLIC ADMINISTRATORS

In the midst of the raging debate, public administrators must continue to deal with nondiscrimination and affirmative action issues. This section reviews the basics of employment policies that probably will not be affected by whatever political decisions are made. Details differ on policies relative to the rest of the 160 plus programs in the Dole Report and to nondiscrimination provisions, but the concepts are common to most if not all of them.

Nondiscrimination

Intentional discrimination as such is not involved in the mainstream of the raging debate. In theory, at least, few policymakers overtly advocate intentional discrimination.

The administrative steps to address intentional discrimination issues also are clear. They include:

1. A strong commitment by management to oppose discrimination
2. Clear communication to supervisors and employees that discrimination will not be tolerated (including antidiscrimination statements in employee handbooks or personnel rules)
3. An open line of communication to management for persons perceiving themselves to be victims of discrimination
4. Prompt appropriate action to deal with persons found to have discriminated illegally

Persons perceiving themselves to be victims of discrimination can file complaints with the EEOC. Under "deferral" agreements, complaints may be referred to state civil rights commissions for processing and disposition. Cooperation with reasonable requests of EEOC investigators is a useful approach; it tends to allay suspicions that the employer has something to hide. If commission investigators wish to interview persons who might have knowledge of the alleged discrimination, the employer is entitled to have a representative present if the employee is a policymaker or a confidential aide to a policymaker, such as a private secretary. Management representatives may not be present when employees or others are being interviewed. Management can and should object if requests for information or treatment by commission investigators are unreasonable. The main thing to remember is not to be "spooked" by EEOC charges being filed. The percentage of "probable cause" findings is low.

Besides low probable-cause findings, another major characteristic of an EEOC investigation is that it is very slow. It is useful to meet the requested deadlines (or to file a request for an extension to a specific date), but once a reply has been filed, forget about the case; it probably will be many months before another communication is received. The EEOC was notoriously slow even before 1991, when the agency was made responsible for the enforcement of the Americans with Disabilities Act (ADA) of 1990. Between the effective date of the Civil Rights Act of 1991 and the end of 1994, more than 45,000 complaints under the ADA were received by the EEOC. President Clinton indicated that the agency received more than 90,000 discrimination complaints in 1994 alone (Clinton, 1995b). The overload at the EEOC is common knowledge and is the subject of the current debate over individual discrimination concerns.

Discrimination in Selection

Standards for selection differ to some degree, depending on whether the employer or educational institution is public or private. Private organizations are not subject to the constitutional requirements relating to equal protection under the laws. Accordingly, they are only subject to the legislative requirements of the Civil Rights Acts.

Issues in selection are whether or not the selection device or devices used are (1) related to the essential duties of the job, and (2) predictive of success on the job. Some degree of flexibility is needed in evaluating these issues. For instance, one city required candidates for firefighter to lift a folded hose and place it on an overhead storage rack in a fire station. Apparently this would meet the criteria, but the test had the effect of screening out the female candidates. Unsuccessful candidates challenged the test and won when they showed that they could have passed the test by standing on a low step stool. An ongoing evaluation of tests, including comparable application rates, selection participation rates, pass rates, appointment rates, and retention rates, provide the data needed to document compliance with selection requirements.

Parenthetically, essential duties of the job also need to be identified for classification and pay plans, employee performance appraisal, skills and knowledge training, and compliance with the Americans with Disabilities Act of 1990.

Affirmative Action Without Specific Victims

Federal programs commonly are the source of requirements for affirmative action. Over the last thirty years, inevitable abuses of the equal employment/affirmative action system have arisen. This is the center of the raging debate.

President Clinton's policy campaign slogan in 1995 was "Amend it, don't end it." After completion of the attorney general's study of the impact of the *Adarand* decision (Dillinger, 1995), the president issued a memorandum to the federal department heads (Clinton, 1995a) directing that all federal programs be evaluated in light of the attorney general's analysis. As a guide, he stated that "the policy principles are that any program must be eliminated or reformed if it (a) creates a quota; (b) creates preferences for unqualified individuals; (c) creates reverse discrimination; or (d) continues even after its equal opportunity purposes have been achieved" (p. 2). This may eventually result in changes in federal requirements.

Meanwhile, the requirements continue in place. The legal criteria for state and local affirmative action programs and for federal programs based on executive orders or regulations are: (1) Is there a compelling government interest to be met (that is, to eliminate present discriminatory practices or to overcome the lingering effects of past discrimination)? and (2) Is the remedy narrowly tailored to meet that interest?

The U.S. Supreme Court decision in *City of Richmond v. J. A. Croson Company* (1989) is instructive on what to avoid in developing an affirmative action program. In this case, the city instituted a 30 percent set-aside program to encourage capacity building for minority construction contractors. Among the problems identified by the Supreme Court were:

1. Absence of any evidence that the city had discriminated on the basis of race in letting contracts, or that its prime contractors had discriminated in selecting subcontractors

2. Absence of a factual basis for requiring a 30 percent set aside (the city used the proportion of blacks in the population rather than the proportion of minority construction contractors in the community)

3. Beneficiaries expressly included contractors from anywhere in the country

4. Beneficiaries included Spanish-speaking, Oriental, Indian, Eskimo, and Aleut persons, although there was no evidence that they had suffered from discrimination by the city or its contractors

5. Absence of past unsuccessful efforts to resolve the problem by "race neutral" means

The opinion added that a legislative finding that the classification was "benign" and that the program was "remedial" was insufficient because "the mere recitation of a 'benign' or legitimate purpose is entitled to little or no weight." The Court also observed that the views of plan proponents that racial discrimination existed in the industry were "of little probative value in establishing identified discrimination in the Richmond construction industry" (p. 500).

As the opinion in *Adarand* (1995) points out, the Court is not holding that affirmative action programs are ruled out; that is a decision for Congress, acting as the national legislature. Rather, the affirmative action program using a racial classification must be thoroughly documented to show that

1. Actions of the jurisdiction or its agents created a problem of present or past discrimination, including the problem's magnitude and cause (Office of Federal Contract Compliance Programs, 1995).

2. Race-neutral solutions to overcome the problem have been tried and found to be ineffective.

3. The proposed solution is demonstrably designed to overcome or reduce the problem as defined and nothing else.

4. The program is subject to periodic evaluation.

5. The program has a built-in termination once its objectives have been achieved.

By using a few synonyms, such as "sunsetting programs" or "built in termination," these requirements should be as familiar to public administrators as the same elements in such systems as management by objectives. As F. Arnold McDermott, past national president of the International Personal Management Association and Denver personnel administrator, often observed, a properly designed and executed affirmative action program is nothing more than sound management.

Cases Cited

Adarand Constructors, Inc. v. *Pena,* 132 L.Ed. 158; 67 F.E.P. Cases 1828 (1995).

City of Richmond v. *J. A. Croson Company,* 488 U.S. 469 (1989).

Fullilove v. *Klutznick,* 448 U.S. 448 (1980).

Griggs v. *Duke Power Company,* 401 U.S. 424 (1971).

Johnson v. *Santa Clara Department of Transportation,* 480 U.S. 469 (1987).

Lorance v. *AT&T Technologies,* 490 U.S. 900 (1989).

Martin v. *Wilkes,* 490 U.S. 755 (1989).

Metro Broadcasting v. *FCC,* 497 U.S. 547 (1990).

Patterson v. *McLean Credit Union,* 491 U.S. 164 (1989).

Price Waterhouse v. *Hopkins,* 490 U.S. 228 (1989).

Regents of the University of California v. *Bakke,* 438 U.S. 265 (1978).

Texas Department of Community Affairs v. *Burdine,* 450 U.S. 248 (1981).

Wards Cove Packing Company v. *Antonio,* 490 U.S. 642 (1989).

References

"Affirmative Action: A Symbol Under Siege." *Wilson Quarterly,* 1995, *19*(3), 127–128.

Birnbaum, J. "Turning Back the Clock," *Time,* Mar. 20, 1995, pp. 36–37.

Bureau of National Affairs. "NAACP, 1989." *Labor Relations Reporter,* Nov. 17, 1989, p. 401.

Bureau of National Affairs. "Affirmative Action After Adarand: A Legal, Regulatory, Legislative Outlook." *Labor Relations Reporter,* 68 FEP Cases, No. 6, Special Supplement, Aug. 7, 1995, pp. S-25–S-30.

Clinton, W. J. "Memorandum for Heads of Departments. Subject: Evaluation of Affirmative Action Programs." White House Press Office, #1786, *US Newswire General Directory,* July 19, 1995a, pp. 1–15.

Clinton, W. J. "Transcript of President Clinton's Remarks on Affirmative Action." White House Press Office, #1790, *US Newswire General Directory,* July 19, 1995b, pp. 1–14.

Congressional Research Service. "Memorandum to Honorable Robert Dole from American Law Division: Compilation and Overview of Federal Laws and Regulations Establishing Affirmative Action Goals or Other Preferences Based on Race, Gender or Ethnicity." Washington, D.C.: Congressional Research Service, 1995.

Dillinger, W. "Memorandum to General Counsel re *Adarand.*" In Bureau of National Affairs, *Fair Employment Practices: Text of Policy Statements,* No. 776. Washington, D.C.: U.S. Justice Department, 1995, vol. 405, pp. 221–248.

Equal Employment Opportunity Commission. "Guidelines on Affirmative Action Appropriate Under Title VII of the Civil Rights Act of 1964 as Amended," 29 CFR Part 1608. Washington, D.C.: Equal Employment Opportunity Commission, 1979.

Equal Employment Opportunity Coordinating Council. "Uniform Guidelines on Employee Election Procedures," 29 CFR Part 1607. Washington, D.C.: Equal Employment Opportunity Commission, 1995.

General Accounting Office. "Immigration Reform: Employer Sanctions and the Question of Discrimination." GAO/GGO-90-62. Washington, D.C.: General Accounting Office, 1990.

Lacago, R. "A New Push for Blind Justice." *Time,* Feb. 20, 1995, p. 39.

Loury, G. "Testimony of Glenn C. Loury, University Professor and Professor of Economics, Boston University." Hearings on Affirmative Action in Employment. Subcommittee on Employer-Employee Relations, Committee on Economic and Educational Opportunities, U.S. House of Representatives. Serial No. 104–14. Washington, D.C.: U.S. Government Printing Office, Mar. 24, 1995, pp. 108–116.

Office of Federal Contract Compliance Programs. "Utilization Analysis," 41 CFR Part 60-2. *Affirmative Action Programs,* sec. 2.11, Required Utilization Analysis, 1995.

Pace, J., and Smith, Z. "Understanding Affirmative Action from a Practitioner's Perspective." *Public Personnel Management,* 1995, *24,* 139–147.

Page, C. "Race Preferences Have Their Place." *Rocky Mountain News,* June 29, 1995, p. 63A.

Patrick, D. L. "Testimony of Deval L. Patrick, Assistant Attorney General for Civil Rights." Hearings on Affirmative Action in Employment, Subcommittee on Employer-Employee Relations, Committee on Economic and Educational Opportunities, U.S. House of Representatives. Serial No. 104–14. Washington, D.C.: U.S. Government Printing Office, July 24, 1995, pp. 43–62.

Wilson, P. "Executive Order to End Preferential Treatment and to Promote Individual Opportunities Based on Merit." Executive Order W–124–95. Sacramento, Calif.: State of California, Executive Department, 1995.

CHAPTER NINETEEN

Gender Issues in the Workplace

Compensation, Reproductive Safety, Family Obligations, and Sexual Harassment

Mary E. Guy
Stacey Simpson Calvert

E ven though employers talk of "personnel" in gender-neutral terms, the women and men of the workforce are anything but gender neutral. Societal expectations of women's and men's roles are reflected in workplace practices. As changes occur in societal norms, they also occur in the workplace—accompanied by pushing and shoving. The issues, laws, and court cases that trace these changes, and the tensions these changes create, are discussed in this chapter. Tables are used to illustrate cases pertaining to selected issues.

PRINCIPAL NATIONAL LEGISLATION

Many workplace practices were developed on several now-outdated assumptions: that most employees were men who were married to wives who worked only at home and took care of the family; that women who worked outside the home did so to supplement their husbands' incomes and therefore did not need wages as high as those of men; and that higher paying, more powerful jobs were simply not suited for women. This conflation of economic privilege, gender, and lifestyle has been in a state of transition for several decades. Most women of working age are now in the workforce and rely on their incomes, just as men do, to support their families. In fact, each successive cohort of American women from 1886 forward has entered the labor market in greater numbers and with greater persistence.

Well over 65 percent of women born between 1956 and 1965 and almost 65 percent of women born between 1946 and 1955 are currently in the labor force (Evans and Nelson, 1989). From 1955 through 1985, six out of every ten new workers entering the labor force were female (Hutner, 1986). Table 19.1 shows the steady increases in entry of women into the workplace.

Caught between the pedestal and the cage, women have relied on the legislative process to protect themselves from gender-based discrimination and have turned to the courts to seek redress when laws do not work. Legislation to ensure fair employment practices, reinforced by case law, provides benchmarks for the changed standards of the contemporary workplace. The following national laws have had the most enduring impacts on balancing the economic playing field so that both women and men may pursue careers of their choice and earn fair wages. A brief description of each law follows the list.

- Equal Pay Act of 1963
- Civil Rights Act of 1964
- Executive Order 11375
- Equal Employment Opportunity Act of 1972
- Pregnancy Discrimination Act of 1978
- Civil Service Reform Act of 1978
- Civil Rights Act of 1991
- Family and Medical Leave Act of 1993

Equal Pay Act of 1963. This amendment to the Fair Labor Standards Act of 1938 requires employers to pay equal wages for work that is substantially equal unless the employer can show that a difference in wages is attributable to some factor other than gender.

Civil Rights Act of 1964. The right to equal pay for equal work is also addressed in the provisions of the Civil Rights Act of 1964. According to Title VII, employers may neither refuse to hire nor discharge any person on the basis

Table 19.1. Women in the Labor Force.

Year	As a Percentage of the Total Labor Force	As a Percentage of All Women of Working Age
1960	34.5	37.7
1970	38.1	43.3
1980	42.5	51.5
1990	45.3	57.5

Source: U.S. Department of Commerce, 1961; U.S. Department of Labor, 1993.

of color, race, sex, national origin, or religion. They may not discriminate with respect to compensation, terms, conditions, or privileges, nor may they limit, segregate, or classify employees or applicants in any way that deprives them of employment opportunities or otherwise adversely affects their employment status.

Despite the inclusion of sex discrimination in the 1964 Civil Rights Act, the primary attention of 1960s-era civil rights legislation was on race, not gender. Indeed, some members of Congress urged a ban on sex discrimination in the 1964 act not so much because of their support for the idea but rather in an effort to defeat the bill. The strategy of some southern conservatives was based on their belief that northern and border state legislators would be less inclined to press an end to racial segregation in the South if they faced an end to gender discrimination in their own backyards. That is one reason why this act and the Equal Employment Opportunity Commission (EEOC), the agency designed to facilitate implementation of the act, have been better suited to addressing racial issues than gender concerns.

Executive Order 11375. This order was issued by President Lyndon Johnson in 1967 and extended the protections to women that were afforded to minorities in Executive Order 11246, which he had issued in 1965. It requires nondiscrimination and positive action by federal contractors on behalf of women, including recruitment and training, employment, and upgrading.

Equal Employment Opportunity Act of 1972. The women's movement gained momentum in the late 1960s and crystallized with support for the Equal Rights Amendment in the early 1970s. It was both the problems of the earlier statutes and the growing pressure for action that brought the Equal Employment Opportunity Act of 1972, which was an amendment to the Civil Rights Act that strengthened the EEOC. Among other things, the 1972 act gave the EEOC the ability to go to court when necessary for direct enforcement action.

Pregnancy Discrimination Act (PDA) of 1978. Discrimination against pregnant women is prohibited by Title VII of the 1964 Civil Rights Act, as amended by the PDA of 1978. It became clear in the 1970s that the Supreme Court was unlikely to address gender inequality in constitutional terms. Three critically important actions set the stage for attention by Congress. First, the Court refused to find classifications based on gender to be inherently suspect. Although it appeared for a time that the Court might take that important step (*Frontiero* v. *Richardson*, 1973), and even though it offered some heightened degree of scrutiny when government treats people differently on the basis of gender (*Craig* v. *Boren*, 1926), the Court was willing to invoke equal protection as a barrier only in relatively extreme cases (*Mississippi University for Women* v. *Hogan*, 1982). Second, the court indicated that it would take constitutional action if, and only if, the government took discriminatory steps not merely in spite of the knowledge that women would be disadvantaged but because of a specific intent to injure them (*Personnel Administrator of Massachusetts* v. *Feeney,* 1979). Third, the court rejected the assertion that differential treatment on the basis of pregnancy was gender discrimination, suggesting that it was a self-inflicted wound (*Geduldig* v. *Aiello,* 1974). The 1978 act, passed in response to the Court's rulings, prohibits discrimination on account of pregnancy by stating that "women affected by pregnancy, childbirth, or related medical conditions shall be treated the same for all employment-related purposes, including receipt of benefits under fringe benefits programs, as other persons not so affected but similar in their ability or inability to work" [42 U.S.C. 2000e(k)].

The Civil Rights Act of 1964 has also been interpreted as prohibiting sexual harassment. The Equal Employment Opportunity Commission, which was created by the act to administer the employment provisions of the law, issued guidelines in 1969 on sex discrimination. The guidelines barred hiring based on stereotyped characterization of the sexes, classifying jobs as men's or women's, and advertising under male and female listings. As amended in 1972, the law covers the federal government, state and local governments, and most companies of at least fifteen employees. Despite the pent-up demand for legal remedies, the courts allowed class actions and class relief in only 13 percent of all sex discrimination cases brought under Title VII between 1965 and 1976 (Blum, 1991).

Civil Service Reform Act of 1978. Although not directly related to gender, the Civil Service Reform Act of 1978 called for a federal workforce that reflects the nation's diversity. Toward that end, it effectively codified the push to diversify the federal workforce and make the bureaucracy representative of the population, both horizontally and vertically. With women severely underrepresented, this act served to heighten employers' sensitivity to the absence of women in civil service posts, especially at the middle and upper ranks.

Civil Rights Act of 1991. This act sets standards for employers when they attempt to justify discriminatory actions or policies based on business necessity, shifts the burden of proof to the employer after the plaintiff has established a *prima facie* case, and provides the right to a jury trial. It also puts more teeth in remedies. Under Title VII of the 1964 Civil Rights Act, prevailing parties could recover only back pay and attorney's fees (public entities are exempt from liability for punitive damages). The Civil Rights Act of 1991 added a provision to permit victims of intentional discrimination to recover compensatory and punitive damages in addition to back pay and attorney's fees. Punitive damages are allowed when the defendant is found to have engaged in discriminatory practices with malice or reckless indifference to the federally protected rights of the plaintiff. Compensatory damages are allowed for future pecuniary losses, emotional pain, suffering, inconvenience, mental anguish, loss of enjoyment of life, and other nonpecuniary losses. Damages are capped at $100,000 for employers with fewer than two hundred employees and $300,000 for larger employers.

These caps do not extend to back pay or other relief originally authorized under Title VII.

Family and Medical Leave Act of 1993 (FMLA). The FMLA covers all employers with fifty or more employees who are employed for at least twenty weeks during a calendar year. Under this law, employees are entitled to up to twelve weeks of unpaid leave during any twelve-month period (1) for the recent birth or adoption of a child; (2) to care for a seriously ill child, spouse, or parent; or (3) for the employee's own serious health condition that precludes working.

In combination with one another, these laws serve as levers that women are able to use to pry open the doors of economic opportunity and to maintain reasonable working conditions once inside. Demands for these laws resulted from discrimination in a variety of forms: unfair salary disparities; denial of promotion opportunities; penalties for pregnancy, childbearing, and child rearing; and sexual harassment. These problems have arisen because workplace policies have treated all employees as if they were men and have penalized women for their nonmale characteristics, including childbearing, child rearing, and gendered roles.

CONTINUING DISADVANTAGES TO WOMEN

Despite thirty years of laws, there are conditions that continue to disadvantage women. These include job segregation, which depresses women's earnings; pay scales that value traditional "men's" jobs as opposed to "women's" jobs; reproductive safety that is interpreted in ways that impose special burdens on women; family obligations based on traditional views of parental obligations; and sexual harassment, in which sex is used to exploit the power imbalance that women face in the workplace.

Job Segregation

Gender equality is not yet a reality in the workplace. A dual labor market with a dual set of wages persists because of job segregation. Until passage of the Civil Rights Act of 1964, employment ads could be categorized by sex so that the employer could specify which sex was preferred. By custom, some positions are still reserved primarily for women and some for men. Researchers have found that 80 percent of women work in occupations in which at least 70 percent of the employees are women (Aaron and Lougy, 1986; Hale, 1996; Himelstein, 1996). That figure has changed little since 1900.

Women are most often found in service and support jobs while directive jobs and machine operation are still dominated by men. The highest concentrations of women are found among secretaries, office clerks, cashiers, registered nurses, bookkeepers, bank tellers, elementary school teachers, child care workers, and nursing aides (Reskin and Hartmann, 1986; U.S. Merit Systems Protection Board, 1996). Reskin and Roos (1990) explain occupational composition as the result of a matching process in which top-ranked workers get the most attractive jobs and lower-ranked workers end up in jobs that others reject.

Table 19.2 shows the persistence of job segregation. It also shows, in the case of lawyers and judges, a precipitous increase in the proportion of women. The table shows that the rate of change varies across occupations, with some showing gradual change while others show more dramatic increments.

Equal Pay and Benefits

Job segregation contributes to the disparity between women's and men's earnings. While equal pay for substantially equal work has been the law of the land for a third of a century, women have suffered economically at the hands of market forces that undervalue women's work compared to men's (Aaron and Lougy, 1986; Glass Ceiling Commission, 1995). The Equal Pay Act of 1963 was the first federal law to bar gender discrimination in terms of wages. That statute makes unlawful the payment of different wages to women and men for performing work in the same establishment and under similar conditions and

Table 19.2. Women's Work.

Occupation	Women as a Percentage of All Workers in Each Occupation		
	1950	1970	1990
Lawyers/judges	3.5	4.8	24.4
Physicians	6.1	9.2	20.7
Registered nurses	97.6	97.3	94.3
Teachers (primary and secondary)	74.5	70.3	74.6
Teachers (college and university)	23.2	28.4	40.5
Engineers	1.2	1.6	9.2
Public administrators (federal, state, and local)	7.1	19.0	45.6
Writers, artists/entertainers	38.2	30.1	48.4
Sales managers	24.5	23.8	34.8
Bank tellers	44.8	73.5	89.8
Bookkeepers	77.1	82.0	89.6
Cashiers	81.1	83.7	79.1
Secretaries/typists	94.4	97.6	98.0
Shipping and receiving clerks	7.0	14.5	29.0

Source: U.S. Department of Commerce, Bureau of the Census, 1953, 1961, 1976, 1990.

that requires substantially equal skill, effort, and responsibility. For example, job pairs, such as nurses' aides and orderlies, and janitors and maids, warrant equal pay. Exceptions to this requirement exist when pay is unequal in order to accommodate a seniority system, a merit system, a system measuring earnings by quantity or quality of production, or any other factor other than gender (Lee, 1989).

Title VII of the Civil Rights Act of 1964 also contains prohibitions against unequal pay for equal work. It provides three grounds for gender-based wage discrimination challenges: (1) unequal pay for equal work, (2) unequal pay for work of comparable worth, and (3) unjustified pay disparity for comparable work. Comparable worth requires equal pay for jobs of comparable value to the employer. "Value to the employer" refers to the skills, efforts, and responsibilities required. Cooks and painters, and secretaries and campus police officers, for example, are often equated to perform work of comparable worth to employers (Willborn, 1986).

Job evaluations, classification systems, rankings, and factor comparison methods all have as their goal to objectify job tasks and develop a classification and compensation system that provides comparable pay for comparable work. Regardless of the "objectivity" of a classification and compensation system, however, job evaluation systems reflect dominant cultural values (Payton, 1988). For example, supervisory jobs pay more than nonsupervisory jobs, jobs that are responsible for lots of money or expensive equipment pay more than jobs that are not, jobs that have more discretion pay more than jobs that have little discretion, and jobs that require dangerous, dirty, or heavy physical effort pay more than those that do not. Most of these higher-paying jobs have historically been performed by men (see *Johnson* v. *Transportation Agency of Santa Clara County,* 1987).

The Equal Pay Act and the Civil Rights Act have had limited impact on women's earnings. When comparisons are made across the board, women make somewhere between 60 and 65 percent of men's earnings (Glass Ceiling Commission, 1995; Willborn, 1986). Since 1955, the average annual earnings gap between men and women in full-time, year-round positions has hovered around 60 percent. It has been as low as 57 percent, in 1973 and 1974, and as high as 65 percent, in 1987 (National Committee on Pay Equity, 1989; U.S. Department of Labor, 1976). By 1985, women working for the federal government made only 63 percent of what their male colleagues made, women in the private sector were paid 56 percent of what men were paid, and the less than 40 percent of women who made up the federal workforce held 90 percent of all jobs in the six lowest pay grades (Payton, 1988).

This continuing pay gap is partially accounted for by the continuing rise in women's labor force participation, which has resulted in a larger proportion of women in or near the entry level. But the dynamic rise in labor force participation by women occurred more than twenty years ago, and the wage differential continues to this day despite equivalent training, time in rank, and work experience (Guy, 1992). Table 19.3 traces the wage disparity over twenty years.

Table 19.4 lists cases that illustrate women's efforts to eliminate pay disparities. Based on these cases, employers must be sensitive to the pay differential that exists between those job classifications that are overwhelmingly filled by women and those that are overwhelmingly filled by men.

Affirmative Action

If affirmative action is nothing more, it is a response to the need to have a workforce that is representative of the citizenry. Affirmative action is discussed in Chapter Twenty, so mention of it here is restricted to its impact on women. Put in place by an executive order and boosted by the Civil Service Reform Act of 1978, affirmative action has helped to open doors. Executive Order 11375 (1967) spelled out what has come to be known as affirmative action for women. Rather than requiring quotas, the order calls for goals and timetables. It does not specify that particular numbers be hired or that less qualified candidates be given preference. It simply requires that special efforts be made to recruit women who are as qualified as men when women are underrepresented in the employee pool (Blum, 1991).

Surveys of public administrators reveal that many dislike affirmative action (Naff, 1995). However, a chronological look at women's advancement into top-level positions in federal agencies shows that since the beginning of affirmative action standards, women have made strides—from 2.1 percent of top jobs in 1968 to as many as 17.2 percent in 1994 (Bayes, 1995). Keeton (1994) reports that in 1992, 34.8 percent of federal managers at the GS 11 pay grade were women. This marked an increase from 9.5 percent in 1970.

Gender discrimination works both ways. In recent developments, reverse discrimination has become an issue for employers. In early 1995, the U.S. Department of Justice filed suit against Illinois State University because of its policy of admitting only women and minorities to a special educational program for janitorial workers (Mills, 1996).

Table 19.3. Women's Wages: Median Weekly Earnings of Full-Time Workers.

	1972		1982		1992	
	Men	Women	Men	Women	Men	Women
16–24 years old	$118	$ 96	$221	$189	$284	$275
25 years and older	$178	$110	$407	$258	$540	$402

Source: U.S. Department of Labor, 1975, 1983, 1993.

Table 19.4. Equal Pay and Benefits Cases.

Case	Year	Issues	Decision
Schultz v. Wheaton Glass Company, 421 F.2d 259 (3rd Cir.)	1970	Pay differential for different sexes in same jobs	Employer violated Equal Pay Act by paying men 10 percent higher rate than women in same job.
Corning Glass v. Brennan, 417 U.S. 188	1971	Use of "market theory" defense in equal pay cases	Defendant claimed that market forces, not sex discrimination, caused male-oriented jobs to be assigned higher wages than female-oriented jobs; court held that jobs need not be identical to be covered under Equal Pay Act.
McDonnell Douglas Corporation v. Green, 411 U.S. 792	1973	Use of disparate treatment theory in discrimination cases	Rejecting a qualified employee is disparate treatment; case created test to establish a *prima facie* case of racial discrimination; later applied to sex discrimination cases.
Christensen v. Iowa, 563 F.2d 353 (8th Cir.)	1977	Comparable worth in male- and female-dominated jobs	Plaintiff's claim rejected; since all jobs were open to both sexes, intent was not discriminatory.
Los Angeles Department of Water and Power v. Manhart, 435 U.S. 702	1978	Sex discrimination in retirement benefits	Pension plan requiring greater contributions by females is unlawful, regardless of actuarial statistics.
County of Washington v. Gunther, 452 U.S. 161	1981	Supreme Court ruling on equal pay/equal work	Gender-based wage discrimination claims are actionable under Title VII without having to meet equal work standard in Equal Pay Act; thus jobs that are comparable but compensated unequally support a claim of discrimination.

Table 19.4. *(continued).*

Case	Year	Issues	Decision
Norris v. *Arizona Governing Commission,* 671 F.2d 330 (9th Cir.)	1982	Sex discrimination in retirement benefits; upheld by Supreme Court in 1983	Equal annuity payments must be paid to male and female retirees.
AFSCME v. *State of Washington,* 770 F.2d 1401 (9th Cir.)	1985	Sex discrimination in female-dominated government jobs	Lower court found intentional sex discrimination based on comparable worth theory; later reversed by appellate court because all jobs were open to both sexes; employer could not be held responsible for free market effects on wages.
Bazemore v. *Friday,* 478 U.S. 385	1986	Supreme Court ruling on admissibility of multiple regression statistics as evidence of discriminatory policies	Court allowed plaintiff to use multiple regression statistics to raise the presumption of intentional gender discrimination.
Gandy v. *Sullivan County, Tennessee,* 24 F.3d 861 (6th Cir.)	1994	Equal pay issues in merit system occupations	Appellate court upheld lower-court decision that the county violated the Equal Pay Act by paying a female supervisor substantially less than her male predecessor who had performed essentially equal work but with a different job title.
Irby v. *Bittick,* 44 F.3d 949 (11th Cir.)	1995	Legitimacy of seniority systems as a defense in equal pay challenge	Court ruled that a seniority system must be applied systematically to justify gender-differential pay. Plaintiff had been in the job longer than her higher-paid male coworkers, so seniority alone could not be a defense. However, prior salary and experience could be factors in establishing higher pay.

Veterans Preference Policies

A prevalent form of gender-based affirmative action that receives little criticism is veterans preference policies. Veterans have received preferential employment in civil service positions since 1865 (Hyman, 1986; U.S. Merit Systems Protection Board, 1995a). A number of veterans preference statutes and regulations have been in effect since that time, but the Veterans' Preference Act of 1944 was the first comprehensive, full-scale preference law ("Veterans Preference Act," 1965). The act remains the statutory basis for preference in federal employment to service-disabled veterans, to veterans who served in wartime, and to their wives or widows. Preference applies to nearly all civilian jobs in all agencies, bureaus, and departments of the executive branch of the federal government, except those positions requiring Senate confirmation.

Those eligible for preference are veterans with service-connected disabilities; veterans who served in any war or in a peacetime campaign for which a badge or service medal was authorized, or the widows of such veterans; and the wives of service-disabled veterans if the veterans are so disabled as to preclude their taking civil service appointments. Among others, the preference consists of the following advantages: a nondisabled veteran automatically has five points added to his score on a civil service examination, a service-disabled veteran automatically has ten points added, and wives and widows also receive these points. When a veteran's actual civil service examination score is below the normal passing grade of seventy, the veteran can nevertheless win placement on the eligible list for jobs if his actual score added to his five- or ten-point preference totals seventy or more. Once he is on the eligible list, a veteran with a ten-point preference automatically has his name moved to the top of the list. The names of veterans with five-point preferences are not moved to the top of the list but are placed on the list in order of their augmented ratings ahead of nonveterans having the same rating. Veterans are also given preference over nonveterans in retention during reductions-in-force, in reinstatement to positions, and in reemployment.

Consistent with prior veterans preference legislation, in 1974 Congress designated affirmative action for Vietnam veterans. The legislation requires employers to take affirmative action to employ veterans and disabled veterans (Northrup, 1977). The Vietnam Era Veterans' Readjustment Assistance Act of 1972, further amended in 1974, requires government contractors to take affirmative action to hire and promote both disabled veterans and veterans of the Vietnam War (Northrup, 1977).

Keeton (1994) argues that the political popularity of veterans preference policies has historically disguised the discriminatory aspects of those policies. Because veterans preference causes a veteran's job qualification score to be raised five to ten points, it disproportionately advantages men, and both male and female job applicants who are nonveterans with credentials equal or superior to veterans lose to men and women who are veterans. Keeton argues that a policy of veterans preference discriminates against most women who apply for civil service positions. Such policies violate most accepted tenets of merit system employment by favoring a select group and disregarding skills, knowledge, and abilities. Since the nation's armed forces are 89.7 percent male, these policies disproportionately and negatively affect women by reserving many public service opportunities for mostly male veterans (Keeton, 1994). However, these policies have generally been upheld in the courts.

In *Anthony* v. *Massachusetts* (1976), a federal court decided that the state's policy of absolute preference for veterans violated the equal protection clause of the Fourteenth Amendment because it deprived women of significant employment opportunities in public service. Other federal courts have upheld these policies, however, including courts in Pennsylvania, Minnesota, California, Illinois, and New Jersey. In *Personnel Administrator of Massachusetts* v. *Feeney* (1979), the Supreme Court took up the constitutionality of such policies and found that because no gender-based discriminatory purpose shaped the policy, it cannot be found to violate the Fourteenth Amendment. Table 19.5 illustrates the mixed decisions that result from veterans preference cases.

Table 19.5. Veterans Preference Cases.

Case	Year	Issues	Decision
Anthony v. *Massachusetts,* 415 F.Supp. 485 (D. Mass.)	1976	Whether veterans preference policies in employment violate equal protection clause in Fourteenth Amendment	Impact of state's absolute veterans preference statute was to deprive women of significant public employment opportunities; this was found to violate the equal protection clause.
Personnel Administrator of Massachusetts v. *Feeney,* 442 U.S. 256	1979	Supreme Court ruling on veterans preference policies	Court held that absolute veterans preference policy does not discriminate against women per se and, since it was neutral in its application, did not violate the Constitution despite disproportionate hiring of men.

Reproductive Safety

Reproductive safety and family law are areas of recent development. By custom, women have been viewed as marginal workers and as more physically vulnerable than men. While employers have accommodated the safety needs of men, they have barred women from jobs that might be hazardous (Bertin, 1989). In fact, workers should have the right to remain fertile without negative economic consequences regardless of their gender. According to Bertin, "an employer's best protection is to prevent foreseeable injury. The employer who conscientiously monitors the workplace environment, informs employees fully, abates known hazards, and when necessary offers voluntary transfer without loss of pay or benefits will be best insured against an adverse judgment" (p. 295).

The Rise of Fetal Protection Policies. In the late 1970s and through the 1980s, many large American corporations created fetal protection policies that attempted to prevent women from working in jobs that were considered high risk for causing birth defects. These jobs, often involving chemical or radiation exposure, were generally high-paying, male-dominated occupations. Women in "female" occupations, such as nurses, beauticians, computer terminal operators, and garment factory workers, were not discouraged or prevented from working in these fields by government or corporate fetal protection policies, despite the frequent exposure to workplace dangers and toxins associated with these jobs (Faludi, 1991).

Often, exposure to toxins or other dangerous substances caused fertility problems or related birth defects for males as well as females. However, policies did not similarly restrict males from holding these high-risk jobs (Faludi, 1991). The Occupational Safety and Health Act of 1970 places a duty on employers to provide a hazard-free workplace, but it lacks specific guidelines for fetal protection.

The question of the legality of fetal protection policies under Title VII came to the attention of the Supreme Court in 1991, with the *International Union (UAAAIW)* v. *Johnson Controls, Inc.* case. The Court found that because Johnson Controls' fetal protection policy was not facially neutral—that is, it did not apply to both male and female workers, who were equally at risk for exposure to toxins—it was in violation of the PDA of 1978 and was therefore illegal. Fetal protection policies have been upheld, however, where they can be demonstrated to be facially neutral and applied for legitimate business reasons. The EEOC and Department of Labor in 1980 issued "Interpretive Guidelines on Employment Discrimination and Reproductive Hazards," stating that sex discrimination was prohibited in hiring or employment in work environments posing reproductive hazards. Under the guidelines, differential policies based on ability to bear children would constitute disparate treatment barring a *bona fide occupational qualification* justification.

In 1988, the EEOC issued "Policy Guidance on Reproductive and Fetal Hazards." This document declares that any policy or practice that denies employment opportunities to one sex because of a reproductive or fetal hazard is unlawful under Title VII if the policy or practice does not similarly bar the other sex from these opportunities. If this denial occurs, it must be justified by substantial, objective, scientific evidence that demonstrates significant risk to employees or their offspring. A "mere suspicion of risk" does not protect the employer from liability for discriminatory policies that exclude one sex from certain jobs or opportunities (Sculnick, 1989, p. 79).

Reproductive Issues. According to the EEOC, pregnancy discrimination complaints are on the rise after a period of decrease. In late 1993, complaints were nearly back to 1987 levels (more than 3,600 complaints), after falling to about 3,100 in 1991. This trend can be attributed to many things: the passage of the FMLA in 1993, which made women more aware of their rights regarding maternity leave; rising numbers of working women having children; and the recently acquired right, via the Civil Rights Act of 1991, to compensatory and punitive damages and a jury trial for victims of sex bias. Juries have historically been generous to plaintiffs in sex discrimination suits alleging wrongful discharge, sometimes making multimillion-dollar awards (Shellenbarger, 1993).

Family and Medical Leave

From 1950 to 1981 the workforce participation rate of mothers with children under age eighteen more than tripled, going from 18.4 percent in 1950 to 58.1 percent in 1981. By 1981, 67 percent of women in their twenties were in the workforce, as were 65 percent of women in their thirties and forties (Radford, 1987). The fact that women remain in the labor force during their child rearing years and that men are participating more actively in child care dictates that employers accommodate family obligations. In 1978, Title VII of the Civil Rights Act was amended by the PDA of 1978, which clarified that discrimination on the basis of sex includes discrimination because of pregnancy, childbirth, or related medical conditions. The FMLA of 1993 provides in part for parental leave, which is paid or unpaid leave granted by an employer to male or female wage earners in connection with the birth, adoption, or fostering of a child (Radford, 1987). Table 19.6 presents cases that relate to reproductive safety and pregnancy discrimination.

Although the FMLA was not enacted until 1993, the social and political factors leading up to its passage have influenced the public agenda for decades. By the late 1980s, fully half of all mothers with children under age six were working; this represented a striking change from the 20 percent of working mothers reported in the 1960s (Steinbach, 1987). Other social changes that came to public attention in the 1980s were the rise in single-parent families and the

Table 19.6. Reproductive Safety Cases.

Case	Year	Issues	Decision/Impact
La Fleur v. *Cleveland Board of Education*, 465 F.2d 1184 (6th Cir.)	1972	Constitutionality of compulsory maternity leave policies	Court found that the school board's policy of placing pregnant teachers on mandatory leave five months prior to due date violated the Fourteenth Amendment's equal protection clause; affirmed by Supreme Court.
General Electric Company v. *Gilbert*, 429 U.S. 125	1976	Whether denial of pregnancy-related benefits for pregnant workers constitutes sex discrimination	Court ruled that discrimination against pregnant workers is not the same as sex discrimination under Title VII; this ruling counteracted by passage of the Pregnancy Discrimination Act of 1978.
Wright v. *Olin Corporation*, 697 F.2d 1172 (4th Cir.)	1982	Whether the company's policy of classifying jobs according to their potential risk to fetuses should be considered discriminatory toward female employees	Court held that fetal protection policies are permissible under Title VII when the company has a business interest in protecting its employees' children and potential children from harm.
Hayes v. *Shelby Memorial Hospital*, 726 F.2d 1543 (11th Cir.)	1984	Whether a pregnant X-ray technician may be placed on mandatory maternity leave to protect her fetus from radiation exposure	Court held that the business necessity defense did not extend to protection of fetuses to avoid liability; the hospital did not adequately pursue less discriminatory alternatives; pregnancy did not impair job performance.
California Federal Savings and Loan Association v. *Guerra*, 479 U.S. 272	1987	Whether states may pass maternity leave statutes that are more generous than the Pregnancy Discrimination Act requires	Court ruled that California's law did not conflict with Title VII; therefore, the state law granting preferential treatment should prevail.

Table 19.6. *(continued).*

Case	Year	Issues	Decision/Impact
International Union (UAAAIW) v. *Johnson Controls, Inc.,* 499 U.S. 187	1991	Supreme Court ruling on the legality of fetal protection policies under Title VII; employer prohibited all women from working in certain manufacturing jobs with high lead exposure	Court unanimously ruled that employers cannot exclude fertile women from jobs; providing fetal protection is not a *bona fide occupational qualification* because the interests of unconceived fetuses cannot be considered essential to the business.
Troupe v. *May Department Stores,* 20 F.2d 734 (7th Cir.)	1992	Whether termination of a pregnant worker on the day before her maternity leave began because of excessive tardiness due to morning sickness is discriminatory under Title VII	Court upheld firing; said plaintiff must show not only that her termination was pregnancy-related but also that the employer treated her differently than other, nonpregnant employees with similar tardiness records.
Armstrong v. *Flowers Hospital,* 33 F.3d 1308 (11th Cir.)	1994	Whether a pregnant health care worker may be discharged for refusing to treat HIV-positive patients in order to protect her fetus	Court of Appeals ruled that the worker had no case under the Pregnancy Discrimination Act. Her discharge for refusing to treat the HIV patient was not discriminatory, since the employer's policy was clearly stated in the employee handbook and applied to all employees.

increasing numbers of three-generation households. High divorce rates and large numbers of mothers raising children without help from fathers contributed to the growing number of working parents attempting to provide for their families. By 1988, 23 percent of all families with children were headed by a single parent ("Family and Medical Leave Legislation," 1993). These developments brought to national attention the increasing level of conflict between work and family responsibilities.

The issue of discrimination due to pregnancy-related disabilities was addressed by Title VII of the Civil Rights Act of 1964, as amended by the PDA of 1978. However, the PDA requires only that all employees be treated equally; if pregnancy or pregnancy-related leave were denied to all employees, male and female, then there could be no claim of discrimination under the law. The FMLA attempted to fill this gap ("Family and Medical Leave Act," 1993). The FMLA was a landmark piece of legislation in that it was the first law Congress had passed mandating the provision of such fringe benefits by employers (Burstein and Lindahl, 1988).

At this writing, there is a small but growing body of case law regarding the FMLA and its application in the workplace. Because the act was intentionally couched in somewhat vague terms, only partially clarified by the final regulations promulgated by the Department of Labor in 1995, employers must look to the courts for guidance in complying with the FMLA; the courts, in turn, look to legislative intent. The purposes of the act include the following: (1) to balance the demands of the workplace with the needs of families and to promote stability and economic security in families; (2) to entitle employees to take a reasonable amount of leave for medical reasons; for the birth, adoption, or fostering of a child; or to care for a child, spouse, or dependent parent with a serious health condition; and (3) to accommodate the legitimate interests of employers.

Most cases that have reached the courts so far have dealt primarily with the issues of what is to be considered a "serious health condition" and how employees may invoke the act's protection. An example of the confusion encountered in trying to interpret the act is one court's noting that "the regulation excludes specific illnesses such as the flu, while providing protection to those that are arguably less serious" (*Brannon* v. *Oshkosh B'Gosh, Inc.*, 1995). Despite some early victories, employers will need to monitor carefully judicial decisions on these and other FMLA issues to determine whether their policies fit with the interpretation of the courts.

A 1994 District Court decision, *Seidle* v. *Provident Mutual Life*, granted summary judgment against a plaintiff who was absent from work for four days to care for a child with an ear infection accompanied by fever. The court determined that according to Congressional intent the child's illness did not constitute the serious health condition required by the FMLA for an employee to be granted leave under the act. Despite this early victory for employers, future decisions are likely to be made against employers who, through a lack of understanding or unwillingness to comply with the FMLA, deny employees leave for legitimate purposes. The other major unresolved issue likely to emerge is the question of elder care as the population increases in age and looks to adult working children to assist in their parents' later years.

Sexual Harassment

Sexual harassment is a relatively new area of law, full of rough edges, anomalies, and uncertainties. Much of what is written about it is a snapshot of a moving picture, since the legalities surrounding it continue to evolve as employers and employees search for clarification of what constitutes harassing behavior. While Title VII made discrimination on the basis of sex illegal, there was no discussion of whether behavior such as sexual harassment constituted sex discrimination as such. When the EEOC issued guidelines on the subject, it concluded that harassment was discrimination under the statute and went on to define what kinds of behavior were included. The U.S. Supreme Court concurred with that reading of the Civil Rights Act and upheld the EEOC guidelines, as well as its definitions of harassment in *Meritor Savings Bank* v. *Vinson* (1986).

The Equal Employment Opportunity Commission has defined sexual harassment as unwelcome sexual advances, requests for sexual favors, and other verbal or physical conduct of a sexual nature when one of the following three conditions exists: (1) submission to such conduct is either explicitly or implicitly made a term or condition of an individual's employment; (2) submission to or rejection of such conduct by an individual is used as the basis for employment decisions adversely affecting such an individual; or (3) such conduct has the purpose or effect of unreasonably interfering with an individual's work performance or creating an intimidating, hostile, or offensive work environment (Hunter College Women's Studies Collective, 1995).

The bottom line is that there are two basic kinds of harassment: *quid pro quo* harassment is that in which a direct demand is made for sexual favors in return for jobs, promotions, pay raises, or the like; *hostile environment* harassment applies where no direct *quid pro quo* has been demanded but where conditions are permitted or encouraged by superiors that cause the employee to feel pressured into tolerating or participating in sexual behaviors.

Indeed, there is a gradation of offending behaviors:

- Gender harassment, which often involves sexist statements and behavior designed not to elicit sexual cooperation but to convey insulting, degrading, or sexist attitudes toward women or homosexuals
- Seductive behavior of an unwanted, inappropriate, and offensive nature

- Physical or verbal sexual advances
- Sexual bribery, which is solicitation of sexual activity or other sex-linked behavior by promise of reward
- Sexual coercion, which is coercion of sexual activity or other sex-linked behavior by promise of reward or penalty
- Sexual assault and/or rape (Hunter College Women's Studies Collective, 1995; Lee and Greenlaw, 1995)

Many employers seem unaware that women frequently experience degrading and insulting remarks about their gender.

The EEOC issued "Guidelines on Sexual Harassment" in November 1980. To prove sexual harassment, the plaintiff must show that (1) the employee belongs to a protected group; (2) the employee was subject to unwelcome sexual harassment; (3) the harassment was based on sex; (4) the employee was harassed concerning tangible job benefits, which altered the conditions of employment and created an abusive work environment; and (5) the employer was liable for the harassment (Greenlaw and Kohl, 1992).

A scan of claims shows a wide variety of harassment activity:

- Women were subjected to a dress code by their supervisor so that he could admire their legs (*Dias* v. *Sky Chefs*, 1990).
- An employee of a county sheriff's office was taken for a drive in the country by the sheriff and told that she and her mother could keep their jobs only if she started "seeing him" (*Simmons* v. *Lyons*, 1984).
- A waitress's supervisor repeatedly exposed himself to female employees and gave choice working assignments to waitresses who cooperated with his sexual advances (*Priest* v. *Rotary*, 1986).
- The employer of a machine operator in a Connecticut print shop refused to discipline a supervisor who subjected the machine operator to repeated sexual solicitation (*Maturo* v. *National Graphics, Inc.*, 1989).
- A student in a New York City police academy had to fight off the assault of a male student by hitting him with a box of ammunition, and had her breasts fondled from behind by her instructor as she tried to fire her weapon (*Watts* v. *New York City Police Department*, 1989).

This area of the law has been slow to develop. For example, in 1975 in *Corne* v. *Bausch & Lomb, Inc.*, two female employees claimed involuntary resignations as a result of physical and verbal sexual advances by their supervisor. The Arizona Federal District Court said that the 1964 Civil Rights Act did not pertain to such circumstances because holding such activity actionable under Title VII would result in a potential federal lawsuit every time any employee made amorous or sexually oriented advances toward another (Woerner and Oswald, 1992). Not until 1976 did courts' attitudes change in regard to the 1964 act's coverage of sexual harassment. In *Williams* v. *Saxbe* (1978), the District of Columbia Federal Court held that sexual harassment was actionable and that retaliatory acts on the part of a male supervisor toward a female employee for refusing sexual advances constituted sex discrimination. For the first time, the courts held the employer responsible for the acts of its supervisory personnel.

The law against sexual harassment is a practical attempt to stop exploitation. Allegations of sexual harassment must be treated seriously, especially when claims of physical contact are involved (Brown and Germanis, 1994). Because punitive damages may now be pursued as a result of the Civil Rights Act of 1991, employers should take complaints seriously and act on them. In *Weeks* v. *Baker & Mackenzie* (1994), a California law firm was faced with a $6.9 million dollar punitive damages award under the state's fair employment practices statute (Woo, 1994). Although the award was later reduced on appeal, it is clear that juries have few qualms about punishing employers monetarily for failing to stop or deter sexual harassment. In this case, the fact that complaints of harassment were kept in the personnel files of the accusers rather than in the files of the harasser's demonstrated that the law firm showed little sensitivity to sexual harassment (Woo, 1994).

It is not enough to draft an organizational policy prohibiting sexual harassment (Brown and Germanis, 1994). Many cases, such as *Yates* v. *Avco Corporation* (1987) and *Robinson* v. *Jacksonville Shipyards* (1991), have turned not only on the existence of a sexual harassment policy but also on the policy's effectiveness and accessibility to employees and the swiftness with which the policy is implemented when a complaint is made. Organizations that have policies with these characteristics have prevailed in the courts.

The 1994 case of *Smith* v. *City of Mobile* demonstrates that an employer must walk a fine line between a sexual harassment lawsuit and charges of wrongful discharge on the part of the accused (Smith, 1995). Faced with serious charges of sexual misconduct by one of the city's supervisors, the city took immediate action in transferring the accuser to another department at her request so that the alleged harassment would be stopped without delay. A thorough investigation by an objective third party, although it did not bear out the charges of sexual harassment, included testimony from coworkers of both the alleged victim and the alleged harasser. Not finding sufficient cause to dismiss the alleged harasser, due to lack of corroborative evidence, the city "took the remedial action of reissuing its sexual harassment policy and ordered it to be posted conspicuously in each department. The court recognized the benefit of this action" (Smith, 1995, p. 16).

Not until the mid-1980s did courts uphold claims of harassing behavior and legitimize the concept of hostile work environments. Rapid developments followed as sexual harassment became better defined and understood. A 1990 decision, *Andrews* v. *Philadelphia,* represents a defining moment in this evolution by acknowledging the different views that women and men use to judge harassing behavior. The decision applied the standard of a "reasonable woman's judgment" rather than that of a "reasonable man's judgment" to evaluate a woman's claim of harassment.

The difference that gender makes in identifying harassing behavior is noted in a report by the U.S. Merit Systems Protection Board (1995b). Based on surveys of federal employees, the report notes that while 91 percent of women consider a supervisor's suggestive looks and gestures as harassment, only 76 percent of men consider it harassment. Large differences such as these explain the gender gap that exists when women and men discuss sexual harassment. Consequently, we can anticipate that the continued development of case law pertaining to sexual harassment, and gender harassment in general, will reflect the tension inherent in gender relations in the workplace. Table 19.7 traces the evolution of court decisions regarding sexual harassment and reflects the give-and-take of men's and women's viewpoints.

IMPLICATIONS FOR PUBLIC MANAGERS

Women will continue to press for their equal place at the economic table. When employers permit an adversarial relationship to develop between women and men in their employ rather than fostering a constructive atmosphere that focuses attention on worker skills instead of on worker gender, the result is a dysfunctional workplace and legal conflict.

There is a continuing need for employers to restructure classification and compensation schedules so that women's skills, knowledge, abilities, and performance are compensated at the same levels as men's. Job designs and descriptions must be reassessed voluntarily or they will be done under legal sanction. Career path assumptions that are based on outdated stereotypes are not valid under existing law because they are clearly based on what the Supreme Court has termed archaic and overbroad generalizations.

Qualified women deserve to be offered promotions, even when they require relocation. It should be the employee's choice, not the employer's assumption, that determines the acceptance or rejection of advancement opportunity. When women enter male-dominated fields, employers must be on the lookout for sexual harassment incidents. The record shows that the most pronounced cases occur when women number only a few in a traditional man's job, such as in transportation, public safety, and public works. Clear policies prohibiting sexual harassment and ensuring speedy responses to complaints are essential.

As lifestyles change, so do workplaces. Employers should position themselves to accommodate requests for family leave not only from women but also from

Table 19.7. Sexual Harassment Cases: A Chronology of Major Decisions.

Case	Year	Issues	Decision/Impact
Barnes v. *Train,* 13 F.E.P. Cas. (BNA) 123 (D.C.)	1974	Female employee's job abolished after refusing supervisor's sexual advances	Court rejected claims; held that supervisor's behavior was not sex discrimination, merely poor personal judgment.
Corne v. *Bausch & Lomb, Inc.,* 390 F.Supp. 161 (D. Ariz.)	1975	Legality of supervisor's unwanted sexual advances toward female subordinates	Court rejected plaintiffs' claims; ruled that supervisor's conduct was not sex discrimination under Title VII.
Tomkins v. *Public Service Electric and Gas Company,* 568 F.2d 1044 (3rd Cir.)	1977	Female employee's physical safety and job security threatened by spurned supervisor	Court rejected; ruled that Title VII was not intended to provide tort remedy for supervisor's physical attack motivated by sexual desire; decision later reversed.
Gan v. *Kepro Circuit Systems,* 28 F.E.P. Cas. (BNA) 639 (E.D. Mo.)	1982	"Welcomeness" of harasser's conduct	Plaintiff's claim denied; court ruled that plaintiff's own sexual aggressiveness and participation in explicit conversations prompted propositions by coworkers.
McKinney v. *Dole,* 765 F.2d 1129 (D.C. Cir.)	1985	Whether sexual harassment conduct must be clearly sexual	Court ruled that conduct need not be explicitly sexual; other harassment or unequal treatment based on the sex of the employee is illegal under Title VII.
Meritor Savings Bank v. *Vinson,* 477 U.S. 57	1986	First Supreme Court ruling on sexual harassment	Three key rulings: sexual harassment unlawful under Title VII; plaintiff must show that conduct is unwelcome through words or actions; to define "hostile environment," must ask whether harassing acts

Table 19.7. *(continued)*.

Case	Year	Issues	Decision/Impact
			occurred in the course and scope of employment. Employer not shielded from liability in *quid pro quo* cases by lack of knowledge of harassment.
Rabidue v. *Osceola Refining Company,* 805 F.2d 611 (6th Cir.)	1986	Establishment of hostile environment	Claim denied; comments and behaviors not severe enough to cause injury or affect psychological well-being.
Yates v. *Avco Corporation,* 819 F.2d 630 (6th Cir.)	1987	Using existence of policies prohibiting sexual harassment as a defense	Policies must be specific, implemented consistently, and enforced effectively to shield employer from liability.
Waltman v. *International Paper Company,* 875 F.2d 468 (5th Cir.)	1989	Establishing a "continuing violation" to prove the existence of a hostile environment	Alleged series of acts must show a pattern of the same type of sex discrimination; acts must make employee aware of rights violations.
Steele v. *Offshore Shipbuilding, Inc.,* 867 F.2d 1311 (11th Cir.)	1989	Liability of employers in *quid pro quo* and hostile environment cases	Employer is liable for acts of employee (harasser) in *quid pro quo* cases; in hostile work environment cases, employer not liable unless it knew or should have known of harassment and failed to take remedial measures.
Weinsheimer v. *Rockwell International Corporation,* 754 F.Supp. 1559 (M.D. Fla.)	1990	Establishing unwelcomeness of harassing behavior; upheld by 11th Cir. in 1991	Plaintiff who previously took part in sexual conversations must tell coworkers that such conduct is no longer welcome.

Table 19.7. *(continued).*

Case	Year	Issues	Decision/Impact
Andrews v. *Philadelphia*, 895 F.2d 1469 (3rd Cir.)	1990	Judging the harassing conduct using a "reasonable woman" standard	Court said harassment should be viewed from the perspective of a reasonable person of the same sex to determine if hostile environment exists.
Ellison v. *Brady*, 924 F.2d 878 (9th Cir.)	1991	Applying "reasonable woman" standard to establish hostile environment	Court elaborated on reasonable woman standard; rejected a sex-blind "reasonable person" standard due to a tendency for the standard to be male-biased.
Robinson v. *Jacksonville Shipyards*, 760 F.Supp. 1486 (M.D. Fla.)	1991	Sufficiency of employer's sexual harassment policies	Defendant's policy found to be insufficient; only one channel for reporting was provided to employees.
Candelore v. *Clark City Sanitation District*, 975 F.2d 588 (9th Cir.)	1992	Relevance of off-work activities to establishing hostile environment	Court rejected plaintiff's claim that a coworker's romance with a supervisor created a hostile work environment.
Burns v. *McGregor Electronic Industries, Inc.*, 989 F.2d 959 (8th Cir.)	1993	Welcomeness of harassing conduct by plaintiff based on non-work activities	Court found that plaintiff's posing nude for a magazine in off-work hours was not basis to find that harassing conduct was welcomed at work.
Harris v. *Forklift Systems*, 510 U.S. 17	1993	Supreme Court re-examined hostile environment standards	Plaintiff may establish hostile work environment without showing severe psychological injury. Factors to consider: frequency of harassing conduct; severity

Table 19.7. *(continued)*.

Case	Year	Issues	Decision/Impact
			of conduct; whether conduct is physically threatening or humiliating or an offensive utterance; whether conduct interfered with employee's work performance.
Weeks v. *Baker & McKenzie,* 1994 WL 774633 (Cal. Super.)	1994	Awarding of punitive damages for sexual harassment cases	Plaintiff awarded multimillion dollar damages for sexual harassment, one of the largest punitive awards ever in California.
Smith v. *City of Mobile,* Civ. Act. No. 94–0236–B-S	1994	Sufficiency of employer's sexual harassment policies and procedures in hostile environment case	City could be held liable only if it knew or should have known of harassment and failed to take action. Because of its swift investigation and action to stop it, the city avoided liability even though it did not discipline the harasser.
Klessens v. *U.S. Postal Service,* 66 F.E.P. Cas. (BNA) 1630	1994	Victim's role in establishing a hostile or abusive work environment	Female worker who participated in off-color language and after-hours socializing with coworker could not make a sexual harassment case against him. Court found that the victim's acceptance of the conduct outside of work failed to show the work environment to be abusive.
Fuller v. *City of Oakland,* 47 F.3d 1523 (9th Cir.)	1995	Sufficiency of employer's sexual harassment policies and procedures	Police department conducted an internal affairs investigation, offered plaintiff a transfer (she refused),

Table 19.7. *(continued).*

Case	Year	Issues	Decision/Impact
			and the harassment later stopped voluntarily. Court found that employer's actions did not express strong disapproval of sexual harassment and therefore could not avoid liability.
Cross et al. v. *State of Alabama,* 49 F.3d 1490 (11th Cir.)	1995	Personal liability of public employees in harassment cases	Court ruled that state mental health official and two supervisors found guilty of sexual harassment may be held personally, although not officially, liable for monetary damages.

men. Likewise, employers must accommodate the safety needs of both women and men. Gone are the days when employers could accommodate men's needs and simply exclude women workers rather than accommodating them.

In conclusion, laws and court decisions are like a wind sock, indicating the direction that the winds of custom are blowing. Changes are gradual and somewhat halting, as a wind sock in a breeze rather than in a stiff gust. When the breeze blows, it does so toward an integration in the workplace that will provide both women and men with equal opportunities. To accommodate this integration, employers must reexamine their practices and be sensitive to the barriers to women's career opportunities that were taken for granted for decades. If they do not, the courts surely will.

Cases Cited

AFSCME v. *State of Washington,* 770 F.2d 1401 (9th Cir., 1985).

Andrews v. *Philadelphia,* 895 F.2d 1469 (3rd Cir., 1990).

Anthony v. *Massachusetts,* 415 F.Supp. 485 (D. Mass., 1976).

Armstrong v. *Flowers Hospital,* 33 F.3d 1308 (11th Cir., 1994).

Barnes v. *Train,* 13 F.E.P. Cas. (BNA) 123 (D.C., 1974).

Bazemore v. *Friday,* 478 U.S. 385 (1986).

Brannon v. *Oshkosh B'Gosh, Inc.*, 897 F.Supp. 1028, 1036 (M.D. Tenn., 1995).

Burns v. *McGregor Electronic Industries, Inc.*, 989 F.2d 959 (8th Cir., 1993).

California Federal Savings and Loan Association v. *Guerra*, 479 U.S. 272 (1987).

Candelore v. *Clark City Sanitation District*, 975 F.2d 588 (9th Cir., 1992).

Christensen v. *Iowa*, 563 F.2d 353 (8th Cir., 1977).

Corne v. *Bausch & Lomb, Inc.*, 390 F.Supp. 161 (D. Ariz., 1975).

Corning Glass v. *Brennan*, 417 U.S. 188 (1971).

County of Washington v. *Gunther*, 452 U.S. 161 (1981).

Craig v. *Boren*, 271 U.S. 323 (1926).

Cross et al. v. *State of Alabama*, 49 F.3d 1490 (11th Cir., 1995).

Dias v. *Sky Chefs*, 919 F.2d 1370 (9th Cir., 1990).

Ellison v. *Brady*, 924 F.2d 878 (9th Cir., 1991).

Frontiero v. *Richardson*, 411 U.S. 677 (1973).

Fuller v. *City of Oakland*, 47 F.3d 1523 (9th Cir., 1995).

Gan v. *Kepro Circuit Systems*, 28 F.E.P. Cas. (BNA) 639 (E.D. Mo., 1982).

Gandy v. *Sullivan County, Tennessee*, 24 F.3d 861 (6th Cir., 1994).

Geduldig v. *Aiello*, 417 U.S. 484 (1974).

General Electric Company v. *Gilbert*, 429 U.S. 125 (1976).

Harris v. *Forklift Systems*, 510 U.S. 17 (1993).

Hayes v. *Shelby Memorial Hospital*, 726 F.2d 1543 (11th Cir., 1984).

International Union (UAAAIW) v. *Johnson Controls, Inc.*, 499 U.S. 187 (1991).

Irby v. *Bittick*, 44 F.3d 949 (11th Cir., 1995).

Johnson v. *Transportation Agency of Santa Clara County*, 480 U.S. 616 (1987).

Klessens v. *U.S. Postal Service*, 66 F.E.P. Cas. (BNA) 1630 (1994).

La Fleur v. *Cleveland Board of Education*, 465 F.2d 1184 (6th Cir., 1972).

Los Angeles Department of Water and Power v. *Manhart*, 435 U.S. 702 (1978).

Maturo v. *National Graphics, Inc.*, 722 F.Supp. 916 (D. Conn., 1989).

McDonnell Douglas Corporation v. *Green*, 411 U.S. 792 (1973).

McKinney v. *Dole*, 765 F.2d 1129 (D.C. Cir., 1985).

Meritor Savings Bank v. *Vinson*, 477 U.S. 57 (1986).

Mississippi University for Women v. *Hogan*, 458 U.S. 718 (1982).

Norris v. *Arizona Governing Commission*, 671 F.2d 330 (9th Cir., 1982).

Personnel Administrator of Massachusetts v. *Feeney*, 442 U.S. 256 (1979).

Priest v. *Rotary*, 634 F.Supp. 571 (N.D. Cal., 1986).

Rabidue v. *Osceola Refining Company*, 805 F.2d 611 (6th Cir., 1986).

Robinson v. *Jacksonville Shipyards*, 760 F.Supp. 1486 (M.D. Fla., 1991).

Schultz v. *Wheaton Glass Company,* 421 F.2d 259 (3rd Cir., 1970).

Seidle v. *Provident Mutual Life,* 871 F.Supp. 239 (1994).

Simmons v. *Lyons,* 746 F.2d 265 (5th Cir., 1984).

Smith v. *City of Mobile,* Civ. Act. No. 94–0236–B-S, 1994, U.S. Dist. LEXIS 192541, at #15 (S.D. Ala., Dec. 29, 1994).

Steele v. *Offshore Shipbuilding, Inc.,* 867 F.2d 1311 (11th Cir., 1989).

Tomkins v. *Public Service Electric and Gas Company,* 568 F.2d 1044 (3rd Cir., 1977).

Troupe v. *May Department Stores,* 20 F.2d 734 (7th Cir., 1992).

Waltman v. *International Paper Company,* 875 F.2d 468 (5th Cir., 1989).

Watts v. *New York City Police Department,* 724 F.Supp. 99 (S.D.N.Y., 1989).

Weeks v. *Baker & Mackenzie,* 1994 WL 774633 (Cal. Super., 1994).

Weinsheimer v. *Rockwell International Corporation,* 754 F.Supp. 1559 (M.D. Fla., 1990).

Williams v. *Saxbe,* 413 F.Supp. 654 (D.C., 1976), reversed on other grounds, 587 F.2d 1240 (D.C. Cir., 1978).

Wright v. *Olin Corporation,* 697 F.2d 1172 (4th Cir., 1982).

Yates v. *Avco Corporation,* 819 F.2d 630 (6th Cir., 1987).

References

Aaron, H. J., and Lougy, C. M. *The Comparable Worth Controversy.* Washington, D.C.: Brookings Institution, 1986.

Bayes, J. H. "Evaluating the Effectiveness of Affirmative Action Policies in Top Federal Administrative Positions for Women and Minorities, 1968–1994." Paper presented at the Annual Meeting of the Western Political Science Association, Portland, Oreg., Mar. 16–18, 1995.

Bertin, J. E. "Reproductive Hazards in the Workplace." In S. Cohen and N. Taub (eds.), *Reproductive Laws for the 1990s.* Totowa, N.J.: Humana Press, 1989.

Blum, L. M. *Between Feminism and Labor.* Berkeley: University of California Press, 1991.

Brown, B. B., and Germanis, I. L. "Hostile Environment Sexual Harassment: Has Harris Really Changed Things?" *Employee Relations Law Journal,* 1994, *19,* 567–578.

Burstein, J. A., and Lindahl, J. A. "Parental-Medical Leave: A New Trend in Labor Legislation." *Employee Relations Law Journal,* 1988, *14,* 303.

Evans, S. M., and Nelson, B. J. *Wage Justice: Comparable Worth and the Paradox of Technocratic Reform.* Chicago: University of Chicago Press, 1989.

Faludi, S. *Backlash: The Undeclared War Against Women.* New York: Doubleday, 1991.

"Family and Medical Leave Act of 1993: Law and Explanation." *Labor Law Reports,* 1993, *547*(2).

"Family and Medical Leave Legislation." *Congressional Digest,* 1993, *72,* 5.

Glass Ceiling Commission. *Good for Business: Making Full Use of the Nation's Human Capital.* Washington, D.C.: U.S. Government Printing Office, 1995.

Greenlaw, P. S., and Kohl, J. P. "Proving Title VII Sexual Harassment: The Courts' View." *Labor Law Journal,* 1992, *40,* 164–171.

Guy, M. E. *Women and Men of the States: Public Administrators at the State Level.* Armonk, N.Y.: Sharpe, 1992.

Hale, M. M. "Gender Equality in Organizations: Resolving the Dilemmas." *Review of Public Personnel Administration,* 1996, *16*(1), 7–18.

Himelstein, L. "Shatterproof Glass Ceiling." *Business Week,* Oct. 28, 1996, p. 55.

Hunter College Women's Studies Collective. *Women's Realities, Women's Choices.* New York: Oxford University Press, 1995.

Hutner, F. C. *Equal Pay for Comparable Worth: The Working Woman's Issue of the Eighties.* New York: Praeger, 1986.

Hyman, H. M. *American Singularity.* Athens: University of Georgia Press, 1986.

Keeton, K. B. "Women's Access to Federal Civil Service Management Positions: The Issue of Veterans' Preference." *Southeastern Political Review,* 1994, *22*(1), 37–49.

Lee, R. D., and Greenlaw, P. S. "The Legal Evolution of Sexual Harassment." *Public Administration Review,* 1995, *55,* 357–364.

Lee, Y. S. "Shaping Judicial Response to Gender Discrimination in Employment Compensation." *Public Administration Review,* 1989, *49,* 420–428.

Mills, J. "New Court Decisions." *United States Law Week,* 1996, *65,* 2328–2329.

Naff, K. C. "The Politics of Representative Bureaucracy." Paper presented at the Annual Meeting of the Western Political Science Association, Portland, Oreg., Mar. 16–18, 1995.

National Committee on Pay Equity. *The Wage Gap, Briefing Paper No. 1.* Washington, D.C.: National Committee on Pay Equity, 1989.

Northrup, J. P. *Old Age, Handicapped and Vietnam-Era Antidiscrimination Legislation.* Philadelphia: University of Pennsylvania Press, 1977.

Payton, C. R. "Every Work into Judgment." In G. M. Vroman (ed.), *Genes and Gender: Women at Work—Socialization Toward Inequality.* New York: Gordian Press, 1988.

Radford, M. F. *Parental Leave: Judicial and Legislative Trends; Current Practices in the Workplace.* Brookfield, Wis.: International Foundation of Employee Benefit Plans, 1987.

Reskin, B. F., and Hartmann, H. I. (eds.). *Women's Work, Men's Work: Sex Segregation on the Job.* Washington, D.C.: National Academy Press, 1986.

Reskin, B. F., and Roos, P. A. *Job Queues, Gender Queues: Explaining Women's Inroads into Male Occupations.* Philadelphia: Temple University Press, 1990.

Sculnick, M. W. "Key Court Cases." *Employment Relations Today,* 1989, *16,* 75–79.

Shellenbarger, S. "As More Pregnant Women Work, Bias Complaints Rise." *Wall Street Journal,* Dec. 6, 1993, pp. B1, B2.

Smith, K. "Mobile Wins Sexual Harassment Lawsuit." *Alabama Municipalities Journal,* Mar. 1995, pp. 16–19.

Steinbach, C. F. "Women's Movement II." *National Journal,* Aug. 29, 1987, p. 2147.

U.S. Department of Commerce, Bureau of the Census. *Census of Population, 1950,* Vol. 2, Pt. 1. Washington, D.C.: U.S. Government Printing Office, 1953.

U.S. Department of Commerce, Bureau of the Census. *Census of Population, 1960,* Vol. 1, Pt. 1. Washington, D.C.: U.S. Government Printing Office, 1961.

U.S. Department of Commerce, Bureau of the Census. *Census of Population, 1970,* Vol. 1, Pt. 1. New York: Arno Press, 1976.

U.S. Department of Commerce, Bureau of the Census. *Detailed Occupation and Other Characteristics from the EEO File for the United States,* CP-S-1–1. Washington, D.C.: U.S. Government Printing Office, 1990.

U.S. Department of Labor, Bureau of Labor Statistics. "Earnings Trends Among Major Labor Force Groups." Press Release USDL 75–493, Sept. 12, 1975.

U.S. Department of Labor, Bureau of Labor Statistics. *Employment and Earnings.* Washington, D.C.: U.S. Government Printing Office, 1983.

U.S. Department of Labor, Bureau of Labor Statistics. *Employment and Earnings.* Washington, D.C.: U.S. Government Printing Office, 1993.

U.S. Department of Labor, Employment Standards Administration, Women's Bureau. *Earnings Gap Between Women and Men.* Washington, D.C.: U.S. Government Printing Office, 1976.

U.S. Merit Systems Protection Board. *The Rule of Three in Federal Hiring: Boon or Bane?* Washington, D.C.: U.S. Government Printing Office, 1995a.

U.S. Merit Systems Protection Board. *Sexual Harassment in the Federal Workplace.* Washington, D.C.: U.S. Government Printing Office, 1995b.

U.S. Merit Systems Protection Board. *Fair and Equitable Treatment: A Progress Report on Minority Employment in the Federal Government.* Washington, D.C.: U.S. Government Printing Office, 1996.

"Veterans Preference Act." *Congress and the Nation, 1945–1964,* Vol. 1. Washington, D.C.: Congressional Quarterly, 1965.

Willborn, S. L. *A Comparable Worth Primer.* Lexington, Mass.: Heath, 1986.

Woerner, W. L., and Oswald, S. L. "Sexual Harassment in the Workplace: A View Through the Eyes of the Court." *Labor Law Journal,* 1992, 40, 786–793.

Woo, J. "Baker & McKenzie Is Told to Pay Punitive Damages." *Wall Street Journal,* Sept. 2, 1994, p. B3.

CHAPTER TWENTY

Public Law in the Changing Civil Service

Lloyd G. Nigro

It is impossible, of course, to evaluate specific public personnel policies and issues without an understanding of the relevant law, court rulings, and administrative rules and regulations. The authors of the other chapters in Part Five of this book make these important connections. This chapter performs the related task of providing a brief commentary on public law as a driving force in the historical development of the civil service in the United States. To do this, it uses something new and something old. The new is a 1996 Georgia state law that rather dramatically illustrates how definitions of merit may be affected by civil service reforms. The old is the seminal work of Max Weber on the sociology of law and bureaucracy, which addresses an enduring question regarding civil service law, namely, How may that law be implemented and reliably enforced?

A CHANGING CIVIL SERVICE

The civil service at all levels of government in the United States is changing, but that is nothing new. The history of American public administration traces a constantly emerging civil service, one undergoing a continuous transformation both in its ideals and in its administration. The reasons for change are many and interrelated. They include powerful social, economic, and technological forces, such as the rise of the welfare state, unionization of public employees, and electronic computers. Ideas about the proper role and purposes of public personnel administration reflect trends in public opinion about government and may therefore be expected to shift over time as the makers of public policy adjust to new or emerging political realities.

In all of this, the pervasive presence and importance of public law is difficult to ignore. As Dwight Waldo pointed out some forty years ago, however, law has not been the lens through which civil service has been studied in America. If public administration is understood to be a legal system, then it "appears primarily as a complex of legal norms or framework of rights and obligations, and when one 'studies administration' what he focuses upon is an official definition of proper relationships between persons and bodies within the system and those outside. The 'law proper' and court systems are the concrete images in such a person's mind when he approaches administration" (Waldo, 1956, pp. 28–29). Waldo noted that while this approach predominated in Western Europe and elsewhere, it was not popular in the United States, and he emphasized that lawyers and public administrationists "offer competing perspectives and skills" (p. 30). Waldo was hopeful that law and public administration might forge a productive partnership: "I wonder if public administration is not now mature enough and strong enough to pay more attention to legal aspects of administration" (p. 30).

For the most part, public administration education and training has emphasized a managerial and social-science perspective on public personnel policy and administration. It would appear, however, that many of today's students of public administration are more likely to undergo some systematic exposure to the legal aspects of administration than was the case as recently as twenty years ago. They should be prepared to add a substantial and needed legal dimension to public administration's perspective on the civil service, a dimension that should improve understanding of the civil service's past as well as its prospects.

In its application to public personnel administration, public law plays several important roles. These roles are often obscured by or filtered through what has come to be called human resources management (HRM), a framework for understanding the human dimension of public administration that emphasizes a managerial point of view. This frame of reference tends to treat law and the legal system as an external constraint or environmental factor that must be understood and addressed appropriately by public managers. In so doing, the HRM perspective understates the importance of public law in several regards. First, in varying degrees of detail and specificity the law makes possible the civil service. Indeed, the civil service is a legal creation. Public personnel administration, therefore, is part of a general effort to realize the rule of law and, in so doing, to protect the dignity of the individual and promote the common good.

Public law has also been a leading cause of changes in the structuring values and day-to-day practices of civil service. An example of this leading role is the profound impact of federal civil rights and equal employment opportunity laws of the 1960s and 1970s on many aspects of public personnel administration at all levels of government. In many jurisdictions, collective bargaining laws have transformed the manner in which the rules of the workplace are made and administered. Recently, the Americans with Disabilities Act of 1990 has affected testing and selection processes and required employers to meet "reasonable accommodations" standards (Kellough and Gamble, 1995, pp. 252–256). Another way of putting this is to say that public law has acted upon the civil service and public personnel administration in such a way as to force significant, and at times profound, changes in policy and behavior (Ingraham, 1995, pp. 55–91).

Public law has also played a supporting role by responding or adapting to (through new or amended laws, regulations and executive orders, or judicial interpretations) new or altered realities presented by the socioeconomic, political, or technological environment of the civil service. In this way, law often legitimizes and facilitates effective governmental responses to new or changing challenges and demands. There are many examples. The extension of Title VII protection to cover sex-based discrimination and sexual harassment has been in no small part a response to the increasing participation of women in the public workforce, in combination with their growing political power on the national scene (*Meritor Savings Bank* v. *Vinson*, 1986; *Harris* v. *Forklift Systems*, 1993). The main provisions of the 1978 Civil Service Reform Act, such as the creation of the Merit Systems Protection Board and the Office of Personnel Management, were at the time anything but radical departures from state-of-the-art thinking about the public personnel function and how to solve the "problem" of bureaucratic responsiveness and accountability to the chief executive (Ingraham and Ban, 1984; Ingraham, 1995, pp. 73–81).

In other cases, public law has served to block or to redirect toward more productive ends efforts to realize popular enthusiasms and the ideological agendas of interest groups and elected executives. The well-known effects of this role include statutes, court rulings, and regulations that have frustrated (or at least made illegal) efforts to exclude AIDS victims from the workplace (Connolly and Marshall, 1990). Attempts to impose universal mandatory drug testing on public employees have been blocked in the federal courts (Thompson, Riccucci, and Ban, 1991). Beginning in 1976, a series of Supreme Court rulings seriously undermined the legitimacy of long-standing patronage systems in state and local governments (Nigro and Nigro, 1994, pp. 20–21).

While change has been continuous, major phases or periods are identifiable in the history of the civil service in the United States. These phases are defined by dominant social values and norms, signature statutes and court decisions, and hallmark public policies and organizational practices. They include the era of systematic spoils and party control (1830–1890), the civil service reform movement and neutral competence (1890–1945), the period of so-called positive personnel and technical staff administration (1945–1960), the rise of unionization and bilateralism (1960–1975), the civil rights movement and equal employment opportunity (1964–1980), and, most recently, managerialism and the empowerment of political executives and their staffs (1980–present).

Each of these phases has brought with it much concern, conflict, and confusion as it has emerged, challenged, and finally transformed the old order. Once established, new orders, such as commission-based merit systems, have in turn developed, elaborated, and finally exhausted their creative potential and capacity to address new generations of problems. They have been overtaken by discrete events, broad social and political forces, their own limitations and internal contradictions, and new ideas and values in currency.

Throughout this evolution, the influence of public law in its various roles and forms is not hard to find. It is important, even when law is being violated or evaded. Max Weber (1978), in his analysis of legitimate order in society, wrote:

> It is possible for action to be oriented to an order in other ways than through conformity with its prescriptions, as they are generally understood by the actors. Even in the case of evasion or disobedience, the probability of their being recognized as valid norms may have an effect on action. This may, in the first place, be true from the point of view of sheer expediency. . . . But apart from this limiting case, it is very common for violation of an order to be confined to more or less numerous partial deviations from it, or for the attempt to be made, with varying degrees of good faith, to justify the deviation as legitimate [p. 32].

If ever a field of human endeavor has existed that illustrates Weber's point, it is public personnel administration in the United States over the past two centuries.

Typically, a new order incorporates still-valued aspects of the old but sets them in a new frame of reference or interpretive matrix. Take, for example, the evolution (some might say metamorphosis) of the meaning of the merit principle that has taken place in the United States over the past fifty years. The policies and practices that have given the concept of merit substance have changed greatly since the 1950s. The meaning of merit has been formed by the choices, calculations, and actions of people in a variety of social settings, including political parties, administrative organizations, legislative bodies, and courts. The state of Georgia offers a clear example of how law may promote the emergence of a new definition of merit by creating a changed organizational context for personnel administration rather than by setting forth a formal redefinition.

MERIT AND CIVIL SERVICE REFORM IN THE STATE OF GEORGIA

Georgia Governor Zell Miller signed legislation in 1996 that should put effective control over much of the state's personnel function, including regulatory authority, firmly in the hands of the state's administrative agencies. In the long term this legislation will do away with the classified civil service as a large proportion of state employment. Currently, about 63,000 workers (45 percent of state employees) are in the classified service. With this legislation, Governor Miller is in a position to implement the recommendations of a statewide task force composed of agency heads, line managers, personnel directors, and a representative from a private sector consulting firm.

The task force chair, who currently heads Governor Miller's Commission on Privatization, observed that "the main thing we want to accomplish here is to make the Georgia State government's system of personnel administration more responsive to the needs of the agencies it is supposed to serve and support. There is no doubt that this is a critical system and agencies cannot be saddled with one that has outlived its purpose. Agency heads need the tools to get the job done for the citizens of this State" (Burkhalter, 1996, p. 1).

This kind of official language is, of course, nothing new. Versions of it are heard regularly in many states and cities. Similar rhetoric has been a hardy perennial at the federal level since 1976, when President Jimmy Carter initiated the process that would culminate in the Civil Service Reform Act of 1978. Under the old law, the Georgia classified service was under a five-member State Personnel Board and a Merit System Commissioner appointed by the governor in consultation with the board. The State Personnel Board was the policymaking body for the State Merit System, and its responsibilities and powers were typical for boards of this kind. The Commissioner of Personnel Administration, acting as the chief executive officer of the Merit System, was "charged with administering the rules and regulations of the State Personnel Board and assuring compliance by all agencies which have covered employees. Additionally, he or she must ensure compliance with all applicable state and federal laws and regulations concerning discrimination in employment, personnel administration, and related matters" (Jackson and Stakes, 1988, p. 88). During recent years, the old Georgia system has been criticized as producing a classified civil service that is guilty of the traditional "bureaucratic" vices. It has been regularly castigated for being insulated and unresponsive to public opinion and executive leadership, procedurally rigid and rules-oriented, and a barrier to efficiency and effectiveness (Governor's Commission on Effectiveness and Economy in Government, 1992).

The new law does not explicitly call for a new definition of merit. In fact, it enumerates six principles that should guide the treatment of employees in classified and unclassified positions. These principles are, without exception, the normative staples of a conventional merit system. The law mandates the creation of a "system of personnel administration which will attract, select, and retain the best employees *based* on merit, free from coercive political influence." In addition to a personnel system based on merit, the stated intent is to establish a system that "will provide technically competent and loyal personnel to render impartial service to the public at all times and to render such service according to the dictates of ethics and morality; *and which will eliminate unnecessary and inefficient employees. It is specifically the intent of the General Assembly to promote this purpose by allowing agencies greater flexibility in personnel management so as to promote the overall effectiveness and efficiency of state government*" (SB 635/HCSFA, House substitute to Senate Bill 635, LC 14 6635-EC, 1996, pp. 1–2, emphasis in original).

A crucial change is likely to occur in the institutional and organizational context through which the meaning of merit must be established and given life. The State Personnel Board and the Commissioner of the Merit System will have their powers and jurisdictions essentially limited to technical support for personnel administration in the state's administrative agencies. Authority over the normative core of merit is to be turned over to agency heads and their personnel offices. Agencies of the state government will assume general responsibility for, among other things:

1. Assuring fair treatment of applicants and employees in all aspects of personnel administration without regard to race, color, national origin, sex, age, disability, religious creed, or political affiliations. This "fair treatment" principle includes compliance with all state and federal equal employment opportunity and nondiscrimination laws.

2. Assuring that employees are protected against coercion for partisan political purposes and are prohibited from using their official authority for the purpose of interfering with or affecting the result of an election or nomination for office (SB 635/HCSFA, 1996, p. 3).

With regard to employees in the state's unclassified service, agencies must "develop policies to ensure compliance with all applicable employment related state and federal laws" (p. 5).

To this point, the Georgia initiative resembles many similar efforts to re-create state and local personnel systems in forms that are believed to offer more responsiveness to managerial needs and executive leadership by empowering agency heads and personnel offices within a general framework of guiding merit principles and law. In the federal personnel system, for example, since 1978 these principles may be enforced by the Merit Systems Protection Board (MSPB) if the Office of Personnel Management (OPM) and the federal agencies are found wanting in this respect. In other words, the Civil Service Reform Act of 1978 establishes the MSPB as one of several staffs authorized to interpret and enforce various aspects of that legislation.

There is, however, an unusual feature of the Georgia law. It sets the stage for the gradual elimination through attrition of the classified civil service. "The classified civil service . . . shall consist of all positions *filled by agencies prior to July*

1, 1996, except those included by law in the unclassified service." And the unclassified service will include "all positions *filled on or after July 1, 1996.*" Finally, "the unclassified service . . . shall consist of all positions in the departments of state government not included in the classified service . . . and these positions shall not be subject to the rules and regulations of the *State Personnel Board*" (SB 635/HCSFA, 1996, p. 10).

It seems certain that the state agencies (several of which are run by elected commissioners who are not necessarily inclined to agree with the governor on all matters) and the office of the governor will have greatly increased control over policy choices about what merit means in Georgia's civil service. The resulting personnel actions on the agency level should establish the meaning of merit in day-to-day practice. What is entirely unclear, of course, is what meaning or meanings will emerge from this institutional setting and become the basis for agency practices in such areas as selection, career development, pay and benefits, terminations, and the interface between career employees and political appointees.

In the foreseeable future, Georgia promises to be a setting in which moderating external influences and controls on agency administrators and state executives will be relatively weak, since Georgia's employees do not bargain collectively and the federal government is in the process of scaling back its activity in these areas. If Georgia's past as a state where patronage was the norm until 1940 (the 1935 federal Social Security Act limited but did not come close to eradicating spoils) is to be used as a guide, a return to widespread spoils and political coercion might be anticipated. There are, of course, many reasons why such an outcome should be less than probable, including social, technical, political, and legal forces and constraints on agency heads and elected executives that did not exist in the 1930s. It is rather unlikely that most Georgia public executives (be they Republicans or Democrats) would see much self interest in a return to the "good old days" of blatant political patronage or the discriminatory practices of the past, even if they could get away with them. But who in Georgia state government will have the mandate and authority to enforce the merit-values and fairness-principles set forth in the 1996 law?

This question has to be asked because the new Georgia law says nothing specific about enforcement beyond a sweeping delegation of legal authority and responsibility to state agencies. In so doing, it raises an enduring question about the relationship between law and administration in civil service. Is it possible to establish a rule of law without creating an administrative staff dedicated to enforcement, a staff with the authority and resources needed to exercise the coercion that may be required to ensure compliance and to punish violations of the law?

On the one hand, it is clearly a fool's errand to pass a law without some provision for its enforcement (the administrative "teeth" side of the equation). On the other hand, as many a public manager will argue, to create a separate staff with the authority to control the details of personnel administration is likely to be self-defeating in technical and political terms. The Georgia "reform" is an explicit, indeed dramatic, example of the currently popular answer to this question: that the law can and should be implemented according to legislative intent by agency heads and their personnel departments without a central rulemaking body, such as the Georgia State Personnel Board, or a central staff with regulatory powers, such as the Georgia Merit System.

IS AN ADMINISTRATIVE STAFF REQUIRED?

In his sociological analysis of law, Weber points out that law is different from social customs or conventions because "it is externally guaranteed by the probability that physical or psychological coercion will be applied by a *staff* of people in order to bring about compliance or avenge violation (Weber, 1978, pp. 34–35). He goes on to say that "law consists essentially in a consistent system of abstract rules" that are applied to specific cases by administrators pursuing the interests or goals set forth in the "orders" creating and governing their organizations (p. 217). Under the rule of law, "the typical person in authority, the 'superior,' is himself subject to an impersonal order by orienting his actions to it in his own dispositions and commands" (p. 217).

For much of its history, civil service reform in the United States has been marked by struggles to establish "impersonal legal orders" under which those in authority will obey the law in a positive and calculable way. The early civil service reformers soon came to believe that supportive social customs and professional or organizational conventions, while necessary, were not sufficient to provide an adequate foundation for a merit system. In other words, the administrative implementation of a "consistent system of abstract rules" called merit principles required "a bureaucratic administrative staff" or "specifically designated group of persons" able to ensure a high probability of "legal coercion" in support of legal authority (Weber, 1978, pp. 220, 313–315). The widespread creation on all levels of government of such administrative staffs in the form of civil service commissions, labor relations boards, offices of equal employment opportunity, and other rulemaking and "law finding" entities is the concrete manifestation of this belief.

The new Georgia civil service law is a concrete manifestation of another belief, one that today is very influential in public administration circles: that too much bureaucratic staff and impersonal legal order has seriously limited the capacity of public administrators to manage human resources effectively and efficiently in the public interest. This point of view encourages broad delegations of authority over personnel matters to line managers, largely on the assumption that this authority will be used responsibly, and as part of a larger governmental effort to improve performance. Centralized personnel administration, particularly regulatory efforts, it is argued, should be limited to the bare minimum needed to ensure that merit principles and other statutory requirements will be upheld.

Answers vary to the question of what constitutes an acceptable organizational and resources minimum. The response provided by the Georgia General Assembly and the governor to the organizational side of the question is that agency personnel units are sufficient, with department heads being accountable to the governor, who in turn is accountable to public opinion. On the resources side, it must be assumed that the funds and positions needed to implement the legislation will be included in an agency's budget. The resources directed to oversight and enforcement should reflect the priorities of agency executives and other powerful actors in the state's budgetary process. These priorities may be expected to shift over time. On the federal level, for example, the budgets and staffing levels of the OPM and the MSPB have mirrored the policy orientations of presidential administrations. Between 1978 and 1988, for example, the OPM went from 3,907 to 1,903 employees, while the MSPB went from 311 to 256 (U.S. Office of Management and Budget, 1978–1988).

Advocates as well as opponents of the Georgia approach might find Weber's commentary on this issue instructive. Weber observed that public administrators seek to expand their discretion under the law: "For all state activities that fall outside the field of law creation and court procedure, one has become accustomed to claims for the freedom and paramountcy of individual circumstances. General norms are held to play primarily a negative role, as barriers to the official's positive and 'creative' activity which should never be regulated" (Weber, 1978, p. 979). This idea is now expressed thus: let managers manage by removing unnecessary rules and regulations administered by personnel departments, civil service commissions, and other obstacles to the creative management of human resources.

Weber goes on to describe the rationale for such bureaucratic discretion in terms that are remarkably similar to those used by modern advocates of decentralization and deregulation: "The rule and the rational pursuit of 'objective' purposes, as well as devotion to these, would always constitute the norm of conduct. Precisely those views which most strongly glorify the 'creative' discretion of the official accept, as the ultimate and highest lodestar of his behavior in public administration, the specifically modern and strictly 'objective' idea of *raison d'état*" (Weber, 1978, p. 979). The contemporary version would be something like this: today's public administrator is a trained professional who may be trusted to honor the spirit of the law and apply it in a manner designed to protect and advance the public interest. The authors of one very popular book on "reinvention" put it in these terms: "It is time to listen to our public entrepreneurs and replace a civil service system designed for the nineteenth century with a personnel system designed for the twenty-first (Osborne and Gaebler, 1992, p. 130).

Weber goes on to summarize in general terms the concerns of today's skeptics and critics of current trends toward extensive delegations of authority in personnel matters to agencies and line managers. He noted that bureaucrats normally should be expected to define public interest in ways that serve (or at least do not undermine) the political and material interests of their agencies (Weber, 1978, p. 979). Based on his writings about legal-rational bureaucracy, there is no reason to believe that he would have exempted Georgia state administrators from this general observation.

Some might argue that the Georgia civil service reform is intended to establish a personnel system for the twenty-first century. Others might reasonably ask if the rule of law can be enforced under these conditions. The Georgia act does not provide for an enforcement staff, and it appears to make very questionable assumptions about the rational calculations and behavior of bureaucrats, especially if we are to believe Weber's observation that administrators are prone to see "reasons of state" in policies and actions that sustain and expand their power (Weber, 1978, p. 979).

CONCLUSION

On March 15, 1996, the Georgia House passed Governor Miller's "merit system legislation." The expected resistance to a law that would allow managers to hire and fire future employees as they see fit did not materialize, as Republicans and Democrats joined together to ensure easy approval. For better or worse, it seems unlikely that the state's employees will have much difficulty seeing a connection between public law and their working conditions.

As if to hammer home the point that state employees in unclassified positions should not look beyond their agencies for assistance in personnel-related matters, the House "defeated an amendment that would have allowed employees to appeal a job termination to an administrative law judge—in effect reinstituting the legal barriers that now inhibit firing" (Foskett, 1996, p. C1). As the number of unclassified positions grows over the coming years, the impact of this law on the meaning of merit in Georgia's state government will become clear. These developments, whatever they might be, should provide yet another interesting case study in public law and the changing civil service.

The current enthusiasm in the United States for civil service reforms that minimize the regulatory role of a central administrative staff and expand public management's discretion in personnel matters might have been viewed with considerable skepticism by Max Weber. He did, after all, conclude that legal-rational bureaucracy had emerged because it was technically superior to "any other form of organization" (Weber, 1978, p. 973). Weber's approach to the relationship between law and administration tended to emphasize the contributions of law to the creation and maintenance of technically proficient and efficient organizations staffed by experts who serve their political masters in a disinterested manner.

The point of view associated with Weber's writings has played a major role in the history of the American civil service. It is not, however, the only influential perspective on law and civil service. The Georgia reform is a reminder of the strong (and often turbulent) relationships among democracy, law, and civil service. In this context, the words of Alexis de Tocqueville ([1835] 1969) are relevant: "Democracy . . . does not display a regular or methodical form of government. . . . Democracy does not provide . . . the most skillful of governments, but it does that which the most skillful government often cannot do: it spreads throughout the body social a restless activity, superabundant force, and energy never found elsewhere, which, however little favored by circumstance, can do wonders" (p. 244).

Dwight Waldo is well known for raising important questions about the study of public administration. The one he asked in 1956 about the field's capacity to "pay more attention to legal aspects of administration" (p. 30) while not treating public administration as simply a legal system is certainly one of them. For the study and practice of public administration, understanding clearly and evaluating fairly events such as the 1996 Georgia civil service reform requires the maturity and strength that Waldo wondered about.

Cases Cited

Harris v. *Forklift Systems,* 510 U.S. 17 (1993).

Meritor Savings Bank v. *Vinson,* 477 U.S. 57 (1986).

References

Burkhalter, P. "Gov. Miller Proposes Legislation to Phase In Unclassified Service." *Georgia Merit System State Personnel News,* 1996, *20*(1), 1.

Connolly, W., and Marshall, A. "An Employer's Legal Guide to AIDS in the Workplace." *St. Louis University Law Review,* 1990, *9,* 561–585.

Foskett, K. "Miller Wins on Merit System." *Atlanta Constitution,* Mar. 15, 1996, p. C1.

Governor's Commission on Effectiveness and Economy in Government. *Final Report.* Atlanta: Office of the Governor, Jan. 8, 1992.

Ingraham, P. W. *The Foundation of Merit: Public Service in American Democracy.* Baltimore: Johns Hopkins University Press, 1995.

Ingraham, P. W., and Ban, C. *Legislating Bureaucratic Change: The Civil Service Reform Act of 1978.* Albany: State University of New York Press, 1984.

Jackson, E. L., and Stakes, M. E. *Handbook of Georgia State Agencies.* (2nd ed.) Athens: Carl Vinson Institute of Government, University of Georgia, 1988.

Kellough, J. E., and Gamble, R. C. "The Americans with Disabilities Act: Implications for Public Personnel Management." In S. W. Hays and R. C. Kearney (eds.), *Public Personnel Administration: Problems and Prospects.* (3rd ed.) Upper Saddle River, N.J.: Prentice Hall, 1995.

Nigro, L., and Nigro, F. *The New Public Personnel Administration.* (4th ed.) Itasca, Ill.: Peacock, 1994.

Osborne, D., and Gaebler, T. *Reinventing Government: How the Entrepreneurial Spirit Is Transforming the Public Sector from Schoolhouse to Statehouse, City Hall to the Pentagon.* Reading, Mass.: Addison Wesley Longman, 1992.

Thompson, F., Riccucci, N. M., and Ban, C. "Drug Testing in the Federal Workplace: An Instrumental and Symbolic Assessment." *Public Administration Review,* 1991, *51,* 515–525.

Tocqueville, A. de. *Democracy in America.* (G. Lawrence, trans.; J. P. Mayer, ed.). New York: Anchor Books, 1969. (Originally published 1835.)

U.S. Office of Management and Budget. *Budget of the United States Government: Fiscal Years 1978–1988.* Washington, D.C.: U.S. Government Printing Office, 1978–1988.

Waldo, D. *Perspectives on Administration.* University Park: University of Alabama Press, 1956.

Weber, M. *Economy and Society.* (G. Roth and C. Wittich, eds.). Berkeley: University of California Press, 1978.

PART SIX

ACCOUNTABILITY

Law Against Management?

No discussion of public law is complete without attention to issues of accountability. The chapters in Part Six consider the relationship between law and ethics, the fishbowl phenomenon and its legal analogue of privacy protection and freedom of information, the debate over tort liability as a mechanism of accountability and remediation, the use of equitable decrees to address problems in a range of settings from prisons to schools, and the broad problem of ensuring adequate judicial review without interfering in the basic purposes of public administration.

In Chapter Twenty-One, William D. Richardson grounds the discussion of accountability in a fundamental but often overlooked fact: law and ethics are two essential components in attempts to ensure accountability in a constitutional democracy, but they are neither identical nor enough by themselves to achieve the goal. Richardson explains why Americans so often tie discussions of accountability to the rule of law, and he recalls some of the benefits of that approach.

Richardson warns, however, that just as important as "who rules and how" is what the body of written rules says. In that respect, ethical standards of American public leadership include those attributes of character that the constitutional framers thought essential to durability of the republic. Also, Richardson contends, it is equally important to understand that law is no substitute for essential attributes of character in the citizenry. Since negative tendencies endure in human nature, efforts to build a foundation for governing require both understanding of human behavior and simultaneous attempts to educate for responsible citizenship.

In the final analysis, Richardson argues, codes of ethics and legal constraints are understandable enough and often even laudable. Nevertheless, they are in themselves insufficient to ensure both the maintenance of a regime of law and an ethical public administration.

Historically, at least since the Progressive Era, a tested assumption has been that one of the best guarantors of accountability for government institutions and officials is the disinfectant quality of sunlight: open availability of information about politics and government serves to deter abuses and to aid in redressing those that occur. In Chapter Twenty-Two, Lotte E. Feinberg addresses in depth the complexities of life in the fishbowl under contemporary freedom of information laws.

Feinberg, like most authors in this volume, operates within an acknowledged set of competing values. Clearly, needs exist for openness, but it is also necessary to limit dissemination of potentially harmful information. Moreover, given the widely varying information needs of different types of agencies, it has been difficult to write government-wide legislation without simultaneously providing sets of exceptions that have sometimes been used to avoid the primary purposes of the statutes. Added to this complexity, managers must understand that there is a tendency in governments to want as much information as possible from others and to disclose as little as possible to them. This tendency toward secrecy is at the heart of much modern debate over government information practices.

Feinberg points out that as administration of information policy has moved from individual agencies to government-wide bodies like the Office of Management and Budget, the General Services Administration, and the National Archives and Records Administration, the problems have become more, not less, complex. Focusing on the implementation and amendments of the Freedom of Information Act over time, she demonstrates how these competing tensions have been addressed across the federal government and indicates as well the role played by courts as participants in the process of information policy development.

Despite the fact that ethical commitments and the threat of disclosure under open government laws ought to act as deterrents to maladministration, there is evidence that people need and expect external legal checks to ensure accountability. One of the most important sets of such checks in the past three decades has been the availability of tort suits brought against units and officials of government to recover money damages for violations of constitutional or statutory rights. In Chapter Twenty-Three, Judge Bruce S. Jenkins and attorney Russell C. Kearl provide one of the most comprehensive summaries available anywhere of the state of the law on tort liability.

Jenkins and Kearl address the many facets of the law of government liability in tort, but they anchor their discussion in the basic concern about who should bear the burden of an injury that comes from government conduct that violates accepted standards of care in the performance of public functions. Each time a court renders a ruling that answers that question in a much different setting, the authors contend, it is making an important policy decision about government responsibility. In so doing, the judge bears a special burden to weigh the problem of the loss suffered by persons affected by government action against the need to avoid a situation in which public managers cannot act because of fear that simple mistakes might subject them to devastating damage judgments.

With that in mind, Jenkins and Kearl turn to a thorough discussion of sovereign immunity and the protection it accords to units of government sued for tortious action at the various levels of government. Much of their commentary explains how the federal government and the states have granted exceptions to the sovereign immunity doctrine, making themselves subject to tort suits with certain limitations. The authors then turn to the official immunity enjoyed by individual public officials and limitations on that protection. In the end, they warn, public administrators must remember that they are creatures of the law and bound to know and obey it.

Another set of mechanisms for addressing problems comes in the form of injunctions—remedial orders issued by courts that do not call for damages to be paid but instead demand that illegal practices be stopped and corrections be undertaken. While there has been much argument against courts, and even finger-pointing, by public managers, the plain fact is that nothing is new about cases in which money damages are not adequate to remedy maladministration. And although the U.S. Supreme Court has told lower courts in no uncertain terms to limit interference with administrative operations unless absolutely necessary, there is every reason to expect that remedial orders will be an ongoing and important fact of life for public managers. This is the subject of Chapter Twenty-Four by Phillip J. Cooper.

Cooper structures the discussion in terms of answers to three important questions: (1) Why are remedial orders issued? (2) How do they come about, and what happens after issuance? and (3) What are some of the important lessons of the past that can help a manager face the possibility of remedial orders in his or her agency? The chapter considers cases in which these orders have been applied to schools, prisons and jails, mental health facilities, and other highly publicized examples. It also cautions that the remedial orders inherited by many administrators when they take a new position are often not the results of mandates by judges; many come, instead, from the provisions of consent decrees that were agreed to by all parties to a dispute and entered under the authority of a court.

The remainder of the chapter explores ways in which the Supreme Court has moved to constrain what is often termed "judicial intervention" in administrative operations through remedial orders. That discussion clearly demonstrates that it has become much harder to get a court to invoke its injunctive power. If it does, the scope of any action taken must be limited and not used as a wild card to undertake judicially mandated policy change. When it becomes demonstrable that the purposes, individually or collectively, for which the order was initially issued have been accomplished, then judges ought to terminate their supervisory jurisdiction.

Of course, injunctive relief and tort liability compensation are but two of the mechanisms by which courts play important roles in the maintenance of public administration accountability. Judicial review, the process by which courts hold themselves available to conduct statutory and constitutional oversight of administrative agencies in properly formulated cases is the most comprehensive approach. That process is addressed by Rosemary O'Leary and Paul Weiland in Chapter Twenty-Five.

At the root of this discussion is a theme common to several of the preceding chapters as well. It is the problem faced by judges in maintaining a proper degree of deference to administrative expertise and experience, on the one hand, and accountability under the law, on the other. The first half of the chapter explores several of the most common issues in judicial review, while the second part emphasizes the particular difficulties that arise in review of administrative decisions concerned with information policy and rulemaking, two sets of common and complex review categories. The authors accept the contention that a necessary partnership exists between courts and administrators, but they argue that courts are strong partners and that the roles of the courts are crucially important in administrative life.

CHAPTER TWENTY-ONE

Law Versus Ethics

William D. Richardson

"The rule of law" is such an oft-used phrase nowadays that it no longer inspires the awe that is quite properly its due (but see Chapter One of this book for a discussion of the rule of law). As participants in the world's oldest democratic republic, Americans should perhaps not even pretend to be surprised at this. After all, a regime founded on a "new science of politics" comes into being with an inherent suspicion about ancient ways and ideas (Hamilton, [1787] 1961). Nevertheless, it takes little observation of the contemporary world since 1989 to realize that political neighbors, those many fragile democracies and republics of every continent, are struggling so mightily precisely because one of their key deficiencies is any kind of tradition in which law (rather than men or force) truly rules. Considering the lack of that particular tradition, it is hardly surprising that the complementary tradition of "law-abidingness" is similarly absent among those who not so very long ago were subjects rather than citizens.

It is law that establishes the foundation that permits a culture to flourish. This is especially the case with democratic republics, in which the citizens are intended to play a role in affairs of the regime. The character or ethical standards of these citizens are in turn largely a cultural product resulting from the interaction of a complex array of forces, including family, education, religion, and the leadership of public servants. Because a large portion of public servants must of necessity exercise varying degrees of discretion in the course of implementing the laws of the regime, the goodness of laws is in many crucial ways dependent upon the goodness of those who are applying them. It is this link between law and ethics that is the focus of this chapter.

LEGITIMACY: WHO SAYS?

Before law can become the awe-inspiring "rule of law" that is accepted and obeyed by members of a regime, it must first be promulgated. And before that can occur, lawmakers must be prepared to give a definitive answer to a rather irreverent but most fundamental question: Who says? That is, who says that I or anyone else should voluntarily defer to the laws? The answer to this question is politically all-important and, not surprisingly, varies both over time and from regime to regime. The source of one's power over another determines, among other important consequences, whether a lawgiver is a legitimate or illegitimate ruler, or just a wielder of power.

Historically, one of the most obvious sources of such power has been force: subjects obey because the ruler is clearly more powerful than the ruled and their lives hang in the balance (Locke, [1690] 1947). Once a ruler has conquered, he generally discovers that the extent of acquiescence is directly proportional to the visibility of the threat of force. Fear may be a powerful motivator, but it needs to be continually nourished.

If the ruler is extraordinarily successful at maintaining the force that is the foundation of such rule, rather soon he or she may find that advancing age dictates a search for a successor. Historically, the search has often gone no farther than the ruler's eldest son, who assumes the mantle of ruler by virtue of heredity. If he in turn is similarly adept at ruling by the sword, there may well come a time when the illegitimate rule by force comes to be seen as a legitimate hereditary power passed down from generation to generation. From a regime's standpoint, a major advantage of such hereditary rule may lie in its peaceful transfer of power from father to son or daughter. The ranks of the claimants here are few and, because of blood ties, indisputable.

At times a ruler has helped to cement a claim to rule by assuming a level of unchallengeable superiority. For mere human beings, what could be better than claiming that the entitlement to rule rests on divine right, that is, on the fact that God has determined who shall rule? Indeed, such claims have an ancient lineage at least partly because the very nature of the assertion is so difficult to deny. Despite the fundamental difficulties of establishing its bona fides, up until just three hundred years ago divine right was the ultimate source of almost every monarchial claim to rule. Indeed, as the theocratic regime established by Ayatollah Khomeini and his successors in Iran attests, the allure of divine right sometimes seems irresistible even today.

While there are other credible but less persuasive ways of securing the voluntary deference of others (such as the demonstrated superiority of virtue possessed by Mother Teresa), the longevity and prominence of the American regime in the world has certainly helped to ensure the supremacy of today's democratic alternative: the selection of rulers by majoritarian elections. From rule by the strongest sword, the nearest in blood, and the closest to God, claims of legitimacy have come to be grounded on the approval of the greatest number. Hence, now all but the most entrenched of tyrants eventually find it prudent from an international if not a domestic standpoint to hold elections in order to demonstrate their standing with the ruled. These elections do not necessarily have to be competitive or even "fair"; in the basest sense of the word, it is the *process* that is important.

WHO RULES AND TOWARD WHAT ENDS?

As the dominant means of conferring legitimacy, elections reflect the late-twentieth-century triumph of one kind of regime: democracy. While it is possible to maintain a nondemocratic regime while submitting to the democratic process of elections—Iran being an obvious case in point—the very fact that rulers feel compelled to utilize them represents a powerful concession to democracy's potent allure. Having conceded that the ruler's legitimacy is dependent upon at least the appearance of democratic means, such regimes are probably not good candidates for resisting the other democratic pressures that may be brought to bear against them over the long term. However, in very fundamental ways, both the rulers and the elections by which they are chosen are still mere *means*. In other words, the majority's selection of certain rulers reflects a perception that those individuals will better pursue certain *ends*. The triumph of the democratic regime, however, is unquestionably one of ends, for unlike other regimes it properly pursues the greatest good of the greatest number. While the greatest good of *the whole* is the grandest of ideals—and is the fullest meaning of the "common good"—the lesser mark of the greatest good of the greatest number seems to be the best that human beings are really capable of achieving.

Within a democratic regime, the electorate is continually challenged to select as a ruler one of several potential contenders who hold forth with different ideas or policies for achieving the desired end. Under different conditions, these claimants might have used the very basis of their claim—virtue, wisdom, and so on—as a source of legitimacy. The triumph of current majoritarian elections, however, reduces them to mere contenders for the electorate's favor. One such claim is made by "the Wise," whose justification for being given political power rests on the quite undemocratic principle of inequality—in this case, their possession of superior or expert knowledge that sets them apart from ordinary citizens. Well-ingrained within the American regime, this claim, of course, also became a fundamental defense for the powers wielded by nonelected administrators. Indeed, the claims of "meritocracy" were rather proudly stressed by large numbers of public administrators from the time of the debates over the Pendleton Act to the era of the "best and brightest" in Franklin Roosevelt's New Deal and John Kennedy's Camelot. From one perspective, however, the somewhat hubristic appropriation of the name of the grandest of aristocracies was probably not the wisest of tactics in the grandest of democracies.

Competing and somewhat intertwined claims to rule on behalf of the electorate are also advanced in democratic regimes by the wealthy. Having amassed a great deal of a scarce good that is widely admired within the contemporary regime, the wealthy reasonably contend that they alone know best how to improve everyone's earthly lot. That such claims resonate with the electorate as readily today as they did at the time of the founding of the nation seems obvious in an era when Ross Perot and Steve Forbes have been able to generate impressive followings by, among other things, spending copious quantities of their own money.

Additional claims are advanced by still others, such as military heroes; the poor, who relatively speaking comprise the largest portion of the regime; and even advocates of various virtues who propose to save either secular lives or immortal souls. It becomes readily apparent how easily a democratic regime can be wafted about by one or another of the competing claimants. With their intimate understanding of the peril that such claimants can pose to the long-term health of a democratic regime, prudent founders promote the claim of one additional potential ruler over all others, namely, the law.

LAW AND ETHICS

In a very fundamental way, democracies are among the regimes best suited to the rule of law and, paradoxically, least able to do without it. In such regimes, the rule of law is chosen as much for what it does as for what it prevents. First, a law by definition is universal rather than particular, that is, it is designed to encompass as many members of the regime as possible. Ideally, a law should exclude no one, applying as readily to the behavior of the *lawmakers* as to the behavior of the *law-abiders*. Second, a law by definition embodies an understanding of the principles undergirding the regime and should advance them (Rohr, 1986, 1988). Thus, because a democracy has as one of its most important principles the general preference of equality over inequality (especially in public matters), democratic laws cannot stray too far from that principle without coming into conflict with it. Third, a properly crafted law helps to ensure uniformity of treatment across time, connecting the previous generations to the present and future generations. This in turn serves as an obvious restraint on what can be done in the present. Fourth, and perhaps most important, a law fulfilling the previous three requirements serves as a substitute for the "rule of men." While it is possible that a ruler could be chosen who is just, temperate, courageous, and wise, such an individual would rule for only a relatively short time. With such individuals, perhaps no laws are needed, for their word could be the law and it would be just. But what about after their rule? History teaches that such rulers are extraordinarily rare. Indeed, the ruler whose word is constrained by no higher law has historically proved to be a source of the greatest tyranny. Among the advantages of living in the twentieth century is that one does not have to cast about very much in search of illustrative cases. Joseph Stalin, Adolf Hitler, Mao Tse-tung, Fidel Castro, Idi Amin, and Saddam Hussein come readily to the fore as examples of totalitarians unconstrained by the existing laws of their regimes.

While law has all of these powerful reasons to recommend it, there are some troubling deficiencies in its actual rule. Perhaps the greatest of these deficiencies arises from that all-encompassing universality that makes it such a powerful constraint on both the ruled and the rulers. The greater the number and variety of citizens that a law is intended to encompass, the more general it must be in its language. (Ponder for a moment the succinctness of that great divine law, "Thou shalt not steal!") Conversely, the smaller the number and the greater the similarity of the citizens who are intended to be affected, the more specific and particular a law can be. Such precision matters not only because it limits the interference with liberty by making clear just what the ruler seeks to prohibit and then leaves other behavior unrestrained. Clarity also allows adequate notice so that those affected can bring themselves into compliance. Indeed, America's founders were so concerned about this aspect of law that they devised a constitutional prohibition against bills of attainder, which are aimed at only one person.

The problem, however, is that human behavior, far from being universal, is wondrously and even maddeningly particular. The universal law cannot possibly provide in its black-letter text for every imaginable variant of human conduct that conceivably would come within its purview. For this reason, laws are intended to be interpreted by the law-abiding citizen, the law enforcer, and especially the judge who attempts to determine whether a particular behavior was contemplated by a particular law. At every stage, numerous opportunities arise for a seemingly universal law to be applied differently according to the particularities of the circumstances. Accordingly, the rule of law focuses on processes that are essential to justice rather than on fixed substance.

It is at this point that the importance of the *character* or *ethos* of the individuals applying the law becomes obvious. Because the application of the law to a particular case requires *disciplined discretion,* opportunities exist for even a well-crafted law to be judiciously or injudiciously enforced. Thus the child welfare caseworker who personally shepherds a heartrending case out of the queue and expedites it is exercising discretion. There has even been a backlash against officials for failing to use discretion in such situations (see *De Shaney* v. *Winnebago Department of Social Services,* 1989). Similarly, the regulatory agency that decides not to launch an investigation and enforcement action is exercising discretion (see *Heckler* v. *Chaney,* 1985). However impractical the expectation, an ideal persists about who should be wielding these unavoidable discretionary powers, namely, individuals whose character is at least faintly reminiscent of the just, temperate, prudent, and wise philosopher-king. It is this mix of universal law, particular applications, discretionary power, and the quest for exemplary characters to exercise those powers that has brought the regime to its contemporary emphasis on ethics.

THE HIGHER LAW OF THE CONSTITUTION

As well read, even classically educated individuals, the founders of the American regime understood that one of the greatest causes of earthly unhappiness had been the persistent attempts to create good human beings by formally linking the political entities of the world with the precepts of one or another of the world's religions (Locke, [1690] 1947; Jefferson, [1787] 1972). The resulting succession of political failures convinced the founders that there was one indispensable foundation for their contemplated democratic republic: take human beings as they *really are,* not as one might wish them *to become.* This meant preparing a regime that was institutionally and constitutionally able to endure in the face of the baser aspects of human behavior.

To accomplish this feat, the founders made the *channeling* of the baser elements of human nature one of the bedrock foundations of the new regime. Since self interest is an inevitable ingredient in the motivation of most people most of the time, they decided to *encourage* it! They fostered a commercial regime that would multiply the opportunities for such behavior by vastly increasing the "kinds and degrees" of property that is the focus of citizen self interest so that the self interest of one political faction would serve to check that of another (Hamilton, [1788] 1961). Then, in direct opposition to those Anti-Federalists who wanted to nurture character in the then-traditional democratic way (by utilizing shame to habituate appropriate conduct in relatively small, homogeneous, self-sufficient farming communities), the founders encouraged the dispersion of these self-interested citizens throughout a large land area (Hamilton, [1788] 1961; Jefferson, [1787] 1972). By so doing they hoped to retard the ability of these groups not only to come together in one place but even to identify easily those who had similar interests. Finally, the channeling devices of a large land area and a commercial regime were married to a particular kind of democracy: a republic that would *re-present* the self-interested views of the citizenry through the filtered medium of elected officials. These same officials were in turn subdivided *horizontally* into three separate branches and *vertically* into a federal system of distinct governments. The incorporation of these and other channeling mechanisms into the Constitution of 1787 provided the new regime with its highest secular law, one that was intended to guide and govern the establishment of all future laws.

The multiplicity of governments, branches, and offices created or ultimately required by this new constitution was animated by a number of additional principles. First, there was the presupposition that the protection of individual liberties was far more important than efficiency in operations. Indeed, the new constitution was calculated to ensure inefficiencies precisely because they would help impede the potential abuses of political power by the rulers. At the same time, the Constitution provided more opportunities for the citizenry to learn about their liberties by vigilantly having to protect them. Second, while the founders did not premise the proper operation of the new regime on the continual presence of virtuous rulers, they did have reason to expect that the multiple government offices would encourage the isolation and checking of overly ambitious rulers. Indeed, it was even hoped that these diverse offices would help nurture the appropriate skills and habits in each succeeding generation's crop of new officeholders. Some influential members of that era even contemplated a careful culling of the young in hopes of identifying those deemed most fit by character, temperament, and education for potential rule (Jefferson, [1787] 1972; Pangle and Pangle, 1993).

THE PREPARATION OF DEMOCRATIC CITIZENS

The constitutional plan of the late eighteenth century thus envisioned a regime of numerous divided governments that were balanced and checked both internally and externally. The citizens in turn were to be divided in numerous informal and formal ways in the expectation that they would more often than not effectively check one another before one faction could come to wield too much political power. Accordingly, it was realistic for the founders to expect that the great bane of democracies, a tyrannical faction wielding dominant political power, would be reduced to the status of a minor threat (Hamilton, [1788] 1961). With the people thus divided by self interest, it was likely that the only proposals that could bridge the self interests and unite a substantial number of the individualistic citizens would be temperate ones. Obviously there would always be a small number of broad, common interests—such as war against outsiders, increases or decreases in national taxes, and limitations on new immigration—that could still serve to unite the divided citizenry into dominant factions. Absent these issues, however, the likelihood was that rulers seeking majoritarian approval would have to make moderate, centrist proposals.

This encouragement of centrist proposals from the rulers had its counterpart among the citizens as well. The channeling of self-interested behavior was intended to nurture a concern for one's private affairs. This preoccupation worked best if one was not distracted by passionate attention to the affairs, political views, or religious beliefs of one's fellow citizens. In other words, a certain *tolerance* went a long way toward facilitating domestic harmony. Indeed, it is sometimes useful to recall that tolerance was not readily present at the founding or summoned forth at the stroke of a pen on parchment. The Constitution's expectations regarding this political virtue required many precursor events, including the proliferation of religious sects to dampen the historical source of factional strife from that quarter, and the culling out of ambitious demagogues—the traditional destroyers of republics—through, among other things, the multiple governments (Hamilton, [1788] 1961). Only when one's private interests were threatened—such as when there was a proposed widening of the road in front of one's home—or an unusual common interest was formed—wars and taxes—was the ordinary citizen most likely to become politically aroused.

However, because the Constitution established a regime with so many different offices, officeholders, and overlapping or even conflicting powers, it also succeeded in creating one of the world's greatest incubators of democratic citizenship. From one perspective, opportunities to hone the skills necessary for effective self governance have increased in some ways during the past two hundred plus years. This development would undoubtedly please Alexis de Tocqueville ([1835] 1969), who thought that an increase in the number of those wielding political power—especially at the local level—would multiply the opportunities for citizens to have disputes over the implementation of laws and regulations. These disputes in turn would force the citizens to be concerned with something other than their own private self interests. A glance at the regime's current 86,743 political jurisdictions—which, interestingly, are actually little more than half the number of jurisdictions in existence fifty years ago—reveals 511,034 elective offices (U.S. Department of Commerce, 1995). Even under the influence of "reinventing government" (Osborne and Gaebler, 1992), total civilian employment in the public sector has crept past 18,745,000 (U.S. Department of Commerce, 1995). Together, these elected and appointed public servants officially wield all of the political power permitted under the Constitution. In the process of doing so, they inevitably provide innumerable opportunities for citizens to learn the critical requisites of self governance.

Indeed, because of the generally agitated and reactive state of American political affairs, observers (such as Tocqueville) have long understood that a fair number of the laws and regulations promulgated each year will be "retrievable mistakes," that is, flawed instruments that, after having been critiqued by those adversely affected by unintended consequences, can be corrected or withdrawn. For instance, the legislation issuing from the various state legislatures pertaining to intrastate speed limits certainly has all the earmarks of this Tocquevillean phenomenon. The laws are likely to be experiments in which the proper resolution of two conflicting principles—in this case, the efficiency of swift transportation and the safety of those being transported—is subjected to empirical tests.

In the American design of government, the self-interested citizen of the regime is expected to be relatively isolated from his or her fellow citizens. In order to be effective, however, in challenging the substance or application of a law or regulation, this same citizen must engage in some of the very behavior that the regime structurally discourages because of the potential political dangers such behavior could pose. Thus the citizen who is politically aroused for the first time may not only have to master the intricacies of making his or her views known throughout the elected and administrative hierarchies, but may also have to learn how to mobilize like-minded fellow citizens. These are not easy skills to master, but once they are possessed they paradoxically make for a more vigilant, public-minded citizen who may well come to serve as one more check in a myriad number of regime checks on potential abusers of political power.

THE IMPORTANCE OF CHARACTER IN PUBLIC ADMINISTRATION

If the Tocquevillean prescription for inculcating the skills of democratic citizenship continues to be of fundamental importance for the political health of the regime, some of the reforms of the past few years may be beneficial. At a minimum, the impetus to reinvent, redirect, or otherwise devolve power from the national government to the states and localities seems likely to increase the opportunities for citizens to become more acquainted with the affairs of the public world.

In the face of contemporary reactions against large government programs and the agencies that implement them, public servants may find their exercise of discretion to be, once again, a subject of debate. Now, thoughtful administrators have long realized that an exceedingly troubling paradox is attached to discretion. On the one hand, the inherent universalism of laws requires someone to have and wield discretion in order to translate the general language of laws to the particularities of the ordinary citizen's behavior. On the other hand, the mere possession of discretion—and its clear potential for abuse—in a regime that recognizes elections as the primary source of political power all but invites the asking of the irreverent question, Who says? Since their early (and decidedly self-serving) answer of a politics-administration dichotomy, public administrators have struggled to present a response that would be convincing to the democratic citizenry. Given the nature of their responsibilities in this regime, perhaps it was inevitable that most of their major answers would involve claims of some form of superiority. While this response has occasionally been a bit muted, it was even the response when the subject of ethics became the focus of citizen concerns (Frederickson and Hart, 1985). In all fairness, ethics is at the very heart of questions about the exercise of administrative discretion, for here the question Who says? thinly veils a related query: Why should they be trusted?

EXTERNAL RESTRAINTS

Even a casual observer of the contemporary American regime is aware that professional associations and governments at all levels have been busily devising codes of ethics intended to guide their respective members in the use of their discretionary powers. Prominently featured in professional journals, printed in employee manuals, and even emblazoned in artful script in public lobbies, these codes typically have ranged from the "thou shalt not" variety to almost inspirational exhortations about the primary importance of the citizen. This flurry of activity tends, however, to overshadow the realization that governments have long been indirectly involved in superintending ethical conduct, especially at state and local levels, where officials have the task of issuing licenses to certain practitioners. Professional associations, such as the International City/County Management Association, have also exercised direct supervision through the establishment of rules of conduct for public employees, backed by sanctions ranging from censure through expulsion from the association.

Indeed, it is this last area that has seen some of the more prominent reforms. These reforms have consistently focused on the area with the most visible potential for abuse: financial conflicts of interest. On the national level, one of the most visible reforms has been the establishment of the U.S. Office of Government Ethics (OGE), which arose from the 1978 Ethics in Government Act. Severed from the Office of Personnel Management in 1989 and made an independent agency, OGE today issues *Standards of Ethical Conduct for Employees of the Executive Branch,* an eighty-five-page manual intended to guide the conduct of the nearly three million executive branch employees. While a substantial portion of this manual is understandably concerned with financial impropriety, the OGE also has assumed broader responsibilities, such as coordinating and facilitating ethics education within the executive branch (U.S. Office of Government Ethics, 1994, pp. 15, 36). State ethics offices and commissions often assume similar responsibilities.

As devices for moderating and guiding the use of discretion, codes of ethics seldom do harm. They may even do a bit of good. A public organization, after all, is composed of numerous people, some of whom may well be exceptionally wise, virtuous, and temperate, and others who are not. The extent to which the best succeed in setting the tone for the whole unit is largely dependent upon the quality of the organization's leadership. For example, if the leaders are unstintingly observant of the law as well as scrupulously attentive to both fiscal austerity and their responsibilities to the citizenry and their elected representatives, their attitude insinuates itself throughout the organization. Under the best of circumstances, such leadership can inspire emulation that leavens the whole unit. It can also serve as a standard that makes clear what is considered shameful and unacceptable behavior. Conversely, if the leaders become known as skirters of the law or fiscal profligates, those within the organization who are disposed to ignore ethical standards might well conclude that they now have an informal license to do likewise.

INTERNAL RESTRAINTS

Despite the founders' expectation that practical self-interested behavior would dominate, America has long had an admiration for an education steeped in the liberal arts, which encourages wider understandings and values. As some commentators have well recognized, one of the explanations for the latter view derived from an ancient association of wisdom with virtue (Pangle and Pangle, 1993; Richardson, 1997). Whether this view either results from a natural culling in which only those with an innate predisposition for learning go on to acquire it, or is a salutary effect produced by the slow accumulation of a certain kind of knowledge, both experience and political theory have suggested that merit exists in a proper education. Aristotle is undoubtedly the most renowned proponent of producing the appropriate kinds of moral and intellectual virtues in both the citizenry and their rulers by means of careful habituation (Aristotle, [1432] 1975). In other words, the preponderance of character is culturally derived. To greatly simplify, the expectation was that an individual with a proper nature might actually come to possess the desired virtues if a diligent regimen of praise and blame constantly served to reinforce their acquisition. For the admiring democrat, however, there was a major difficulty: this system of praise and blame had little tolerance for a democracy's distinctions between public and private lives—much less for its attachment to material well-being. An Aristotelian approach might well inculcate the desired virtues, but at such a cost to liberties and rights that it might be ill-suited to a democratic regime.

The allure of such culturally induced character formation was not easily relinquished, however. Influential thinkers such as Thomas Jefferson, Benjamin

Franklin, and George Washington long entertained ideas about making a special place within the regime for a sort of aristocracy based on talent whose members would be educated from the earliest of ages for the rigors of rule (Jefferson, [1787] 1972; Pangle and Pangle, 1993; Richardson, 1997). This education would focus on the acquisition of knowledge appropriate to future republican rulers (such as law, history, engineering, and the works of John Locke). Not surprisingly, it was quite consistently linked with the establishment of a special academy.

For good or for ill, the establishment of such an academy has never come to pass. In one of its most idealized forms, this academy was intended to emulate the military service academies in prestige and purpose. In recent times, one of the main inspirations for this idea has been the aristocratic French National School of Public Administration. Such an aristocratic model has little chance of being implanted within the mature American democratic republic. However, the goal of more directly cementing the linkage between technical competence and ethical fitness as important determinants of one's fitness to rule never seems to stray too far from the horizon. While Americans are unwilling to emulate the now-modified British practices, which traditionally approached civil service staffing with the Aristotelian view that an excellent liberal arts education alone is the primary prerequisite, we should still be able to take some small comfort from the willingness of commentators to suggest the kinds of ethical knowledge that should be taught to pre-service and in-service public servants (Catron and Denhardt, 1994; Hejka-Ekins, 1988, 1994; Kavathatzopoulos, 1994; Marini, 1992; Pratt, 1993; Richardson and Nigro, 1987; Rohr, 1978, 1986, 1988; Taylor, 1992; Torp, 1994).

CONCLUSION

An understanding of the intertwined relationship between the rule of law and ethics in America is admittedly difficult, for it is complicated by issues of legitimacy, competing claims to rule, discretion, and moral fitness to rule. The vivid prospect of a realignment in the current powers of the various governments is likely to increase, not decrease, both the importance of the rule of law and the attention given to ethics. At both state and local levels, elected and appointed officials may well be wielding more visible political powers that will increase the potential for clashes with the citizenry of the regime. While such clashes may inspire a sense of real civic responsibility among the affected citizens and advance the task of teaching them important political skills, it also will almost certainly redirect attention to the uses and abuses of administrative discretion. The historical justifications for this power—a politics-administration dichotomy, efficiencies, superiority of wisdom—were not overly persuasive in the past. They will be even less so in the shadow of the present view that majoritarian elections are *the* indisputable source of political legitimacy.

The issue of the *character* of those wielding administrative discretion will continue to be an appropriate subject for inquiry. While the proliferation of codes of ethics and ethical training is unlikely to do harm from the standpoint of character—aside from the possibility that certain ethically challenged individuals might become more clever through their training in situational ethics—there is currently little persuasive evidence to demonstrate that it does a great deal of good in terms of improving ethical behavior. The prospects for such training are further complicated by the fact that it is expensive because for existing public servants it usually takes place during the normal workday. In times of fiscal austerity, this approach will have to demonstrate that it is accomplishing its mission—which to date it has been hard pressed to do.

Given both the nature of the regime itself and the contemporary emphasis on the dominance of majoritarian approval, there may be more appropriate ways of bolstering the interdependent relationship of law, character, and discretion. For instance, among the more fruitful of such approaches is the resurgence of discussion about the roles to be played in the regime by citizen boards. While there are potentially significant differences among boards whose members are appointed by elected officials, those filled by administrators, and others that are community based or staffed by volunteers, such boards may be effective devices for advising administrative units and, yes, even reviewing their actions. On the local level, citizen bodies composed of self-interested parents are blossoming in school districts as a way of checking and guiding the power of professional educators. Such entities have long served as politically important checks on controversial actions by local police. Now they are also being extended into the realm of child welfare as state agencies for children and family services find their critical but politically volatile actions under progressively greater scrutiny. Under these conditions, the necessary exercise of administrative discretion can be bolstered and, if need be, checked by its direct linkage to the ultimate source of democratic power, the citizenry. Furthermore, citizens participating in these ways have opportunities to hone the skills so admired by Tocqueville. At the same time, fellow citizens observing and being served by affected administrative units are given some democratic reassurance about the ways in which the government's discretionary powers may be wielded.

Whatever the long-term merits of such activities, they are only some in a long line of attempts to lessen the inherent tensions between democratic and undemocratic elements of the regime. However, if such forms of citizen involvement are successful in more firmly linking the practical necessity of administrative discretion with the democratic foundations of majoritarian political power, such regime virtues as temperance and law-abidingness may prove to have been well served.

Cases Cited

De Shaney v. *Winnebago Department of Social Services,* 489 U.S. 189 (1989).

Heckler v. *Chaney,* 470 U.S. 821 (1985).

References

Aristotle. *Nicomachean Ethics.* (H. Rackham, trans.). Cambridge, Mass.: Harvard University Press, 1975. (Originally published 1438.)

Catron, B. L., and Denhardt, K. G. "Ethics Education in Public Administration." In T. L. Cooper (ed.), *Handbook of Administrative Ethics.* New York: Dekker, 1994.

Frederickson, H. G., and Hart, D. K. "The Public Service and the Patriotism of Benevolence." *Public Administration Review,* 1985, *45,* 547–553.

Hamilton, A. *The Federalist Papers.* (C. Rossiter, ed.). New York: New American Library, 1961. (Originally published 1788.)

Hejka-Ekins, A. "Teaching Ethics in Public Administration." *Public Administration Review,* 1988, *48,* 885–891.

Hejka-Ekins, A. "Ethics in In-Service Training." In T. L. Cooper (ed.), *Handbook of Administrative Ethics.* New York: Dekker, 1994.

Jefferson, T. *Notes on the State of Virginia.* (W. Peden, ed.). New York: Norton, 1972. (Originally published 1787.)

Kavathatzopoulos, I. "Training Professional Managers in Decision-Making About Real-Life Business Ethics Problems: The Acquisition of the Autonomous Problem-Solving Skill." *Journal of Business Ethics,* 1994, *13,* 379–386.

Locke, J. *Two Treatises of Government.* (T. I. Cook, ed.). Riverside, N.J.: Hafner Press, 1947. (Originally published 1690.)

Marini, F. "The Uses of Literature in the Exploration of Public Administration Ethics: The Example of *Antigone.*" *Public Administration Review,* 1992, *52,* 420–426.

Osborne, D., and Gaebler, T. *Reinventing Government: How the Entrepreneurial Spirit Is Transforming the Public Sector from Schoolhouse to Statehouse, City Hall to the Pentagon.* Reading, Mass.: Addison Wesley Longman, 1992.

Pangle, L., and Pangle, T. *The Learning of Liberty: The Educational Ideas of the American Founders.* Lawrence: University Press of Kansas, 1993.

Pratt, C. B. "Critique of the Classical Theory of Situational Ethics in U.S. Public Relations." *Public Relations Review,* 1993, *19,* 219–234.

Richardson, W. D. *Democracy, Bureaucracy, and Character: Founding Thought.* Lawrence: University Press of Kansas, 1997.

Richardson, W. D., and Nigro, L. G. "Administrative Ethics and Founding Thought: Constitutional Correctives, Honor, and Education." *Public Administration Review,* 1987, *47,* 367–376.

Rohr, J. A. *Ethics for Bureaucrats: An Essay on Law and Values.* New York: Dekker, 1978.

Rohr, J. A. *To Run a Constitution: The Legitimacy of the Administrative State.* Lawrence: University Press of Kansas, 1986.

Rohr, J. A. "Bureaucratic Morality in the United States." *International Political Science Review,* 1988, *9,* 167–178.

Taylor, H. *The Statesman.* (D. L. Schaefer and R. R. Schaefer, eds.). New York: Praeger, 1992.

Tocqueville, A. de. *Democracy in America.* (G. Lawrence, trans.; J. P. Mayer, ed.). New York: Anchor Books, 1969. (Originally published 1835.)

Torp, K. H. "Ethics for Public Administrators." *National Civic Review,* 1994, *83,* 70–73.

U.S. Department of Commerce. *Statistical Abstract of the United States, 1995.* Washington, D.C.: U.S. Government Printing Office, 1995.

U.S. Office of Government Ethics. *Third Biennial Report to Congress.* Washington, D.C.: U.S. Government Printing Office, 1994.

CHAPTER TWENTY-TWO

Open Government and Freedom of Information

Fishbowl Accountability?

Lotte E. Feinberg

The fundamental issue of balancing access, privacy, and secrecy—of determining which government records should be public, which should be private, and which the government should be privileged to conceal—is as pressing and unsettled today as it was in 1966 when the Freedom of Information Act (FOIA) was enacted, in 1974 and 1986 when major substantive amendments were adopted, and in 1996 when the FOIA was again amended to bring it into the information and electronic age while also addressing a number of administrative concerns. Moreover, it is an issue that has been integral to debates about the definition of democracy and the nature of government. These questions were grappled with before the Constitution of the United States was written; they were implicit in the debates framing the Constitution; they have been critical in defining government actions through much of the twentieth century; and they show little sign of ever being settled.

Two central tenets govern much of this debate, both explicitly and implicitly: (1) the demand for accountability, particularly of appointed and career public servants in the executive branch; and (2) the need to operate under the constitutional commitment to separation of powers. Accountability is inextricably entwined with definitions of democracy. From James Madison, Thomas Jefferson, and Patrick Henry to Supreme Court Justice Louis Brandeis (see Brandeis and Warren, 1890) and into the present, despite divergent views on many aspects of government, there is an unshakable belief that democracy depends on an informed electorate. For democracy to work, citizens must have access to information about what their government is doing and how decisions have been reached. The great difficulty is that the information sought for accountability is often that which government wants least to reveal.

Through all these debates, the courts have generally been exempt from comparable requirements for public access to the process of decision making, despite sporadic and infrequent proposals. Most striking is the fact that while statutes govern preservation of and access to records of presidents, federal agencies, and Congress, there is nothing equivalent for papers of Supreme Court Justices. Although the courts regularly make decisions about what should be available from officials and offices in the other two branches of government, they themselves are not subject to disclosure beyond the limits of their published work.

Separation of powers focuses primarily on the never-ending balancing act among the three branches, particularly on adjusting power between Congress and the president. The struggle is joined at irregular intervals by Supreme Court decisions that at times have strengthened the presidency and at other times have strengthened the powers of Congress.

IMPOSING ACCOUNTABILITY WHILE BALANCING COMPETING VALUES

It was expanding demand for executive branch accountability, a demand that redefined *access* over the last sixty years, that led to the passing of the Federal Register Act of 1935, which created the *Federal Register* in 1936. This demand also produced the Administrative Procedure Act of 1946, the FOIA of 1966, the Federal Advisory Committee Act of 1972 (which was amended and codified in 1976), and the Government in the Sunshine Act of 1976. Most of these laws resulted from long, hard-fought battles based on shifting alliances of individuals and groups in and out of government.

The demand for increased executive branch accountability has been one of the central struggles of twentieth-century American public administration and governance. Major efforts began in the 1930s and continued in the 1940s, a result of the almost stunning proliferation of new agencies and their attendant regulatory powers during the first years of the Roosevelt administration. Enactment of the National Industrial Recovery Act of 1933 and Franklin Roosevelt's attempt to regulate seemingly everything from the amount of oil produced in Texas to the employment of newspaper delivery boys was viewed with alarm, as a new form of tyranny, by those who did not share Roosevelt's New Deal philosophy. There were strong objections to this "infinitude of rules promulgated by Government bureaus at their own discretion as law" (Edmonds, 1940). These objections were brought dramatically into focus when businesses were called to answer in court for violating rules that had never been published (*Panama Refining Company* v. *Ryan*, 1935, and *Amazon Petroleum Corporation* v. *Ryan*, 1935). The cry for limitation of and control over government actions was mounted by members of the legal profession (individual lawyers, law professors, the American Bar Association, and some members of Roosevelt's own administration), journalists (the American Society of Newspaper Editors and the American Newspaper Publishers Association), and members of Congress, as well as Supreme Court justices.

The results, over time, were three important, interrelated pieces of legislation: the law creating the *Federal Register*, the Administration Procedure Act, and the Freedom of Information Act. The creation of the daily *Federal Register* (which began publication in 1936) was the first groundbreaking step, requiring publication of all proposed and final agency rules, with opportunity for timely public comment as rules were being developed. By the 1990s, the *Federal Register* had become a massive compendium of almost all the activities of executive branch agencies, running more than sixty thousand pages annually. Since 1993, under the Government Printing Office Electronic Information Access Enhancement Act, it has been available by law electronically (on-line, on CD-ROM, or on disk), as well as in print and microfiche.

The Administrative Procedure Act (APA) of 1946 was designed "to improve the administration of justice by prescribing fair administrative procedure." Congress specified agency rulemaking and adjudication procedures, as well as mechanisms for making available agency rules, opinions and orders, and public records, and it expanded what was to be published in the *Federal Register*.

While one intent of the APA was to make government records available to the public, the actual language—such as "persons properly and directly concerned" or "information held confidential for good cause found"—permitted agencies instead to interpret the law as a "withholding" statute, giving them broad discretion to refuse to release records. Additionally, there was no mechanism for reviewing agency decisions. This changed when the public records section of the APA was rewritten and amended 1966 by the FOIA. Congress provided more explicit guidelines in that legislation for agency release of records to requesters, administrative appeal of denials, and judicial review of those decisions, along with penalties against agencies for records improperly withheld.

Government secrecy has been an even thornier problem. The demand for secrecy has been addressed not only by legislation but by the often fiercely guarded concept of executive privilege, by promulgation of executive orders governing classification, as well as by such "secret" presidential decisions as national security directives (NSDs, NSDDs, PDDs). This complex issue has shaped the handling of atomic and nuclear energy, as well as general classification and declassification of information. It led to the Uniform Trade Secrets

Act of 1905, and it provided the impetus for the Central Intelligence Information Act of 1984, which exempted the Central Intelligence Agency from much of the FOIA requirements, and for reconfiguration of part of the FOIA in 1986, reducing public access to government records of law enforcement and intelligence activities.

The issue of privacy—initially, the general "right to be let alone" by government (Brandeis and Warren, 1890)—has become more broadly directed to the need to protect individual privacy, a need increasingly challenged by the explosive growth of information technology in the 1990s. Since the 1970s, concerns for protecting privacy have led to the Privacy Act of 1974, and later to the Computer Matching and Privacy Protection Act of 1988 (which amended the Privacy Act). Other privacy statutes created protections for individuals' educational, financial, and credit records, as well as for their cable subscriptions. These statutes include the Federal Family Education Rights and Privacy Act of 1974, the Right to Financial Privacy Act of 1978, the Fair Credit and Reporting Act of 1982, and the Cable Communications Policy Act of 1984. The FOIA also contains privacy protections for individuals' records, as do a variety of agency regulations.

AGENCY-LEVEL WORK:
COMPLEX QUESTIONS, DETAILED ANSWERS

Decisions affecting the handling of government information spill out well beyond the boundaries of the three broad areas that have traditionally been seen as the framework of information policy—access, privacy, and secrecy. Another set of laws and guidance addresses agency management, including governing the records agencies must retain, the formats of those records, and the length of time they are kept. Included are statutes, such as the Paperwork Reduction Act of 1980 and its 1986 amendment and the Federal Technology Transfer Act of 1986 and its amendment of 1989, as well as executive branch guidance in the form of Office of Management and Budget (OMB) circulars. The electronic information revolution is leading to other challenges, as reflected in the Electronic Freedom of Information Act Amendments of 1996 (popularly known as the EFOIA), the first FOIA amendments in a decade. Commissions, services, and programs are targeted to help solve information problems, such as the Commission on Federal Paperwork, which functioned from 1974 to 1979, and the General Services Administration's Information Resource Management Service and its Government-Wide Information Resources Management Assistance programs. The Defense Department even established an Information Resources Management College in March 1990 as part of its National Defense University, which offers graduate-level courses and workshops in managing information resources.

Statutes regulating both the National Archives and presidential papers and records, as well as the libraries holding them after presidents have left office, add yet another dimension. These statutes are also relatively recent and not fixed. For example, the Presidential Records Act of 1978 applies to presidential papers and documents of former presidents (beginning in 1981), with access following general FOIA guidelines. However, as a result of the 1992 President John F. Kennedy Assassination Records Collection Act, courts have been asked to consider whether requests for records should be handled under the FOIA or according to the less restrictive terms of the Kennedy Assassination Records Collection Act.

Taken together, the issues of access, privacy, and secrecy, in their many guises, form the evolving field of information policy, a complex tangle of competing and conflicting statutes, regulations, and agency guidance (typically, the Justice Department, the OMB, and the Office of Personnel Management), along with case law and the vagaries of congressional oversight.

At the fulcrum of decision making in information policy are the public managers who are responsible for exercising discretion as they implement, manage, and shape this policy. The task is especially difficult, and often thankless, because there is not, and has not been, a consistent government-wide approach to these issues. At times, contradictory messages have emanated from the executive branch (the White House, the Justice Department, and specific agencies, for example) and from Congress about how to balance access, privacy, and secrecy. Not only has the extent of congressional oversight of the FOIA varied, depending on the interests of those leading particular committees, but there have also been fundamental disagreements of statutory interpretation among members, even as they have voted to enact or amend the statute. In addition, the judiciary has interpreted and reinterpreted the statute, and at times has even created new rights and standards not considered by Congress.

Fluctuating White House Policy and Judicial Responses

The access balance has also shifted in response to specific administrations. Presidents have framed the values while the Justice Department has issued memoranda and guidance, held training sessions, and importantly, set the legal standard for when they would defend agency withholding decisions in court. For example, President Jimmy Carter initially urged agencies to emphasize access when interpreting the FOIA, while President Ronald Reagan's administration encouraged a narrower statutory interpretation with expanded use of existing exemptions as a way of restricting access. The FOIA pendulum swung back toward increased openness with President Bill Clinton. In a 1993 memorandum, he called on his department and agency heads "to renew their commitment to the FOIA, to its underlying principles of openness," and to do so by handling requests for information "in a customer-friendly manner." But even in this case, the message has been mixed. For example, while advocating increased FOIA access, President Clinton nonetheless retained as directors of the Justice Department's Office of Information and Privacy the same two men from the Reagan-Bush administrations who were instrumental in helping to narrow interpretation of the FOIA.

A key question is when the Justice Department should defend in court an agency's decision to withhold records. The standard changed three times between the Carter and Clinton administrations. Under Carter, the Justice Department would defend an agency "only when disclosure is demonstrably harmful, even if the documents technically fall within the exemptions of the Act" (Bell, 1976). In contrast, under Reagan, the Justice Department would "defend all suits" that challenged a denial, unless there was no "substantial legal basis" or the denial presented "an unwarranted risk of adverse impact on other agencies' ability to protect important records" (Smith, 1981). Clinton's attorney general reversed the Reagan policy, moving closer to the Carter position. The current standard is to defend "only in those cases where the agency reasonably foresees that disclosure would be harmful to an interest protected by that exemption" (Reno, 1993, p. 1).

Along with the executive and legislative branches, the courts have played a key role in interpreting the FOIA. That role grew significantly as a result of the 1974 amendments, but as with the other two branches, some court decisions expanded public access to records while other decisions supported agency efforts to restrict access. In one unusual instance, in 1973 Congress objected strenuously to a Supreme Court decision (*EPA* v. *Mink*) and took almost immediate legislative action to reverse that decision. Congress specifically rewrote one of the FOIA exemptions to leave no doubt that the legislature intended the courts to have a broad role in reviewing and being able to overturn executive branch decisions that assign secrecy classifications to documents by executive order. As of September 1994, the Justice Department listed 3,831 federal judicial decisions (published as well as unpublished) that dealt with an array of FOIA and privacy issues (Maida, 1996). This is a conservative count, since many of these citations actually involve multiple judicial decisions.

Unforeseen Events Shape Policy and Administration

A final factor that must be understood as a preface to the larger debate over balancing access, privacy, and secrecy decisions is the uncontrollable and unanticipated political environment. For example, much of the bipartisan congressional drive to amend the FOIA in 1974 was linked to Watergate, President Richard Nixon's resignation, and the resulting public and political demand to understand the events and hold "government" accountable.

Uncontrollable events can also produce intense policy clashes within an administration over setting boundaries between openness and secrecy, as occurred with President Clinton's position on national security classification. On April 17, 1995, after much internal White House debate, Clinton issued Executive Order 12958, on classified national security information, which was designed to replace President Reagan's more restrictive Executive Order 12356, issued in 1982. The president's goal, he said, was to shift the balance away from secrecy; "doubtful calls about classification" would be resolved "in favor of keeping the information unclassified." Employees would be not only "encouraged and expected to challenge improper classification" but "protected from retribution" for so doing; more stringent standards would have to be met before information could be designated as classified (Clinton, 1995, p. 1).

Within just two days, much of this philosophy of openness appeared to change. On April 19, 1995, the nation was shocked by the devastating bombing of the Murrah Federal Building in Oklahoma that killed 168 people and injured more that 500 others. In the wake of this bombing, by Americans and not by foreign terrorists, the president and many others began to call for a dramatic expansion in the intelligence gathering activities of the Federal Bureau of Investigation (FBI) and other law enforcement agencies. Almost exactly a year later, Clinton signed into law the sweeping Antiterrorism and Effective Death Penalty Act of 1996. Among other things, government law enforcement and investigatory powers were expanded and, inevitably, access to some government records was decreased.

Violent external events have influenced other information policies. Reagan's classification guidance not only evolved out of fundamental values about the importance of protecting government records—values shared by his senior administration members—but were also shaped by international terrorist activities. During 1980 and 1981, when these policies were being developed, they were influenced by the toppling of the Shah of Iran and the rise to power of Ayatollah Khomeini, by the Iranian hostage situation that had paralyzed the Carter administration, and by threats in Afghanistan and the Middle East.

Although protecting intelligence and law enforcement agency activity is different from classification decisions, executive branch policies about access and classification have often been linked by a common philosophical approach to information and its control. Executive orders on classification also intersect directly with the FOIA; the very first exemption [5 U.S.C. 552(b)(1)] permits agencies to withhold "matters" that are "specifically authorized" by executive order "to be kept secret in the interest of national defense or foreign policy."

The question, then, is, Where does a career professional start in seeking to understand and respond to the competing, conflicting demands of information policy? The answer is that the professional must accept working within the fuzzy confines of ambiguity. Information policy has been and is likely to remain a negotiated combination of statute, regulation, executive branch guidance, congressional oversight, and case law.

CREATING AND MANAGING THE FOIA

The FOIA has been the single piece of federal legislation that has closely defined the concept of "open government" for more than a quarter of a century. But the statute's language, its legislative history, and the case law that has followed it demonstrate the complexity of setting a single standard. The statute rests on a philosophy of open government as an essential condition for democracy, and it provides specific remedies (including financial compensation) to those improperly denied access to records. At the same time, it offers agencies discretionary opportunities to withhold records, first through categories of records that may be exempt, and second through the potentially powerful tool of fees and fee waivers, those statutory charges that can be assessed or waived for a requester seeking records.

The FOIA is grounded on the premise that any person may request government records held by executive branch agencies. Most important, the agency decision to release or withhold those records rests on the nature and content of the records, not on who the requester is or the use to which those records might be put. Administrative and judicial remedies are provided for people whose requests for records have been denied. Administratively, each agency must create an appeal process for internal review of a decision that denies release of records. If the denial is sustained, the statute permits the requester to appeal to the courts. Judicial remedies include the right to have a U.S. district court review the request *de novo* (to review all the issues from the beginning) and the records *in camera* (to look at requested records privately), and the right to receive reasonable attorney fees and other litigation costs if the court finds that the complainant has substantially prevailed.

The statute favors the requester in court in several ways. Unlike review of other agency decisions in which the agency has only to show that its actions were not arbitrary or capricious, under the FOIA the agency has the burden of sustaining its action, that is, demonstrating why the records should be withheld or the fee waiver denied. In addition, the requester may "shop" for the district court of choice, choosing from among four locations: where he or she resides, where his or her principal place of business is located, where the agency records are located, or in the District of Columbia. During the 1990s, "shopping" has begun to increase as a number of requesters who previously chose the D.C. Circuit as the court of preference have looked to other appellate courts, such as the Ninth Circuit, which are now viewed as more likely to be sympathetic to their concerns.

The statute not only specifies avenues of appeal and redress, but since 1974, agencies have been required to respond to requests within strict time limits. Until 1996, a requester had to be informed within ten working days whether or not the agency would comply with the request and the reasons for a negative decision. One of the long-running agency complaints, however, was that this was insufficient time and generally unworkable. The 1996 amendments responded to this first by increasing the notification period for most requesters to twenty working days and then by permitting agencies to set up both a multi-tracking system to routinely separate relatively simple requests that could be handled quickly from lengthy, complicated ones, and a process for expediting some requests. Requests accepted for expedited processing must still be answered in ten working days.

Also since 1974, requesters have had to be informed of their right to appeal an adverse decision. If the request is denied, the agency has twenty working days within which to decide the appeal and notify the requester. Under "unusual circumstances," specified in the statute, the agency may extend either the initial decision or the appeal decision within ten days. If a decision is made to release records, the agency must make them available "promptly." In reality, these strict guidelines have been used with considerable flexibility: unusual circumstances have often been broadly and loosely defined, and a number of agencies have had response backlogs of months and even years. This is another aspect that the 1996 amendments sought to address both by defining unusual circumstances and by requiring agencies to report more publicly and in greater detail about their backlogs.

From the outset, there was general congressional agreement that some records would have to be exempted from release. While those on the House subcommittee that originally crafted the statute had hoped to limit these exemptions to three categories, the number crept steadily upward to nine for the final statute. That number has remained in place since 1966, but several of the categories have been either tightened or significantly expanded over time.

Although many members of Congress involved in writing the original 1966 statute and the 1974 amendments viewed the nine exemptions as permissive and not mandatory, over time agencies, including the National Archives, have tended to interpret the exemptions as mandatory, requiring that records falling within the exemptions not be released. This interpretation is mediated to some extent by the statute. The FOIA requires that "reasonably segregable" portions of documents be released after the exempt portions have been removed.

The nine categories of records that may be exempt include the following:

- National defense or foreign policy matters specifically authorized under criteria established by executive order and properly classified

- Internal agency personnel rules and practices as well as inter- or intra-agency memoranda, which are not normally available without litigation

- Personnel or medical files, release of which would be a "clearly unwarranted invasion of privacy"

- Financial or commercial information that is a trade secret, privileged, or confidential

- Law enforcement records or information, broadly defined

- Reports related to the work of agencies regulating or supervising financial institutions

- Geological and geophysical information and data

In addition, one exemption applies to matters that are specifically exempted from disclosure by other statutes. These are typically referred to by their numbers, (b)(1) through (b)(9).

THE 1974 AMENDMENTS

The history of the FOIA is a study of expansions and contractions of access through statute, administrative discretion, and case law. At times, agency response has been closely monitored by members of Congress, by inter groups such as journalists and public interest advocates seeking records, or corporate interests, who are often seeking to restrict access to their records while obtaining the records of their competitors. At other times, issues of access have seemed more routine or less pressing, and Congress has accepted executive branch arguments for limiting certain kinds of access.

The 1974 amendments, a source of expanding access, resulted from three factors. First, as amply demonstrated during lengthy House and Senate hearings, the act clearly was not working as Congress had intended. Serious efforts to amend the FOIA began in the early 1970s with hearings conducted by both houses. The hearings produced a litany of horror stories, such as requests ignored, long delays of up to 180 days in getting records, and exorbitant charges for copies of documents (as much as $1.00 per page).

Second, not only did the 1973 Supreme Court decision *EPA* v. *Mink* interpret the Court's role in reviewing one category of records very narrowly, but Justice Potter Stewart's sharp, terse, concurring opinion also helped galvanize members of the House of Representatives into make a bipartisan response in rewriting that section of the act and overturning the Supreme Court's decision. The issue was President Nixon's decision to conduct underground atomic tests at Amchitka Island, off Alaska. Some of his executive branch agencies questioned the wisdom of the testing. Patsy Mink, Democratic Congresswoman from Hawaii, tried both to stop the tests and to get copies of the agencies' views. When both efforts failed, she made an FOIA request. It was denied, citing FOIA exemption (1), records that were classified "secret," or "top secret," by executive order. Even though the tests were conducted, Congresswoman Mink decided to seek judicial review and was joined in her unsuccessful appeal to the Supreme Court by some thirty members of the House of Representatives. Justice Stewart wrote that Congress had "built into" the FOIA an exemption that provided "no means to question an Executive decision to stamp a document 'secret,' however cynical, myopic, or even corrupt that decision might have been" (*EPA* v. *Mink,* p. 95). And it was this blunt opinion that contributed to the rewriting of the statute.

Third, questions about presidential power and accountability raised by Watergate, the resignation of President Nixon, and his subsequent pardon by President Ford forged the bipartisan coalition in the House and Senate that not only voted for the 1974 amendments but that quite swiftly and resoundingly overturned President Ford's veto of the bill. The veto was the result of a short, intense fight. As a Congressman, Ford had voted for the initial statute in 1966, but as President he now found himself on the opposite side. His advisors on the FOIA veto were a combination of old Nixon hands who remained at the White House, members of the new Ford administration, and a Harvard Law professor, Phillip Areeda, brought on board during the transition and given management of the FOIA as one of his first assignments. During the spring and early summer of 1974, as President Nixon moved inexorably to resignation and then as Ford abruptly assumed the presidency, several unsuccessful attempts were made by members of Congress and the White House to negotiate a compromise on the proposed FOIA amendments.

In fact, White House memos show that President Nixon was opposed to vetoing the bill. By the end of the summer, however, his attention was elsewhere and attempts at negotiating a compromise had broken down.

The Nixon staff holdovers had been and remained fiercely opposed to the bill. The Ford people argued strenuously at the outset against any veto. Within the Ford camp, however, it was Areeda who opposed the act and persuaded Ford's advisors, one by one, to shift their positions and join in recommending that the president veto the bill.

The political environment in which this decision was made was critically important. On May 9, 1974, the House Judiciary Committee had begun hearings to consider impeachment. On July 30, three articles of impeachment were voted against the president. Little more than a week later, on August 9, 1974, President Nixon resigned. President Ford pardoned him on September 8, 1974, to resounding national criticism that was especially sharp in the House of Representatives. It was against this background that, on October 17, 1974, President Ford vetoed the FOIA amendments. That same day, in an unprecedented move, President Ford appeared before the House Subcommittee on Criminal Justice, joined by the House Committee on the Judiciary, for two hours to explain his decision and answer questions about the pardon.

A national outcry arose over the veto of the FOIA amendments, with editorials criticizing the decision appearing in newspapers across the country. Within a month, the veto had been decisively overridden by the House and Senate on roll call votes. Once it had been overridden, Ford moved promptly to ensure compliance with the amended statute. Within four months, the Justice Department issued a memorandum to provide agencies with guidance for implementing the changes. Reflecting Ford's philosophy, it stated that "it is the mission of every agency to make these Amendments effective in achieving the important purposes for which they were defined" (Levi, 1975, p. iii). During the next several years, the number of FOIA requests and the volume of documents released increased dramatically. This policy toward openness was further encouraged during the first two years of the Carter administration, with agency access officers frequently suggesting, "If in doubt, give it out." Toward the end of the Carter administration, however, that balance toward access had begun to shift, and a wholesale retreat began with the Reagan administration, using the tools of administrative discretion and guided by the Justice Department.

One of the first things William French Smith did as attorney general was establish the Office of Legal Policy and ask for a thorough study of how the FOIA was working and being administered. Law enforcement records were his major concern, but he began with the general belief that under Carter there had been "an unbalancing" in administration of the act. By the end of his four years as attorney general, Smith was pleased that they changed the administration of the act. Although it would be another four years until the FOIA statute was amended, he had succeeded through administration and guidance in shifting the executive branch balance toward greater restrictions.

THE 1986 AMENDMENTS

By 1986, the political climate had changed substantially from that of the 1970s, and the FOIA amendments reflected much of this. They were introduced not as a separate piece of legislation but as one of 107 disparate amendments to the Omnibus Anti–Drug Abuse Act of 1986. There were neither public hearings nor committee reports. Instead, the amendments were the product of House and Senate negotiations engaged in five years earlier that had previously failed to gain sufficient support in either House for enactment. Whereas the country had been focused on Watergate and the changing of the guard in the White House in 1974, in 1986 the major changes were taking place voluntarily and quietly in

Congress. In the House, Speaker Thomas ("Tip") O'Neill announced his retirement after thirty-four years (ten as Speaker); and in the Senate, six of the senior members also retired (Senators Thomas Eagleton, Barry Goldwater, Gary Hart, Paul Laxalt, Russell Long, and Charles Mathias).

The 1986 amendments produced some significant changes, making it less expensive for some requesters to get records but more difficult for others. The major revisions dealt with fee waivers, categories of requesters, and exemptions for law enforcement records. In addition, the OMB was given a new role, providing guidelines for uniform fee schedules and guidance in applying the fees. Also, both the role of the courts and the immediacy with which FOIA cases would be addressed in courts were scaled back.

The first revision concerned requesters, costs, and fee waivers. Until 1986, requesters were viewed as one undifferentiated group; their normal FOIA request costs were limited to "uniform" and "reasonable" fees charged by the agency for searching for and duplicating records. The amendments, in contrast, created three categories of requesters, each with different rights. Requesters in the first category, those making requests for commercial (profitmaking) reasons, can be charged for search, duplication, and importantly, for the potentially time-consuming and expensive document review that determines whether or not records can be released. Requesters in the second category, a loose agglomeration encompassing "representatives of the news media," as well as "an educational or noncommercial scientific institution whose purpose is scholarly or scientific research" (P.L. 99–570, title 1, 1801–1804), can be billed only for reasonable document duplication costs as long as the request is not for commercial use. The third category consists of everyone else: public interest and nonprofit groups as well as people seeking records for personal reasons. They can be charged for both search and duplication, but not for review. For those in the second and third categories, the first two hours of search time are free, as is copying the first one hundred pages of documents. Additionally, there is no charge if it costs more to collect the fees than to provide the documents. These provisions do not apply to commercial requesters.

The fee waiver policy was also changed. There had always been a statutory public interest fee waiver or fee reduction, but the definition of *public interest* changed between 1974 and 1986. The 1974 standard was, again, relatively broad, with fees to be waived or reduced when agencies determined that the information requested was considered as primarily benefiting the general public.

With the 1986 amendments, determining public interest became more complicated. It thus became more difficult for a requester to qualify for a fee waiver. To meet the new statutory standard, agencies had to find that the information was "likely to contribute significantly to public understanding of the operations or activities of the government" and that it was "not primarily in the commercial interest of the requester" [5 U.S.C. 552(a)(4)(A)(ii)(II)]. As with the other revisions, the terms *likely, significantly,* and *public understanding,* all became potential discretionary battlegrounds. To help agencies interpret these terms, the Justice Department in 1987 replaced its 1983 five-step fee waiver guidelines with new policy guidance specifying six complex conditions (termed "factors") that a requester had to meet to qualify for a waiver or reduction in fees. The effect was to set a still higher hurdle for anyone seeking a fee waiver. For example, an agency could refuse to grant a fee waiver by finding that there were already a number of publications available on the subject and, therefore, in the agency's judgment the new requester's work would not be likely to make a significant contribution. Similarly, proposing to disseminate records through a library or records repository would be insufficient to meet the test of "contributing to the understanding of the public at large" (Markham, 1987).

The judiciary's role was narrowed as well. Courts still review agency decisions to withhold records *de novo* and *in camera.* But in fee-waiver questions, the court's *de novo* review is now limited to the record before the agency. Instead of making an independent judgment on whether a fee waiver should be granted (based on hearing both sides), the court decides only on whether the agency followed its procedures in arriving at its decision. Another significant change relates to the scheduling of FOIA court cases. Under the 1974 statute, the FOIA cases were to take precedence on the docket over all other cases, with hearing, trial, or argument being expedited, unless the district court found other cases to be of greater importance. This was repealed in 1986.

One of the most extensive and controversial revisions in 1986 dealt with the (b)(7) exemption for law enforcement records, which pitted those concerned with protecting records against those concerned with access and accountability. It has now become more difficult to gain access to an array of records. The threshold for the exemption was lowered in almost all cases, making it easier to apply. The kinds of materials that could be included under the exemption were broadened, and selected categories of records normally subject to the FOIA could be excluded for an indeterminate period. For example, the 1974 exemption applied specifically to investigatory "records that were compiled for law enforcement purposes." The 1986 amendment deleted the word *investigatory* and expanded what could be exempt to include records or *information.* The new exemption standard became any "records or information compiled for law enforcement purposes."

More categories of records could now be exempted, and it became easier to meet the exemption standard. The threshold in 1974 rested on a relatively narrow standard of what "would" cause harm, as in interfere with, disclose, or be an unwarranted invasion. In 1986, the standard in most cases became the far more discretionary "could reasonably be expected to" interfere with, disclose, or endanger. Several subsections were also added, covering criminal violations, foreign intelligence, counterintelligence, and terrorism records, which permit an agency under a number of conditions to treat these records as "not subject to" the FOIA.

ELECTRONIC FOIA: THE 1996 AMENDMENTS

The 1996 amendments clearly state that the FOIA applies to agency records maintained "in any format, including an electronic format." The Electronic Freedom of Information Act Amendments differed significantly in tone and purpose, however, from the initial FOIA and the 1974 and 1986 amendments. From 1966 to 1986, crafting the exemptions, especially for law enforcement records, was one of the major sources of contention, along with debates over such issues as uniform fees, fee waiver standards, timely responses to requests, and the role of the courts.

In 1996, no changes were made in the exemptions. Rather, efforts were directed at technology and administration, making it easier to obtain records electronically and to monitor agency compliance through changes in reporting to both Congress and the general public. Nonetheless, while the amendments solved some problems, they also raised a number of new issues, failed to address some critical ones, and may well have opened the door for unintended litigation.

The EFOIA, a rare bipartisan effort in a partisan Republican Congress stridently at odds with a Democratic president, was rushed into law shortly before the 104th Congress adjourned. Although Democratic Senator from Vermont Patrick Leahy, a long-time FOIA champion and advocate for some form of electronic amendment, had developed and moved a bill along in the Senate well before the House had such a bill, it was the House version that was passed and accepted by the Senate with no changes. A number of factors coalesced to ensure speedy enactment. Three of the House sponsors—Steven Horn, Republican from California; Carolyn Maloney, Democrat from New York; and Randy Tate, Republican from the state of Washington—and their key staffers had a strong interest in the bill. Horn, chairman of the House Government Management, Information and Technology Subcommittee, had been elected in 1992, as had Maloney. Tate, one of the freshmen swept into office with the 1994 "Gingrich revolution," represented a district with leading information technology corporations. The issue also appealed substantively and politically to Speaker Newt Gingrich. He wanted to make more government information of all kinds available electronically (as he had already done with congressional records), and he was also concerned with supporting vulnerable freshman Republicans—in this case Tate, who needed to demonstrate legislative skills to interested constituents. The press and requester communities supported action, and it was understood that the president would sign the bill.

Horn's subcommittee conducted two days of hearings in June 1996 and marked up the bill in July; the House voted on it 402 to 0 on September 17. The next day, the Senate voted for the House version on a voice vote, and President Clinton signed the bill into law on October 2. As a footnote to history, despite the bill's enactment, Tate lost his November reelection bid.

Broadening Electronic Access

A major thrust of the 1996 legislation is to make agency records released under the FOIA and their annual reports widely available electronically, preferably through computer telecommunications. A second goal is to make it easier for a requester to learn what records an agency has and where these records are located.

One of the potentially far-reaching changes deals with the records an agency decides to release. Under the EFOIA, once this decision has been made, an agency must also make those records available for public inspection and copying, and it must do so electronically, if it determines that the records "have become or are likely to become the subject of subsequent requests for substantially the same records."

The requester, not the agency, is to choose the form or format in which the requested record is provided (if that requested format is readily reproducible). This legislation specifically overturns two previous court cases, *Dismukes* v. *Department of the Interior* (1984) and *SDC Development Corporation* v. *Mathews* (1976), which had held that the format of requested records was an agency decision and (in *Dismukes*) that the agency "had no obligation . . . to accommodate the plaintiff's preference" (p. 763).

Agencies must now index and describe all of their major information systems as well as their record locator systems and make these available by computer telecommunications by December 31, 1999.

Another concern of requesters was that, especially with electronic records, they often could not determine how much had been denied or deleted ("redacted") from a request. As a result of the EFOIA, agencies must "make a reasonable effort to estimate" the amount omitted, and when there are deletions they must provide this information where it occurs, if technically feasible. Agencies need not do this, however, if they claim harm under one of the nine exemptions.

Agencies are also to make "reasonable efforts" to maintain and search for records in electronic form. As with the estimates, however, electronic search may be avoided "where these efforts would significantly interfere" with the agency's automated information system. This could become a problem for requesters because the statute does not define "significantly interfere with" and this issue has never been raised when considering paper records.

Administrative Accountability and Procedure

Among the administrative and procedural changes made by the EFOIA are those in the content and dissemination of the agencies' required annual reports on FOIA activities. To provide new measures of accountability, agencies must for the first time list the total number of FOIA requests received and processed each year, along with the median time for processing and the number of staff assigned to handle these requests. As before, agencies must report the number of times they denied records and the number of times these decisions were overturned in court. In addition, they must now list the statutes other than the FOIA that they cited in denials [(b)(3) denials], as well as whether the courts upheld their use of these statutes.

The annual reports are to be made widely and more easily available to Congress and the general public, with the attorney general assigned new dissemination requirements. In Congress, the reports are now to be sent not just to the House Speaker and Senate Majority Leader for them to distribute to the appropriate committees, but also to the chairmen and ranking minority members of specified House and Senate committees. In the House, this is the Committee on Government Reform and Oversight; in the Senate, it is the Committees on Governmental Affairs and the Judiciary. Each agency is to make its report available electronically, preferably by computer telecommunications, and the attorney general is responsible for making all these electronic reports available "at a single electronic access point."

The 1996 amendments continue a trend, begun in 1986, away from treating all requesters and requests equally. Under the EFOIA, instead of responding on a first-come, first-served basis, agencies may now set up multitracking systems for different types of requests, although the statute does not specify the number of tracks or the notification process, if any, for those assigned to different tracks. Requesters with large, complex requests would have the option of narrowing their requests in order to move to a different track. Agencies may also provide for "expedited" processing for requesters who "certify" that they have "a compelling need," as defined by statute.

Statutory Uncertainties and Unfinished Business

Some analysts fear that, absent further clarification—for example, by the OMB—several of these changes could lead to a number of problems for requesters. For example, they might be pressured into reducing their requests to qualify for faster processing, and they might be penalized in an appeal process for failing to do so; some tracks might dramatically increase the time it takes to receive requests; and in a worst-case scenario, a person "certifying" a compelling need to receive expedited processing might be subject to criminal investigation if the claim's veracity were challenged (Gellman, 1996).

As Congress raced to enact this bill, two "hot button" items fell by the wayside. First, members of Congress and the requester community have disagreed with a 1989 Supreme Court decision (*Department of Justice* v. *Reporters Committee for Freedom of the Press*), arguing that it distorted the congressional intent of the FOIA by holding that the FOIA had a "core purpose" of accountability and hence could be used only to "shed light on government activities and operations" (Leahy, 1996, p. 60). In the Senate report that accompanied the EFOIA, Senator Leahy wrote that the Court's "core purpose" construct "imposes a limitation on the FOIA which Congress did not intend and which cannot be found in its language and distorts the broader import of the Act in effectuating Government openness" (p. 40). However, since this did not make it into the bill, the statement, though clear, is not in any way binding on any court (Hammitt, 1996).

The second issue was a last-minute effort to overturn a 1996 D.C. Circuit Court decision that the National Security Council (NSC) was not an agency and therefore not subject to the FOIA (*Scott Armstrong et al.* v. *Executive Office of the President et al.*), even though it had repeatedly been considered by the government to be an agency. The effort to add three words to the bill specifying that the NSC was in fact subject to the FOIA failed at the last moment; there was concern that any change in the bill would break the agreement reached by the House and Senate subcommittees and the White House and would jeopardize the enactment of the entire bill.

Clearly, as with any new piece of legislation, a number of old and new issues must be negotiated. How well the EFOIA will work must await the experience of requesters and submitters; the oversight of Congress, the OMB, and the Justice Department; the development and implementation of agency regulations; and the judgment of the courts.

JUDICIAL PARTNERS IN FOIA DEVELOPMENT

The judiciary has been a full partner in shaping FOIA administration and use, as Congress intended from the earliest House subcommittee meetings in the fifties. Courts have rendered decisions on some of the most fundamental concepts introduced but not initially defined by Congress, such as the definitions of *agency* and *record*. They have also considered fee waiver requests and attorneys' fees, and reviewed whether an agency has adequately searched for records or correctly applied a particular exemption.

The courts' role is so potent because of their ability, for the most part, to examine an entire issue *de novo* and *in camera*, and with the exception of fee-waiver cases and expedited processing, they are not restricted to reviewing just an agency's record or procedure. Congress expected the courts to scrutinize agency claims for withholding and built in the tools for rendering independent judgment. Because the court has the right to review all the issues *de novo* instead of reviewing only the administrative procedure by which the agency handled the request, the court can make its own determination as to whether the records should be released or withheld. The court's right to look at the requested records *in camera* permits judges to weigh the merits of each side's argument without risking harm from public release of those records. However, since the 1980s, often in split decisions the courts have steadily narrowed the definition of *agency record* (and therefore what is subject to release under the FOIA), *public interest,* and even *agency.* Justice William Brennan, in a sharp dissent over the definition of *agency records* (*Forsham* v. *Harris,* 1980), warned that "the Court's approach must inevitably undermine FOIA's great purpose of exposing Government to the people" (p. 190).

Several examples illustrate the power, reach, and role of the judicial branch. Two of the most important cases came relatively early. The first (*Vaughn* v. *Rosen,* 1973) spelled out what information an agency must provide to help requesters challenge an agency's decision to withhold records. Prior to this case, a requester had been at a disadvantage in trying to overturn an agency's decision to withhold records because the typical requester did not know what records the agency was withholding or why they were being withheld and hence could not argue effectively in appealing the decision.

The case began when Robert Vaughn, a professor engaged in research on the Civil Service Commission, made a FOIA request for reports. After both his request and appeal were denied, he filed suit. In *Vaughn,* the Court ruled that the agency had to produce what became known as a "Vaughn Index": an itemized, indexed list of those documents and portions of documents that it was and was not releasing, demonstrating why each exemption was being claimed. The description had to be "sufficiently specific" so that "a reasoned judgment" could be made as to whether the material was really exempt. Subsequently, Vaughn indexes have been requested routinely, although they may be replaced as a result of the 1996 requirement that agencies describe and index all their major information and record locator systems.

In *Chrysler Corporation* v. *Brown* (1979), the Supreme Court created a right, not found in the FOIA, for businesses ("submitters") to have a court review an agency's decision to release to a FOIA requester that corporation's records held by the agency. The general issue arose because private firms routinely submit data about their operations to various government agencies. Some data may be required by law, while some must be submitted if a firm is seeking a government contract. In either case, under the FOIA, when a third party (often a competitor) requested that information, it was up to the agency holding the records to decide whether they should be released or withheld. The decision would usually be based on the agency's interpretation of FOIA exemption (b)(4), which was designed to protect "trade secrets and commercial or financial information obtained from a person" that was "privileged or confidential," and on the Trade Secrets Act of 1905 (a criminal statute). Congress had made no provision for notifying submitters of commercial or financial information that anyone had requested their records or that the agency had decided to release those records, and submitters had no voice in the agency's decision. That changed as a result of *Chrysler* and a subsequent executive order.

In *Chrysler,* the corporation sought to prevent the Defense Department from releasing to a FOIA requester the workforce compliance records that Chrysler had been required to submit in bidding for a government contract. The Court held unanimously that even though Chrysler had "no private right of action" (no right to file a lawsuit) under either the FOIA (which was "exclusively a disclosure statute") or the Trade Secrets Act, it *did* have the right to judicial review under a separate provision of the APA. Under APA Section 10(a), "[a] person suffering legal wrong because of agency action . . . is entitled to judicial review thereof." This was a landmark decision; even though Chrysler lost its case, it won what was actually sought—the right to file a "Reverse FOIA" suit. Specifically, the court held that a business did have a right to file suit to stop an agency from releasing its records to a FOIA requester, and a court would then have to review the agency's decision. However, in contrast to the broad *de novo* court review of FOIA cases, subsequent circuit court decisions have generally limited the scope of review in Reverse FOIA cases to the agency's administrative record.

Eight years after *Chrysler,* President Reagan issued Executive Order 12600 in 1987. It outlined administrative procedures that agencies must establish to advise commercial submitters about how to protect their "confidential commercial information," and it specified that they must be notified with opportunity to comment if the agency has decided to release the records or the requester has filed suit.

Determining what constitutes agency records (essential because the FOIA applies only to agency records) and deciding when these may be exempted from release have long been a source of struggle. The Supreme Court began to answer the first question in *Forsham* v. *Harris* (1980). The issue was whether raw research data from a research project funded entirely by the federal government but carried out by a private organization was subject to the FOIA. The Court held 7 to 2 that the records should remain private; neither federal funding nor federal participation in generating data was sufficient to turn a private grantee's data into agency records.

Businesses have argued that under a (b)(4) exemption their commercial and financial records should not be released. Two important D.C. Circuit Court cases, seventeen years apart, tackled this issue. The first, *National Parks and Conservation Association* v. *Morton* (1972) proposed a two-pronged test as an objective measure needed to determine when these records could be held confidential. If release would impair the government's future ability to obtain necessary information or would "cause substantial harm to the competitive position" of the submitter, the records could be protected.

This standard was substantially revised when the D.C. Circuit Court ruled 7 to 4 that industry safety reports submitted to the Nuclear Regulatory Commission could be withheld because they had been submitted "voluntarily" (*Critical Mass Energy Project* v. *NRC,* 1992). The court reached its decision by creating two new categories of financial or commercial records: those submitted "voluntarily" (and "not customarily released to the public" by the submitter) and those "mandated" for submission by the government (hence subject to the FOIA). Dissenting, Judge Ruth Bader Ginsburg said that with this decision "there will be no objective check on, no judicial review alert to" government or business officials' "temptation" to claim confidentiality whenever the government requests information.

In another major curtailment of the FOIA, the Supreme Court expanded the privacy exemption and narrowed the definition of *public interest* (*Department of Justice* v. *Reporters Committee for Freedom of the Press,* 1989). Citing invasion of privacy, the Court unanimously rejected journalists' request for rap sheets from the FBI's computerized databases on an alleged organized crime figure who had received government contracts. The justices held that release of the rap sheets did not contribute to the core purpose of the act, which the Court defined as contributing significantly to public understanding. They also held that, especially with computerized criminal records, an individual's privacy rights outweigh public interest in disclosure. Further, when balancing individual privacy against public interest, a majority of the justices encouraged developing categories rather than doing case-by-case analysis. Critics have said that the narrow public interest definition contravenes congressional intent, which called for a very broad interpretation, and that the public interest standard for fee waivers was improperly applied to cover the entire act. Nonetheless, this decision has substantially changed the way the FOIA privacy exemptions are applied, and despite discussion in Senate and House committee reports, it has not been overturned with the 1996 amendments.

Clearly, each of the three branches has had an essential role in defining the FOIA and shaping its administration, although interpretations have often tugged the statute in opposing directions. However, as one justice noted, "Congress remains free to alter what we have done" (*Critical Mass Energy Project* v. *NRC,* 1992, p. 875).

STATE ACCESS LAWS

Open records, open meetings, and privacy issues have been as hotly debated at the state level as at the national level. While there has been a tendency to link concepts of freedom of information to the federal government, states and localities collectively also possess vast stores of information of potential value to citizens, and in some states there is no less tension among the branches than at the federal level, with the added twist that state attorneys general are often independently elected officials who may have an eye on the governorship.

While some states enacted access laws long before the federal statute was passed (such as Florida in 1915 and 1919), and while others moved more slowly, all fifty states as well as the District of Columbia, Guam, and the Marianas Islands now have open records laws, with case law in many ways paralleling case law at the national level. Judges in the 1990s are still ruling on the definition of *public interest,* on who is subject to FOIA, and on whether specific mailing lists and directories can be released.

At the state level, efforts to ensure access to government records have not stopped with the enactment of statutes. In many states, assistance in understanding and using existing law is provided by government organizations, press associations, universities, or public interest groups. As of October 1995, the Society of Professional Journalists had identified twenty-six states operating freedom-of-information (FOI) hotlines through press associations or councils (such as the Arizona First Amendment Coalition and the Wyoming FOI Hotline) and three other states—Massachusetts, New York, and Texas—served by state-sponsored groups. Several hotlines have toll-free numbers, and a growing number have Internet addresses ("Primer on States' Access Laws," 1995). As of 1996, there are government and professional associations in every state and the District of Columbia that provide FOI information ("State Access Laws and Contacts," 1996).

SUMMARY

Freedom of Information Act legislation (both federal and state) has been a powerful tool for increased understanding of and accountability from the executive branch of government, despite controversy and valid criticisms. Journalists, biographers, public interest groups, historians, and private individuals have all used the act, as have numerous members of the business community. Hundreds of newspaper articles, books, and television reports have resulted from or been enhanced by records obtained under the FOIA. It is estimated that in 1995 there were approximately six hundred thousand federal FOIA requests, and requests could reasonably top one million annually by the turn of the century. But this does not mean that the old debates over how to balance access, secrecy, and privacy have been resolved or that there is not legitimate concern that access to government records has been diminished.

Information policy, in all its guises, remains one of the most complex, controversial, dynamic aspects of American government. The rapid changes in electronic communications, with e-mail, hypertext, and hypermedia, have made legislating a balance between access and protection even more difficult. For the administrator, deciding how to handle requests for records is almost always a high-wire balancing act over competing demands. Decisions must constantly be renegotiated. Rarely have all three branches simultaneously shared the same philosophy. Just as often, each branch has sent out mixed signals, reflecting a lack of consensus among its own members. The point at which agreement begins and ends is with the vision of the founding fathers, that an effective democracy depends on an informed electorate. How these terms are defined and achieved is centered in the ongoing multilevel debate that is fundamental to constitutional democracy.

Cases Cited

Amazon Petroleum Corporation v. *Ryan,* 293 U.S. 338 (1935).

Chrysler Corporation v. *Brown,* 441 U.S. 281 (1979).

Critical Mass Energy Project v. *NRC,* 975 F.2d 871 (D.C. Cir., *en banc,* 1992) ("*Critical Mass II*"), cert. denied, 113 S.Ct. 1579 (1993).

Department of Justice v. *Reporters Committee for Freedom of the Press,* 489 U.S. 749 (1989).

Dismukes v. *Department of the Interior,* 603 F.Supp. 760 (D.D.C., 1984).

EPA v. *Mink,* 410 U.S. 73 (1973).

Forsham v. *Harris,* 445 U.S. 169 (1980).

National Parks and Conservation Association v. *Morton,* 351 F.Supp. 404 (D.D.C., 1972), rev'd, 498 F.2d 765 (D.C. Cir., 1974), appeal after remand sub nom., 547 F.2d 673 (D.C. Cir., 1976).

Panama Refining Company v. *Ryan,* 293 U.S. 388 (1935).

Scott Armstrong et al. v. *Executive Office of the President et al.,* No. 95–5057 (consolidated with No. 95–5061), U.S. Court of Appeals for the District of Columbia Circuit, Aug. 2, 1996.

SDC Development Corporation v. *Mathews,* 542 F.2d 1116 (9th Cir., 1976).

Vaughn v. *Rosen (I),* 484 F.2d 820 (D.C. Cir., 1973), cert. denied, 415 U.S. 977 (1974).

References

Bell, G. "Department of Justice Guidelines on Freedom of Information Act." Letter to heads of all federal departments and agencies. Washington, D.C.: Office of the Attorney General, Mar. 2, 1976.

Brandeis, L. D., and Warren, S. D., Jr. "The Right to Privacy." *Harvard Law Review,* 1890, *4,* 193–220.

Clinton, W. J. "Memorandum for Heads of Departments and Agencies on the Freedom of Information Act." Washington, D.C.: Office of the President, Oct. 4, 1993.

Clinton, W. J. "Statement by the President to Accompany Executive Order 12958." Washington, D.C.: Office of the President, Apr. 17, 1995.

Edmonds, S. E. "Pro and Con on the Logan-Walter Bill." *St. Louis Post-Dispatch,* Feb. 16, 1940.

Gellman, R. "The New EFOIA Law: One Person's View." *Access Reports,* 1996, *22*(20), 3–8.

Hammitt, H. "Will EFOIA Amendments Affect *Reporters Committee?" Access Reports,* 1996, *22*(20), 1–3.

Leahy, P. "Additional News of Senator Leahy." U.S. Senate Judiciary Committee Report No. 104–272, May 15, 1996, pt. 9.

Levi, E. H. "Attorney General's Memorandum on the 1974 Amendments to the Freedom of Information Act." Washington, D.C.: Office of the Attorney General, Feb. 1975.

Maida, P. (ed.). *Freedom of Information Case List.* Washington, D.C.: U.S. Government Printing Office, 1996.

"Primer on States' Access Laws." *Quill,* Oct. 1995, pp. 42–53.

Reno, J. "Attorney General's Memorandum for Heads of Departments and Agencies Regarding the Freedom of Information Act." Washington, D.C.: Office of the Attorney General, Oct. 4, 1993.

Smith, W. F. "Attorney General's May 4, 1981, Memorandum on the Freedom of Information Act to Heads of All Federal Departments and Agencies." Washington, D.C.: Office of the Attorney General, 1981.

"State Access Laws and Contacts." *Quill,* Oct. 1996, pp. 64–71.

CHAPTER TWENTY-THREE

Problems of Discretion and Responsibility

The Debate over Tort Liability

Bruce S. Jenkins
Russell C. Kearl

In his oft-quoted *Commentaries on the Law of England,* Sir William Blackstone observed that "besides the attribute of sovereignty, the law also ascribes to the king, in his political capacity, absolute *perfection.* The king can do no wrong. . . . The king, moreover, is not only incapable of *doing* wrong, but even of *thinking* wrong" ([1765] 1979, pp. 238–239). No longer insulated by the cloak of divinity and, by definition, the inability to err, the king (in modern dress, the state) can and does err.

Early in Anglo-American jurisprudential history, the courts crafted rigid doctrines of sovereign and official *immunity* that favored the interests of government in the power to act—and to err—over the interests of citizens in being free from injury to person or property caused by governmental actions. More recently, courts and legislatures have endeavored to strike a more thoughtful balance between the needs of the state to make policy and to govern effectively, and the personal and property interests of its citizens.

This is a remarkable advance on the accommodation that occurred at Runnymede, when it was decided that the king himself was subject to law—law enacted by someone other than the king—and that the king was not the law.

Recognition of the legitimacy of lawful governmental power survives today, as does state and individual immunity from suit by parties adversely affected by the legitimate exercise of that power. There is growing recognition, however, that when government officials and public servants commit either intentional wrongs or negligent wrongs that have private consequences (that hurt someone or someone's property), those public officials or servants, and even the state itself, should often be answerable in court to the person hurt, much the same as a private person would be. Enlightened legislators and courageous judges have tried to make law that provides that the state should be responsible for the harmful private consequences to persons and property of its public errors and the errors of its officers and servants. The questions then become: *How* responsible? and *Who* decides?

TORT LAW AND PUBLIC POLICY

Tort law defines the law's protection of three distinct groups of interests:

1. Interests of *personality*—"the sum total of a human being," most often physical well-being
2. Interests of *property*
3. Interests in *relations* with other persons

Tort law defines and protects these interests through *judicial remedies*: the remedy of compensation (and sometimes, punishment) in the form of an award of money *damages,* or preventive remedies such as an *injunction* or other affirmative court order or decree. Traditionally, tort law represents a variation on "a much stricter moral principle, found in the early history of the common law and other systems of law, that if one hurt another he must make recompense for the hurt" (Green and others, 1977, pp. 2–3).

Tort law recognizes that in everyday life human conduct creates risks. Tort law endeavors to determine the proper allocation of those risks. When harmful private consequences of public acts are evident, tort law asks in each instance: *Should a private individual be required to bear the burden of an injury or loss flowing from risk-creating governmental conduct?* Where the law says yes, an immunity, or exemption from legal liability, exists and the burden of a harmful private consequence remains upon the injured party. Otherwise, the tort law proceeds to weigh a variety of factors in deciding who should ultimately bear the cost of the particular harm.

Much like the legislative and administrative processes, the tort process is a public policy process. Tort actions and the standards of conduct that give rise to them "are imposed by law, and are based primarily on social policy, and not necessarily based on the will or intention of the parties," as would be the case, for example, in an action for breach of contract (*Tameny* v. *Atlantic Richfield Company*, 1980, p. 176).

Indeed, in tort law, as Green (1959) explains, "'We the People' are a party to every lawsuit and it is our interest that weighs most heavily in its determination"

(p. 1). "We the people" are represented in each case by "those whom we invest through the *political* process with power to deal with the problems epitomized in a 'case' brought to a court for determination—primarily lawyers, judges, and jurors to whom fall the responsibility of shaping and making decisions. It is their translation of our desires and needs which influences so greatly the disposition of the case as between the parties" (p. 2).

The tort process does not treat each case in isolation, but as part of a larger decisional framework in which both the immediate interests of the parties and broader considerations of the public interest—economic, administrative, ethical, and remedial factors—weigh in the balance. The judicial method in tort cases is characterized by a thoughtful and searching inquiry into facts, the formulation of issues for decision (fact or law), the definition and application of standards of human conduct, and the fashioning of appropriate remedies where relief appears warranted. The court, as an institution, relies on the judge's own human judgment in evaluating the important ethical, economic, practical, and remedial factors that must be balanced in each case. Whether a plaintiff will be granted the law's protection and whether a defendant will be required to have met a specified standard of conduct or to be answerable in damages represents "a policy decision in purest form" (Thode, 1977, p. 10).

Some public administrators, already sensitized to regimes of legal constraints—rulemaking procedures, notice and hearing requirements, judicial review—may view tort law as nothing more than another regime of legal "rules" needlessly burdening the administrative process. Some may imagine themselves the potential target of greedy plaintiffs claiming fanciful injuries and self-interested lawyers pressing exaggerated claims, and may view the tort process as an unwarranted and unwelcome intrusion by the judiciary into an agency's functions and an administrator's prerogatives.

In fact, the tort process calls for a public accounting of the true costs of government, costs that may not find reflection in a legislative appropriation or an agency budget. Tort law's emphasis on cause and consequence, conduct and compensation, and risk and prevention serves as a wellspring of the current emphasis on "risk assessment" and "risk management" in the legislative and administrative policy and planning processes.

The tort process reminds public administrators that government has limits, that persons have rights, and that power begets responsibility. Tort law expects that government, in doing its work, will routinely observe the same duties and standards of care that the law demands of everyone else. An informed administrator feels confident in possessing the power to decide, the power to plan, and the power to act, knowing all the while that the power to act does not include authority to act carelessly, excessively, or maliciously in performing tasks and achieving results.

The tort process nurtures public trust by imbuing the administrative process with a sense of accountability on an immediately personal level. A citizen need not fear being crushed under the wheels of a royal official's coach without any hope of redress in the king's courts. Tort law and the tort process play an important part in realizing fundamental American constitutional ideals concerning the rule and role of law, in reaffirming that no one, not even government itself, is above the law. A return to the sunny meadows of Runnymede!

This chapter addresses the integration of one public policy process, the tort process, with another, the administrative process. It examines past and present efforts to balance the public interest in providing compensation for government-caused injuries to persons and property with the public interest in efficiency, cost-effectiveness, and the sound exercise of discretion in doing the work of government. The current patchwork of governmental tort liability theories, immunity doctrines, and statutory exceptions poses some knotty problems for public administrators, the public they serve, and the courts to whom people turn seeking to resolve controversies of conduct and consequence.

SOVEREIGN IMMUNITY

In the first century of American history, the principle that government—federal, state, and municipal—was immune from all species of tort liability appears largely to have been taken for granted. In the early 1800s, the king could still do no wrong.

The Federal Government

In *Cohens* v. *Virginia* (1821), a well-known case vindicating the appellate jurisdiction of the Supreme Court over state criminal proceedings, Chief Justice John Marshall observed that "the universally received opinion is, that no suit can be commenced or prosecuted against the United States; that the judiciary act does not authorize such suits" (pp. 411–412; see also *Hill* v. *United States,* 1850).

Judicial pronouncements half a century later seem no less sweeping: "No government has ever held itself liable to individuals for the misfeasance, laches, or unauthorized exercise of power by its officers or agents," that is, for "the unauthorized acts of its officer, those acts being in themselves torts." Government "does not undertake to guarantee to any person the fidelity of any of the officers or agents whom it employs, since that would involve it in all its operations in endless embarrassments, and difficulties, and losses, which would be subversive of the public interests" (*Gibbons* v. *United States,* 1868, p. 274). In the Court's view, "public service would be hindered, and the public safety endangered, if the supreme authority could be subjected to suit at the instance of every citizen, and consequently controlled in the use and disposition of the means required for the proper administration of the government" (*The Siren,* 1868, p. 154).

In 1855 Congress created the U.S. Court of Claims, authorizing it to hear claims against the United States based on express or implied contracts. No corresponding expansion of governmental tort liability was to be implied: "The creation by act of Congress of a court in which the United States may be sued, presents a novel feature in our jurisprudence. . . . The language of the statutes which confer jurisdiction upon the Court of Claims, excludes by the strongest implication demands against the government founded on torts" (*Gibbons* v. *United States,* 1868, p. 275). As to tort claims against the federal government, the doctrine thus articulated would remain essentially intact for another eighty years.

State Governments

States likewise shared the blanket immunity from tort liability inherited by the United States from the English crown. After the U.S. Supreme Court held states vulnerable without consent to lawsuits by private individuals (*Chisholm* v. *Georgia,* 1793), the states rushed the Eleventh Amendment through ratification by 1795. However, the states responded more rapidly to currents of change than the federal government. State legislators and state court judges have taken significant steps toward more responsive treatment of the private consequences of erroneous governmental conduct.

In *Bernardine* v. *City of New York* (1945), the New York Court of Appeals (that state's highest court) construed a 1929 New York statute as abolishing the common-law immunities of both the state and local governments in that jurisdiction, except in very limited respects. Other state legislatures and state courts soon followed suit. By 1986, one could generalize that "virtually all jurisdictions, either judicially or by legislative fiat, have abolished or substantially abridged the doctrine of government immunity" (Isham, 1986, p. 24).

In the wake of judicial decisions abrogating traditional common-law immunity, many states adopted "tort claims acts" that redefined the scope and extent of governmental tort liabilities. Governmental immunity persists in many states for "discretionary" governmental functions, or under the "public duty" doctrine, or according to some similar formulation set forth in particular state statutes or case precedent (American Law Institute, 1982, pp. 256–266; Shepard's Editorial Staff, 1992, pp. 1–299).

Local Governments

The exemption of local county and municipal governments from tort liability derived less from attributions of royal infallibility than from more practical considerations: courts assumed that such entities likely had no funds from which to pay a judgment on a tort claim and that the mere prospect of liability would result in endless litigation; the problem of private remedy would be better addressed by the legislature. For the most part, later rationales offer variations on these themes.

The blanket immunity of local governments soon began to be eroded. Beginning with New York in 1842, some courts drew a distinction between "governmental" and "proprietary" functions, the latter being rendered vulnerable to tort liability. Other courts pointed to the purchase of liability insurance as a waiver of immunity, at least to the extent of the coverage.

In *Hargrove* v. *Town of Cocoa Beach* (1957), a case involving a prisoner who died in a fire in a jail left unattended, the Florida Supreme Court abandoned the common-law immunity doctrine outright, terming it "an Eighteenth Century anachronism" (p. 133). Other jurisdictions soon joined in abrogating the doctrine, by court decision, statute, or both (Prosser, 1971, pp. 979–985).

As creatures of state law, and particularly of the state legislature, counties and municipalities typically fall within the scope of state statutes or court decisions abolishing or modifying traditional governmental immunity doctrines. For that reason, local governmental tort liability may parallel that of state agencies in a particular jurisdiction.

Foundations of the Doctrine

The confidence with which the doctrine of sovereign immunity was asserted in the nineteenth century cloaked its uncertain, almost apocryphal origins (see Jaffe, 1963). Conceding that "the principle has never been discussed or the reasons for it given," the Court in *United States* v. *Lee* (1882, p. 207), observed that sovereign immunity "has always been treated as an established doctrine." Writing a century later in *Owen* v. *City of Independence* (1980), Justice William Brennan revisited the roots of the doctrine:

> Although it has never been understood how the doctrine of sovereign immunity came to be adopted in the American democracy, it apparently stems from the personal immunity of the English Monarch as expressed in the maxim, "The King can do no wrong." It has been suggested, however, that the meaning traditionally ascribed to this phrase is an ironic perversion of its original intent: "The maxim merely meant that the King was not privileged to do wrong. If his acts were against the law, they were *injuriae* (wrongs). Bracton, while ambiguous in his several statements as to the relation between the King and the law, did not intend to convey the idea that he was incapable of committing a legal wrong." Borchard, Government Liability in Tort, 34 Yale L.J. 1, 2, n. 2 (1924) . . . [p. 645, n. 28].

A reasoned foundation for the doctrine of sovereign immunity has proved elusive. Justice Felix Frankfurter, the archetypical conservative jurist, suggested that "this immunity from suit is embodied in the Constitution," although the constitutional text remains wholly silent on the subject (*Kennecott Copper Corporation* v. *State Tax Commission*, 1946, p. 580, dissenting opinion). Justice Oliver Wendell Holmes, the renowned legal realist, offered a remarkably positivist justification for the doctrine: "A sovereign is exempt from suit, not because of any formal conception or obsolete theory, but on the logical and practical ground that there can be no legal right as against the authority that makes the law on which the right depends" (*Kawananakoa* v. *Polyblank*, 1907, p. 353).

Whatever its origins, the American doctrine of sovereign immunity contemplated that the proper remedy for a governmental tort would be a legislative one: "In such cases, where it is proper for the nation to furnish a remedy, Congress has wisely reserved the matter for its own determination" (*Gibbons* v. *United States*, 1868, pp. 275–276).

Historically, legislative relief has been dispensed most often in the form of a private bill providing for payment of an individual claim. Private bills follow much the same path through the legislature as bills dealing with broader topics and make their own demands on the time and attention of legislators (see Holtzoff, 1942).

THE FEDERAL TORT CLAIMS ACT

At the federal level, Congress grew weary of granting private remedies; between 1939 and 1942, some 6,300 private bills were introduced in Congress, many of which involved compensation for tort injuries. Legislative fatigue, coupled with unrelenting scholarly criticism of the doctrine itself, led to the enactment of the Federal Tort Claims Act as part of the Reorganization Act of 1946 (Green and others, 1977, p. 215).

Though characterized almost as much by its exceptions as by its rule, the Federal Tort Claims Act established the general proposition that the United States should be held liable in money damages "for injury or loss of property or personal injury or death caused by the negligent or wrongful act or omission of any employee . . . while acting within the scope of his office or employment, under circumstances where the United States, if a private person, would be liable to the claimant in accordance with the law of the place where the act or omission occurred" [28 U.S.C. 2672, 1994]. Thus the government itself becomes liable for the "negligent or wrongful" conduct of its employees "in the same manner and to the same extent as a private individual under like circumstances" [28 U.S.C. 2674, 1994].

Congress qualified the expansive language of the Federal Tort Claims Act by incorporating a series of exceptions to liability. Two exceptions are particularly broad, excluding (1) any claim "based upon an act or omission of an employee of the Government, exercising due care, in the execution of a statute or regulation, whether or not such statute or regulation be valid"; or (2) any claim "based upon the exercise or performance or the failure to exercise or perform a discretionary function or duty on the part of a federal agency or an employee of the Government," regardless of whether the discretion was abused [28 U.S.C. 2680(a) (1994)]. In general, then, the Federal Tort Claims Act extended the tort process to reach negligent governmental conduct not involving a "discretionary function."

In addition to the exceptions made by Congress, the Supreme Court has fashioned two more of its own: (1) the so-called *Feres* doctrine, which excludes injuries to members of the armed forces that are "incident to service" (*Feres* v. *United States*, 1950); and (2) an exclusion of claims based on theories imposing strict liability, such as liability for ultrahazardous activities (*Laird* v. *Nelms*, 1972). While both of these judicial exceptions have been roundly criticized, both persist.

The Discretionary Function Exception

In 1946 Congress took the giant step of consenting to suit when government servants have acted negligently or wrongfully, excepting acts involving the exercise of a "discretionary function." The discretionary function exception marks a critical boundary between those governmental activities Congress chose to expose to a suit for damages by private individuals and those it did not. Yet fifty years of experience under the Federal Tort Claims Act has not produced a clear distinction, a "bright line" test identifying which governmental functions are discretionary and which are not.

Determining what function is truly discretionary proves, of course, to be a quest for boundaries, for definition. The word finds meaning only in context, and contexts vary as much as the people who engage in the activities of government. The Supreme Court speaks of "judgment of the kind protected by the discretionary function exception" *(Berkovitz* v. *United States*, 1988, p. 536). What kind of judgment is that?

Discretionary Function Defined

Discretion is the power to make decisions, to choose from valid alternatives, to decide what is to be done, and to do it or cause it to be done (Jaffe, 1965, p. 240). "Conduct cannot be discretionary unless it involves an element of judgment or choice" (*Berkovitz* v. *United States*, 1988, p. 536). State law definitions often parallel evolving federal definitions (*Tango* v. *Tulevech*, 1983, p. 41). Policy decisions—the exercise of the power of public policy choice—result in no liability in court. The policymaker is simply doing what a policymaker is entitled to do. Discretion of this kind may well be insulated, and indeed should be. As the Supreme Court now reads the statute, the discretionary function exception "protects only governmental actions and decisions based on considerations of public policy," that is, "legislative and administrative decisions grounded in social, economic, and political policy" where an officer or public administrator has been afforded room for independent judgment (*Berkovitz* v. *United States,* 1988, p. 537). Conversely, where a statute, regulation, or policy prescribes a course of action to be followed, where an officer or administrator acts to carry a prescribed policy into effect, that activity—and choices made in carrying on that activity—may not be insulated from liability, and indeed should not be.

The question of what constitutes "the permissible exercise of policy judgment" really combines *two* distinct inquiries:

1. Whether the action was a matter in which judgment or choice by the agency official, public administrator, or employee was *permissible—* that is, whether the agency, administrator, or employee was invested with *the power to choose,* either by statute, rule, regulation, or established policy. "If the employee's conduct cannot appropriately be the product of judgment or choice, then there is no discretion in the conduct for the discretionary function exception to protect."

2. Whether the government agency or public administrator exercised judgment or choice "based on considerations of public policy," that is, judgment "of the kind that the discretionary function exception was designed to shield" (*Berkovitz* v. *United States,* 1988, pp. 536–537).

The first inquiry anticipates three possible outcomes:

1. If statute, regulation, or policy mandates a particular action and the government employee complies, the conduct remains protected from liability as action "in furtherance of the policies" underpinning the regulation.

2. If the employee violates that mandate, "there will be no shelter from liability because there is no room for choice."

3. If the statute, regulation or policy affords the employee "the necessary element of choice," it may at least be presumed that the employee's actions "are grounded in policy when exercising that discretion"—a matter to be determined through the second inquiry (*Gaubert* v. *United States,* 1991, pp. 323–324).

The second inquiry focuses not on the employees' mental processes in exercising the discretion but on "the nature of the actions taken and on whether they are susceptible to policy analysis" (*Gaubert* v. *United States,* 1991, p. 325). Whether the conduct in question involves protected discretion—choice "grounded in the social, economic, or political goals of the statute" (p. 323)— turns on the nature of the action when considered in a generalized sense rather than on a fact-intensive exploration of the actual decision-making process in each particular case. The second inquiry asks whether the action "is one which *we would expect* inherently to be grounded in considerations of policy" (*Baum* v. *United States,* 1993, p. 721, emphasis added). In at least one case, the exception has been held not to apply where no decision was made. In affirming the trial court's finding that the navy negligently failed to warn family members of a naval shipyard worker of risks of exposure to asbestos dust from the employee's clothing, the U.S. Court of Appeals for the First District ruled that the discretionary function exception did not apply (*Dube* v. *Pittsburgh Corning,* 1989, p. 797). Similarly, some state courts have refused to find conduct to be discretionary when choice or judgment was required but no policy choice or judgment was in fact made (*Haddock* v. *New York,* 1990, p. 485).

Discretionary Functions and the "Duty" Issue in Tort Law

Tort law deals with standards of human conduct, with duties of care in relation to risk-creating conduct. Whatever the kind of tort, tort law asks four questions concerning a plaintiff's claim:

1. Is there a factual connection between plaintiff's injury and defendant?

2. Does the legal system's protection extend to the interest that plaintiff seeks to vindicate, and if some protection is afforded, what standards of care does the legal system impose on the defendant?

3. Was that standard of care breached by the defendant?

4. What are the damages? (Thode, 1977, p. 1).

All four queries must be decided in the plaintiff's favor in order for the plaintiff to obtain a judicial remedy.

The second query, dealing with the scope of the law's protection, is often characterized as *the duty issue,* that is, it asks whether the law imposes a duty upon the defendant to conform to a particular standard of conduct toward another, particularly the plaintiff. To say that a defendant owes a duty to the plaintiff is a shorthand way of saying that the plaintiff's interests are entitled to legal protection against conduct by the defendant that falls short of a legally defined standard (Prosser, 1971, pp. 324–325).

Whether governmental conduct involves a discretionary function speaks to the duty issue. Discretionary function serves as a specific basis for determining that no duty exists. The District Court of Appeals of Florida explained it this way: "Discretionary acts do not give rise to liability because they are not tortious. By definition, *one who has discretion to act has no duty to act*" (*Penthouse, Inc.* v. *Saba,* 1981, p. 458, n. 2, emphasis added). Congress has said, in effect, that government officers who exercise discretion in making policy judgments and policy choices owe no duty of care to avoid negligent or other wrongful injury to the public. The injured party bears the harmful private consequences of discretionary public acts.

If the court determines that a particular action was not discretionary, this does not necessarily mean that a duty of care was owed to a particular plaintiff. Rather, the court proceeds to examine the duty issue in light of the facts of the particular case, weighing the economic, administrative, ethical, and preventative factors that bear upon the question of allocation of risk.

Is government responsible for the private consequences of public action? The court decides.

Tort Law and the Separation of Powers

The public policy process of tort law clashes most directly with the processes of public administration where discretionary functions of government are at issue. Where the decision to act or not to act has been entrusted to the processes and the judgment of a government agency or officer, it seems inconsistent to revisit that same decision by substituting the processes and judgment of another agency or officer, albeit a judicial one, through the mechanism of a civil lawsuit. Indeed, "the crux of the concept embodied in the 'discretionary function' exception is that of separation of powers" (*Payton* v. *United States,* 1981, p. 143).

Separation of powers finds its roots in the Constitution of the United States and its fracturing of the powers of government into three great divisions—legislative, executive, and judicial. The most fundamental determination as to who gets to decide is found in the famous case of *Marbury* v. *Madison* (1803), in which the Supreme Court "declared the basic principle that the federal judiciary is supreme in the exposition of the law of the Constitution" (*Cooper* v. *Aaron,* 1958, p. 18) and in which Chief Justice John Marshall wrote that "it is emphatically the province and duty of the judicial department to say what the law is" (*Marbury* v. *Madison,* 1803, p. 177).

One of the important innovations of the U.S. Constitution in the early view of separation of powers expressed in Book Eleven of Montesquieu's *The Spirit of Laws* ([1750] 1949) was the idea of a *coequal* and *independent* judiciary. Even so, the Supreme Court remains cautious about "judicial second-guessing of legislative and administrative decisions grounded in social, economic and political policy through the medium of an action in tort" (*Gaubert* v. *United States,* 1991, p. 323). Considerations of constitutional separation of powers inform a court's deliberation on the duty issue in cases involving governmental torts, regardless of the particular wording of a federal or state tort claims statute.

While the fracturing of governmental power into the three great divisions flowed from the genius of the founding fathers informed by classical learning and British history, there has arisen in this country a fourth great branch of government—an aggregation of administrative agencies—that, because of the inability or reluctance of Congress to legislate with particularity as to some subjects, has combined anew the powers once divided by the Constitution. Agencies have been empowered by Congress to make law (to *legislate*, through "rule-making"), to enforce those self-enacted rules with respect to particular persons or events (to *execute*, through agency investigations and enforcement actions), and to interpret and apply those same rules to parties appearing before administrative tribunals (to *adjudicate*, to pronounce or decree judicially). Thus one sees the phenomenon of an agency making, enforcing, and interpreting law, combining in one location the power that the framers envisioned as being forever partitioned. One need only compare the sheer physical bulk of the current *Code of Federal Regulations* with that of the current *United States Code* to grasp the extent of the explosion of lawmaking by agencies other than Congress—virtually all of which has occurred pursuant to statutory mandates from Congresses more than willing to delegate legislative powers and responsibilities to others.

In an ordered society, pockets of discretion are created and efforts are made to patrol the shifting borders between pockets of power through the legislature, the agencies, and ultimately through the courts. Generally speaking, those who act well within their pockets of power by following reasonable procedures and proceeding in accordance with reasonable standards have been treated as immune from suit.

Continuing exemption of discretionary actions of government officers from damages liability in private lawsuits, then, vindicates separation of powers principles. Allowing for the protected exercise of discretion acknowledges the legitimate reach of legislative, executive, and administrative powers within their own spheres. It acknowledges the fundamental differences between legislative fact-finding aimed at policymaking, and judicial fact-finding used to resolve disputes, as well as clarifying the role of each in the processes of government. This protection also acknowledges the legitimacy of the political and administrative processes as appropriate checks on abuse of power by officers and administrators in making policy decisions.

Indeed, the Federal Tort Claims Act entrusts all federal tort claims to agency decision-making processes in the first instance; all claims must first be presented to the agency involved, which is afforded an opportunity to resolve the matter before a lawsuit may be filed. The requirement is said to be "jurisdictional," that is, it sets a defined limit on the courts' own pocket of power to decide claims.

Trouble can arise for the official, the public servant, or the state itself when a public actor exercises unauthorized power, stepping beyond a well-defined border that limits his power and in doing so hurting someone or someone's property. Trouble can arise when the official exercises power within his or her sphere—but in a fashion that is careless, negligent, or even malicious, or that uses unreasonable force or zeal such that someone gets hurt. In either instance, tort law would impose liability in damages on the government official, the servant, or even the state itself—not only to compensate the person injured by governmental excess or carelessness, but to reaffirm the boundaries of official pockets of power and remind government of its own limits.

The task here is to alert public administrators that limits exist on the exercise of governmental power. The state, its officials, and its servants may be answerable in damages for either the unauthorized exercise of power or the negligent exercise of power that causes private hurt. Tort law "sets forth standards of conduct which ought to be followed. The penalty for failing to do so is to pay pecuniary damages" (*Riss* v. *City of New York,* 1968, p. 590, Keating, J., dissenting). The tort process advances separation of powers principles by taking a "second look" at administrative agency actions in an independent *judicial* forum outside of the fourth branch.

The Discretionary Function Exception in Perspective

Many federal tort claims arise out of recurrent fact patterns that do not raise discretionary function issues. Vehicle collisions, injuries in and around federal buildings and structures, medical malpractice by government physicians, law enforcement officers' use of excessive force—these cases all involve fact patterns (wrongful death, personal injury, property damage) familiar to courts in traditional common-law tort cases and generally do not implicate the public policy process.

Discretionary function more likely arises as an issue in cases involving military activities, foreign relations matters, government inspection, licensing and regulatory activities, or large-scale operations such as flood control. More recently, claims involving workplace safety for government contractors, injuries in parks or wilderness areas, and public exposure to toxic materials have raised discretionary function issues (Zillman, 1995, pp. 373–378).

In carrying out the policy of a statute, the Forest Service ranger may drive a government vehicle carelessly and hurt someone. A ranger may construct a wooden walkway and negligently fail to maintain it, or operate a cafeteria that serves tainted food to tourists. It is in the category of day-to-day, operational decisions that most answerable acts take place.

Conversely, a ranger may decide that, as a matter of policy, placing warning signs may detract from maintaining the wilderness character of a trail. Bears may be in an area without warnings of their presence. Limited resources may be allocated to patch and repair some roads through forest land but not others. Campers may be allowed to traverse an area known to have frequent flash floods. These actions may reflect the necessary element of policy choice, a weighing of policy considerations, and may be deemed discretionary.

DISCRETIONARY FUNCTIONS, "PUBLIC DUTY," AND STATE GOVERNMENTS

Many states also exempt discretionary governmental conduct from tort liability—by express statutory exception in at least twenty-nine states, by judicial interpretation of general statutory language (*Haddock* v. *New York*, 1990), or as an exception to judicial abrogation of common-law immunity (*Dover* v. *Imperial Casualty & Indemnity Company*, 1990) in several more states (Shepard's Editorial Staff, 1992, pp. 99–108, 215–218).

In addition, some states refer to a public duty doctrine, which shelters government officers and administrators against private lawsuits based on a duty that is owed to the general public, such as providing police or fire protection. According to the public duty doctrine, in effect a duty owed to everyone does not equate with a duty of care owed to a particular person. Tort liability must be based on some special duty of care owed to a particular individual, usually because of some special relationship. The police, for example, in responding to a particular 911 emergency call, may owe a duty of care at least to arrive at the correct address (*De Long* v. *County of Erie*, 1983). Courts following the public duty doctrine commonly apply it where the injured party claims that government, usually the police, failed to protect against injury inflicted by another person—an error of omission. A young woman terrorized and ultimately maimed by a rejected suitor who made repeated threats may have no claim for damages arising from the city's failure to provide police protection (*Riss* v. *City of New York*, 1968). However, if government undertakes to act and acts negligently, the public duty doctrine finds no application, such as when a state agency solicits a housing placement for a mental patient fascinated with setting fires but fails to furnish sufficient information to the owner of the rooming house to enable her or him to protect the property (*Onofrio* v. *Department of Mental Health*, 1990).

Some state courts view the public duty doctrine with great skepticism. Where a home burned because the fire department did not respond due to lack of an on-duty fire engine driver, the Alabama Supreme Court rejected the notion that the department's duty to put out fires was owed only to the public and not to an individual homeowner. The court retorted, "Does this mean that the whole town has to be on fire before the fire department responds to a call?" (*Williams* v. *City of Tuscumbia*, 1983, p. 825).

The public duty doctrine may best be understood as a variation on the protections afforded to discretionary governmental actions, particularly where courts explain that the amount of police, fire, or other protection "is limited by the resources of the community and *by a considered legislative-executive decision* as to how those resources may be deployed. For the courts to proclaim a new and general duty of protection in the law of tort . . . would inevitably determine how the limited police resources of the community should be allocated" (*Riss* v. *City of New York*, 1968, pp. 581–582, emphasis added).

OFFICIAL IMMUNITY AND PERSONAL LIABILITY OF GOVERNMENT OFFICERS

Sovereign immunity itself does not insulate government officers, public administrators, or agency employees from personal liability for actions taken within the scope of their employment. Indeed, "when federal, state, and local governments were not liable for their torts, liability of public employees was often used as a substitute. The law of liability of public employees has probably been distorted because of immunity of the governments. When private principals are liable in tort, their agents are seldom sued; [but] when public principals are not liable because of sovereign immunity, their agents are often sued" (Davis, 1984, p. 9).

Official immunity—the concept of the immunity of government officers from personal liability for their official acts—springs from the same root considerations as the doctrine of sovereign immunity. Official immunity "apparently rested, in its genesis, on two mutually dependent rationales: (1) the injustice, particularly in the absence of bad faith, of subjecting to liability an officer who is required, by the legal obligations of the position, to exercise discretion; and (2) the danger that the threat of such liability would deter his willingness to execute the office with the decisiveness and the judgment required by the public good" (*Scheuer* v. *Rhodes*, 1974, p. 240).

Official immunity, then, is grounded in public policy designed to prevent public officials and administrators from feeling constrained in the performance of their official duties by the threat of personal liability, and to preserve the independent judgment of public officers who might otherwise be influenced by the threat of retaliatory lawsuits. Official immunity spares public administrators the burden of diverting valuable time and resources to defending what may be frivolous litigation (Koch, 1985, p. 227).

To some extent, the roots of official immunity can be found in constitutional text. Article I, Section 6 of the U.S. Constitution grants absolute immunity to members of both houses of Congress with respect to any speech, debate, vote, report, or action done in session. The Speech and Debate Clause "was intended to secure for the Legislative Branch of the Government the freedom from executive and judicial encroachment which had been secured in England in the Bill of Rights of 1689 and carried to the original Colonies (*Scheuer* v. *Rhodes*, 1974, pp. 240–241; see also *Hutchinson* v. *Proxmire*, 1979).

In contrast, official immunity as it pertains to the executive and judicial branches remains largely a matter of judicial doctrine.

Absolute Immunity Versus Qualified Immunity

"Judicial officers"—judges, prosecutors, witnesses—those who are "integral parts of the judicial process," have traditionally been afforded *absolute immunity* from suit for actions taken as part of the judicial process (*Briscoe* v. *La Hue,* 1983, p. 335). Such immunity of prosecutors is limited to their judicial role; only *qualified immunity* shields such other roles as investigation and administration (*Buckley* v. *Fitzsimmons,* 1993). Absolute immunity bars liability where the acts complained of were negligent, intentional, or even malicious. In 1978, the Supreme Court extended absolute immunity to administrative law judges and hearing examiners: "We think that adjudication within a federal administrative agency shares enough of the characteristics of the judicial process that those who participate in such adjudication should also be immune from suits for damages" (*Butz* v. *Economou,* 1978, pp. 512–513). The same immunity also extends to those agency personnel with discretion to initiate administrative proceedings, and to agency attorneys who conduct a hearing, trial, or similar proceeding (pp. 515–516).

Absolute immunity also shields the president of the United States against claims "for damages predicated on his official acts" (*Nixon* v. *Fitzgerald,* 1982, p. 749) and insulates executive officers and public administrators engaging in discretionary functions against most kinds of tort claims. At one time, the Supreme Court had indicated that absolute immunity from traditional tort claims extended to all public officers acting within the scope of their authority and within the line of duty (*Barr* v. *Matteo,* 1959). However, in *Westfall* v. *Erwin* (1988), the Supreme Court explained that absolute immunity from traditional tort claims "should be available only when the conduct of federal officials is within the scope of their official duties *and* the conduct is discretionary in nature" (pp. 297–298).

On the state level, besides applying to legislators, judges, prosecutors, and court functionaries, absolute immunity generally extends only to the highest executive officers of state government. State laws afford most public administrators and agency employees only a qualified immunity against tort liability for actions taken within the scope of their employment. Generally, qualified immunity bars a lawsuit where a government officer or public administrator acted within the scope of his or her authority or employment to carry out a discretionary rather than a ministerial function in good faith—that is, without malice, fraud, or other corrupt motive (Shepard's Editorial Staff, 1992, pp. 315–329).

Where the conduct violates a federal constitutional right, or another right protected by federal law, qualified immunity may give way to liability if a government officer, public administrator, or agency employee knew or should have known that the action would invade the plaintiff's clearly established constitutional rights, regardless of the actor's good faith. This is true of those engaged in discretionary activities as well: "government officials performing discretionary functions generally are shielded from liability for civil damages insofar as their conduct does not violate clearly established statutory or constitutional rights of which a reasonable person would have known" (*Harlow* v. *Fitzpatrick,* 1982, p. 818). Whether a plaintiff asserts a "clearly established" right becomes a threshold issue to be decided by the court before an officer or administrator is further burdened with the costs of defending "a long drawn out lawsuit" (*Siegert* v. *Gilley,* 1991, pp. 232–233).

Whether absolute or qualified, an immunity or privilege from liability for damages afforded to a public official or servant "is not a badge or emolument of exalted office, but an expression of a policy designed to aid in the effective functioning of government" (*Barr* v. *Mateo,* 1959, pp. 572–573). The purpose of official immunity "is not to protect an erring official, but to insulate the decision making process from the harassment of prospective litigation" (*Westfall* v. *Erwin,* 1988, p. 295). As the Supreme Court explained in *Scheuer* v. *Rhodes* (1974, p. 242), "Implicit in the idea that officials have some immunity—absolute or qualified—for their acts, is a recognition that they may err. The concept of immunity assumes this and goes on to assume that it is better to risk some error and possible injury from such error than not to decide or act at all."

Official immunity should not encourage official error. The law makes this point with even greater emphasis where violations of the Constitution are concerned.

Bivens and Constitutional Torts

One of the most fruitful and instructive areas of governmental tort liability is of course in the area of *constitutional torts,* in which persons claim deprivation of rights guaranteed them by the U.S. Constitution. The right must be found in the Constitution, and the vindication of the right must be accomplished through a private lawsuit based on federal civil rights legislation, or directly through the Constitution itself.

Official immunity does not protect government officers, public administrators, or agency employees who violate the Constitution. In *Bivens* v. *Six Unknown Named Agents* (1972), the Supreme Court held that a private person may bring a lawsuit for damages alleging a violation of the Constitution itself against individual government officers or employees. In *Bivens,* the plaintiff claimed that federal narcotics agents entered his home and arrested him without a warrant or probable cause in violation of the Fourth Amendment's guarantee against unreasonable searches and seizures.

Following *Bivens,* in a series of cases involving constitutional claims arising out of a variety of factual contexts, the Supreme Court has reaffirmed that constitutional rights may be vindicated through a private lawsuit for damages brought directly under the Constitution itself, at least where there are not "special factors counselling hesitation," or where Congress has not "provided what it considers adequate remedial mechanisms for constitutional violations that may occur in the course of [the] administration" of a government program (*Schweiker* v. *Chillicky,* 1988, p. 423)—in other words, where Congress has not provided an alternative damages remedy (*McCarthy* v. *Madigan,* 1992). Where an officer asserts a qualified immunity, the plaintiff must establish at the outset that the right claimed to have been violated is clearly established; a ruling adverse to a claim of qualified immunity on this issue may be immediately appealable (*Behrens* v. *Pelletier,* 1996). A *Bivens*-style constitutional tort claim may not be brought against the federal government itself or a specific federal agency (*Federal Deposit Insurance Corporation* v. *Meyer,* 1994).

To recover damages against a government officer, administrator, or employee, a *Bivens* plaintiff must also prove that he or she suffered actual injury or loss as a result of the wrongful conduct. Damage awards on constitutional claims, like other tort claims, should be governed by the principle of compensation (*Carey* v. *Piphus,* 1978).

Some critics charge that a constitutional tort claim too often serves as "a tool of harassment and vengeance" (Kratzke, 1996, p. 1177), that many traditional common-law tort claims may easily be "framed in constitutional terms," and that under *Bivens* official immunity "disappears at the very moment when it is needed" to deflect vexatious claims (*Butz* v. *Economou,* 1978, pp. 520, 526, Rehnquist, J., dissenting). Views differ. At a minimum, the *Bivens* constitutional tort doctrine serves as a reminder to government officers and public administrators that "our system of jurisprudence rests on the assumption that all individuals, whatever their position in government, are subject to federal law" (*Butz* v. *Economou,* p. 506).

Insurance, Indemnity, and Substitution

Ultimately, the extent to which the governmental unit answers for wrongful acts of its officials has been treated as a question of public policy, to be decided by the legislature. The answers vary both in quantity (breadth of coverage) and quality (limitations on responsibility, such as damage caps or exclusions of exemplary remedies for intentional or malicious acts). Many states authorize the purchase of insurance covering employee liability for injury or loss resulting from government activities. Some states promise to indemnify public officers, administrators, and employees who may be held personally liable for their official acts (though few states undertake to do so where punitive damages are concerned). Some substitute a claim against the state for a claim against an individual employee, shifting both the cost of defending a claim and the cost of paying a possible damages award to government and, ultimately, the taxpayers (Davis, 1994, pp. 203–207).

The Federal Employee Liability Reform and Tort Compensation Act of 1988, also known as the Westfall Act, makes the United States the only party against whom a private lawsuit for damages resulting from the tortious conduct of its officers, agents, and employees may be brought. In substituting Federal Tort Claims Act liability for tort damages remedies against individual employees, Congress decided that the United States as a nation should shoulder the financial responsibility for its official errors, at least for its common-law torts. The act expressly excepts *Bivens*-style constitutional torts or any claim of violation of a statute that specifically authorizes lawsuits against individual officers for such violations. Further, the United States stands in place of its errant employees as defendant in a lawsuit only after the attorney general certifies that the employee was acting within the scope of his or her employment "at the time of the incident out of which the claim arose" (see *Gutierrez de Martinez* v. *Lamagno*, 1995).

The policy question that needs to be decided by each governmental entity or by the courts if given the opportunity is, To what extent should the government entity be held responsible for acts of its officials and servants that if done by a private person would result in liability for tortious injury? If persons should be responsible for damages done to another through fault, then good policy reasons exist for extending that concept from the persons in general and artificial persons such as corporations to the state itself and its actors.

The concept of evenhandedness finds application, as does the concept of consistency and the concept of fairness. The concept of compensation through risk shifting also finds application, with the state standing in the shoes of an insurance company and the cost borne by the taxpayers rather than by the payers of insurance premiums. As Schwartz (1984) observes:

> The state has increasingly been making itself into a mutual insurance company against accidents and distributing the burden of its citizens' mishaps among all its members. . . .
>
> From the point of view of the injured plaintiff, the movement from common-law officer liability to governmental risk liability is most desirable, for it will result in compensation in virtually all cases. But a system of complete governmental responsibility will mean the practical elimination of personal liability of officers. Even in those cases not covered by the trend toward officer immunity . . . plaintiffs will prefer to sue the government concerned, since execution of judgments against it need never run the hurdle of defendant's inability to pay.
>
> Such an extension of governmental liability removes personal liability as a check upon public officers. The officer who has to pay victims of his own torts out of his own pocket is less likely to act wrongfully than one who feels that he is acting only as an impersonal government agent [pp. 574–576].

The Federal Employee Liability Reform and Tort Compensation Act of 1988 strikes a balance between entity and officer liability. It places the burden of liability for most common-law torts on the government, while individual officers, administrators, and employees remain personally liable for their constitutional torts. Yet lines are imprecisely drawn, as in *Carlson* v. *Green* (1980), in which the director of the Federal Bureau of Prisons was held personally liable for negligent treatment of an asthmatic inmate. State and local governments may choose to strike similar or different balances.

SUMMARY

As Justice Robert Jackson once suggested, "it is not a tort for government to govern" (*Dalehite* v. *United States,* 1953, p. 57, dissenting opinion). The tort process nevertheless plays a key role in reconciling competing interests in government discretion and government responsibility. The question asked by tort law persists: *Who should bear the burden of risk-creating governmental conduct?*

In the name of separation of powers, American courts have departed from the common-law ideal of their English counterparts that "every official, from the Prime Minister down to a constable or a collector of taxes, has the same responsibility for every act done without legal justification as any citizen" (Schwartz, 1984, p. 558). Yet everyone concedes that traditional doctrines of sovereign and official immunity offer answers to the tort question that today prove largely inadequate to the task. Where remnants of state infallibility endure, an absence of state accountability to private persons for state actions, good or bad, also endures. "It is," wrote Abraham Lincoln in his first annual message to Congress, "as much the duty of government to render prompt justice against itself, in favor of citizens, as it is to administer the same, between private individuals. The investigation and adjudication of claims, in their nature belong to the judicial department" (1989, p. 287).

Tort law holds government accountable for its errors. The tort process evaluates risk-creating government conduct using an agency's own lawful authority and policymaking discretion as its yardstick. No matter whether plaintiff or government prevails, the tort process lends legitimacy to public administration because an independent judiciary has taken a second look at government conduct believed to be unlawful and to have caused private injury. In applying tort law standards of conduct to governmental activities, courts help weave the work of public administrators into the legal fabric of day-to-day life. The government officer, like the average citizen, must act with reasonable care.

Where matters of agency power and discretion remain unclear or even contradictory, or where confusion reigns as to the reach of agency authority, the extent of private rights, or the facts surrounding an event resulting in injury, courts may be of assistance in defining boundaries and standards and in resolving disputed questions of law or fact, always in the fact-specific context of a particular case. Where agency and citizen disagree as to boundaries, or as to event, the court decides.

As a practical matter, courts deciding governmental tort liability cases do not make policy decisions for public administrators. To the extent that a person's injury or loss results from government's failure to meet a minimum standard of conduct in public administration, "public officials are presented with two alternatives: either improve public administration or accept the cost of compensating injured persons" (*Riss* v. *City of New York,* 1968, p. 589, Keating, J., dissenting). In this sense, ultimately the public administrator decides. The court's role through the tort process is simply to "require officials to weigh the consequences of their decisions" (*Riss* v. *City of New York,* 1968, p. 589).

A check and balance not found in the organic document of the federal system—*financial responsibility*—requires serious study and thought by those who make policy decisions and those who carry out policy decisions once they have been made. The prospect of bearing financial responsibility for subjecting persons to risk resulting in injury may well be the most effective check on overzealous governmental actions having harmful consequences to people. So often, injury and liability may be avoided by simply paying heed to the Constitution, the statutes, the regulations, and established policies—the limitations that exist.

The government official, the public administrator, and the agency employee must always be concerned with the boundaries of power, with what decisions may be made, with when discretion may be exercised. Staying within the authorized pocket of power demands attention and effort—not solely out of fear of lawsuits and being answerable in court, but in trying to do the right thing simply because it is the right thing to do.

Likewise, a public administrator would be well served to remain aware of the constitutional rights of persons, particularly those specific rights that at this point appear clearly established and that may bear directly upon the actions of officers and employees carrying out a policy or program. A person establishing a career in public service should always remember that "no man in this country is so high that he is above the law. No officer of the law may set that law at defiance with impunity. All the officers of the government, from the highest to the lowest, are creatures of the law, and are bound to obey it" (*United States* v. *Lee,* 1882, p. 220).

Cases Cited

Barr v. *Matteo,* 360 U.S. 564 (1959).

Baum v. *United States,* 986 F.2d 716 (4th Cir., 1993).

Behrens v. *Pelletier,* 116 S.Ct. 834 (1996).

Berkovitz v. *United States,* 486 U.S. 531 (1988).

Schweiker v. *Chillicky,* 487 U.S. 412 (1988).

Siegert v. *Gilley,* 500 U.S. 226 (1991).

The Siren, 74 U.S. (7 Wall.) 152 (1868).

Tameny v. *Atlantic Richfield Company,* 27 Cal.3d 167, 164 Cal. Rptr. 839, 610 P.2d 1330 (1980).

Tango v. *Tulevech,* 61 N.Y.2d 34, 459 N.E.2d 182 (1983).

United States v. *Lee,* 106 U.S. 196 (1882).

Westfall v. *Erwin,* 484 U.S. 292 (1988).

Williams v. *City of Tuscumbia,* 426 So.2d 824 (Ala., 1983).

References

American Law Institute. *Restatement of the Law (Second): Torts 2d.* Appendix §§ 841 to End. St. Paul, Minn.: American Law Institute Publishers, 1982.

Blackstone, W. *Commentaries on the Laws of England.* Vol. 1: *Of the Rights of Persons.* Chicago: University of Chicago Press, 1979. (Originally published 1765.)

Borchard, E. M. "Government Liability in Tort." *Yale Law Journal,* 1924, *34,* 1, 129.

Borchard, E. M. "Government Liability in Tort." *Yale Law Journal,* 1925, *35,* 229.

Davis, K. C. *Administrative Law Treatise.* Vol. 5. (2nd ed.) San Diego: Davis, 1984.

Davis, K. C., and Pierce, R. J., Jr. *Administrative Law Treatise.* Vol. 3. (3rd ed.) New York: Little, Brown, 1994.

Green, L. "Tort Law Public Law in Disguise." *Texas Law Review,* 1959, *38,* 1.

Green, L., and others. *Cases on the Law of Torts.* (2nd ed.) St. Paul, Minn.: West, 1977.

Holtzoff, A. "The Handling of Tort Claims Against the Federal Government." *Law and Contemporary Problems,* 1942, *9,* 311.

Isham, J. L. "Annotation, Validity and Construction of Statute or Ordinance Limiting the Kinds or Amounts of Actual Damages Recoverable in Tort Action Against Governmental Unit." *American Law Reports, Fourth Series,* 1986, *43,* 19.

Jaffe, L. L. "Suits Against Governments and Officers: Sovereign Immunity." *Harvard Law Review,* 1963, *77,* 1.

Jaffe, L. L. *Judicial Control of Administrative Action.* New York: Little, Brown, 1965.

Koch, C. H., Jr. *Administrative Law and Practice.* Vol. 2. St. Paul, Minn.: West, 1985.

Kratzke, W. P. "Some Recommendations Concerning Tort Liability of Government and Its Employees for Torts and Constitutional Torts." *Administrative Law Journal of the American University,* 1996, *9,* 1105.

Lincoln, A. *Abraham Lincoln: Speeches and Writings, 1859–1865.* (D. E. Fehrenbacher, ed.). New York: Library of America, 1989.

Montesquieu, C. L. de S. *The Spirit of Laws.* (T. Nugent, trans.). Riverside, N.J.: Hafner Press, 1949. (Originally published 1750.)

Prosser, W. L. *Handbook of the Law of Torts.* (4th ed.) St. Paul, Minn.: West, 1971.

Schwartz, B. *Administrative Law.* (2nd ed.) New York: Little, Brown, 1984.

Shepard's Editorial Staff. *Civil Actions Against State and Local Government: Its Divisions, Agencies, and Officers.* Vols. 1 and 2. (2nd ed.) New York: McGraw-Hill, 1992.

Thode, E. W. "Duty-Risk v. Proximate Cause and the Rational Allocation of Functions Between Judge and Jury." *Utah Law Review,* 1977, *1,* 10.

Zillman, D. N. "Protecting Discretion: Judicial Interpretation of the Discretionary Function Exception to the Federal Tort Claims Act." *Maine Law Review,* 1995, *47,* 365.

CHAPTER TWENTY-FOUR

Court Involvement in Operations of State and Local Institutions

Injunctions and Other Remedies for Maladministration

Phillip J. Cooper

Stories of cases in which courts have reportedly intervened in the operation of administrative agencies of state and local governments have grown to mythic proportions (Horowitz, 1977). And as astute observers of public administration have observed, such epic stories, however inaccurate or overblown many may be, still have great power (Kelly and Maynard-Moody, 1993). It is true that there have been many situations in which courts have issued orders mandating the reform of jails, prisons, mental hospitals, local housing policies, and police departments, though such orders are far fewer now than they were a decade ago. It is also true that these so-called *remedial decrees* can have significant impacts on the operations of the agencies to which they are directed (Di Iulio, 1990; Wood, 1990).

Sadly, fear and frustration can arise in cases in which ignorance or understandable sensitivity against judicial intervention has been exploited by political and academic commentators (see, for example, Graglia, 1976). However, judicial response to illegal operation of institutions becomes considerably less frightening and a great deal more understandable when the actual experience of remedial orders is examined closely and dispassionately. No one thinks that it is a good idea for courts to be operating jails, hospitals, or schools, and that plainly includes judges who have been called upon to do so (Cooper, 1988). There are, however, answers to several important questions about remedial orders that it is important for public managers to know. These questions include (1) Why are remedial orders issued? (2) How do they come about and what happens after issuance? and (3) What are some of the important lessons of the past that can help a manager face the possibility of remedial orders in his or her agency?

NATURE AND OPERATION OF REMEDIAL COURT ORDERS

Essentially, courts are involved in four ways in maintaining accountability of administrative agencies. The rarest form of involvement is the criminal trial of officials indicted for corruption, malfeasance, or some other alleged violation of criminal law. Fortunately, such trials are an infrequent phenomenon and one that most public managers never witness during an entire career. The second form of involvement is the use of judicial review to determine whether a decision issued by an administrative agency (1) is within the statutory authority of the agency, (2) complies with the requirements of the Constitution (state, federal, or both), (3) meets the procedural requirements imposed by the Administrative Procedure Act or other applicable statutes, (4) is arbitrary and capricious, or (5) is without substantial evidence on the record as a whole to support the finding. The third form of involvement are cases brought as tort suits—civil suits that seek cash damages for an injury that was committed in violation of some legal obligation. Finally, there are cases that seek equitable relief in the form of an injunction mandating or prohibiting some kind of official action. These are the cases that are at the root of this discussion of remedial orders.

The Character of Equitable Remedies

To understand remedial decrees, which are often referred to as *equitable remedies,* it is necessary to understand the concept of equity and the development of equity jurisprudence in the British system, which was later adopted by American courts.

The idea of equity dates back to Aristotle. Since any law made by human beings is subject to fallibility and the limitations of humanity, flexibility is needed in fashioning punishments or remedies for legal violations so that justice can be done. In essence, equity is the idea that to facilitate justice some cases should be treated on their special characteristics. It is a principled exception to the normal rule of equal justice under law.

In Britain, the position of lord high chancellor was created to take care of this need to do equity. Although the king was anointed with perfect truth and perfect justice, the judges of the realm were not. There was always a chance that their applications of the law might result in injustices. The chancellor was known as the Lord Keeper, meaning that he was the keeper of the king's conscience. He would sit in equity to mitigate injustices and produce equitable rulings that solved the problems. When that happened, the judge was said to be engaged in a *weighing of the equities,* the factors that must be considered if a judgment is to be rendered that will resolve the problem and avoid injustices or unnecessary hardships.

Over time, the equity practice was institutionalized in what are called *chancery courts.* Still later, other courts were empowered to render decisions at law and judgments in equity. Indeed, the Constitution of the United States provides that "the judicial Power shall extend to all Cases, in Law and Equity, arising under this Constitution, the Laws of the United States, and Treaties made, or which shall be made, under their Authority" (Article III, Section 2).

It is also important to know that many cases seeking remedial orders are brought as *class actions,* meaning that one or a few parties who are representative of a class of persons who feel injured by an alleged violation of law go into court to represent the entire class. Thus, two children were identified as the plaintiffs in a case challenging Georgia's state statute governing the institutionalization and treatment of mentally ill or developmentally disabled children. The two represented all children then institutionalized in the state's facilities (*J.L.* v. *Parham,* 1976). As a legal device, the class action suit is neither new nor an outgrowth of modern American consumerism or civil rights politics. It dates back to the sixteenth century and was originated as a device by which to make more efficient the handling of similar claims by large numbers of people. It was far simpler to have in court a few representative parties rather than all of those facing the same problems. It is true that the device has been used by civil rights organizations, prisoner advocacy groups, environmentalists, and others to advance their causes, but the class action has also been employed by stockholders, land owners, and conservative interest groups.

In many cases, the plaintiffs seek not only a declaration of their legal status or rights but also an order directing offending parties to honor those rights in the future. Thus, equitable decrees often address the particular problems of the past that gave rise to the legal violation, but they may also mandate actions or impose constraints on behavior in the future.

The kinds of tools that judges have available to them to bring about equitable remedies are what are termed *prerogative writs.* The best known of these is the *injunction,* an order by which a court orders or prohibits some kind of action. These devices are called prerogative writs because the judge has great discretion in determining when and how to use them. Courts may also issue decrees as orders that are agreed to by the parties and submitted to the judge. These orders are called *consent decrees.* Once the court makes the agreement a decree of the court, it is enforceable by the contempt power. At some later point, the parties may return to the court on a motion to show cause why the other parties who are believed to be in violation of the decree should not be held in contempt.

Why Are Remedial Orders Issued?

Courts have used their equity powers for generations in such private law settings as bankruptcy proceedings, corporate reorganizations, stockholders suits, and even divorces, but what has prompted most of the contemporary debate about equitable remedies has been the use of court orders in public law cases such as *Brown* v. *Board of Education of Topeka, Kansas* (1954, 1955), which mandated school desegregation, and later civil rights matters.

Remedial orders are issued for two basic reasons. First, many of the problems raised in these cases cannot be remedied with money damages. That is true, for example, in school desegregation, mental health institution, or jail cases. The remedy for a suit about prison conditions is not to reward the prisoner with money but to require the state involved to operate its penal institutions in a manner that does not violate Eighth Amendment prohibitions against cruel and unusual punishment. The institutionalized child requires not discharge into a community unwilling or unable to provide for his or her needs but an assurance that if the state is going to operate a mental health facility it will do so in conformity with the law.

Second, long lists of varied court findings have been ignored or even openly resisted by state and local governments. The classic case, of course, is the campaign of "massive resistance" launched by southern states (see *Cooper* v. *Aaron*, 1958; *Green* v. *County School Board*, 1968; *Alexander* v. *Holmes County, Mississippi*, 1969; *Swann* v. *Charlotte-Mecklenburg Board of Education*, 1970). Similar resistance has been encountered in some gender discrimination cases and in police-community relations disputes. A classic example of both is former mayor Frank Rizzo's refusal to address persistent policy abuse and gender discrimination cases in Philadelphia's police department (Cooper, 1988). In the case of prison conditions and mental health institution settings, the problem has less often been outright resistance to compliance than the inability of these relatively weak interests to break through state legislative politics to obtain funding and other necessary policy changes (see Harriman and Staussman, 1983).

While many corrections administrators and mental health professionals react against the history of remedial orders issued by courts in their fields, most also readily acknowledge that it would have been virtually impossible to make needed improvements in their professional practice without the many court orders (see, for example, Wood, 1990; Cooper, 1988). The rulings not only forced states and localities to address problems that they had ignored for years, but also put others on notice that there were minimum standards and they would be enforced.

How Do Remedial Decrees Come About, and What Happens After They Do?

There is a tendency to think that remedial decree cases are the result of well-planned interest group litigation. That has been true in some cases, but more often it is not. Many of the most important cases involving schools, prisons, mental hospitals, and the like were not planned. A case, such as the now-famous example of *Wyatt* v. *Stickney* (1971), which shaped the issue of rights in the area of mental institutions, often picks up importance as it develops and interest groups and governments become aware of the potential impact of a judgment in the matter. Thus one of the most important prison conditions cases in history (*Rhodes* v. *Chapman,* 1981) developed when a prisoner's lawyer who did not want to handle a case talked a law professor into taking on the litigation as a semester clinical law project. Once the district court and circuit court of appeals in this case had outlawed the double-celling practice in a prison designed to have one inmate to a cell, all fifty state attorneys general came together to prepare a brief encouraging the Supreme Court to hear the case and reverse the lower courts. They were successful in that effort.

It is also not always true that these cases are complex, at least in terms of deciding whether there has been a violation of law. Indeed, in many cases it was clear from the outset that the law had been violated; the only question was how to fashion a remedy to address the problem. Thus when the mayor of an Ohio city said in an open council meeting that the real reason the city was blocking a low- and moderate-income housing project was to keep African Americans from other parts of the Cleveland area from moving in, there was no question that the law had been broken, and it should have been no surprise that the Civil Rights Division of the U.S. Department of Justice moved in to take action against the city (*United States* v. *City of Parma, Ohio,* 1980). The same was true when the state of Michigan moved to block a voluntary desegregation plan developed by the Detroit School Board (*Milliken* v. *Bradley,* 1974).

In more recent times, the liability questions—the question of whether there has been a violation of law sufficient to justify a remedy—have often become more difficult, because the Supreme Court has become more restrictive in giving guidance to lower courts. Another factor is that progress has been made in prison conditions, mental health policy, and in some communities at least, police behavior. Thus the circumstances giving rise to the litigation are often not as extreme as, for example, in the early prison cases (see, for example, *Holt* v. *Sarver,* 1969). It is useful to consider how these cases develop once they are, for whatever reason, launched.

What Is the Life Cycle of a Remedial Decree?

The process by which remedial cases develop and are worked out roughly follows several stages, which include the trigger phase, the liability phase, the remedy phase, and the post-decree phase. The idea is not so much to think chronologically but to see these as analytically distinct portions of the process.

Often, legal challenges result when a series of possible controversies meets some kind of triggering event that prompts someone to make the decision to launch litigation. When that happens, it is common for others to seek to join the battle on one side or the other and for all of the other tensions that have been building up over time to come pouring out in court. Thus, when suits were filed against Philadelphia police practices, the attorneys were overwhelmed by telephone calls from other people who had had bad experiences with the police department and wanted to be included in the suit or at least have their abuses considered.

The fact that a suit seeking an equitable decree remedy is launched is no indication that it will succeed. Indeed, a host of barriers stand in the way of efforts by students, prison inmates, or interest groups even to get to trial, let alone to succeed. These barriers range from procedural requirements, such as the need to demonstrate standing to sue, to the burden of demonstrating the actual substantive legal violations that are alleged.

Conversely, on many occasions the officials who were ultimately at the heart of these legal challenges knew, or should have known, that they were likely to be sued and, given the realities they faced, likely to lose. That has been true, for example, in many jail or prison cases in which it was clear that overcrowding, unhealthy conditions, or a lack of basic services like medical care virtually guaranteed a suit. In such cases, the smart move is to face the obvious and move to remediation before being forced to do so by a court. Few situations are more frustrating to judges than to be put in the position of having to do from the bench what virtually all knowledgeable observers knew should have been done in the legislature or the governor's office.

The liability stage is far more dynamic than being merely the point in the process at which the court determines whether the plaintiff has proved his or her case. For public administrators, how the participants behave is as important as what the outcome may be. While it is true that judges have substantial discretion with respect to equitable remedies when the case reaches that later stage of the process, it is also true that their discretion is circumscribed by the way the parties conduct themselves during the trial portion of the case. If the lawyers for the parties do not present the case in such a way as to provide a solid record with a full consideration of the critical issues, that constrains what the judge can do later. Such failures at the liability stage also lay the basis for continuing appellate battles rather than providing a foundation for constructive action. For example, when the state of Michigan refused to present a case in the Detroit school desegregation issue, it ensured an inadequate record in the case and refocused attention on the city when the case had really been concerned with the actions of the state government all along (*Milliken* v. *Bradley,* 1974).

If the court rules in favor of the plaintiffs, the case moves to the remedy-crafting stage and the parallel appeals process that often accompanies it. The remedy-crafting process itself consists of a planning and negotiation phase and a formal decision phase. Generally, a judge attempts to play a facilitative role during the planning and negotiation stage by encouraging the parties to settle on an agreement that the judge can approve. However, a judge's ability to play that role is limited by the willingness of the parties to participate. If the parties reach a settlement, if one or more of the parties refuses to negotiate, or if the parties reach an impasse, then the court must take a more direct and formal role. Where possible, the judge usually acts as a validating official who accepts or rejects proposals submitted by the parties. If the parties have a full agreement, the judge merely decides whether to accept it as a consent decree that will henceforth be enforced under the contempt power of the court. If the parties do not have an agreement, then the judge must work through the elements of remedy piece by piece. Contrary to the impression given by some commentators, judges rarely create the remedies or even portions of them themselves. Rather, they grant or deny the requests of the plaintiffs or defendants.

Typically, judges have a variety of options from which they can choose and that parties offer to the court as remedies. These include process remedies that may avoid specifying what the government must do but may establish committees to make those determinations or create dispute resolution bodies to address particular issues that must be addressed. The advantage is that such an approach keeps the court at arms length from the detailed decisions and implementation of remedial measures, a very attractive idea to many judges. Alternatively, the court may order performance standards in which the defendants are ordered to achieve certain outcomes but have discretion as to how to do so. Finally, in those cases in which the defendants are either unwilling or unable to cooperate, the court may order particular actions that not only establish specific targets but also specify how they are to be reached. This is the least attractive approach to most judges because it virtually ensures that the court will be kept involved for some time.

Once a remedy is issued, if any level of dispute remains between the parties an immediate appeal will normally be pursued. If the trial court's ruling establishes novel doctrine or carves out a new remedial approach, it is common for the judge to move slowly on pressing for implementation of the decree until an appeals court has ruled in the court's favor. The classic case is Judge Frank Johnson's ruling in an Alabama mental health case (*Wyatt* v. *Stickney,* 1971). Once Judge Johnson received a clear affirmation from the Circuit Court of Appeals, he was more willing to respond to the plaintiffs' calls for assistance with implementation.

The post-decree phase consists of implementation, evaluation, and refinement of the remedy. The way courts interact with administrators after a remedy is ordered depends on a number of factors. First, if the defendants comply with the order, little or no reason exists for the judge to become involved further. However, if implementation problems arise, the judge may be asked either to fine-tune the remedy to the circumstances by modifying some of the terms or take enforcement action if the parties are recalcitrant.

The role of the judge in implementation also varies depending on whether she or he has kept the day-to-day responsibility at the court or has chosen to use a third party in that role. Traditionally, courts may employ three types of outside assistance. First, monitors may provide the court with information about the level and nature of compliance. Second, courts may use a special master to whom some degree of independent decision making may be delegated. The master becomes an active and responsible party, providing the judge with some degree of distance. Finally, in extreme cases a court may even mandate a receiver, which is a concept not unlike the idea of a receiver in bankruptcy. This was done in the Alabama mental health cases when, after years of failure to provide treatment, both sides concluded that authority was needed to break through state rules and politics that blocked progress. Judge Johnson ordered the receivership but made the governor of the state the receiver (Cooper, 1988).

Relationships of courts to managers involve two sensitive dimensions. The first is the deference paradox and the second is conflict conversion. The *deference paradox* arises because, on the one hand, judges know that if their opinions are not strong enough an appeals court may very likely overturn their liability judgments and throw out the remedies. On the other hand, judges often try to avoid writing harsh opinions (which administrators may see as adversarial) in an attempt to encourage a cooperative atmosphere. It is a difficult balance to maintain.

If, however, local politicians or administrators portray the judge as the enemy, there may be a process of *conflict conversion,* in which the adversary process is less between the plaintiffs and the government and more between the administrators and the judge. When that happens, there is every reason to expect continuing battles throughout the implementation process.

Finally, an effort is required to reach disengagement, the point at which the court terminates its jurisdiction in a case. Three sets of problems are involved for the court in this situation. Some state and local governments have fought implementation and stalled for a lengthy period, finally claiming that the courts have been involved for too long and, therefore, that the remedial supervision should be terminated (see *Pasadena Board of Education* v. *Spangler,* 1976, Marshall, J., dissenting). When implementation stretches out over a long period of time, circumstances change from those under which the original case was brought and it becomes quite complex to determine the level of compliance with the order as it was issued in the first instance. For example, in *United States* v. *City of Parma, Ohio* (1980), the city claimed that it could not take some of the actions originally provided for in the remedy because the federal funding had been cut in the program. What the city did not say, of course, was that it had used every means at its disposal to stall the case to that point (Cooper, 1988).

It may also be the case that plaintiffs wish to use the existing remedy process to address new problems. Thus, in a Detroit schools case, teachers sought to use the court's remedial process to ensure school disciplinary procedures that would provide better protections for teachers. That was, of course, a very different issue than the desegregation case that prompted the remedy in the first place.

Finally, the administrators involved may not really want a court order terminated. They may, rightly or wrongly, see the court's continuing involvement as a way to obtain needed funds and support from state legislatures or local communities that would not be forthcoming without such judicial leverage.

THE MOVE TO TRIM JUDICIAL REMEDIES

Although political commentators and some academicians seek to convey the message that there is a growing or at least continuing trend toward judicial use of remedial orders in administration, the reality is quite clearly to the contrary. It is true that many correctional facilities, a variety of mental health programs, and numbers of school districts are still operating under remedial orders. However, beginning in the mid-1970s, the U.S. Supreme Court began a series of rulings that have become increasingly strong over the years warning federal courts, at least, to limit their involvement in the day-to-day operations of state and local institutions. Judges must act within three sets of constraints: applicability, scope, and duration of remedial orders.

Limitations on Applicability: Restricting When Courts Can Intervene

The Supreme Court has repeatedly reminded courts that they are not to invoke their remedial powers unless an actual violation of law has been proved. It has also made proving such cases far more difficult than they were before.

In cases concerning allegations of race or gender discrimination, the Court has made it quite clear that plaintiffs must prove the existence of intentional discrimination (*Washington* v. *Davis,* 1976). While a number of types of evidence can be used to demonstrate that intent (see *Arlington Heights* v. *Metropolitan Housing Development Corporation,* 1977), such proof is extremely difficult because those who discriminate rarely admit that they are doing so (see *Memphis* v. *Greene,* 1981). In one case, the Court held that it is not enough to show that policymakers acted with the knowledge that their plans would have a clearly discriminatory effect. They must have acted not merely in spite of that discriminatory effect but because of it (*Personnel Administrator* v. *Feeney,* 1979).

While some statutes provide for lower standards of proof, the Court has generally discouraged judicial intervention on grounds of deference to local control of schools and other institutions.

The Supreme Court has been most adamant about restricting the receptivity of lower courts to suits brought by prisoners claiming violations of the Eighth Amendment's cruel and unusual punishment provisions. The Court clearly discouraged rulings based solely on overcrowding in *Rhodes* v. *Chapman* (1981). Following that victory, the superintendent of the prison involved announced that the irony was that he had just won the right to operate a prison with more than twice the number of inmates, the hardest inmates in the system, for which that facility was designed. He foresaw the bloody riot that was to come some years later at the Southern Ohio Correctional Facility due in no small measure to the overcrowded conditions. More recently, the Court moved to restrict cases concerned with prison services such as medical care, finding that for prisoners to prevail they must demonstrate the prison administrator's intent to cause pain (*Wilson* v. *Seiter*, 1991). That does not mean that no such opportunities exist; the Court has held that some inmates had grounds to seek relief from continuing exposure to cigarette smoke in a confined space that led to serious health effects (*Helling* v. *McKinney*, 1993).

In fact, the Court has generally sent the message that the preferred means to obtain redress for maladministration is a suit for money damages against the offending officer (*Rizzo* v. *Goode*, 1976). The Court has made it quite clear, however, that such suits should be targeted at individual officers or perhaps at local governments, but the doctrine of sovereign immunity will be invoked if there is an effort to move against the state (*Seminole Tribe of Florida* v. *Florida*, 1996).

Boundaries Around the Scope and Nature of Remedial Orders

Even if a basis for a remedy exists, the Court has repeatedly warned over the past twenty years (and with even greater intensity during the 1990s) that remedies should be no more expansive than is needed to address the specific legal violation involved. That emphasis really began in 1974 when the Court rejected a metropolitan area–wide remedy to desegregate the Detroit schools. In its second ruling on that case, the Court wrote: "Federal-court decrees must directly address and relate to the constitutional violation itself. Because of this inherent limitation upon federal judicial authority, federal-court decrees exceed appropriate limits if they are aimed at eliminating a condition that does not violate the Constitution or does not flow from such a violation" (*Milliken* v. *Bradley*, 1977, p. 282). That is a command the Court has repeated with increasing vigor since then (see *Board of Education of Oklahoma City* v. *Dowell*, 1991). The Court has repeatedly warned that the character of a violation determines the scope of a remedy, that is, a remedy is justifiable only insofar as it alleviates the constitutional violation presented (*Freeman* v. *Pitts*, 1992).

Even though it has occasionally upheld some remedial orders, such as portions of the Florida state court injunction limiting the behavior of protesters at abortion clinics, the Court has warned that it will give careful attention to matching an injunction's objectives and restrictions to ensure that the relief is no more burdensome to the defendants than required to relieve the plaintiffs (*Madsen v. Women's Health Center, Inc.*, 1994). Even in extreme cases, the Court has pressed trial judges to demonstrate that they had not employed remedies that were more intrusive on the local political process than was necessary to accomplish the task at hand (*Spallone v. United States*, 1990).

The Court has also warned that a district court cannot do indirectly what it lacks the authority to mandate directly. In the Kansas City school desegregation case, the Court found that the wide-ranging orders concerning teacher pay raises, capital expenditures, and other programs exceeded the proper scope of the court's remedial authority (*Missouri v. Jenkins*, 1995).

Restrictions on Duration of Remedies: Limits to How Long Courts May Remain Involved

The most commonly debated issue in recent years has been when courts must terminate their jurisdiction over agencies. Just as the scope of remedies was allowed to be broad until the mid-1970s, so the Court's direction to lower courts was to ensure that the remedial task was fully accomplished (*Green v. County School Board*, 1968, p. 248). However, following the urging of Justice William Rehnquist, the Burger Court began to move to assert local control as a critical value and called for the earliest feasible elimination of judicial supervision.

In *Pasadena Board of Education v. Spangler* (1976), the school board had begun to implement a desegregation remedy but its members were turned out at the next election largely by a group of candidates who pledged to contest the court's ruling. The new board not only moved to delay further implementation activities but also returned to the courts to get the jurisdiction of the trial court terminated. In the face of evidence of the clear likelihood of resegregation, the Supreme Court ruled in the favor of the board. The Court concluded that it was enough that a neutral attendance pattern had been initially implemented. In 1991, the Court reversed a court of appeals ruling and upheld the termination of jurisdiction in an Oklahoma City case, warning that federal supervision was always intended to be temporary and that compliance with a court order "for a reasonable period of time" was sufficient for the federal court to terminate jurisdiction, particularly in light of the importance of deference to local control (*Board of Education of Oklahoma City v. Dowell*, 1991). In a 1992 Georgia case, the Court upheld the discretion of the district court to terminate portions of a remedial decree even if other parts of the remedy remained to be accomplished (*Freeman v. Pitts*, 1992). After all, as the Court warned in the Kansas City case, it has two goals: to end the violation and to restore local control (*Missouri* v. *Jenkins*, 1995).

LESSONS FOR THE MANAGER

The fact that the trend of rulings by the U.S. Supreme Court is clearly in the direction of restricting the use of remedial decrees does not mean that managers can ignore the subject. Other factors counsel continued awareness and caution. First, opportunities remain for new challenges that can bring remedial orders. Second, it is not uncommon to find upon taking a position that one is inheriting pending remedial orders. Finally, other lessons need to be learned about working with the courts.

Continuing Sources of Remedial Decrees

There are two continuing sources of remedial orders: state court rulings based on state law, and what might be termed the problem of unfunded mandates. Many of the most visible cases involving remedial orders developed in federal courts. That is not surprising since many of them were brought under provisions of the Constitution or federal civil rights statutes. However, as the federal courts began to be more restrictive, some litigants called on state courts to do under state law what the federal courts would not do. Indeed, some federal judges even encouraged that strategy (Brennan, 1986). Probably the best-known example of this phenomenon is in the area of school finance litigation. Although the Supreme Court refused in 1973 to use the Constitution to strike down property-tax-based school finance systems on grounds of discrimination (*San Antonio Independent School District* v. *Rodriguez*, 1973), numerous states, including Texas, have done so since then using state law. There have also been state rulings in such other areas as jail conditions and mental health institution reform. It is therefore possible that new rulings may come from the state courts even as the federal courts are drawing back.

One of the difficult areas that on occasion brings demands for remedial orders results from unfunded mandates imposed by higher levels of government. Thus when the federal government or state legislatures mandate delivery of services but fail to appropriate sufficient funds to cover the requirements, there is every chance that the gap will provoke a suit. Recent examples have included situations such as the Individuals with Disabilities Education Act, the current version of what used to be called the Education for All Handicapped Children Act. In recent years, the Supreme Court has allowed parents who claimed that local governments had not met their obligations to provide services under the act to take their children to private schools and then collect the tuition and fees from the local community (*Florence County School District Four* v. *Carter*, 1993). While that is an award of money rather than a remedial decree, it has the effect of ordering the communities to find ways to finance Individualized Education Plans whether or not they have the assistance of the state or federal governments, on pain of having to pay a much higher bill for a private school. Conversely, the Supreme Court has ruled in a mental health case that although mentally retarded residents or patients in a state institution could sue for minimally adequate conditions, they could not seek to collect a damages judgment against the physicians in charge of their cases or the institution if the clinicians failed to deliver adequate services because of budget constraints (*Pennhurst State School and Hospital* v. *Halderman,* 1981). In sum, where a legal obligation to provide services exists in statute or from some other source and insufficient funds are provided to meet the obligation, the pressure seems to be to move to seek remedial orders. That may very well be a growing phenomenon given contemporary fiscal trends.

Inheriting Consent Decrees and Remedial Orders

Quite apart from the possibility of new remedial decrees, any number of administrators step into new positions only to find that they have inherited consent decrees or remedial orders from an earlier time. It is even worse not to know that such orders exist and to learn about them when someone sues for their enforcement. In one Minnesota prison case, involving an earlier decree calling for improvements in medical care, it appeared that some of the administrators involved were caught unaware when an inmate sued for violation of the decree because of exposure to tuberculosis and failure to test for and treat that disease in a timely and effective manner (*De Gidio* v. *Pung,* 1989).

One of the interesting issues that arises from the use of consent decrees, especially those entered into without a trial and specific finding of liability, is that years later the decree may continue after those who originally negotiated it are gone from the scene. In the absence of a clear set of findings from a well-developed trial record, it can be difficult to know what to do when circumstances have changed and the question arises whether to continue with the consent agreement or suggest that it is no longer applicable.

At a minimum, administrators who work in education, corrections, housing, elections, or human resources management need to be alert to the possibility that their organization may have such agreements in place. If so, processes are required to ensure compliance. Discussions are also needed to determine the status of the order and to make judgments about whether some change is needed or even whether it would be appropriate to move for termination.

Working Relationships with Courts

If an administrator is facing an existing order or the possibility of a new one, some points are worth remembering from past experiences. First, it is not true that most judges do not know or care about the problems that may result from the implementation of a remedial decree. The evidence is that where a reasonable effort is made to show a good faith effort to comply with the task but a strong case can be made as to what difficulties need to be addressed, judges are willing to listen and to act on that information (Cooper, 1988). The problem is often a disconnection between the lawyers arguing the cases or handling the negotiations and the administrators who have the technical knowledge and expertise needed to understand what precisely is at issue. Close communication between administrators and attorneys is crucial. Merely turning the case over to the lawyers can produce results that are problematic for both the administrator and the court.

Second, it is virtually always foolish and counterproductive to engage in conflict conversion. Making the judge out to be the problematic party and acting as though the court is the enemy may be useful to some politicians but it does not result in an effective working relationship between courts and state or local governments. It is not helpful merely to repeat many times the frustration a community has with an order of the court. Doing so only damages communications and conveys a sense, whether it is accurate or not, of recalcitrance on the part of defendants who have already lost a suit. Such behavior also fails to serve the public interest because it is not in the public interest to be in violation of the law. Finally, such behavior by public officials encourages law breaking by others in the community, for as Justice Louis Brandeis was fond of repeating, government is an ever-present teacher. If public administrators are seen to be disrespectful toward judges or contemptuous of their orders, the lesson may be learned by citizens who may be less hesitant to violate the law themselves.

CONCLUSION

Remedial orders have existed for many years in a variety of cases under both state and federal law. Contrary to some political commentary, it is not true that the courts have been engaged in an ever-expanding use of such decrees. In fact, the Supreme Court has led a continuing effort since the mid-1970s to force lower courts to limit the occasions when remedial orders are granted, to restrict the scope of orders that are issued, and to limit the duration of judicial supervision of state and local units of government.

Conversely, clear reasons exist why remedial decrees have been issued and will continue to be used, if in more limited ways than before. When that occurs, the process is neither mysterious nor intrinsically hostile to administrators, especially if they bring informed attitudes to the process and avoid needless confrontation. Taking a positive and cooperative attitude to the process not only ensures the likelihood of a more workable relationship with the judicial system but teaches important lessons about law-abiding behavior to the citizens of the community.

Cases Cited

Alexander v. Holmes County, Mississippi, 396 U.S. 1218 (1969).

Arlington Heights v. Metropolitan Housing Development Corporation, 429 U.S. 252 (1977).

Board of Education of Oklahoma City v. Dowell, 498 U.S. 237 (1991).

Brown v. Board of Education of Topeka, Kansas, I, 347 U.S. 483 (1954).

Brown v. Board of Education of Topeka, Kansas, II, 349 U.S. 294 (1955).

Cooper v. Aaron, 358 U.S. 1 (1958).

De Gidio v. Pung, 704 F.Supp. 922 (D.Minn., 1989).

Florence County School District Four v. Carter, 510 U.S. 7 (1993).

Freeman v. Pitts, 503 U.S. 467 (1992).

Green v. County School Board, 391 U.S. 430 (1968).

Helling v. McKinney, 509 U.S. 25 (1993).

Holt v. Sarver, 300 F.Supp. 825 (EDAR, 1969).

J.L. v. Parham, 412 F.Supp. 112 (MDGA, 1976).

Madsen v. Women's Health Center, Inc., 129 L.Ed.2d 593 (1994).

Memphis v. Greene, 451 U.S. 100 (1981).

Milliken v. Bradley, 418 U.S. 717 (1974).

Milliken v. Bradley, 433 U.S. 267 (1977).

Missouri v. Jenkins, 132 L.Ed.2d 63 (1995).

Pasadena Board of Education v. Spangler, 427 U. S. 424 (1976).

Pennhurst State School and Hospital v. Halderman, 451 U.S. 1 (1981).

Personnel Administrator v. Feeney, 442 U.S. 256 (1979).

Rhodes v. Chapman, 452 U.S. 337 (1981).

Rizzo v. Goode, 423 U.S. 362 (1976).

San Antonio Independent School District v. Rodriguez, 411 U.S. 1 (1973).

Seminole Tribe of Florida v. Florida, 134 L.Ed.2d 252 (1996).

Spallone v. United States, 493 U.S. 265 (1990).

Swann v. Charlotte-Mecklenburg Board of Education, 402 U.S. 1 (1970).

United States v. City of Parma, Ohio, 494 F.Supp. 1049 (NDOH, 1980).

Washington v. Davis, 426 U.S. 229 (1976).

Wilson v. Seiter, 501 U.S. 294 (1991).

Wyatt v. Stickney, 325 F.Supp. 781 (MDAL, 1971).

References

Brennan, W. J., Jr. "The Bill of Rights and the States: The Revival of State Constitutions as Guardians of Individual Rights." *New York University Law Review*, 1986, *61*, 535–553.

Cooper, P. *Hard Judicial Choices*. New York: Oxford University Press, 1988.

Di Iulio, J. *Courts, Corrections, and the Constitution: The Impact of Judicial Intervention on Prisons and Jails*. New York: Oxford University Press, 1990.

Graglia, L. *Disaster by Decree*. Ithaca, N.Y.: Cornell University Press, 1976.

Harriman, L., and Staussman, J. "Do Judges Determine Budget Decisions? Federal Court Decisions in Prison Reform and State Spending for Corrections." *Public Administration Review*, 1983, *43*, 343–351.

Horowitz, D. *Courts and Social Policy*. Washington, D.C.: Brookings Institution, 1977.

Kelly, M., and Maynard-Moody, S. "Policy Analysis in the Post-Positivist Era: Engaging Stakeholders in Evaluating the Economic Development Districts Program." *Public Administration Review*, 1993, *53*, 135–142.

Wood, R. *Remedial Law*. Amherst: University of Massachusetts Press, 1990.

CHAPTER TWENTY-FIVE

The Balancing Act of Judicial Review

Ensuring Enough Deference to Administrators and Enough Accountability

Rosemary O'Leary
Paul Weiland

One of the pivotal issues in contemporary American public administration is the scope of judicial review of an agency's action or lack of action. The purpose of judicial review of administrative decision making, generally, is to ensure minimum levels of fairness. This area of law is formed through a blending of statutory, constitutional, and judicial doctrines, and thus it is a complex mix of sometimes inconsistent decisions and doctrines. It has been said that the scope of review for a specific administrative decision may range from 0 to 100 percent, meaning that depending on the issue in question, a reviewing court may have broad or narrow powers to decide a case—or something in-between.

This chapter provides a broad integrative view of the role of judicial review in contemporary American public administration. It highlights judicial review of agency information gathering and dissemination activities as well as rulemaking, and it discusses the problems that all judges face in walking the line between ensuring adequate review to maintain accountability while avoiding interference in areas where deference ought to be accorded.

MAJOR CATEGORIES OF JUDICIAL REVIEW

When an agency makes a decision, it usually does three things. First, it interprets the law in question; second, it collects facts concerning a particular situation; and third, it uses discretionary power to apply the law to the facts. The review by a judge of an agency's actions is very different in each of these three areas. At the same time, it must be acknowledged that separating an agency's actions into three discrete categories can be difficult, as when questions of law and fact are mixed. Nevertheless, for the sake of the immediate discussion, each type of judicial review of agency action is discussed separately.

Legal Interpretation

An agency's interpretation of the law usually demands a strong look by a reviewing court. Whereas the determination of facts lies clearly within an agency's scope of expertise, the courts have relative independence to review and scrutinize questions of law. When constitutional issues are of concern, judges rarely defer to administrative interpretations. However, when an agency's interpretation of its own regulation is at issue, it is said that deference is "more clearly in order" (*Udall* v. *Tallman*, 1965). The general practice is that a judge gives less deference to an agency's legal conclusions than to its factual or discretionary decisions. This emphasis stems primarily from the Administrative Procedure Act (APA) [5 U.S.C. 551 *et seq.*], first adopted in 1946 and often amended since then. The APA is the chief federal legislation that establishes procedural standards governing how administrative agencies must perform their regulatory tasks. Among the reasons listed in the APA for when an agency's decision may be reversed are two that deal solely with questions of law: whether the Constitution has been violated [sec. 706(2)(B)], and whether the agency has exceeded its statutory authority [sec. 706(2)(C)].

At the same time, judges have shown deference to administrative interpretations of the law. The archetypal case that illustrates this point is *Chevron U.S.A., Inc.* v. *Natural Resources Defense Council* (1984). The *Chevron* case concerned the Environmental Protection Agency's "bubble concept" enacted pursuant to the Clean Air Act of 1977. Under the bubble concept, the EPA allowed states to adopt a plantwide definition of the term *stationary source.* Under this definition, an existing plant that contained several pollution-emitting devices could install or modify one piece of equipment without meeting the permit conditions if the alteration did not increase the total emissions from the plant. This allowed a state to treat all of the pollution-emitting sources within the same industrial group as if they were encased within a single bubble. As long as the total emissions under the bubble met national standards, individual violations of the standards would be ignored.

Environmentalists sued the EPA, asserting that this definition of stationary source violated the Clean Air Act. Although it acknowledged that the Clean Air Act at that time did not explicitly define what Congress envisioned as a stationary source, and that the legislative history of the act was not helpful, the Court of Appeals held that the EPA's definition was "inappropriate" given the purpose of the relevant section of the Clean Air Act (which addressed requirements under the nonattainment program), namely, to improve rather than merely maintain present air quality. Upon appeal to the Supreme Court, the pivotal issue, given the fact that Congress had not directly spoken on the issue, was whether the EPA's definition was based on a permissible construction of the statute.

In a unanimous decision, the Supreme Court held that the EPA's definition was a permissible construction of the statutory term *stationary source.* Included in the rationale of the Justices were the following: First, an examination of the legislation and its history showed that Congress did not have a specific opinion about the applicability of the bubble concept to these cases. Second, the legislative history of this part of the Clean Air Act plainly showed that in the permit program Congress sought to accommodate the conflict between economics and the environment. Third, while the EPA's policy at one time was virtually identical to the view espoused by the Court of Appeals, a new administration had reevaluated the policy and concluded that the definition would be appropriate. Fourth, the wording of both the statute and the legislative history of the act indicated that Congress generally intended to give the EPA broad discretion in implementing the act. Overall, the Court wrote, the EPA's interpretation of the statute represented a reasonable accommodation of manifestly competing interests and was entitled to deference.

The *Chevron* doctrine, however, is complex and not easily implemented by judges on a consistent basis given the variety and varying complexities of individual court cases. In determining whether an agency's interpretation of the law is appropriate, a judge examines several factors, including the "plain meaning" of the statute, the statutory context, the congressional intent as ascertained through legislative history, the public policy context as ascertained from case law and other statutes, the persuasive authority, any parallel statutes, and scholars' interpretations. These factors often can provide support for conflicting determinations regarding agency interpretation of the law, thus making the job of the judge difficult.

The case *Industrial Union Department, AFL-CIO* v. *American Petroleum Institute* (1980) was concerned with the authority of the Occupational Safety and Health Administration (OSHA) to promulgate regulations for toxic materials in the workplace that were designed to create a risk-free environment for workers. This is an example of a case in which the legislative history and the general purpose of the legislation were relied upon by the judge to make a decision that the agency action in question was not in line with congressional intent. Both the Court of Appeals and the Supreme Court struck down the regulations in this 1980 case primarily because the secretary of labor had not made pertinent findings as required by the Occupational Safety and Health Act of 1970.

In another case, *Continental Airlines* v. *Department of Transportation* (1988), the reviewing court clarified that for the court to find an agency's interpretation of the law "unreasonable," the plaintiff must demonstrate that the agency's interpretation would actually frustrate congressional goals. In this case the pivotal issue was whether the U.S. Department of Transportation had correctly interpreted a portion of the International Air Transportation Competition Act of 1979. Finding that the agency's interpretation was not "patently inconsistent" with the statutory mandate, the reviewing court upheld the agency's actions.

Substantial Evidence Review

An agency's fact-finding usually demands less scrutiny by reviewing judges than legal issues. Section 706(2)(E) of the APA states that an agency's decision may be reversed if it is unsupported by substantial evidence. Further, section 706(2)(F) states that an agency's decision may be reversed if it is unwarranted by the facts "to the extent that the facts are subject to trial de novo by the reviewing court." At the same time, however, judges generally acknowledge that an agency fact finder who has heard the testimony of witnesses and who has been immersed in a case may be in a better position than the judges to ascertain facts. Tied in with this is the simple truth that it would be inefficient, costly, and time-consuming for a court to duplicate an agency's collection of factual information every time there is an appeal.

Judicial review of an agency's discretionary powers is usually deferential to a point, while maintaining an important oversight role for the courts. A judge is to evaluate the reasonableness of an agency's findings of fact and not collect the "truth" itself. This usually amounts to a judge making sure that the agency has done a careful job of collecting and analyzing information, that it has taken a hard look at the important issues and facts. The judge must look at all the evidence for and against the agency and decide whether the agency's findings are reasonable under the totality of the evidence.

Abuse of Discretion Review

Even if a reviewing court decides that the agency correctly understood the law involved and concludes that the agency's view of the facts was reasonable, it may still negate the decision if the activity of the agency is found to be "arbitrary, capricious, an abuse of discretion, or otherwise not in accordance with the law" [APA sec. 706(2)(A)]. Such a decision can involve legal, factual, or discretionary issues. This type of review has been called several things: a "rational basis" review, an "arbitrariness" review, and an "abuse of discretion" review.

Some common reasons that a reviewing judge may hold that an agency has abused its discretion include the following:

- An agency administrator's decision may be a deviation from agency precedent, without adequate explanation.
- An agency administrator's decision may clash with the agency's own rules.

- An agency administrator's decision may violate principles of judge-made law, including equitable estoppel.

- An agency administrator's decision may be overly harsh.

- The judge may become "aware, especially through a combination of danger signals, that the agency has not really taken a 'hard look' at the salient problems and has not genuinely engaged in reasoned decision-making" (*Greater Boston Television Corporation* v. *FCC*, 1970, p. 851).

Remand

One common mechanism for a judge to use to encourage an agency to rethink its decision is a remand for fuller explanation. At times the motivation behind a remand is to obtain information about the agency's reasoning that supported the decision. At other times the remand is an indirect way in which the court may voice its disapproval of the agency's decision. A classic example of the use of the remand is the case of *Citizens to Preserve Overton Park, Inc.* v. *Volpe* (1971), in which the pivotal issue was why the secretary of the U.S. Department of Transportation had approved a highway route through Overton Park. In this case the Supreme Court held that the reviewing court must make an inquiry into the agency's rationale, either by obtaining affidavits from the agency decision makers or by holding a hearing in court to gather testimony. The lower court responded by holding a twenty-five-day trial. Where an agency does provide a valid explanation for its decision, that decision must be taken at face value by a reviewing judge unless the plaintiff clearly can show bad faith or improper behavior.

Judicial Discretion

When examining judicial review of agency actions in the categories discussed earlier, it is important to understand that judges retain an immense amount of discretion. Determining whether "substantial evidence" exists to support an agency's conclusions or whether an agency's actions were an "abuse of discretion" can be a highly subjective process or may depend unconsciously on a judge's particular view of the subject matter. As Judge Patricia Wald put it: "Despite much protestation to the contrary, a judge's origins and politics will surely influence his or her judicial opinions. Judges' minds are not compartmentalized: their law-declaring functions cannot be performed by some insulated, apolitical internal mechanism. However subtly or unconsciously, the judge's political orientation *will* affect decisionmaking" (Wald, 1987, p. 895).

A study by O'Leary (1993) that examined the EPA concluded that many accusations that judges were either too active or too passive towards the agency were inaccurate and unfair generalizations. O'Leary found instead a continuum of judicial review, from passive to overly intrusive judges. Most judges agree that judicial review of agency actions is necessary as a check against potentially misguided bureaucrats who are unelected but must still be held accountable to the principles of constitutional democracy.

REVIEW OF INFORMATION GATHERING AND DISSEMINATION

Administrative agencies collect and disseminate millions of bits of information daily. In general, most administrative agencies enjoy wide discretion to require the disclosure of information, as long as they have satisfactory delegation in their enabling statutes, follow their own procedures, and obey the Constitution, specifically the Fourth and Fifth Amendments. It is in this area that the judiciary has actively engaged in oversight to prevent abuse of discretion.

The judge's task of assessing the legality of an agency's information-gathering activities, however, is not a simple task, for two primary reasons. First, many of the constitutional protections applied in these cases were designed for criminal proceedings, and most agency actions are not criminal. Hence, the application of constitutional principles to the administrative setting is not always a straightforward task. Second, many agency actions take place outside of formal proceedings. These informal actions utilize a wide variety of information-gathering methods and procedures, ranging from inspections to report writing, from the seizure of goods to the inspection of records.

The APA and case law generally lay out several rules that must be followed by agencies seeking information. First, the investigation must be commissioned by law and carried out for a genuine reason. Second, the information pursued must be germane to the legal investigation. Third, the request for information must be reasonably precise and not place an unreasonable hardship on the entity that is the subject of the investigation. Finally, the data requested may not be privileged.

When an agency gathers information through searches and inspections, those actions must not violate the Fourth Amendment's prohibition against unreasonable searches or seizures, which includes a provision that search warrants may be issued only upon a demonstration of probable cause. In the early days of administrative law the general rule was that the constitutional warrant rule did not apply to administrative inspections. In the 1960s this changed through a series of judicial decisions (*Camera* v. *Municipal Court,* 1967; *See* v. *City of Seattle,* 1967). Because of this judge-made law, the general rule today is an adaptation of the criminal standard to administrative law. Specifically, in the

Camera and *See* cases the courts held that satisfaction of reasonable legislative or administrative standards is necessary for conducting an area inspection before an administrative search warrant may be issued.

Freedom of Information

In the area of agency disclosure of information, the most important and pervasive statute is the 1966 Freedom of Information Act (FOIA). The general rule is that an agency must make records available promptly to any person who requests them, unless the material falls within a listed exemption. Examples of exemptions include classified information, internal personnel information, trade secrets, and medical records. Refusals of such requests are reviewable in district court, where the government has the burden of explaining its rationale for withholding such information.

An example of the impact of the judiciary on administrative agency behavior under FOIA can be seen in the case of *Cohen v. EPA* (1983). In the early 1980s, in response to a lawsuit by a journalist, the EPA changed its policy concerning the disclosure of the names and recipients of notices sent under the Comprehensive Environmental Response, Compensation and Liability Act (CERCLA or Superfund) of 1980. Under Administrator Anne Gorsuch, the EPA had taken the position that hazardous waste was essentially under control and that excessive regulation of industry, not pollution, was the most significant problem the EPA needed to address. Therefore, when journalist Neil J. Cohen filed requests with the EPA under FOIA to acquire copies of Superfund letters sent to individuals, corporations, and government agencies, the agency essentially refused to cooperate. The EPA released the body of letters to Cohen but maintained that the identities of the addressees were exempt from disclosure under FOIA. The EPA said that release of such information would be an "unwarranted invasion of privacy" and would reduce the cooperation of those parties in voluntary cleanup of hazardous wastes (*Cohen v. EPA*, p. 1377). Cohen sued, arguing that disclosure would have the opposite effect because public opinion would force the responsible parties into action.

Judge William B. Bryant of the U.S. District Court for the District of Columbia disagreed with the EPA and found in favor of Cohen. Bryant said that the EPA had failed to prove that the release of the information in question would interfere with the EPA's enforcement function by "resulting in concrete adverse consequences" (p. 1377). The judge also disagreed that releasing the names would be an invasion of privacy. The case had the effect of changing EPA policy concerning the release of the names of potentially responsible parties under CERCLA.

Advisory Committees and the Disclosure of Information

Another important statute with regard to agency disclosure of information is the 1994 Federal Advisory Committee Act (FACA). This statute regulates the activities of federal government advisory committees and mandates that meetings of such committees must generally be held in public, with certain exceptions. The FACA recently was invoked in a lawsuit concerning the Clinton Administration (*Northwest Forest Resource Council* v. *Espy,* 1994). In response to the long-standing controversy between environmentalists and the timber industry concerning the use of federal forest lands, President Clinton formed FEMAT—the Forest Ecosystem Management Assessment Team. The purpose of FEMAT was to study the federal forest conflict and generate options for the president. On July 1, 1993, Clinton announced his Forest Plan for a Sustainable Economy and a Sustainable Environment, which was based significantly on Option 9 developed by FEMAT. Sixteen days later the Forest Service released the FEMAT report, as well as a draft Environmental Impact Statement that analyzed only FEMAT-sanctioned options and put forth Option 9 as the preferred alternative.

Members of the forest products industry sued, alleging in part that FEMAT's activities in advising the president violated the FACA. FEMAT, they argued, constituted an official advisory committee under FACA, which entitled the timber industry and the public to have been privy to and to have participated in FEMAT's proceedings. Judge J. Jackson of the U.S. District Court for the District of Columbia found that FEMAT was indeed an advisory committee subject to FACA. Further, the judge found that FEMAT was convened and did its work in violation of FACA. For example, FEMAT refused to open its meetings to the public, failed to publish notice of meetings in the *Federal Register,* failed to make its records and other documents available for public inspection, and failed to keep detailed minutes of meetings, as well as violating FACA in other ways. Despite these rulings for the plaintiffs, however, the judge refused to enjoin the executive branch from relying upon the FEMAT report to promulgate regulations implementing the forest plan. In a decision that is a classic example of the problem that all judges face in walking the line between ensuring adequate review to maintain accountability while avoiding interference in areas where deference ought to be accorded, Judge Jackson reasoned that it would be improper to instruct the president concerning what he can and cannot consider in executing the duties of his office.

JUDICIAL REVIEW OF ADMINISTRATIVE AGENCIES: RULEMAKING

Since the establishment of the U.S. government, one of the most significant actions carried out by public agencies has been the formulation of policy by promulgating rules. It is perhaps in this area of administrative law that the judiciary has had the greatest impact on public administration, especially since the early 1970s. While Congress has encouraged administrative rulemaking through the creation of a multitude of enabling statutes, judges have stimulated liberal use of rulemaking authority primarily by erring on the side of finding agency authority to proceed by rulemaking.

In the case of *National Petroleum Refiners Association* v. *FTC* (1973), for example, the pivotal issue was whether the Federal Trade Commission (FTC) was empowered under the Trade Commission Act of 1914 to promulgate substantive rules of business conduct called *trade regulation rules.* Two trade associations and thirty-four gasoline refining companies protested the regulations on several grounds, including an assertion based on a narrow reading of the statute that the Trade Commission Act mentioned only adjudication, not rulemaking, as the means of enforcing statutory standards. Relying on the legislative history of the act, as well as on the plain language of section 6(g) of the statute, which gave the FTC the authority to "make rules and regulations for the purpose of carrying out the provisions" of certain portions of the act, the Court of Appeals held that the FTC was authorized to promulgate such rules. To do otherwise, the Court wrote, "would render the Commission ineffective to do the job assigned it by Congress" (p. 697).

An area of rulemaking in which the courts have played a pivotal role is "hybrid" rulemaking. Hybrid rulemaking generally imposes participatory procedures on agencies that, for the sake of fairness, are over and above the norm for that particular form of rulemaking. These participatory procedures generally fall into two camps.

First, judges have pushed public organizations to release data on which certain rules were based in order to foster greater dialogue about the rules in question. For example, in the case of *United States* v. *Nova Scotia Food Products Corporation* (1977), the Court of Appeals held that the U.S. Food and Drug Administration's failure to disclose to interested parties the scientific data on which it relied in promulgating a regulation establishing time-temperature-salinity prescriptions for smoked whitefish was procedurally erroneous. It is interesting to note that the process was an informal one, and that the court did not use the APA to support its decision (although it did cite case law and the agency's own rules and regulations). Rather, the court used sentiments based on fairness and logic, such as, "There is no reason to conceal the scientific data relied upon" (p. 251), "We can think of no sound reasons for secrecy" (p. 251), and "The scientific material which is believed to support the rule should be exposed" (p. 252).

Second, judges have remanded rulemaking cases ordering agencies to allow cross-examination, even though APA rules did not mandate such action by the agencies. An example is the case of *Mobil Oil Corporation* v. *FPC* (1973), in which the Federal Power Commission (FPC) set minimum rates required to be charged by natural gas pipelines for transportation of certain liquid and liquefiable hydrocarbons merely by giving public notice and an opportunity to comment on the rate. The FPC argued that the Natural Gas Act of 1938 allowed the making of orders and rules that are "necessary or appropriate to carry out the provisions" of the act and that the setting of rates in this instance was not formal rulemaking under the APA (p. 1254). Although the Court of Appeals agreed that the agency's actions did not constitute formal rulemaking under the APA, the court lambasted the agency for allowing "artificial distinctions based upon the language of the APA" to determine which procedure should be followed in this instance (p. 1252). Reasoning that the APA provides only the outer boundaries of administrative procedures, the court said that a final determination of what procedures are appropriate depends on the totality of the circumstances, including in this instance an analysis of the regulatory scheme envisioned by Congress in passing the Natural Gas Act. Upon further examination of the Natural Gas Act, the court concluded, among other things, that the FPC did not permit a testing of evidence by procedures sufficiently adversarial in nature to provide a reasonable guarantee of its reliability.

Perhaps the most famous of the hybrid rulemaking cases—a case with a holding opposite in part to the previously discussed cases—is *Vermont Yankee Nuclear Power Corporation* v. *Natural Resources Defense Council* (1978). Among the important issues in this case was the legality of rules promulgated in 1974 by the Atomic Energy Commission (AEC; later the Nuclear Regulatory Commission) involving the environmental effects associated with the uranium fuel cycle in nuclear power reactors. A court of appeals held that although it appeared that the AEC employed all the procedures required by the APA, and more, the rulemaking proceedings were inadequate. The Court of Appeals overturned the rule as well as the AEC's granting of a license to a nuclear power plant and remanded the case for further proceedings.

The Supreme Court reversed the decision of the Court of Appeals. Included in the Court's rationale was the fact that the Court of Appeals had engrafted its own notion of proper proceedings upon the agency. The Court wrote that nothing in the APA, the 1969 National Environmental Policy Act (NEPA), the circumstances of the case, the nature of the issues being considered, past agency practice, or the AEC's enabling statute permitted the Court of Appeals to review and overturn the rulemaking proceeding on the basis of procedural devices employed, as long as the agency used at least the statutory minimum. In this instance, the agency clearly met the statutory minimum.

Since *Vermont Yankee,* judges have reduced their supervision of the regulatory process. However, they remain active in the rulemaking process, primarily by rigorously enforcing APA requirements.

CONCLUSION

More than two decades ago, D.C. Circuit Court of Appeals Judge David Bazelon wrote, "We stand on the threshold of a new era in the history of the long and fruitful collaboration of administrative agencies and reviewing courts" (*Environmental*

Defense Fund v. *Ruckelshaus*, 1971, p. 597). Today that collaboration has grown into what some call a partnership between judges and public administrators (see, for example, Rosenbloom, 1987). It is important to recognize, however, that the judiciary has been and will continue to be the dominant partner in this relationship (see O'Leary and Wise, 1991). In fact, some scholars have criticized the role of the judiciary in the partnership (for example, Melnick, 1985).

While the partnership is likely to continue to be unequal, it need not be untenable. The attractiveness of the partnership is threefold. First, it forwards a notion of governmental entities working with rather than in opposition to one another. Second, it delineates an important role for the judiciary in the American political system, which is characterized by the separation of powers (see, for example, Cooper, 1988). Although the structure of the judicial decision-making process is not amenable to the development of broad statements of policy, the courts provide a forum for dealing with the cases and controversies that have been brought to them. Third, the partnership does not include a strong predetermined view of public administration. It incorporates the recognition that in some cases oversight is necessary and in some it is not. Clearly the challenge for the judiciary is to strike the appropriate balance between restraint and activism in order to provide for a partnership that ensures enough deference to administrators and enough accountability.

Cases Cited

Camera v. *Municipal Court*, 387 U.S. 523 (1967).

Chevron U.S.A., Inc. v. *Natural Resources Defense Council*, 467 U.S. 837 (1984).

Citizens to Preserve Overton Park, Inc. v. *Volpe*, 401 U.S. 402 (1971).

Cohen v. *EPA*, 19 ERC 1377 (1983).

Continental Airlines v. *Department of Transportation*, 843 F.2d 1444 (D.C. Cir., 1988).

Environmental Defense Fund v. *Ruckelshaus*, 439 F.2d 584 at 597 (D.C. Cir., 1971).

Greater Boston Television Corporation v. *FCC*, 444 F.2d 841, 850–852 (D.C. Cir., 1970), cert. denied, 403 U.S. 923 (1971).

Industrial Union Department, AFL-CIO v. *American Petroleum Institute*, 448 U.S. 607 (1980).

Mobil Oil Corporation v. *FPC*, 483 F.2d 1238 (D.C. Cir., 1973).

National Petroleum Refiners Association v. *FTC*, 482 F.2d 672 (D.C. Cir., 1973), cert. denied, 415 U.S. 951 (1974).

Northwest Forest Resource Council v. *Espy*, 846 F.Supp. 1009 (1994).

See v. *City of Seattle*, 387 U.S. 541 (1967).

Udall v. *Tallman*, 380 U.S. 1, 16 (1965).

United States v. *Nova Scotia Food Products Corporation*, 568 F.2d 240 (1977).

Vermont Yankee Nuclear Power Corporation v. *Natural Resources Defense Council,* 435 U.S. 519 (1978).

References

Cooper, P. J. *Hard Judicial Choices.* New York: Oxford University Press, 1988.

Melnick, R. S. "The Politics of Partnership." *Public Administration Review,* 1985, *45,* 653–660.

O'Leary, R. *Environmental Change: Federal Courts and the EPA.* Philadelphia: Temple University Press, 1993.

O'Leary, R., and Wise, C. "Public Managers, Judges, and Legislators: Redefining the New Partnership." *Public Administration Review,* 1991, *51,* 316–327.

Rosenbloom, D. "Public Administrators and the Judiciary: The 'New Partnership.'" *Public Administration Review,* 1987, *47,* 75–83.

Wald, P. M. "Some Thoughts on Judging as Gleaned from One Hundred Years of the *Harvard Law Review* and Other Great Books." *Harvard Law Review,* 1987, *100,* 895.

PART SEVEN

LAW IN PUBLIC POLICY

Part Seven engages critical facets of the relationship between law and public policy, a subject too often ignored in existing literature. In particular, it considers who represents government and why that representation is important, what the interaction of law and public decision-making processes looks like in the toughest of circumstances in real life, how law and legal processes affect budgets and financial management, what forces of law in government services procurement are becoming more important as contracting out increases, and how alternative dispute resolution techniques have been fashioned and implemented to reconcile some of the tensions without destructive conflicts.

Cornell W. Clayton's chapter on legal representation for government units and officials (Chapter Twenty-Six) is another of the chapters in this book that break new ground. It is not enough to know who represents whom, Clayton contends. It is also important to know why the answers to that question matter. Addressing the politics of the legal bureaucracy, Clayton explains that the supposedly obvious idea that governments are represented by attorneys general is not nearly so clear in practice. There is, he argues, a "legal administrative state," and how that structure is shaped and operates has a great deal to do with how policies are formulated, enforced, and ultimately defended in court. It is a complex structure, and it includes all levels of government.

In particular, Clayton explains that many sophisticated managers and analysts tend to picture legal representation in relatively simplistic ways—approaches that they would criticize as naive if used to explain any other kind of organization.

At the federal level, relationships among appointed attorneys general and career-oriented Justice Department lawyers, agency counsel, and special counsels (also known as special prosecutors) are complex and sometimes competitive. Tensions between state attorneys general and governors or state legislative leaders are common, with many of the attorneys general serving as independently elected officials who often see themselves headed for the statehouse.

Thus Clayton explains why it is important to understand how government lawyers operate within government, as well as how they represent government agencies to courts and outside parties. That intragovernmental role has become more significant as the complexities of intergovernmental relations in such areas as regulation have grown. Roles of state attorneys general have also become more interesting as the federal government has deregulated in many areas, leaving more options to states. At the same time, decisions by states to act are made difficult by the increasing complexity of the doctrine of preemption.

Just how important the role of lawyering is, and how it can affect policy in action, is well illustrated in Chapter Twenty-Seven by Charles W. Washington. Like the Nigro chapter on civil service reform (Chapter Twenty), Washington's chapter provides a case study that examines in realistic detail the dynamics and implications of the interactions between law and administration. The author uses efforts to desegregate the Broward County, Florida, school system both to illustrate the interactions of government stakeholders and to demonstrate how people interact with those agencies and officials in the context of decades-long legal, political, and administrative processes.

Washington emphasizes the difficulties that arise when courts must operate under technical legal concepts like *unitary schools*; when citizens work toward desired policy outcomes that are frustrated by technical language that seems to violate commonsense notions of what is right and just; and when administrators must work with diverse stakeholders over time in a complex fiscal and political environment. This is a story of what happens as various stakeholders seek to use the courts to achieve outcomes that they have been unable to realize in other political contexts.

One of the sets of impacts that comes from the interactions between courts and public managers involves budgets and public finance issues. When courts mandate remediation of unconstitutional prison conditions, when they require local governments to reimburse parents for private school expenses if the governments do not otherwise provide for children with special needs, or when they subject state and local employers to the Fair Labor Standards Act's wage and hour provisions, budgets are affected. This is the subject of Chapter Twenty-Eight by Thomas P. Lauth and Phillip J. Cooper.

In addition to the obvious and direct impacts of judicial rulings on budgeting and finance, the authors discuss a range of less apparent ways in which courts affect financial practices and expenditures. These include rulings governing relationships between legislatures and chief executives in the budgetary development process and in budget execution. Another set of judicial rulings that has been virtually ignored in public administration is those that shape the nation's financial infrastructure, such as restrictions on state taxation policy, the ability of states and localities to address corporate mergers and relocations, and decisions defining citizens' rights that constrain governmental regulatory authority in the absence of compensation to affected property holders.

Lauth and Cooper also argue, however, that while the impacts are important and often difficult, they are aspects of a normal and continuing process of public management in which courts are common participants. Indeed, it is possible for administrators to anticipate and understand judicial rulings that will affect budgets in ways that enhance performance and accountability.

One set of interactions between courts and agencies that have important fiscal consequences is the body of law and policy associated with government contracting for public services, a subject addressed by Ruth Hoogland DeHoog in Chapter Twenty-Nine. While most of the literature of the past two decades on government contracting and privatization focuses on normative arguments about whether and how much to contract out, De Hoog takes the reader beyond that point to the management issues that arise when decisions have been made to use contracts to achieve public purposes. Contracting for public services is in many respects even more complex and critical than traditional procurement of hardware and other products. DeHoog discusses the kinds of issues that are considered as part of the decision to contract, the ways in which contracts are awarded, and the nature of relationships that develop after the award, while the terms of the contract are being fulfilled. Additionally, she considers special issues that arise when government rather than a private firm is a party to a contract. These issues include social policy obligations associated with diversity and labor practices, and the great importance of accountability. In all of this, DeHoog demonstrates the mixture of law and management that is at the heart of the contractual relationship.

One of the things that becomes clear from the discussion of increased use of mechanisms like contracting is that the trend is to move away from standard litigation as a first option in law and management relationships and to focus instead on negotiated means to address problems. Lisa B. Bingham writes in Chapter Thirty about the growing use of alternative dispute resolution (ADR) techniques that have at their core efforts to expand negotiation and reduce zero-sum confrontations. The ability to save time and money, as well the opportunity to resolve a problem in a manner that allows parties to leave the table feeling positively about the other stakeholders, is a feature that makes ADR an attractive option.

In the remainder of the chapter, Bingham explores the various types of ADR techniques, including those that involve third parties as mediators or arbitrators, as well as contemporary variations on both of those established procedures. These techniques do not, of course, always resolve disputes, particularly those that are serious or large or in which the parties have visceral commitments to their positions. Even so, techniques are available to narrow and structure conflict, if not actually to resolve it. Despite the limitations of ADR, a knowledge of it is essential to any modern public managers' tool kit.

CHAPTER TWENTY-SIX

Government Lawyers

*Who Represents Government and
Why Does It Matter?*

Cornell W. Clayton

Why are the activities of government lawyers of interest to students and practitioners of public policy? The short answer to this question revolves around the fact that control over a growing number of policy areas has been shifting out of the legislative arena and into the courts and the administrative state. A growing body of scholarship has been devoted to explaining the causes of this shift and its consequences for administrators and judges (Melnick, 1983, 1994; Rabkin, 1989; Shapiro, 1988). Still, relatively little is known about the role of the government lawyers operating at the nexus of this policymaking relationship.

The federal government employs nearly forty thousand attorneys, and thousands more work for state and local governments. Approximately one-fifth of the attorneys in the federal government are in the Department of Justice, and the rest are scattered throughout the various federal offices, agencies, and departments. At the state level, the majority of attorneys work either in the offices of the fifty state attorneys general and respective state departments of law, or in the offices of local prosecutors and county or municipal attorneys.

While attorneys are scattered throughout government, this chapter focuses especially on developments affecting those officers who represent government entities in judicial proceedings or those who frame policy issues by providing legal counsel to administrative officials. That is to say, it is chiefly the political rather than the bureaucratic aspects of legal administration that are examined here, though these concerns can never be entirely separate. In addition, while most studies of government lawyering focus on individualized offices or the policies of particular administrations, this chapter identifies themes and issues common to the work of all government lawyers (Langeluttig, 1927; Cummings and McFarland, 1937; Biddle, 1962; Huston, 1967; Huston, Miller, Krislor, and Dixon, 1968; Richardson, 1976; Navasky, 1977; Bell and Ostrow, 1982; Kleindienst, 1985; Caplan, 1987; Smith, 1991; Fried, 1991; Clayton, 1992; Baker, 1992; Salokar, 1992; Harrigar, 1992; Clayton, 1995). In this sense it treats government lawyers as part of a legal administrative state. Before turning to these themes, however, it is important to trace the major features of government legal administration in the United States.

THE LEGAL ADMINISTRATIVE STATE

Like all other aspects of the American administrative state, legal administration is structured by both federalism and the separation of powers. The chief legal administrative officer at both the state and federal levels is the attorney general. This office was part of the American inheritance from England. During the colonial period, local attorneys were appointed in each colony as representatives of the English attorney general (Edwards, 1964). Following the Revolutionary War, these officers were reestablished as state attorneys general. Unlike the colonial attorneys, however, these new state officers were not local delegates of a central government. Under the Articles of Confederation, there was no federal court system, and no office administered the government's legal work. Not until the new Constitution was ratified and Congress passed the Judiciary Act of 1789, creating the federal court system, was a federal office of attorney general established. Thus state attorneys general prefigured the federal office, and their role has always been more clearly defined.

State Attorneys General and State Lawyering

Today all fifty states have an attorney general or equivalent office. In forty-four states the office is defined in the state's constitution, and in six others (Alaska, Hawaii, Indiana, Oregon, Vermont, and Wyoming) by statute alone. Most states have also created a state department of law, but even where a law department does not exist the office of attorney general comprises a large bureaucracy of lawyers and others. The smallest office is in Montana, where the attorney general supervises thirty-one attorneys and sixteen nonattorneys and has a budget of more than $2 million; the largest is in California, where the attorney general supervises more than 775 attorneys and 955 nonattorneys and has a budget of more than $279 million (Ross, 1993).

In addition to constitutional and statutory powers, state attorneys general possess common-law authority to represent the public interest. Commenting on this politically important discretionary power, the Fifth U.S. Circuit Court of Appeals explained: "The attorneys general of our states have enjoyed a significant degree of autonomy. Their duties and powers typically are not exhaustively defined by either constitution or statute but include all those exercised at common law. There is and has been no doubt that the legislature may deprive the attorney general of specific powers; but in the absence of such restriction he typically may exercise all such authority as the public interest requires" (*State of Florida* v. *Exxon Corporation,* 1976, pp. 268–269).

Although the specific duties of the attorney general vary from state to state, it is possible to identify five broad functions performed by the office: (1) rendering advisory opinions to government officials, (2) representing state legal interests in judicial proceedings, (3) drafting and promoting legislative proposals, (4) administering state expenditures in areas such as contracting and state bonding, and (5) disseminating to the public information on important legal issues.

The relationship between the state attorney general and the three branches of government has been an evolving one. In many states the office was originally established as part of the judicial branch and then later reconstituted as part of the executive branch. In Louisiana, for example, the office was part of the judicial branch until 1974, when a new state constitution reassigned it to the executive branch (Yeager and Hargrave, 1991). Today in most states the attorney general is fixed by constitution or statute as part of the executive branch. Still, a handful of states leave the office's constitutional locus unclear, and in some states it continues to have a close relationship to the judiciary. In Tennessee, for instance, the office is appointed to an eight-year term by the state's supreme court, while in Oregon the attorney general serves as counsel to the supreme court and the state's court administrator.

Unlike at the federal level, only six states (Alaska, Arizona, Florida, Hawaii, Michigan, and New Jersey) make the attorney general a member of the governor's cabinet. In most states the attorney general is elected independently, and it is not uncommon for the governor and the attorney general to be from different parties. This fact also explains the common gubernatorial practice of appointing a personal legal counsel to advise on policy and duties related to the executive prerogative, such as pardons and appointments. Nevertheless, in most states the attorney general is the exclusive representative of the state in the courts, though in a few states in-house counsels may represent the governor when he or she is sued personally or in a representative capacity. Moreover, while some states employ in-house counsel in major agencies, it is the norm for state agencies to seek legal opinions on major legal matters from the attorney general (Ross, 1990, pp. 61–75).

The most important distinction between state attorneys general and the federal office is the mode of selection and removal. In forty-three states the attorney general is elected; in five states (Alaska, Hawaii, New Hampshire, New Jersey, and Wyoming) the attorney general is appointed by the governor; in Maine, selection is by secret ballot of the legislature; and in Tennessee, the attorney general is appointed by the state supreme court. The mode of selection has implications for the power to remove. In thirty-six states there are impeachment provisions in the constitution, though such proceedings are rare. The only recorded impeachment occurred in Arizona in 1947, after the attorney general was convicted of violating state gambling laws. In eight states the attorney general can be removed through a recall, and in the five states where the attorney general is appointed by the governor, removal can be by the chief executive (Ross, 1990, pp. 24–25).

Independent electoral mandates and fixed terms of office alter the political role of state attorneys general. At the federal level, presidential administrations are frequently criticized for "politicizing" the Justice Department or for using federal legal policy to pursue their political agendas. At the state level such criticisms take a different form. The office's election and tenure provide the office-holder with the autonomy to represent those positions that they believe are in the public interest or that are required by the law, regardless of the preferences of the governor or state legislature. Indeed, unlike the federal office, thirty-eight of the fifty state attorneys general possess common-law standing to directly challenge the constitutionality of the laws enacted by the state legislature and the policies of executive branch agencies (Ross, 1990, pp. 27–39).

State attorneys general nevertheless increasingly find themselves criticized for a different kind of politics. As the size and power of the office has grown, it has attracted younger and more ambitious attorneys (Morris, 1987). Individuals such as Elliot Richardson, Walter Mondale, Thomas Eagleton, Jacob Javits, John Danforth, Bruce Babbitt, George Deukmejian, David Souter, and Bill Clinton have used the office to propel themselves into higher state elective office or national-level politics. Critics contend that state attorneys general may often be less concerned with protecting the public interest than with enhancing their own political careers. An article in the *National Law Journal,* for instance, criticized Missouri's former attorney general for an upsurge in petitions to the U.S. Supreme Court during the period in which he was running for governor ("Ashcroft," 1987).

The U.S. Attorney General and the Department of Justice

The relationship between the attorney general and the three branches of government at the federal level also has evolved over time. The Judiciary Act of 1789 failed to fix the office to one of the three branches; early drafts proposed that the officer be appointed by the Supreme Court. The final version, which left appointment authority vague, implied presidential selection. Still, the legislative history of the act and the conditions surrounding the office's early operation led it to be viewed as a quasi-judicial institution. Eventually, custom and common law, and finally statutory reform in 1870, entrenched the office as part of the executive branch establishment (Clayton, 1992, pp. 48–50). But the office's transformation from quasi-judicial to executive has left deep tensions in its relationship to the president (Baker, 1992, pp. 107–125).

The attorney general's relationship to other legal officers has also evolved. Early attorneys general struggled to control the federal government's legal work. The Judiciary Act of 1789 also created U.S. attorneys offices in each of the federal judicial districts, and Congress established legal officers, usually titled "solicitors," in several of the departments and agencies it created. The attorney general had no formal control over the litigating and advising activities of these officers until 1870, when in response to the rising legal costs of defending suits from the Civil War, Congress established the Department of Justice and brought these officers under the nominal control of the attorney general. Although the 1870 act envisioned centralized control of U.S. attorneys, in reality that control remains limited. Although the attorney general establishes broad policies, U.S. attorneys still enjoy considerable latitude in interpreting and applying those policies (Eisenstein, 1978).

Attorneys general have always had to be "learned in the law," the only formal requirement under the Judiciary Act of 1789. Since creation of the Department of Justice they have also had to become skillful politicians and administrators, capable of managing a powerful bureaucracy that now numbers more than 90,000 employees. In administering the Justice Department, the attorney general is aided by the deputy attorney general, an office established in 1953, and the associate attorney general, established in 1977.

Primary responsibility for the federal government's appellate litigation has been delegated to the fourth-ranking officer in the Justice Department, the solicitor general. Established by the act that created the Justice Department in 1870, the solicitor general originally served as a general administrative assistant. Over time the office evolved into an elite barrister, with exclusive responsibility for supervising appeals from lower courts and arguing government cases in the Supreme Court. The office's close relationship to the Court has led some commentators to vest the office with a quasi-judicial status; one even labeled it the "tenth justice" (Caplan, 1987). Others have argued against this characterization and pointed out that solicitors general, while adhering to high professional standards of accuracy, have historically served as mouthpieces for the legal views of the president and his administration (Salokar, 1995).

The remainder of the Justice Department is divided into more than thirty divisions, bureaus, agencies, and offices. Six core legal divisions each handle distinct legal areas: antitrust, civil, civil rights, criminal, environment and natural resources, and tax. There are also offices of the inspector general, intelligence policy and review, legal counsel, justice programs, professional responsibility, and policy and communication. Other administrative functions of the attorney general include supervision of the U.S. attorneys and marshals, the Federal Bureau of Investigation, the Drug Enforcement Agency, the Immigration and Naturalization Service, federal prisons, parole, pardons, and the Board of Immigration Appeals. The department's budget illustrates the dramatic growth in the nation's legal business. In 1920 the budget was a modest $17 million, by 1970 it had grown to $641 million, and by 1980 it stood at $2.64 billion. In 1991 the budget eclipsed $9 billion ("Current Services Budget," 1993). Even controlling for inflation, the budget grew more than 300 percent in actual dollars between 1970 and 1980 and will grow by at least the same amount during the 1990s (Clayton, 1992, p. 28).

Other Federal Law Officers

Much recent controversy surrounding government lawyering has focused on the enforcement of ethics laws. Following the Watergate scandal in the early 1970s, a new regime of federal ethics laws emerged. At the heart of these laws was the Ethics in Government Act of 1978, which created the independent counsel's office (Harrigar, 1995). Independent counsels are appointed by a federal appellate court and are thus buffered from the conflict of interest that Justice Department prosecutors confront when investigating the president or members of his administration. Although constitutional questions about the office were settled by the Supreme Court in *Morrison v. Olson* (1988), the operation of independent counsels has remained controversial.

Critics argue that the office is part of a scandal-style of politics in post-Watergate Washington, in which investigations become weapons for partisan politics (Garment, 1991). Following an independent counsel investigation of the Iran-Contra scandal, for instance, Republican opposition to the counsel statute in Congress prevented its reauthorization in 1992. Two years later, however, with Republican leaders anxious for "independent" investigations of President Clinton's involvement in the Whitewater scandal, the act was reauthorized and Kenneth Starr, a former solicitor general during the Bush administration, was appointed to take over the investigation (Taylor, 1994). While few independent counsel investigations result in actual prosecutions, critics maintain that the mere appointment of a prosecutor and the media coverage it generates is enough to seriously damage any administration (Eastland, 1990).

The post-Watergate regime of ethics and the scandal-style of politics associated with it has also transformed the work of the White House legal counsel. The office was originally created by Franklin Roosevelt in 1941. Until the 1970s, however, counsels advised presidents on policy matters but had no staff and no regular law-related functions. Since the 1970s, the office has assumed a more institutionalized presence. With a staff of more than thirteen associate and assistant counsels, the office today performs a variety of roles, such as advising presidents on the legal implications of legislation or presidential action, managing the administration's judicial selection process, and counseling on ethics. This last function takes up the bulk of the counsel's time. As ethics laws have become more complex, presidents have turned to the counsel to act as an ethics watchdog, to give administration officials legal advice on ethics standards and screen prospective nominees to high-level positions in the administration.

In a system of separated powers, government attorneys must represent and balance competing institutional clients. Congress, the White House, and the courts at times clash over the meaning of the law and the interest of the government in particular cases. The mere styling of cases such as *United States* v. *House of Representatives* (1983) and *United States* v. *United States District Court* (1972) illustrates the problem. In state governments, this problem is usually resolved by giving the attorney general an independent electoral mandate. At the federal level, where government lawyers are appointed, such clashes present a real dilemma. During the Watergate scandal, for example, attorney general Elliot Richardson promised Congress during his confirmation hearings that the Justice Department would conduct a thorough and independent investigation of the Watergate break-in. When President Nixon ordered Richardson to fire the special prosecutor, who had been appointed to keep that promise, a crisis ensued that was resolved only by Richardson's own resignation (Richardson, 1976).

A more common consequence of interbranch conflict, however, is fragmentation in legal services as each branch seeks to employ attorneys loyal to its views. The frequent legal clashes between the president and Congress during the 1970s had precisely this effect; in 1978, Congress established the Senate legal counsel's office and the counsel to the clerk of the House of Representatives to represent its views in court when the Justice Department refuses or is at odds with Congress. Prior to this time, Justice Department refusals to defend Congress and its statutes were quite rare. When they occurred, Congress hired outside counsel on an ad hoc basis or used counsel from such places as Congressional Research Services to write briefs representing its views. But creation of these offices now provides an institutionalized competitor to Justice Department representation (Miller and Bowman, 1979; "Executive Discretion," 1983).

Similarly, the Supreme Court in 1972 created an in-house legal counsel's office. Though the office's primary function is to advise the Court and its members, it has on occasion hired private counsel to represent the Court in litigation. The complexities involved in legal problems confronting the Court became clear when the justices actually ruled against their own security force on a First Amendment claim involving demonstrations at the Court (Winkle and Swann, 1993).

The real fragmentation of the federal legal services, however, has occurred inside the executive branch itself. Congress's creation of the Department of Justice was a response to repeated pleas from presidents for the efficiency and uniformity in legal position that centralization promised (Easby-Smith, 1904; Key 1938). But even after the Justice Department was established, the promise of centralized control remained subject to the ebbs and flows of larger efforts to centralize the emerging administrative state. As with other areas of administration, centralizing control over agency legal work tends to strengthen presidential influence over it. Decentralization, conversely, usually works to enhance the relative influence of Congress and agency bureaucrats (Clayton, 1992, pp. 77–80; Herz, 1995). Thus, despite creation of the Justice Department, Congress continued to allow other agencies to retain legal counsel, and the agencies jealously guarded their independent authority to represent themselves in court. It was not until Franklin Roosevelt (within the context of governmental reorganization surrounding the New Deal) issued an executive order requiring Justice Department management of all government litigation that any semblance of centralized control emerged. Even then, the order, later codified by statute, dealt only with litigation and left legal advising to agency counsel (Horowitz, 1977; Herz, 1995).

Legal scholar Donald Horowitz described this post–New Deal division between Justice Department and agency lawyers as "a division of labor and a divorce of function" (Horowitz, 1977, p. 5). With few exceptions, litigation became the domain of the Justice Department, while advising administrators on the legal ramifications of regulatory programs became the responsibility of the agency counsel. This division of labor allows for specialization that is beneficial to both sides; Justice lawyers become expert litigators adept at shielding agencies' action from judicial review, while agency lawyers become experts in the substantive area of law over which their agency has regulatory responsibility. There are also ongoing disputes over the utility of the division of labor, however. Agency lawyers often complain of having to educate Justice Department lawyers about the substantive legal issues in cases that are litigated, while Justice Department lawyers complain that misadvising agencies early in a case often makes it impossible to litigate it successfully later (Olson, 1985). Nevertheless, the division of labor did reflect an implicit understanding about the separation of powers; litigation is part of the president's constitutional power to execute the law, while advising agency administrators seems more closely associated with the quasi-legislative powers that Congress delegates directly to agency heads.

Justice Department Oversight of Administrative Agencies

Since 1970, the division of labor and the agreement undergirding it has come under pressure from both sides. Faced with an increasingly hostile Congress (usually controlled by the opposite party), presidents began relying heavily on administrative rather than legislative strategies of policymaking (Nathan, 1983; Waterman, 1985). An important goal in such strategies was strengthening White House control over the regulatory process. Consequently, presidents have sought to extend Justice Department oversight of agency litigation and advising, as well as White House control of the Justice Department (Clayton, 1992, pp. 172–220). Perhaps the exceptions to this general trend were the Ford and Carter administrations; though they strengthened Justice Department oversight of agency policymaking, they also sought to reduce contacts between the department and the White House in the aftermath of Watergate (Baker, 1992, pp. 126–165).

Congress and agency bureaucrats, conversely, became increasingly resentful of the threat that Justice Department supervision of litigation posed to agency enforcement autonomy. During the 1970s, Congress became more willing to make statutory exceptions to the Justice Department's litigating monopoly for agencies, such as the Environmental Protection Agency (EPA) and the Department of Labor, and in areas of law vulnerable to White House incursions (Bell, 1978). Thus, as the White House has sought greater influence over agency legal advising, Congress and agency bureaucrats have sought to decentralize litigating authority. The Justice Department has been in the middle, wanting on the one hand to convince Congress that it is professionally independent and politically neutral, but needing on the other hand to reassure White House policymakers that it is loyal (Clayton, 1992, pp. 172–209).

POLITICAL LOYALTY OR POLITICAL ABUSE

The charge that the administration of law has been politicized is a frequent refrain in post-Watergate politics, but what is meant by this charge is often less than clear. The term *politics* usually has more than one meaning in such discussions: politics as a philosophy of government, and politics as partisan abuse of power. While the influence of the latter over the administration of law is clearly improper, the extent to which the former might properly influence it is a matter of debate.

The Clinton administration's handling of the Whitewater investigation is only one of the latest episodes to arouse charges of political abuse of federal law enforcement (Rabkin, 1995). The Bush administration was alleged to have improperly influenced the investigation of influence peddling in the Department of Housing and Urban Development, and it was accused of misconduct in the investigation of the Bank of Credit and Commerce International scandal in the late 1980s (Biskupic, 1989). The Reagan Justice Department was the subject of a series of allegations involving obstruction of justice, including the Iran-Contra scandal and an alleged effort to conceal illegal activity by officials in the EPA (Clayton, 1992, pp. 200–209). Charges of corruption in federal legal administration are not unique to the last two decades, however. The Justice Department has been near or at the center of nearly every political scandal of the twentieth century (Clayton, 1992, pp. 98–107; Baker, 1992, pp. 107–125). By far the most damaging of these scandals was Watergate. Between 1972 and 1975, the conflict consumed five attorneys general, six deputy attorneys general, and two special prosecutors. The scandal, involving a cover-up of illegal campaign activity by members of the Nixon administration, reached a nadir in 1973 when President Nixon fired Attorney General Elliot Richardson for refusing to dismiss the special prosecutor (Jaworski, 1976). Although the president's legal authority to fire the attorney general was never seriously challenged, the controversy surrounding political control of federal prosecution lingered long after Nixon left the White House.

In the wake of Watergate, Congress passed the independent counsel law, but it considered more radical proposals for restructuring the Justice Department to guard against future abuses. In hearings titled "Removing Politics from the Administration of Justice," Senator Sam Ervin's Subcommittee on the Separation of Powers considered a proposal to create an "independent" Department of Justice by buffering the attorney general from the president's removal authority (U.S. Congress, Senate Judiciary Committee, 1974). The Ervin proposal was rejected because it was thought to violate the separation of powers by removing from the president control of functions at the heart of his constitutional duty to "faithfully execute the laws." Indeed, of the seventeen expert witnesses who testified at the hearings, fourteen concluded that the Ervin plan would violate the Constitution.

Critics of the Ervin proposal also questioned whether it was desirable to have federal law enforcement removed from political accountability. This question loomed large in light of a growing fear in the 1970s of "subsystem governments" and "agency capture" by special interests. Finally, critics charged that the assumption that the administration of law could be "depoliticized" by removing it from presidential control relied on an unsophisticated view of politics. The very title of the Ervin hearings illustrated the confusion surrounding the meaning of "politics" in such discussions. It is one thing to say that the president should not obstruct a criminal investigation of his own administration; it is quite another to deny the president any influence over government legal policy. Nixon's intervention into the Watergate investigation is a clear example of impropriety, but not all White House interventions into government legal administration are improper. The problem is that it is next to impossible to erect obstacles to prevent partisan corruption or cronyism that do not also affect political influences of a proper kind.

Two examples illustrate this difficulty. The first occurred when the Justice Department was preparing to file a major antitrust suit against ITT Corporation in 1971. The Johnson administration initiated the suit, and it was ongoing when Nixon was elected in 1968. On the day the suit was to be filed in 1971, however, Attorney General Richard Kleindienst received a call from President Nixon instructing him to drop the case. Kleindienst subsequently called the Antitrust Division and arranged for the suit to be settled out of court. Nixon's intervention in the case may merely have reflected his concern about antitrust enforcement policy; it was a major issue during the campaign and Nixon promised to ease antitrust regulation. Kleindienst learned later, however, that ITT contributed $400,000 to Nixon's reelection campaign in exchange for the out-of-court settlement (Kleindienst, 1985, pp. 90–109).

Contrast this intervention with one that occurred seven years later in the Carter White House. In 1978, in *Regents of the University of California* v. *Bakke,* the Court was asked whether race-conscious affirmative action programs at state universities violated the Equal Protection clause of the Fourteenth Amendment and Title IX of the 1964 Civil Rights Act. The position of the federal government, which intervened in the suit as amicus curiae, was bound to influence the Court. Solicitor General Wade McCree originally drafted a brief arguing that race conscious treatment within a voluntary state program was improper. After learning of the solicitor general's position, President Jimmy Carter called and instructed the attorney general to have McCree rewrite the government's brief. After some protest, McCree did. The government's position softened on affirmative action, arguing only that numerical quotas (not race preferences in general) were objectionable. The brief no doubt influenced the Court, which coincidentally adopted the same position (Bell and Ostrow, 1982).

The tendency to conflate pejorative and affirmative meanings of politics is deeply rooted in the antistatist nature of American political culture. But the confusion that results from that conflation, especially since Watergate, has hindered any effort to reform the administration of justice. Quite apart from the considerations of corruption or abuse, questions about how responsive law enforcement should be to the president's political agenda go to the heart of the rule of law. In the *ITT* and *Bakke* cases, the White House intervened to change the government's legal posture; but even though Nixon's intervention was inappropriate, it does not follow that the president is not entitled to some say about enforcement of antitrust law. Similarly, because President Carter's mediation in an affirmative action case was not necessarily improper does not mean presidents should have carte blanche to change the government's legal positions. What is clear is that there is no simple answer to either how or where one draws lines between proper and improper political control of the government's law enforcement and legal administration.

SEPARATION OF POWERS, ADMINISTRATIVE DISCRETION, AND THE RULE OF LAW

Controlling administrative discretion is an old problem in the science of government (Culp-Davis, 1971). Unbounded discretion is the very definition of tyranny, the evil that modern constitutions and the idea of rule of law are designed to prevent. The historical origin of this problem is reflected in the words of William Pitt that are carved on the Justice Department building in Washington, D.C.: "Where law ends, tyranny begins." Pitt's pronouncement is, however, too stark. No bright lines mark where legal authority for government action begins or ends. This is particularly the case in the modern administrative state, where Congress and state legislatures have delegated vast amounts of discretion under sweeping, sometimes vaguely written statutes (Eastland, 1992).

Most government action takes place in a twilight zone between what law clearly authorizes and what it clearly prohibits. Within this zone, custom and convention, professional norms and institutional cultures merge together to license and constrain discretionary conduct. The rule of law is thus given content even when no formal legal enactment binds governmental behavior. It is the work of government attorneys, whether in the state or federal system, whether in the Department of Justice, the White House, or in the various regulatory agencies, to construct and define these informal understandings and assist political superiors in navigation through them.

Yet if it is government lawyers who at least initially provide substance to the rule of law, how they should go about this is less clear. The lines produced by convention and professional norms are not clear, and during periods of interbranch conflict those lines become all the more blurred. This is not to suggest that the law is wholly indeterminate. At some point the exercise of discretion ceases to enjoy the color of law. When, for example, members of Ronald Reagan's National Security Council secretly channeled funds from covert arms sales to the Nicaraguan Contras, then misled Congress to cover up their involvement, they violated the law. No theory of administrative discretion can change this conclusion. Not even Terry Eastland, who served in the Reagan Justice Department and defends a broad view of executive discretion, could support the administration's actions in this case (Eastland, 1992, pp. 96–105). The law, in this case the Boland Amendment, which Ronald Reagan himself had signed, may not have been good policy (as defenders of the administration were quick to point out). But disagreement with the wisdom of the law does not justify willful violation of its express commands, even by a president or his immediate staff. Such conduct violates the very idea of the rule of law implicit in the Faithful Execution Clause of Article II of the Constitution (see Clayton, 1992, pp. 187–190).

Still, this is an extreme case. Debates about the legality of administrative action are usually fought on murkier ground, where the commands of law are less clear or where different branches or agencies have honest disagreements about its meaning. Take, for example, the Clean Air Act Amendments of 1990, which required state administrators to hold public hearings before granting air pollution permits. Although it was clear that the law required public scrutiny of new applications for pollution permits, did it require public notice and hearings when granting minor changes in existing permits? The statutory language was unclear on this point. William Reilly, head of the EPA, and the agency's chief legal counsel, Donald Elliot, both thought that such notice and hearings were required, and the EPA drafted regulations to that effect in December 1990. When industry representatives learned of the proposed regulations, they appealed their case to White House counsel Boyden Gray, officials of the Office of Management and Budget (OMB), and members of Vice President Dan Quayle's Council on Competitiveness. After several meetings among Elliot, the OMB, and council members, the EPA changed its position and issued a new draft regulation in April 1991, allowing minor permit modifications without public hearings.

Over the course of the next year, Representative Henry Waxman, a California Democrat, held hearings before the House Subcommittee for Health and the Environment, criticizing the EPA's change and lecturing Elliot and White House officials on their obligations to ensure agency compliance with congressional mandates. In August 1991, Elliot resigned, but he wrote a memorandum to Reilly concluding that the original draft rule, not the latter one, complied with the intent of the statute. Buoyed by Waxman's hearings and Elliot's memo, the EPA returned to its original interpretation of the law and set out to redraft its regulation. In May 1992, the White House secured an opinion from the Justice Department supporting its position. Finally, in June the EPA was forced to retreat, and it promulgated its final rule exempting minor modifications from the public review requirements.

Was the EPA's final rule inconsistent with the law? Members of Congress thought so. The EPA's lead counsel, forced to reverse his own independent interpretation of the law, also thought so. Lawyers in the White House were convinced otherwise, however, as were lawyers in the Department of Justice. One way to answer this question might be to ask what the courts decided. This, however, misses the point that the vast majority of such decisions are never reviewed by any court; and even when they are, courts display great deference to the legal positions advanced by lawyers for the executive. The solicitor general is extremely successful before the courts; recent studies indicate that during the past thirty years the Supreme Court sided with the solicitor general more than 68 percent of the time (Salokar, 1992, p. 21).

The importance of legal decision making in the executive branch is amply illustrated by another episode that began in 1988, when the Department of Health and Human Services (HHS) reinterpreted the meaning of the Public Services Act of 1970 in order to bring it into accord with the Reagan administration's political goal of restricting access to abortion services. Under the twenty-year-old law, federal agencies were prohibited from granting funds to programs where abortion is a method of family planning. Under four different presidential administrations the statute had been interpreted by administrators and judges as restricting abortion services but not abortion counseling. Under the law's new interpretation, however, HHS issued regulations prohibiting federally funded clinics from counseling on abortion as well.

In 1991, in *Rust v. Sullivan,* HHS's new regulation was challenged on First and Fifth Amendment grounds and attacked as an unreasonable interpretation of the statute. After dismissing the constitutional objections, the Court turned to the question of statutory interpretation by agencies. Upholding HHS's reversal, Chief Justice William Rehnquist framed the issue as whether the new regulation could be justified under "any plausible construction" of the statute. Under the *Chevron* standard (*Chevron U.S.A., Inc. v. Natural Resources Defense Council,* 1984), Rehnquist explained, the Court accords "substantial deference" to executive branch interpretations of the law. When a statute is ambiguous, the question for the courts, he asserted, is not whether the agency has adopted the most accurate interpretation but only whether it has adopted a reasonable one (see Starr, p. 283).

Stunned by this reinterpretation of its statute and the Court's deference to it, Congress passed legislation in 1991 that specifically overturned HHS's new regulation. President George Bush vetoed the measure, however, and the House of Representatives fell eleven votes shy of the two-thirds margin required to override. In this case, judicial deference to executive branch interpretations of the law proved so pliant that it permitted not just the reversal of a long-established policy under a statutory law, but a reversal that was specifically rejected by a contemporary majority in Congress. The effect, *The New York Times* pointed out, was the backward making of law: administrators were exercising broad discretion to make policy, and Congress was forced to try to muster a two-thirds vote to stop them (Lewis, 1991).

Cases such as these raise serious questions about government lawyering and the rule of law in a system of separated powers. Few would argue that an administration is bound to a particular interpretation of law simply because it was adopted by a previous administration. Nor would many argue that it is inappropriate for the president to override legal interpretations made by his subordinates. But what should guide administrative interpretation and enforcement of the law, especially when the three branches disagree?

Cases like these are far more common than the Iran-Contra variety. In a system of separated powers, the relationship between administrative action and the rule of law, rather than being delineated by bright lines, is more like a continuum: at one end are administrative actions that enforce a clear understanding of the law; at the other are administrative actions that violate that understanding. In between are many shades of legality, where the commands of law are more or less explicit, more or less consistent, and exist in a context that produces more or less controversy over their interpretation. Government lawyers are asked to distinguish and navigate between these shades.

POLITICS AND THE INTERGOVERNMENTAL
CONTEXT OF GOVERNMENT LAWYERING

A final development affecting the political role of government lawyers is the unfolding of recent trends in state-federal relations. A central thrust of the "New Federalism" of the 1970s and 1980s was regulatory retrenchment and devolution of the administrative state (Bowman and Pagono, 1990; Peterson, 1984). During this period, Congress was led by both presidential commitment to deregulation and fiscal imperatives to shift to states the responsibility for administering federal mandates and policies (Fix and Kenyon, 1990). According to one study, by 1990 Congress had in twenty years enacted more than forty-seven major statutes that imposed sweeping new regulatory responsibilities on states (Conlan, 1991). A good example of these trends is in the area of environmental protection. Prior to 1970, states played only a minor role in environmental regulation. Since then, however, Congress has enacted at least twelve major pieces of legislation that impose major enforcement responsibilities on state attorneys general. These laws include the Clean Air Act Amendments of 1990 and 1970; the Ocean Dumping Ban Act of 1988; the Lead Contamination Control Act of 1988; the Water Quality Act of 1987; the Safe Drinking Water Act Amendments of 1986; the Hazardous and Solid Waste Amendments of 1984; the Comprehensive Environmental Response, Compensation and Liability Act (the Superfund law) of 1980; the Federal Insecticide, Fungicide, and Rodenticide Act of 1978; the National Environmental Policy Act of 1976; the Resource Conservation and Recovery Act of 1976; and the Federal Clean Water Act of 1972. Under most of these statutes, states must establish enforcement programs to implement federal standards, and the full enforcement burdens usually fall on the attorney general; but even when enforcement lies with other state agencies, the attorney general must advise and defend those agencies against lawsuits challenging their actions (see Webster, 1990; Thornburg, 1990).

In addition to devolving or shifting the enforcement burden of federal regulatory statutes, the way federal regulatory retrenchment has been carried out during the past two decades has further complicated the role of state lawyers. Divided government and partisan disputes between Congress and the White House have led presidents to rely increasingly on "administrative retrenchment" and nonenforcement strategies rather than on legislative repeal or disablement (Waterman, 1985). Virtually none of the major deregulatory initiatives since 1980 were accompanied by legislative action (Conlan, 1991). But while administrative strategies of deregulation may have reduced federal activity, they have increased regulatory burdens on the states by leaving intact public demand for regulatory programs while shrinking federal commitment and resources. To fill the void left by federal withdrawal, states have become more aggressive in their own efforts to enforce federal laws and to establish their own regulatory statutes and standards (Nathan and Doolittle, 1987; Bowman and Kearney, 1986; Webster, 1990).

Given the new regulatory responsibilities of states, it is not surprising to find that state attorneys general have become more frequent litigants in the federal courts. Several studies have found that state litigation has trended sharply upward since the 1960s. Kearney and Sheehan (1992), for instance, found that the number of cases in which states were party rose from a low of 20 cases in 1955 to a high of 140 in 1986. Moreover, the number of cases in which states appeared as appellants grew from 7 percent of all cases between 1953 and 1969 to 23 percent of all cases decided by the Court between 1980 and 1988. Similarly, a study of state amicus activity by Morris (1987) also found a sharp upward trend during this period: between 1960 and 1973, states participated as amicus curiae in only 4 percent of the cases before the Supreme Court, compared to 13 percent of cases decided between 1974 and 1983.

More indicative of the changing context of state legal work, however, is the pattern of intergovernmental litigation that has emerged. In contrast to earlier periods when state lawyers were interested in shielding state and local jurisdictions from federal regulatory infiltration, in recent years states have turned to federal courts to compel the federal government to enforce its own laws and regulatory standards. In *Ohio* v. *United States Environmental Protection Agency* (1993), for example, attorneys general from ten states sued the EPA for failure to implement waste-site clean-ups required under the Superfund law of 1980. Similar suits have been brought by states under other federal statutes, especially under the Clean Air Act when states have asked courts to force the EPA to deal with acid rain from neighboring states (*New York* v. *Ruckelshaus*, 1986; *Thomas* v. *State of New York*, 1988).

States have also directly challenged presidential efforts to limit the reach of some federal statutes. In *School Board of Nassau* v. *Arline* (1987), for example, the solicitor general argued that a federal law protecting the handicapped against discrimination only protected those with physical impairments of a non-contagious nature (thus excluding AIDS and other communicable diseases). Attorneys general from five states challenged this view, arguing that federal antidiscrimination law should be broadly construed. The Supreme Court agreed. Citing the states' brief in a footnote, the Court said that the broader interpretation would actually assist local health officials by lessening the reluctance of infected persons to report their condition. Another example is found in *City of Cleburne, Texas* v. *Cleburne Living Center* (1985). In this case, twenty-four states joined in four separate amici briefs to urge the Court to overturn a city ordinance that required a permit for the operation of a group home for the mentally retarded. The solicitor general had filed an amicus brief arguing that the permit requirement was not in violation of federal law or the Due Process Clause of the

Fourteenth Amendment. The Court, however, sided with the amici states and voided the ordinance as lacking a rational basis.

State attorneys general have also increasingly sought their own direct enforcement authority over federal statutes. In the area of consumer protection, for instance, the National Association of Attorneys General (NAAG) has lobbied Congress to ensure that any new federal legislation specifically authorizes states to bring direct enforcement actions. NAAG credits its efforts for securing state rights of action under the Telephone Consumer Protection Act of 1991, the 900 Services Act of 1992, and in recent amendments to the Consumer Credit Protection Act of 1971, among others (Clayton, 1994).

When states are unsuccessful in securing enforcement of federal statutory standards, they may respond by passing their own regulatory statutes that mirror federal standards. Since 1970, for example, twenty-seven states have authorized their attorneys general to enforce "little RICO" laws that mimic the Racketeer Influenced and Corrupt Organizations Act, fifteen have adopted "mini-Superfund" statutes, and forty-nine have adopted statutes mirroring the Federal Trade Commission Act (Clayton, 1994). The impact of mirror statutes on public policy can be enormous. When the Reagan Justice Department was attempting to restrain the reach of federal civil rights laws, for example, states used mirror antidiscrimination statutes to pressure private companies and organizations, like the Jaycees and Rotary clubs, to become more open. In *Roberts* v. *U.S. Jaycees* (1984), for instance, Minnesota's attorney general used a state antidiscrimination statute barring discrimination in "places of public accommodation" to enjoin the national organization of the Jaycees over its refusal to admit women. After losing this case, and after similar conflicts with the attorneys general of New York and California, the Jaycees changed their national membership policy. Three years later, California's attorney general used the state's antidiscrimination statute to force the Rotary International to admit women (*Rotary International* v. *Rotary Club of Duarte,* 1987). California's brief as an intervenor was supported with amici from Minnesota and eleven other states.

Where the new style of intergovernmental litigation is most prominent, however, is in the area of federal preemption, where states wishing to fill regulatory voids left by federal retrenchment have had to overcome federal objections. In *Louisiana* v. *Federal Communications Commission* (1986), for instance, thirty-five states filed briefs challenging the FCC's effort to prevent them from regulating rate and price competition by companies providing intrastate telecommunication services. The solicitor general argued that state authority to regulate had been preempted by the Communications Act of 1934 and added that "the heart of the case is whether . . . federal policy of increasing competition in the [telecommunications] industry will be thwarted by state regulators who have yet to recognize or accept this national policy." Nonetheless, the Court rejected the federal government's argument. Noting the large number of states involved in the case, Justice

William Brennan denied that Congress gave the FCC "power to dictate to the States" its preference for deregulating the telecommunication services market (p. 375).

Similarly, in 1986, in *California* v. *Granite Rock Company*, attorneys general from twenty states signed a brief supporting a California statute regulated mining activities on federal lands. The solicitor general had intervened on behalf of the mining company, arguing that California's authority over activities on federal property had been preempted by the Mining Act of 1872 and other federal land management acts. Nonetheless, the Court rejected the solicitor general's assertion of federal preemptory authority. Federal land management statutes, the Court concluded, only preempted state efforts aimed at comprehensive management of federal property, not the more narrow application of otherwise applicable state environmental regulations over activities carried out on that property.

Not all state legal efforts to thwart federal deregulatory efforts have been successful. In *Morales* v. *TWA* (1992), for example, a majority of the Court struck down a Texas statute regulating the airline industry and chastised the National Association of Attorneys General for thwarting federal airline deregulation efforts. Nor has the federal government attempted to withdraw from many areas of regulatory control. Nevertheless, it is clear that the political context for intergovernmental legal administration has become an increasingly complex one. States no longer react reflexively to federal regulatory intrusions, and the federal government no longer exclusively controls national regulatory standards. This has at once complicated the work of federal lawyers and given lawyers who represent states a new national policymaking role.

CONCLUSION

Government lawyers have received relatively little scholarly attention despite their importance in a system in which public policy is increasingly made in the courts and the administrative state. This chapter has described some of the major features of government legal administration in the United States, and the offices responsible for it. It has also identified some common issues and developments shaping the work of government lawyers: the conflict between political loyalties and the commitment to the rule of law, the importance of the separation of powers in establishing the political context of government legal work, and how trends in intergovernmental relations have changed the relationship between state and federal lawyers.

It has not, nor could it, examine all of the many roles played by government lawyers in modern American government. Nearly thirty years ago, Miller (1968) wrote that government lawyers operate in an environment of "great complexity when seen in its entirety. What gets public attention is usually only the tip of the iceberg, underneath which may be discerned a vast number of ways in which [these lawyers] function within the governmental framework" (p. 41). This statement is even more true today, and this chapter has charted only a small portion of the underside of that iceberg.

Cases Cited

California v. *Granite Rock Company*, 480 U.S. 572 (1986).

Chevron U.S.A., Inc. v. *Natural Resources Defense Council*, 467 U.S. 837 (1984).

City of Cleburne, Texas v. *Cleburne Living Center*, 473 U.S. 432 (1985).

Louisiana v. *Federal Communications Commission*, 476 U.S. 355 (1986).

Morales v. *TWA*, 112 S.Ct. 2031 (1992).

Morrison v. *Olson*, 108 S.Ct. 2597 (1988).

New York v. *Ruckelshaus*, 21 ERC 1721; 14 Envtl L.Rep. 20,873 (D.C. Cir., 1986).

Ohio v. *United States Environmental Protection Agency*, 997 F.2d 1520 (D.C. Cir., 1993).

Regents of the University of California v. *Bakke*, 438 U.S. 265 (1978).

Roberts v. *U.S. Jaycees*, 486 U.S. 609 (1984).

Rotary International v. *Rotary Club of Duarte*, 481 U.S. 537 (1987).

Rust v. *Sullivan*, 111 S.Ct. 1759 (1991).

School Board of Nassau v. *Arline*, 480 U.S. 273 (1987).

State of Florida v. *Exxon Corporation*, 526 F.2d 266 (1976).

Thomas v. *State of New York*, 802 F.2d 1443 (D.C. Cir., 1988).

United States v. *House of Representatives*, 556 F.Supp. 150, D.D.C. (1983).

United States v. *United States District Court*, 407 U.S. 297 (1972).

References

"Ashcroft." *National Law Journal*, Jan. 28, 1985, p. 30.

Baker, N. *Conflicting Loyalties: Law, Politics and the Attorney General's Office.* Lawrence: University Press of Kansas, 1992.

Bell, G. "The Attorney General: The Federal Government's Chief Lawyer and Chief Litigator, or One Among Many." *Fordham Law Review*, 1978, 46, 1049.

Bell, G., and Ostrow, R. *Taking Care of the Law.* New York: Morrow, 1982.

Biddle, F. *In Brief Authority.* New York: Doubleday, 1962.

Biskupic, J. "Thornburgh's Bumpy Start." *Congressional Quarterly*, 1989, 26, 2215–2218.

Bowman, A., and Kearney, R. *The Resurgence of States.* Upper Saddle River, N.J.: Prentice Hall, 1986.

Bowman, A., and Pagono, M. "The State of American Federalism." *Publius,* 1990, *20,* 1.

Caplan, L. *The Tenth Justice: The Solicitor General and the Rule of Law.* New York: Knopf, 1987.

Clayton, C. W. *The Politics of Justice: The Attorney General and the Making of Legal Policy.* Armonk, N.Y.: Sharpe, 1992.

Clayton, C. W. "Law, Politics, and the New Federalism: State Attorneys General as National Policymakers." *Review of Politics,* 1994, *56*(3), 525–553.

Clayton, C. W. (ed.). *Government Lawyers: The Federal Legal Bureaucracy and Presidential Politics.* Lawrence: University Press of Kansas, 1995.

Conlan, T. "And the Beat Goes On: Intergovernmental Mandates and Preemption in an Era of Deregulation." *Publius,* 1991, *21,* 43.

Culp-Davis, K. *Discretionary Justice: A Preliminary Inquiry.* Urbana: University of Illinois Press, 1971.

Cummings, H., and McFarland, C. *Federal Justice.* Old Tappan, N.J.: Macmillan, 1937.

"Current Services Budget Authority by Agency." *Budget of the United States Government, Fiscal Year 1993.* Washington, D.C.: U.S. Government Printing Office, 1993.

Easby-Smith, J. *The Department of Justice: Its History and Functions.* Washington, D.C.: Lowdermilk, 1904.

Eastland, T. "The Independent Counsel Regime." *Public Interest,* 1990, *100,* 68.

Eastland, T. *Energy in the Executive: The Case for the Strong Presidency.* New York: Free Press, 1992.

Edwards, J. *The Office of the Crown.* London: Sweet & Maxwell, 1964.

Eisenstein, J. *Counsel for the United States.* Baltimore: Johns Hopkins University Press, 1978.

"Executive Discretion and the Congressional Defense of Statutes." *Yale Law Journal,* 1983, *92,* 970.

Fix, M., and Kenyon, D. *Coping with Mandates: What Are the Alternatives.* Washington, D.C.: Urban Institute, 1990.

Fried, C. *Order and Law: Arguing the Reagan Revolution.* New York: Simon & Schuster, 1991.

Garment, S. *Scandal: The Culture of Mistrust in American Politics.* New York: Random House, 1991.

Harrigar, K. *Independent Justice: The Federal Special Prosecutor in American Politics.* Lawrence: University Press of Kansas, 1992.

Harrigar, K. "Independent Justice: The Office of the Independent Counsel." In C. W. Clayton (ed.), *Government Lawyers: The Federal Legal Bureaucracy and Presidential Politics.* Lawrence: University Press of Kansas, 1995.

Herz, M. "The Attorney Particular: The Governmental Role of the Agency General Counsel." In C. W. Clayton (ed.), *Government Lawyers: The Federal Legal Bureaucracy and Presidential Politics.* Lawrence: University Press of Kansas, 1995.

Horowitz, D. *The Jurocracy.* Lexington, Mass.: Heath, 1977.

Huston, L. *The Department of Justice.* New York: Praeger, 1967.

Huston, L., Miller, A., Krislor, S., and Dixon, R. *Roles of the Attorney General.* Washington, D.C.: American Enterprise Institute, 1968.

Jaworski, L. *The Right and the Power: The Prosecution of Watergate.* Houston: Gulf, 1976.

Kearney, R., and Sheehan, R. "Supreme Court Decisionmaking: The Impact of Court Composition on State and Local Government Litigation." *Journal of Politics,* 1992, *54,* 1008.

Key, S. "The Legal Work of the Federal Government." *Virginia Law Review,* 1938, *25,* 165.

Kleindienst, R. *Justice.* New York: Praeger, 1985.

Langeluttig, A. *The Department of Justice of the United States.* Baltimore: Johns Hopkins University Press, 1927.

Lewis, A. "How Freedom Died." *New York Times,* Nov. 22, 1991, p. A–15.

Melnick, S. R. *Regulation and the Courts: The Case of the Clean Air Act.* Washington, D.C.: Brookings Institution, 1983.

Melnick, S. R. *Between the Lines: Interpreting Welfare Rights.* Washington, D.C.: Brookings Institution, 1994.

Miller, A., and Bowman, J. "Presidential Attacks on the Constitutionality of Federal Statutes." *Ohio State Law Review,* 1979, *40,* 51.

Morris, T. "States Before the Federal Courts." *Judicature,* 1987, *70,* 298–305.

Nathan, R. *The Administrative Presidency.* New York: Wiley, 1983.

Nathan, R., and Doolittle, S. *Reagan and the States.* Princeton, N.J.: Princeton University Press, 1987.

Navasky, V. *Kennedy Justice.* New York: Atheneum, 1977.

Olson, S. "Comparing Justice and Labor Department Lawyers: Ten Years of Occupational Safety and Health Litigation." *Law and Policy,* 1985, *7,* 287–303.

Peterson, G. "Federalism and the States: An Experiment in Decentralization." In J. Palmer and I. V. Sawhill (eds.), *The Reagan Record.* Washington, D.C.: Urban Institute, 1984.

Rabkin, J. *Judicial Compulsions: How Public Law Distorts Public Policy.* New York: Basic Books, 1989.

Rabkin, J. "White House Lawyering: Law, Ethics, and Political Judgments." In C. W. Clayton (ed.), *Government Lawyers: The Federal Legal Bureaucracy and Presidential Politics.* Lawrence: University Press of Kansas, 1995.

Richardson, E. *The Creative Balance.* London: Hamish Hamilton, 1976.

Ross, L. *States Attorneys General: Powers and Responsibilities.* Washington, D.C.: National Association of Attorneys General, 1990.

Ross, L. *Statistics on the Office of Attorney General.* Washington, D.C.: National Association of Attorneys General, 1993.

Salokar, R. M. *The Solicitor General and the Politics of Law.* Philadelphia: Temple University Press, 1992.

Salokar, R. M. "Politics, Law, and the Office of the Solicitor General." In C. W. Clayton (ed.), *Government Lawyers: The Federal Legal Bureaucracy and Presidential Politics.* Lawrence: University Press of Kansas, 1995.

Shapiro, M. *Who Guards the Guardians: Judicial Control of Administration.* Athens: University of Georgia Press, 1988.

Smith, W. F. *Law and Justice in the Reagan Administration.* Stanford, Calif.: Hoover Press, 1991.

Starr, K. "Judicial Review in the Post-*Chevron* Era." *Yale Journal on Regulation,* 1986, *3,* 283–312.

Taylor, A. "Schedule for Hearings Is Unclear as Starr Takes Over Probe." *Congressional Quarterly Weekly Report,* Aug. 13, 1994, p. 23.

Thornburg, L. "Changes in the State's Law Firm." *Campbell Law Review,* 1990, *12,* 343.

U.S. Congress, Senate Judiciary Committee. *Ervin Hearings: Removing Politics from the Administration of Justice.* 93d Cong., 1st Sess., 1974.

Waterman, R. *Presidential Influence and the Administrative State.* Knoxville: Tennessee University Press, 1985.

Webster, W. "The Emerging Role of State Attorneys General." *Washburn Law Journal,* 1990, *30,* 1.

Winkle, J. W., III, and Swann, M. "When Justices Need Lawyers: The U.S. Supreme Court's Legal Counsel." *Judicature,* 1993, *76,* 244.

Yeager, C., and Hargrave, L. "The Power of the Attorney General to Supersede a District Attorney." *Louisiana Law Review,* 1991, *51,* 733–754.

CHAPTER TWENTY-SEVEN

Race, Education, and the Legal and Administrative Systems

Perpetual Tensions

Charles W. Washington

In the mid-nineteenth century, Alexis de Tocqueville ([1835] 1972), commenting on his observations of democracy in the United States, noted the uniqueness of the "Anglo-Americans," those of British origin, who dominated the American population: "The people are . . . the real directing power; and although the form of government is representative, it is evident that the opinions, the prejudices, the interests, and even the passions of the people are hindered by no permanent obstacles from exercising a perpetual influence on the daily conduct of affairs" (p. 61).

American democracy, observed Tocqueville, is characterized by three centers of power (legislative, executive, and judicial), citizen participation in the political process with interim accountability checks, representative government, and a range of diverse opinions, prejudices, and interests in which majority preference is the decision rule. But what if the majority, which Tocqueville called the "Anglo-Americans," develops public policies that restrict the right of participation by others in the governance process and ignores the intrinsic value of every individual?

This is the type of philosophical and political question addressed by James Madison at the Constitutional Convention in 1787. Madison, as critiqued by Dahl (1956, pp. 4, 34, 90–91), envisioned a democracy characterized by compromise, political equality, popular sovereignty, rule by majority, and a sensitivity to the intensity of the preferences of the minority such that there are institutionally built-in and inherent inclinations to prevent tyranny of the minority by the majority and tyranny of the minority against the majority. Political equality suggests popular participation by both the majority and the minority. Political equality and popular sovereignty, articulated primarily through vocal factions that have differential access to the policymaking process and the day-to-day administrative apparatus, will result in differential influence on the types of policy outcomes (Dye and Zeigler, 1990).

Madison's concerns are particularly relevant to the implementation of public education policies in systems employing an appointed school superintendent who manages through school principals in a decentralized management system. Conscious efforts must be made to provide opportunities for citizens to participate in the policymaking and administrative decision-making processes of local school systems. Citizens must be able to participate in the election of school board members, or of those who appoint school board members, and to express opinions about the qualifications and appointment of a school superintendent. Bureaucratic processes and mechanisms must be sufficiently flexible and open in order to permit, if not invite, public participation in the processes for proposing and deciding school board policies. In an urban, independent school district, these policies are likely to address such issues as attendance boundaries; student assignments; school openings, closings, or repurposing; special attractor programs such as magnet schools or programs; choice and controlled choice zones; busing; neighborhood schools; staff assignments; facilities location; and curricula. These issues elicit and reflect varying levels of public emotions and sensitivity.

The most serious challenges to school board policies, after policy approval or during implementation, often occur in a court of law (Cooper, 1988). This type of challenge has been the history of public K–12 education in this country with respect to achieving desegregated education and equal protection under the law for minorities, especially African Americans, under provision of the Due Process and Equal Protection Clauses of the Fifth and Fourteenth Amendments to the U.S. Constitution (Cooper, 1988).

This chapter focuses on the K–12 public policy quadrangle, in which the tensions between democracy and bureaucracy are manifested. The public policy quadrangle is circumscribed by four walls of influence: (1) policymakers—the elected or appointed school board, (2) executive leadership by the superintendent and the bureaucracy, (3) participation by and opinions of the general public and special interest groups, and (4) the role of the courts. Of course, no contemporary picture of the tensions between bureaucracy and democracy in K–12 public education is complete without acknowledging the role played by the media. For present purposes, the role is acknowledged as one of communicating the actions of school boards, the opinions of political activists, interest groups, and editors, and the decisions of intervening courts. The media is not a focus of this chapter, however.

This analysis focuses on a contemporary case study concerning the School Board of Broward County, Florida. The principles and problems discussed may be applicable to many school systems across the country. However, some of the specifics may not apply to dependent school districts that do not have the independent taxing, borrowing, and policymaking authority that is possessed by Florida's countywide school systems.

The central issue is the tension between democracy and bureaucracy in the provision of quality K–12 public education by local, independent school boards or systems in a desegregated, multicultural context. This fundamental issue can be decomposed into more discrete issues: (1) What constitutes quality K–12 public education in a desegregated setting? (2) What constitutes equal protection under the law and school board policies in order to achieve equality of educational opportunity? and (3) To what extent do decisions of the courts create, clarify, or confuse the actions of policymakers, the superintendent, and the bureaucracy in efforts to achieve quality K–12 public education in a desegregated, multicultural environment?

QUALITY K–12 PUBLIC EDUCATION IN A DESEGREGATED SETTING

The answer to the question "What constitutes quality K–12 public education in a desegregated setting?" is rooted in the history of American constitutional democracy. As the Supreme Court said in *Brown* v. *Board of Education of Topeka, Kansas* (1954), "Education is perhaps the most important function of state and local governments" (p. 493). This fundamental nature of education has made it a critically important focus of constitutional discussion for years. The relationship between education and race is deeply rooted in the legal system.

Thirty days after Lincoln issued the Emancipation Proclamation on January 1, 1863, the Thirty-Eighth Congress proposed the Thirteenth Amendment to the legislatures of the several states for approval. Designed to abolish slavery and involuntary servitude (except as a punishment for a crime), the amendment was ratified by the end of 1865 (*Guide to Congress,* 1976, p. 224). A number of the southern states responded with the passage of "Black Codes," which limited severely the rights of freed slaves following the Emancipation Proclamation. In response, the Thirty-Ninth Congress proposed to all the states the ratification of the Fourteenth Amendment and also passed the Civil Rights Act of 1866. The Fourteenth Amendment was designed to provide citizenship and to guarantee equal protection under the law and due process to free blacks as well as to former slaves. The Civil Rights Act was designed to make void the U.S. Supreme Court's decision in *Dred Scott* v. *Sandford* (1857), which denied Dred Scott his freedom, ruling that slaves were property and protected as such by the Constitution. The Fourteenth Amendment was ratified on July 28, 1868. The intended effect of these two amendments and the Civil Rights Act of 1866 was to grant free blacks and former slaves full U.S. citizenship and to entitle them to due process and equal protection under the law.

Separate but Equal Doctrine

These actions were preludes to the first significant U.S. Supreme Court decision to link race and education. A century ago, in *Plessy* v. *Ferguson* (1896), the U.S. Supreme Court made at least two key education rulings. It ruled that it was *reasonable* for the state to pass a law that would require Plessy, a citizen who alleged he was seven-eighths Caucasian and one-eighth African blood, to sit in "separate but equal" railway passenger cars for the colored race rather than with whites. In rendering the Court's decision, Justice Henry B. Brown referenced an 1849 decision in the state of Massachusetts (*Roberts* v. *Boston*) and reasoned:

> The object of the [fourteenth] amendment was undoubtedly to enforce the absolute equality of the two races before the law, but, in the nature of things, it could not have been intended to abolish distinctions based upon color, or to enforce social, as distinguished from political, equality, or a commingling of the two races upon terms unsatisfactory to either. Laws permitting or requiring their separation, in places where they are liable to be brought into contact, do not necessarily imply the inferiority of either race to the other, and have generally, if not universally, been recognized as within the competency of the state legislatures in the exercise of their police power. *The most common instance of this is connected with the establishment of separate schools for white and colored children, which have been held to be a valid exercise of the legislative power by courts of states where the political rights of the colored race have been longest and most earnestly enforced* [*Plessy* v. *Ferguson*, 1896, p. 544, emphasis added].

Justice Brown reiterated the relevance of the state's right to provide separate but equal education when he rendered his "reasonableness" explanation of a state's use of its police powers to pass such legislation as that affecting Plessy. He stated:

> In determining the question of reasonableness, [the state] is at liberty to act with reference to the established usages, customs, and traditions of the people, and with a view to the promotion of their comfort, and the preservation of the public peace and good order. Gauged by this standard, we cannot say that a law [the 1890 Louisiana law] which authorizes or even requires the separation of the two races in public conveyances is unreasonable, *or more obnoxious to the Fourteenth Amendment than the acts of Congress requiring separate schools for colored children in the District of Columbia*, the constitutionality of which does not seem to have been questioned, or the corresponding acts of state legislatures [*Plessy*, 1896, p. 551, emphasis added].

Clearly, quality K–12 education was not defined to include the education of blacks and whites in the same setting.

Education in the South between the *Plessy* (1896) and *Brown* v. *Board of Education* (1954) decisions can hardly have been described as being of equal quality for blacks and whites. As Myrdal (1944) observed in *An American Dilemma,* the foundations of the public schools for both blacks and whites were laid during Reconstruction. Soon thereafter, Myrdal observed, as under restoration governments, the "Negroes were severely discriminated against" and "in many parts of the South Negro education deteriorated for decades" (p. 888).

The *Brown* Era: Invalidating the Separate but Equal Doctrine

The separate but equal doctrine remained healthy until *Brown* v. *Board of Education of Topeka, Kansas* (1954), sometimes referred to as *Brown I.* It took more than half a century for the U.S. Supreme Court to get to this revisitation of the race-and-education relationship. In *Brown I,* the Court decided that it would address frontally the question of whether the separate but equal doctrine of *Plessy* should endure. Noting that all the cases that had been brought before it from the states of Kansas, South Carolina, Virginia, and Delaware had adhered to the *Plessy* doctrine, the Court stated: "We come then to the question presented: Does segregation of children in public schools solely on the basis of race, even though the physical facilities and other 'tangible' factors may be equal, deprive the children of the minority group of equal educational opportunities?" The Court answered: "We believe that it does" (p. 493). In arriving at its decision, the Court consciously went beyond consideration of the fact that in some of the state cases there was evidence of efforts to equalize conditions in white and black schools with respect to buildings, curricula, teachers' qualifications and salaries, and other tangible indicators. The Court chose to consider the *effect* of segregation itself on public education. Drawing on psychological research and on reasoning in six of its earlier education-related cases (*Cummings* v. *Richmond County Board of Education,* 1899; *Gong Lum* v. *Rice,* 1927; *Missouri ex rel. Gaines* v. *Canada,* 1938; *Sipuel* v. *Oklahoma,* 1948; *Sweatt* v. *Painter,* 1950; and *McLaurin* v. *Oklahoma State Regents,* 1950), the Court concluded:

> Today, education is perhaps the most important function of state and local governments. Compulsory school attendance laws and the great expenditures for education both demonstrate our recognition of the importance of education to our democratic society. It is required in the performance of our most basic public responsibilities, even service in the armed forces. It is the very foundation of good citizenship. Today, it is a principal instrument in awakening the child to cultural values, in preparing him for later professional training, and in helping him to adjust normally to his environment. In these days, it is doubtful that any child may reasonably be expected to succeed in life if he is denied the opportunity for

an education. Such an opportunity, where the state has undertaken to provide it, is a right which must be made available to all on equal terms [*Brown* v. *Board of Education of Topeka, Kansas,* 1954, p. 493].

The Court held that the doctrine of separate but equal had no place in public education, that "separate educational facilities are inherently unequal. Therefore, we hold that the plaintiffs and others similarly situated for whom the actions have been brought are, by reason of the segregation complained of, deprived of the equal protection of the law" (p. 493).

Brown II (*Brown* v. *Board of Education of Topeka, Kansas,* 1955) considered the remedies for the deprivation found in *Brown I,* and the Court established the linkage to policymaking and administration. Recognizing that primary responsibility for solving the problems of inequality rested with local school authorities, the courts would have to consider whether the actions taken by school boards constituted good faith implementation of the policies consistent with constitutional principles inherent in the Fourteenth Amendment. In *Brown II,* as remedies were fashioned the Court went beyond the notion of "equal" in search of equal protection under the law and embraced the concept of equity. The Court also made it clear that remedies were not to be without plans and immediate action. It stated: "In fashioning and effectuating the decrees, the courts [referring to the federal appellate and district courts] will be guided by equitable principles. Traditionally, equity has been characterized by a practical flexibility in shaping its remedies and by a facility for adjusting and reconciling public and private needs" (p. 349). With respect to plans, the Court stated: "[The district courts] will also consider the adequacy of any plans the defendants may propose to meet these problems to effectuate a transition to a racially nondiscriminatory school system. During this period of transition the courts will retain jurisdiction of these cases" (p. 301).

The Court required the defendants to make a prompt start toward full compliance with its ruling. It remanded the cases to appellate and district courts "to take such proceedings and enter such orders and decrees consistent with this opinion as are necessary and proper to admit to public schools on a racially nondiscriminatory basis *all deliberate speed* the parties to these cases" (p. 301). This phrase was deliberately ambiguous. It was drawn from equity practice that meant moving carefully, deliberately, and with due concern for problems. In *Brown II,* the Court indicated that district courts "should consider problems related to administration, arising from the physical condition of the school plant, the school transportation system, personnel, revision of school districts and attendance areas into compact units to achieve a system of determining admission to the public schools on a nonracial basis and revision of local laws and regulations which may be necessary in solving the foregoing problems" (p. 349).

` Three things are apparent from *Brown I* and *Brown II*: (1) equality of educational opportunity was not possible in the eyes of the Court if provided in a segregated setting, and if it was provided in such a setting, blacks were not being provided equal protection under the law; (2) equality of education in settings with whites was equated with "quality" education in so far as it was assumed that white students, in white schools, received quality education; and (3) it was not clear that the Court was embracing education in a culturally diverse environment, but it was clear that students' competencies to deal effectively with their environments and to be aware of cultural values were part of the thinking expressed by the Court.

EQUAL PROTECTION UNDER THE LAW AND SCHOOL BOARD POLICIES

The Supreme Court's decision in *Brown I* and *Brown II* set the parameters for what constitutes equal protection under the law. The Court's rulings were unambiguous with respect to whether segregated education by law constitutes equal protection under the law. It does not. However, with respect to state laws and local school board plans designed to remedy the segregation problem, the Court mandated continued involvement or supervision by the courts. Typically this meant federal or district court orders for desegregation plans or court-approved consent decrees between plaintiffs and local school boards.

Consent decrees may be accompanied by (or may require the development of) a desegregation plan and may be quite specific with respect to what local school boards are required or plan to do. In some cases, consent decrees require corrective or remedial actions. In other cases, they require the equal application of policies, procedures, and mechanisms to achieve desegregation.

Court supervision is maintained to hear complaints by plaintiffs as well as to order appropriate relief, or to make decisions with respect to specific administrative or policy actions by local school boards if brought before the court by complaining plaintiffs. Judges may also take action at the request of court-ordered monitors or special masters. The courts may, if appropriate, release the local school district from supervision, depending on the extent to which the school district has met the terms of its own desegregation plan and other conditions specified by the court. So, what constitutes equal protection under state law, local policies, and rules and regulations is a function of the extent to which policies and actions are consistent with court-approved desegregation plans or consent decrees agreed to by the parties and covered by the U.S. Supreme Court's rulings.

The courts have tended to both create and clarify local school boards' and local bureaucracies' functions. Court decisions have also contributed to confusion at times. The implementation of local school boards' desegregation plans requires compliance with both general principles and specific conditions laid down by the relevant case law as determined by the respective courts having supervision. In some cases a judicial decision at the appellate level has served to clarify points of dispute over desegregation plans resulting from decisions rendered at the district court level. In other instances the court's involvement has imposed requirements on local school boards:

1. To develop desegregation plans (*Brown v. Board of Education,* 1955)

2. To eliminate vestiges of discrimination found in such areas as student assignment, faculty, staff, transportation, extracurricular activities, and facilities—the so-called "Green Factors" (*Green v. School Board of New Kent County,* 1968)

3. To redesign or modify student assignments, employ busing, and use stand-alone schools, such as the "Finger Plan" in Oklahoma, to achieve desegregation (*Dowell v. Board of Education of Oklahoma City Public Schools,* 1972)

4. To correct certain educational deficiencies attributable to segregation (*Milliken v. Bradley,* 1977)

5. To comply with the specific terms of a consent decree, such as equal application of methods to ensure that integration will be shared by both black and white students (*Rae Smith and Raymond Smith, Jr., et al. v. William McFatter, Superintendent of Schools, Broward County, Fla., et al.,* 1987)

6. To demonstrate that current racial imbalances are not related to prior segregation (*Mills v. Polk County Board of Public Instruction,* 1993; *Jacksonville Branch NAACP v. Duval County School Board,* 1989)

7. To consider quality of education as a factor in analyzing the vestiges of segregation (*Freeman v. Pitts,* 1991)

In more recent cases, the U.S. Supreme Court and other federal courts have rendered decisions that may confuse as much as clarify what their intentions are with respect to equal educational opportunity and constitutional actions of local school boards and administrative bureaucracies. An example of this is the decision of the Fifth Circuit Court of Appeals that race cannot be taken into consideration as a factor in affirmative action admissions policies for graduate professional schools. In *Hopwood v. Texas* (1996), the court also "rejected diversity as a compelling interest justifying race-conscious admission practices" (Hogan and Hartson, 1996). Although the appeals court's decision in *Hopwood* clearly rejects race as a consideration in admissions decisions, it raises questions about the relevance of the "narrow tailoring" prong (the other prong being serving a compelling government interest) of the "strict scrutiny" standard applied to affirmative action decisions by the courts in *Regents of the University of California v. Bakke* (1978) and *Adarand Constructors, Inc. v. Pena* (1995).

The denial of a writ of certiorari by the Supreme Court on July 1, 1996, did little to clarify the meaning and applicability of the *Hopwood* decision to K–12 school desegregation policies. However, the Fifth Circuit Court's judgment in that case has been considered by some to be applicable to K–12 desegregation cases, especially to those districts that are released from court supervision and are unitary. The confusion lies in the relevance of, and how to demonstrate, "narrow tailoring" and "compelling government interest" with respect to desegregation or diversity.

CITIZEN PARTICIPATION AND BROWARD COUNTY SCHOOL DESEGREGATION

No point in the policy quadrangle is more fragile and susceptible to abuse or capable of exerting significant influence than where citizen participation and input occur or are taken into consideration. One or two false starts by policymakers or by the superintendent, based on misinterpretation of the will of the public, can mean the end of an elected school board member's tenure or public upheaval over the actions of a superintendent and, perhaps, his or her dismissal. Waldo (1971) notes that no term can really be placed in direct opposition to *participation*. Participation refers to those centrifugal forces working on and within the organization, "seeking to draw authority and power downward (in a hierarchical sense) and outward (in a special sense)" (p. 26).

Citizen participation in the policy formation process in Broward County has been fairly open, especially at school board meetings. However, input at this stage is usually too late to make major differences, especially with respect to "big ticket" policy items such as school location, special program planning decisions, boundary changes, and student assignment and reassignment. Yet citizen participation and input about the disparate impact of political decisions on minorities in the system are valuable when sought by the school board. Such participation opportunities also include citizen committees and task forces.

In 1987, the School Board of Broward County and the attorney for the plaintiff in a 1983 school desegregation case worked out terms of agreement in a consent decree about how to proceed to achieve racial desegregation of the Broward County schools (*Smith v. McFatter*, 1987). This consent decree required specific actions on the part of the school board and specific roles to be played by a biracial committee, in addition to ongoing and recurring consultation with the attorney for the plaintiffs in the case.

In October 1993, operating under the 1987 consent decree, the retiring superintendent of the Broward County schools appointed, with the approval of the school board, the Boundary Task Force. This task force was charged with four responsibilities: (1) to determine the extent to which the School Board of Broward County had complied with the 1987 consent decree with respect to its desegregation efforts, (2) to analyze the Multicultural Education Training Advocacy Agreement, (3) to analyze boundaries for student assignments, and (4) to determine the unitariness of the school system.

In January 1994, to avoid confusion over the scope of responsibility of the existing, staff-dominated Boundary Committee within the district, which had traditionally developed and proposed recommendations to the school board for boundary changes, the Boundary Task Force was renamed the Desegregation Task Force (Morgan, 1994). Shortly after a new superintendent was appointed the name was changed again to the Superintendent's Desegregation Task Force. The new superintendent met with the members of the task force and expanded its charge to include a comprehensive review of all district policies related to desegregation and boundaries and their relationship to growth, innovative programs, and budget priorities. The task force was asked to make specific recommendations that could be implemented administratively by the superintendent or that needed policy approval by the school board (Petruzielo, 1994). The task force, cochaired by a Hispanic female and an African American male, was composed of seventeen citizens representing the racial, ethnic, religious, gender, and geographic diversity of the county. It was nearly evenly divided by gender, and nearly every member at the time of appointment currently or previously had a child enrolled in the Broward County public schools.

The results of the thirteen-month effort of the Superintendent's Desegregation Task Force were more than two hundred recommendations addressing each of the factors outlined by the Supreme Court in the *Green* (1968) case: student assignment, facilities, faculty and staff, educational achievement, extracurricular activities, transportation, and an additional item, magnet programs. The task force also addressed the degree of unitariness of the school district. The final recommendations of the task force were made to the school board on January 30, 1995.

ROLE OF THE COURTS

The role of the courts, the fourth wall of the policy quadrangle, in decreasing or increasing the tensions between democracy and bureaucracy is apparent from the nature of the decisions rendered by the judges with respect to equal educational opportunity. The decision of individual judges, however, may not necessarily reflect the theoretical role of the judiciary as an institution. The judge or judges in a particular case can moderate or intensify the tensions between democracy and bureaucracy. The 1987 Broward County consent decree provides the reference point for illuminating the extent to which judges' decisions have had policymaking and administrative implications.

In 1970, sixteen years after the *Brown* decisions and seventeen years prior to the 1987 consent decree, a local attorney, W. George Allen, filed a class action suit on behalf of his son and others similarly situated, alleging that the school board operated a dual system that discriminated against black students and violated their constitutional right to equal protection under the law (*Allen et al.* v. *Board of Public Instruction of Broward County, Florida,* 1970). The School Board of Broward County (SBBC) admitted to its actions and policies, and the district court "found that the school district had been unconstitutionally operating a segregated school system" (Hogan and Hartson, 1994, p. 4). The district court ordered the school board to develop a desegregation plan that would make certain adjustments in the board's admissions policies and attendance boundaries, to use pairing and clustering in elementary schools, and to desegregate its faculty, among other changes. The school district's initial desegregation plan was adopted by order of the district court on April 30, 1970, but elements were appealed by the plaintiffs. The Fifth Circuit Court of Appeals, in its order of August 18, 1970, affirmed in part and reversed in part the lower court's ruling. The circuit court approved adjustments in the plan with respect to clustering of elementary schools. The school district had by then changed its name to the Board of Public Instruction of Broward County. Its desegregation plan was adopted, with revisions, by orders issued in April, August, and September 1970.

Assessing Adherence to a Democratic Principle

The following spring, the plaintiffs filed a motion in district court challenging implementation of the 1970 desegregation plan (*Allen et al.* v. *Board of Public Instruction, Broward County, Florida,* 1971). The district court ordered that the plan be amended with respect to the assignment of kindergarten children to schools serving their neighborhoods, the desegregation of a previously all-black high school, the adjustment of boundaries of several adjoining high schools, and the further adjustment of elementary school clustering. Of particular importance in this ruling were factors that bore significantly on the nature and character of the public policies of the SBBC and on the administrative policies, rules, and regulations implemented by the superintendent. Judge Ted Cabot's ruling included a finding that "the Broward County School Desegregation *Plan* as adopted by orders of the court of April 30, August 28, and September 4, 1970, and this order, constitutes a unitary school system in accordance with the United States Constitution" (p. 252). Judge Cabot added, however: "The court reserves jurisdiction of the parties and the cause to assure that the school system is operated *as a unitary system in accordance with the United States Constitution* (p. 252, emphasis added).

It is, of course, one thing to assert that if the plan were fully and effectively implemented it would produce a unitary system, and quite another to assume that just because the plan theoretically should produce a unitary system it would do so in practice. Judge Cabot died that year, and the petitioners were concerned that the plan might suffer the same fate. The plaintiffs petitioned Judge Joe Eaton for a declaration of contempt of court by the SBBC. Judge Eaton held a conference with the parties to brief them on the status of the case and to express some philosophical views about the proper role of the judicial branch. The court indicated that it would not insert itself into the planning of *future* actions on the part of a school board, nor would it render an opinion on the possible legality of planned actions of the board. The court explained that it could not act at that time on either the petition for a declaration of contempt of court by the plaintiff, or the school board's request to modify the appeals court's order.

Perhaps the most important aspects of the conference with Judge Eaton, though they were not considered such at the time, were the judge's multiple references to the unitary status of the Broward County school district. Eaton stated, "The point is that the 1971 judgment said, 'Alright [*sic*]; what was a segregated system is now a unitary system. If you do this there will be a unitary system, if it works.'"(*Allen et al.* v. *Board of Instruction of Broward County, Florida*, 1972, p. 22). A second reference was to the fact that "if [the Broward County School System] is a unitary system it is because the Courts said it was, and, if so, then there is no requirement that the Court start over, because Judge Cabot died, and get involved in relitigating it to see if you can integrate more" (p. 24). Judge Eaton stated: "It is the Court of Appeals that handed down the mandates that required integrated school systems. When those same Courts of Appeals say this one is a unitary system, then it is, because that is also the law. Now this case is like the other case; it has been litigated. It is res judicata; it says to me, 'judge, whatever you think, the courts have ruled on this. This is now a unitary system'" (p. 34).

In closing the conference, Judge Eaton dismissed the plaintiffs' petition and did not rule on the school board's request for the right to modify its desegregation plan with respect to pairing and clustering. He invited the attorney for the plaintiffs to resubmit, if he chose to, a more specific and narrowly tailored motion for contempt, leaving out those matters over which the court has no jurisdiction, such as reopening a particular school or making the school district more unitary.

For the next eight years, the SBBC desegregation issue lay dormant before the court. In 1979, Judge Eaton relinquished the court's jurisdiction over the case "without making precise findings on the school district's compliance with prior orders, success in eliminating vestiges of segregation to the extent practicable, or good faith commitment to its constitutional obligations. Instead, the court merely noted that 'eight years [had] passed since the entry' of the last remedial order" (Hogan and Hartson, 1994, p. 5). The court held no evidentiary hearing related to unitariness prior to its decision. Also, because there was no appeal of Judge Cabot's 1971 order, the court appeared to have linked the decision only to the matter of the length of time that had passed and to an assumption that the school district had acted in good faith to remedy the constitutional violation admitted to in the 1970 *Allen* case. However, Judge Cabot issued no "precise statement that the constitutional violation [in *Allen*] had been remedied" (Hogan and Hartson, 1994, p. 5).

The 1987 Consent Decree and Administrative Implications

In 1981 the attorney for the original plaintiffs sought an injunction to restrain the SBBC from operating a neighborhood-based, segregated school system (see *Rae Smith and Raymond Smith, Jr., et al.* v. *William McFatter, Superintendent of Schools, Broward County, Fla., et al.,* 1982). This suit, dismissed in 1982 but refiled in 1983, alleged that the SBBC had failed to follow through on its obligations under the court orders in the *Allen* case (*Rae Smith and Raymond Smith, Jr., et al.* v. *William McFatter, Superintendent of Schools, Broward County, Fla., et al.,* 1983). The case was settled in a consent decree that required the school district to take specific steps to ensure the maintenance of a unitary system. Judge Kenneth L. Ryskamp, who had assumed this case following the 1982 dismissal by Judge Eaton of the same parties' earlier case, indicated that "the court does not find that the School Board of Broward County, Florida, violated any of the laws of the State of Florida, or the Florida Constitution, or the laws of the United States or the United States Constitution" (*Smith* v. *McFatter*, Order, 1987, p. 2). The court did not specifically find that the prior constitutional violations found in *Allen* (1970) had been remedied, but it stated that the "settlement between the Plaintiffs and the Defendant [the SBBC] is for the purposes of improving the educational system and to ensure the maintenance of a unitary system of education for the school system of Broward County, Florida" (p. 2).

The 1987 court order imposed additional obligations on the school district but contained no specific time limit, nor did it state any time frame for the court's jurisdiction or supervision. The order mandated ten specific requirements. For example, equal application of methods was required "to ensure that integration will be shared by both black and white students within Broward . . . and that the utilization of Magnet Programs, other voluntary programs, and feasible and practical boundary changes will be implemented to achieve such equal application" (p. 2). The decree also required the establishment of a biracial committee (specifically requiring representation from the NAACP) to review all boundaries, all student transfer or reassignment policies, all magnet programs and where they are located "to insure that the policies promote the maintenance of a unitary school system" (p. 3). The biracial committee was required to make reviews annually and report to the school board (not the superintendent). The school board was to provide the biracial committee with an annual analysis and review of all proposed school closings prior to final actions.

In addition, the consent decree required that specific affirmative action and equal employment opportunity responsibilities should be fulfilled. It required "that the Office of Equal Opportunity shall be staffed, upgraded, and report and answer directly to the superintendent and shall monitor and implement all programs, laws, rules, regulations, and policies affecting equal access for the Broward County school system" (p. 3). There should also be an annual review of the district's affirmative action plan, evaluating its effectiveness in the system.

The decree required that "minimally, a designated month of the school year should be identified by the superintendent and/or Board, wherein the superintendent would report to the Board as to the progress of the implementation of an effective Affirmative Action Plan" (p. 3). Amendments to the affirmative action plan were permitted at any time, provided that they were based on data received as a result of implementing the plan. The decree also required that the racial mix of faculty and staff, including principals, assistant principals, and guidance counselors, "should be the same racial mix of the total county population when feasible and practical" (p. 4). To accomplish this goal, the school board was required to set goals for training and upgrading minorities to those positions, to reestablish individual school profiles, and to "establish a procedure whereby the Office of Equal Opportunity and the Personnel Office will prepare and distribute a profile for those positions in the instructional fields to be filled" (pp. 4–5). The profiles would represent a goal to be achieved as soon as practicable.

The final substantive provision was that "school facilities in traditionally Black areas will continue to be upgraded, renovated and maintained assuring that the curriculum offered, the activities provided, the physical plant, and all other amenities provided by the School Board will be essentially equal to all other school facilities in traditional white areas" (p. 5).

The 1987 decree set the parameters for the administrative and policy agenda for the school board until the establishment of the Desegregation Task Force in 1993. During this six-year interim period, policy decisions and changes by the SBBC were made in consultation with the attorney for the plaintiffs in *Smith* v. *McFatter.*

POST-CONSENT DECREE, POST-TASK FORCE DILEMMA, AND UNCERTAINTY

The superintendent and the school board accepted most of the recommendations of the Superintendent's Desegregation Task Force, but a crisis emerged with respect to three key recommendations. This crisis set in motion a new era of tensions. The three recommendations were (1) that the school board, armed with the task force's report and its recommendations, along with other relevant data and information, should seek a declaration by the court whether the district was unitary; (2) that the practice of "starbursting" (the incoherent busing or "scattering" of black children from their neighborhoods to multiple white neighborhoods for the purpose of desegregation) be discontinued *unless white and black children shared equally the burden of desegregation*; and (3) that the school board modify or eliminate its rule that no child who is in the minority at a given school can be granted a reassignment to another school in which the child's race is in the majority if the move negatively affects the racial composition of the school the child is leaving or the school to which she or he is being assigned.

The board rejected the first and third recommendations but, after much public outcry, acquiesced to the second. On the advice of Hogan and Hartson, a law firm specializing in desegregation law, the board declined to petition the court for a declaration of unitariness. The consequences of delay and resistance to the recommendations became apparent. The rejection of the recommendation to seek a declaration of unitariness and the failure to modify or reject the "adverse impact" rule became key factors in a new lawsuit filed against the district. Likewise, the delay in eliminating starbursting gave impetus to the creation of an activist citizens' group, Citizens Concerned About Our Children (CCC), which also filed suit against the district (see *Citizens Concerned About Our Children et al. v. School Board of Broward County,* 1995). In the heat of the controversy following the Desegregation Task Force Report, including severe criticism in the black press, the attorney for the plaintiffs in the original *Allen* (1970) and *Smith* v. *McFatter* (1987) cases withdrew from representing *Smith et al.* The *Smith* case was assumed by a team of younger attorneys with less experience in desegregation cases.

Unitary or Not?

In 1992, prior to the establishment of the Desegregation Task Force, five white parents using the fictitious names Washington, Adams, Madison, and others filed a federal civil rights suit on behalf of their children against the school board of Broward County, its attorney, and the former superintendent (see *Washington et al.* v. *School Board of Broward County, Fla.,* 1992) alleging that their children were victims of unconstitutional racial discrimination when the board denied the requests of the parents for a boundary change. That boundary change would have sent their children from their existing elementary school, Harbordale (an integrated school according to the district's own standards), to Sunrise Middle School (40 percent black, 60 percent white) rather than to Rogers Middle School (43 percent black, 57 percent white).

In a hearing before the district court judge in January 1995, the plaintiffs argued that the denial was race based in view of the fact that the effect on the receiving school's ratio of blacks to whites would have changed only marginally.

Sunrise Middle School would have become eight-tenths of 1 percent blacker, and the ratio at the sending school, Harbordale, would have remained essentially the same (*Washington et al.* v. *School Board of Broward County, Fla.*, transcript, 1995, p. 4). The rationale offered for the allegation consisted of three key arguments:

1. Because the SBBC was unitary in 1992, the school board could not claim as a defense that it was bound by the 1987 consent decree.

2. If the school district was dual, the use of the rule was arbitrary, unfair, and unequally applied to the schools in the eastern corridor that were already desegregated and not to the newly built and opened schools in the western part of the county (p. 6).

3. The court lacked jurisdiction in the *Smith* case in 1987 to issue the consent decree, given that the district had been previously declared unitary (p. 11).

Given the facts, however, the district would have a difficult time demonstrating that it was not dual under the Green factors. The plaintiffs' attorney warned that if "a de novo review would be made of the school district today, . . . employing the Green factors, the court would probably be horrified to find that the system has not met the goals; that today, if anything, we believe the situation is much worse than existed at the time of the original order in 1970" (*Washington et al.* v. *School Board of Broward County, Fla.*, transcript, 1995, p. 12). The attorney continued: "I'm saying that if the court had to go through a de novo review, if it [the school district] is not unitary or had not been declared unitary, and this was considered a hearing to determine whether it was unitary under the Green factors, I don't think the county could meet the constitutional test. . . . If I have to go forward with the evidence, I think I could make a compelling case to show it is a dual system, it's intentionally dual, that there is a misapplication of the laws and there is no equal protection" (p. 13).

The school board's attorney took the position that the school district was neither dual nor unitary. Rather, it was characterized as partially unitary:

The Supreme Court has said that unitary is not a concept that is given to such an easy kind of definition that he [plaintiffs' attorney] is trying to give it. . . . He says that as a matter of law this school system is unitary and basically has been since 1971, and he uses unitary in its ultimate sense that a court has made a full determination of all the issues of the Green factors, or maybe there is even a seventh, student performance, and that the court has found this [the school district] to be a unitary school system.

If there is such a finding, if this [school district] has been unitary since 1971, . . . then race cannot be considered. . . . We consider race because race is relevant unless the school [district] has been declared to be a totally unitary system. . . . There is a point at which one can become unitary, but that . . . *depends upon discrete factual findings,* [that have] not occurred in this case [pp. 15–16, emphasis added].

In August 1995, Judge Ryskamp ruled on three questions: (1) Was the district court's 1971 declaration that the Broward system was unitary clear and unambiguous? (2) Did an issue of material fact exist as to whether the court relinquished jurisdiction of the case in 1979? and (3) What impact did the *Smith* v. *McFatter* (1987) consent decree have on the status of the Broward County school system? Judge Ryskamp granted summary judgment for the plaintiffs, finding that "there is no genuine issue of material fact that Judge Cabot's unappealed 1971 Order and Judge Eaton's unappealed 1979 decision to relinquish jurisdiction over the School Board together constitute a clear and binding declaration by this Court that the Broward County school system has attained full unitary status as of 1979. Because there is no evidence that Broward County's school system ever lost its unitary status, the Court finds that the school system was unitary when plaintiffs instituted their action in 1992 and remains so to this day" (*Washington et al.* v. *School Board of Broward County, Fla.,* 1995, p. 10).

The 1995 judgment and order did not explicitly address the status of the 1987 consent decree. However, the court stated, "Although the Court recognizes that retention of court jurisdiction is indeed incompatible with a finding of full unitary status it nonetheless cannot agree with defendants [the School Board]" (p. 8). For the school board, this position constituted a catch–22. Because full unitary status was attained as of 1979, when the court relinquished jurisdiction, the school board would have had to demonstrate that it lost its unitary status by purposefully adopting policies that were segregative. The catch–22 was that the school board had not done and could not do this because in the 1987 *Smith* v. *McFatter* consent decree the court stated: "The Court does not find the School Board of Broward County, Florida violated any laws of the State of Florida, or the Florida Constitution, or the laws of the United States, or of the U.S. Constitution" (p. 2). The situation was described clearly in the *Washington* case: "Since no precedent constitutional violation occurred, no basis for federal intervention into the School Board's policy decisions exists. . . . Consequently, the 1987 consent decree, to the extent that it states that jurisdiction over the parties has been retained, is nothing more than a retention to enforce an agreement between the parties to settle the litigation. This Court made no finding of a constitutional violation which would vest jurisdiction in the Court" (*Washington et al. v. School Board of Broward County, Fla.,* Order Granting Partial Summary Judgment, 1995, p. 9).

Race-Based Decisions and Equal Protection Violation

In January 1996, the district court ruled against the plaintiffs in the *Washington* case with respect to unconstitutional race-based discrimination when the requested boundary change was denied by the SBBC. The court found that the materials submitted by the plaintiffs did not support summary judgment. It did not find sufficient evidence of purposeful racial discrimination when the board denied a boundary change, and thus did not grant summary judgment. However, counsel for the school board and the plaintiffs in the *Washington* case did negotiate a settlement agreement that was approved by the school board. The board made several concessions in return for (1) dismissal of the charges of discrimination and conspiracy against the SBBC, (2) the plaintiffs' agreement to jointly file a stipulation informing the court that a settlement had been reached, and (3) the plaintiffs' agreement to join the SBBC in asking that a final order of dismissal from the court be entered within thirty days of when the court became informed that the parties had reached an agreement on fees and costs. In return, the board guaranteed anonymity to the infant plaintiffs; agreed that there would be "no retaliation against any student, parent, teacher, principal or school arising from any issue asserted in this litigation with the Board" (p. 2); agreed to award damages of $2,500 per family unit to the plaintiffs; and agreed to stipulate that the plaintiffs prevailed on their claim seeking a declaration that the school district was unitary, obtained the student assignment relief they sought, and were therefore entitled to reasonable attorney fees.

The agreement also granted, effective in the 1996–97 school year, the reassignment or boundary changes necessary for students attending Harbordale to attend Sunrise Middle School, and it agreed that the revised middle and high school boundaries would continue unless a demonstrated educationally appropriate need is found for new boundaries consistent with policies and practices within Broward County. Further, the processes used to achieve any future boundary changes would be in compliance with federal, state, and local laws. The agreement assured the five family plaintiffs (the children) and/or their siblings the option to be assigned to Sunrise Middle School and/or Ft. Lauderdale High School regardless of any subsequent boundary changes, as long as they live in the current geographic boundary of Harbordale Elementary School and are enrolled in the Broward County School System.

Washington Case: Final Judgment

The conclusion of the *Washington* case came on March 11, 1996, when Judge Ryskamp declared the Broward County School District to be a unitary. An unresolved issue remained, however—the 1987 consent decree. Much of the litigation and all of the major controversy about the school board's policies and administrative procedures related to desegregation were linked to that decree. What was the status of the 1987 consent decree given the final judgment that the school district is unitary?

Depending on one's viewpoint about the value of the 1987 consent decree as the conscience of the law operating to motivate and encourage the school district to desegregate, the action of the new attorneys for the defense in the *Smith* case in 1996, and the motion by the CCC to intervene, can be characterized as baffling, strange, or extraordinarily optimistic. The attorneys moved to terminate the consent decree, but it was the only real tool the plaintiffs possessed to leverage action from the school board in search of real desegregation.

The judge asked the attorney for *Smith*, the plaintiff who challenged inequality of educational opportunity in 1983, about the mood of the black community regarding the breakdown in neighborhoods in efforts to achieve diversity and get back to neighborhood schools. The response given may strike one as either a call for equal protection under the law or a sense of déjà vu recalling the U.S. Supreme Court's reasoning in *Plessy* v. *Ferguson* in 1896. The attorney said: "We want the focus to be more on making the schools in the African-American community equal to the schools in the western communities. . . . If the Consent Decree was standing in the way of the school board having the ability to do that which would be equal for all of the citizens of the community, that's really why he [Rae Smith] was in agreement with vacating and moving from this order, so that everybody could move on towards accomplishing the goals that hopefully everyone wants to see accomplished (*Smith v. McFatter*, Transcript of Hearing, 1996, p. 28).

Was this a call for a return to separate but equal, or an appeal for equality of educational opportunity and equal protection under the law consistent with valued principles of democracy? While the answer to this question may not be crystal clear, it is apparent, when the two statements are taken together, that quality education and equality of educational opportunity were both values subscribed to with a hope that "everybody could move on towards accomplishing the goals that, hopefully, everyone wants to see accomplished" (*Smith v. McFatter*, Transcript of Hearing, 1996, p. 28).

The motive behind the school board attorney's seeking a dismissal of the 1987 court order was fear of potential liability under the suit filed by the CCC (see *Citizens Concerned About Our Children et al.* v. *School Board of Broward County*, 1995). The CCC suit was filed in June 1995, and the Court declared on March 11, 1996, that the school district is unitary and had been since 1971. It was therefore unitary at the time of the filing of the 1992 *Washington* case. This judgment would make race-based decisions made since 1971, certainly since 1992, unconstitutional and illegal. There was reason for the school board's attorney to fear that the board would be liable for damages in civil suits for any race-based actions taken pursuant to the 1987 consent decree. The CCC suit alleged such actions, including "starbursting . . . [and] denying black students access to magnet programs; adopting practices that led to increased segregation; and administering resources to cause predominantly black schools to have lower quality educational materials, curricula, and facilities, and in hiring and staffing practices" (*Citizens Concerned About Our Children et al.* v. *School Board of Broward County*, 1995; see also *Smith v. McFatter*, Order of Dismissal and Termination of

Jurisdiction, 1996, p. 5). The CCC filed a motion to intervene and to quash or vacate the 1987 consent decree, and that motion was denied by the court.

In rendering his June 13, 1996, judgment on the status of the 1987 consent decree, Judge Ryskamp commented: "The parties to this action, case no. 83–6086, have . . . filed a Joint Stipulation for Order of Dismissal. The parties agree that, in light of this Court's August 16, 1995 Order declaring the Broward County school system to be unitary, it is appropriate to dismiss this action (*Smith* v. *McFatter*, Order of Dismissal and Termination of Jurisdiction, 1996, p. 6).

The court found that the provision in the 1987 consent decree (paragraph K) that retained jurisdiction to the court "simply retained jurisdiction by this Court to enforce the agreement reached in the settlement between the parties to that action, case no. 83–6086" (p. 7). The second finding of the court was that "the parties to the settlement agreement embraced in the 1987 consent order, specifically the defendant School Board of Broward County, have been operating under an ongoing duty to comply with the 1987 consent order, up through the time that the Court issued its Order declaring the Broward County School System to be unitary on August 16, 1995" (p. 7). Further, the court ruled that "all actions that were taken by the School Board to comply with the 1987 Consent Order were taken in good faith and in an effort to avoid being held in contempt of court for noncompliance" (p. 7). Thus, "having declared the Broward County School System to be unitary by Order dated August 16, 1995, the Court finds that the 1987 Consent Order is vacated as of August 16, 1995" (p. 7).

CONCLUSIONS AND IMPLICATIONS

The status of desegregation policies in the school board of Broward County at the outset of 1997 was one of high uncertainty. Given the June 13, 1996, rulings of Judge Ryskamp, it would appear that the court's finding of unitary status gave the court no further basis for jurisdiction. Thus the court's interest would be irrelevant under the law. However, the ruling of unitariness showed little appreciation for the work done by the Desegregation Task Force and put the school district in uncharted waters, assuming that it willed to and would be able to act unitarily when in fact its entire history in practice had not been unitary, though some positive steps had been taken in that direction. Indeed, the problem facing the district remains how to achieve and maintain desegregated K–12 public schools given a number of difficult constraints that lend themselves to lawsuits from those who feel that their constitutional rights are being violated. These constraints include demographic changes (that is, greater ethnic and racial diversity); the residual effects of an entrenched, historical pattern of segregated neighborhoods in parts of the county; emergent integrated neighborhoods; and western population growth in neighborhoods that are predominantly white.

The ruling of the district court judge has provided relief for a limited number of citizens and essentially makes moot the claim of those who have filed on behalf of the many African American children who continue to attend schools in which educational achievement levels, physical facilities, instructional programming, and faculty composition and sensitivity remain controversial issues.

The issues that confront the district are several, but the most critical appear to be the following:

1. How does the district embrace desegregation as a system priority in light of the court's ruling and the pressures to make its policies race-neutral? Moreover, what does *race-neutral* mean in light of remedial policies employed to date to achieve the level of desegregation and equality of educational opportunity that has been attained? Can the concept of diversity, employed by some other districts but brought into question in *Hopwood* v. *Texas* (1996) become a viable alternative for desegregation and be equally or more effective in providing quality equal educational opportunity in a diverse environment of multiple cultures, ethnic groups, and races?

2. Can the district, in the wake of *Hopwood* v. *Texas*, adequately craft its diversity policies such that they meet the criteria to be "narrowly tailored" and "show a compelling government interest"? Perhaps more fundamental, does the ruling in the *Hopwood* case even apply to the district and K–12 educational policies?

3. Will the district be bold and confident enough (a) to accept itself as unitary, based on its own assessment and knowledge of its policies, practices, and programs that have produced the degree of desegregation that is presently realized; (b) to move ahead and provide quality education and not be limited by traditional constraints in terms of racial thoughts and practices, being free to work with its communities to celebrate the individuality and diversity associated with each student and faculty member; and (c) to facilitate the achievement of quality education in a less than perfectly integrated environment, based on a clearly stated justification for diversity as a compelling governmental and educational interest?

4. How does the district maintain its commitment to both quality education and equal educational opportunity that goes beyond separate but equal while persuading the public that differential (equitable) allocation of resources is necessary to correct the existence of inequality in facilities and educational achievement within the system, and that diversity in staffing need not be limited to some artificially established cutoff point?

5. A long shot: Could the district bring itself to appeal the decision of the district court on grounds that the decision reflects an error in law; that there never was sufficient airing of the facts; that the interpretation of past rulings, in isolation from the facts, introduces uncertainty in place of the guidance and agreement provided in the 1987 court order; and that the judgment does little

in the way of ensuring equal protection of the law under the fourteenth amendment for all of its students? Black children, administrators, and faculty continue to be adversely affected by the residuals of past de jure segregation in housing and the remnants of some dual school system board policies, practices, and most seriously, attitudes.

From a review of the facts, opinions, judgments, strategies, policies, and processes that constitute the public education policy quadrangle, using Broward County's school system as an example, the tensions persist between fundamental principles of democracy in the policymaking quadrangle and the day-to-day bureaucratic or administrative requirements to operate an efficient, effective, economical, quality, and politically acceptable school system. Such tensions are often heightened or ameliorated by the orders and judgments of the courts. The results show clear winners and losers; unfortunately, throughout these long, drawn-out proceedings, the winners and losers are always the same.

Perhaps it is time for policymakers and superintendents in unitary K–12 public education systems to consider the relevance of the philosophical concepts of Immanuel Kant with respect to determining right action. Kant's Categorical Imperative provides a well-known formula for preserving equal educational opportunity if policymakers and administrators in unitary school systems accept it: "One ought to act such that the principle of one's act could become a universal law of human action in a world in which one would hope to live; and one ought to treat others as having intrinsic value in themselves and *not* merely as a means to achieve one's ends" (Kant, [1788] 1952, p. 7).

With respect to race and the legal system, the experience of the Broward County schools illustrates realities that are both greatly troubling and sometimes encouraging. Most clearly, at the least, the *search for reasonableness* that ideally characterizes the jurisprudence of constitutional democracy is exceedingly lengthy and run through with complexities. Two generations of searching since *Brown* v. *Board of Education* may lead an observer to conclude that constitutional fundamentals are often lost in the realities of present-day practice of law and politics. But the search endures, in hopes of reasonableness in support of the fundamental values of human dignity and a rule of law.

Cases Cited

Adarand Constructors, Inc. v. *Pena*, 115 S. Ct. 2097 (1995).

Allen et al. v. *Board of Public Instruction of Broward County, Florida*, 315 F.Supp. 1127 (S.D. Fla., 1970).

Allen et al. v. *Board of Public Instruction, Broward County, Florida*, 329 F.Supp. 251 (S.D. Fla., 1971).

Allen et al. v. *Board of Public Instruction of Broward County, Florida*, No. 70–31–Civ-J. (S.D. Fla., May 4, 1972).

Board of Education of Oklahoma City Public Schools v. *Dowell,* 498 U.S. 237 (1991).

Brown v. *Board of Education of Topeka, Kansas (Brown I),* 347 U.S. 483 (1954).

Brown v. *Board of Education of Topeka, Kansas (Brown II),* 349 U.S. 294 (1955).

Citizens Concerned About Our Children et al. v. *School Board of Broward County,* No. 95–6517–Civ-Ryskamp (S.D. Fla., June 1995).

Cummings v. *Richmond County Board of Education,* 175 U.S. 528 (1899).

Dowell v. *Board of Education of Oklahoma City Public Schools,* 338 F.Supp. 1256 (N.D. Okla., 1972).

Dred Scott v. *Sandford,* 60 U.S. (19 Howard) 393 (1857).

Freeman v. *Pitts,* 503 U.S. 492 (1991).

Gong Lum v. *Rice,* 275 U.S. 78 (1927).

Green v. *School Board of New Kent County,* 391 U.S. 430 (1968).

Hopwood v. *Texas,* WL 120235 (5th Cir., 1996).

Jacksonville Branch NAACP v. *Duval County School Board,* 883 F.2d 945 (11th Cir., 1989).

McLaurin v. *Oklahoma State Regents,* 339 U.S. 637 (1950).

Milliken v. *Bradley,* 433 U.S. 267 (1977).

Mills v. *Polk County Board of Public Instruction,* No. 92–2832 (11th Cir., 1993).

Missouri ex rel. Gaines v. *Canada,* 305 U.S. 337 (1938).

Plessy v. *Ferguson,* 163 U.S. 16 (1896).

Rae Smith and Raymond Smith, Jr., et al. v. *William McFatter, Superintendent of Schools, Broward County, Fla., et al.* No. 81–6200–Civ-JE (1982).

Rae Smith and Raymond Smith, Jr., et al. v. *William McFatter, Superintendent of Schools, Broward County, Fla., et al.* No. 83–6086–Civ-Ryskamp (1983).

Rae Smith and Raymond Smith, Jr., et al. v. *William McFatter, Superintendent of Schools, Broward County, Fla., et al.* Order. No. 81–6200–Civ-Ryskamp (Apr. 29, 1987).

Rae Smith and Raymond Smith, Jr., et al. v. *William McFatter, Superintendent of Schools, Broward County, Fla., et al.* Transcript of Hearing Before Hon. Kenneth L. Ryskamp, U.S. District Judge, in West Palm Beach, Florida. No. 83–6086. (S.D. Fla., Feb. 23, 1995).

Rae Smith and Raymond Smith, Jr., et al. v. *William McFatter, Superintendent of Schools, Broward County, Fla., et al.* Transcript of Hearing Before Hon. Kenneth L. Ryskamp. No. 83–6086–Civ-Ryskamp (May 30, 1996).

Rae Smith and Raymond Smith, Jr., et al. v. *William McFatter, Superintendent of Schools, Broward County, Fla., et al.* Order of Dismissal and Termination of Jurisdiction. No. 83–6086–Civ-Ryskamp (June 13, 1996).

Regents of the University of California v. *Bakke,* 438 U.S. 265 (1978).

Roberts v. *Boston,* 5 Cush. 198 (1849).

Sipuel v. *Oklahoma,* 332 U.S. 631 (1948).

Sweatt v. *Painter,* 339 U.S. 629 (1950).

Washington et al. v. *School Board of Broward County, Fla.* No. 92–6177-Civ-Ryskamp (1992).

Washington et al. v. *School Board of Broward County, Fla.* Transcript of Hearing Before Hon. Kenneth L. Ryskamp. No. 92–6177–Civ-Ryskamp (S.D. Fla., Jan. 26, 1995).

Washington et al. v. *School Board of Broward County, Fla.* Order Granting Partial Summary Judgment. No. 92–6177–Civ-Ryskamp (S.D. Fla., Aug. 16, 1995).

Washington et al. v. *School Board of Broward County, Fla.* Order Denying Plaintiffs' Motion for Partial Summary Judgment on Counts I and V, No. 92–6177–Civ-Ryskamp (S.D. Fla., Jan. 5, 1996).

Washington et al. v. *School Board of Broward County, Fla.* Final Judgment. No. 92–6177–Civ-Ryskamp (Mar. 11, 1996).

References

Caiden, G. E. "Excessive Bureaucratization: The J-Curve Theory of Bureaucracy and Max Weber Through the Looking Glass." In A. Farazmand (ed.), *Handbook of Bureaucracy.* New York: Dekker, 1994.

Cooper, P. J. *Hard Judicial Choices: Federal District Court Judges and State and Local Officials.* New York: Oxford University Press, 1988.

Dahl, R. A. *A Preface to Democratic Theory.* Chicago: University of Chicago Press, 1956.

Dye, T., and Zeigler, H. *The Irony of Democracy: An Uncommon Introduction to American Politics.* (8th ed.) Pacific Grove, Calif.: Brooks/Cole, 1990.

Guide to Congress. Washington, D.C.: Congressional Quarterly, 1976.

Hogan and Hartson Law Firm. "Letter to Virgil L. Morgan, Superintendent, Broward County Schools, re Unitary Status Issues," Jan. 27, 1994.

Hogan and Hartson Law Firm. "Memorandum to Superintendent re *Hopwood v. Texas,*" May 20, 1996.

Kant, I. *Preface to the Metaphysical Elements of Ethics.* In R. M. Hutchins (ed.), *Great Books of the Western World.* Chicago: Encyclopaedia Britannica, 1952. (Originally published 1788.)

Morgan, V. L. "Memo to Rod Sasse re Renaming of the Boundary Task Force," Jan. 4, 1994.

Myrdal, G., with Richard, S., and Rose, A. *An American Dilemma: The Negro Problem and Modern Democracy.* New York: HarperCollins, 1944.

Petruzielo, F. R. "Letter to Sadie Witmore, Subject: Case #RE-0491484," Apr. 14, 1994.

Tocqueville, A. de. *Democracy in America.* (A. Hacker, ed.). New York: Washington Square Press, 1972. (Originally published 1835.)

Waldo, D. *Public Administration in a Time of Turbulence.* Novato, Calif.: Chandler & Sharp, 1971.

CHAPTER TWENTY-EIGHT

Legal Impacts on Budgets and Finance

Anticipating Problems and Reacting to Realities

Thomas P. Lauth
Phillip J. Cooper

February 19, 1985, was a day like most other days for many city managers and county administrators. Like any other Tuesday morning, it began with conversations around the coffee pot and discussions of priorities, along with the usual concerns about immediate problems to be solved. But by lunchtime, things had changed. It was no longer an ordinary workday, because during the morning the U.S. Supreme Court had rendered a decision in the case of *Garcia* v. *San Antonio Metropolitan Transit Authority* (1985), which held that the provisions of the Fair Labor Standards Act (FLSA) did indeed apply to local government employees. In so doing, the Court overturned a 1976 decision that held that it did not apply (*National League of Cities* v. *Usery*, 1976).

Administrators were, to quote an earlier reaction to a Supreme Court justice's presentation (Douglas, [1940] 1969, p. 33), "shocked into a state of profound grumpiness" by the *Garcia* ruling, because it meant a major effort to reconsider their personnel and pay practices, as well as the likelihood of significantly increased costs. Not only that, but state and local government managers reacted vehemently to the fact that they had been caught unawares by an apparently feckless Court that failed to honor settled law. After all, had the Supreme Court not ruled in precisely the opposite direction only ten years earlier?

But no one should have been surprised by the *Garcia* ruling, at least not if they had been paying attention to the legal context within which they operated. In the first place, the 1976 ruling that had barred FLSA application to local government employees had itself reversed a 1968 precedent (*Maryland* v. *Wirtz*) and substantially undermined others as recent as 1973 (*Fry* v. *United States*). The *Usery* ruling was a dramatic departure from a number of decisions on the relationship between federalism and national regulatory authority under the Constitution's Commerce Clause.

Not only was nothing settled about that area of law, but the *Usery* ruling was itself an extremely shaky opinion authored by one of the most ideologically driven justices in recent Supreme Court history. Then Associate Justice William Rehnquist's opinion was a questionable argument based on a combination of old intergovernmental tax immunity doctrine and a novel reading of the Tenth Amendment to produce the notion that even if some kind of activity was regarded as within congressional authority to regulate commerce, there was nevertheless a bar to the application of federal regulation to states and localities. Not only was that approach a dramatic switch from recent precedents, but it also flew in the face of rulings more than a quarter-century old (see *United States* v. *California*, 1936; *New York* v. *United States*, 1946) and even substantially challenged opinions from the nineteenth-century era of Chief Justice John Marshall as well as the Constitution's Supremacy Clause.

From a more pragmatic perspective, Rehnquist's opinion represented anything but well-settled law. For one thing, he had only a bare majority of five in support of his argument. Moreover, Justice Harry Blackmun, who gave Rehnquist the critical fifth vote in *Usery*, warned in a concurring opinion that his agreement was limited to a very narrow set of circumstances. And if it was possible to question that Blackmun meant what he said, that doubt was soon to be removed. From 1981 through 1983, the Court issued a number of decisions raising serious concerns about the *Usery* doctrine, with Blackmun now leading the Court toward reversing the 1976 ruling (*Hodel* v. *Indiana*, 1981; *Hodel* v. *Virginia Surface Mining Association*, 1981; *Federal Energy Regulatory Commission* v. *Mississippi*, 1982; *EEOC* v. *Wyoming*, 1983).

Thus, from the beginning, governments should never have assumed that the *Usery* ruling on FLSA was firm. Further, the Court had warned public managers over a three-year period that it was preparing to overturn *Usery*. If any question remained before, certainly by 1983 informed observers were on notice that change was coming.

In the face of all that, how could so many managers have been caught so unprepared for what was obviously going to happen? Answers to that question tell a good deal about some dangerous views of the role of courts in fiscal matters. They show why more attention is required to understand how judges interact with and affect public finance and budgeting.

First of all, many administrators liked Rehnquist's ruling, not because it was good law (in fact, most who complain about the *Garcia* decision overturning *Usery* have never even read Rehnquist's ruling, or for that matter, the *Garcia* opinion itself), but because the outcome seemed to favor them. Not only that, the ruling seemed to be a case where the Court was declaring in loud tones why it was not only leaving the local governments alone but also protecting them against the intrusion of the national government. Staying out was a good idea to many administrators who already felt themselves overwhelmed by federal regulation. The ruling also promised to be helpful to their fiscal situation, protecting them from increases in personnel expenditures, already the largest item in many budgets.

But understanding why many public managers liked *Usery* does not explain why so many failed to see the *Garcia* decision coming. There are two basic problems. The first is that courts are often regarded not as normal participants in the ongoing discussion of the task of governing but as outside interlopers who impose on, intervene in, or interfere with important management decisions. While such a reaction is understandable, it is neither accurate nor helpful. Judges are, and always have been, at least in the United States, normal participants in public policy and administration. One of the important innovations in the U.S. Constitution was the inclusion of the judiciary as a coequal branch of government, subordinate to neither the legislative nor the executive branch. That model was in fact borrowed from state governments, whose courts had used the powers of judicial review to overturn actions by other state officials even before the U.S. Constitution was drafted (see *Holmes* v. *Walton,* 1780; *Trevett* v. *Weeden,* 1786; *Bayard* v. *Singleton,* 1787).

Quite apart from the basic tensions between administrators and courts, however, many administrators fail to monitor important judicial rulings that affect their activities. Many rely entirely on others to do that. Often the assumption is that the actions of courts are matters for attorneys, not managers. Nothing could be further from reality.

This chapter indicates why and how the decisions of courts affect the fiscal processes of government at all levels and shape the relationships between government and not-for-profit organizations that provide many public services under contract. It argues that while judicial involvement in budgetary and financial management practices may appear frustrating, it is a normal factor that needs to be considered not only at the time that budgets are developed and adopted but also in fiscal planning activities, whether they involve capital expenditures or operating budgets.

In general, courts influence budgeting and financial management in three ways. First, some rulings define, constrain, or facilitate budgetary processes. Second, courts issue specific rulings that directly affect spending. Third, some varieties of decisions indirectly drive fiscal processes.

EFFORTS TO CONTROL BUDGETARY AUTHORITY: NATIONAL-LEVEL ISSUES

Many of the most important fiscal arguments over the years have been about who controls decisions about appropriations and expenditures. At both national and state levels, these issues have often involved continuing debates between the legislature and the chief executive. These debates are about budgetary provisions that permit, mandate, or prohibit spending. They take the form of specific clashes over fiscal control but are in reality separation-of-powers debates.

The executive budget in the twentieth century traces its roots to the early Progressive Era and the so-called economy and efficiency movement (see Shuman, 1988). At the national level, it goes back to the Taft Commission that was authorized by Congress in 1910 and reported in 1912. The Budget and Accounting Act of 1921 came out of that movement. Not long thereafter, during the Great Depression, Franklin Delano Roosevelt and his Democratic congressional colleagues worked together to battle the economic collapse and then found themselves facing a world war. When political parties mattered more than they do today and when both branches were under the same partisan control, disputes over budget policy were more internal and less concerned with legal, even constitutional, debate. Indeed, there was often doubt that the budgetary function was being given the attention that it deserved (Key, 1940).

However, with more divided government and with Congress frustrated by an apparent aggrandizement of presidential powers on virtually all fronts, the stage was set by the 1970s for more open challenges (Shuman, 1988; Sundquist, 1981). Moreover, when the Nixon administration moved significantly to alter the system of costs and benefits of public programs through a shift to block grants and revenue sharing, the scene was set for conflict (Reagan, 1972). Efforts were made to move away from more tightly controlled categorical programs and to decentralize some control over the expenditure of dollars raised through federal taxes.

Not only that, but President Richard Nixon asserted a wide range of fiscal powers. One action was imposition by executive order of wage and price controls (*Amalgamated Meat Cutters & Butcher Workmen of North America* v. *Connally*, 1971). The administration also engendered a broad and intense conflict when it insisted, through impoundment of funds, that it could play a direct and unilateral role in the budget process by having, in effect, a second bite of the apple. According to the White House, not only was the president entitled to control budget preparation, but he also had power under the general executive authority to refuse to expend funds he thought inappropriate or unnecessary. This so-called budget impoundment power not only triggered litigation (noted later in this chapter), but also involved an interbranch battle when Congress enacted the Congressional Budget and Impoundment Control Act.

Additionally, the effort by the administration to politicize the Office of Management and Budget (Berman, 1979) led Congress to create its own fiscal analysis capability in-house with the establishment of the Congressional Budget Office, which has been the dominant fiscal analysis organization in the national government since its creation. The role of fiscal institutions like the Federal Reserve also became more important as the administration moved the dollar off the gold standard and into the international monetary exchange marketplace. Of course, as was often the case, these battles did not culminate until after Nixon had been driven from office by the Watergate scandal.

The Watergate episode was important for many reasons. The so-called imperial presidency had reached a point at which Congress was prepared to fight back to regain power. The Congressional Budget and Impoundment Control Act was adopted as a part of a larger body of legislation that included an expansion of the Freedom of Information Act, the Right to Privacy Act, the War Powers Resolution, and the National Emergencies Act. This general challenge to the rise in powers claimed by the president was supported by the Supreme Court's ruling in the Watergate tapes case (*United States* v. *Nixon,* 1974). The Court took a strong and unanimous position that a limit exists beyond which presidential claims about the meaning of Article II or Article I of the Constitution are limited—the kind of ruling that had been avoided for many years.

The next year the Supreme Court for the first time addressed the budget impoundment issue in *Train* v. *City of New York* (1975). Largely for reasons of policy disagreement with a Democratically controlled Congress, Nixon refused to make available for obligation funds appropriated by Congress for more than one hundred programs. Various cabinet officers were subsequently sued to release the appropriated funds. The administration offered a variety of justifications for impoundments, including the president's statutory authority under the Anti-Deficiency Act of 1905, his duty to manage the economy and control the national debt, the inherent powers of the president under Article II of the Constitution, and his executive responsibility to execute the budget. These obligations, the administration said, required the president to implement appropriations legislation without expending funds in inefficient and inappropriate ways. Commentators pointed out that prior presidential impoundments of funds ranged from Jefferson's refusal to expend funds appropriated for gunboats in 1803 to Roosevelt's constraints on public works projects, Truman's refusal in 1949 to use $700 million for the expansion of the Air Force, Eisenhower's decision on the Nike-Zeus missile program, and Kennedy's impoundments with respect to the B–70 bomber.

Critics also insisted, however, that most of the precedents cited were in military and foreign affairs, fields in which presidents are accorded unusual deference by the other branches (see *United States* v. *Curtis Wright Export Corporation*, 1936), or occurred during the financial emergency of the Great Depression. Moreover, earlier presidential impoundments had not been litigated. There were, however, decisions at the lower court levels that suggested that executive interpretations did not enjoy quite that much latitude (see *City of Los Angeles* v. *Coleman*, 1975; *National Council of Community Mental Health Centers* v. *Weinberger*, 1973; *People ex rel. Bakalis* v. *Weinberger*, 1973).

In the Congressional Budget and Impoundment Control Act of 1974, Congress moved to constrain the president's ability to defer expenditures and made impoundments subject to congressional review under two categories: rescissions or permanent cancellation of budget authority, and deferrals or temporary withholding of budget authority within the fiscal year. In later years, however, the Supreme Court's ruling overturning one-house legislative vetoes (*Immigration and Naturalization Service* v. *Chadha*, 1983) placed the validity of portions of the 1974 act in some doubt. Hence, while the statute remains in place, later Congresses have avoided pressing for its use where, as was the situation in the Reagan years, the administration seemed likely to use the opportunity to seek Supreme Court review of the statute's constitutionality.

On at least two occasions since then, the Supreme Court has sent signals that while it was not particularly interested in intervening where the White House and Capitol Hill were in agreement, there are limits to creativity, even if it appears to arise from compromise rather than conflict. Thus the Court warned that jointly appointed regulatory commissions, with some members selected by the president and others by Congress violated the Appointments Clause of Article II of the Constitution (*Buckley* v. *Valeo*, 1976). The more direct admonition, however, came in the dispute over the Gramm-Rudman-Hollings Budget Deficit Reduction Act.

Gramm-Rudman was one of many schemes that, it was claimed, would force a balanced budget. It was also one of a series of efforts, like military base closings, in which the players tried to divert the political heat away from themselves by creating a device that forced action but avoided the need for either the president or members of Congress to take direct responsibility for specific spending cuts. The machinery depended on a finding by the comptroller general (head of the U.S. General Accounting Office) that the statutory spending limits had been exceeded, based on figures submitted by the Office of Management and Budget. Whenever the comptroller general reached such a finding, he would issue the finding to the president, in effect ordering him to sequester funds from both the domestic and the military and foreign affairs sides of the budget. Not surprisingly, there was heavy opposition to the legislation, such that an understanding had to be reached even to get the bill to the floor for a final vote. Under that agreement, it was understood that an immediate challenge to the new budget-limiting device would be launched, with an expedited appeal to the Supreme Court in order to get a ruling before the process moved too far downstream.

Indeed, such a challenge was immediately launched with the cooperation of then Congressman Michael Synar, and it quickly found its way to the Supreme Court. In *Bowsher* v. *Synar* (1986), the Court struck down the mechanism on grounds that the comptroller general was a legislative officer who was, in effect, authorized by the statute to order the president not to spend money that had already been appropriated. Put differently, a decision was being made to nullify properly adopted appropriations legislation, passed in accord with Article I and signed into law by the president. Even in a time when the Court was willing to tolerate a variety of experiments (see *Thomas* v. *Union Carbide Agricultural Products,* 1985; *Commodity Futures Trading Commission* v. *Schor,* 1986; *Mistretta* v. *United States,* 1989; *Morrison* v. *Olson,* 1988), the Gramm-Rudman process went too far.

Questions about what the courts might do also caused considerable concern in 1995 and 1996, when the government was shut down because of budget conflicts and a so-called train wreck loomed on the horizon. With a refusal to adopt continuing resolutions, a threat not to extend the debt limit, and the presence of the Anti-Deficiency Act to block unauthorized spending existing simultaneously with various statutory entitlement programs and billions of dollars of outstanding contracts, the dangers of pushing many aspects of fiscal life into the courts was more than a little frightening. Quite apart from specific judgments affecting policy, rulings from such challenges might very well have reopened basic separation-of-powers issues. Although that did not come to pass, even the threat of it was sobering to decision makers at both ends of the avenue.

EFFORTS TO CONTROL BUDGET AUTHORITY: ISSUES IN THE STATES

At the state level, efforts at controlling budget authority have taken the form of controversies over (1) separation of powers in budget preparation, approval, and execution; (2) the limits of impoundment; (3) the chief executive's prerogative to reduce spending when faced with a revenue shortfall; (4) use of the line-item veto; and (5) the status, scope, and format of appropriations legislation.

Separation of Powers

Most state governments have an executive budget system in which governors are responsible for recommending to the legislature a budget for the next fiscal period. The executive budget is a comprehensive document that not only verifies the accuracy of agency estimates and the soundness of agency requests, but weighs their importance in relationship to each other and assesses their compatibility with the policy goals and program objectives of the governor. In such a system, budget preparation and execution are executive branch responsibilities, and budget approval or enactment is the responsibility of the legislative branch (Abney and Lauth, 1989). This separation of powers typically is anchored in the state constitution and usually is kept in balance by political adjustments between the branches. Occasionally, however, individuals or groups representing the interest of one of the branches, turn to the courts in an effort to alter the relationship.

Such was the case in Mississippi in 1983 when the state supreme court declared unconstitutional the long-standing practice of state legislators serving on boards and commissions that have executive responsibilities. Prior to 1983 the Commission on Budget and Accounting, an eleven-member body including the governor as nonvoting chairperson and legislative leaders from each chamber, prepared the budget and submitted it to the legislature. "The legislative leaders, who controlled the Budget Commission, made the major budget decisions during the budget preparation, legislative approval and budget execution phases" (Clynch, 1991, p. 125). In a case initiated by then Attorney General and later Governor Bill Allain, the Mississippi Supreme Court prohibited legislative involvement in budget execution through service on boards and commissions, but it did not require the state's legislative leadership to abandon its practice of developing a budget for submission to the legislature (*Alexander* v. *Mississippi,* 1983). Following the court decision, Mississippi created an executive branch agency with responsibility for budget preparation and execution. Today, Mississippi has an executive Department of Finance and Administration and a Joint Legislative Budget Committee. The Mississippi legislature receives two budget proposals, one from the governor and one from the legislative leadership. The *Alexander* decision is credited by Professor Edward Clynch with moving the state toward "a more executive-centered system" within a framework of separation of powers (see Clynch, 1986, 1991).

Limits of Impoundment

Impoundment, the executive act of withholding and not making available for obligation funds appropriated by the legislature, happens at the state level as well as in Washington. Motives for impoundment may be largely managerial, to achieve efficiency or to avoid deficiency in spending, or essentially political, to serve the policy objectives of the chief executive. In the context of separation of powers, the practice of impoundment raises the question of whether appropriations enacted by the legislature are permissive or mandatory for the executive. Two cases serve to illustrate the issue.

As noted earlier, almost from the beginning of the republic, presidents have engaged in limited impoundments. It was not, however, until President Nixon's aggressive use of impoundment between 1969 and 1973 that impoundment became an issue for adjudication. In *Train v. City of New York* (1975), cited earlier, the Supreme Court avoided the constitutional issues between Congress and the president. However, in the absence of statutory authority permitting impoundment, the Court directed the administration to make available to states funds appropriated by Congress for water pollution control.

The New York State Court of Appeals was more definitive in asserting that the governor of that state possesses no inherent or implied power to impound funds that have been appropriated by the legislature (*County of Oneida v. Berle*, 1980). The 1977 New York executive budget contained a $12 million item for the sewage works reimbursement program. The legislature added $14 million. Of the $26 million appropriated, the Division of Budget withheld $7 million and made available for obligation $19 million. Oneida County maintained that it had been improperly denied reimbursement for the operation and maintenance of its sewage treatment works. In defense, the state argued that the governor has a constitutional obligation to maintain a balanced budget and that the power to impound follows from that obligation. The court disagreed, holding that the governor does not have a constitutional power to impound funds and has responsibility only to propose and not to maintain a balanced budget (Axelrod, 1989, p. 66, and Zimmerman, 1981). Zimmerman (1981) reports that gubernatorial use of the line-item veto, which had been infrequently used prior to this decision, substantially increased following it.

Authority to Reduce Spending

Related to the issue of executive impoundment of appropriated funds is the chief executive's prerogative to reduce spending when faced with a revenue shortfall. In one set of cases, at least, the outcome seems to have depended on selecting the proper rationale for the action. In the spring and early summer of 1991, Georgia revenue collections were substantially behind the rate of growth on which the state's 1992 fiscal year budget had been projected. In July 1991, less than two weeks into the 1992 fiscal year, Governor Zell B. Miller ordered a one-day-per-month furlough for all state employees. The furlough plan, which was expected to save the state $8 million per month, was subsequently disallowed by a state superior court (*Georgia State Employees Union, Local No. 1985 v. Miller*, 1991; *Georgia Association of Educators v. Miller*, 1991).

The Fulton County Superior Court held that if the governor had based the furlough plan on a stated desire to produce efficiency in state government, the action probably would have been legal because the 1962 state Budget Act allows the governor to supervise and manage the Office of Planning and Budget. However, because the governor presented the plan as an effort to bring about a temporary budget cut before the convening of a special session of the General Assembly approximately one month later, the action amounted to an infringement of the General Assembly's authority to amend the appropriations act and therefore was a violation of the state constitution. A lesson for budgeters is that the legality of budgetary decisions sometimes depends on the proffered justification. In short, expressed intent is basic.

Wisconsin faced a similar set of circumstances in the 1980–1981 fiscal year. A projected deficit led the Wisconsin secretary of administration to direct all agencies to reduce allotments by 4.4 percent. The Department of Instruction informed school districts that state aid would be cut. Municipalities also were informed of reductions in local assistance payments. In *City of Milwaukee* v. *Linder* (1981) (and its companion case, *School District of La Farge* v. *Linder*), the court ruled that although the secretary of administration had authority to reduce allotments for state operating agencies and programs, aid for education and local assistance payments was not an appropriation subject to allotment. Proper responses to a financial crisis might include legislative revision of statutes or appropriations, but not abuse of discretion by the state budget office. These cases affected the budget process by (1) more narrowly defining the executive's budget authority, (2) limiting the scope of the executive's ability to deal with budget shortfalls, and (3) defining the share of the budget that is comprised of formula-driven programs and entitlements (J. Montgomery, chief of budget operations, Department of Administration, State of Wisconsin, personal communication, 1986).

The Wisconsin and Georgia responses to revenue shortfalls illustrate differences in the approaches and perhaps even in the values that administrators and judges bring to decision making. As noted earlier, in Wisconsin the executive branch proposed a 4.4 percent across-the-board budget reduction, and in Georgia the governor proposed a one-day-per-month furlough for all state employees. On the face of things, both proposals seem like reasonable decisions aimed at responding quickly to fiscal crises and distributing the burden of the decision equally to all agencies and programs. However, in each instance administrators seem to have ignored or at least misperceived the importance of issues that judges determined to be important. In Georgia, the court perceived the proposed action as a violation of separation of powers, and in Wisconsin the court perceived the proposed action as an abuse of executive authority. At the risk of oversimplification, it appears that administrators were concerned with outcomes to the neglect of relationships of intent and processes, while the judges emphasized authority of institutions and related processes. In both instances the state lost, not because it was pursuing inappropriate outcomes, but because the executive branch exceeded its authority or did not adhere to correct process. Public financial managers should not only obey the law in their day-to-day operations, but also be mindful of the ways in which courts and judges are likely to assess their policy decisions.

The Line-Item Veto

The line-item veto is the power of chief executives to veto lines or items of an appropriations bill without having to negate the entire bill. This power developed in the states in part because the executive veto was ineffective when dealing with wasteful and pork barrel spending in appropriations bills. Unlike other bills, appropriations bills are not constitutionally limited to one subject, represent a wide variety of compromises, and typically contain many items favored by the governor as well as a few objectional items added to the executive budget by the legislature. Vetoing such a bill is always extremely difficult and usually unthinkable for governors. The line-item veto was intended to restore the governor's ability to protect the executive budget by being able to veto objectional elements of appropriations bills.

The line-item veto is not only used to eliminate appropriation items (dollars). It also may be directed against nonmonetary provisions that impose conditions or limitations on items of expenditure, or against nonmonetary provisions of appropriations bills that constitute general purpose legislation (Abney and Lauth, 1997).

Substantial litigation has involved use of the line-item veto. Unfortunately, cases often have been quite fact-specific, and court decisions have resulted in numerous inconsistencies among the states. Richard Briffault's (1993) analysis of the item veto in state courts provides the best guidance to this litigation.

What is an appropriations bill? Briffault reports that state courts have answered this question in three ways: (1) by limiting the availability of the item veto to those bills that have the primary purpose of making appropriations (*Bengzon* v. *Secretary of Justice of the Philippine Islands,* 1937), (2) by considering any bill that contains an appropriation to be an appropriations bill (*State ex rel. Kleczka* v. *Conta,* 1978), and (3) by reviewing each bill to determine "whether the bill contains an appropriation which could significantly affect the governor's budgeting responsibility" (*Junkins* v. *Branstad,* 1989, p. 1199). Briffault argues that the "any appropriation" standard is the easiest standard to apply and most consistent with the purpose of the item veto.

What is an appropriation? Even though entitlements and formulae funding have impacts on state spending, Briffault reports that state courts have generally excluded them from definitions of appropriations if they do not actually appropriate state funds (*Harbor* v. *Deukmejian,* 1987; *Karcher* v. *Kean,* 1984).

What is a vetoable item? In some states, governors are permitted to veto general legislation that the legislature incorporates into an appropriations bill (*State ex rel. Turner* v. *Iowa State Highway Commission,* 1971), but in other states governors are limited to vetoing monetary items (*Jessen Associations, Inc.* v. *Bullock,* 1975).

The level of specificity at which vetoes are permitted varies across the states. Some courts permit the governor to break up a legislative section, while other courts do not. For example, vetoing specific salaries within an appropriation for wages and salaries was permitted in Florida (*Green v. Rawls,* 1960), but in Massachusetts the court did not permit the governor to veto parts of what the legislature structured as a broader single item (*Opinion of Justices,* 1981).

Briffault reports that most state courts permit governors to veto nonmonetary words and phrases as long as the effect is not to create new legislation that the legislature did not pass (for example, *Brown v. Firestone,* 1980; *Colorado General Assembly v. Lamm,* 1985).

In Wisconsin, the Supreme Court interpreted the state's item veto provision broadly to permit the governor to veto words, phrases, letters from words, and digits from numbers—as long as what remains is a "complete and workable" law (*State ex rel. Wisconsin Senate v. Thompson,* 1988). However, the Wisconsin constitution was amended in 1990 to prevent the governor from making new words by striking letters, but it remains silent on making new numbers by striking digits (Briffault, 1993, p. 1197). At stake in many of the state cases is the relative power of legislatures and governors to influence appropriations outcomes. Briffault suggests that the legislature's power is enhanced if only broad appropriations categories can be vetoed by governors, and the governor's power is enhanced if he or she is permitted to separate from broadly defined items specific subitems to be vetoed. Presumably this is because governors may be less willing to veto broadly defined items that include a combination of preferred as well as objectional subitems.

At stake also, Briffault observes, is the extent to which gubernatorial use of the item veto amounts to the creation of new legislation that the legislature did not pass. Of course, if this were not the case to some extent, the basic purpose of the line-item veto to protect the executive budget against legislative particularism would be defeated. Nevertheless, state courts seem to have been cautious (except perhaps in Wisconsin) to limit gubernatorial use of the item veto to negating legislative actions while not permitting governors to cross over too far into legislative terrain by using the item veto to create legislation that the legislature is unlikely ever to have enacted.

Finally, the item-reduction veto is a special form of the line-item veto possessed by governors in eleven of the forty-three item-veto states—ten as constitutional provisions and one by state supreme court interpretation (*Commonwealth ex rel. Attorney General v. Barnett,* 1901). Emergence of the reduction veto resulted from failure of the ordinary item veto to achieve its objectives. Legislatures began to bundle objects of expenditure into broad appropriation categories so as to make the negation of particular projects or items difficult, if not impossible. The item-reduction veto is an attempt to protect the ordinary line-item veto from legislative countermeasures.

A legislated form of presidential line-item veto went into effect on January 1, 1997, based on perceptions of state experiences. A constitutional challenge by six congressional foes of this legislation was rejected June 26, 1997, when the Supreme Court ruled that they lacked standing to sue (*Raines* v. *Byrd*, 1997).

Appropriating Federal Funds

State legislatures have constitutional authority to appropriate state funds, including state funds that provide a match for federal grants. But do state legislatures have authority to appropriate in detail the federal funds that are received by state agencies? This is an important question because federal funds may amount to as much as 25 percent of the budget in many states.

In the mid-1970s, the Pennsylvania General Assembly decided to exercise over federal funds the full control that it exercises over state funds by requiring that all federal funds coming into the Commonwealth be deposited in the General Fund. Monies allotted to Pennsylvania by the Law Enforcement Assistance Administration were involved. The case raised two questions: (1) Does the General Assembly's authority over state funds extend to federal funds? (2) Does the executive or the legislature have authority to control the expenditure of federal funds?

The Pennsylvania Supreme Court held that funds that Pennsylvania receives from the federal government do not belong to officers or agencies of the executive branch but to the Commonwealth, and that the General Assembly has constitutional authority to appropriate in detail all funds, including federal monies that flow through the Commonwealth treasury (*Shapp* v. *Sloan*, 1978). The court noted that the Commonwealth is not free to use funds obtained from the federal government for its own purposes but must use them pursuant to agreements with the federal government. It also found no evidence that Congress considers such state legislative involvement in appropriations of federal funds an encroachment on the supremacy of the federal government. This case suggests to fiscal managers that budgeting issues sometimes involve larger issues of separation of powers and federalism.

Status, Scope, and Format of Appropriations

What is the status of a budget act? Budget acts usually are the most important pieces of legislation enacted in a legislative session. The budget act provides spending authorization for state agencies and programs and, unlike general purpose legislation, which typically is limited to a single subject, the budget act encompasses the entire range of state government functions. In Kentucky the budget has been held to be a "bill" rather than a resolution; when enacted, it is incorporated into Chapter 47 of the Kentucky Revised Statutes and completely revised each legislative session with passage of the budget bill for the next biennium (Hackbart, 1991). Further, *Armstrong v. Collins* (1986) held that the budget bill is superior to other bills and overrides other existing state statutes.

What may be contained in a budget act? Courts usually give legislatures wide latitude regarding content as long as legislatures adhere to their own procedures when enacting legislation. That only seems appropriate for the most populous branch of government in a democratic society. However, a 1995 Pennsylvania case suggests limits to what may be contained in an appropriations act (Feustel, 1996). The Pennsylvania constitution requires that general appropriations bills "embrace nothing but appropriations for the executive, legislative and judicial departments of the Commonwealth, for the public debt and for the public schools" (p. 8). In *Common Cause v. Commonwealth* (1995), the court held that appropriations to civic and community groups were not permitted. The Commonwealth argued that the appropriations in question were being made to state agencies. The court held, however, that agencies themselves could not use some of the money that was appropriated and that by identifying groups, not agencies, as the recipients of the appropriations, the legislature was usurping the executive branch's spending prerogatives. Although the court allowed most of the legislature's appropriations to stand, items that did not fall into the five allowable categories for a general appropriations act were disallowed. The lessons for budgeters from this case are that courts may not tolerate legislative infringement of executive branch spending prerogatives, and that it is safer to earmark appropriations for government agencies than for nongovernmental groups.

LEGAL RULINGS THAT MANDATE FISCAL ACTIONS

Varied judicial actions directly affect budgetary and financial management matters. Examples include remedial decrees that mandate spending for various types of programs, personnel-related decisions that may influence what is often the largest single category of spending in many budgets, and regulatory and condemnation-related proceedings that have significant impacts on planning and capital expenditures.

Remedial Orders

Chapter Twenty-Four dealt in detail with orders issued by courts in a wide range of fields from prison and jail conditions to school desegregation and mental health treatment. While the Supreme Court, as that chapter indicated, has warned federal courts to restrain any temptation to impose sweeping injunctions that would impose excessively broad or unjustified burdens on state and local governments, there remain many jurisdictions that continue under the obligations of remedial decrees. In many cases, the decrees are not the result of judicial findings following trial but the consequences of negotiated agreements that take the form of consent decrees.

While there have long been protests by administrators against these orders that have so often been labeled as judicially imposed burdens, the fact is that it is not uncommon for managers to encourage litigation against their institutions in an effort to obtain court-ordered support for their needs (see Wood, 1990). While there have been arguments about whether remedial orders have brought as many resources as some assume they have, and about the level of costs and burdens that have accompanied those judgments (see Di Iulio, 1990; Harriman and Staussman, 1983), no corrections or mental health practitioner with many years of experience will doubt that many of the reforms and improvements that have come in those fields have followed judicial rulings. They know that when county schools compete for resources with county jails, state health care programs compete with state prisons, or mental health programs compete with transportation programs, there has historically been little doubt as to likely outcomes.

The other criticism of remedial decrees centers on the fact that, on the one hand, court orders place restrictions on administrative choices. On the other hand, no public official ever legally possessed the discretion to violate the Constitution.

Quite apart from this more visible debate over remedial decrees, there are less well understood but important dimensions for those concerned with budgets, both operating and capital. First, it is important for newly arriving administrators in a jurisdiction or agency to know whether they are inheriting obligations under existing court orders or consent decrees. It has happened in areas of high turnover, such as corrections administration, that current administrators have seemed completely unaware of old commitments and suits have been brought challenging the administration's failure to implement policies that were contained in consent decrees issued years before.

Another concern arises because it may take a considerable amount of time to carry out remedial obligations, particularly where new facilities are required, as is often the case with respect to jail conditions. Questions arise about how to balance the need for long-term financing of capital projects while carrying sufficient expenditures in current budgets to maintain facilities, albeit at inadequate levels, until the new facilities are ready.

An additional issue is presented where remedial orders are accompanied by requirements to support a court-ordered monitor or special master. While these situations are less common than they were in the 1970s or early 1980s, they still arise from time to time. The problem is not only the need to pay the costs of the special master, but also to provide sufficient mechanisms of accountability to protect the community against possible fiscal abuses.

More recently, many financial issues have arisen in connection with school finance litigation. For example, local school boards have been required to reimburse parents for private school tuition when parents have unilaterally judged that the local district was not adequately honoring the Individualized Education Plan established for their child under the Individuals with Disabilities Education Act (*Florence County School District Four* v. *Carter,* 1993).

Personnel-Related Rulings

Personnel decisions may be less visible and create less commotion than court-ordered institutional reform or school finance rulings, but they may have fiscal consequences that are at least as important. Thus there is no doubt, whatever the argument on the merits, that the *Garcia* ruling discussed at the beginning of this chapter has had important implications for local governments. But there can be other less visible rulings with even greater consequences. Thus when the Supreme Court ruled that retirement annuity programs could not pay women different payback rates or charge different monthly contributions than for men, the impact was substantial (*Los Angeles Department of Water and Power* v. *Manhart,* 1978).

Of course, many of the rulings concerned with human resources issues are neither regulatory nor civil rights matters but contract issues. While it is clear that traditional collective bargaining agreements have produced contracts that have been the basis for many important rulings, a recent new dimension is important. As increased contracting is done for social services, many new issues need to be considered (see Ruth Hoogland DeHoog's discussion in Chapter Twenty-Nine of this book). Thus, the General Accounting Office's (GAO) director of education and employment issues, Linda G. Morra, wrote to Senator Paul Simon, Democrat from Illinois: "Private sector firms receive billions of dollars annually in federal government contracts for goods and services. While these firms generally profit from their business with the federal government, some also violate federal laws that protect the rights of employees to bargain collectively" (U.S. General Accounting Office, 1995, p. 1). Specifically, GAO found some eighty firms receiving a total of more than $23 billion in federal contracts that had violated the National Labor Relations Act. That figure represented approximately 13 percent of the total of $182 billion expended in federal contracts in 1993 (p. 1).

Regulatory Takings

Labor laws represent only one of many kinds of regulatory programs for which government at all levels is responsible. At the same time that legislators and administrators face pressures to protect the environment and public health, they must also operate in a contemporary context in which citizens are aware that they are protected by the Fifth and Fourteenth Amendments to the U.S. Constitution against the taking of private property without due process, including just compensation. Courts play an important role in addressing the potential tension between these two facts of public life: they have been asked with increasing frequency to expand the situations in which compensation is required, and to reconcile changes with potentially significant fiscal impacts.

Traditionally, an important distinction has been drawn between regulations and the taking of property. Thus, when it becomes necessary to cut diseased trees in a neighborhood to prevent spread of damage, that is a matter of regulation that can be implemented by states and localities under so-called police power—the authority to regulate in matters of health, safety, or public welfare, under the Tenth Amendment to the Constitution. As Justice William O. Douglas wrote, regulation generally entails a cost; it is part of the cost of maintaining the society (*Day-Brite Lighting* v. *Missouri,* 1952). In that case, the Court rejected a challenge to a Missouri law that required employers to give their people four hours off with pay on election day. A quarter century before that, the Court had rejected challenges to emerging zoning laws on grounds that they represented barriers to the use and enjoyment of private property (*Euclid* v. *Ambler,* 1926). Even some of the justices who had the strongest commitments to individual rights in history have upheld regulations on private property. Thus, for example, Justice Douglas wrote for the Court upholding a Long Island ordinance that limited residents in private homes to family members (*Village of Belle Terre* v. *Borass,* 1974).

Conversely, the Court has not allowed regulatory powers to be used in any way that government sees fit without limits or penalties. Thus, when East Cleveland, Ohio, attempted to limit the definition of the term *family* for purposes of its zoning ordinances to what amounted to the nuclear family, the Court drew the line (*Moore* v. *East Cleveland,* 1977). The Court would not permit a community effectively to exclude from residential areas group homes for mentally retarded residents (*City of Cleburne, Texas* v. *Cleburne Living Center,* 1985).

More specifically, the Supreme Court has issued rulings indicating a willingness to look more carefully at purported regulations to determine whether they cross the line and become uncompensated takings of property (see, for example, *Nollan* v. *California Coastal Commission,* 1987). In a South Carolina case involving restrictions on coastal development, the Court suggested that where the subject to be regulated does not reach the rough equivalent of a nuisance, government may be engaged in a taking of property for which compensation is required rather than a regulation (*Lucas* v. *South Carolina Coastal Council,* 1992). But moving in that direction takes the Court back to an approach in which it becomes extremely difficult to make regulations that cover many people or situations in a coherent planning process. The Court gave notice of its general inclination, apparent in the South Carolina case, to further constrain regulation and force compensation for what amounted to regulatory takings in *Dolan* v. *City of Tigard* (1994). In that case, the Court struck down a Tigard, Oregon, community development code that had a 15 percent open space requirement and a demand for developers to dedicate land for pedestrian pathways, and in certain places a greenway adjoining the flood plain amounted to a taking of property. The dissenting justices pointed out that the majority had shifted from the idea that government actions are presumed to be lawful to a situation under which local governments are faced with a very substantial burden of proof in crafting important policies. There are continuing efforts to expand the concept of regulatory takings and to constrain regulation (see Fischel, 1995). The fiscal implications of such moves are obvious and severe.

Governments as Regulators and as Market Participants

Government is more than a regulator of property and the marketplace in which it is bought and sold. Increasingly, governments are major market participants. And when government changes roles by moving from power to contract as a mode of action, its legal character may change, along with the processes by which it accomplishes its goals. Thus, when South Dakota, which operated a cement plant, gave preferences to in-state buyers, the Supreme Court upheld the state against a challenge that claimed a violation of interstate commerce restrictions. Writing for the majority, Justice Harry Blackmun observed that the critical distinction was the fact that the state was acting as a market participant rather than as a market regulator (*Reeves* v. *Stake,* 1980). In 1983, the Court upheld, against a Commerce Clause challenge, a Boston requirement that 50 percent of employees in city contracts had to be city residents (*White* v. *Massachusetts Council of Construction Workers,* 1983), again citing the market participant theory.

Many uncertainties arise as public sector organizations increasingly enter the marketplace. Thus the very year after the Court upheld the Boston contract requirements, it struck down a Camden, New Jersey, ordinance modeled on the Boston provision. This time the Court ruled that while the market regulator versus market participant idea held with respect to the Commerce Clause, it did not bar challenges based on other portions of the Constitution (*United Building Trades Council* v. *Camden,* 1984), in this case the Privileges and Immunities Clause. In that same year, the Court struck down an Alaska timber sales program that required as a part of the contract that state-owned timber be processed in Alaskan mills before it could be exported from the state (*South Central Timber Development* v. *Wunnicke,* 1984). Rejecting the state's argument that it was merely a seller of timber, Justice Byron White wrote for the plurality: "The market-participant doctrine permits a State to influence 'a discrete identifiable class of economic activity' in which it is a major participant. Contrary to the State's contention, the doctrine is not carte blanche to impose any conditions that the state has the economic power to dictate, and does not validate any requirement merely because the State imposes it upon someone with whom it is in contractual privity" (p. 96).

These are only some of the dimensions of life in the new world of markets that shape the ways in which governments can raise and expend funds and purchase or vend goods and services, activities at the very heart of the fiscal life of those public sector organizations.

INDIRECT INVOLVEMENT IN FISCAL MANAGEMENT

While many direct implications of public law are important in budgeting and public finance, there is also a range of indirect but crucial impacts. Therefore, in addition to giving attention to the more obvious interactions between fiscal managers and judges, public administrators should observe the courts as ongoing participants in policy and management processes.

The courts have issued rulings in a wide array of cases that have helped to shape and reshape the fiscal infrastructure. Cases like those discussed earlier that reconsider the roles of government in the economy, as regulators and as market participants, are but a part of a much larger body of law based on challenges to traditional assumptions about the essential elements of fiscal life. Related is the continuing conversation about the structure of government and the powers and limits in the various parts of the public sector—another important field in which contemporary tensions in law and management have played out.

Reshaping the Fiscal Infrastructure: Structures, Powers, Limits

Decisions that affect the fiscal infrastructure and the structures and limits of power clearly set conditions and control assumptions on which decisions about public finance, budget preparation, and budget execution are made. Thus when the Supreme Court ruled that states could not tax corporations doing mail order business in a state but not operating warehouses or trucking firms there, despite the fact that the firm involved was one of the largest retailers vending products to the citizens of North Dakota, it was a decision of far greater importance than just what would happen with the Quill Corporation (*Quill Corporation* v. *North Dakota*, 1992). With more and more businesses no longer operating their own warehouses and trucking operations but relying on shipping firms to provide the warehouse services, and operating through computer or telephone-based ordering systems rather than through stores or sales representatives, limitations on the ability to tax a very significant aspect of retail business is of crucial importance. That is particularly true at a time when consumption-based taxes are playing increasingly important roles in the economy. Similarly, when courts define the boundaries of states' authority to impose so-called severance taxes on shipment of oil, gas, or minerals to other states or foreign countries, they limit what are sometimes otherwise weak fiscal players from obtaining revenue from their natural resource bases (*Maryland* v. *Louisiana*, 1981; *Commonwealth Edison* v. *Montana*, 1981).

Determinations about the jurisdiction and authority of states and localities to regulate or tax corporate operations also have critical consequences for communities in which those firms do business. This is a growing challenge in this era of national and multinational firms that move millions of dollars around the world overnight and frequently restructure themselves and the markets in which they do business. Firms have been changing so rapidly that it is often difficult for states to determine how to tax the profits associated with their transactions. For example, one state was told that it could not tax a corporation from another state that sold the stock of a firm that operated within the state to finance an acquisition of a third firm (*Allied Signal* v. *Director, Division of Taxation*, 1992). Conversely, the Supreme Court has not been willing to strip states of all regulatory authority in situations involving corporate mergers or moves (see, for example, *CTS Corporation* v. *Dynamics Corporation*, 1987).

The issue of regulation of markets by states or their subdivisions is equally important. The Supreme Court has decided many cases dealing with the so-called silent Commerce Clause, the provision of Article I of the U.S. Constitution that gives Congress the power to regulate interstate commerce and places limitations on actions by states that discriminate against or substantially impair the operation of interstate commerce. Thus the Court has struck down attempts to control shipment of solid or hazardous waste into states on grounds that such regulations interfere with interstate commerce (*Fort Gratiot Landfill* v. *Michigan Department of Natural Resources*, 1992; *Chemical Waste Management* v. *Hunt*, 1992).

Indeed, the impact of these rulings can be direct, in addition to their long-term and less visible significance as forces shaping the financial context of government. For example, the Supreme Court held that forcing haulers of solid waste to dump at designated trash plants is an unconstitutional burden on interstate commerce (*C. & A. Carbone* v. *Town of Clarkstown*, 1994). The City of Savannah, Georgia, which operates a resources recovery facility to which local haulers were required to take their loads, estimates that the *Carbone* decision resulted in approximately $800,000 per year in lost revenue, which has to be made up through general government revenue (C. Morrill, Budget Director, City of Savannah, Georgia, personal communication, Nov. 17, 1995).

Attempts by states to force firms to do business with them, with an eye toward the states' competitive positions relative to neighboring states, have also been constrained (*Brown-Foreman Distillers* v. *New York State Liquor Authority*, 1986); *Healy* v. *Beer Institute*, 1989). States are even challenging each other with respect to the marketplace, as when Wyoming successfully attacked an Oklahoma requirement that public utilities use a percentage of Oklahoma fuel as opposed to coal imported from elsewhere (*Wyoming* v. *Oklahoma*, 1992).

Of course, intergovernmental conversations continue about congressional authority to reach into states and localities either directly by commerce clause regulation (*United State* v. *Lopez*, 1995) or indirectly through requirements attached to federal funding (*South Dakota* v. *Dole,* 1987). A number of justices have indicated a desire to restore a stronger position for states in those debates (*Seminole Tribe of Florida* v. *Florida,* 1996).

Risk Management: A Fiscal Reality with a Murky Future

The Supreme Court ruling in the *Seminole Tribe* case of 1996 (which concerned the immunity of states from certain kinds of legal challenges) brings to mind risk management as another important dimension of judicial impacts on the fiscal affairs of governments. There has been a dramatic and important national dialogue concerning the degree to which the national government, states, localities, and public officials as individuals ought to be more accountable for tort liability damages. The details of that debate are ably conveyed in Chapter Twenty-Three.

In addition to the obvious direct and indirect costs of risk management, there are also potential and actual costs associated with the need for increased legal assistance. It is not simply a question of managing litigation expenses, which is itself complex, but also the need to ensure sufficient legal consultation at important stages of decision making to minimize risk. In that sense, and because of the size and nature of the fiscal threats, the issue is not merely one of paying for insurance; it is essential to understand the impacts of risk analyses on day-to-day decision making.

LIVING WITH JUDICIAL PARTICIPATION
IN FISCAL MANAGEMENT

The purpose here is not to paint a dark picture of the roles of law and courts in fiscal affairs. Rather, it is to make clear why it is important to pay attention to these forces, to understand them as common aspects of public administration, to learn more about them, and to watch developments arising in the courts just as managers monitor other developments.

Irene Rubin (1997) has written that budgets go well beyond mere technical documents; "they are also intrinsically and irreducibly political" (p. 1). She could just as well have added that they are just as clearly and unalterably legal documents. She correctly stressed that budgets "reflect the relative power of different individuals and organizations" (p. 2). Courts and judges and the litigators who invoke their participation are among those power players.

In the end, then, public administrators should not have been surprised by the ruling in the *Garcia* (1985) case. Indeed, they should have anticipated it. Ample warning had been given by the courts to prepare for the impact of such a decision. In a way, the fact that administrators were unprepared says more about public administration than it does about courts. It is time to integrate public law into public finance and budgeting in a more central way than has been experienced to date, and to do so in practice, not merely academically.

Cases Cited

Alexander v. Mississippi, 441 So.2d 1339 (MS, 1983).

Allied Signal v. Director, Division of Taxation, 504 U.S. 768 (1992).

Amalgamated Meat Cutters & Butcher Workmen of North America v. Connally, 337 F.Supp. 737 (D.D.C., 1971).

Armstrong v. Collins, 709 S.W. 2d 437 (KY, 1986).

Bayard v. Singleton, 1 N.C. (Mart.) 5 (NC, 1787).

Bengzon v. Secretary of Justice of the Philippine Islands, 299 U.S. 410 (1937).

Bowsher v. Synar, 478 U.S. 714 (1986).

Brown v. Firestone, 382 So.2d 654 (FL, 1980).

Brown-Foreman Distillers v. New York State Liquor Authority, 476 U.S. 573 (1986).

Buckley v. Valeo, 424 U.S. 1 (1976).

C. & A. Carbone v. Town of Clarkstown, 511 U.S. 383 (1994).

Chemical Waste Management v. Hunt, 504 U.S. 334 (1992).

City of Cleburne, Texas v. Cleburne Living Center, 473 U.S. 432 (1985).

City of Los Angeles v. Coleman, 397 F.Supp. 547 (D.D.C., 1975).

City of Milwaukee v. Linder, 301 N.W. 2d 196 (WI, 1981).

Colorado General Assembly v. Lamm, 704 P.2d 1371 (CO, 1985).

Commodity Futures Trading Commission v. Schor, 478 U.S. 833 (1986).

Common Cause v. Commonwealth, No. 320, (MD, 1995).

Commonwealth Edison v. Montana, 453 U.S. 609 (1981).

Commonwealth ex rel. Attorney General v. Barnett, 48 A. 967 (PA, 1901).

County of Oneida v. Berle, 411 N.Y.S. 407 (NY, 1980).

CTS Corporation v. Dynamics Corporation, 481 U.S. 69 (1987).

Day-Brite Lighting v. Missouri, 342 U.S. 421 (1952).

Dolan v. City of Tigard, 129 L.Ed.2d 304 (1994).

EEOC v. Wyoming, 460 U.S. 226 (1983).

Euclid v. Ambler, 272 U.S. 365 (1926).

Federal Energy Regulatory Commission v. Mississippi, 456 U.S. 742 (1982).

Florence County School District Four v. Carter, 510 U.S. 7 (1993).

Fort Gratiot Landfill v. Michigan Department of Natural Resources, 504 U.S. 353 (1992).

Fry v. United States, 421 U.S. 542 (1973).

Garcia v. San Antonio Metropolitan Transit Authority, 469 U.S. 528 (1985).

Georgia Association of Educators v. Miller, No. D–91117, July 25, 1991.

Georgia State Employees Union, Local No. 1985 v. Miller, No. D–91116, July 25, 1991.

Green v. Rawls, 122 So.2d 10 (FL, 1960).

Harbor v. Deukmejian, 742 P.2d 1290 (CA, 1987).

Healy v. Beer Institute, 491 U.S. 324 (1989).

Hodel v. Indiana, 452 U.S. 314 (1981).

Hodel v. Virginia Surface Mining Association, 452 U.S. 264 (1981).

Holmes v. Walton, 4 Historical Review 456 (NJ, 1780).

Immigration and Naturalization Service v. Chadha, 462 U.S. 919 (1983).

Jessen Associates, Inc. v. Bullock, 531 S.W.2d 593 (TX, 1975).

Junkins v. Branstad, 448 N.W.2d 480 (IA, 1989).

Karcher v. Kean, 479 A.2d 403 (NJ, 1984).

Los Angeles Department of Water and Power v. Manhart, 435 U.S. 702 (1978).

Lucas v. South Carolina Coastal Council, 120 L.Ed.2d 798 (1992).

Maryland v. Louisiana, 451 U.S. 725 (1981).

Maryland v. Wirtz, 392 U.S. 183 (1968).

Mistretta v. United States, 488 U.S. 361 (1989).

Moore v. East Cleveland, 431 U.S. 494 (1977).

Morrison v. Olson, 487 U.S. 654 (1988).

National Council of Community Mental Health Centers v. Weinberger, 361 F.Supp. 897 (D.D.C., 1973).

National League of Cities v. Usery, 426 U.S. 833 (1976).

New York v. United States, 326 U.S. 572 (1946).

Nollan v. California Coastal Commission, 483 U.S. 825 (1987).

Opinion of Justices, 428 N.E.2d 117 (MA, 1981).

People ex rel. Bakalis v. Weinberger, 368 F.Supp. 721 (NDIL, 1973).

Quill Corporation v. North Dakota, 504 U.S. 298 (1992).

Raines v. Byrd, No. D–96-1671, WL 348141 (1997).

Reeves v. Stake, 447 U.S. 429 (1980).

Seminole Tribe of Florida v. Florida, 134 L.Ed.2d 252 (1996).

Shapp v. Sloan, 391 A.2d 595 (PA, 1978).

South Central Timber Development v. Wunnicke, 467 U.S. 82 (1984).

South Dakota v. Dole, 483 U.S. 203 (1987).

State ex rel. Kleczka v. Conta, 264 N.W.2d 539 (WI, 1978).

State ex rel. Turner v. Iowa State Highway Commission, 186 N.W.2d 141 (IA, 1971).

State ex rel. Wisconsin Senate v. Thompson, 424 N.W.2d 385 (WI, 1988).

Thomas v. *Union Carbide Agricultural Products,* 473 U.S. 568 (1985).

Train v. *City of New York,* 420 U.S. 35 (1975).

Trevett v. *Weeden,* (RI, 1786).

United Building Trades Council v. *Camden,* 465 U.S. 208 (1984).

United States v. *California,* 297 U.S. 175 (1936).

United States v. *Curtis Wright Export Corporation,* 299 U.S. 304 (1936).

United States v. *Lopez,* 131 L.Ed.2d 626 (1995).

United States v. *Nixon,* 418 U.S. 683 (1974).

Village of Belle Terre v. *Borass,* 416 U.S. 1 (1974).

White v. *Massachusetts Council of Construction Workers,* 460 U.S. 204 (1983).

Wyoming v. *Oklahoma,* 502 U.S. 437 (1992).

References

Abney, G., and Lauth, T. P. "The Executive Budget in the States: Normative Idea and Empirical Observation." *Policy Studies Journal,* 1989, *17,* 829–840.

Abney, G., and Lauth, T. P. "Line-Item Veto." In J. Shafritz (ed.), *The International Encyclopedia of Public Policy and Administration.* New York: Henry Holt, 1997.

Axelrod, D. *A Budget Quartet: Critical Policy and Management Issues.* New York: St. Martin's Press, 1989.

Berman, L. *The Office of Management and Budget and the Presidency.* Princeton, N.J.: Princeton University Press, 1979.

Briffault, R. "The Item Veto in State Courts." *Temple Law Review,* 1993, *66,* 1171–1204.

Clynch, E. J. "Budgeting in Mississippi: Are Two Budgets Better Than One?" *State and Local Government Review,* 1986, *18,* 49–55.

Clynch, E. J. "Mississippi: Does the Governor Really Count?" In E. J. Clynch and T. P. Lauth (eds.), *Governors, Legislatures, and Budgets: Diversity Across the American States.* Westport, Conn.: Greenwood Press, 1991.

Di Iulio, J. *Courts, Corrections, and the Constitution: The Impact of Judicial Intervention on Prisons and Jails.* New York: Oxford University Press, 1990.

Douglas, W. O. *Democracy and Finance.* Port Washington, N.Y.: Kennikat Press, 1969. (Originally published 1940.)

Feustel, B. "The Fiscal Perspective: Pennsylvania Budget Violates State Constitution." *Fiscal Letter,* 1996, *18,* 8–9.

Fischel, W. *Regulatory Takings: Law, Economics, and Politics.* Cambridge, Mass.: Harvard University Press, 1995.

Hackbart, M. M. "Kentucky: Transitions, Adjustments and Innovations." In E. J. Clynch and T. P. Lauth (eds.), *Governors, Legislatures, and Budgets: Diversity Across the American States.* Westport, Conn.: Greenwood Press, 1991.

Harriman, L., and Staussman, J. "Do Judges Determine Budget Decisions? Federal Court Decisions in Prison Reform and State Spending for Corrections." *Public Administration Review,* 1983, *43,* 343–351.

Key, V. O. "The Lack of a Budgetary Theory." *American Political Science Review,* 1940, *34,* 1137–1140.

Reagan, M. *The New Federalism.* New York: Oxford University Press, 1972.

Rubin, I. *The Politics of Public Budgeting.* (3rd ed.) Chatham, N.J.: Chatham House, 1997.

Shuman, H. E. *Politics and the Budget: The Struggle Between the President and the Congress.* (2nd ed.) Upper Saddle River, N.J.: Prentice Hall, 1988.

Sundquist, J. L. *The Decline and Resurgence of Congress.* Washington, D.C.: Brookings Institution, 1981.

U.S. General Accounting Office. *Worker Protection: Federal Contractors and Violations of Labor Law.* Washington, D.C.: U.S. Government Printing Office, 1995.

Wood, R. *Remedial Law.* Amherst: University of Massachusetts Press, 1990.

Zimmerman, J. F. "Rebirth of the Item Veto in the Empire State." *State Government,* 1981, *54*(2), 51–52.

CHAPTER TWENTY-NINE

Legal Issues in Contracting for Public Services

When Business Does Government

Ruth Hoogland DeHoog

C ontracting out for public services has been promoted in the public management literature as a solution to the ills of government for more than twenty years now. For most purposes, the early debate about this alternative to traditional public service delivery focused on ideological and economic arguments in the broader discussion of privatization (President's Commission on Privatization, 1988; Savas, 1987). More recently, scholars have examined many of the issues of management and implementation in specific program areas, such as human services (DeHoog, 1984; Demone and Gibelman, 1989; Schlesinger, Dorwart, and Pulice, 1986), correctional facilities (Geis, 1987; Shichor, 1995), wastewater treatment facilities (Heilman and Johnson, 1992), refuse collection (Savas, 1977, 1981), parks (Allen, 1989), public education (Brown and Hunter, 1995; Russo, Sandidge, Shapiro, and Harris, 1995), and public transportation (Luger and Goldstein, 1989; Perry and Babitsky, 1986; Teal, 1988). While some of these efforts have focused on cost savings that might be realized, analysts are increasingly concerned about the effects on service quality, service distribution, and public accountability.

Unfortunately academic perspectives on these services often give scant coverage of the legal issues involved in contracting. This chapter calls attention to the interplay between the management and legal perspectives, and allows highlighting of the most salient concerns. Some of these concerns raise broad, critical questions on the nature of the state and legal accountability, while others are more narrowly focused on the contracting process. For example, fundamental constitutional and civil rights issues call attention to the question of whether to privatize certain services, while problems in contract bidding and administration raise questions about how to improve the contracting process to avoid legal pitfalls. In all these areas, however, it is necessary to understand that the decisions favoring privatization not only require considerable research about costs and benefits but also often require some statutory and administrative regulatory changes to provide sufficient legal safeguards (Russo, Sandidge, Shapiro, and Harris, 1995). In addition to these legal issues, since contracting has become more commonplace, greater attention should be devoted to the complicated interorganizational and interpersonal relationships on which these contractual interactions depend.

This chapter cannot review all the intricacies of case law that deal with each phase of the contract decision-making process, from the decision to contract for a service to the evaluation of performance. However, the first section outlines some of the key conceptual and general management issues, followed by highlights of some of the most critical legal issues in contracting. These highlights begin with the question of whether to contract out, and end with some of the thorniest implementation problems.

KEY CONCEPTUAL AND MANAGEMENT ISSUES

The shift to privatization as a general policy of federal, state, and local governments in recent years has necessitated a change in the way public officials think about service delivery and their relationships with private organizations. Although governments have always bought some goods and services from the private sector, in the last fifteen years privatization has become a mantra as well as a public policy preference of elected officials. Thus symbolic, political, and ideological issues often overshadow management concerns. In a rush to satisfy voters and adopt popular innovations, policymakers, at their peril, may overlook key legal and implementation problems when they promise privatization as a solution to public problems.

Several key terms require definition for the subsequent discussion. First, privatization often refers to a wide range of options in which services are delivered by private agents. These include not only contracting but also vouchers, load-shedding, coproduction, volunteers, franchises, and subsidies (Savas, 1987). Contracting, in which the government writes a service contract with an outside supplier and pays the contractor directly, can involve not only private firms but other public entities as well. In this chapter, the primary focus is on contracting with private agents, both for-profit and nonprofit organizations. In the human services, for example, public agencies, nonprofits, and for-profit companies might compete for the same awards. While similar management issues are found in all three sectors, each set of entities may face somewhat different accountability and reward structures affecting their public contracts.

Another distinction must be made in contracting, between the production (delivery) and the provision (arranging and financing) of services (Kolderie, 1986; Savas, 1987). Thus a government unit can decide to provide a service itself, but it may contract with private suppliers to produce it. (Unfortunately, the nonprofit literature adds an element of confusion when service agencies are referred to as service providers, even when acting under a public contract.) The government (or principal) specifies the service delivery methods, advertises the contract, chooses the contractor (agent), and pays for the service in some way—usually either on a per unit basis (as in many human services) or with a lump sum. The government monitors contract compliance and performance, and if dissatisfied, can decide not to renew the contract.

Advocates have argued that contracting out yields three primary benefits: (1) *a reduction of costs*, due to economies of scale, efficient management practices, circumvention of public personnel constraints, lower wage and benefit packages, and/or competition for contracts; (2) *an improvement of service quality*, because of better management, service specialization, and/or access to a more qualified labor market; and (3) *a reduction in the growth and dominance of the public sector*, due to shifting labor, funding, and service delivery to a more efficient private sector.

The empirical evidence suggests that in some services (such as garbage collection) significant savings are realized with contracting (Savas, 1987). Not all of the research agrees, however, and the results are even more mixed when service quality and efficiency are at issue (Hirsch, 1995). (Note that cost savings do not imply that efficiency has improved when, for example, wages are cut.) It is apparent that certain services, methods, and localities are more likely to achieve these benefits. More recent experience with contracting in city governments (such as Phoenix and Charlotte) suggests that competition for contracts, and not necessarily characteristics of the sectors themselves, produces cost and service quality advantages.

The third benefit of contracting, reduction in the size and growth of government, is the hardest to measure and agree upon with much objectivity, since it assumes that the public sector is too large. Nonetheless, it should be noted that under contracting specifically, the government agency's budget may not necessarily be reduced even though the number of public employees is. Employee skills and tasks may differ, however, under more widespread contracting—that is, negotiation, monitoring, and evaluation needs are greater when government buys from the private sector. And oversight and accountability become even more complicated and critical when multiple suppliers are used. Thus, while direct service costs may decline, transaction costs, as economists call them (Williamson, 1985), will increase and may require more professional skills.

LEGAL ISSUES IN DECIDING TO CONTRACT FOR SERVICES

Public managers responsible for contracting for services are critical to the realization of cost and quality benefits. Their knowledge and skill in planning, implementing, and monitoring contracts may be the key to a successful contracting process and its outcomes. Before a contract can be open for bid, however, many prior management decisions must be made. As Collett (1981) observed about federal contracting, "one of the most serious deficiencies in planning for contracting is that program officers frequently fail to consider first the elements essential to a decision on whether or not to contract. They do not evaluate their goals, the resources (personnel and funds) required, their in-house capability vs. that of contractors, a cost analysis (in-house vs. contractor), timing, and legal parameters. Only if consideration of these and other factors leads program officers to decide that contracts are necessary and cost-effective should the process itself begin" (p. 8).

The first step in service contracting should be ascertaining whether the service can and should be purchased. Certainly the federal government has few legal restrictions on its contracting; the famous Office of Management and Budget Circular A76 and its subsequent versions require the use of outside suppliers whenever possible. In fact, under the National Performance Review (1993), the Federal Acquisition Streamlining Act of 1994, and Executive Order 12931 (Federal Procurement Reform, Oct. 13, 1994), the federal process has been improved, decentralized, and simplified to encourage more private sector procurement. State and especially local governments, however, may encounter some restrictions, whether in constitutional or statutory forms. State constitutions restrict the freedom of municipalities to provide certain services as they wish. In some states, for example, only public agencies can produce certain services, such as jail management. Sometimes the legal basis for contracting can be quite murky, and can itself discourage risk taking by local governments.

Some scholars argue that beyond specific legal restrictions on contracting, certain types of contracting should be avoided for other fundamental reasons. Moe (1987), among others (Kettl, 1988, 1993; U.S. General Accounting Office, 1991), is concerned about the widespread use of contracting, as well as other privatization methods. He suggests that the distinctive role of government as the sovereign limits what can properly be assigned to private organizations. For example, maintaining the legal use of coercive force as a unique characteristic of the state is a fundamental doctrine that many scholars suggest should not be extended to other parties, even under a contract that preserves clients', inmates', or citizens' civil rights. In addition, some services (such as defense, air traffic control, and social security) are so critical to society or the economy that any interruption or failure would create a major crisis.

The threat to constitutional rights of both employees and clients in contracting is an especially serious matter, according to some legal scholars (Sullivan, 1987). While the U.S. Constitution protects citizens from *government* infringement of their rights under the State Action Doctrine, they are not necessarily protected when public services are contracted out to private agencies. Two key Supreme Court cases, *Rendell-Baker* v. *Kohn* and *Blum* v. *Yaretsky,* both decided in 1982, spelled out how private organizations are exempt. As one commentator read these rulings, "even when government retains responsibility, through funding or regulation for provision if service delivery or production is privatized, both clients and employees generally lose rights which they would have had were production kept in public hands. When both provision and production are privatized, only those activities which have been both traditionally and exclusively public functions are subject to constitutional restraints" (Sullivan, 1987, p. 464). Thus employees' freedom of speech, freedom of assembly, or right to due process are protected if employed by a public agency, but it is not entirely clear how much protection is available when they are performing the same job with state funds in a private entity.

In human services contracting, a critical concern involves the constitutional rights of dependent populations in prisons, mental health facilities, halfway homes, and so on (Shichor, 1995; Sullivan, 1987). As crime and incarceration levels have increased over the last decade, private firms have become interested not only in building and financing facilities but also in managing and operating prisons and jails (Palumbo, 1986; Shichor, 1995). Questions have been raised, however, about contracting out for these facilities, whether for juveniles, adults, or aliens. Should social control functions of government be delegated to private firms that may have to use deadly force in their work? Who is legally liable should an inmate be hurt or killed by an employee? And is privatization more unattractive simply because inmates or residents are held against their will, and thus obviously have no choice of providers? While most scholars (Robbins, 1986; Shichor, 1995) conclude that constitutional issues do not present a serious obstacle to prison management contracts, "the ultimate legal responsibility for the private prison will remain with the government" (Shichor, 1995, p. 108). To protect themselves against private bankruptcy, which might occur following a large lawsuit, governments may have to require high levels of liability insurance for prison firms to cover the potential costs of civil suits. In addition, contracts may have to spell out clearly the constitutional safeguards for inmates.

One of the most difficult obstacles facing jurisdictions that consider privatization is labor opposition (Chandler and Feuille, 1991; Naff, 1991). The American Federation of State, County, and Municipal Employees, the largest public labor union, along with many other federal, local, and specialized unions, has argued that public employees and the public lose when contracting out is used.

Pay and benefit levels, as well as job security, are often reduced when public services go private. Some observers have argued (Suggs, 1986) that minorities and women are disporportionately affected by job losses, primarily because frequently targeted services (such as housekeeping, garbage collection, and landscaping) employ these workers. However, at least one scholar (Murin, 1985) has asserted that minority contractors may be more effective at meeting human service needs if they are more familiar with the target populations.

Some of the disputes have involved direct political action (such as strikes, walkouts, and pickets), while others have spawned legal battles (Naff, 1991). The courts have been concerned about employee rights and collective bargaining agreements. For example, in *Independent School District No. 88, New Ulm, Minnesota* v. *School Service Employees Union Local 284* (1993), the Minnesota Supreme Court ruled that when a school district contracted out for food services, "the district was required to submit to binding arbitration over the impact of its action" (Russo, Sandidge, Shapiro, and Harris, 1995, p. 131). However, at the federal level at least, the courts "have consistently upheld management's right to make the decision to contract out and generally have prevented the union from interfering with that decision" (Naff, 1991, p. 26). The exception to this rule is where Congress has included labor protections in legislation (see, for example, Luger and Goldstein, 1989).

What do these labor issues mean for public managers who are considering contracting for services? First, it is incumbent upon management to consider carefully the effect of privatization on workers, especially the disparate impact on minorities and low-wage earners in their agencies. Second, managers should be encouraged to protect workers, including allowing city workers and departments to bid on government contracts along with private firms, as has been successfully done in some public services in Phoenix, Charlotte, and Minneapolis. If outside firms win the awards, managers should attempt to incorporate in the agreements as many employee (and client) protections and benefits as possible to obtain comparable outcomes as in government production. For example, some contracts require employment of public workers for a period of six months to a year at certain pay and benefit levels, with dismissal for cause following that period. In any case, the perceived fairness of the process and outcomes for employees may be a key element in ensuring public satisfaction with contracting.

THE PROCESS OF AWARDING CONTRACTS

When contracting is chosen as an alternative to public production, the process of awarding, managing, and evaluating contracts is critical—and often commands less attention than the decision to contract out. Yet some scholars

(DeHoog, 1984; Kettl, 1993; Thayer, 1987) suggest that private firms have incentives to cheat, lie, and shirk responsibilities unless the system develops strict requirements, penalties, and monitoring devices. Private organizations may also be willing to use their political connections to obtain lucrative contracts when other competitors are involved (DeHoog, 1984; Hanrahan, 1983). Where the consequences of mistakes involve direct services to human beings, as in public education, corrections, or social services, the importance of these controls looms larger than where government purchases supplies or consulting services. According to *State and Local Government Purchasing* (Council of State Governments, 1988), the primary principles of public procurement are competition, impartiality, efficiency, and openness. Of these, competition and impartiality are probably held most sacred in the purchasing system to ensure a beneficial outcome as well as to promote public accountability in the process. The standard practice for awarding contracts is through the competitive sealed bid process, which includes public advertisement of the government's needs, invitations to bid containing specifications, a public bid opening, and an award to the lowest responsive and responsible bidder (Council of State Governments, 1988; Zemansky, 1987). To be effective and efficient, this process must not only occur within a competitive environment (there must be at least two responsible bidders), but also include a set of clear specifications and allow sufficient time for contractors to prepare the bids. Unwise, hasty decisions can be made when government officials lack information about services, clients, costs, and potential management problems.

Most of the legal issues surrounding the formal bidding process are fairly straightforward, because government regulations, state statutes, or local ordinances clearly spell out the bidding process. However, public procurement officials must be aware of the potential threats to the process—primarily corruption, collusion, fraud, and conflict of interest. These threats become particularly troublesome for public administrators when elected officials are involved in the process of awarding bids. Certain safeguards built into the system (such as sealed bids, disclosure of investments by officials, and accounting requirements) are often mandated by federal, state, or local laws, but vigilance is still necessary to ensure a clean process that strictly adheres to all relevant regulations, statutes, and ordinances. Protests and lawsuits from disgruntled bidders are not only costly, but they may also delay the start of services or programs with the selected contractor.

Instead of the formal bidding process, informal methods of awarding service contracts (DeHoog, 1984; MacManus, 1992) are often used for professional services, highly specialized services, small contracts, emergency needs, or social programs (for example, for small businesses or those owned by women or minorities). These efforts are not always meant to be strictly competitive, because they attempt to balance (or reduce) the importance of competition with other goals—rapid response, reduced bidding costs, or social and economic purposes (MacManus, 1992).

The request for proposal (RFP) may be used to ensure some level of competition and to obtain a complete proposal for service delivery. A more rapid tool, the request for quote (RFQ), provides a method for obtaining an oral or written price quote without involving the lengthy RFP process. The sole source negotiation process (DeHoog, 1990) is primarily relied on for services that can be purchased from only one supplier, or where the government's expertise and information are incomplete.

Public managers and contractors usually prefer more flexible approaches that reduce their time and costs, but these approaches may open government agencies to criticisms about competition, impartiality, and openness. Obviously the professionalism, competence, and skill of the government contracting officials (Cooper, 1980) is even more critical here than where the process and award criteria are more clear-cut in the formal bidding procedures. Various types of abuses may occur, including "wired" or "sweetheart" solicitations, the division of large contracts into small noncompetitive ones, repetitive sole source contracts, and favoritism in providing information to contractors (Collett, 1981). In this more informal process, the relationship between the individuals on both sides of the contracting equation is of paramount importance. Because purchasing officers may be at an information disadvantage and often only one firm may have the technological, professional, or capital capacity to produce the service, these situations may lead to abuse by potential contractors.

While state and local governments have become increasingly sophisticated in their purchasing policies and procedures (MacManus, 1992), a potential problem area is ascertaining whether the bidders are responsible, to ensure that the chosen contractor will in fact be capable of carrying out the terms of the contract in a timely and effective manner. This can be a sticky area, especially when the government employees themselves are not experts in the service, or when competition is limited to a single source or to a small number of newer contractors. Where state statutes or local ordinances require awards to the lowest bidder, purchasing officers are often concerned about the likelihood of contract compliance, but they are only able to throw out bids when provided evidence of nonresponsibility. Even when such rewards are not required, officials may feel strong pressures on large or sensitive projects to award bids to low bidders, because explaining nonresponsiveness or nonresponsibility to the media, elected officials, and the public is a daunting task.

Writing a tight, clear, and complete set of specifications, performance standards, and penalties (and perhaps incentives) into the contract is absolutely critical to protecting public services. The expertise of the government agency and officials is, of course, essential in preparing the bid announcement and specifications, advertising in the appropriate outlets, providing bidders with information in pre-bid conferences, and making awards. Unfortunately, the bidders themselves may have an informational advantage over the government. Increasingly in complex high-tech or scientific procurement, consultants are hired to assist public agencies in the preparation of the RFP. These relationships, however, may themselves produce potential conflicts of interest, because a consultant on one project may become a bidder on another.

Another risk reduction method in services contracting is to require contractors to be bonded or insured against bankruptcy, as has long been the practice for construction contracts. Nonetheless, reliance on previous contractors with strong reputations for performance is a common pattern in service contracting, at least when some discretion is allowed by officials.

When abuses or major errors occur, they are often uncovered after some damage has already been done. The legal remedies of financial penalties and/or debarment to punish illegal behavior and prevent future bids by these firms is costly, time-consuming, and not entirely effective, especially in large projects and services. These tools are understood as discouraging or catching only the most egregious of the contracting abuses. In addition, legal action or debarment in one municipality or state may not necessarily mean that the responsible officers will be prevented from bidding on contracts in other governments, either as the same organization or with a new name or type of ownership. For example, in 1996 the North Carolina Department of Corrections allowed a firm to receive a low-bid award on a private state prison construction and operation project, even though the contracting officials knew that the firm had been debarred in another state ("Former Prison Builders," 1996).

TENSIONS IN CONTRACTING RELATIONSHIPS

One of the management issues in contracting services is who should be responsible for the bidding process—the department or agency that requires the service, or a central purchasing agency? As MacManus (1992) found in her survey of state governments, the states are increasingly centralizing purchasing functions, while the federal government continues to use a more complex, decentralized system. This complexity, as well as extensive reporting and monitoring requirements, can discourage firms and agencies from competing in the process. The advantage of centralization obviously is that purchasing officers know the law, policies, and procedures; they can review the bids and contracts for legal errors, as well as make changes to improve the outcomes. Conversely, the advantages of decentralization may include a speedier process, a greater emphasis on the services to be delivered, and perhaps better communication with the suppliers during the entire process. These agency professionals, who are probably more familiar with the likely service suppliers, might also be able to generate enhanced competition through their contacts in the event of few interested bidders.

Quite naturally, conflicts can occur between the line and staff functions in purchasing, with each side having somewhat different goals in the process (DeHoog, 1986). These conflicts draw attention to a broader question in contracting. Which is more effective: ensuring contractual compliance by developing strict purchasing procedures, contractual safeguards, and accountability requirements, or by giving public administrators more discretion to develop contracts and accountability methods tailored more to the particular service and contractors? Certainly most purchasing procedures must comply with certain standard legal requirements, and every contract writing process involves common "boilerplate" provisions that protect the government as well as the contractor. But beyond these methods, how much managerial discretion is beneficial to ensure good quality services? This remains an open question, because the legal requirements themselves may lead to less desirable outcomes, such as being required to choose a contractor that a manager believes will not be as effective as another one.

Inherent tensions also exist between the differing goals of government and contractors, in addition to their obvious differences in pursuing the public interest or their business interest in profit. Firms and nonprofit agencies prefer long-term contracts, or at least an assurance of renewals, to buffer themselves against the vagaries of political and administrative change and to allow them to make certain capital and human resources investments. In seeking to reduce their uncertainty, contractors generally prefer long-term, sole-source contracts, reduced competition, and a negotiated rather than open competitive bidding process (DeHoog, 1990). Government officials may also share these goals, because their administrative (or transaction) costs are reduced as a result, and they can develop a trusting, professional relationship with key private participants (DeHoog, 1990; Williamson, 1985). As Kelman (1990) argues in his study of federal procurement of computer equipment and services, the quality of the services provided by suppliers may be significantly better when an enduring relationship of loyalty, service, and information exchange is established between the two sides of the contract.

Several forces, however, may militate against public agencies developing these contracts and relationships with contractors. Not only are short-term (often one year) service contracts required in some jurisdictions, but governments may also be constrained by competitive requirements that emphasize fairness and objectivity in contracting, to prevent corruption, cozy relationships, and information advantages that accrue to long-term contractors. Agencies may also prefer to retain some flexibility to alter service methods, to switch to a more responsive contractor, or to end the service altogether. Officials themselves may believe that service quality will be maintained best when contractors operate under conditions of uncertainty and do not assume they have a permanent contract. Thus both legal and management pressures may combine to discourage long-term relationships, whether or not they may be useful for certain kinds of contracting.

CONTRACTING WITH MINORITY BUSINESSES: GOALS AND SET-ASIDES

The process of contracting usually focuses on ensuring competition, fairness, efficiency, and accountability, as discussed earlier. However, concerns about social equity also arise. Should contracting or purchasing decisions sometimes be made to achieve certain social purposes? When governments spend increasingly larger amounts of their budgets on contracting, the economic impact of these contracts on employment, profitability, and local communities becomes increasingly important. Recognizing that the playing field in the contract competition may not always be level for everyone, the federal government in the 1970s led the way in developing programs to assist traditionally disadvantaged firms—that is, minority- and female-owned businesses. State and local governments also established set-aside programs for minority business enterprises and/or women business enterprises to ensure that certain percentages of the total number of government contracts and subcontracts would be allocated to these two types of contractors, often but not exclusively in construction contracts.

These programs became quite controversial, both because of some abuses by white-owned firms that passed themselves off as minority business enterprises, and because of the accusations of preferential treatment. The issue of the constitutionality of the set-asides were addressed in three Supreme Court decisions: *Fullilove v. Klutznick* (1980), *City of Richmond v. J. A. Croson* (1989), and *Metro Broadcasting, Inc. v. Federal Communications Commission et al.* (1990). Following *Fullilove v. Klutznick,* in which the Court upheld federal set-asides contained in a federal statute, set-aside programs for minority-owned businesses were established in many state and local governments, as well as in federal contracts. The decision in the *Croson* case, however, turned the tide of set-asides, when the Court declared unconstitutional the City of Richmond's set-aside program (30 percent of the city construction contract dollars) because it violated the Equal Protection Clause of the Fourteenth Amendment. Nonetheless, within a year, the Court upheld the federal set-asides at the Federal Communications Commission in *Metro Broadcasting,* exempting congressional requirements to improve minority participation. As Rice (1991, p. 115) asks: "When may government be *color conscious* rather than *color blind?*" The answer to this question currently appears to be twofold: (1) when Congress requires it, or (2) when a state or local government can prove that minorities and minority-owned firms have been discriminated against in prior contracting.

Since *Croson,* state and local governments have closely scrutinized their set-aside programs. As a result, many have revised them to pursue either race-neutral approaches (for example, antidiscrimination policies) or race-conscious approaches (La Noue and Sullivan, 1995). In the latter, some have replaced set-asides with goals in awarding contracts or subcontracts to minority firms. A few have developed disparity studies (MacManus, 1990; Rice, 1992) that document how minorities have been discriminated against in public contracting. These efforts require significant research and clear evidence of disparities in contract awards between white and minority-owned firms.

CONTRACT ADMINISTRATION, MONITORING, AND EVALUATION

Contracting, like any other public management function, must be carefully implemented and monitored. Contracting does not avoid the problems of bureaucracy. Monitoring, accountability, and control problems may become more difficult, because at least two sets of bureaucracy are involved—the public bureaucracy that organizes and oversees contracting, and the private bureaucracy, or in many cases, bureaucracies, that operate a service. Many outrageous examples of abuse, waste, and fraud can be cited (Hanrahan, 1983) when contractors are used. Failures to perform according to contracts, or the possibility of contractors going bankrupt, are additional concerns that have legal implications.

Several different types of contract administration controls can be used to avoid many of these problems. Client complaints (directed to public agencies), contractor reports, and regular random monitoring for contract compliance (especially service approaches) are critical methods that can detect potential problems early enough to take corrective action. Financial audits, while necessary and usually required of contractors above certain limits, are less valuable because they often come too late, following at least one full year of a contract. Audits can sometimes be effective, however, in providing convincing evidence of wrongdoing that can be used to terminate a contract. In the human services, program evaluation studies can usefully focus on outputs and outcomes as much as on the service delivery procedures, but their findings may provide information that comes at a high cost and rather late in the program implementation stage. In addition, performance clauses, while beneficial in many hard services, are difficult to enforce in the human services because of external forces (for example, economic conditions) outside the control of the contractors (DeHoog, 1984; Donahue, 1989). Nonetheless, if these oversight methods can be carefully designed and effectively executed, they can provide a variety of useful information to improve future contracts and services. They may also deter some unethical firms and agencies from bidding for contracts or abusing their agreements.

Critical questions that go beyond monitoring methods and techniques for managing the process are Who are selected as monitors? and Who supervises them? As with writing contract specifications and agreements, the knowledge and skills of the individuals, as well as their organizational location, may be important. These responsibilities may be filled by a central procurement office's contract managers or by line personnel in the service departments, or they may be shared by both offices. As one scholar (Rehfuss, 1990, p. 47) observes, "selecting the person or persons to monitor contracts requires judgments about several issues, such as the complexity of the contract, the size and diversity of the agency, the nature of the service or project being contracted out, and the training and experience of the program officials. No one organizational arrangement is appropriate to every setting."

Yet the consequences of elaborate monitoring, reporting, and evaluation systems—increased costs of contracting and discouragement of some worthy firms and nonprofits from competing for government contracts—are important to understand.

The first of these outcomes is fairly obvious. While the costs of self reporting by contractors and of responding to citizen-initiated complaints may not be high, these sources of information may not be reliable or valid measures of contract compliance and performance. Therefore, objective monitoring of service delivery and performance outcomes by public officials becomes necessary. Yet according to the limited research on this subject (DeHoog, 1984; Donahue, 1989; Kettl, 1988; Rehfuss, 1990), this part of the contracting process may be given short shrift, primarily because of the high costs involved. Once again, the skills of public officials can be critical in dealing with the task of both collecting objective evidence and communicating the results and recommendations to the contractors. Certainly the government goal is not to terminate contracts because of minor infractions or noncompliance; it is primarily to improve services and compliance to the agreed standards.

The second outcome of extensive oversight mechanisms may be more troublesome for those who believe that contracting succeeds largely because of competitive conditions. From the standpoint of contractors, government controls over services and operations may also complicate certain management issues, and they may reduce the potential benefits of competition. Certainly the contracting red tape, restrictions, reporting requirements, and payment delays (MacManus, 1991) may prevent some contractors from competing. As Ferris (1993) and Smith and Lipsky (1993) have discussed, nonprofits sometimes are reluctant to enter into public contracts because they face a critical question: Are they willing to sacrifice some of their independence for government control? Government contracts require nonprofit agencies to alter certain policies, procedures, and services to obtain the funds. In doing so, they add yet another layer of accountability that may sometimes produce conflicts with their missions or with other influences on these organizations, such as their boards of directors, clients, foundations, or donors. Receiving multiple contracts from different public sources requires agencies to increase their administrative personnel and costs, with less attention given to direct service delivery. This may change the character and goals of the agency from independence and service to being an extension of government and having greater dependence upon public funding. The reluctance of some nonprofits, as well as for-profit firms, to compete for contracts thus has implications for the degree of competition in purchasing certain services.

LEGAL ISSUES INVOLVING CONTRACTORS' RIGHTS AND RESPONSIBILITIES

When government contracts with firms for public services, and when the firms perform those services within clear specifications, what legal protections do these private agents have for their actions? Several legal issues that affect management procedures have been raised, including intellectual property rights in research and development, Freedom of Information Act exemptions for contractors, tax exemptions, and immunity from liability.

One of the thorniest of these legal problems in contracting, mentioned earlier in the discussion of prisons, involves contractor liability for defective equipment, unsafe procedures, or harmful results when the contractor creates a product or performs a service according to government specifications (Nero, 1989). The critical issue is whether the contractor acts merely as an agent of the state or federal government, and thus is immune from liability (Ellsworth, 1988). Two principles apply here: first, that "the government has a unique federal interest in getting its work done" (Nero, 1989, p. 769); and second, that a contractor acts as an agent of the government without using its own discretion. Thus, in public works projects, military weapons systems, and other contracts in which the contractor lacks discretion in the design or performance of the contract, contractors are extended the same liability protection as state and federal officials. Contractors are liable, however (with some exceptions in military procurement), if any discretion is involved in administrative rulemaking, implementation, or service delivery decisions. In certain areas, such as lawsuits against prison contractors, this liability may provide a lucrative incentive for litigants and lawyers to take action against major corporations. If these firms declare bankruptcy, however, the government may have to pay the judgments (Shichor, 1995).

CONCLUSION

When governments decide to contract for services, especially direct services to citizens, they must be aware of both the legal and management issues involved. Not only must they have the legal authority to contract for a service, but they must also carefully weigh the costs and benefits of using outside suppliers for service delivery. Legal liability and labor issues may loom large for certain services, and these should be considered carefully prior to the decision to contract out.

Once government officials decide to purchase a service, they face additional problems in the contract bidding, award, and administration phases. While most jurisdictions have clear legal requirements and policy guidelines, they must follow them carefully to avoid violations, challenges by contractors, or unwise awards. A basic tension exists between the legal requirements and management concerns, however. Measures to increase legal compliance and accountability may also increase complexity, costs, reporting requirements, and consequently, contractor dissatisfaction. Ultimately this may lead to contractor reluctance to compete for government contracts, which in turn may reduce competition.

In sum, the contracting alternative for services is not as straightforward for public managers as some have assumed. Problems in maintaining fairness to potential service suppliers and the chosen contractors must be balanced with the desire for quality services for clients at a reasonable cost to taxpayers. As with many management issues, the success of this innovation largely hinges on the knowledge and ability of the public manager to make wise choices. Nonetheless, the design of the contracting system itself, as well as the influence of political participants, can play critical roles in how well services contracting works.

Cases Cited

Blum v. *Yaretsky,* 457 U.S. 991 (1982).

City of Richmond v. *J. A. Croson,* 488 U.S. 469 (1989).

Fullilove v. *Klutznick,* 448 U.S. 448 (1980).

Independent School District No. 88, New Ulm, Minnesota v. *School Service Employees Union Local 284,* 503 N.W.2d 104 (1993).

Metro Broadcasting, Inc. v. *Federal Communications Commission et al.,* 497 U.S. 547 (1990).

Rendell-Baker v. *Kohn,* 457 U.S. 830 (1982).

References

Allen, J. W. "Use of the Private Sector for Service Delivery in State Parks and Recreation Areas." In J. W. Allen (ed.), *The Private Sector in State Service Delivery: Examples of Innovative Practices.* Washington, D.C.: Urban Institute Press, 1989.

Brown, F., and Hunter, R. C. "Privatization of Public School Services." *Education and Urban Society,* 1995, *27,* 107–113.

Chandler, T., and Feuille, P. "Municipal Unions and Privatization," *Public Administration Review,* 1991, *51*(1), 15–22.

Collett, M. J. "The Federal Contracting Process." *Bureaucrat,* 1981, *10*(2), 7–12.

Cooper, P. J. "Government Contracts in Public Administration: The Role and Environment of the Contracting Officer." *Public Administration Review,* 1980, *40*(5), 459–468.

Council of State Governments and the National Association of State Purchasing Officials. *State and Local Government Purchasing.* (3rd ed.) Lexington, Ky.: Council of State Governments, 1988.

DeHoog, R. H. *Contracting Out for Human Services: Political, Economic, and Organizational Perspectives.* Albany: State University of New York Press, 1984.

DeHoog, R. H. "Evaluating Human Services Contracting: Managers, Professionals, and Politicos." *State and Local Government Review,* 1986, *18,* 17–44.

DeHoog, R. H. "Competition, Negotiation, or Cooperation?" *Administration and Society,* 1990, *22,* 317–340.

Demone, H. W., Jr., and Gibelman, M. (eds.). *Services for Sale: Purchasing Health and Human Services.* New Brunswick, N.J.: Rutgers University Press, 1989.

Donahue, J. D. *The Privatization Decision: Public Ends, Private Means.* New York: Basic Books, 1989.

Ellsworth, J. E. "Extending Immunity to Private Contractors on Government Contracts." *Brigham Young University Law Review,* Fall 1988, pp. 835–847.

Ferris, J. M. "The Double-Edged Sword of Social Service Contracting." *Nonprofit Management and Leadership,* 1993, *3,* 363–376.

"Former Prison Builders Face Own Legal Problems," *News and Record* (Greensboro, N.C.), July 10, 1996, p. B2.

Geis, G. "The Privatization of Prisons." In B. J. Carroll, R. W. Conant, and T. A. Easton (eds.), *Private Means, Public Ends: Private Business in Social Service Delivery.* New York: Praeger, 1987.

Hanrahan, J. D. *Government by Contract.* New York: Norton, 1983.

Heilman, J. G., and Johnson, G. W. *The Politics and Economics of Privatization: The Case of Wastewater Treatment.* Tuscaloosa: University of Alabama Press, 1992.

Hirsch, W. Z. "Contracting Out by Urban Governments: A Review." *Urban Affairs Review,* 1995, *30,* 458–472.

Kelman, S. *Procurement and Public Management: The Fear of Discretion and the Quality of Government Performance.* Washington, D.C.: American Enterprise Institute Press, 1990.

Kettl, D. F. *Government by Proxy: (Mis?)Managing Federal Programs.* Washington, D.C.: Congressional Quarterly Press, 1988.

Kettl, D. *Sharing Power: Public Governance and Private Markets.* Washington, D.C.: Brookings Institution, 1993.

Kolderie, T. "The Two Different Concepts of Privatization." *Public Administration Review,* 1986, *46,* 285–291.

La Noue, G. R., and Sullivan, J. C. "Race-Neutral Programs in Public Contracting." *Public Administration Review,* 1995, *55,* 348–356.

Luger, M. I., and Goldstein, H. A. "Federal Labor Protections and the Privatization of Public Transit." *Journal of Public Policy Analysis and Management,* 1989, *8,* 229–250.

MacManus, S. A. "Minority Business Contracting with Local Government." *Urban Affairs Quarterly,* 1990, *25,* 455–473.

MacManus, S. A. "Why Businesses Are Reluctant to Sell to Government." *Public Administration Review,* 1991, *51,* 328–344.

MacManus, S. A. *Doing Business with Government: Federal, State, Local, and Foreign Government Purchasing Practices for Every Business and Public Institution.* New York: Paragon House, 1992.

Moe, R. C. "Exploring the Limits of Privatization." *Public Administration Review,* 1987, *47,* 453–460.

Murin, W. J. "Contracting as Method of Enhancing Equity in the Delivery of Local Government Services." *Journal of Urban Affairs,* 1985, *7,* 1–10.

Naff, K. C. "Labor-Management Relations and Privatization: A Federal Perspective." *Public Administration Review,* 1991, *51*(1), 23–30.

National Performance Review. *Reinventing Federal Procurement.* Washington, D.C.: U.S. Government Printing Office, 1993.

Nero, C. T. "Constitutional Law: Legal Windfalls for Government Procurement Contractors." *Wake Forest Law Review,* 1989, *24,* 745–779.

Palumbo, D. J. "Privatization and Corrections Policy." *Policy Studies Review,* 1986, *5,* 598–605.

Perry, J. L., and Babitsky, T. T. "Comparative Performance in Urban Bus Transit: Assessing Privatization Strategies." *Public Administration Review,* 1986, *46,* 57–66.

President's Commission on Privatization. *Privatization: Toward More Effective Government.* Washington, D.C.: U.S. Government Printing Office, 1988.

Rehfuss, J. "Contracting Out and Accountability in State and Local Governments: The Importance of Contract Monitoring." *State and Local Government Review,* 1990, *22,* 44–48.

Rice, M. F. "Government Set-Asides, Minority Business Enterprises, and the Supreme Court." *Public Administration Review,* 1991, *51,* 114–122.

Rice, M. F. "Justifying State and Local Government Set-Aside Programs Through Disparity Studies in the Post-*Croson* Era." *Public Administration Review,* 1992, *52,* 482–490.

Robbins, I. P. "The Legal Dimensions of Private Incarceration." *American University Law Review,* 1986, *3,* 531–854.

Russo, C. J., Sandidge, R. F., Shapiro, R., and Harris, J. J. "Legal Issues in Contracting Out for Public Education." *Education and Urban Society,* 1995, *27,* 127–135.

Savas, E. S. "An Empirical Study of Competition in Municipal Service Delivery." *Public Administration Review,* 1977, *37,* 714–717.

Savas, E. S. "Intracity Competition Between Public and Private Service Delivery." *Public Administration Review,* 1981, *41,* 46–52.

Savas, E. S. *Privatization: The Key to Better Government.* Chatham, N.J.: Chatham House, 1987.

Schlesinger, M., Dorwart, R. A., and Pulice, R. T. "Competitive Bidding and State Purchase of Services: The Case of Mental Health Care in Massachusetts." *Journal of Policy Analysis and Management,* 1986, *8,* 245–259.

Shichor, D. *Punishment for Profit: Private Prisons/Public Concerns.* London: Sage, 1995.

Smith, S. R., and Lipsky, M. *Nonprofits for Hire: The Welfare State in the Age of Contracting.* Cambridge, Mass.: Harvard University Press, 1993.

Suggs, R. E. "Minorities and Privatization: Issues of Equity." *Public Management,* 1986, *69,* 14–15.

Sullivan, H. J. "Privatization of Public Services: A Growing Threat to Constitutional Rights." *Public Administration Review,* 1987, *47,* 461–467.

Teal, R. F. "Contracting for Transit Service." In J. C. Weicher (ed.), *Innovations in Public Transit.* Washington, D.C.: American Enterprise Institute for Public Policy Research, 1988.

Thayer, F. C. "Privatization: Carnage, Chaos, and Corruption." In B. J. Carroll, R. W. Conant, and T. A. Easton (eds.), *Private Means, Public Ends: Private Business in Social Service Delivery.* New York: Praeger, 1987.

U.S. General Accounting Office. *Government Contractors: Are Service Contractors Performing Inherently Governmental Functions?* GGD–92–11. Washington, D.C.: U.S. Government Printing Office, 1991.

Williamson, O. *The Economic Institutions of Capitalism: Firms, Markets, Relational Contracting.* New York: Free Press, 1985.

Zemansky, S. D. *Contracting Professional Services.* Falls Church, Va.: National Institute of Government Purchasing, 1987.

CHAPTER THIRTY

Alternative Dispute Resolution in Public Administration

Lisa B. Bingham

"Most cases settle." Approximately 90 percent of all lawsuits actually filed in court settle without a trial. Beyond that, untold numbers of disputes never result in a filed complaint. These too settle, although no hard data exist on how many of these there are, or the rate at which they are resolved. Public administrators spend much of their careers resolving disputes. How can one make sure that a dispute gets settled instead of resulting in years of litigation? What are the different ways to achieve settlement? In the past two decades, a vast array of new and recycled techniques has emerged under the general heading *alternative dispute resolution*, or ADR, all marketed as ways to avoid court. This chapter examines the legal framework within which ADR operates, surveys ADR techniques, and explains how they work and circumstances in which they are useful.

WHY USE ALTERNATIVE DISPUTE RESOLUTION?

Although systematic evaluation is difficult and in its earliest stages (see Galanter, 1988; Esser, 1989, contains a comprehensive review of the evaluation literature through its date of publication), the evidence tends to show that administrators can save time and money by using ADR. Most studies have been concerned with procedures that state or federal courts supervise, but commentators have recognized the ready application of experience from the courts to agencies that have heavy adjudication case loads (Harter, 1987). It is certainly clear that parties report higher satisfaction with the process for resolving disputes when they have more control over it (Wall and Lynn, 1993; Lind and others, 1990). Moreover, the evidence shows that negotiated settlements are implemented at higher rates—that is, they stick (McEwen and Maiman, 1984).

Some evidence shows that *mandatory* mediation or arbitration may actually slow down case processing, by diverting cases that would otherwise settle bilaterally through direct negotiation between the parties. In other words, if the parties can plan on ADR as a necessary step, they tend to delay attempts at settlement and instead wait for the mediator or arbitrator to assist them (MacCoun, 1991). However, when parties cannot plan on access to a mediator but can only request voluntary mediation or arbitration when it is clear that direct negotiation will be inefficient or ineffective, then there is no evidence of additional delay. A variety of federal agencies have reported cost savings through their use of ADR. However, these estimates generally are based on the hypothetical cost of a fully litigated case instead of on an actual controlled experiment (Administrative Conference of the United States, 1995; Costantino, 1992; Schuyler, 1993). In its report to Congress, the Administrative Conference of the United States (ACUS) indicated that the Federal Deposit Insurance Corporation (FDIC) estimated that it saved more than $10 million in legal fees and expenses over a three-year period by using ADR rather than litigation in liquidation and litigation matters. The Department of Labor estimated that it saved between 7 and 19 percent in enforcement cases and between 18 and 64 percent in case-processing time in a regional mediation pilot program. The U.S. Air Force estimated that it saved $4 million in Equal Opportunity Employment (EEO) case processing costs using mediation for more than one hundred EEO complaints (Administrative Conference of the United States, 1995, p. 37).

AUTHORITY TO USE ALTERNATIVE DISPUTE RESOLUTION

Public administrators have always resolved a variety of disputes voluntarily through settlement (Harter, 1987, p. 150). Recently, legislatures and commentators have come to acknowledge the role that settlement can play in making an agency more effective and efficient. In general, agency authority to use ADR may derive from any one of a number of sources. The agency may either infer its authority or have express statutory authority to use ADR, stemming from a general ADR statute or from a specific mandate to that agency.

Implied Authority

State and local agencies may infer their authority to use ADR from the state Administrative Procedure Act (APA). Often these statutes provide for informal proceedings and the resolution of complaints by settlement. Agencies may also imply their authority from a general enabling statute that gives the agency the power to enter into contracts. This implied authority is generally adequate for all the consensual processes discussed in this chapter, because the agency cedes no decision-making power to a private party. It merely uses a different technique to negotiate a settlement, something agencies have always done.

There may, however, be questions regarding an agency's authority to use one form of ADR, specifically, binding arbitration. Some have argued that binding arbitration represents an unlawful or unconstitutional delegation of lawmaking power. For example, in the federal sector, the comptroller general issued early rulings prohibiting federal agencies from using binding arbitration outside of labor relations on the theory that agencies could not lawfully turn over lawmaking power to a private third party who is not accountable to the people through constitutional governmental processes (see 32 Comp. Gen. 333, 1953, and 19 Comp. Gen. 700, 1940; and Breger, 1991). However, later statutes authorized federal agencies to use binding arbitration (see later discussion). On the state level, opponents of arbitration have raised this argument in connection with interest and grievance arbitration of labor disputes, sometimes with success. In some states, legislative bodies have responded with frustration to awards where they believe the arbitrator has "split the baby," that is, rendered a compromise award instead of ruling on the merits for one party or the other. In some instances, they have refused to appropriate funds to implement the award. For this reason, many states have enacted general purpose public sector labor relations statutes authorizing, among other things, binding arbitration. Court decisions regarding an agency's ability to use arbitration often are found under interpretations of a state arbitration statute—for example, the Uniform Arbitration Act—when someone challenges the arbitrator's award as outside the scope of his or her authority or contrary to public policy. In general, however, the trend is toward recognizing agency authority to use binding arbitration.

Direct Authority

Federal agencies now also have direct or express statutory authority to use ADR. In part to codify existing federal practice, and also to encourage its expansion, Congress enacted the Administrative Dispute Resolution (ADR) Act of 1990 and the Negotiated Rulemaking Act (NRA) of 1990 (Bingham and Wise, 1996; Susskind, Babbitt, and Segal, 1993). Both the ADR Act and the NRA provisions were made permanent parts of Title V by the Administrative Dispute Resolution Act of 1996 (P.L. 104–320). (The NRA Act is discussed in Chapter Thirteen of this book.) State legislatures have begun to pass similar statutes. The ADR Act encourages federal sector administrators to use ADR techniques in appropriate cases (Harter, 1987). Prior to the passage of the ADR Act, some agencies had engaged in ADR without explicit authorization, inferring their authority from statutes other than the APA, while other agencies took a narrow view of their powers and declined to use these techniques (Administrative Conference of the United States, 1987; Breger, 1987; Riggs and Dorminey, 1987). The ADR Act had broad, bipartisan support; Republicans reason that it would reduce litigation costs for both parties, and Democrats support it on the theory that it would promote better outcomes, including higher participant satisfaction with the process of government decision making (Grassley and Pou, 1992; Hatch, 1987; and U.S. Senate, Government Affairs Committee, 1990). The National Performance Review has encouraged agencies to use their authority under the ADR Act (National Performance Review, 1993, p. 47, and Gore, 1993, p. 119).

The ADR Act has given direct authorization to all federal government agencies to use ADR in any type of dispute—whether between the government and private parties, interagency or intra-agency, or between labor and management. The intent of the act is to provide federal agencies with an "inexpensive means of resolving disputes as an alternative to litigation in the Federal courts" (ADR Act, sec. 2). The ADR Act defines ADR as "any procedure that is used in lieu of an adjudication as defined in [the APA], to resolve issues in controversy, including but not limited to settlement negotiations, conciliation, facilitation, mediation, fact finding, minitrials, and arbitration, or any combination thereof" (sec. 2). The ADR Act does not define these procedures but leaves agencies to define them (for some suggested definitions, see Administrative Conference of the United States, 1992). All ADR use is voluntary for both parties.

The ADR Act gives the agency complete, unreviewable discretion in deciding whether to use ADR. This means that an agency may decide not to use ADR, and its decision is not subject to appeal or review under the APA. The ADR Act requires agencies to consider using ADR, but it does not mandate its use. It requires each agency to develop a policy on ADR, in consultation with ACUS and the Federal Mediation and Conciliation Service (FMCS), but it does not set a deadline for adopting the policy. The ADR Act directs the agency to examine ADR in connection with formal and informal adjudications, rulemaking, enforcement actions, issuing and revoking licenses or permits, contract administration, litigation brought by or against the agency, and other agency actions. It also requires an agency to appoint a senior official to serve as a dispute resolution specialist, with responsibility for implementation of the agency policy.

The ADR Act recognizes that some disputes may not be suitable for negotiation. Just as the prosecutor will not plea bargain with a serial killer against whom she has a strong case, the public administrator considering an enforcement action may choose to make an example of an open and egregious violator. Similarly, agencies may choose not to settle a case because an important legal principle or precedent is at stake (for a detailed discussion of cases inappropriate for settlement, see Edwards, 1986, and Fiss, 1984). The statutes give administrators the discretion to make these choices. Agencies may use ADR in any kind of proceeding, but they are admonished that ADR may not be appropriate when there is need for an authoritative precedent, when the matter involves significant questions of policy, when it is important to maintain established policies consistently, when the matter affects persons not parties to the ADR proceeding, when a full public record is important, or when the agency must maintain continuing jurisdiction over the matter [5 U.S.C. 572]. If administrators exercise this discretion appropriately, they may resolve most disputes and at the same time achieve greater public participation in the decision-making processes of government (Stephenson and Pops, 1991; Manring, 1994).

The ADR Act of 1996 authorizes the FMCS to establish procedures to expedite cases and to assist agencies in hiring neutrals. The act provides certain limited confidentiality for the parties.

THE RANGE OF ADR PROCESSES

Processes in ADR fall into three general categories: unassisted negotiation, consensual processes involving third parties, and adjudicatory processes involving third parties. Agencies may use these processes internally or to resolve conflicts outside the agency (Costantino and Merchant, 1995).

Negotiation

Certain approaches to negotiation are considered to fall on the ADR continuum, specifically, principled or interest-based negotiation and partnering.

Principled or Interest-Based Versus Competitive Negotiation. The terms *principled negotiation* and *interest-based bargaining* represent an approach to bargaining advocated by the Harvard Negotiation Project (Fisher, Ury, and Patton, 1991; Fisher and Brown, 1988; Ury, 1991; Ury, Brett, and Goldberg, 1989) that includes as well collaborative or win-win bargaining (Cohen, 1991). These approaches are at the opposite end of the continuum from positional, confrontational, competitive, or adversarial bargaining (Koren and Goodman, 1991).

The Harvard Negotiation Project formulation of principled negotiation entails four steps: (1) separate people from the problem; (2) focus on interests, not positions; (3) invent options for mutual gain; and (4) use objective criteria (Fisher, Ury, and Patton, 1991, p. 13). The win-win formulation suggests seven analogous steps: (1) establish trust, (2) obtain information, (3) meet their needs, (4) use their ideas, (5) transform relationships to collaboration, (6) take moderate risk, and (7) get their help (Cohen, 1991, pp. 176–177). Generally these steps provide a shorthand for describing and structuring a process that takes place among a group of people. No one step exists in isolation, but rather each is part of a dynamic and evolving interpersonal relationship. The goal is to achieve agreements that contain mutual gains (for a more detailed discussion of negotiation for public administrators, see Bingham, 1996).

Cohen (1991) characterizes adversarial negotiation as "winning at all costs . . . Soviet style" (p. 119). In competitive negotiation, the parties often get caught up negotiating over a series of artificial positions instead of addressing the true needs and interests underlying the dispute. Principled negotiation finds its easiest application where the parties have an ongoing relationship, for example, a manufacturer, an agency and its supplier, or a labor union and the employer (Lax and Sebenius, 1986). However, a negotiator can also use principled negotiation effectively to bargain a one-shot deal, with certain caveats.

For a number of reasons, public administrators should make every effort to use principled, not positional, negotiation. First, public administrators potentially face continuing relationships with every regulated entity or former employee; each party is a member of the public that the agency serves. In public service, very often the how of what is done is as important as what is accomplished. Unfortunately, most press coverage seems to focus on the how, and not the what, of agency business. In other words, principled negotiation is good public relations. Second, principled negotiation is ethical practice. A reputation for integrity is a negotiator's, and an administrator's, greatest asset. Principled negotiation is a step-by-step recipe for negotiating integrity. Third, public administrators hold positions of public trust. The public has high expectations and holds public administrators to high standards of personal conduct. It would violate that trust to knowingly mislead a party to a negotiation, and a member of the public might construe many of the standard hard-bargaining ploys as intentional deception. There is no hard evidence that a competitive negotiating style is any more effective than principled negotiating (Boskey, 1993, p. 10, citing Williams, 1983).

In the public sector, however, an administrator's authority to negotiate is often circumscribed. An administrator may make a commitment in negotiation only to find it countermanded by a superior. In the federal sector, some administrators have expressed concern about oversight by the inspector general. When they settle a case, they must make certain that the inspector general's office will view the settlement as reasonable and not as collusive or sacrificing the public interest (Bingham and Wise, 1996). Moreover, not all negotiating partners are willing to use a principled approach (for suggestions on how to handle this problem, see Ury, 1991). Principled negotiation skills are an important tool, as long as they are used in the service of the public interest.

Partnering as a Dispute Avoidance Process. In the area of procurement and government contracting, many agencies have begun to use a process called *partnering.* This process is intended to build a strong, collaborative working relationship between contracting parties before disputes arise, and to set up channels of communication that parties will use immediately upon the first sign of a dispute. The chief executive officer or top management of the contractor and the top public administrators responsible for the project go on a retreat, generally lasting for several days, during which they discuss their expectations for the contract and the means through which it will be executed. They set up avenues of communication and processes for handling disputes as soon as they arise. In addition, they simply get to know each other better. After the retreat, they have regular troubleshooting meetings to catch any problem early in its development. The process is one of dispute avoidance. However, not all disputes are avoidable. While the partnering process may reduce the need for litigation, administrators may nevertheless need to maintain an arm's length relationship with contractors to ensure effective oversight of the public interest.

Consensual Processes Involving a Third-Party Neutral

There is a constantly evolving array of processes in which the parties bring in a third party to aid in settlement (as a general reference, and for tables on key elements of various processes, see Goldberg, Sander, and Rogers, 1992, pp. 4–5). The hallmark of all these processes is that the third party has no power to impose a settlement on the parties. The process simply aids the parties in reaching their own agreement. If they do, that agreement often takes the form of a contract that is enforceable in court. The differences among these processes stem from the third party's degree of activism. Often the third party is referred to simply as the neutral, although considerable disagreement exists among scholars as to whether the third party should be neutral in the literal sense of not leaning harder on one party than on the other in pursuit of a resolution. Frequently, a neutral finds it necessary to aid the weaker party to redress a serious imbalance of power in the discussions. Some scholars suggest that "impartial" is the better characterization.

This section examines the processes referred to as facilitation, conciliation, mediation, early neutral evaluation, minitrial, and summary jury trial. It is important to recognize that all of these terms are imprecise, and there is considerable local variation in how the neutral actually carries out his or her responsibilities.

Facilitation. Facilitation is a process common to negotiated rulemaking and to complex environmental or public disputes. City councils have also used it for agenda and goal setting and in budget deliberations with public participation. The Negotiated Rulemaking Act defines a facilitator as "a person who impartially aids in the discussions and negotiations among the members of a negotiated rulemaking committee to develop a proposed rule" [5 U.S.C. 562 (4)]. In general, the multiple parties retain a facilitator as the neutral third party. In negotiated rulemaking other than that where this task is performed by a convener, the facilitator may first engage in an assessment of whether the dispute is "mediable," that is, whether there is any prospect of reaching a settlement within a reasonable amount of time (Hamilton, 1991). The facilitator is then responsible for helping the parties negotiate a protocol for the succeeding negotiation (Cormick, 1989), which includes setting ground rules on meeting times, places, press releases, and expert assistance, and determining a time frame and some structure for the process. The facilitator chairs all meetings and orchestrates discussion by asking problem-solving questions in an effort to help the parties identify underlying shared interests and to brainstorm possible ideas for settlement. In general, a facilitator is less activist than a true mediator, but instead makes it possible for the parties to conduct direct discussions.

In environmental and public policy disputes, the facilitator must also manage the problems posed by the presence of multiple parties, with varying levels of commitment to resolving the dispute. Sometimes the facilitator must break a large group representing diverse constituencies into smaller working groups, each with a narrower charge. Often there are concerns about the ability of a representative to deliver the support of the constituency. Some scholars have criticized the leveling effect of facilitation, which with its emphasis on consensus may give a recalcitrant party undue influence over the outcome. Conversely, it may be difficult to exclude that party without putting the settlement at risk of litigation. Lastly, some have criticized the up-front investment in time and resources that a complex public policy negotiation entails.

Conciliation. Conciliation is a term used in Title VII of the Civil Rights Act of 1964, and in that context it refers to the agency's role after it has conducted a preliminary investigation and determined existence of reasonable cause to believe that prohibited discrimination occurred. The Equal Employment Opportunity Commission (EEOC) investigator may then assist the parties in exploring possible ideas for settlement of the complaint, by confidentially communicating with each disputing party. Since the EEOC investigator has made a finding of reasonable cause, he or she is not entirely neutral. Outside the Title VII context and more generally, conciliation has referred to settlement of labor disputes without a strike, as in the FMCS. In this context, conciliation is the same as mediation.

Mediation. Mediation is the single most popular ADR technique in government (Bingham and Wise, 1996). Mediation is also the most activist form of third-party intervention for consensual dispute resolution (for more on mediation, see Kolb and Associates, 1994, and Bush and Folger, 1994). Usually, parties may retain an outside neutral mediator through a government board or panel, such as the Federal Mediation and Conciliation Service; a private provider such as the American Arbitration Association, the Center for Public Resources Institute for Dispute Resolution, JAMS-Endispute, or United States Mediation and Arbitration; or one of numerous other independent neutrals. Recently, some agencies (including the U.S. Department of Labor; see Schuyler, 1993) have attempted to train employees to mediate disputes involving other employees or members of the public; these mediators are often termed in-house neutrals. Federal agencies have also signed a compact to institute a shared-neutrals program, by which they train employees in their own agency to mediate disputes in a different agency (Administrative Conference of the United States, 1994).

Mediation is a voluntary process (see Goldberg, Sander, and Rogers, 1992, pp. 103–189). The mediator may not impose a solution and may only assist parties to reach a mutually agreeable voluntary settlement. Mediation is an extension of negotiation between the parties. The mediator provides a safe avenue for communicating interests the parties are unwilling or unable to share directly. Mediation is also a confidential process. All communications from the parties to the mediator are kept confidential to encourage fullest exploration of possible solutions. Mediators usually have a privilege against being called as a witness in the event of a legal proceeding, and offers of settlement are generally inadmissible as evidence in any event (see Nolan-Haley, 1992, pp. 90–100). However, the specifics of the privilege (for example, whether the parties or the mediator hold it) and its extent may vary from state to state. In general, mediators from the FMCS hold the privilege and may invoke it against the parties to a labor dispute (*NLRB* v. *Joseph Macaluso, Inc.*, 1980). In addition, the parties may enter into a contract agreeing to confidentiality.

The mediator screens the case, explains the mediation process to the parties, assists the parties with exchanging information, helps the parties to brainstorm new ideas to resolve the dispute, and assists the parties in defining and drafting the agreement (Nolan-Haley, 1992, pp. 60–78). The first step in screening the case is a mediability assessment (Hamilton, 1991), that is, determining whether the issue is properly the subject of mediation and whether the parties are ready for the process. The mediator attempts to ascertain whether there is a good faith desire to settle. He or she generally explains the process in joint session and addresses issues, including his or her credentials, ground rules, a protocol for mediation (Cormick, 1989), neutrality and impartiality, the process, the fact that there is no imposed agreement, the mechanics (generally a joint meeting and exchange of statements, followed by shuttle diplomacy, followed by a joint meeting to explain the settlement and initial it), confidentiality, and the rule that mutual respect is required (Nolan-Haley, 1992, pp. 60–78).

The mediator assists with information exchange and bargaining by conducting separate sessions in which he or she collects pertinent information, frames issues, isolates points of agreement and disagreement, generates options (brainstorming), encourages compromise, and brings parties to closure (Nolan-Haley, 1992). Essential mediator skills include active listening, which includes acknowledging the legitimacy of the parties' emotional responses and paraphrasing a party's comments to validate the speaker and demonstrate whether the mediator understood the speaker's concerns. Active listening also includes questioning—specifically, using open-ended questions and problem solving (who, what, where, when, why, why not, and how) instead of leading questions ("When did you stop breaking the law?"), and also using questions that clarify a speaker's statements. The mediator must observe how the parties behave in private caucus and must interpret nonverbal communication.

Typical mediator tactics for breaking impasse include separating the parties, accumulating agreements on smaller points, setting a deadline after which the mediator threatens to withdraw assistance, keeping the parties negotiating for a prolonged session or around the clock, reality testing by revealing each side's best alternative to a negotiated agreement to the other side, engaging in informal early neutral evaluation (see later discussion), making a mediator's proposal for settlement, having the parties select a limited number of priority issues, negotiating conditional "package agreements" that are contingent upon approval of a complete settlement, allowing each side to vent and have a voice, and other methods.

Agencies have used mediation with success in environmental disputes (Peterson, 1992), hydropower disputes (Moore, 1991a, 1991b), farmer-lender credit disputes (Riskin, 1993), equal employment opportunity or discrimination complaints (Edwards, 1993; Office of Personnel Management and Equal Employment Opportunity Commission, 1994), and procurement and government contracting disputes (Brittin, 1989; Crowell and Pou, 1990; Interagency ADR Working Group, 1994). The FDIC has an active mediation program for credit disputes (Costantino, 1992, 1993, 1994; Costantino and Kaplow, 1994). The Forest Service has used mediation for planning purposes and public participation (Manring, 1994). These are only a selection of recent reports.

The strengths of mediation include its consensual nature. Public administrators report less fear of loss of control with mediation than with arbitration (Bingham and Wise, 1996). Parties find it a more satisfying process than litigation; they perceive it as more fair (Lind and others, 1990; Tyler, 1994). If the parties do reach a settlement, they have certainly saved transaction costs. The primary weakness of mediation is the lack of finality if the parties fail to reach an agreement. Other scholars have also criticized it for taking what may be public issues and privatizing them with confidential, off-the-record settlements, thus impoverishing the body of judicial precedent that regulates society (Edwards, 1986; Fiss, 1984; Galanter, 1988).

Early Neutral Evaluation. Early neutral evaluation is a service often performed informally by mediators, but it is also a process the parties can use for any kind of dispute to negotiate their own resolution. A neutral third party with substantive expertise listens to each party informally present its interests and positions in the dispute. The neutral then gives the parties a preliminary opinion on the merits of the dispute. In other words, the process operates as a reality check. For the first time, some objective person to whom the parties have ceded authority tells them the likely outcome of the case should the parties not settle but instead proceed to adjudication, whether through the administrative process or the courts. The purpose of this process is to foster further, more realistic negotiation. In dispute-system design parlance, this is called a loop-back to negotiation (Ury, Brett, and Goldberg, 1989). The early neutral evaluator has no authority to bind the parties to a particular solution, and generally his or her opinion on the dispute is not admissible in a trial. Moreover, the early neutral evaluator generally does not mediate the dispute but returns the parties to their own negotiation. The Internal Revenue Service has used this process with great success for a number of years to resolve disputes over the valuation of property that is claimed as a deduction for charitable contributions. A related process uses dispute resolution panels to perform the same function (for an evaluation of such panels in discrimination disputes, see Knishkowy, 1994).

Minitrials. Minitrials are commonly used to resolve litigation over complex commercial disputes. The Army Corps of Engineers made pioneering use of minitrials in major contract litigation (Edelman, Carr, and Creighton, 1989). In a minitrial, each party is represented by counsel and generally by a chief executive officer (CEO) or high-ranking executive with authority to settle the dispute on the spot. The parties' lawyers each present abbreviated versions of the evidence and argument on their case, generally directing their presentation to the CEO of the opposing party. They generally present evidence in summary form, not through testimony, and in this sense a minitrial is not a trial at all. At the conclusion of the evidence and argument, the CEOs attempt to negotiate a settlement of the dispute. More often than not, they excuse their lawyers. The parties hire a neutral with substantive expertise and high prestige—for example, a retired federal court judge—to supervise the process and answer questions of procedure. This differs, however, from early neutral evaluation in that the neutral has no authority to decide or even to give an opinion on the dispute. Occasionally the parties may ask the neutral to become an early neutral evaluator if they reach an impasse.

Summary Jury Trials. These are also used to resolve complex civil litigation. In a summary jury trial, the parties actually go so far as to impanel a real jury, the members of which usually believe they are participating in a real trial. However, the parties present short versions of the evidence. The jury deliberates and makes findings of fact and liability, after which the judge releases them. The parties use this information to negotiate a settlement. They are not bound by the jury's findings; these are merely advisory (although usually, the jury does not know that). In other words, this too is a loop-back to negotiation.

Adjudicatory Processes Involving a Third-Party Neutral

A number of processes resemble an administrative agency adjudication. They are generally varieties of arbitration. Arbitration is an ancient practice, dating back at least as far as Roman law. Most generally, it is a process in which parties hire a private judge to decide their dispute. Although historically the parties define the authority of the arbitrator, since World War II various public sector labor-relations statutes have authorized state-appointed arbitrators to resolve labor disputes; sometimes these statutes define the scope of the arbitrator's authority.

There are some basic categories for arbitration. Arbitration may be of rights or interests. Rights arbitration is the retrospective adjudication of who is entitled to what under an existing contract that one side says the other has breached. It may also be arbitration of statutory rights, as when employer and employee agree to submit a discrimination claim under an existing statute to an arbitrator. The key fact is that the arbitration focuses on past events. Interest arbitration is the prospective adjudication of who will be entitled to what under some future contract. In an interest arbitration, the arbitrator takes evidence for the purposes of determining the parties' interests and evaluating how to combine them to structure their future relationship; the arbitrator may write a contract for the parties. Rights arbitration is quasi-adjudicative, and interest arbitration is quasi-legislative.

In addition, arbitration may be binding or nonbinding. Binding arbitration produces an award that the winning party may enforce in court and convert into a court judgment. Nonbinding arbitration produces an award that is advisory only and serves as a loop-back to negotiation if the parties choose not to accept it. Both rights and interest arbitration may be binding or nonbinding.

Lastly, since arbitration first enjoyed success in this country in the context of labor relations, there is a tendency to categorize arbitration as labor or "everything else" (for comprehensive guides to labor arbitration, see Elkouri and Elkouri, 1991, and Schoonhoven, 1991). "Everything else" may be lumped together under the heading "commercial." For example, the American Arbitration Association has a labor arbitrator panel and a commercial arbitrator panel. Within the commercial panel, there are experts on architects' contracts, construction, divorce, environmental disputes, consumer contracts, commercial sales contracts, nonunion employment contracts, and so forth. Each expert represents a subcategory within the commercial panel.

In all arbitration, as in an administrative adjudication, neither the decision maker nor the parties are bound by the rules of evidence used in a court of law (Schoonhoven, 1991, p. 231). It is a matter of routine for an arbitrator to admit hearsay evidence "for what it is worth," subject to parties' later briefs on relevance. The hearings are generally held in conference rooms, either at the agency or at a neutral site such as a hotel. However, the hearings themselves generally follow the adjudicatory model. The parties make opening statements. The party with the burden of proof (generally a civil preponderance-of-the-evidence test) proceeds to present its case, with its witnesses subject to cross-examination. The other party presents the case in rebuttal. Generally, cross-examination is not limited to the scope of the direct examination, and other procedural legalisms and niceties are ignored. It is common for parties to use nonlawyer representatives in arbitration, and for there to be no record of the hearing except perhaps a tape recording. The parties may make closing statements or submit written briefs arguing their cases. In expedited arbitration, all the same rules apply, except that the arbitration hearing is usually scheduled within weeks of the demand, there are no written briefs, and the arbitrator must render an award on an abbreviated time schedule, usually two weeks. Sometimes the parties ask the arbitrator to render an award from the bench.

Fact-Finding. In labor relations, fact-finding is a term of art that really means nonbinding interest arbitration. The arbitrator is called a fact finder and listens to presentations of evidence and argument on each disputed clause or article in a proposed new or successor collective bargaining agreement. The fact finder then evaluates the evidence and issues an award, often called a report, in which he or she proposes specific contract language or benefits on each disputed issue. The fact finder also explains the evidence and rationale for his or her conclusions. The parties generally are not bound by the report unless they fail to reject it within a certain period specified in the state labor-relations statute, for example, thirty days. Usually, they reject it as a matter of course, but use it to return to the bargaining table and cut a deal that varies in some ways from what the fact finder proposed. Often the parties may request mediation for this round of negotiations. In other words, fact-finding is yet another "loop-back to negotiation" (Ury, Brett, and Goldberg, 1989).

More recently, some parties have used fact-finding more literally, to define the facts of a disputed case so that the parties may jointly use these facts to negotiate a settlement, or as in negotiated rulemaking, a proposed regulation. Fact-finding of this variety entails presentations of evidence to a subject matter expert, who may have highly technical scientific or engineering knowledge. The fact finder then decides the disputed questions of fact. Generally the parties are bound by the decision in this variant of fact-finding. This process is particularly useful in environmental disputes, for example, where the parties may disagree over the scientific evidence of risk or toxicity.

Nonbinding Rights Arbitration. The parties may use arbitration as another loop-back to negotiation. In that event, they may agree that the arbitrator's award is nonbinding, or merely advisory. In labor relations, perhaps as many as 10 percent of all grievance procedures have advisory arbitration as a final step for grievances over breach of contract. Generally, the parties abide by the terms of the arbitration award; it has great moral force and suasion. However, for political or other reasons, management may be loathe to delegate full authority to the arbitrator to decide the grievance. By analogy, other disputing parties may agree by contract to submit a dispute to nonbinding arbitration (for a useful case study on the Army Corps of Engineers' nonbinding arbitration of a construction contract dispute, see Edelman, Carr, Lancaster, and Creighton, 1990).

Many courts have adopted this technique as a way of reducing the cases on the docket. Often this "court-annexed" arbitration is a mandatory step before a trial. The advantage of nonbinding arbitration is that it serves as a reality check for parties headed toward trial. Its disadvantage is its lack of finality; if the parties reject the award and litigate the case anyway, they may end up spending more in transaction costs than they would have without the interim step. This is why some critics suggest that mandatory nonbinding arbitration actually limits access to courts, by imposing additional costs on those who can least afford it. Moreover, one scholar found that mandatory nonbinding arbitration actually slowed the clearing of a court's docket, by diverting cases away from settlement negotiation; the parties simply waited until the arbitration before they thought about settling (MacCoun, 1991).

Binding Arbitration

Varied binding arbitration approaches are used. In all varieties, the parties are bound by the arbitrator's decision and may appeal to court only on very limited grounds. This policy of deferral to arbitration is strongly established. In its *Steelworkers Trilogy* (1960), the Supreme Court held that federal courts should resolve doubts in favor of enforcing labor agreements to arbitrate grievances; moreover, federal courts should enforce any labor arbitration award that draws its essence from the collective bargaining agreement (Elkouri and Elkouri, 1991, p. 25–31). Recently the Supreme Court extended its policy of deferral to arbitration agreements outside the context of labor relations; it held it would enforce a predispute agreement to arbitrate statutory rights—in this case, age-discrimination claims—unless Congress indicated in the statute that such claims should not be submitted to arbitration (*Gilmer* v. *Interstate/Johnson Lane Corporation*, 1991).

Interest Arbitration in Labor Relations. In the public sector, there is a tendency to associate binding arbitration with a specific subcategory of arbitration, namely, binding interest arbitration in the context of labor relations. This is arbitration generally mandated by statute in some states to resolve protracted public sector bargaining disputes, where the parties have attempted to negotiate a new collective bargaining agreement for a prolonged period of time and have failed to agree. The state intervenes to solve the dispute by offering binding interest arbitration in lieu of the private sector right to strike. This can take several forms. The statute may use an issue-by-issue approach or a total package approach. In issue-by-issue arbitration, the arbitrator rules on each disputed clause or article of the contract separately; one party may win on some of the issues and lose on others, as the arbitrator attempts to create a package that, overall, balances the interests of the parties. In a total package approach, the arbitrator has a single discussion of the total contract; it may result in winner-take-all. In addition, arbitration may be a last best offer, also known as final offer arbitration, or it may be somewhat open. In last best offer, the arbitrator must choose between the final offers of labor and management; the arbitrator has no authority to shape a compromise. The theory is that the arbitrator will choose the most reasonable alternative, and this will force the parties to make more reasonable final offers than they were willing to make to each other across the table. In its more open form, the arbitrator is not constrained by the offers of the parties but may draft a compromise that neither party has proposed. The end result of any of these forms, in any of their combinations, is a binding, enforceable contract governing the future collective bargaining relationship of the parties during the contract term. Interest arbitration includes, for example, salary arbitration in professional baseball. It is conceivable that contracting parties could use it to structure a relationship outside the context of labor relations, but this is rare.

Grievance Arbitration in Labor Relations. This other variant of binding arbitration in labor contracts is rights arbitration over a claim of breach of an existing contract. It directly substitutes for state or federal court litigation over the meaning of the collective bargaining agreement as a contract. Generally there are two categories of grievances: discipline and contract interpretation. In discipline cases, management has the burden of proof to show facts justifying the discipline, generally to a just cause standard. In contract interpretation cases, the union has the burden of proof to show that management misinterpreted or misapplied the contract. This system of industrial justice has been very successful in providing a relatively quick, inexpensive means of providing final decisions in contract disputes.

Employment Arbitration. This is a form of rights arbitration. The Model Employment Termination Act proposes to substitute arbitration for litigation of all employment dismissal cases; the arbitrator would take the place of a judge in wrongful discharge and discrimination cases. This remedy is somewhat controversial. At present, it has been adopted by some nonunion employers in personnel manuals or employment contracts. The courts are enforcing these arbitration agreements, although whether the employee has "voluntarily" agreed to them is open to question. Its advantage is that it provides a prompt, inexpensive forum for the employee who might have no other day in court. Its disadvantage is that outside the union context, the employee may lack adequate representation and preparation for the hearing.

Commercial Arbitration. Arbitration has been a method for resolving commercial contract disputes for centuries; it dates back to the Middle Ages. In the modern era, it is common to find "form contracts" with arbitration clauses, particularly in the areas of construction, architects' services, sales, international business transactions, automotive lemon laws, securities dealer disputes, and so forth. Commercial arbitration is generally a form of rights arbitration, used when disputes arise during an existing relationship to determine the relative rights of the parties.

Med-Arb. Med-Arb is a relatively new procedure in which a neutral first mediates the dispute, and then, if mediation fails, the neutral goes on to arbitrate the dispute. It does not represent pure mediation, because the mediator has the power to compel acquiescence of the parties. Its advantage is that it ensures finality, and it is efficient in its use of neutrals; the arbitrator already knows a great deal about the case from the mediation. Its disadvantage is that the parties may be reluctant to confide their bottom line to the mediator for fear he or she will use it against them in the later arbitration. This inhibition of disclosure of information may interfere with voluntary settlement.

Enforcement of ADR

With respect to consensual processes, choice of a means to enforce a settlement depends on the form of the settlement. In the vast majority of cases, a settlement is converted into a settlement agreement, which is a form of contract, and it is subject to the contract law of the appropriate jurisdiction. If the parties fail to reduce their agreement to a contract, they may nevertheless have recourse under contract law where one party has relied to its detriment on the other party's representations regarding the settlement. There are also circumstances in which the parties simply rely on each other's good faith, and there is no enforcement mechanism other than to return to the original litigation, if this is still possible under a statute of limitations. In labor relations, refusal to implement a grievance settlement or an arbitration award is an unfair labor practice, for which there are state and federal administrative remedies.

Consent Decrees. If parties reach a settlement after a lawsuit is instituted, their settlement may take the form of a consent decree or consent judgment of the court (for an extensive discussion of consent decrees, see Levine, 1993). This means that their settlement is not simply a valid contract, it is a judgment or order that the court will enforce through its contempt powers. It is not a judgment on the merits, and hence not precedent for other cases. It is not subject to appellate review, with very limited exceptions. Public administrators should ensure institutional memory of consent decrees, so that new administrators do not violate their terms through ignorance of their existence. Consent decrees may remain in force for many years, and conditions giving rise to them may change; these decrees are subject to modification by the court in appropriate circumstances (Levine, 1993).

Review of Arbitration Awards. The scope of review for a binding arbitration award is very limited. Both the Uniform Arbitration Act adopted by most states and the Federal Arbitration Act require a prompt motion to vacate the award (usually within thirty days). Courts will only vacate an award if there has been fraud, undue influence, evident bias, an incomplete award, an award that exceeds the submission or the scope of the arbitrator's authority, or an award that violates public policy. These standards are narrower than the APA standards for judicial review of most other kinds of agency action. Courts will generally overturn agency action if it is arbitrary or capricious, lacks substantial evidence on the record as a whole, is unconstitutional, was made on unlawful procedure, or is affected by an error of law. The ADR Act of 1990 added a provision for federal agencies; they may simply vacate an arbitration award by rejecting it within thirty days after the arbitrator issues it. This essentially renders arbitrations with federal agencies binding on only one party—the other side. This may be one reason why it has not caught on in the federal government (Bingham and Wise, 1996).

CONCLUSION

Public administrators have a variety of useful tools in ADR. Interest-based negotiation applies to much of the daily business of an agency. Facilitation can improve public participation in meetings. Mediation can produce more mutual solutions and reveal hidden common interests to disputing parties. Arbitration, in its many forms, may provide the parties with decisions they need at a much lower cost than litigation. These processes produce solutions that are enforceable as contracts, or in court. Public administrators can save time and money through the appropriate use of ADR.

Cases Cited

Gilmer v. Interstate/Johnson Lane Corporation, 500 U.S. 20 (1991).

NLRB v. Joseph Macaluso, Inc., 618 F.2d 51 (9th Cir., 1980).

Steelworkers Trilogy: United Steelworkers v. *American Manufacturing Company,* 363 U.S. 564 (1960); *United Steelworkers* v. *Warrior & Gulf,* 363 U.S. 574 (1960); *United Steelworkers* v. *Enterprise Wheel & Car Corporation,* 363 U.S. 593 (1960).

References

Administrative Conference of the United States. "An Overview of Federal Agency Use of Alternative Means of Dispute Resolution." In "A Colloquium on Improving Dispute Resolution: Options for the Federal Government" (symposium). *Administrative Law Journal,* 1987, *1,* 405–426.

Administrative Conference of the United States, Office of the Chairman. *Implementing the ADR Act: Guidance for Agency Dispute Resolution Specialists.* Washington, D.C.: Administrative Conference of the United States, 1992.

Administrative Conference of the United States. *Interagency Pilot Project on Sharing Neutrals.* Washington, D.C.: Administrative Conference of the United States, 1994.

Administrative Conference of the United States. *Toward Improved Agency Dispute Resolution: Implementing the ADR Act.* Washington, D.C.: Administrative Conference of the United States, 1995.

Bingham, L. B. "Negotiating to Achieve Public Objectives." In J. L. Perry (ed.), *Handbook of Public Administration.* (2nd ed.) San Francisco: Jossey-Bass, 1996.

Bingham, L. B., and Wise, C. R. "The Administrative Dispute Resolution Act of 1990: How Do We Evaluate Its Success?" *Journal of Public Administration Research and Theory,* 1996, *6,* 383–414.

Boskey, J. B. "Blueprint for Negotiations." *Dispute Resolution Journal,* Dec. 1993, pp. 8–19.

Breger, M. J. "Introduction." In "A Colloquium on Improving Dispute Resolution: Options for the Federal Government" (symposium). *Administrative Law Journal,* 1987, *1,* 399–404.

Breger, M. J. "Realizing the Potential of Arbitration in Federal Agency Dispute Resolution." *Arbitration Journal,* 1991, *46,* 35–40.

Brittin, A. J. "Alternative Dispute Resolution in Government Contract Appeals." *Public Contract Law Journal,* 1989, *19,* 210–232.

Bush, R.A.B., and Folger, J. P. *The Promise of Mediation: Responding to Conflict Through Empowerment and Recognition.* San Francisco: Jossey-Bass, 1994.

Cohen, H. *You Can Negotiate Anything: How to Get What You Want.* New York: Citadel Press, 1991.

Cormick, G. W. "Strategic Issues in Structuring Multi-Party Public Policy Negotiations." *Negotiation Journal,* 1989, *5,* 125–132.

Costantino, C. A. "FDIC Uses Spectrum of ADR Options to Resolve Disputes: Finding New Ways to Decrease Costs, Speed Resolutions, and Maximize Recoveries." *Federal Bar News and Journal,* 1992, *39,* 524–527.

Costantino, C. A. "Summary of FDIC ADR Creditor Claims Pilot Project April 1993." Paper presented at the 1993 Conference of the Society for Professionals in Dispute Resolution, Toronto, Oct. 20–23, 1993.

Costantino, C. A. "How to Set Up an ADR Program." *Government Executive*, 1994, *26*, 44–45.

Costantino, C. A., and Kaplow, C. M. "FDIC Criteria for Neutrals Depend on Experience." *Alternatives to the High Cost of Litigation*, 1994, *12*(7), 85, 93–94.

Costantino, C. A., and Merchant, C. S. *Designing Conflict Management Systems: A Guide to Creating Productive and Healthy Organizations.* San Francisco: Jossey-Bass, 1995.

Crowell, E. H., and Pou, C., Jr. "Appealing Government Contract Decisions: Reducing the Cost and Delay of Procurement Litigation with Alternative Dispute Resolution Techniques." *Maryland Law Review*, 1990, *49*, 183–254.

Edelman, L., Carr, F., and Creighton, J. L. *The Minitrial: Alternative Dispute Resolution Series, Pamphlet 1.* Fort Belvoir, Va.: U.S. Army Corps of Engineers, 1989.

Edelman, L., Carr, F., Lancaster, C., and Creighton, J. L. *Nonbinding Arbitration: Alternative Dispute Resolution Series, Pamphlet 2.* Fort Belvoir, Va.: U.S. Army Corps of Engineers, 1990.

Edwards, A. O. "Eye on EEO." *ADR Network*, 1993, *1*(1), 8.

Edwards, H. T. "Alternative Dispute Resolution: Panacea or Anathema?" *Harvard Law Review*, 1986, *99*, 668–684.

Elkouri, F., and Elkouri, E. *How Arbitration Works* (4th ed.) *and 1985–1989 Cumulative Supplement.* Washington, D.C.: Bureau of National Affairs, 1991.

Esser, J. P. "Evaluations of Dispute Processing: We Do Not Know What We Think and We Do Not Think What We Know." *Denver University Law Review*, 1989, *66*, 499–562.

Fisher, R., and Brown, S. *Getting Together: Building Relationships as We Negotiate.* New York: Penguin Books, 1988.

Fisher, R., Ury, F., and Patton, B. *Getting to Yes: Negotiating Agreement Without Giving In.* New York: Penguin Books, 1991.

Fiss, O. M. "Against Settlement." *Yale Law Journal*, 1984, *93*, 1073–1090.

Galanter, M. "The Quality of Settlements." *Journal of Dispute Resolution*, 1988, pp. 55–84.

Goldberg, S. B., Sander, F.E.A., and Rogers, N. H. *Dispute Resolution: Negotiation, Mediation and Other Processes.* (2nd ed.) New York: Little, Brown, 1992.

Gore, A., Jr. *From Red Tape to Results: Creating a Government That Works Better and Costs Less.* Report of the National Performance Review. Washington, D.C.: U.S. Government Printing Office, 1993.

Grassley, C. E., and Pou, C., Jr. "Congress, the Executive Branch and the Dispute Resolution Process." *Journal of Dispute Resolution*, 1992, pp. 1–24.

Hamilton, M. S. "Environmental Mediation: Requirements for Successful Institutionalization." In M. K. Mills (ed.), *Alternative Dispute Resolution in the Public Sector.* Chicago: Nelson-Hall, 1991.

Harter, P. "Points on a Continuum: Dispute Resolution Procedures and the Administrative Process." *Administrative Law Journal*, 1987, *1*, 141–211.

Hatch, O. G. "A View from Congress." In "A Colloquium on Improving Dispute Resolution: Options for the Federal Government" (symposium). *Administrative Law Journal*, 1987, *1*, 427–440.

Interagency ADR Working Group. "Agencies Sign OFPP Pledge to Use ADR in Contract Disputes." *ADR Network*, 1994, *2*(1), 1–3.

Knishkowy, J. *USDA Dispute Resolution Board Pilot Project Evaluation: Final Report.* Washington, D.C.: U.S. Department of Agriculture, 1994.

Kolb, D. M., and Associates. *When Talk Works: Profiles of Mediators.* San Francisco: Jossey-Bass, 1994.

Koren, L., and Goodman, P. *The Haggler's Handbook: One Hour to Negotiating Power.* New York: Norton, 1991.

Lax, D. A., and Sebenius, J. K. *The Manager as Negotiator: Bargaining for Cooperation and Competitive Gain.* New York: Free Press, 1986.

Levine, D. I. "The Modification of Equitable Decrees in Institutional Reform Litigation: A Commentary on the Supreme Court's Adoption of the Second Circuit's Flexible Test." *Brooklyn Law Review*, 1993, *58*, 1239–1278.

Lind, E. A., and others. "In the Eye of the Beholder: Tort Litigants' Evaluations of Their Experiences in the Civil Justice System." *Law and Society Review*, 1990, *24*, 953–996.

MacCoun, R. J. "Unintended Consequences of Court Arbitration: A Cautionary Tale from New Jersey. *Justice System Journal*, 1991, *14*, 229–243.

Manring, N. J. "ADR and Administrative Responsiveness: Challenges for Public Administrators." *Public Administration Review*, 1994, *54*, 197–202.

McEwen, C., and Maiman, R. "Mediation in Small Claims Court: Achieving Compliance Through Consent." *Law and Society Review*, 1984, *18*, 11–50.

Moore, C. W. *Corps of Engineers Uses Mediation to Settle Hydropower Dispute.* Alternative Dispute Resolution Series Case Study No. 6. Washington, D.C.: U.S. Army Corps of Engineers, 1991a.

Moore, C. W. *Mediation.* Alternative Dispute Resolution Series Pamphlet No. 6. Washington, D.C.: U.S. Army Corps of Engineer, 1991b.

National Performance Review. *Improving Regulatory Systems: Accompanying Report of the National Performance Review.* Washington, D.C.: Office of the Vice President, 1993.

Nolan-Haley, J. M. *Alternative Dispute Resolution in a Nutshell.* St. Paul, Minn.: West, 1992.

Office of Personnel Management and Equal Employment Opportunity Commission. *Alternative Dispute Resolution: A Resource Guide.* Washington, D.C.: Office of Personnel Management and Equal Employment Opportunity Commission, 1994.

Peterson, L. "The Promise of Mediated Settlements of Environmental Disputes: The Experience of EPA Region V." *Columbia Journal of Environmental Law*, 1992, *17*, 327–380.

Riggs, D. A., and Dorminey, E. K. "Federal Agencies' Use of Alternative Means of Dispute Resolution." *Administrative Law Journal*, 1987, *1*, 125–139.

Riskin, L. L. "Two Concepts of Mediation in the FMHA's Farmer-Lender Mediation Program." *Administrative Law Review*, 1993, *45*, 21–64.

Schoonhoven, R. J. (ed.). *Fairweather's Practice and Procedure in Labor Arbitration.* Washington, D.C.: Bureau of National Affairs, 1991.

Schuyler, M. L. *A Cost Analysis of the Department of Labor's Philadelphia ADR Pilot Project.* Washington, D.C.: U.S. Department of Labor, 1993.

Stephenson, M. A., Jr., and Pops, G. M. "Public Administrators and Conflict Resolution: Democratic Theory, Administrative Capacity, and the Case of Negotiated Rule-Making." In M. K. Mills (ed.), *Alternative Dispute Resolution in the Public Sector.* Chicago: Nelson-Hall, 1991.

Susskind, L. E., Babbitt, E. F., and Segal, P. N. "When ADR Becomes the Law: A Review of Federal Practice." *Negotiation Journal*, 1993, *9*, 59–75.

Tyler, T. R. "Governing amid Diversity: The Effect of Fair Decision Making Procedures on the Legitimacy of Government." *Law and Society Review*, 1994, *28*, 809–831.

Ury, F. *Getting Past No: Negotiating with Difficult People.* New York: Bantam Books, 1991.

Ury, F., Brett, J., and Goldberg, S. B. *Getting Disputes Resolved: Designing Systems to Cut the Costs of Conflict.* San Francisco: Jossey-Bass, 1989.

U.S. Senate, Government Affairs Committee. *Committee Report on Administrative Dispute Resolution Act of 1990.* Report. No. 101–543. *Congressional Record*, 136, Oct. 19, 1990.

Wall, J. A., Jr., and Lynn, A. "Mediation: A Current Review." *Journal of Conflict Resolution*, 1993, *37*, 160–194.

Williams, G. R. *Legal Negotiation and Settlement.* St. Paul, Minn.: West, 1983.

CONCLUSION
Present and Future Challenges

This book's final chapter is principally about the future. Examining present developments, it looks forward into the dynamics of relationships between law and public administration, both domestic and international.

Charles R. Wise highlights important forces that are driving and changing these relationships. He finds devolution and decentralization, redefinition of the public and private spheres, and the internationalization of public administration to be critical factors that are affecting a wide range of long-accepted ideas and practices. At the same time that these forces are reshaping institutions and the processes by which they interact, there are concomitant changes in the rights and expectations on those institutions that are presented by individual citizens. What all this means, he cautions, is that public administration and public law need to be more connected in the minds of managers than ever before in matters both procedural and substantive.

Public administrators do not have a choice as to whether law and the courts will be important factors in day-to-day life. Thus Wise argues that issues on the public law agenda must be in full partnership with other matters in public managers' work. Managers may not be able to shape some of the law and management issues that affect them, but they do have the opportunity to understand those interactions better. As a result of that understanding, they will be able to position themselves and their organizations more effectively to mitigate the negative aspects and shape possible positive changes in the years to come. Awareness and education are the first stages of the movement toward a more fruitful and effective working relationship in the twenty-first century.

CHAPTER THIRTY-ONE

The Future of Public Law

Beyond Administrative Law and National Borders

Charles R. Wise

Public law has experienced a renaissance in the field of public administration in recent years. This is not to say that all the complex relationships between law and administration have been worked out or that lawyers and managers are working smoothly together to further advance common goals in public affairs. A true partnership has still not evolved (O'Brien and Wise, 1985), even though much has happened in legal doctrine and managerial practice. Both the centrality and the difficulty of the relationships between law and administration have nonetheless impressed themselves on the field of public administration, in large part because in practice legislators, judges, and administrators have been increasingly thrust upon one another in legal arenas, with profound impacts on the conduct and outcomes of public services (see O'Leary and Wise, 1991). In an important sense, the academic attention to public law has not been fueled by the wide acceptance of any new theoretical breakthrough but rather, for many in the field, by a belated recognition that law matters because judges can and do exercise real power that has significantly rearranged administrative reality (Diver, 1979). This has not come as a surprise to scholars, who have long studied relationships between law and administration (many of these scholars are represented in this book), but it has forced a reconsideration by others who were convinced that the paths to greater administrative understanding lie largely with economic, psychological, or sociological variables.

As Martin Shapiro (1993) has pointed out, in political science, under the impact of the "behavioral revolution," the study of law was deemphasized and the remaining remnant became largely unidimensional, focusing on constitutional law. Concomitantly, public administration scholarship became oriented to administrative behavior and organization, with administrative law as a remnant treated as one of several formal screens that investigators had to penetrate in order to discover real political behavior (p. 365). The difficulty with that *de minimis* view of law is that it missed both the fundamental importance of administrative law for furthering governmental goals, and the impacts that administrative law has on administrative performance, both positive and negative. As Cooper (1996, p. 118) has observed, the supremacy of law is a central element of American constitutional government; modern administrative law has evolved with a sense of the need to maintain the ideal of the supremacy of law and also to temper it with the recognition of administrative reality.

Thus the study and practice of administrative law remains a vital arena within public law and administration. Much needs to be done to understand the dynamics of its operation in government and to adapt it to new pressures in public affairs. Thus the subtitle of this chapter, "Beyond Administrative Law and National Borders" is not meant to recommend an end to research and teaching about the various facets of administrative law or even administrative law at the national level. On the contrary, a fair argument can be made that, given the outpouring in the last thirty years of domestic legislation that has been the source of new regulations and adjudication, administrative law is a bigger enterprise than ever. It represents an important research venue in public law. An examination of just one administrative law element in one venue, say rulemaking at the national government level (Kerwin, 1994), is enough to demonstrate needs for both research and adaptation of rulemaking enterprises in order to achieve more effective public policy.

Nonetheless, other public law venues also deserve the attention of public administrators and require additional research. Public law has shown itself to be much broader than administrative law, and public administrationists need to be focusing on a multidimensional public law agenda if they are to deal effectively with the evolving relationships of public law and public administration. Public administration should not be in an exclusively reactive mode. In fact, a useful perspective for public administration's future is to approach the issues on the agenda of public law as a full partner. That is, public administration potentially has a great deal to offer the development of public law in various areas. For one thing, research and experience with program implementation and administrative execution are necessary to ground other values of public law in behavioral reality to make it possible for those other values to be made manifest. For example, it is one thing for a judge to decree equality of treatment, and quite another to achieve it. Without the full range of administrative action seeking the same goal, the decree is less than meaningful.

For public administration to realize its potential as a contributor, however, practitioners and scholars must be attentive to several trends that are having an impact on the field of public administration. These are (1) devolution and decentralization, (2) the redefinition of the intersection of public and private spheres, and (3) internationalization.

DEVOLUTION AND DECENTRALIZATION

The United States is going through a turn in the centralization-decentralization cycle, with emphasis on decentralization and devolution since the 1980s. While there are multiple explanations, from resource scarcity to ideological preferences to public distrust of big government, the branches of the federal government are responding by shifting responsibilities to the states.

The Reagan administration began the hard push toward governmental decentralization. President Bill Clinton, who began his term proposing a national centralization of health care, declared in his fourth State of the Union message that "the era of big government is over."

Congress has already cut many federal domestic programs, with responsibilities passing to the states. Although Congress and the president adopted a new welfare reform law, which ended the national government guarantee to individuals and turned the welfare program into a block grant program with much more control over program structure and operations delegated to the states, the jockeying over the desirability of devolution of responsibility to the states is not over. Questions of state capacity to provide service and fairness to those eligible will continue to be asked and debated as the reform is implemented. In short, while a consensus has been achieved that devolution is desirable, significant debate continues over the shape that it will or should take. Undoubtedly, a significant part of the debate will take place in the courts. Nonetheless, change in welfare law is but one example of the notable shift in the assumptions concerning federal policy. Direct operation of services by the federal government is largely not preferred by either Congress or the president. The working assumption is that decentralized operations, with some state and local government leadership, are to be preferred.

The judicial branch, too, is doing its part to further the devolution movement. Recently the Supreme Court has taken pains in several cases to reinvigorate its Tenth Amendment jurisprudence. The harbinger of this trend was, perhaps, Justice Sandra Day O'Connor's opinion in *Gregory* v. *Ashcroft*, in which the Supreme Court denied a federal statutory challenge to a provision of Missouri's constitution on Tenth Amendment grounds. In that opinion, Justice O'Connor went to extraordinary lengths to set out a renewed position on the importance of state sovereignty in the American governmental framework. Justice O'Connor continued the expansive dissertation on the constitutional principles of federalism in invalidating a portion of a federal environmental statute that mandated state action in *New York* v. *United States* (1992).

In *United States* v. *Lopez* (1995, p. 581), the majority reaffirmed "first principles" and quoted *Federalist* No. 45: "The powers delegated by the proposed Constitution to the federal government are few and defined. Those which are to remain in the State governments are numerous and indefinite." In *Lopez*, the opinion invalidated a federal statute that the U.S. Justice Department sought to justify based on the Commerce Clause. The Court acknowledged that it's previous opinions may have "taken long steps down that road" to "convert congressional authority under the Commerce Clause to a general police power of the sort retained by the states." However, the majority stated, "we decline to proceed any further." Instead, the majority invalidated the statute and signaled that it would also be more circumspect in interpreting the Commerce Clause in future cases.

The argument here is not that the Supreme Court has adopted a clear preference for state power. No clear federalism doctrine prevails even in a single policy area (Wise and O'Leary, 1997). However, in the aftermath of the decision in *Garcia* v. *San Antonio Mass Transit Authority* (1985), many commentators feared that the Court's role in upholding federalism in any case was over. This has not happened (Wise and O'Leary, 1992). Rather, the Court has shifted from a long period of almost never upholding state power against federal power to one of more selectively upholding federal power and sometimes upholding state power. In the same term that the Supreme Court upheld state power in *Lopez*, it upheld federal power in *U.S. Term Limits, Inc.* v. *Thornton et al.* (1995). Thus no monolithic preference supports state power. Yet the Court's recent stance implies more deference to the states than before and creates more policy space within which the states can experiment and provide leadership.

The decentralization movement poses significant challenges for public law and public administration. Public law is becoming a more diverse and complex enterprise. Further devolution of program operations or policymaking does not necessarily mean a simplification of legal relationships among levels of government. For example, while states are freer to create new services as they see fit, once they create them, individual recipients are entitled to federal due process guarantees that can be vindicated in federal courts (see Wise, 1996). In addition, while decentralization of some program operations for several federal programs has been occurring, the law of federal preemption has become more rather than less complex during the past two decades (see Wise and O'Leary, 1992). Also, state-local legal relations are not necessarily being either decentralized or simplified. At the same time that national policymakers are increasingly responding to concerns about unfunded mandates placed on the states by the national government, states have been increasing unfunded mandates on local governments

(Zimmerman, 1995). To understand trends will require a shift in focus from national preoccupation to analysis of fifty state systems in interaction with each other within the federal system.

One jurisprudential area that requires more attention is state constitutional law. State constitutional rights law has been getting more attention as several state supreme courts have been deciding cases based on statements of rights included in state constitutions, such as free speech. The U.S. Supreme Court has validated the practice and declared that a previous Supreme Court decision does not necessarily "limit the authority of the State to exercise its police power or its sovereign right to adopt in its constitution individual liberties more expansive than those conferred by the Federal Constitution" (*Pruneyard Shopping Center* v. *Robins*, 1980, p. 81). Jurisprudence of state constitutional rights is premised on the principles that the U.S. Constitution provides a minimum or floor for the protection of individual rights and that the states are free to grant greater rights to their citizens (Fisher, 1989). State constitutions are often more precise and sweeping in protecting rights that are also included in the U.S. Constitution, such as speech and assembly. Also, some state constitutions include additional rights not included explicitly in the federal Constitution, such as right to privacy, right to participation, right to know, and right to pure water. In interpreting these rights, state courts are more likely to look to each other than to the U.S. Supreme Court.

It may be argued that state constitutions allow different communities of citizens to formulate different solutions to problems affecting the nation and to resolve problems peculiar to their states (Kincaid, 1988). Nonetheless, interpretations of a much more diverse set of constitutions bearing on the implementation of public policies and operation of state and local programs pose a real challenge to the field of public law. It is no longer sufficient to depend on following the line of jurisprudence being developed in the federal courts and the pronouncements of the Supreme Court as guides to administrative action. Instead, public administrators need to understand applicable state constitutional precedents, and that involves a much more diverse line of cases.

Also, as the devolution of regulatory and programmatic authority continues, the states will increasingly play significant legislative roles with respect to policy development. For example, the area of environmental regulation began as a highly centralized regulatory enterprise within the Environmental Protection Agency (EPA) (Crampton, 1984). Subsequently, a consensus emerged in Congress and elsewhere that a larger state and local role was preferable, especially with regard to enforcement (Manley, 1987). By 1984, the states were characterized by EPA's director of management systems as "the primary operational arm of a national network for environmental protection" (Crampton, 1984, p. 5). In addition, several states have been actively legislating their own, more stringent environmental laws, such as California's statute mandating that automobile companies market some pollution-free cars in California before they will be allowed to continue to market any cars after 1997.

While Congress and the president continued wrangling over the degree of devolution that is appropriate for policymaking and administration of Medicaid in the future, by 1996 the Department of Health and Human Services had granted waivers from federal regulations to twenty-four states. As a result, state legislatures in those states are in a position to structure state responsibilities to a much greater extent than before. In fact, one reason for the waivers is to allow and encourage state experimentation to achieve more effective and cost-efficient programs. If state medical assistance policies and implementation are to be understood, comparative analysis of state law and administrative practices that provide the framework for this experimentation is now essential.

All of the pertinent state legislative activity is not coming as a result of devolution and decentralization of federal programs, of course. States are increasingly acting in their own right, and interest groups of many types have focused legislative efforts increasingly at the state level to achieve policy goals. As Walker (1995, pp. 256–257) has pointed out, over the past two decades states have engaged in pioneering efforts in consumer protection, campaign finance, "sunset" legislation, coastal zone management, hospital cost control, enterprise zones, foreign trade, universal health care, and educational reform. Through their independent policymaking processes, the states reflect differing approaches to servicing preferences, governmental accountability, and social legislation.

As a result of all of this legislative and administrative rulemaking activity at the state level, more administrative behavior actually will be regulated, directed, and constrained by state laws than by federal laws as the action moves to lower levels of government in major areas of public policy. Concomitantly, statutory interpretation as undertaken by state courts will be more significant. To understand what is happening on a national basis, more comparative analysis is needed about how these courts are defining rights and responsibilities in the several areas of public policy within the orbit of states.

In addition, with so many services and functions being governed by state and local agencies, the administrative law systems at subnational levels will be tasked to a greater extent than ever before. Public law scholars will need to revisit the structure and processes of state administrative law to assess how they are evolving in response to the accelerated decentralization taking place. Concomitantly, the legal capacity of state and local line agencies will require more attention. Not only will state agencies become more involved in service delivery and regulation, but they will necessarily become more deeply involved in policymaking and dispute resolution. Capacity considerations include not only the availability of legal counsel and legal training for line managers, but also the need for education and skills in the processes and training for alternative dispute resolution (ADR). In regard to the latter, research done with respect to the national government demonstrates that federal agencies are only beginning to use ADR techniques, and mostly for internal administrative matters rather than for external operations that would have more direct impact on streamlining relationships with the public. If state agencies are to do any better at implementing ADR techniques, then, concerted management training is likely to be required and attention will need to be paid to designing state systems of dispute resolution to permit and encourage ADR (see Bingham, 1996b).

With respect to the availability of legal counsel, many line agencies in all but the largest states have relatively little legal counsel that they can call their own. Instead, they must rely on offices of state attorneys general, which are almost always headed by elected officials, and which may or may not be oriented toward assisting state agencies directly. In short, the legal capacity issue for state and local governments is multifaceted and will require increasing attention.

REDEFINITION OF THE INTERSECTION OF PUBLIC AND PRIVATE SPHERES

Throughout its development, public administration has been concerned with defining the differences and relationships between public and private management (Urwick, 1957; Sayre, 1958; Rainey, Backoff, and Levine, 1976; Allison, 1982). Discerning the nature of "publicness" and its implications for management practice, research, and education has been a significant component of the academic enterprise of public administration. At the current juncture, multiple public sector reform proposals are based on premises of once again redefining the public-private nexus.

For example, the exercise has been reinvigorated by the privatization movement and the ensuing debate over the nature of and appropriate roles for privatization. Even the critics of privatization among public law specialists have acknowledged the movement and accorded it credit for forcing a discussion of the issue of the assignment and management of functions with a public character (Moe, 1987, p. 455).

As I have discussed elsewhere, public services in the United States are seldom the sole responsibility of a single public agency; instead they are the responsibility of public service configurations. The interorganizational field of any given sector of public activity consists of a variety of different types of organizations, public and private (Wise, 1990, p. 148).

Nonetheless, the current period is characterized by "reform" proposals that are premised on the desirability of increasing even further the involvement of the private sector in the provision of public services. It has been a commonplace in public administration for many years to refer to public-private partnerships.

Far from Big Government "doing it all"—as in building the Great Society during the 1960s—the rallying cry of policy innovation since the 1970s and especially since the 1980s has been to build effective public-private partnerships (Committee for Economic Development, 1982; Coleman, 1989) and/or to create "better government" by promoting competition among government service providers and making government more entrepreneurial (Osborne and Gaebler, 1992). Increasingly, management of public services is more involved with networks that are linked by contracts than with bounded hierarchical organizations. These networks span the public sector, the private sector, and the nonprofit sector (Milward, 1996, p. 78).

While it is true that government has always, to an important extent, contracted with private business, the current period is characterized by calls for an expansion in size and prominence of the contract state. In public administration, thus far, more effort has gone into seeking out additional opportunities to contract for services and charting possible cost savings from doing so than has gone into specifying the management imperatives necessary to develop and manage the contracts successfully. The field has increasingly turned attention to the more specific issues and problems of managing in the contract state. Public law potentially has much to contribute to the analysis and the development of management strategy. For example, it is clear that contracting for services exacerbates the problem of control. Specifying exactly what a nonprofit or private agency must provide to public clients is not an easy task. Additionally, carrying out a threat to cancel a contract for nonperformance can leave the government without a service provider (Milward, 1996, pp. 81–85). In fact, information needed to monitor contracts is sometimes difficult to obtain (Kettl, 1993). Collusion, conflicts of interest, abuse of contract terms, and lack of competition are all potential problems (Prager, 1994; Goldstein, 1992; MacManus, 1992). This is especially a concern as traditional arms-length principles are displaced by collaboration, as espoused by the National Performance Review of the Clinton administration (Gore, 1993). Thus the drafting, execution, and monitoring of contracts has become more important than ever. The type of contract has to be appropriate for the type of performance sought, contract terms have to be clear, the desired sequence of activities has to be clearly delineated where possible, alternative processes must be defined, performance assessment measures have to be specified, and performance and audit dates have to be set (O'Leary, 1996).

Thus, a greater need exists for public law specialists to examine and analyze the approaches and provisions included in contracts in order to discern the implications for the capacity of public agencies to fulfill their governing responsibilities while managing contractors effectively. It is not appropriate to assume that the same contract approaches and terms will fit all service and other public situations. For example, DeHoog's (1984, pp. 134–136) study of human services in Michigan showed that the social and employment services were intended to be effective in changing the lives of clients and not only to give them some temporary services. Quality and effectiveness were more important than lowest cost, and the nonprofit agencies involved operate under different pressures and incentives than firms such as those providing garbage collection services. In addition, in social services multiple actors are involved with different responsibilities for specifying and interpreting different sets of applicable regulations in the contracting process. Also, the courts have long been active in defining protections for the customers and clients of public social service agencies, and they are unlikely to take a hands-off approach merely because an agency contracts for the service with a private party (see Rosenbloom and O'Leary, 1997, pp. 117–150).

Kettl's (1993) analysis of the contract state has led him to call for a new class of government officials trained to handle the realities of contracting today. They need to be skilled at drafting clear and enforceable standards, managing information, monitoring and auditing, and negotiating. Public law needs to be involved in analyzing contract standards, monitoring and auditing provisions, discerning information requirements, and negotiating approaches in order for the field to produce the knowledge base that such training requires.

In addition, as I have discussed elsewhere (Wise, 1989), changes in service arrangements brought about by increased contracting have implications beyond drafting the terms of contracts for public administration. Contracting is not a panacea for inadequate government organizational capacity. When government retains a role in service provision while relying on private production of public services, important public responsibilities must still be organized and managed by public agencies. The expanded use of contracting requires government organizations to be able to manage interdependencies with an array of private, nonprofit, quasi-governmental, and other organizations at various levels of government. This requires increasingly sophisticated government organizations to possess the technical, fiscal, and human resources capacities within structures that are legally endowed to permit them to pursue public goals in the complex field of interorganizational relationships (Wise, 1990, p. 147). Public law has an important role in analyzing the legal and administrative attributes of public organizational capacity required to manage public responsibilities in increasingly complex interorganizational networks.

THE REEMERGENCE OF PROPERTY RIGHTS IN REGULATORY DEBATE

Another aspect of the redefinition of public and private spheres is the rearrangement of rights and responsibilities of government and private owners with respect to property. This wide-ranging rearrangement is taking place in at least two important venues: the federal courts and the state legislatures. This policymaking is still at the beginning stages, and public law potentially has much to contribute both to the policy debates and deliberations surrounding the issues involved, and to the implications for regulatory and programmatic implementation that will continue to unfold.

With respect to the federal courts, an important line of cases affecting public administration has come along since 1987 by way of reinvigorating the doctrine of regulatory taking (see Wise, 1994; Wise and Emerson, 1994). The regulatory taking doctrine has been developed by the courts based on the Fifth Amendment's provision that property may not be taken for public use without just compensation. Although Justice Oliver Wendell Holmes first enunciated the concept in 1922, stating that the "general rule at least is, that while property may be regulated to a certain extent, if regulation goes too far, it will be recognized as a taking" (*Pennsylvania Coal* v. *Mahon,* p. 415), the federal courts did not get very serious in filling out the doctrine and applying it significantly to regulatory activities until the late 1980s. In *Nollan* v. *California Coastal Commission* (1987), however, in which a landowner appealed a state regulatory decision, the Supreme Court held that the state agency must be prepared to prove in court that a "legitimate state interest" is "substantially advanced" by the state regulation, and that an "essential nexus" exists between the "end advanced" (or the enunciated purpose of the regulation) and the "condition imposed" by the application of the regulation to the property that restricted the owner's use of it (p. 836). This has meant and will continue to mean a higher level of federal judicial scrutiny of the adequacy and relationship of regulatory methods used by federal, state, and local governments.

Public officials to this point have received only minimal guidance from the federal courts regarding the criteria they will employ, and thus administrative action directed at avoiding a successful challenge to a regulatory action is accompanied by great uncertainty. The Supreme Court has been definitive for two situations by stating that there are two categories in which regulators would have to pay regardless of other factors: (1) where the regulation results in physical occupation, and (2) where the regulation denies "all economically viable use" (*Lucas* v. *South Carolina Coastal Council,* 1992). For all other regulatory situations, which lead to the majority of cases, the lower courts are directed to engage in "ad hoc factual inquiries" balancing such factors as "the economic impact of the regulation," "the extent to which it has interfered with distinct investment-backed expectations," and "the character of the government action" (*Penn Central Transportation* v. *New York City,* 1978, p. 124). With respect to the character of the government action, the jurisdiction has the burden of meeting the "essential nexus" test of *Nollan.*

The Court has now stated something more about the degree of connection the jurisdiction must demonstrate between the "end advanced" and the "condition imposed" by a regulatory action. In *Dolan* v. *Tigard* (1994), the Court enunciated a new test of "rough proportionality" and stated: "No precise mathematical calculation is required, but the city must make some sort of individualized determination that the required dedication is related both in nature and extent of the impact of the proposed development" (p. 2323). As a result, there can be little doubt that the lower courts will become more involved in defining the types of evidence that state and local regulators must produce in order to successfully meet the test of "rough proportionality." This means that administrators will need to change their processes and come up with additional information to meet the new requirements, and this will affect many regulatory decisions. Public law analysts will be scrutinizing these unfolding elements of doctrine regarding government regulation of private property for years to come.

The rearrangement of rights and responsibilities in regard to property is not confined to the regulatory area. For example, the Supreme Court has now entered into laying down conditions under which property may be confiscated pursuant to the forfeiture laws. In *United States* v. *James Daniel Good Real Property* (1993), the Court employed its due process analysis, enunciated in *Matthews* v. *Eldridge* (1976), to declare that unless exigent circumstances are present, the Due Process Clause requires the government to afford notice and meaningful opportunity to be heard before seizing real property subject to civil forfeiture. In order to demonstrate exigent circumstances, the government must establish that less restrictive measures would not suffice to protect the government's interests in preventing the sale, destruction, or continued unlawful use of the property.

As the dividing lines between public and private continue to blur and meld into each other, substantial adaptations of administrative processes will continue to be required. Laws are clearly evolving as relationships change among government, nonprofit, and private organizations. The relationships have always been complex, with government serving as promoter, regulator, customer, and service provider in relationships with private organizations, sometimes simultaneously. The complexity is being expanded in the current era, and public law will be changing to keep up with the new dynamics that are evolving.

INTERNATIONALIZATION

It is now widely recognized that internationalization constitutes a dynamic that affects every sort of institution. Nonetheless, it is incumbent on public law scholars to consider how this dynamic affects the field of public law and what opportunities are being opened as a result. The triumph and spread of democracy, the integration of international financial, production, and trading systems, and the communication and transportation revolutions are all affecting how people think and feel about their governments and what they expect from them. A new wave of constitutionalism is evident as people look to constitute new governmental arrangements.

Opportunities for analysis of both international and comparative legal developments are presented to public law scholars. With regard to the comparative agenda, perhaps at no other time in world history have so many new national systems of law been in creation at the same time. This is largely a result of the dissolution of the Soviet empire, the establishment and reestablishment of nations in central and eastern Europe, including the newly independent states of the former Soviet Union. New constitutions are being written and modified and new systems of law, including regulatory and administrative law, are being developed.

As one observer of the scene put it: "The momentum for establishing constitutional government is abroad, not just in one nation, but in many, and it is supported by most of the world" (Varat, 1992, p. 178). It is important to understand that positive factors supporting constitutional reform in these countries coexist with negative factors that stand in the way (Sajo, 1995). Nonetheless, public administration has long been concerned with the development of new public institutions, and the legal dimension in general and the expansion of constitutionalism in particular cannot be ignored in the new democracies. Public administration has a contribution to make as these countries seek to transform strong-state bureaucracies that were constructed under dictatorships as instruments of the elites into bureaucracies that are subordinated to the rule of law in service of the development of democratic government. Western nations have a common interest in seeing eastern bureaucracies successfully transformed, if for no other reason than that their national security interests are involved in the successful adjustment of eastern European countries to constitutional democracy. Public law and administration scholars have an interest in being involved in the analysis and construction of such democratic administrative systems not only for the knowledge that will be gained during such momentous transitions, but also from the standpoint of contributing to the rule of law and its implications for democracy and peaceful interaction on an international scale.

In western European countries, the importance of constitutional judicial review is spreading, with significant implications for public law. There are certainly significant differences between systems in which institutionally independent courts with coercive powers exercise judicial review in concrete cases, such as in the United States, Canada, Germany, and Greece, and other continental constitutional courts, which stand apart from the ordinary courts and only examine the constitutionality of laws in the abstract. Nonetheless, courts in both systems are addressing similar kinds of civil rights issues that are intimately involved with government policy and regulation. For example, constitutional courts in Austria, France, Germany, and Italy have boldly and almost contemporaneously entered into consideration of the constitutionality of abortion legislation (Capelletti, 1989, p. 162). German, French, and other continental courts have issued wide-ranging decisions on basic constitutional issues, often drawing on unwritten or historical principles and values (Schwartz, 1992, p. 745).

In addition, the European Court on Human Rights is active in rendering decisions based on the European Convention for the Protection of Human Rights and Fundamental Freedom. Fourteen of the twenty-one European Community nations have accepted a clause of the European Convention allowing their citizens to attack before the European Commission on Human Rights and, potentially, the European Court of Justice any violation of the Convention by any sort of state action, whether judicial, legislative, or administrative. In effect, this is a form of judicial review at the transnational level (Capelletti, 1989, p. 168). Clearly, an international civil rights jurisprudence is developing and confronting many contemporary issues that affect the rights of individuals and the responsibilities of governments generally. Just as modern nations have many insights to gain from each other in other aspects of governance, comparative analysis could yield valuable insights in the area of judicial review and its impacts on administration.

Interesting developments in judicial review are not to be found only in western European countries. The advent of constitutional courts in Eastern and Central Europe, as in Russia, Hungary, Poland, the Czech Republic, Bulgaria, and Romania, have brought decisions based on these countries' new constitutions. While it is too early to draw firm conclusions, evidence exists of decisions that defend constitutional principles and human rights against legislative and executive encroachments (Schwartz, 1992). Whether these courts can continue in this vein and withstand drives aimed at abandoning democracy and the rule of law remains to be seen. The extent to which these constitutional courts establish legitimacy and judicial power in nations that are unaccustomed to an independent judiciary will contribute to the staying power of democratic government. The interaction of these courts and the executives will be fertile ground for analysis for years to come.

Of course, Europe is not the only region that requires the attention of public law scholars. Asian countries represent the fastest developing economic region in the world, and societal and governmental changes, including changes in legal systems, are sure to follow.

Developments in international affairs are blurring distinctions between domestic and international law, including old national boundaries between regulation and administration. New international combinations involve legal arrangements with which administrators at all levels have to contend.

A prominent example is the treaty of the European Union (EU). The European Court of Justice has established doctrines that affect administration in every member government. For example, the court's judgment in *Van Gend &*

Loos NV v. *Commission of the European Communities* (1984) established the doctrine of direct effect, which applies to all EU treaties and legislation. The doctrine held that where a provision is clear, complete, and in need of no further implementation, it can be relied upon by an individual or business against the state. For one thing, in terms of public human resources policy, as soon as an EU labor law directive is due to be implemented, all its directly effective provisions can be relied upon by public sector employees. Thus, public human resources management is directly affected by EU action.

Also, the European Court of Justice has established a government liability principle available for individuals to employ against their national governments to guarantee the enforcement of EU laws and regulations. It the case of *Andrea Francovich* v. *Italian Republic* (1991), the court held that a state must be held liable for the loss and damage caused to individuals as a result of breaches of European Court law for which the state can be held responsible. In addition, the court held that, in the case of the nonimplementation of an EU directive by a member state, damages would be available for any loss that resulted. The liability principle holds for any case in which a member state violates EU law, regardless of which organ of the state is responsible.

Given the increasing predilection of modern nations to enter into international agreements that affect domestic policy in areas from trade to environmental protection, it should be expected that there will be increasing experimentation with new forms of transnational dispute resolution and that officials at various levels of government will be called upon to participate. Public law and public administration potentially have much to contribute to the construction and analysis of these new institutional arrangements. In particular, public law analysts must be concerned with political and administrative factors and not only with the legal issues involved if workable institutional arrangements are to be derived from such agreements.

If law is viewed in part as a societal problem-solving instrument, then modern nations can also potentially gain insights from comparative analysis of key bodies of law aimed at solving priority public predicaments. For example, most industrialized nations are facing similar kinds of environmental problems and are attempting to institutionalize various types of regulatory regimes to deal with them. Structures and approaches may be similar or different, but taken as a whole, such nations can be said to be conducting an international field experiment in environmental protection and restoration. Potentially, environmental policymakers and regulators can learn from the different approaches being taken and their successes and failures.

Public law and public administration must be involved in the comparative analysis of such key regulatory areas. The administrative and policy approaches imbedded in the laws require analyses of the interaction of institutions, behaviors, and policies with which scholars of public law and administration are accustomed to dealing. For example, environmental regulation in few countries can be wholly a responsibility of the central government; it is most likely to be a set of shared responsibilities of jurisdictions at various levels of government. Beyond recognizing that fact, it must also be realized that environmental law is in part about structuring the relationships among various governmental jurisdictions and officials. Numerous issues arise in discerning optimal arrangements for the different responsibilities. How much power should be allocated to the central government to set minimum standards? What powers need be allocated to the center to provide for a minimum harmonization of product standards and to prevent the creation of unnecessary barriers to trade? Which standards are locality-specific and dependent on the physical and geographical characteristics of the region or state? Which standards have transboundary implications? Policymakers may gain insight into such issues of environmental federalism by comparing various approaches, but the analyses must be informed by the real similarities and differences that exist in the laws and the institutional structures (Kimber, 1995).

Another reason for engaging in such comparative analysis is for international policymaking purposes. While it has now been recognized that many environmental problems are really global problems requiring international solutions, implementation of such policies requires national legislation and implementation. Treaties, such as the United Nations Convention on Biological Diversity, are not self executing. Modern industrialized nations must take the lead in addressing the imperatives of the Convention. Many such nations contain federal arrangements that must be worked through and/or adjusted. For example, one analyst finds in comparing the environmental policies and federal structures of the United States and Germany that Germany puts too much emphasis on implementation by state and local governments and the United States, too little. The finding is that Germany and the United States need to recognize more fully the complex regional and interjurisdictional character of pollution (Rose-Ackerman, 1994, p. 1622).

CONCLUSION

Decentralization, the redefinition of public and private spheres, and internationalization are all multiplying the relationships with which public officials and public agencies have to contend. Concomitantly, these dynamics are rearranging the rights and responsibilities of numerous parties with stakes in various facets of the public agenda. As a result, public law is becoming an even more multifaceted enterprise.

While the complexity of the public law enterprise is increasing, it is also generating an environment in which much experimentation and innovation can take place. Whether the focus is on the creation of many new constitutions in Central and Eastern Europe, or on the innovations in state law dealing with devolved authority over welfare, medical aid for the poor, or environmental protection, the variations being created constitute policy laboratories that cry out for comparative analysis. Public law analysts should anticipate a demand from policymakers and public administrators to do systematic evaluations of both substantive and procedural aspects of these laws. The political and administrative implications need attention as well. Policymakers need such information because, as with past administrative or policy changes, significant debates are now under way over the effectiveness, equity, and efficiency of many new arrangements. Public law and public administration analysts need to combine forces to address the multitude of fascinating questions that characterize the contemporary debates.

Cases Cited

Andrea Francovich v. *Italian Republic,* E.C.R. C–6/90, C9/90 (19 Nov. 1991).

Dolan v. *Tigard,* 114 S.Ct. 2309 (1994).

Garcia v. *San Antonio Mass Transit Authority,* 469 U.S. 528 (1985).

Gregory v. *Ashcroft,* 111 S.Ct. 2395 (1991).

Lucas v. *South Carolina Coastal Council,* 505 U.S. 1003 (1992).

Matthews v. *Eldridge,* 424 U.S. 319 (1976).

New York v. *United States,* 505 U.S. 144 (1992).

Nollan v. *California Coastal Commission,* 483 U.S. 825 (1987).

Penn Central Transportation v. *New York City,* 435 U.S. 920 (1978).

Pennsylvania Coal v. *Mahon,* 260 U.S. 393 (1922).

Pruneyard Shopping Center v. *Robins,* 447 U.S. 74 (1980).

U.S. Term Limits, Inc. v. *Thornton et al.,* 115 S.Ct. 1842 (1995).

United States v. *James Daniel Good Real Property,* 510 U.S. 43 (1993).

United States v. *Lopez,* 514 S.Ct. 549 (1995).

Van Gend & Loos NV v. *Commission of the European Communities,* E.C.R. 98, 230/83 (13 Nov. 1984).

References

Allison, G. "Public and Private Management: Are They Fundamentally Alike in All Unimportant Respects?" In R. Lane (ed.), *Current Issues in Public Administration.* (2nd ed.) New York: St. Martin's Press, 1982.

Bingham, L. B., and Wise, C. R. "The Administrative Dispute Resolution Act of 1990: How Do We Evaluate Its Success?" *Journal of Public Administration Research and Theory,* 1996, *6,* 383–414.

Capelletti, M. *The Judicial Process in Comparative Perspective.* Oxford: Clarendon Press, 1989.

Coleman, W. G. *State and Local Government and Public-Private Partnerships.* Westport, Conn.: Greenwood Press, 1989.

Committee for Economic Development. *Public-Private Partnerships: An Opportunity for Urban Communities.* New York: Committee for Economic Development, 1982.

Cooper, P. J. "Understanding What the Law Says About Administrative Responsibility." In J. L. Perry (ed.), *Handbook of Public Administration.* (2nd ed.) San Francisco: Jossey-Bass, 1996.

Crampton, L. "Helping the States Carry a Bigger Load." *EPA Journal,* 1984, *10*(1), 4–5.

DeHoog, R. H. *Contracting Out for Human Services.* Albany: State University of New York Press, 1984.

Diver, C. "The Judge as Political Powerbroker: Superintending Structural Change in Public Institutions." *Virginia Law Review,* 1979, *65*, 43–106.

Fisher, L. "How the States Shape Constitutional Law." *State Legislatures,* 1989, *14*, 37–39.

Goldstein, M. *America's Hollow Government.* Burr Ridge, Ill.: Irwin, 1992.

Gore, A., Jr. *From Red Tape to Results: Creating a Government That Works Better and Costs Less.* Report of the National Performance Review. Washington, D.C.: U.S. Government Printing Office, 1993.

Kerwin, C. *Rulemaking.* Washington, D.C.: Congressional Quarterly Press, 1994.

Kettl, D. F. *Sharing Power: Public Governance and Private Markets.* Washington, D.C.: Brookings Institution, 1993.

Kimber, C.J.M. "A Comparison of Environmental Federalism in the United States and the European Union." *Maryland Law Review,* 1995, *54*, 1658–1690.

Kincaid, J. "State Constitutions in the Federal System." *Annals of the AAPSS,* 1988, *496*, 12–22.

MacManus, S. A. *Doing Business with Government.* New York: Paragon House, 1992.

Manley, R. E. "Federalism and Management of the Environment." *Urban Lawyer,* 1987, *2*, 661–681.

Milward, H. B. "The Changing Character of the Public Sector." In J. L. Perry (ed.), *Handbook of Public Administration.* (2nd ed.) San Francisco: Jossey-Bass, 1996.

Moe, R. C. "Exploring the Limits of Privatization." *Public Administration Review,* 1987, *47*, 453–460.

O'Brien, D., and Wise, C. R. "Law and Administration." *Public Administration Review,* 1985, *45*, 641.

O'Leary, R. "Managing Contracts and Grants." In J. L. Perry (ed.), *Handbook of Public Administration.* (2nd ed.) San Francisco: Jossey-Bass, 1996.

O'Leary, R., and Wise, C. R. "Public Managers, Judges, and Legislators: Redefining the New Partnership." *Public Administration Review*, 1991, *51*, 316–327.

Osborne, D., and Gaebler, T. A. *Reinventing Government: How the Entrepreneurial Spirit Is Transforming the Public Sector from Schoolhouse to Statehouse, City Hall to the Pentagon.* Reading, Mass.: Addison Wesley Longman, 1992.

Prager, J. "Contracting Out Government Services: Lessons from the Private Sector." *Public Administration Review*, 1994, *54*, 176–184.

Rainey, H., Backoff, R., and Levine, C. "Comparing Public and Private Organizations." *Public Administration Review*, 1976, *36*, 233–244.

Rose-Ackerman, S. "Environmental Policy and Federal Structure: A Comparison of the United States and Germany." *Vanderbilt Law Review*, 1994, *47*, 1587–1622.

Rosenbloom, D. H., and O'Leary, R. *Public Administration and Law.* New York: Dekker, 1997.

Sajo, A. "On Old and New Bottles: Obstacles to the Rule of Law in Eastern Europe." *Journal of Law and Society*, 1995, *22*, 97–103.

Sayre, W. "Premises of Public Administration: Past and Emerging." *Public Administration Review*, 1958, *18*, 102–105.

Schwartz, H. "The New East European Constitutional Courts." *Michigan Journal of International Law*, 1992, *13*, 741–785.

Shapiro, M. "Public Law and Judicial Politics." In A. W. Finifter (ed.), *Political Science: The State of the Discipline II.* Washington, D.C.: American Political Science Association, 1993.

Urwick, L. "Public Administration and Business Management." *Public Administration Review*, 1957, *17*, 77–82.

Varat, J. D. "Reflections on the Establishment of Constitutional Government in Eastern Europe." *Constitutional Commentary*, 1992, *9*, 171–187.

Walker, D. B. *The Rebirth of Federalism.* Chatham, N.J.: Chatham House, 1995.

Wise, C. R. "Whither Federal Organizations: The Air Travel Challenge and Federal Management's Response." *Public Administration Review*, 1989, *49*, 17–28.

Wise, C. R. "Public Service Configurations and Public Organizations: Public Organization Design in the Post-Privatization Era." *Public Administration Review*, 1990, *50*, 141–155.

Wise, C. R. "Regulatory Takings." In D. H. Rosenbloom and R. Schwartz (eds.), *Handbook of Regulation and Administrative Law.* New York: Dekker, 1994.

Wise, C. R. "Understanding Your Liability as a Public Administrator." In J. L. Perry (ed.), *Handbook of Public Administration.* (2nd ed.) San Francisco: Jossey-Bass, 1996.

Wise, C. R., and Emerson, K. "Regulatory Takings: The Emerging Doctrine and Its Implications for Public Administration." *Administration and Society*, 1994, *26*, 305–336.

Wise, C. R., and O'Leary, R. "Is Federalism Dead or Alive in the Supreme Court? Implications for Public Administrators." *Public Administration Review*, 1992, *52*, 559–571.

Wise, C. R., and O'Leary, R. "Intergovernmental Relations in Environmental Management and Policy." *Public Administration Review*, 1997.

Zimmerman, J. F. *State-Local Relations: A Partnership Approach.* (2nd ed.) New York: Praeger, 1995.

NAME INDEX

A

Aaron, H. J., 318, 319, 341
Abney, G., 510, 513, 526
Adamany, D., 67, 74
Adams, J. S., 248–249, 252
Agnew, S., 10
Aleinikoff, T. A., 94, 103
Alexander, S., 249, 252
Allain, B., 510
Allen, J. W., 528, 542
Allen, W. G., 489
Allison, G., 575, 584
Amin, I., 365
Anthony, R., 34, 39
Appleby, P., 106, 119
Areeda, P., 386
Aristotle, 371, 372, 374, 425
Axelrod, D., 511, 526

B

Babbitt, B., 460
Babbitt, E. F., 548, 566
Babitsky, T. T., 528, 544
Backoff, R., 575, 586
Baird, J., 287, 297
Baker, N., 458, 461, 465, 475
Ball, H., 60–61, 90, 93, 96, 102
Ballard, W. D., 145n

Ban, C., 275, 283, 286, 289, 298, 346, 355
Barnes, J. A., 45, 55
Barr, S., 52, 55
Bayes, J. H., 321, 341
Bazelon, D., 449–450
Beam, D. R., 153, 157
Beer, S. H., 165, 180
Bell, G., 381, 398, 458, 465, 467, 475
Berman, L., 507, 526
Berring, R. C., 84, 88
Bertin, J. E., 326, 341
Best, S., 171, 182
Bickel, A., 93, 102
Biddle, F., 458, 475
Bingham, L. B., 455–456, 546, 548, 551, 553,
    555, 562, 563, 575, 584
Birnbaum, J., 303, 312
Bish, R., 165, 182
Biskupic, J., 465, 475
Black, H. L., 95, 96, 102, 261
Blackmun, H. A., 269, 270, 271, 504, 520
Blackstone, W., 400, 422
Blanchard, K. H., 246, 252
Blum, L. M., 317, 321, 341
Bockanic, W. N., 241, 252
Borchard, E. M., 405, 422
Boskey, J. B., 551, 563
Bowman, A., 471, 472, 475–476

SUBJECT INDEX

A

Abood v. Detroit Board of Education, 263–264, 271

Access to information, 377–380, 383–386, 391, 396–397

Accommodation of coordinate construction, 133–134

Accountability: administrative, 156; aspects of, 357–451; and democracy, 376–377; and information policies, 376–399; and judicial review, 440–451; and law, 361–375; overview of, 357–360; political and economic, 53; and remedial orders, 424–439; and tort liability, 400–423

Act to Prevent Pernicious Political Activities. *See* Hatch Acts

Adarand Constructors, Inc. v. Pena: and equality, 303, 304, 305, 310, 311; and executives, 207, 209; and strict scrutiny, 487, 500

Adjudication: in alternative dispute resolution, 557–559; as management tool, 110, 115–116; in public management, 36–38

Adler v. Board of Education, 266, 271

Administration: culture of, 16–22; policy distinct from, 106–118. *See also* Public administration; Street-level administration

Administrative Conference of the United States (ACUS): and alternative dispute resolution, 547, 549, 554, 563; and negotiated rulemaking, 226–227, 229, 230, 235

Administrative Dispute Resolution (ADR) Act of 1990, 548, 562

Administrative Dispute Resolution (ADR) Act of 1996, 548–550

Administrative Procedure Act (APA) of 1946: and alternative dispute resolution, 547, 549, 562; and authority, 78–79, 80; and information policy, 377, 378, 395; and judicial review, 441, 443, 445, 448–449; and remedial orders, 425; and rulemaking, 31, 34, 38, 39, 109, 112, 227, 230

Administrative procedures laws, as tools, 108, 111

Administrative support and management laws, as tools, 108

Advisory Committee on Human Radiation Experiments, 201

Advisory committees, and judicial review, 446–447

Affirmative action: abuses of, 309–311; debate on, 302–305; evaluation of, 306–308; and executive orders, 190, 193, 207; and gender issues, 321; judicially imposed, 306; remedies under, 305–306

AFGE v. Reno, 280, 285

Afghanistan, and terrorism, 382

599